ARTHURIAN STUDIES IX

THE RETURN OF KING ARTHUR

ARTHURIAN STUDIES

THE RETURN OF
KING ARTHUR

British and American
Arthurian Literature
since 1900

BEVERLY TAYLOR
& ELISABETH BREWER

D. S. BREWER . BARNES & NOBLE

First published 1983 by
D. S. Brewer
240 Hills Road, Cambridge
an imprint of Boydell & Brewer Ltd
PO Box 9, Woodbridge, Suffolk IP12 3DF
and by
Barnes and Noble Books
81 Adams Drive, Totowa, New Jersey 07512

ISBN 0 85991 1365
US ISBN 0-389-20278-9

British Library Cataloguing in Publication Data

The return of King Arthur.—(Arthurian studies
ISSN 0261-9814; 9)
1. Arthur, *King*
I. Title   II. Brewer, Elisabeth
398'.352   DA152.5.A7

ISBN 0-85991-136-5

Printed in Great Britain by
St Edmundsbury Press, Bury St Edmunds, Suffolk

CONTENTS

PREFACE

This book describes and analyses British and American Arthurian literature published since 1800, paying close attention to the writers' uses of source material and their relationship to Arthurian tradition, while also assessing the accomplishment and relative literary merit of individual works. Though surveys have been made of British Arthuriana published prior to 1835 by James Douglas Merriman, and of British and American works published between 1900 and 1950 by Nathan Comfort Starr, the Arthurian literature of British Victorians, nineteenth-century Americans, and writers on both sides of the Atlantic since World War II has received slight attention.

In this volume we have concentrated particularly on Arthurian literature of the nineteenth century, for two reasons. First, these works demonstrate what elements of the legend, through what sources, were known to the age. They illustrate the combination of tradition with invention which restored the legend to literary prominence. Second, the more obscure works (such as those by John Thelwall and Henry Hart Milman, for example) are increasingly less accessible, and full treatment here will preserve for future Arthurians a sense of these texts and their role in the literary recovery of Arthur. As far as works published in the last two decades are concerned we have aimed principally to describe these, since their large number makes fuller analysis impracticable within the scope of this volume.

Throughout this study we have cited Caxton's edition of Malory (in the Everyman edition published by J. M. Dent in 1906) as the version of the *Morte Darthur* most widely known to nineteenth- and twentieth-century writers. We have normalised the widely varied spellings of Arthurian names, as far as possible, when we speak of the traditional figures (Lancelot and Guenevere, Tristram and Iseult), but when we discuss particular literary texts, we use the writers' designations for their own characters.

The Prologue, chapters 5, 7, and 8, and the full bibliography were prepared by Elisabeth Brewer; chapters 1, 2, 3, 4 and 6 were written by Beverly Taylor. Both contributed to the final chapter.

Chapel Hill, North Carolina   January 1983
Cambridge, England

PROLOGUE: THE NATURE OF THE ARTHURIAN STORIES

The story of Arthur has been told again and again and has continued to capture the imagination for well over a thousand years, drawing into its orbit other stories of almost equal resonance, such as that of Tristram and Iseult and of the Grail. Each age in which the stories have been told and re-told has found in them the means of expressing something of its own attitudes, ideals and anxieties, and this is as true of the nineteenth and twentieth centuries, with which we are here concerned, as of the Middle Ages, when the great body of Arthurian stories crystallised around the charismatic figure of the Once and Future King. Still they maintain their appeal, as theatre and cinema, historical novels and poems, journalistic allusions, Ph.D. theses and tourist attractions demonstrate, to say nothing of the investigations of archaeologists, historians and occultists. The search for the historical Arthur has been intensified since the Second World War, but it is the element of myth in the stories in which, above all else, their hold over our imaginations consists.

When the Arthurian legend was virtually rediscovered in the nineteenth century, writers and artists gradually became aware of its potential as a new source of symbolism. Though some writers retold the stories for their narrative interest alone, others discovered the means of shaping them so as to give expression to new insights and significances. The enthusiasm for all things medieval which rapidly developed in the nineteenth century may have been largely nostalgic and antiquarian, but, by implicit comparison of imagined past and present reality, it also made possible the revaluation and more precise definition of the contemporary. From the Arthurian legend, writers and artists took the situations, themes and motifs which had most meaning for them, by means of which they could give new and symbolic expression to their own experience.

There would have been no Arthurian revival at all, however, no widespread and continued interest in the Arthurian themes without Sir Thomas Malory's *Le Morte Darthur*.[1] For Malory provided, as he may still provide, not only a very comprehensive and well-structured source of Arthurian material for the later writer, but a version that unlike its counterparts in other languages, was and is readily accessible. The rediscovered *Le Morte Darthur* not only satisfied the nineteenth century's growing interest in the Middle Ages, but satisfied it in a way that few other medieval texts could have done. The power of the stories, the overall structure that holds them together, mounting to the climax of the Table's downfall and the death of the protagonists, the noble prose in which these events are related and evaluated, have made Malory's version the most influential of Arthurian texts in any language. Morris and Burne-Jones as young men, introduced to Malory, discovered 'a world of mystical religion and noble chivalry of action, of lost history and romance'[2], an imaginary world in which they and others of their circle lived. For them, it was a shared experience, as perhaps with many other Victorian readers, for Malory was meant to be, and no

1

doubt often was read aloud. But however *Le Morte Darthur* was read, an audience was gradually created, as in the Middle Ages, who were familiar with the stories and were ready for new versions and new interpretations. Many new retellings for children played their part too in reviving interest in Arthur and his knights, and the ideals to which they were dedicated.

Malory did not need to be translated: his fifteenth-century prose was sufficiently close to modern English, to the language of the Prayer Book and the Bible, to be read without difficulty in the nineteenth century. Moreover, Malory's own interests in *Le Morte Darthur* were of a nature to appeal to the Victorian reader and to make later re-tellings easier: his devotion to the noble ideal of the Round Table, for instance, and his awareness at the same time of the difficulty of living up to it; his perception of how conflicting human passions can destroy a great institution; his interest in character. Malory, the 'Knight Prisoner', over the long years of working with his material, came to know his protagonists as if they had peopled his own world. Lancelot and Guenevere have the individuality and vibrance of living personalities, representative and symbolic figures though they remain. Their joy and suffering, courage and loyalty, jealousy and generosity are true to human experience, so that the annals of these troubled lives readily captured and still do capture the imagination.

It is a further advantage of Malory's version, moreover, that it is set in a world that is in a sense timeless, and certainly without vividly realised settings (unlike, for example, *Sir Gawain and the Green Knight* with its brilliant descriptive detail). Its lack of specific location prevents it from being quaintly medieval and it has the added advantage as a source-book that it allows the later writer or artist to create his own backgrounds, detailed or merely suggested, for the events or the characters. The wide range of differing backgrounds, from the romantic Pre-Raphaelite vision to Tennyson's sometimes more domestic scenes— or indeed to the updated realism of Mark Twain or T. H. White—make apparent the extent to which such free adaptation has been possible.

Similarly, though Malory's earlier books in some ways resemble historical chronicles, Arthurian legend makes the minimum demand for historical accuracy, and so gives greater imaginative freedom to the later writer. The historical novelist must make every effort to get his facts and his background right, to solve the problem of dialogue and to avoid anachronisms of many kinds. The Arthurian writer can satisfy the reader's craving for stories of long ago without encountering such difficulties, because he is dealing in effect with the stuff of myth, not history. In belonging to the remote past but not to a very clearly defined historical period, Arthurian legend had allowed even the medieval writer a similar scope; the author of *Sir Gawain and the Green Knight* placed Arthur's Camelot firmly in a fourteenth-century courtly setting; Malory seems to have imagined his characters as moving in a world distant in date but in other respects similar to the fifteenth century in which he was writing. Though since the Second World War there has been a small spate of historical treatments of the story of Arthur, placing him in post-Roman Britain, these novels represent a new departure in Arthurian literature, and sacrifice the symbolic potential of the story to an attempt to recreate the ancient world in realistic detail.

The richness of Malory's *Le Morte Darthur* as a source for the later writer derived also in some part from its moral and religious dimensions. The noble ideal is founded on the Pentecostal Oath, the high quest is the quest of the Grail; yet Arthur's 'most noble Christian realm' (Book XX, chap. xvii), though it is a realm in which Christian ideals are recognised, gives no descriptive detail about medieval religious practices. *Le Morte Darthur* is non-sectarian, non-doctrinal. Malory has no sermon to preach, only the underlying hope and belief that divine forgiveness and the bliss of heaven await those who have loved well and repented of their sinful lives. The awe-inspiring mysteries of the Grail quest are so deeply symbolic that their Christian trappings fall from them, leaving them to signify, beyond the search for a holy object, beyond a specifically Christian revelation, the unceasing human aspiration towards something more than worldly gratification. As the stories provide a medium for the expression of such aspirations, so they encompass the difficulty of achieving them; the distractions, the conflicts, the jealousies that may make the attainment of ideals impossible. Malory's *Le Morte Darthur* shows the unending struggle for the establishment of the just society, and the factors that war ceaselessly against it. That Malory's society had its basis in Christian ideals and practices rather than in pagan ones, again made it more closely relevant to the concerns of nineteenth-century society in particular. It suggested nostalgically an age of faith untorn by sectarian religious conflict or theological argument, an age of simple trust in God. In turn, this dimension of the Arthurian stories, as with some other elements such as the dominant themes of love and chivalry, lent itself to parodic and 'debunking' reactions as readily in nineteenth-century versions as in twentieth-century ones.

For the nineteenth-century reader, the Arthurian world also contained a recognisable social as distinct from political structure. The 'honourable society', the noble fellowship of good knights bound together by loyalty and high endeavour, had an appeal for highly polarised Victorian society, not least because of its predominantly masculine nature. Morris and Burne-Jones, while undergraduates, inspired by *Le Morte Darthur*, planned to found a little quasi-religious society of their own, to be called the Order of Sir Galahad, to perform noble acts of charity and self-sacrifice in the East End of London, until the Pre-Raphaelite Brotherhood claimed their allegiance instead, and they dedicated themselves to art and lost their enthusiasm for religion. Arthurian society as depicted by Malory was a society of equals, dedicated to a shared ideal. In it, fair play was highly valued, and justice might be made to prevail. It was, furthermore, a society which recognised the ideal of the gentleman, a concept of great importance to the class-conscious Victorians, and which found its embodiment, above all, in Tristram and Lancelot.

In *Le Morte Darthur*, Malory shows us the building up and establishing of a noble institution, and its subsequent destruction as the result of conflicting loyalties. Arthur's dilemma, caught as he is between the duty of maintaining a just rule and a stable realm, cost what it may, and the demands of his private life, can be as well appreciated in modern as it was in medieval times. His lament, when the downfall of the Round Table seems imminent, tersely makes his priorities apparent: '—wit you well my heart was never so heavy as it is now, and much more I am sorrier for my good knights' loss than for the loss of my fair queen; for queens I might have enow, but such a fellowship of good knights shall never be together in no company.' (Book XX, chap. ix.) His total commitment to the kingdom, as events move inexorably towards disaster, is the outcome of the painful choice that he is forced to make between public and private obligations. The situation as Malory presents it reveals the choice that confronts him in startling terms, pushing its implications to their furthest limits, but in Arthur's devotion to the 'fellowship of good knights' and his indifference, ultimately, to his queen, we recognise the timeless problem of balancing professional commitments against personal claims. In Malory's story, the problems of the loveless marriage and of love outside marriage, so troubling to the nineteenth and early twentieth century, could be seen and distanced, in his tolerant and humane vision of the 'love in those days'. His lightness of touch sketches, but sketches brilliantly, the situations, the emotions, the passionate exchanges, as part of the larger whole, the rise and fall of Arthur and the Round Table. The later writer, aware of the modern audience's desire for psychological realism, has been able to explore more fully the states of mind and emotion that the situations might evoke.

The power and appeal of the Arthurian stories also derive from the rich variety of themes embedded in them, and made accessible by Malory. For the nineteenth century the theme of love was particularly important, and Malory's detached and tolerant attitude to the loves of Lancelot and Guenevere, Tristram and Iseult, in his deeper preoccupation with the fortunes of the Round Table as an institution, allowed scope for many different approaches to the situations of the pairs of lovers. Malory's unromantic treatment of the story of Tristram, for example, gives the later writer his opportunity. All Malory has to say of the momentous occasion when the lovers drink the love-potion together is: 'But by that their drink was in their bodies, they loved each other so well that never their love departed for weal neither for woe. . . . And thus it happed the love first betwixt Sir Tristram and La Beale Isoud, the which love never departed the days of their life. So then they sailed. . . .' (Book VIII, chap. xxiv.) The essentials of the story are there, together with an acceptance of the naturalness of love and particularly of its physical expression, uncomplicated by moral censure, and without romantic adornment. The same may be said of the story of Lancelot and Guenevere and of Elaine of Astolat: Malory offered later writers a model from a moral point of view as well as an acceptable means of writing about passionate love in an age of great sensitivity on the subject. Though the misdeeds of Mrs Gaskell's Ruth or Hardy's Tess might cause a minor outcry, it was possible to write about sexual relationships unacceptable to society when they were set in a more remote and morally neutral context, and when the protagonists were not of the present day. The exploration of the unhappy love-situations of Arthurian legend could also provide a corrective to the insipid romances of much contemporary fiction, while it satisfied the popular demand for love-stories.

The theme of loyalty, so important in Malory, linked with that of chivalry, also had a strong appeal for nineteenth-century readers. The conflict of loyalties and its implications, suffered in particular by Lancelot, torn between his duty to his king and to Guenevere, as 'faith unfaithful kept him falsely true', could be well understood. The 'cash nexus' seemed to be obliterating the subtler and traditional loyalties of an earlier society; and the picture of an age when a man owed his obligations to the king, to the man who had made him knight, and to his brothers in arms, in a clear-cut framework of relationships, had a nostalgic appeal. Patterns of male friendship, so strong in the nineteenth century, found their prototype in *Le Morte Darthur*, in such relationships as that of Lancelot with Gareth and Lavayne. The chivalry embodied in the Pentecost oath, which all the members of the Round Table renewed each year, 'always to do ladies, damosels, and gentlewomen succour, upon pain of death', and apparent in such episodes as Lancelot's almost quixotically generous dealing with Meliagaunt, also had a strong imaginative appeal. Though it was obviously a feature of an archaic society, it could still to some extent provide a workable ideal and a model for attitudes to women in a later age, as fact and fiction testify.

The theme of destiny, which binds together all the stories, had attractions for the nineteenth-century reader less strongly felt today, and strengthened the sense of the appropriateness of the stories as a medium for contemporary meanings. Destiny still seemed to be guiding Britain towards a great and glorious future under a powerful monarch, and in an age of strong nationalistic and patriotic feeling, Arthurian literature was in accord with popular sentiment. Malory's Arthur is destined to build a great kingdom and an admirable society, embodying the ideals of his age; but the warnings that the stories also carry as to what imperils such a society could also be seen to have relevance in the nineteenth century. Arthur as national hero embodied for the Victorians the popular masculine ideal, an earlier exponent of 'muscular Christianity'. The tendency to see the hand of God in human affairs must have made more satisfying the strong patterns of destiny in the Arthurian stories, for the prophecies work themselves out as the consequences of wrong-doing do in a Victorian novel. Mordred survives the attempt to drown him with all the children born on May-day, and is cast up, preserved and eventually brought to court 'toward the end of the Death of Arthur'. 'Our deeds determine us'; and there is no escaping the consequences of former evil-doing. Guenevere fulfils Merlin's prophecy that she will not be wholesome for Arthur to take to wife, 'for that Launcelot should love her, and she him again.' Galahad comes at last to bring healing to King Pellam. The doom that befalls the protagonists is not the result of mere ill-fortune, but the direct or indirect consequence of folly or obstinacy or sinful deeds, as with the birth of Mordred. The most powerful stories are those in which the patterns work themselves out in the long-term, in which generations are involved, and in which earlier choices give rise to unpredictable consequences.

Malory's great work made apparent, to a society that prided itself on present achievement, yet looked back yearningly to former glory, ways in which the Arthurian material could be given political, religious and social interpretations for the expression of contemporary public or private meanings. Without the intrinsic power of the stories, which Malory allows us to sense beneath the surface of his narrative, they would not have been worth re-telling; without the elements of myth in them, whether recognised or not, they could not have continued to reverberate in the imagination in their new forms. Arthur is more than other kings; more than simply a national hero. The life of King Alfred, 'England's darling', could indeed outshine Arthur's in splendour of achievement, in courage and wisdom, as in human interest; yet Alfred's life, lacking the dimension of myth, lacks what makes Arthur's of timeless significance. For Arthur is the hero appointed by destiny who, like Tristram and Galahad later, must come to fulfil the divine purpose, whatever man may do to hinder him. Arthur must be conceived and born, despite the attempts of Igraine and her husband to avert their fate. The unknown child, reared in obscurity, later asserts his unique claim to his title, to his kingly function and to the instruments of his power. Consciously or unconsciously we can ourselves identify with the boy who steps forward to show his newly acquired adult competence and status, to claim his place in his society, and to move into the wider world of struggle and responsibility. We recognise the story of the birth of the hero as myth, placing Arthur beside those biblical and classical characters for whom also prophecies decreed a special destiny, which no human contrivance could frustrate, singled out to fulfil a unique purpose. As Charles Kingsley suggests in his story of the Argonauts in *The Heroes*, 'Each of us has a Golden Fleece to seek, and dragons to slay before we win it', and we like to discern the workings of destiny in our own lives through the medium of such stories. Arthur, the Once and Future King, though no one can tell the time and place and manner of his coming again, takes his rightful place among the heroes of myth, not only because of the mystery of his origins, but also because of his death and disappearance. Though his reign ends in the destruction of the realm and in his death, yet his death is not defeat, because it is not extinction. As Malory says, 'here in this world he changed his life'. (Book XXI, chap. vii.)

Myths express inner meaning through outward occurrences. We recognise in the story of Balin and Balan a story of symbolic significance, as Balin the striker of the Dolorous Blow brings death and disaster wherever he goes. There is no escaping the doom that is prophesied, but the destruction that Balin brings about is not random: it results in the death of those who are loved best. To amend the evil unknowingly brought about by Balin, the goodness of Galahad is to become operative, though in ways unforseeable to men. Without such hope as this story holds out, life would be intolerable, yet it is a hope not necessarily dependent on religious faith. The Waste Land may symbolise for us the devastation of the First World War, the ravages of industrialisation, the spiritual poverty of modern society, the totalitarian regime, or the alienation of the individual soul from any kind of spiritual reality or values, but however we interpret the symbol, in looking for deliverance we reinforce our hope through literature.

We recognise in the Grail myth a story of unquestioned power. The elements of the story capture the imagination: the sacred and mysterious object, the vision of which can only be glimpsed fleetingly by most; the mystery that chooses to whom it will reveal itself and that rejects the unworthy, however well qualified they may seem; the final achievement, 'costing not less than everything', of the ultimate merging of the human with the divine. It is the type of every quest that demands total singleness of purpose and indifference to ordinary worldly considerations. It reassures us that the sacrifice is indeed worthwhile, whatever it may be; it consoles us if we fail, for few can succeed, and to have made the attempt, even if unsuccessfully, is its own reward. In the failure of Lancelot, the 'best knyght of the world', to achieve the quest, and his rebuffing and exclusion from full experience of the Grail vision, we recognise the humiliation, disappointment and frustration of our own experience of rejection.

The Grail myth lends itself to refashioning in many different modes: it can assimilate the magical, or take on the religious conventions of the society for whom it is retold, as in the medieval versions. It can draw into itself other myths, as in Charles Williams's *Taliessin through Logres*. It can be fitted into a twentieth-century setting, as in John Cowper Powys's *A Glastonbury Romance*. It can take on private significances, as in the poems of William Morris, and it can survive parody. Whatever its origins, in ancient fertility rite, Celtic myth or Christian tradition, the pattern of the story and the symbols around which it is organised make it a valid mode of expression even for the present day. Indeed, it may be said to be the dominant Arthurian myth of the first half of the twentieth century, for reasons which are not hard to discern.

From the predominantly Christian ethos of the Grail myth we turn to the entirely secular story of Tristram and Iseult, which perhaps more than any other appealed to the late nineteenth and early twentieth century. Part of its appeal lies in our recognition of the chance happenings of real life in the unlucky accident of the drinking of the love-potion, its bittersweet consequences and the inseparability of joy and sorrow, sex and death. The romantic perfection of this overwhelming love is underlined by the irony of its social inacceptability. At a deeper level, too, the story exerts its power over the imagination as a story of frustrated childhood longings.[3] It can be interpreted as a story about the child's subconscious longing for merger with his maternal first love, and his sadness at having to renounce it. Traces of this underlying meaning come to the surface in Arnold's *Tristram and Iseult*, in which Tristram longs for Iseult of Ireland to come to him on his death-bed, like a sick child waiting for his mother; and in which the lovers' simultaneous death unites them at last. Such underlying levels of meaning, apparent in a post-Freudian age, intensify the power of the myth and give it its strongest hold over the imagination. Though of course without perceiving these inherent meanings, the Victorians preferred this love-story to that of Lancelot, and found it more manageable. The love-potion which brought about the misfortunes of Tristram, Iseult and indeed of King Mark, too, to a large extent diminished the responsibility of the guilty lovers, and made their sin easier to condone than that of Launcelot and Guenevere.

The power of the Arthurian stories, their memorability and imaginative appeal, depend not only on the myths that structure them, but also on the motifs and symbols which, though they may originate in a primitive world and belong to an earlier age, yet often still have their modern equivalents. The sword in the stone awaits the child born to be king, who alone can draw it and possess it; each individual's gifts are unique. The incident has its counterpart in many other hero-myths: Perseus is given his winged sandals and other vital equipment with his appointed task by the goddess Athene, for example, but the pattern is similar. The sword that Arthur draws is to defend his land, to maintain right and to establish justice. It is a symbol of manly power attained and assumed, which involves dedication to the task ordained. The power to draw it distinguishes Arthur from his rival Kay: there can be no disputing his superiority now, but the moment of revelation permits the disclosure of Arthur's previously obscure origins in a dramatically effective scene. The larger pattern of destiny within which all have their place now becomes apparent.

Around the figure of Arthur there gather the characteristics needful for a superman. His mysterious origins; his charisma which enables him to draw all good knights to him and to establish the kingdom; the sword and scabbard—emblems not only of his calling but also of supernatural protection—and his final departing in the barge to Avalon make him more than other men. So, more than other kings, he gathers to himself hero-stories as he gathers noble knights to his court. That he does not die, that he will come again, is the fitting end to such a life.

We recognise the 'rite de passage', the graduation ceremony in the drawing of the sword from the stone. In the same way we perceive the symbolic significance of the love-potion, as we respond to the bewildered horror of the irrevocable moment when Tristram and Iseult drink together. Indeed, the symbol of the love-potion has acquired increased imaginative and functional importance in the course of time, since in some earlier versions of the story it did not play a crucial part. The symbols in Arthurian story give pictorial and objective form to inner experience whether emotional, intellectual or spiritual, even if without the conscious intention of the medieval author, and we respond to them intuitively, rather than by a conscious process of decoding. Their meaning may be almost irrecoverable, or may be ambiguous as with the Grail, but we feel the power of the symbol nevertheless. For Malory, as for most medieval writers, the swords wielded by the protagonists may be mere tools of the trade, or they may have magical properties, or they may have symbolic significance, but it is rarely that their meaning is defined, though all swords suggest both martial and sexual prowess or aggressiveness. The acquisition of a sword brings literal and symbolical meanings close together: manliness is put on with it. But, though we may only sense, rather than precisely define, the meaning of the images, their resonance is often increased rather than lessened in consequence.

Traditional stories may work at different levels, whatever form they take, enabling us to objectify and sometimes to conceptualise through imagery, those experiences and impulses of which we are not normally fully aware. Through them, we tell ourselves what we think, whether we bother to decode the message or not. Such stories deal with the deeper recurrent patterns of life and family relationships, often unrecognised or unacknowledged: the sibling rivalries, the resentments and fears, the aggressive impulses and guilts and envyings that we usually endeavour to suppress or deny. These patterns are perhaps more effectively given expression through myth and symbolic imagery than through the realistic, particularising detail or psychological analysis of the modern novel. The form of the Arthurian stories, as distinct from that of epic, or of much modern fiction, can by its very nature more closely represent common human experience through its symbolic patterns. The romantic hero who has still to prove himself, the 'rites de passage' that he undergoes, the quest that he undertakes—as in the stories of Arthur, of Gareth, of the Grail— mirror our own struggles and partial failures, as well as our achievement and recognition.

These stories depend not so much on a simplification of experience as on a penetration to a lower level of consciousness. Like other myths, they are often concerned with self-realisation and with the process of individuation, processes which are most effectively shown symbolically through the adventures of representative figures rather than through the analysis of highly individualised characters. Their universal significances and inner meanings are apprehended through the outer event rather than made explicit, and as with most symbolic stories, our attention is often directed to the relationships between members of different generations. In the dark begettings of Arthur, of Mordred and of Galahad, the sins or at least the actions of the fathers are visited upon the children over a long time span, and usually it is to the child rather than to the father that our attention is directed. Arthur's distress at the untoward event of Mordred's birth is of much less importance than Mordred's consequent enmity and vicious resentment towards his father. Lancelot begets Galahad, and after his recovery from the consequences of his horrified realisation of the trick that destiny has played on him, he is no longer—to all intents and purposes—seen as a father. But his son, by contrast with Mordred, becomes in course of time not a destroyer but a redeemer of his society. He surpasses his father as a son should do, but in his own individual way through holiness rather than in deeds of arms. The uncertain outcome of each begetting is only seen after much time has passed, and with Mordred and Galahad, the one balances the other. The failure to achieve parenthood brings its own troubles: Guenevere's childlessness makes her vulnerable, Arthur's lack of a legitimate heir imperils his kingdom, Iseult's childlessness—as also with Guenevere—imprisons her in that stage of immature, almost adolescent passion in which Elaine of Astolat dies, unfulfilled. The stories show what happens, and how widespread the consequences may be, when the normal life-patterns of love, marriage and parenthood are broken. The sequential, developmental structure of the stories gives them a hidden purposiveness and strength, as the long-term results of earlier actions make themselves apparent.

Since the revival of interest in Arthurian legend, writers have found in it steadily developing and changing possibilities for the expression of symbolic meaning. The nineteenth century needed a new mythology, and found in these stories a comprehensive symbol-system often valid for us still in the late twentieth century, as the diverse art forms that have resulted testify, ranging from Wagner's *Tristan und Isolde* and *Parsifal* in music, Burne-Jones's tapestries and pictures in art, and Tennyson's *Idylls* in verse, to the many modern cinematic versions of today. Arthurian stories in the nineteenth century had the great advantage of being popular, not associated with an aristocratic educational tradition, and so had a special appeal that classical mythology lacked. Arthur's origins, moreover, legendary though they are, have made his figure particularly meaningful for the British, especially in times of heightened national consciousness. The name of Arthur suggests the glorious past, with its chivalry and spiritual idealism. In local tradition, Winchester and Tintagel and Glastonbury have continued to cherish their ancient associations with his story.[4] The national significance of the legend, which has always appealed to the imagination, is emphasised by the superstition that Arthur will come again in time of special need.[5] He still represents a patriotic ideal, stable in its essentials, though shifting in its superficial details through the centuries. For the fourteenth-century poet in *Sir Gawain and the Green Knight*, who looked back to an unspecified but glorious time when Arthur and his court were all 'in their first age', and for Spenser who saw Arthur as the embodiment of all the princely virtues, as for Tennyson who represented him (in the words of Hallam Tennyson in introducing the *Idylls*) as the 'pure, generous, tender, brave, human-hearted Arthur', he was, as he still remains, a significant figure.

In the image of the Round Table with all that it implies, Arthurian legend provides a basis for symbolism that no classical myth can rival. While in Greek mythology, Jason and the Argonauts and Odysseus and his crew are in some ways comparable, since they are both great leaders with courageous bands of warriors, it can be seen that they lack the symbolic potential of Arthur and his knights. They come from a remoter world, a different society, and their fellowship is not based upon a Christian ethic. They are less differentiated; their relationships are strictly limited. The organisation of the Round Table, on the other hand, gives the story of Arthur a firm basis in a recognisable, close-knit social structure, the lives of whose members are inextricably interrelated and sometimes individualised. Arthur's court provides a nucleus, a stable centre from which members of the society can go out to engage in their various adventures. The Round Table is thus a complex yet also adaptable symbol which can be related to modern society, and which is capable of sustaining very diverse variations and drawing to itself many new elements.

The Arthurian stories offer us—now, as they have always done—an alternative world in the modern, particularised sense of the word. It is not simply an imaginary world such as Burne-Jones depicted, whether centred on Camelot,

Mark's court or Sarras, but a world which can accommodate deviations from the generally accepted norm. One can see that in the nineteenth and early twentieth century, for example, the world of Camelot, by allowing the problem of love outside marriage and the changing attitudes to moral questions to be aired, provided a kind of safety valve. The Arthurian stories lend themselves to the creation of liberating fantasies, sometimes embodying ideals, as in Tennyson's *Idylls*, sometimes making it possible to celebrate those features of contemporary life that may actually be seen as ideal in themselves. Conversely, Arthurian literature in such works as Robert Nye's *Merlin*, may also furnish a medium for fantasies of a totally different kind, thus affording a channel for the expression of some less presentable features of modern life. The stories and their themes and motifs can equally readily be adapted to the expression of sexual, political or spiritual experience. Their characters, as human beings for the most part without superhuman powers, whose motivation, conflicts and relationships are still recognisable today, can be transposed into modern situations. Camelot itself has taken on a new significance as a political image in the United States.

The comprehensiveness of the Arthurian themes allows them to accommodate all the passions. Unlike, for example, the world of Tolkien, so brilliantly realised in *The Lord of the Rings*, the Arthurian world finds a place both for *agape* and *eros*; it includes mystical religion, romantic love, parent–child relationships and the faithful devotion of friends, as well as the unbridled demands of lust. Thus even the alternative world that it constructs can take shape in very different, even sharply opposed ways, asserting itself as opposed to social convention in its glorification of illicit love, while also providing a channel for religious idealism. In the Grail episodes, the transcendent religious experience which goes beyond the comprehension or the expectations of conventional, everyday religion can be represented, as in Charles Williams's poems, and in his and C. S. Lewis's novels. Through Arthurian themes, the tension between the ideal and the real finds expression, while Victorian solemnities, medieval absurdities and the exaggerated romanticism of both the nineteenth and the twentieth centuries can be put in their place by burlesque and parody.

The Arthurian stories to which attention has been directed since the mid-nineteenth century are of course selected ones. We cannot use them all. Some seem much more significant, because their symbolic meaning is more flexible or more relevant to our society. We do not make much of Arthur's Roman wars, or of the healing of Sir Urry, and Sir Gareth's story has been neglected by most writers. But the fact that the attention of authors and artists has been drawn to a variety of different stories, from the birth and childhood of Arthur to his death, has meant that the total, cumulative, shared experience of the Arthurian world in our time (as in the Middle Ages) is both extensive and potent. It has been and to some extent yet may be a communal fantasy, of which such motifs as the sword in the stone and the love of Tristram and Iseult, for example, are often still resonant, when many biblical and classical allusions are no longer recognised or meaningful. So comprehensive is the Arthurian world, that we can go in it where we will and take what we will from it.

The search for a new mythology in the nineteenth century which led many writers to Arthurian legend was accompanied by much critical argument about the proper subject matter of poetry. There seems to have been widespread agreement at the mid-century that such topics as would arouse sympathy were to be preferred, and that those which were rich in human interest were most appropriate for the contemporary writer. Arthurian legend could supply these in abundance: Arthur and the problems of his realm, the tragic love of Tristram and Iseult and the dedicated quest of Galahad, for example, provided admirable subjects for psychological exploration through the medium of dramatic monologue, poetic drama or extended narrative. The diversity of the characters—Arthur, Lancelot, Galahad, Mordred, Guenevere, Elaine of Astolat—and the fact that though types, each could be individualised and indeed, even clothed in modern dress, psychologically speaking, offered great advantages. It was not difficult to relate the predicaments of the protagonists to contemporary experience, since they already inhabited a moral world with some of the complexity of real life, a world which went beyond any simple opposition or conflict between the forces of good and evil. This interest in the characters of Arthurian stories was a necessary stage in the evolution towards a recognition of their underlying and wider symbolic significances. In an age increasingly aware of the importance of myth and mythology, the stories eventually came to be recognised as a source of still meaningful myths that could be separated from pseudo-history, romance and trivial fantasy to communicate the insights of twentieth-century poets. The First World War, the Great War to those who fought or lived through it, helped to direct attention to an aspect of the Arthurian legend not previously found significant—the Waste Land. In the desolation and devastation of Flanders it was not difficult to see a Terre Gastée; nor was the term inappropriate for the more metaphorical sterility apparent to such as T. S. Eliot in western society in the nineteen-twenties. The myth of the Grail supplied symbols and structure for entirely new creative work, such as that of John Cowper Powys and Charles Williams, which could use the motifs freely to represent states of mind and of spirit, both individual and communal.

A quite distinct use of Arthurian legend in the twentieth century has developed, furthermore, in the work of such writers as James Joyce and David Jones, who have found in it a fund of motifs and symbols. Though their main concern lies elsewhere, there may be an interwoven strand of Arthurian reference, as in *Finnegans Wake*, the story of Tristram and Iseult weaves in and out, while in David Jones's *In Parenthesis*, Arthurian references (mostly from Malory, but also from the Welsh Triads) are interwoven with biblical allusions to provide both a national historical and a more general background to the experience of trench warfare in 1915. Only with a great and familiar mythology can such reference be both accessible and effective; liberation from the constraints of specific Arthurian narrative produces distinguished work within the familiar tradition.

In the late twentieth century, idealism is out of fashion, or has so shifted its shape as to be less easily recognised. Romance has almost entirely lost its intellectual respectability. Malory's words on the death of Arthur, 'here in this world he changed his life', are true in another sense, however. He is still very much a living figure in such quasi-historical novels as Mary Stewart's trilogy and Catherine Christian's tale, which place him in the context of post-Roman Britain and endeavour to recreate something of the actual background of the fifth century. Though the treatment for the most part represents a return to literalism by contrast with those earlier twentieth-century works which make symbolic use of Arthurian motifs, these very competent novels maintain interest in his story, as did the medieval romances. Increasingly, however, Merlin is the dominant figure in recent Arthurian writing, and this is surely significant of cultural changes: we have left behind not only the idealism of the nineteenth century, but also its insistent matter-of-factness. Though we reject miracles, we accept magic, along with sex and violence, as a conventional ingredient of our popular fictions. Science fiction and horror films have made commonplace what was once incredible and unacceptable. Merlin can do more now than animate mustard-pots, and modern readers do not demand rational explanations. Merlin may be symbolic of the powers of the human mind, with which the popular imagination is now so patently fascinated, as the renewed interest in the occult and in transcendental meditation, for example, demonstrates. As we recognise the need to take account of our power over our environment with its alarming implications, and of those subconscious urges which we can neither fully understand nor control, we tell ourselves new stories. In them, we no longer focus on Arthur as super-ego, but on Merlin as id. Merlin, imprisoned in his cave at the end of the story, indeed, can be seen as an image for the taming of the unbridled power of the subconscious. But as we struggle to explore and to understand our own natures more comprehensively, now often turning towards our evil impulses rather than to our nobler aspirations, the story of Arthur still remains a source of vital symbols, while it awaits another great author or artist to give it renewed life and fresh significance.

1

The Return of Arthur

Nineteenth-Century British Medievalism and Arthurian Tradition

In the final pages of Sir Thomas Malory's late fifteenth-century *Morte Darthur*, King Arthur bids farewell to Sir Bedivere—and to English medieval romance— as he is carried from the battlefield to a barge destined for Avalon, where he may be healed of his wounds. Although Malory records that the king died and was buried at Glastonbury, he also narrates the alternative legend that Arthur survived and awaits return—the once and future king. After three centuries of banishment from literature truly Arthurian in focus and inspiration, Arthur reappeared in England early in the nineteenth century, and he must certainly have felt himself to have chosen an unlikely time and place for his second coming. Industrialisation, urbanisation, utilitarianism, democratisation, along with modern science and rational skepticism, seemed to be extirpating all traces of the world familiar to Arthur or to the writers who celebrated him throughout the Middle Ages. The environmental change is succinctly sketched in Gerard Manley Hopkins' description of the once gracefully medieval Oxford, wearing in the nineteenth century 'a base and brickish skirt' ('Duns Scotus's Oxford', 1879). Long before Hopkins' observation, brickish factories dominated landscapes, and man found himself inhabiting not only a different physical world, but a new and frequently bewildering spiritual realm as well. Hence Matthew Arnold compared modern man to an inexperienced child, shorn of the secure religious faith represented by the Middle Ages, yet lingering fearfully in the shade of the medieval monastery in which he could no longer dwell ('Stanzas from the Grande Chartreuse', 1855).

Despite an external and internal landscape apparently hostile to romance, Arthur returned to English literature after more than three hundred years with an intensity remarkable for both the quality and the quantity of works produced. Even those who avoided specifically Arthurian subjects—Robert Browning, for example—were influenced by Arthurian concepts such as the quest and the chivalric code. From Alfred Tennyson's early Arthurian poems published in the 1830s and 1840s, through William Morris' *Defence of Guenevere* volume published after mid-century, to Algernon Charles Swinburne's *Tristram of Lyonesse* and *The Tale of Balen* appearing in the last two decades of the century, Arthurian materials fascinated important writers throughout the Victorian era. The major literary work achieved by Arthur's return, Tennyson's *Idylls of the King* (1859–85), occupied the poet for more than fifty years and

15

came closer than any other work of the age to being an epic and a national poem.

This Victorian enthusiasm, contrasting sharply with the preceding century's general lack of interest in the Middle Ages (Voltaire acerbically judged the life of medieval men to be of no greater interest than the activities of bears and wolves), vividly signalled Arthur's second coming. Although between Malory's romance, printed in 1485, and Tennyson's publication in 1832, Arthurian works had appeared in England in an inconstant but unbroken flow, these works generally had little connection with medieval tradition other than names or occasional episodes familiar from the Middle Ages. By and large these Renaissance and Enlightenment works, such as Spenser's epic *Faerie Queene*, Dryden's dramatic opera *King Arthur*, or Fielding's play *Tom Thumb*, simply wove Arthur or his famous knights into a tapestry of situations and events remote from Arthurian stories and concerns. Malory's romance, the major collection of Arthurian legends available in English, having appeared frequently between Caxton's edition in 1485 and Stansby's corrupt version of Caxton in 1634, thereafter remained unpublished and was mainly known only to antiquarians until the nineteenth century.

The resurrection of Malory, and of Arthurian legend in general, may be largely credited to the work of such antiquarians as Richard Hurd, Thomas Percy, Thomas Warton, George Ellis, Sir Walter Scott, and the more scholarly Joseph Ritson. Their painstaking labours recovered medieval romance from obscurity and brought it to a large body of cultured readers. While their editing and other studies may be said to have stimulated the first serious historical and linguistic interest in the literary documents of the Middle Ages, they also focused attention on medieval romance as distinguished literature which had influenced the giants—Chaucer, Shakespeare, Milton, and Spenser. Moreover, the eighteenth-century antiquarians made modern writers aware of models other than the classics, thereby expanding the subject matter and stimulating the inventiveness of contemporary literature. Renewed interest in Malory, specifically, may be traced to Thomas Warton's *Observations on the Faerie Queene* (1754, revised 1762), which described Spenser's indebtedness to the *Morte Darthur*, among other medieval romances, for much of the imaginative richness of his epic.[1]

As a result of the antiquarian zeal of the eighteenth century, Malory was rediscovered with such enthusiasm that the *Morte Darthur* appeared in two separate editions in 1816, another in 1817, and a fourth in 1858. Though the printing of 1817, introduced by Robert Southey, was rather expensive, the editions of 1816 were relatively inexpensive and aimed at a popular audience. The effect of these publications was to take Malory beyond the domain of antiquarians, into the hands of poets such as Tennyson and Morris, thus effectively transporting Arthur back from Avalon and restoring him to prominence in English letters.

This revival of interest in Arthur was in Britain the most concentrated literary aspect of the pervasive phenomenon of nineteenth-century medievalism, which registered in the work of linguists and editors, historians, architects, painters, and writers throughout Europe, and to a lesser extent even in America. While the efforts to retrieve the past through studying folklore and literature and emulating medieval plastic arts may be seen as a self-conscious historicism—and even, in the case of Germany, as an attempt to recreate a nationalistic heritage—the broad medievalism of the Romantic period began as varied reactions against neo-classical symmetry, decorum, and order. Ironically, although eighteenth-century novelists, for example, had used medieval (or pseudo-medieval) machinery to intrigue their readers with the exotic or unfamiliar—stimulating terror with dungeons, ancient curses, and haunted castles—aspects of the Middle Ages became increasingly popular and meaningful to the nineteenth-century as they became more familiar, as the influence of medieval architecture visibly testified. Beginning in such eccentricity as Horace Walpole's Strawberry Hill—a plain Georgian house fantastically remodelled after 1750 with battlements, twisted chimneys, and quatrefoil windows—nineteenth-century architectural medievalism soon domesticated the strange Gothic-style banks and railway stations.

Such emulation often created ridiculous and sham effects, as when William Beckford's artificial 'ruin' of a convent on the grounds of Fonthill Abbey promoted a trend in canvas and plaster 'ruins' as fashionable garden adornments. Tastes for picturesque decay were frequently satirised, as in Thomas Love Peacock's novel *Melincourt* (1817), where one half of the family castle is 'fast improving into a picturesque ruin' while the other is 'degenerating, in its interior at least, into a comfortable modern dwelling'. Yet the fad for artificial Gothic attested some significant attitudes toward contemporary life. In Dickens' *Great Expectations* (1861), for example, which explores the effects of materialism on dreams, aspirations, fellowship, and love, Mr Wemmick's Gothicised home symbolically contrasts his private fulfilment with society's general sterility. Efficient, impassive, and impersonal in Mr Jaggers' city offices, Wemmick metamorphoses as he nears his suburban cottage, embellished and fortified like a Gothic castle. With its sham Gothic windows and a Gothic door almost too small to be functional, it flaunts all utilitarian principles. Its most significant feature is a moat spanned by a drawbridge emphatically excluding the mechanical, material values of the city from this medievalised home, within which filial tenderness, love, and good cheer prevail.

When such artificial, even bizarre, experiments with Gothic design and decoration as Strawberry Hill, Fonthill Abbey, and Wemmick's 'castle' evolved into a revival of genuinely Gothic architecture led by figures such as Augustus Welby Pugin, the trend was informed by painstaking study of authentic buildings and decorative design of the sort revealed by John Ruskin's detailed drawings. Most proponents of the Gothic revival were motivated by aesthetic sensitivity and regard for ancestral achievements, but for some, especially toward the end of the century, this enthusiasm for old architecture was only empty nostalgia that belied the devastating changes in modern life. Thus in Thomas Hardy's *Jude the Obscure* (1895) workmen's efforts to preserve the medieval structures of Christminster (Oxford) in a world increasingly crass, ruthless, and uprooted from religious and social traditions seem increasingly ironic. Jude's idealisation of the learning and culture represented by the medieval university begins to change when, on his first morning in the city, he reads the 'architectural pages', seeing in these 'historical documents' the failure of the 'wounded, broken' buildings in the 'deadly struggle against years, weather, and man'. The efforts which became widespread among Victorians to preserve and restore Gothic buildings here appear to be vain endeavours to stop the clock: 'Moreover he perceived that at best only copying, patching and imitating went on here; which he fancied to be owing to some temporary and local cause. He did not at that time see that mediaevalism was as dead as a fern-leaf in a lump of coal; that other developments were shaping in the world around him, in which Gothic architecture and its associations had no place. The deadly animosity of contemporary logic and vision towards so much of what he held in reverence was not yet revealed to him' (II.–ii).

But between the 1830s and the darkening vision of Hardy, writers enthusiastically discussed Gothic design and plastic arts as an aspect of larger philosophical matters, as in Ruskin's famous celebration of medieval variety, originality, and vitality in *The Stones of Venice* ('On the Nature of Gothic', 1853). Pugin's architectural study, *Contrasts: or, a Parallel between the Noble Edifices of the Middle Ages, and Corresponding Buildings of the Present Day; Shewing the Present Decay of Taste (1836)*, implicitly concerned more than 'taste', for his paired illustrations showed that modern social and ethical standards underlay the decline in architectural integrity. As Kenneth Clark observes, in Pugin's juxtaposed drawings of a town in 1440 and in 1840, 'the contrast is brought home with extraordinary ingenuity, not only by the immediately forbidding air of the modern town—its jail well in the foreground, its forest of chimneys where once there rose a forest of spires—but by the most subtle details. Only after some minutes do we notice that the pleasure-ground is made over the hallowed dead, that there are railings round the new monument and a tollgate on the iron bridge.' A second pair of pictures similarly contrasts medieval and modern drinking fountains. 'Freely, from the rich Gothic fountain, a robust young man is drawing a cup of sweet water. But from the foul modern pump a policeman has driven away a wan urchin who has come with his battered can . . . ; while another policeman lounges sardonically in the door of the police-court—and indeed his colleague's action is unnecessary, for the handle of the pump is fastened with an immense padlock.'[2] The altered physical face of England overtly testified to cultural changes less concrete but no less real.

Such cultural change was the subject matter of much of Sir Walter Scott's fiction. His immensely popular metrical romances and 'medieval' novels (more than a half dozen, from *Ivanhoe* in 1819 to his last work, *Castle Dangerous* in 1832), may in part be credited with stimulating the medieval interests of the century, but they must also be seen as his shrewd efforts to tap currents originating elsewhere. To a great extent the popularity of Scott's medieval works grew out of nostalgia—both his and his readers'—a desire to freeze, if only in literature, an essentially familiar way of life which was rapidly changing in the face of shifts from rural to urban dwelling, from agriculture and cottage crafts to mechanised industry, from secure religious faith to profoundly unsettling skepticism, from government centred in the hands of aristocracy and gentry to democracy. Scott's medieval novels memorialise a relatively static society with a defined set of values, which if imperfect, was also a known quantity attractive to nervous skeptics of change because it had survived for centuries. Admittedly, Scott's version of the Middle Ages offered fancy and local colour more than history. As A. O. J. Cockshut has observed, Scott 'was writing for a public ready to be entertained and bewitched by an unreal middle age, a public that had emancipated itself from the stock Augustan prejudices about medieval barbarism, and was now ready to adopt different misconceptions, and to be deceived in new ways.'[3]

Yet Scott's depictions, regardless of historical misrepresentations, were not escapist literature. While some of his characters represent ideals of chivalry—a concept which Scott defined for his age in the *Encyclopedia Britannica* (1818) as an individual's altruistic devotion to his society and religion—others criticised the excesses and misapplications of the chivalric code, as, for example, when Rose in *The Betrothed* questions a knight's automatically claiming marriage to a damsel he has saved. In *Count Robert of Paris* Scott shows the decay of chivalric idealism into jaded pretension. In such a work as *The Antiquary*, where he focuses on a relatively modern period, he criticises his contemporaries' superficial and warped view of the past (by showing, for instance, the discrepancy between Oldbuck's daydreams and actuality), suggesting simultaneously that in some ways the past was superior to the present and that man can probably never fully understand former ages. His depictions of changing society also show the foolish vulnerability of characters (like Arthur Philipson and his father in *Anne of Geierstein*) who fail to adapt to changes or to understand contemporary man and moment. But at the same time, Scott suggests that the past age is in many ways more engaging than the present, not only more picturesque but more noble. In his medieval world, ideals of chivalry and honour thrive, though only in rare individuals. While his romanticised past scarcely reflects the brutal actualities of life in the Middle Ages, it focuses on ideals which from the distance of centuries could be distilled from the adulterating mass of petty details of daily living.

Besides representing the ideals popularised by Scott—chivalrous individual behaviour and a comfortably traditional society—the Middle Ages for other nineteenth-century writers illustrated an ideal social, economic, and political order. Although the actualities of feudalism would scarcely have suited a society which increasingly recognised the evils of slavery and the worth of democracy, the medieval relationship between lord and vassal was easily sentimentalised as a familial bond. The worker who fulfilled his obligations with dignity was in turn succoured by a paternal lord. This envisioned relationship surely contrasted attractively with the contemporary chasm between rapacious captains of industry and exploited workers. In addition to offering the idealised notion of society organised in a secure, hierarchical economic family, the Middle Ages for such figures as John Ruskin and William Morris represented an economy desirably built upon individual craftsmanship and accomplishment rather than on mechanised uniformity, and also built upon the fellowship of trade guilds rather than on cut-throat competition. All of these economic and social notions appealed to Thomas Carlyle, who in *Past and Present* (1842) cites the medieval monastic society of Bury St. Edmunds as an instructive contrast to his age. In his view the monastic order reflected vigorous spirituality and a communal co-operation sacrificed by his own materialistic, competitive society. At the same time, the heroic leadership of the medieval Bishop Samson illustrated the merit of organising a hierarchy behind a strong, enlightened leader. Thus Carlyle's work illustrates the nineteenth-century sense that the Middle Ages could not only represent noble ideals but also offer practical lessons and patterns for modern economic and social organisation.

Many of Carlyle's contemporaries, on the other hand, saw that medieval life was not always noble, practical, or organised. At least one nineteenth-century poet described the Middle Ages not as a more civilised time, but as an age of violence. If order existed, it grew from conflicts between individual desires and visions of right. William Morris's poems based on Froissart's *Chronicle* focus on militaristic values and bloodshed. In 'The Judgment of God' (1858), for example, a knight recalls his father's instructions to slash at his foe's head 'When you catch his eyes through the helmet-slit / . . . And the Lord God give you joy of it!' To cite but one other instance, in 'The Haystack in the Floods' (1858) a damsel watches her jealous lord slay her lover: 'Right backward the knight Robert fell, / And moan'd as dogs do, being half dead, / . . . so then / Godmar turn'd grinning to his men, / Who ran, some five or six, and beat / His head to pieces at their feet.' By portraying such scenes so graphically, Morris in one sense refrained from idealising the Middle Ages. But in another sense, the very coarseness of his portrait idealised the vitality of medieval man. In contrast to Englishmen of the present age—when, Arnold declared, 'The kings of modern thought are dumb; / . . . . They have the grief men had of yore, / But they contend and cry no more' ('Stanzas from the Grande Chartreuse')—the warriors of Morris' Middle Ages acted—fiercely, violently, but more important, dynamically. And even in this vibrant, brutal world, Morris portrayed subtle psychological and emotional states.

Other writers eschewed a sentimental view of the Middle Ages for purposes of satire. Peacock, for example, was one of many who satirised the medieval enthusiasms of his age. *Nightmare Abbey* (1818), like Jane Austen's *Northanger Abbey* (1817), mocks Gothic architecture and the conventions of the Gothic novel; it also mocks the taste of Romantic writers for remote ages and quaint, exotic customs. Far more frequently, however, the medieval period served as a vehicle for satirising the present. Peacock himself seriously studied Welsh language and lore and in his novels translated or emulated medieval ballads and romances to provide aesthetic contrasts to the modern emphasis on fact and figures. In *Crochet Castle* (1831), although Peacock satirises his protagonist's excessively sentimental enthusiasm for the weapons, dress, and customs of the Middle Ages, he also allows this Mr. Chainmail (who may be seen as a parody of Scott) to condemn the commercialism of the modern world by praising the earlier era. In a central episode, characters debate whether the present state of society is inferior or superior to that of the twelfth century. Ultimately the novel resolves this issue by showing modern perspectives, whether pragmatic or transcendental, to be inadequate equipment for coping with growing materialism. Whereas contemporary currents—derisively termed 'the march of the mind'—promote greed, corruption, and loveless marriages, the medieval values of Mr Chainmail underlie his affectionate, familial relationship with his domestics and allow him to achieve genuine love and even a measure of valour.

Mr Chainmail's delight in battle-axes, coats of mail, and other physical trappings of medieval custom, though comic in its excess, suggests another level on which the Middle Ages appealed to the nineteenth century. In the midst of increasingly sombre surroundings, the quaint, remote world of the Middle Ages offered colour, elegance, ritual, and pageantry. While such ritual doubtless appealed to man's desire for order and stability, it also satisfied purely aesthetic hungers. Medieval stained glass windows and illuminated manuscripts could hardly fail to attract artists like Dante Gabriel Rossetti who painted under skies being darkened by industry. The extreme example of the Eglinton Tournament suggests the delight in pageantry and colour afforded by medieval practices. When the coronation of Queen Victoria was modernised and divested of much of its medieval pomp, the disappointed Earl of Eglinton sponsored a chivalric extravaganza complete with a formal procession, medieval costumes, jousting, a Queen of Beauty, and thousands of participants. The event was not just a frolic for the idle rich, for it attracted a crowd of spectators numbering between sixty and eighty thousand, and press coverage—which ranged from mockery to measured admiration—by its volume alone suggests the cultural significance of the tournament. For an age of mass production, urban dwelling, and the consequent blighting of nature's brightness and of human individuality— likewise an age of utilitarianism and sober social customs which prescribed the frock coat and iron corset—the flamboyance of prancing chargers and glinting armour, fluttering pennons and colourful pavilions exerted great attraction. The notion of English gentlemen in 1839 reviving the lapsed customs of the tourney is on one level ludicrous. Trollope satirised such a plan in *Barchester Towers* (1857), where one gentleman eschews tilting at a flour sack to preserve his clothing, while another trips his horse with the unwieldy twelve-foot lance. Yet the very fact that so many participants lavished so much money on accoutrements and so much time in preparing, to be watched by so many spectators who could share the experience only vicariously, testifies that the Eglinton tournament addressed significant needs arising from what Matthew Arnold later termed the deficiency of the 'poetical' in 'the age and all one's surroundings.' To him nineteenth-century England was 'not unprofound, not ungrand, not unmoving:—but *unpoetical*.'[4]

Use of medieval trappings to counter this lack of beauty or imagination frequently resulted in ridiculous anachronisms, for the earlier period was too remote for substantial knowledge and often too much sentimentalised for judicious representation. These amusing incongruities, which flourished in eighteenth-century Gothic fiction (Clara Reeve's novel *The Old English Baron* of 1777 depicts a castle with shutters on the windows), continued throughout the nineteenth century. When Queen Victoria planned a medieval costume ball at Buckingham Palace in 1842, she insisted that her gown be scrupulously patterned on a historical painting, but she refused to sacrifice her corset for a less defined and more authentic medieval silhouette. When rain virtually ruined the anticipated grandeur of the first day of the Eglinton Tournament, spectators opened practical Victorian umbrellas—although as one reporter observed, 'there is nothing chivalrous about an umbrella'—and, as one newspaper reported, heightened the incongruity of the medieval procession: the 'serpentine line of helmets and glittering armour, gonfalons, spear points, and plumes, just surging above the sea of moving unbrellas, had the effect of some gorgeous and bright scaled dragon swimming in troubled waters.'[5]

Despite such frequently ridiculous effects, anachronisms did not always produce discord or laughter. While it was admittedly incongruous for Sir Walter Scott to equip his medieval manor with gas lights, Abbotsford may be seen as his attempt to temper the pragmatic comforts of the modern world with the romance of a bygone era, to be physically enriched but not spiritually impoverished by material progress. Growing up in the age deemed 'unpoetical' by Arnold, young William Morris derived imaginative and spiritual vigour from Scott's historical fiction and also from a miniature suit of armour in which he rode about the countryside. As a student at Oxford, when he, Dante Gabriel Rossetti and Edward Burne-Jones painted Arthurian murals for the new Gothic-style Oxford Union, he tried to create similar delight by commissioning another suit of mail. This antique garb was clearly a source of humour—especially when the visor stuck shut and Morris raged helplessly against a chorus of laughter from the band of artists. But the cause for mirth was as much the failure of the modern workman's technology as the presence of the armour in the nineteenth-century hall, where it was actually much at home with the artistic theories and chivalric notions of Morris and his fellows. More significant than the problem with the helmet is the fate of the Arthurian murals, which almost immediately began to fade. As with the stuck visor, this more serious failure stemmed not from the incongruity of medieval inspiration but from the modern artists' inadequate technical knowledge of how to apply paint to plaster.

While the Middle Ages might awaken the imagination and supply pleasing colours and tones, artists clearly had to face modern technical matters related to their media. In literature this issue received extensive attention from critics who insisted that poets address timely concerns in modern forms and language. In her verse novel *Aurora Leigh* (1857), which dealt with current issues such as materialism, illegitimacy, and prostitution, Elizabeth Barrett Browning stated the argument for contemporaneity. Medieval works tended to exaggerate events and figures of the past, and more important, to diminish awareness of the grandeur of one's own age:

> *All actual heroes are essential men,*
> *And all men possible heroes; every age,*
> *Heroic in proportion . . .*
> *. . . Ay but every age*
> *Appears to souls who live in't (ask Carlyle)*
> *Most unheroic. . . .*
> *. . . That's wrong thinking, to my mind,*
> *And wrong thoughts make poor poems . . .*
> *Nay if there's room for poets in the world . . .*
> *Their sole work is to represent the age,*
> *Their age, not Charlemagne's . . .*
> *[That] spends more passion, more heroic heat,*
> *Betwixt the mirrors of its drawing rooms,*
> *Than Roland with his knights at Roncesvalles*
> *. . . King Arthur's self*
> *Was commonplace to Lady Guenever,*
> *And Camelot to minstrels seemed as flat*
> *As Fleet Street to our poets.*

(Book V, ll. 151–222)

Similarly, Robert Browning's 'Tray' (1879) disparaged modern celebrations of knights written in the archaic style of medieval romances. Such tedious, artificial poems, 'Tray' implies, are decidedly inferior to a realistic story about a heroic dog (concluding with a topical protest against vivisection) recounted in contemporary language.

In a critical climate encouraging modernity and 'relevance', Tennyson's Arthurian poems drew fire for being irrelevant and artificial, in both style and subject matter. As one critic admonished, 'The old epics will probably never be surpassed, any more than the old coats of mail; and for the same reason; nobody wants the article; . . . they are become mere curiosities.'[6] Even Ruskin, who was so much attracted to the creative economic example of the Middle Ages, felt that the 'treasures of wisdom' and incomparable 'word-painting' of Tennyson's *Idylls of the King* were squandered: 'it seems to me that so great power ought not to be spent on visions of things past but on the living present. For one hearer capable of feeling the depth of this poem I believe ten would feel a depth quite as great if the stream flowed through things nearer the hearer.'[7] Although most critics celebrated Tennyson's felicitous language and imagery, they generally concurred that 'to bewitch us with our own daily realities, and not with their unreal opposites, is a still higher task'.[8] In part such objections arose from critics' sense that modern treatments of the Middle Ages distorted actuality. Sentimental views of the past obscured not only distant history, but also the relative merits of the present. Yet many critics conversely recognised that

23

creative distortion of fact could illuminate essential truth. One argued, for example, that 'the events of the chivalric legend are better adapted to sustained and prolonged poetry than the events of . . . the present day . . . because they abound much less in dangerous detail, . . . give us a sort of large-hand copy of life which it is comparatively easy to understand.'[9] Unfettered by petty facts, literature based on medieval matter could reflect universal concerns.

Other critics defended works set in the Middle Ages on grounds that they allowed aesthetic pleasure and free play of the imagination. Despite his own argument for contemporary relevance, Ruskin also recognised an aesthetic appeal inherent in the medieval world but not in his own: 'On the whole, these are much *sadder* ages than the early ones; not sadder in a noble and deep way, but in a dim wearied way,—the way of ennui, and jaded intellect. . . . The Middle Ages had their wars and agonies, but also intense delights. Their gold was dashed with blood; but ours is sprinkled with dust.'[10] Arnold echoed these sentiments when he declared that although the Middle Ages were marked by 'a strong sense of . . . irrationality', they exerted a 'peculiar charm and aroma', 'poetically the greatest charm and refreshment possible for me'.[11]

Though such critics recognised the value of aesthetic escape from pressing contemporary issues and a comparatively drab environment, the important Arthurian works of the nineteenth century do not merely afford temporary diversion or aesthetic relief. While Tennyson, for example, acknowledged the romantic value of remoteness—'it is the distance that charms me in the landscape, the picture and the past, and not the immediate to-day in which I move'[12]—he also insisted that his was not escapist art; it was essentially didactic and aimed at modern problems. He adopted medieval setting and story in part because he felt that men would accept lessons couched in myth and romance.

Ironically, Tennyson, who was criticised for writing about the past rather than the present, was also criticised for not being sufficiently medieval. Reviewers argued that he had merely depicted Victorian characters and concerns in the garb of the early era. Thus Gerard Manley Hopkins termed the *Idylls* 'Charades from the Middle Ages' in which picturesque effects—like 'real lace and good silks and real jewelry' used in a blatantly artificial tableau—never disguised the Victorian presence.[13]

The pressure of this critical debate over setting poetry in the Middle Ages probably prompted Tennyson to frame his early medieval narratives within contemporary scenes. In *The Princess* (1847), for example, a modern episode introduces the timely issue of higher education for women. The subject then develops in a romance vaguely set in the medieval period. This rather daring blend of old and new struck many readers as merely absurd. When Browning heard of the scheme—a female university to be described in a 'fairy-tale'—he declared such anachronistic treatment to be unsuitable for a world in which 'locomotives . . . must keep the very ghosts of [fairies] away'.[14] Although some critics echoed Browning's judgement and held that the medieval ambience and the contemporary concerns blurred each other, Tennyson by pursuing what he termed a 'strange diagonal' between romance and realism, medieval and modern, succeeded in treating the controversial 'woman question' with humour, sensitivity, and detachment. Approaching the contemporary issue through medieval fiction allowed him to convey a complex attitude, to champion the cause of university training for women and to oppose male domination, while simultaneously defending the values of traditional female roles rejected by his educationally ambitious heroine, Princess Ida. In addition, throughout the medieval tale he subtly employed references to modern scientific thought in order to suggest that traditional attitudes must adapt to a new sense of mankind and the world.

Tennyson similarly used a modern frame for the earliest published portion of his Arthurian *Idylls*, embedding the narrative of Arthur's death within 'The Epic' (1842), an English idyl which illustrates customs among the nineteenth-century gentry. The modern frame raises the topic of prevailing critical debate—the value of old literary forms and subject matter for the present century. In the introduction, the host of a Christmas party reads the salvaged fragment of an Arthurian epic which its author had years before cast into the fireplace. The poet had destroyed most of the work because he decided that 'truth / Looks freshest in the fashion of the day' and that the epic form is outmoded—'why should any man / Remodel models?' Moreover, the subject matter—the Round Table society—is extinct, and 'nature brings not back the Mastodon, / Nor we those [heroic] times.' Yet the rescued poetic fragment proves to be no mastodon of verse, for it affects the listeners, particularly the narrator. Stirred by the reading, he dreams of Arthur's returning to nineteenth-century England, freshly dressed—like truth—in the fashion of the day, as 'a modern gentleman / Of stateliest port.' When the narrator awakens to the sound of Christmas bells memorialising another ideal figure who promised a second coming, we fully see the applications of the medieval tale to the modern world described in the frame. This contemporary world has been characterised by one speaker, Parson Holmes, as a declining society: 'all the old honour had from Christmas gone'; schism, geology, and debates over church procedure have rendered a 'general decay of faith / Right through the world.' This modern complaint is echoed in the medieval narrative by Sir Bedivere, who laments Arthur's defeat and the failure of the Round Table order: 'For now I see the true old times are dead, / When every morning brought a noble chance, / And every chance brought out a noble knight.' Bedivere himself links the early promise of Camelot to the birth of Christ: 'Such times have been not since the light that led / The holy Elders with the gift of myrrh.' Thus the culmination of the modern coda, linking the envisioned reappearance of Arthur in the modern world with the tolling of Christmas bells, signals an opportunity for the ideals of Christianity and of medieval chivalry to be restored to the world Parson Holmes has declared moribund. In effect we see that, as King Arthur comments, 'The old order changeth, yielding place to new, / And God fulfills Himself in many ways, / Lest one good custom should corrupt the world.' Each day—even in the nineteenth century—brings a noble chance, and each chance can bring forth a noble knight—although chance, knight, and nobility can be clothed (like Arthur in the narrator's dream) in the fashion of the new order and the new day.

In 'The Epic' Tennyson joins the medieval narrative and its modern frame to suggest two important principles about nineteenth-century medieval works. The first arises from a cyclical concept of history and implies that man may learn from the examples of the past. After suggesting that the Arthurian order recaptured the ideals of early Christianity, the conclusion, which depicts a symbolic second coming of Arthur and memorialises the birth of Christ, implies that the modern world can, despite Parson Holmes' harangue, recapitulate the ideals common to Christian and Arthurian society. As the Round Table order attempted to remodel the model of Christ, the Victorian world may profit from the patterns of the past. The second important principle suggested by the combined modern frame and the framed medieval narrative is that for the contemporary world, literature will provide the enlightened leadership supplied in earlier periods by messiahs and kings, or in more recent time by ministers. In declaring that there is 'no anchor, none, / To hold by,' the Parson in effect betrays his responsibility to represent just such an anchor. The modern parallel to King Arthur—or to the Parson—as a spiritual leader of men is the diffident poet Everard Hall, whose epic fragment inspires the narrator to dream of Arthur and the ideals of Camelot restored to the present age. Whereas Tennyson's combining medieval and modern elements in *The Princess* distances a volatile contemporary issue and permits him simultaneously to commend and to caution against feminist attitudes, the similar combination in 'The Epic' and the 'Morte d'Arthur' establishes the contemporaneity of a superficially remote Arthurian narrative. Throughout the century poets used medieval materials both to focus on modern concerns through the objectifying distance permitted by a medieval setting or myth and to discern in traditional tales emblems meaningful, even instructive, to the present.

This literary preoccupation with the past accompanied a pervasive historicism in the nineteenth century. For the first time history was studied scientifically and recognised as a legitimate academic subject, but historical interest penetrated far beyond academic circles. As Morse Peckham has pointed out, the middle decades of the century witnessed publication of a large number of historical works of 'gigantic scale' read 'in numbers still impressive' by a public which consequently had 'a knowledge of the past such as no human beings had ever had before'.[15] This pursuit of the past was widespread, self-conscious, and increasingly competent. Assistance was provided by improved organisation and publication of archival material in the government Records Office, and most especially, by editions produced by important historical groups such as the Roxburghe (1814), Bannatyne (1823), Maitland (1828), and Abbotsford (1835) Clubs, the Surtees (1834), English Historical (1837), Camden (1838), Aelfric (1843), Caxton (1845), and Early English Text (1864) Societies—more than a dozen were organised between 1834 and 1846. The age produced in the writings of Macaulay, Carlyle, and J. A. Froude some of the finest exemples of literary historicism ever penned. Interest specifically in the Middle Ages produced such scholarly studies as Henry Hallam's *View of the State of Europe During the Middle Ages* (1818), three analytical volumes densely packed with dates, facts, and documentation, as well as such vastly more popular works as Kenelm Digby's *Broad Stone of Honour: or, The True Sense and Practice of Chivalry* (1822). Also subtitled *Rules of the Gentlemen of England*, it offered what the author terms 'a truly philosophic history of chivalry' in an astonishingly lavish tapestry of details from medieval literature and history, compendiously enlivened by anecdotes and quotations from a range of literature encompassing classical poetry and Wordsworth.

More purely literary concerns are not so far removed from such historical analyses of the Middle Ages as they might initially seem, for reviewers of the day contemplated the relationships between current scholarship and fictional or poetic representations of the past. They vigorously debated, for example, whether Scott's historical novels impeded the study of history, and Scott himself dramatised the controversy in an imaginary dialogue between 'the Author' and an antiquarian metaphorically identified as 'Dryasdust'. This Dryasdust argued for factual fidelity and charged that Scott was 'in danger of causing history to be neglected—readers being contented with such frothy and superficial knowledge as they acquire from your works, to the effect of inducing them to neglect the severer and more accurate sources of information' (prefatory letter to *Peveril of the Peak*). 'The Author' denied that he was 'adulterating the pure sources of historical knowledge'; after all, he was entertaining, not writing history: 'A poor fellow, like myself, weary with ransacking his own barren and bounded imagination, looks for some general subject in the huge and boundless field of history . . . —bedizens it with such colouring as his skill suggests—ornaments it with such romantic circumstances as may heighten the general effect . . . and thinks, perhaps, he has done some service to the public, if he can present to them a lively fictitious picture, for which the original anecdote or circumstance . . . only furnished a slight sketch.' Despite such protest, however, Scott elsewhere affirmed the serious value of his looking at the past, primarily for examples of what man should avoid or correct: 'Our ancestors lodged in caves and wigwams where we construct palaces for the rich and comfortable dwellings for the poor. And why is this but because our eye is enabled to look back upon the past to improve on our ancestors' improvements and to avoid their errors. This can only be done by studying history and comparing it with passing events.'[16]

While reviewers quarrelled with Scott's historical misrepresentations, historians who transcended Dryasdust pedantry saw the importance of literary reshapings of the past. Macaulay described the ideal historian as one who would not only accumulate events and facts, but also 'intersperse the details which are the charm of historical romance', and he praised Scott for having 'used those fragments of truth which historians have scornfully thrown behind them'.[17] Whether the poetic licence and unique brand of local colour which caused critics to label Scott's narratives inimical to history caused his readers to neglect the discipline may remain moot, but his novels did stimulate great popular interest in the past, for as Carlyle wrote, Scott communicated that 'the bygone ages of the world were actually filled by living men. . . . Not abstractions were they, not diagrams and theorems; but men, in buff or other coats and breeches, with colour in their cheeks, with passions in their stomach, and the idioms, features and vitalities of very men.'[18] This vital sense of living men was precisely what Carlyle aimed for in his own historical writing, and he evoked a sense of the Middle Ages that was not just romance but human realities: 'No age ever seemed the Age of Romance to *itself*. . . . Roland of Roncesvalles . . . found rainy weather as well as sunny; knew what it was to have hose need darning; got tough beef to chew, or even went dinnerless, was saddle-sick, calumniated, constipated . . . and oftenest felt, I doubt not, that this was a very Devil's world, and he, Roland himself, one of the sorriest caitiffs there.'[19]

Yet the gap between serious historical study and a general sense of life distilled by the imagination may not be so wide as many of Scott's reviewers and his own defence of fancy suggested, for the connections between the serious historicism of the age and the literary medievalism are strong. The availability of manuscript material and the historical consciousness of anterior ages significantly stirred both writers' imaginations and the reading public's responsiveness. When Tennyson as a boy lighted upon Malory's *Morte Darthur*, the work was not widely known. But throughout the first half of the century, the increasing availability of medieval lore—both literary and historical—fed the imaginative fires of the young poet and helped to prepare readers for medieval matter. Antiquarian and scholarly interests during the early decades of the century made accessible to Victorian poets a wealth of potentially inspiring materials which for centuries had been confined to difficult manuscripts in obscure places. Besides the three early editions of Malory—in 1816 the *History of the Renowned Prince Arthur, King of Britain*, published by Walker and Edwards, and *La Mort d'Arthur*, published by R. Wilks and probably edited by Joseph Haslewood; and in 1817 the *Byrth, Lyf, and Actes of King Arthur*, published by Longman with an introduction and notes by Robert Southey, edited by Upcott—the parade of Arthurian editions produced in England glitters impressively. They included such works as the chronicles of Nennius, Geoffrey of Monmouth, and Layamon, the two Welsh Arthurian tales in Lady Charlotte Guest's translation of the *Mabinogion*, and no fewer than twenty-three medieval Arthurian romances. (See Appendix I for a chronological list of Arthurian editions appearing between 1800 and 1850.)

The editing zeal continued into the second half of the century, building a grand structure of Arthuriana on the foundation laid by eighteenth-century antiquarianism. In 1854 San-Marte reproduced Giles' Latin text of Geoffrey of Monmouth. In 1858 still another edition of Malory, edited by Thomas Wright, appeared. The previous year, Francis Child's ballad collection included the 'Legend of King Arthur' and 'King Arthur's Death', which had earlier been published with four other Arthurian ballads ('Sir Lancelot du Lake', 'The Boy and the Mantle', 'The Marriage of Sir Gawain', and 'King Ryence') in Bishop Thomas Percy's *Reliques of Ancient English Poetry* (1765–94). Other eighteenth-century works included John Pinkerton's 1792 publication of two metrical Gawain romances and Thomas Warton's discussion of Arthurian legend (especially the stories of Tristram, Lancelot, and the Grail) in his *History of English Poetry* (1774–81). As significant as the editions of original medieval romances and ballads were works such as George Ellis' *Specimens of Early English Metrical Romances* (1805; revised by J. O. Halliwell in 1848) and John Dunlop's three-volume *History of Fiction* (1814; reprinted in 1816 and 1845), which made the principal Arthurian stories widely available in readable modern English summaries.

The accessibility of Arthurian story to nineteenth-century poets may be illustrated by tracing the avenues by which the Tristram legend, which became the subject of major poems by Arnold, Tennyson, and Swinburne, entered Victorian consciousness. European verse romances treating the story of Tristram and Iseult were not readily available to the English early in the century. The Middle High German edition of Gottfried von Strassburg which appeared in 1785 was poor, though it was followed by better editions in the early 1800s (1821, 1823, 1843). Béroul's Anglo-Norman version was not published until 1823, and only in 1835 did an incomplete edition of Thomas' Anglo-Norman fragments appear. Translations were slower in coming; Gottfried's poem was finally published in English in 1879, whereas the other medieval poems appeared in English only in the twentieth century. But two versions existed in medieval English, Malory's and Scott's edition of *Sir Tristrem* (1804; reprinted 1806, 1811, 1819, 1833, 1848). Though Scott included a glossary, notes, and modern English plot summaries, the narrative probably aroused little interest because of its difficult Northern Middle English, which is complicated by awkward transposition and omission of words, abrupt transitions, and obscure diction; this version scarcely represents the compelling qualities of the traditional love story.

Whereas Scott's edition of *Sir Tristrem* exerted comparatively slight influence on English poets (though it was probably read by Swinburne, and perhaps by Arnold), Scott commented in his preface that Malory's *Morte Darthur* was already 'in the hands of most antiquaries and collectors' (*Sir Tristrem*, p. lxxvi), and the three editions of 1816 and 1817 made the story known to a wider audience. Malory's work was the source of references to Tristram in Arthurian poems published before mid-century by Wordsworth and Reginald Heber. Although Scott's edition and Malory's romance were the literary versions of the legend which helped reintroduce Tristram into English poetry, we should recognise that Arthuriana was in the air, and other references, though far less influential than Malory's work, were promoting familiarity with the legend among English men of letters. The tale was recounted, for example, in John Dunlop's *History of Fiction*, which summarises what his subtitle calls 'the most celebrated prose works of fiction, from the earliest Greek romances to the novels of the present age'. Dunlop includes all the basic elements of the Tristram legend, stripping away the bulky narrative excesses of the medieval prose romances which disperse bits of the story throughout considerations of the entire Round Table society. Periodicals had also picked up the interest in Arthurian materials, and Matthew Arnold, for example, encountered the Tristram legend in articles on the tales of the Round Table written by Théodore de la Villemarqué for the French *Revue de Paris* (1837 and 1841). The legend was also revived in England through the study of Celtic lore. In 1809, Edward Davies' *Mythology and Rites of the British Druids* devoted twenty-two pages to the Tristram figure in the Welsh Triads and in the Middle English *Sir Tristrem*. And although such writers as Dante, Petrarch, and Ariosto did not narrate the legend, allusions in the *Inferno* (V, 67), *Trionfo d'amore* (III, 80), and *Orlando Furioso* (IV, 52 and XXXII, 89) must have piqued the curiosity of literate Englishmen. The point is that while Malory's work was the principal source and inspiration for English writers of the century, the fascinating stories and symbolic potential of Arthurian legend were evoked by works which appealed to a wide range of readers for a variety of reasons, from Celtic national pride to literary snobbishness.

But the reading public was not necessarily so well versed in medieval lore, nor so receptive to it, as the poets of the period. After Arnold published in 1852 the first English Tristram poem of the century, he felt compelled to provide his audience with fuller background and consequently included in the second edition an explanatory preface drawn from Dunlop's *History of Fiction*. Tennyson, it has been argued, in 1842 addressed a public for whom 'Arthurian story was still strange to the ordinary reader', and he must be credited with 'creating the taste by which he was enjoyed'.[20] By 1860, however, the ubiquitousness of Arthurian romance prompted a reviewer for *Fraser's* to insist that for readers of novels, 'a familiarity with the *Morte d'Arthur* has lately become almost indispensable' and a reviewer for *Blackwood's* to remark that the knights of Camelot 'crowd upon us everywhere in prose and poetry'.[21]

What is most significant about readers' and writers' increasing awareness of multiple versions of Arthurian legend is that nineteenth-century Arthurian poets recognised that they were writing in a tradition, that they were selecting tales from various versions and were consciously deleting, adding, and re-arranging details, motifs, and themes. They were consciously crafting new expressions in an already rich and manifold body of literature. This awareness contrasts markedly with the approaches of writers between Malory and Tennyson, who by and large appropriated characters and motifs to works which otherwise had little kinship to Arthurian tradition. In many instances, the nineteenth-century writer measured his own innovations against medieval treatments to emphasise his contribution and either his fidelity to tradition or the independence of his vision. While Tennyson, for example, cited suggestions in Joseph of Exeter, Albéric des Trois-Fontaines, and the *Brut ab Arthur* to justify his portrait of Arthur, he also liked to emphasise the individuality of his Lancelot, his 'own great imaginative knight'.[22] Tennyson specifically proposed to modernise the tales and to show their special relevance to his age. As Hallam Tennyson explained about his father's treatment of Arthurian legends, he 'infused into them a spirit of modern thought and an ethical significance, . . . as indeed otherwise these archaic stories would not have appealed to the modern world at large' (*Memoir*, II, 122). When Tennyson read the suggestion that his Grail narrative echoed medieval treatments, he demurred: 'I can't conceive how the Grail . . . can well be treated by a poet of the 13th century from a similar point of view to mine, who write in the 19th, but, if so, I am rather sorry for it, as I rather piqued myself on my originality of treatment' (*Memoir*, II, 61–2). Although medieval literature provided the fabric from which the *Idylls* were fashioned, the cut and style were to Tennyson's mind his own.

But while Tennyson intended to do something new and contemporary, he also aimed to partake of the rich literary heritage. He based his *Idylls* primarily on Malory's *Morte Darthur* and the *Mabinogion*. Justly noted for the quantity and eclecticism of his reading, however, he also informed his sense of the Middle Ages by investigating not only medieval romance and songs, but also studies of medieval literature, history, and folklore—and some of the material he probably read in Welsh.[23] Swinburne likewise conducted 'research' of sorts for his Arthurian poetry. Before reshaping the Tristram legend, he read all available extant medieval versions of the story, including Malory, Scott's edition of *Sir Tristrem*, and Francisque Michel's *Tristan: Recueil de ce qui reste des poèmes relatifs à ses aventures, composés en français, en anglo-normand, et en grec dans les XII. et XIII. siècles* (1835–39), which includes Béroul and Thomas.

Swinburne may have known Wagner's opera *Tristan und Isolde* (based on Gottfried von Strassburg), the libretto for which was begun in 1857 and finished in 1859, although the opera was not actually performed until 1865. This point raises the issue of Wagner's possible influence on Victorian Arthurians. Tennyson expressed little interest in Wagner's operatic treatment of Arthurian legend. When one enthusiast recommended the subject of his opera on the son of Perceval, the Swan Knight Lohengrin, for a poem, the Laureate brushed the suggestion aside by noting 'what a remarkably sharp nose you've got'.[24] Arnold, who found Wagner's Tristram story interesting although the music was not, felt his own version of the legend, which antedated the opera, to be superior.[25] Swinburne seems to have been alone among Victorian Arthurians in his enthusiasm for the German composer. Discussing his projected *Tristram of Lyonesse*, he wrote that 'Wagner's music ought to abash but does stimulate me.'[26] Although Wagner's operatic reshaping of the Tristram legend represented, in effect, the overwhelming love tragedy of the age, it does not seem to have affected English poets as it did German audiences. Wagner's other Arthurian opera, *Parsifal*, based largely on the *Parzival* of Wolfram von Eschenbach, was his last opera, not performed until 1882 although the libretto was apparently written by 1877, eight years after Tennyson completed the major nineteenth-century version of the Grail story in English.

Swinburne purposefully consulted medieval versions of the Tristram story because he intended to work within established tradition, to create a new poem 'acceptable for its orthodoxy and fidelity to the dear old story'. Although he could not include 'a tithe of the various incidents given in the different old versions', he meant to include 'everything *pretty* that is of any importance, and is in keeping with the tone and spirit of the story'. He also planned to portray the legend more authentically than his contemporaries had: Arnold had 'transformed and recast the old legend, and Tennyson—as usual, if I may be permitted to say so—has degraded and debased it'.[27] We need not agree with Swinburne that Tennyson's 'Morte d'Albert' dressed Victorians in medieval costume and actually represented the modern 'divorce-court' more than a courtly past ('Under the Microscope') in order to recognise that such debate marked a serious interest among Victorian poets in the place of their works in Arthurian tradition.

Clearly not all nineteenth-century writers were so much concerned with literary antecedents. After Arnold read the Tristram story in the *Revue de Paris*, he turned to Malory but found that his own poem 'was in the main formed, and I could not well disturb it'.[28] Except for echoing the summary of the thirteenth-century French Vulgate *Ystoire de Merlin* which prefaces Southey's edition of Malory, and echoing the *Morte Darthur* in the haunting last line, Arnold's *Tristram and Iseult* distinctly resists many traditional elements of the legend. Also countering the general concern with tradition were writers like William Morris, who may be said to have subscribed unconsciously to Scott's theory that 'tradition, generally speaking, is a sort of perverted alchemy which converts gold into lead'.[29] Far from rehashing events in earlier works, Morris, once inspired by Malory, freely invented details and formulated radically independent conceptions of characters.

Yet even the poems of Arnold and Morris fall well within Arthurian tradition. Romancers of the Middle Ages, who used basic legends again and again, frequently altered plot, recombining narrative details and familiar motifs to create many different versions of a single legend. Variety in plot, literary form, and style have always marked Arthurian literature, as versions of the Tristram legend ranging from Béroul's twelfth-century poem to Malory's late fifteenth-century prose attest. Whether a writer—like Gottfried and Swinburne—linked Tristram's death to the classical motif of the black and white sails; or—like Malory and Tennyson—described Mark's ignoble stroke; or—like Arnold—adapted no medieval version, the legend allowed a variety of archetypal and symbolic effects. What Arnold, Morris, Tennyson, and Swinburne shared with medieval writers, whether or not they followed narrative details, was recognition of the expressive, didactic, and symbolic potential of Arthurian legends. Even the earliest medieval versions are set in the distant past or the long-ago of fairy tale and myth. That they may initially have derived from historical events and actual customs notwithstanding, the tales became in medieval romances meaningful emblems rather than slices of life. The most encompassing symbolic potential lies in the idea of Camelot as an ideal order. The concept of the Round Table inextricably combines social, political, ethical, and religious ideals in a society which flourished yet ultimately failed. Thus Arthurian story provided for nineteenth-century writers a broad canvas and crowded palette with which to delineate significant contemporary concerns and to paint either brightly optimistic pictures of human potential or darker possibilities.

As the key which unlocked the treasury of Arthurian legend for the nineteenth century, Malory's *Morte Darthur* can scarcely be emphasised sufficiently. His style—curiously diffuse for modern readers—was not always admired. Scott, celebrating the 'high tone of chivalry', nevertheless described the work as 'extracted at hazard, and without much art or combination' (preface to *Sir Tristrem*). Tennyson thought the *Morte Darthur* 'much the best' of chivalric romances. Even though it contained 'very fine things', however, they were 'all strung together without Art' (*Memoir*, I, 194). Yet in these 'very fine things' distilled from Malory's voluptuous presentation, Tennyson found the heady essence for his own greatest work. This essence, curiously, is conflict. The *Morte Darthur* depicts a world of conflict ranging from the physical encounters of international battles and civil wars, tournaments, and the almost incessant jousting of individual knights; to the emotional clashes of illicit love, adultery, and jealousy; to the spiritual conflict of religious faith belied by action, the hope of eternal salvation jeopardised by awareness of immediate sin. Stories of King Arthur and the Round Table appealed to Victorian poets because, for all their remoteness and quaintness, they deal with ethical, moral, and emotional problems that transcend custom, place, or time.

In 1853 Charlotte Yonge memorialised the influence of the *Morte Darthur* when the hero of *The Heir of Redclyffe*, Guy Morville, commended the romance for its high moral tone ('the depth, the mystery, the allegory—the beautiful characters of some of the knights')—it was his 'boating–book for at least three summers' (ch. 10). By 1860, however, the same novelist described a younger generation who no longer 'moulded their opinions and practice on the past': 'Chivalry had given way to common sense, romance to realism, respect for antiquity to pitying patronage, the past to the future' (*Hopes and Fears*, II, ch. xv). Yonge's sense of changing times did not, however, signal the second demise of Arthur. Although her young heroines of 1860 did not absorb the medievalism of Scott and Pugin, this 'new generation' looked to the poetry of Tennyson, in whose hands Arthurian legend would once again achieve literary eminence. A survey of British and American Arthurian literature in the hundred and twenty years following this pronouncement that 'chivalry had given way' may tell us little about the ascendancy of 'common sense', but it clearly establishes the continuing vitality of the matter of Britain.

2

Reawakening Tradition

British Literature, 1800–1830

After reaching its peak in Malory's stately compression of the massive story cycle, Arthur's literary fortunes declined over the next three centuries—slowly, but almost as dramatically as the fortunes of his Order decline in the pages of the *Morte Darthur*. For 150 years after Caxton's printing of Malory, Arthurian story reappeared in works by respected poets. But the political controversies of the seventeenth century increasingly narrowed the usefulness of a legend long associated with royalist sentiments, and the rationalism of the eighteenth century nearly extinguished the appeal of Arthurian matter. By this time, most works which used Arthurian characters were either subliterary or totally unconnected with traditional story except by proper names. Yet the legend which has survived the battle of Camlan survived these exigencies as well. Even though no truly important Romantic work featured Arthurian material, antiquarians and poets revived Arthurian legend and re-established its suitability for belles lettres. By 1830, Arthur's promised return had become assured.[1]

When Renaissance and early seventeenth-century writers used Arthurian story and characters primarily to embody nationalistic and royalist attitudes, they were emphasising a political bias early built into the legend: Geoffrey of Monmouth's *Historia Regum Britanniae* had endowed the new Norman kings with a British heritage; Malory's *Morte Darthur* had praised the supposed ancestor of the ascendant Tudor monarchs; and Spenser's Arthurian references celebrated the greatest Tudor as his Gloriana. Subsequent, but less distinguished, works affirmed the Stuarts' claims to the throne by invoking their Arthurian ancestry, thus emphasising the political implications of the legend and nearly eliminating other thematic concerns.

This intimate association of Arthur with the concept of monarchy and with the Stuart kings clearly limited the appeal of the legend during the political upheaval of the seventeenth century. Milton, for example, having served as Latin Secretary for the Commonwealth government, rejected the Arthurian subject on which he had planned to base an epic. Later treatments such as John Dryden's opera *King Arthur; or, the British Worthy* (1691) and Richard Blackmore's epics, *Prince Arthur* (1695) and *King Arthur* (1697), praised the restored Stuart, Charles II, and the Stuarts' replacement, William III. This application of Arthurian story to so specific and controversial a political theme doubtless diminished its attractiveness for full literary treatment.

As the thematic uses of Arthurian works narrowed, writers' consciousness of antecedent tradition (and in most cases, their artistry) also dwindled. The works of both Dryden and Blackmore, for instance, owe virtually nothing to medieval tradition other than the names of characters. The most revealing illustration of this tendency to appropriate names of Arthurian characters to a situation totally remote from traditional story is not a political work, but a burlesque of bombastic, overwrought Restoration tragedies—Henry Fielding's *Tragedy of Tragedies; or the Life and Death of Tom Thumb the Great* (1730, 1731), which marries Arthur to Dollallolla, gives him a daughter, Huncamunca, and narrates the heroics of a pygmy knight.

Throughout the seventeenth and eighteenth centuries, Arthurian matter was known less as literature than as popular history or folklore, largely the province of children's reading. Moreover, traditional episodes of Arthurian story were less familiar than characters' names. Generally remembered for a few dominant traits or adventures, these characters readily became caricatures of their medieval prototypes. Merlin, for example, appeared in seventeenth and eighteenth-century publications more often than any other Arthurian character, but he had become nothing more than a stereotyped prophet. Divorced from medieval story, his name lent interest to cheap pamphlets of prognostication and to such works as John Partridge's predictions published annually as the *Merlinus Liberatus* (1689–1707).

The traditional stories had become problematical for a variety of reasons besides Arthur's associations with the Tudor and Stuart monarchies. Notwithstanding Caxton's assertion that his romance was morally didactic—'all is written for our doctrine, and for to beware that we fall not to vice nor sin; but to exercise and follow virtue' (Caxton's preface)—the patent moral lapses of Malory's characters elicited criticisms such as those of Queen Elizabeth's former tutor, Roger Ascham. He objected that 'the whole pleasure of . . . [the *Morte Darthur*] standeth in two speciall poyntes, in open mans slaughter, and bold bawdrye' (*The Scholemaster*, 1570). Unlike Ascham, Renaissance and Restoration poets did not necessarily measure literary interest in terms of morality, but the 'bawdrye' of Arthurian story would generate misgivings among critics and poets well into the nineteenth century.

Even for writers who did not require virtue in the central characters, however, the fabulous, obviously fictional aspects of the legend proved troublesome. Cervantes, in satirising the disastrous effects of Don Quixote's reading chivalric romances, reflects a mistrust of fancy which became more pronounced in the Age of Reason. To the eighteenth century, the barbaric, superstitious Middle Ages were peopled by primitives whose stories offered little useful to civilised men. Arthurian matter was significant so long as it could be read as history, but once viewed as legend or myth—once read as romance rather than chronicle—it lost its value.

Rejection of Arthurian and other medieval story by later writers must also be seen as the complement of Renaissance and Neoclassical enthusiasm for classical literature. The stuff of great poetry, as every schoolboy knew from his curriculum, was classical myth and craftsmanship, not the rude, unpolished, digressive matter and manner of medieval romance. As the basis for learning, the Bible and classical literature provided the common coin for educated writers and readers, and this standard was intensified by the religious controversy of the sixteenth and seventeenth centuries and by the Neoclassical emphasis on decorum, restraint, symmetry, and rationality.

When the cultural currents culminating in Romanticism opened new aspects of human experience to literary treatment, writers not only handled Biblical and classical tradition in new ways, but also looked elsewhere for stories and characters to embody their themes. British Romantics turned to medieval material less frequently than did their European counterparts, yet the works of leading English poets reflect the growing taste for representations of the Middle Ages. Generally, these stemmed not so much from direct acquaintance with medieval literature itself (other than Chaucer) as from a sense of the Middle Ages transmitted by Spenser and by Italian writers such as Petrarch and Boccaccio, Ariosto and Tasso.

British Romantics did not often use traditional medieval stories or characters; instead, they aimed for medieval 'atmosphere'. In such works as 'The Ballad of the Dark Ladie' (written about 1798, published 1834) and *The Eve of St Agnes* (1819), Coleridge and Keats achieved a 'medieval' ambience through vibrantly coloured tapestries, quaint castles, minstrel songs, and elegant lords and ladies. These two poets also derived particularly fine effects from their sense of medieval supernatural, Coleridge in the shape-shifter Geraldine in *Christabel* (begun by 1797, published 1816) and Keats in the motif of a mortal enchanted by a fairy lover in 'La Belle Dame Sans Merci' (1819). Despite such interest in medieval ambience and motif, Romantic poets did not turn to Arthurian lore to any significant extent. Even though medieval Arthurian literature cannot be described as widely available by the time the great Romantics were writing, Arthuriana was increasingly in the air, and at least Wordsworth and Keats read Malory.[2] But of the major Romantics, only Wordsworth composed an Arthurian work; it is hardly equal to his greatest poetry, and *The Egyptian Maid* disappoints any expectation for a grand Romantic restoration of Arthur. Although Wordsworth, like Milton, had early considered writing a substantial nationalistic work on Arthur, Coleridge later declared that the legend was no longer suitable for a national epic, for it had become too remote from contemporary human concerns: 'an epic poem must either be national or mundane. As to Arthur, you could not by any means make a poem on him national to Englishmen. What have *we* to do with him? Milton saw this, and . . . took a mundane theme—one common to all mankind.' Coleridge also identified an aspect of Arthurian romance which may have lessened its appeal to Romantic writers, who increasingly explored subjective experiences of both their characters and themselves. He observed that characters in romances manifested traditional traits so consistently that Tristram, who was 'always courteous', or Lancelot, always 'invincible', could easily be lifted from one metrical ballad or chronicle and inserted into another. Such figures permitted expression of neither 'a subjectivity of the *persona*' (as in Shakespeare's multifaceted characters) nor 'a subjectivity of the poet' (as in Milton's presence 'in everything he writes').[3]

Though romance material may not have seemed to offer Romantic poets fertile possibilities for characterisation, it did suggest some fine images; especially inspiring was Merlin, the single Arthurian figure cited in the poetry of Shelley, Coleridge, and Keats. Whereas Shelley in an early drama uses the concept of Merlin's prophetic vision in a compact, though not especially effective, image (*Charles the First*, II, 368–70), Coleridge achieves more complex effects by referring to the legend, used in Spenser's *Faerie Queene* (III, ii, 18–19), of Merlin's magic glass, which reflects whatever the gazer longs to see:

> For still there lives within my secret heart
> The magic image of the magic Child,
> Which there he made up-grow by his strong art,
> As in that crystal orb—wise Merlin's feat,—
> The wondrous 'World of Glass', wherein inisled
> All long'd for things their beings did repeat;—
>
> ('The Pang More Sharp than All', ll. 36–41)

Through he ironic contrast between the craft of the wizard and the 'strong art' of the guileless child, Coleridge deftly suggests the creative power of innocence and love.

Keats similarly achieves multiple effects through his Arthurian allusion in *The Eve of St Agnes*. Apparently referring to Merlin's fatal infatuation, Keats not only associates his lovers' union with enchantment, but also hints that disaster lurks among the delights of love: 'Never on such a night have lovers met, / Since Merlin paid his Demon all the monstrous debt' (ll. 170–1). Of all the major Romantic poets, Keats would seem to have been the one most likely to write a significant Arthurian poem. In an early fragment imitating Spenser, he declared 'I must tell a tale of chivalry', 'revive the dying tones of minstrelsy, / Which linger yet about lone gothic arches' ('Specimen of an Induction to a Poem', wr. 1817). This fragment of 68 lines boasts some promising passages and imagery, suggesting that as a more mature and less derivative poet, Keats could have produced a worthier chivalric story than his 162-line scrap of 'Calidore: A Fragment' (1817), which introduces a youth 'burning / To hear of knightly deeds' and a knight apparently ready to tell of some.

Although neither Keats nor any other important Romantic poet successfully fulfilled this promise to 'tell a tale of chivalry', Wordsworth's predecessor as Poet Laureate did use Arthurian legend in more extended allusions than those of Shelley, Coleridge, and Keats. The context of Robert Southey's references, however, hardly offered Arthur a promising re-entry into British poetry: *Madoc* (1805) features the unlikely situation of a twelfth-century Welshman who sailed to America and there converted to Christianity some Aztec Indians emigrating from 'Aztlan' to Mexico. After recruiting 'a fresh supply of adventurers' in Wales, Madoc was never heard from again. Within this incongruous situation,

Southey refers to King Arthur as a standard of heroism. Madoc, sprung from 'immortal Arthur's line' (II, 207), early learned 'to lisp the fame of Arthur' (XI, 142) and to emulate him. Arthurian material figures prominently in Southey's description of a bardic song which speculates about the fate of Merlin: 'Whither sail'd Merlin with his band of Bards, / Old Merlin, master of the mystic lore?' (XI, 105–6). Whatever the appeal of Southey's fancy that Merlin may yet be singing with a mermaid beneath the sea (117–23), Arthurian story was hardly likely to regain stature by being insinuated into a tale of Welsh and Aztec involvements in twelfth-century America.

Southey's influence in restoring Arthurian legend to literary prominence stemmed not from his poetry but from his activity as antiquarian and editor. Seriously interested in medieval literature, he approached it from something of a scholar's perspective. Undertaking to complete an edition of the *Morte Darthur* (when the first contracted editor 'decamped with another man's wife'), he conducted fairly extensive research. The preparatory reading mentioned in his letters includes the 'S. Greaal', the 'Italian "Trystans" and the "Life of Merlin",' 'the Perceval', ballads, Geoffrey of Monmouth, Scott's *Sir Tristrem*, 'the two long poems of Luigi Alemanni', and French romances in the impressive library of the noted book collector, Richard Heber. Southey's correspondence, like Sir Walter Scott's, reflects a lively exchange of inquiries and information with antiquarians and Welsh scholars about the sources, analogues, historicity, and literary qualities of medieval literature. As Southey described his expertise for editing Malory, 'Were there an Academy of the Round Table, I believe myself worthy of a seat there in point of knowledge.'[4]

This serious interest in medieval literature shared by men like Southey and Scott is the key to the revival of Arthurian legend as something more than the extracurricular reading of schoolboys. Although, for example, Southey, Tennyson, Morris, and Swinburne first encountered the *Morte Darthur* in boyhood, by 1886 Swinburne unabashedly listed it among the works he would keep 'if compelled to choose' only one hundred books or authors.[5] Substantial credit for this resurrection must go to antiquarians and scholars such as George Ellis who encouraged study of medieval literature. Their pursuits in turn stimulated new poems, derived not just from popular notions of stereotyped characters or folk history, but from traditional Arthurian materials. In the first three decades of the century, the major Arthurian poems written in England came from a coterie of antiquarians who scouted out manuscripts of little-known medieval literature, edited—or contemplated editing—these rarities, and corresponded animatedly about their investigations. At the hub of this activity was Ellis, whose *Specimens of Early English Metrical Romances* made stories of Arthur, Lancelot, and Merlin available in modern English summaries. He corresponded with Scott and Southey (both of whom planned to edit Malory) about matters Arthurian, and they all consulted Richard Heber's impressive collection of rare early books. Like Scott, Heber's brother Reginald would write a new Arthurian poem, as would Reginald's intimate friend Henry Hart Milman. Still another close associate of Ellis, John Hookham Frere, who also exchanged Arthurian commentary with Scott, would write an Arthurian poem early in the century. With the exception of three writers—John Thelwall, whose drama, the first Arthurian work of the century, follows eighteenth-century precedents in being almost totally divorced from Arthurian tradition; Wordsworth, whose work comes last in order of publication; and Thomas Love Peacock, who wrote from a very personal interest in Welsh lore—the authors of original Arthurian works of the Romantic period were associated with George Ellis' erudition, Richard Heber's library, and a keen interest in medieval literature.

That the literary productions of the period began in antiquarian and historicist impulses is most obviously true in the case of Walter Scott. Nationalistic pride in Scotland prompted him to edit *Sir Tristrem*, for he held the incorrect theory that the romance was written by a Scot, Thomas the Rhymer or Thomas of Ercildoune. He also insisted that the story of Tristram was founded in fact: 'I have all along thought [that] a person of this name really swallowed a dose of cantharides intended to stimulate the exertions of his uncle.' When Scott proposed to edit Malory, he acted less out of literary than antiquarian or historicist enthusiasm, 'merely to preserve that ancient record of English chivalry'.[6] By approaching medieval material more as historical records than as imaginative creations, Scott probably inhibited his own poetic abilities to work with the stories. In fact, as literature none of the original Arthurian poems by the friends of Ellis and Scott really succeeds. They are all important in varying ways, however, as part of the process of recovering traditional Arthurian story. So long as a writer merely peopled a freely invented episode with stereotyped characters bearing Arthurian names, the product could command little interest except through its own thematic and stylistic features. But when writers re-established traditional story as a background for their innovations, their works could enjoy the additional richness afforded by traditions resonating through new versions, or by departures from the familiar generating surprise. Moreover, although Scott looked to medieval material for history, antiquarian scholars exhumed not historical artifacts, but legend. Only when Arthurian story was free of historicist cobwebs would it achieve fulfilment as imaginative literature. The Arthurian works written and published between 1800 and 1830 reflect the halting process of recovering this tradition.

i. John Thelwall, *The Fairy of the Lake: A Dramatic Romance in Three Acts* (1801)

Of the faint stirrings which anticipated Arthur's literary reawakening in nineteenth-century Britain, the earliest, by John Thelwall, a lecturer on elocution and revolutionary politics, follows the example of eighteenth-century works in using Arthurian names but little otherwise related to medieval tradition. The result in *The Fairy of the Lake* is unintentionally ludicrous. This verse 'dramatic romance in three acts', originally intended for staging but later described by Thelwall as a closet drama, features Arthur, Guenever, and Tristram in a tale contrived in the spirit of Gothic theatre, combining supernatural shocks and spectacle with a melodramatic plot and flat characters. Beyond the names and a few details suggested by medieval chronicle, the characterisation of the three principal Arthurian figures and all aspects of the plot are Thelwall's own. Published as one of the *Poems Chiefly Written in Retirement*, the drama expresses none of the radical political sentiments which filled Thelwall's many political pamphlets (and gained him the notoriety of standing trial for sedition). It aims to be nothing more than titillating entertainment.

At the opening of the drama, Vortigern, inflamed by incestuous desires, has abducted his daughter, Guenever, who is betrothed to Arthur. Vortigern's wife, the sorceress Rowenna—similarly inflamed by adulterous desire for Arthur—enchants Arthur's men to foil his rescue of Guenever, but the Lady of the Lake frees them. Ultimately Rowenna kills Vortigern and has her men set fire to the tower where Guenever and Tristram await rescue. After looking on helplessly, Arthur finally burns Rowenna and her castle, yet he remains powerless to aid Guenever. Rescue comes from the magical Lady of the Lake (the 'Fairy' of the title), who suddenly transforms the burning structure into a pool of water and takes Guenever and Tristram safely into her swan-drawn chariot. The drama ends with Arthur's coronation as king.

This synopsis scarcely conveys the ghastly quality of the melodrama. Triteness stems from Thelwall's inept alteration of Arthurian tradition, his weak characterisation, and his ineffective mingling of Arthurian figures from chronicle history with Teutonic mythology and Gothic 'horror'. There is no evidence that Thelwall knew Malory, although the instance of Arthur's being cast asleep by enchantment and rescued from danger by the Lady of the Lake bears faint resemblance to the King's encounters with Morgan le Fay and Accolon in the *Morte Darthur* (IV, x). Thelwall seems to have taken the situation of Vortigern's marriage to Rowenna, the heathen daughter of the Saxon Hengist, from Nennius' *Historia Britonum* (sections 37–47). In linking Nennius' account of the villainous king Vortigern and sorceress Rowenna to the fortunes of Arthur, who in Nennius appears a bit later, and Guenever, whom Nennius does not mention, Thelwall took one of the 'liberties for which', he wrote, 'as a Poet, I hope to be pardoned' (p. 207). Infinitely less pardonable than such liberty with chronology is Thelwall's liberty in combining Arthurian figures with supernatural beings from Northern mythology. Notwithstanding scholarship suggesting that the legendary Arthur may have originally derived from a Celtic deity, the Arthur of the chronicles bears no relationship to Thelwall's supernatural beings: Hela, Queen of the Infernal Regions; the Fatal Sisters; the Giants of Frost; Demons of the Noon; and Incubus, a frozen demon. Although Thelwall suggested that 'the Cambrian superstitions harmonise so readily with those of the Northern nations; and the mixed and illegitimate christianity of those times borders so closely upon paganism, that, I trust, the combination will not destroy the *poetical probability* of either' (p. 207), the mixture yields neither 'poetical probability' nor poetic enjoyment.

The weakest aspect of the work is its flat characterisation and the remoteness of its Arthurian figures from their traditional natures. Thelwall offers probably the blandest Arthur ever recorded. In keeping with the chronicle tradition, the king is initially described as a hero who has routed the Saxons: 'In horrid grace, / Wrathful he strode the field' (pp. 9–10). Unfortunately, Arthur achieves this formidable stature offstage, and from the time he appears (one-third of the way through the drama), he is largely ineffective, unresourceful, and unappealing. His greatest talent is for inaction; for example, after discarding his helmet, shield, and enchanted sword as worthless, he sits 'in a disconsolate attitude' and 'continues to pore upon the ground, in vacant agony' (p. 51). During the final battle Arthur primarily gazes helplessly (often exclaiming 'Distraction!') as Guenever calls pathetically. This Guenever is scarcely developed, except when Arthur enumerates her perfections in conventional language: 'Oh! Sweet of Sweets! / Personified perfection!—tint! and form!' (p. 48). The number of exclamation points in his praise reveals much about the character of Arthur and the flavour of the drama as a whole.

The most interesting Arthurian figure in Thelwall's work is his ale-swilling Tristram, who bears little relationship to his medieval namesake. His buffoonery provides an inane Bacchic counterpoint to Arthur's misery. As the chieftain laments 'disastrous Guenever' (one of his many infelicitous phrases), Tristram irreverently bemoans his empty wine flask (p. 39). Though Tristram later redeems his buffoonery by trying to rescue Guenever, his bravery remains undeveloped, and we last see him extolling 'valiant Cwrw' [ale] (p. 85).

The stilted speeches of Thelwall's characters provide no match for his envisioned scenic effects. Before the climax the audience is treated to mist, thunder, lightning, meteors, and hailstones; fantastic dances by phantoms and fairies; caverns suddenly opening from nowhere; and an icy throne guarded by deformed giants. Because the play was not performed, we can only speculate on the probable success of these special effects. But even when read as descriptive elements in a closet drama, the stage directions and setting seem more compelling than the actions and dialogue. Wedded to these 'horrors' smacking of eighteenth-century Gothic fiction (which also inspired the central concern with incest) are several limp efforts at comic relief provided by Tristram and by Rowenna's jocularly malevolent Incubus, a frosty monster who sprinkles his speeches with racy colloquialisms and anachronistic references to the nineteenth century. The combination of such vapid humour with colourless dramatis personae and ineffective Gothic horror yields a work which by itself would have suggested that Arthurian matter, like sleeping dogs, should be left alone.

ii. Henry Hart Milman, *Samor, Lord of the Bright City: An Heroic Poem* (1818)

Slightly more readable is another work based on the chronicle story of Vortigern and Rowenna entitled *Samor, Lord of the Bright City*. Unlike Thelwall, who took the material as the subject of melodrama, Henry Hart Milman saw the story of Vortigern's betraying Britain and Uther Pendragon's rising to power as the stuff of a serious nationalistic work. He modestly termed it 'an heroic poem', but its twelve-book structure and elevated style, along with his indication that passages were modelled on 'the poets of Greece and Italy' (Preface), suggest that he, like Milton, discerned epic possibilities in the legendary chronicles of early Britain. Although Milman, a clergyman and fellow of Brasenose College, professor of poetry at Oxford from 1821 to 1831, he is justifiably known less for his poetic accomplishments than for his translations of Sanskrit materials, his edition of Edward Gibbon's *Decline and Fall of the Roman Empire*, and his *History of the Jews* and *History of Latin Christianity*. While far less distinguished than these later scholarly works, his attempt at a British epic nevertheless interested him for years. Begun at Eton and nearly completed at Oxford, *Samor* underwent extensive revision even after publication in 1818, with a second edition following in the same year.

The poem deals with the period before Arthur's reign, but in one late episode features Arthur as an infant warrior who begins to fulfil the prophecies of Merlin. For his story, Milman discreetly follows the Vortigern episodes as recounted by Geoffrey of Monmouth's *Historia Regum Britanniae* rather than the more titillating version in Nennius, which apparently provided Thelwall with the shock of incest so necessary to his Gothic theatrical.[7] In general Milman's remains close to Geoffrey's version. King Vortigern consorts with enemy Saxons led by Hengist and Horsa, marries Hengist's daughter Rowenna, and yields control of British lands to the heathens. The threat of Saxon domination ends when Uther Pendragon, son of the good king Constantine, unites the petty kings of Britain to defeat their common foe. On this skeletal plot Milman fleshes out a story about his fictitious hero, Samor. Unabashedly called 'the Avenger', Samor almost singlehandedly raises Uther to power and saves Britain from the Saxon fiends. Milman's preface cites authorities for his characters and plot (Gibbon's *Decline and Fall* and John Whitaker's eighteenth-century *History of Manchester*) and for his hero, whom he claims appears in 'the chronicles', in William Harrison's sixteenth-century *Description of Britain*, and in William Dugdale's seventeenth-century *Baronage of England*. Nevertheless, as Milman's specifically Arthurian passages illustrate, he spins a lengthy romantic adventure from a great skein of his own imaginings and only a few threads of chronicle tradition.

As in a long section of Geoffrey's chronicle (VII, 3–4), which is an expanded version of the earlier *Prophetiae Merlini*, Milman's Merlin prophesies the future of Britain after Vortigern's reign. Unlike the medieval account, where Merlin rather ominously describes his prophetic vision to Vortigern, Milman's poem depicts Merlin encouraging the hero Samor by revealing to him Britain's grand future. In language that occasionally echoes the riddling imagery of Geoffrey, the nineteenth-century 'prophecy' encapsulates famous events associated with British monarchs (Bk. VIII). Obviously affected by the general revulsion from the execution of Louis XVI and subsequent excesses of the French Revolution, Milman celebrates such English rulers as Alfred the Great and the Tudors (especially Elizabeth), gives a sympathetic view of Charles I, and suggests not only the horror of regicide but the failure of government without monarchy. To consecrate this view of history, Milman has his prophet Merlin derive fore-knowledge not from wizardry, but from divine revelation. According to Milman's tale, all the greatness recorded in this synopsis of British history flowers from the seed bed of Arthur's Round Table society, which replaced the fragmented and warring Britain of Vortigern's reign (VIII, 304–12).

Whereas the radical Jacobin Thelwall had found nothing in Arthurian story to express his revolutionary politics, Milman like Geoffrey of Monmouth, Malory, and Spenser, found the material a useful vehicle for royalist sentiments and Arthur a proud symbol of nationalism. But unlike Malory and Spenser, Milman excites little aesthetic interest. Some passages are spirited; most are tedious and sentimental. Least appealing are Milman's liberties with traditional Arthurian story, which emasculate the power of early versions and create laughable improbability. Uther's pursuit of Igerna (Arthur's mother), for example, is in Geoffrey's chronicle and Malory's romance an intense, raw conflict. In the hands of Milman the clergyman, it becomes less shocking to propriety but also less effective. Whereas in medieval tradition Uther lusts for Igerna, the wife of Gorlois, so much that he enlists Merlin's magic to help him lie with her disguised as her husband, in Milman's poem Uther is Igerna's husband and Gorlois her abductor. Samor the Avenger restores Igerna (presumably un-sullied) to Uther.

In this mawkish scene Arthur appears as a babe in arms who is attracted to his father's ostentatious helmet. This interest in armour is not just childish delight, but evidence of his military inclinations. Although the *enfances* of mythological heroes traditionally include miraculous feats, this Arthur is no mere Hercules strangling serpents in the security of his crib. In the battle between the Britons and the Saxons, the infant takes to horse and rallies Uther's troops (XI, 514–23). Predictably, the hero Samor escorts the child safely back to his anguished mother, but not before the world has glimpsed the promise of 'Arthur of Bretagne'.

Milman's tale celebrates the origins of nationalistic consciousness in Britain and, as lodestars of national grandeur, the noble monarchs who have ruled in the tradition of the first great king, Arthur. In passing, it also anticipates the appeal of Arthurian stories of love and spiritual quests. While announcing that his poem tells about the generation before Arthur—'The fathers of that fam'd chivalric race / Of knights and ladies, glorious in old song'— Milman suggests the scope of the Arthurian cycle, including stories such as those of 'White-handed Iseult, Launcelot of the Lake, / Chaste Perceval, that won the Sangreal quest' (XI, 399–402). Because Milman himself vitiated the vitality and emotional appeal of Arthurian story, we may be grateful that he left untold the tales of Iseult and Launcelot, which derived not from the chronicle tradition out of which he worked, but from romance. Milman must have known some of this romance material through his intimate friendship with Reginald Heber, who in the decade preceding publication of *Samor* was using Malory as the basis of his own Arthurian poem. Before publication of Heber's work in 1830, however, Arthurian material would inspire not the epic conceptions which appealed to Milman, but satire and burlesque.

iii. Sir Walter Scott, *The Bridal of Triermain* (1813)

Although Sir Walter Scott's adventurous verse romances do not generally fall under the heading of social satire, his Arthurian episode in *The Bridal of Triermain* offers a fairly interesting satiric use of legendary figures. The light-hearted satire may seem a bit surprising in Scott's sole use of Arthurian lore. On the basis of his serious enthusiasm for medieval tales, his close friend and assistant in compiling and transcribing material for *The Minstrelsy of the Scottish Border*, John Leyden, had suggested as early as 1803 that Scott would be the poet of a 'mightier hand' who would revive Arthurian story and peal 'proud Arthur's march from Fairyland'. This passage from Leyden's long poem *Scenes of Infancy*, which commemorates the past and the landscape around Teviotdale, implies that Scott would treat Arthurian material with the dignity found in Leyden's own allusions to Celtic lore about 'haunted Merlin' and 'victorious Arthur'.

Indeed nineteenth-century British readers might well have expected a substantial Arthurian work from Scott, their authority on romance and chivalry. His essays on these subjects for supplements to the *Encyclopedia Britannica* (1814 ánd 1823) testified to his prolonged and lively study of romance literature. As early as the first year of the century he had begun corresponding with George Ellis regarding stories of the Round Table,[8] and at least nine years before the editions of Malory appeared in 1816, he contemplated editing the *Morte Darthur*. Although he deferred to Southey in a characteristically gallant gesture when he learned that the future Poet Laureate (in whose favour he would decline that title in 1813) planned a similar project,[9] Scott helped to make his readers familiar with Malory even before he published in 1813 his single Arthurian poem, *The Bridal of Triermain*. In his metrical romance *Marmion* (1808), a highly popular 'Tale of Flodden Field' set in the sixteenth century, he alluded to Arthurian incidents and in notes provided long extracts from Malory to acquaint his readers with the story of the Chapel Perilous and Lancelot's quest for the Grail. The introduction to this work describes the continuing appeal of medieval romance, 'How on the ancient minstrel strain / Time lays his palsied hand in vain.' Having remarked the interest of chivalric romance for poets such as Spenser, Milton, and Dryden, Scott affirmed that he himself would 'Essay to break a feeble lance, / In the fair fields of old romance' (Intro. to Canto I). Unfortunately, *The Bridal of Triermain* fulfils this vow rather literally, for it proves to be a 'feeble lance' when entered in the lists with such a work as the *Faerie Queene*.

In his poem Scott invents an Arthurian episode in a spirit generally faithful to medieval romance, while also preserving folklore and documenting allusions in a manner that recalls his eclectic procedures as an antiquarian collector and editor of medieval ballads and romance. His enthusiasm for authentic ballads, which extended back to his boyhood reading of Percy's *Reliques*, did not inhibit his poet's impulse to reshape his material as he prepared the *Minstrelsy* (1802–3). His 'editing' involved free conjectural emendation: He 'improved' diction, filled lacunae, rearranged stanzas, borrowed and excluded episodes, invented transitional passages, and fashioned poems out of as many as ten different medieval versions. In the second and third editions of the *Minstrelsy* (1803, 1806) he also published poems which he had written in the manner of the old ballads. When he edited the incomplete manuscript of *Sir Tristrem*, Scott acknowledged that he composed passages to fill in gaps and, especially, to provide a conclusion, but he did not specifically identify his additions. They are on the whole so successful that few readers can tell where the medieval romancer leaves off and Scott begins. Thus practised in emulating old style and tone while embroidering new material into an authentically medieval tapestry, Scott wrote a fairly readable Arthurian tale in *The Bridal of Triermain*. In three cantos of 113 irregular stanzas, he frames his invented Arthurian episode within a narrative (based on the Sleeping Beauty fairy-tale) which occurs some five hundred years later; he sets both of these stories within a contemporary frame. The poem fails, by and large, because the three tales yield an unwieldy and ultimately rather pointless mix. While the Arthurian episode bears on the other two levels of narrative in occasionally interesting ways, it is essentially gratuitous. It nevertheless remains the most engaging of the three components of the poem.

The work begins in the nineteenth century with a lover of modest means, Arthur, protesting at the pride of his beloved Lucy in rank and wealth. To illustrate her error, he begins a tale 'Of errant knight and damozelle; / Of the dread knot a wizard tied, / In punishment of maiden's pride' (Introduction, viii). His narrative actually involves two stories, one following the quest of Roland de Vaux of Triermain and the other providing the background of the lady this knight seeks. In Plantagenet England, the gallant Sir Roland dreams of a fair lady and awakens determined to marry her—if she exists. He seeks information from the ancient sage Lyulph, who was 'sprung from druid sires, / And British bards that tuned their lyres / To Arthur's and Pendragon's praise' (I, vi). Lyulph tells a story 'handed down from Merlin's age' about the lady of Sir Roland's dream. 'Lyulph's Tale' is the Arthurian portion of Scott's work.

Once King Arthur, seeking adventure, chanced upon a magical castle inhabited by frolicsome damsels. There he became enamoured of their princess, Guendolen. After dallying for three months, Arthur began to regret neglecting his kingdom, and he returned to Camelot after promising Guendolen that if she bore him a daughter, the girl should wed the 'best and bravest' knight proved in the lists. Fifteen years later, when Gyneth interrupted Arthur's Pentecostal feast, the king honoured his vow by proclaiming a tournament. With some foreboding he charged Gyneth to stop the contest if it became too bloody. When his knights, desiring the maiden and her handsome dowry, transformed the joust from sport to deadly combat, Gyneth refused to halt the bloodshed. Finally, after Merlin's young kinsman fell dead, the magician halted the strife and imposed penance on Gyneth. She would lie in enchanted sleep for centuries, until awakened by a knight 'for feats of arms as far renowned / As warrior of the Table Round' (II, xxvi). Here ends Lyulph's Arthurian tale, which explains the lady in Roland de Vaux's dream, and we return to the time when Roland sets out to awaken Arthur's enchanted daughter.

In Canto III, after Scott's modern narrator has wed his Lucy, he resumes the tale of Roland de Vaux to satisfy her curiosity. At Gyneth's castle the knight withstands various temptations and finally awakens the princess with a kiss; lightning flashes, thunder roars, and the enchanted castle vanishes. The narrator concludes by emphasising the didactic purpose of his two old stories: 'Adventure high of other days / By ancient bards is told, / Bringing, perchance, like my poor tale, / Some moral truth in fiction's veil' (Conclusion, ii).

Scott, grafting his new story of the liaison of King Arthur and Guendolen and the disastrous tournament onto traditional matter, worked much as medieval romancers must have done, expanding the Arthurian cycle through accretion of new episodes. But he violated this organic and traditional growth process by uneasily joining stories set in different 'ages'. This awkward combination proves to be the weakest aspect of the poem, not because medieval and modern episodes cannot work together successfully (as they do in Tennyson's 'The Epic' and 'Morte d'Arthur'; see ch. 1), but because Scott's connections, while functioning as sophisticated structuring devices, lack sufficient thematic significance.

But at the same time that Scott freely invents an episode, he remains faithful to the large outlines of Arthurian legend, as when he refers to Lancelot, Tristram, and Caradoc, who refuse to vie for Gyneth's hand: 'There were two who lov'd their neighbours' wives / And one who loved his own' (II, xviii). Scott also alludes to the final battle with Mordred at Camlan, which was nearly circumvented by the calamitous tournament. To forestall this thwarting of the legendary destiny, Scott supplies a properly awesome Merlin, who conjures whirlwind and earthquake to halt the tournament bloodshed (II, xxv–xxvi).

Besides alluding to such elements in Arthurian legend, Scott builds the stories of both King Arthur and Sir Roland upon motifs standard in medieval romance: the knight's amorous adventures in a magical castle full of lovely ladies (as in the stories of Lancelot and Perceval); the appearance of an unknown youth, begotten by an errant knight, to claim recognition at court (as in the story of the Fair Unknown, Galahad); the lady on a white palfrey who interrupts a feast at Camelot (as in Malory's account of Arthur's wedding feast); the quest for a lady in a dream (as in Chaucer's *Tale of Sir Thopas*, which Scott cites in his epigraph). Other links to medieval literature appear in allusions to pieces in Percy's *Reliques* (for example, the reference to Caradoc's chaste wife in the ballad of 'The Boy and the Mantle'). Scott's notes explain such allusions as well as references to folklore generally related to Arthur, as when he identifies 'the Round Table' at Penrith, a land configuration associated in folk memory with chivalric contests. His Arthurian world reflects standard romance depictions. At Caerleon or Camelot or Carlisle (Scott offers all the alternatives) 'wine and mirth did most abound, / And harpers play'd their blithest round' (II, xiv), and 'glee and game / Mingled with feats of martial fame' (II, xii). Yet the Round Table also represents religious and social order: 'all who suffered causeless wrong, / From tyrant proud or traitour strong, / Sought Arthur's presence to complain, / Nor there for aid implored in vain' (II, xi).

Significantly, into these traditional descriptions Scott injects an irreverent view of Arthur and his courtiers. Arthur himself thirsts for excitement and behaves irresponsibly. Not content to remain at court with Guenever, he prefers errant adventuring. When he encounters Guendolen, however, he readily exchanges adventure for the delights of the boudoir. Though Arthur in medieval romance sometimes manifests boyish enthusiasm for game and adventure (as in *Sir Gawain and the Green Knight*), early literature offers little precedent for Scott's king as so errant a knight or so cavalier a husband. Malory's Arthur, for example, enjoys several liaisons (one of which, of course, produces Mordred), but this philandering occurs only before he marries. Scott's treatment may have been suggested by medieval tales of the 'false Guenever', which George Ellis mentions in his *Specimens*. These versions, in the Vulgate *Merlin* and *Lancelot*, depict Arthur's setting aside his wife for another woman named Guenever (thus permitting the queen to remain with Lancelot), until he is forced by needs of the realm to resume his rightful marriage. In using the name Guendolen for the king's paramour, a name which in medieval romance sometimes designates Guenever (as in the late thirteenth-century Latin prose romance, the *Historia Meriadoci*), Scott in effect creates the doubling at work in the stories of a true and a false Guenever.

Throughout his story of Arthur's adultery, Scott maintains a blithe, irreverent tone, offering comedy and satire rather than tragedy or moral instruction. His light-hearted description of the bevy of boisterous beauties who welcome the king to Guendolen's castle illustrates this tone (I, xvii). Nor does he evaluate Guenever's affair harshly. While Arthur amuses himself elsewhere, 'the frank hearted monarch full little did wot, / That she smiled, in his absence, on brave Lancelot' (I, xi). Scott's Arthurian story at times approaches the satire of human foibles found in a comedy of manners, as in the scene where Gyneth appears at court, giving evidence of Arthur's earlier vagrancy. The situation affords some entertaining interplay among the characters. While the king welcomes his heretofore unknown daughter, he furtively checks Guenever's reaction. Free of jealousy, she shows amoral good cheer and enjoys the scene as a license for her own indiscretions: 'But she, unruffled at the scene, / Of human frailty construed mild, / Looked upon Lancelot, and smiled' (II, xv).

This ironic detachment and wry humour with which Scott, like Guenever, mildly regards the human frailty of his Arthurian world contrasts with his more typical sense of propriety, which is illustrated in an editorial controversy about his *Sir Tristrem*. When John Leyden had discovered, one thousand lines into transcribing the manuscript of the romance, an explicit reference to the female anatomy, he refused to affix his name to the edition. Scott, who thought that 'the extreme antiquity of the language is a complete fig-leaf',[10] nevertheless published the work without the offending line—except in a dozen copies he termed 'uncastrated', which he sent to fellow antiquarians.[11] Even though he would submit to delicate sensibilities despite his scholar's impulse, in *The Bridal of Triermain* he could also suspend reticence for purposes of satire. This treatment was possible because Camelot does not exist in the later Middle Ages which Scott treated with consistent dignity elsewhere in his verse and novels. He imbues the framing story of Sir Roland de Vaux, set in the twelfth century, with moral earnestness, celebrating the knight's courage, honour, and purity. In the modern passages, on the other hand, he adopts a lightly satiric stance, deriding nineteenth-century snobbishness and the pretensions of sportsmen and artists, 'lordings and witlings' (II, i). This modern sense of human nature—not an idealised chivalry—is what Scott projects through the coy machinations of Guendolen's seductive damsels or the exaggerated alacrity with which Arthur's knights ignore their ladies' pleading glances in order to compete for Gyneth's large dowry. In 'Lyulph's Tale' even though the Round Table represents chivalric principles, close-ups of individuals consistently reveal a comic sense of human weakness detached from any specific age or culture.

We should also keep in mind the importance of different voices in the poem, all of which is 'spoken' by the contemporary suitor Arthur. He is lecturing his Lucy against pride, but just as important, he is flirting and trying to amuse her more than his more fashionable rivals do. Cannily, this narrator attributes the slightly amoral, comic perspective of the Arthurian world to the ancient sage, Lyulph, and reserves for his own speaking voice the orthodox morality of Roland's story. Although the Arthurian section of *The Bridal of Triermain* is by far more entertaining than the narrative of Roland's idealised quest for his Sleeping Beauty, ultimately it palls because it accomplishes so little.

But perhaps we should not expect too much from this type of poetry. Entertainment seems to have been the primary purpose behind Scott's original conception of the work. It began as a spoof, as a fragmentary parody of his own writing style published along with parodies of George Crabbe and Thomas Moore in the *Edinburgh Register* of 1809 (pub. 1811) as the work of 'Caleb Quotem'. Apparently the unfinished verse seized Scott's imagination, so he developed the story. But even when he published the completed work, he maintained anonymity and actually sought through 'systematic mystification' to imply that it was the work of his friend William Erskine. Although he later claimed that this elaborate ruse was intended to test the reviewers, who too often evaluated the name of the author rather than the merit of the work, he may actually have been exploring new narrative tactics—and a newly satiric tone—

under protective anonymity, as well as testing the taste of the reading public, which increasingly preferred Lord Byron's verse romances to his own.[12] *The Bridal of Triermain* was less successful than Scott's other metrical romances. The fact that it soon inspired two insipid theatrical productions (Ellerton's operetta *Triermain*, 1831; and Isaac Pocock's *King Arthur and the Knights of the Round Table: A New Grand Chivalric Entertainment, in Three Acts*, 1834) testifies less to the impact of the poem than to the lucrative value of associating Sir Walter Scott's name with any enterprise.

In *The Bridal of Triermain* Scott's narrator, assuming the sprightly voice of Lyulph, declares the pre-eminence of the chivalric age in qualities which inspire great tales: 'The attributes of those high days / Now only live in minstrel lays, / . . . / Strength was gigantic, valour high, / And wisdom soar'd beyond the sky' (II, xix). Yet Scott soon turned altogether from 'minstrel lays' or verse romances and also abandoned Arthuriana for more congenial material. While his exceedingly popular novels retain a chivalric and romantic spirit regardless of their chronological settings, Scott was more at home with the quasi-historical subject matter and local colour afforded by a past and a society somewhat closer to his own world than was the realm of Arthur. His medieval novels are set more comfortably near the age of Sir Roland de Vaux than the remote legendary past of King Arthur. Though *The Bridal of Triermain* holds a relatively insignificant place in Scott's literary career, it is significant in the development of nineteenth-century Arthurian literature, for it illustrated that Arthurian material could serve as a vehicle for comedy and satire without itself being dismembered. To an ironic perspective, the frankly fabulous legends offered human personalities and situations eminently susceptible to satiric probing. This possibility, hinted by Scott's poem, would prove the basis of effective satire in the Arthurian work soon to be written by Thomas Love Peacock and, later, by Mark Twain.

iv. John Hookham Freere, *The Monks and the Giants* (1817, 1818)

Nearly a decade before Scott published his partly Arthurian romance, he had received a letter from George Ellis discussing the nature of romance. Ellis and another devotee of medieval literature, John Hookham Freere, had concurred that 'The *only* thing *essential* to a romance was, that it should be *believed* by the hearers.'[13] While Scott's Arthurian episode may be said to be as 'believable' as romances ever were, Freere's work involving Arthurian characters, familiarly called *The Monks and the Giants*, patently aims at comic absurdity. Freere had early attracted the attention of Scott with his Middle English version of an Old English heroic poem, *The Battle of Brunanburgh*, and in turn greatly admired Scott's edition of *Sir Tristrem*.[14] Despite this serious interest in medieval literature, however, Freere, unlike Scott, did not attempt to join a new episode to the larger framework of existing Arthurian legend. Instead, he merely began his burlesque (of over two hundred *ottava rima* stanzas) with a tale ostensibly about

Arthurian knights, but soon shifted concern to monks, giants—and nothing Arthurian in sight.

The formal title for Cantos I and II, published in 1817, and again for Cantos III and IV, published in 1818, intentionally generates false expectations among readers, for it claims to be *A Prospectus and Specimen of an Intended National Work, by William and Robert Whistlecraft, of Stow-Market, in Suffolk, Harness and Collar-Makers. Intended to Comprise the Most Interesting Particulars Relating to King Arthur and His Round Table*. The descriptive title is as ironic as the ruse of the fictitious poets Whistlecraft. Only the first two cantos are Arthurian—in that they use traditional characters—and the story itself has no medieval antecedents. In promising to offer a 'national work' comprising 'the most interesting particulars relating to King Arthur', the saddlers would seem to be undertaking the national epic which both Milton and Wordsworth had considered and rejected. The joke lies in the harness makers' inadequate sense of what constitutes a national poem, an epic manner, or even 'interesting particulars'. Frere intended to illustrate what he called 'the burlesque of ordinary rude uninstructed common sense' by showing the pedestrian minds of his 'thoroughly common' authors working with the 'lofty and serious subjects' of medieval romance.[15] To do so, as an early editor observed, 'he had to revive the Arthurian subject as well as to vulgarise it'.[16] Consequently he had his harness makers employ Arthurian knights in a tale of their own invention wherein little happens, and interest derives from the banal perspective and lively colloquial style of these 'narrators' as they 'rub down the Round Table' and 'put a coat of varnish on the Fable' (Proem, xi).

Cantos I and II relate the conflict between Arthurian knights and a band of giants. The tale begins at Arthur's Christmas feast at Carlisle, which is interrupted by news that some fair ladies have been abducted by giants (II, v). Arthur's knights set out to rescue the women. After locating the giants' fortress, Sir Tristram rather unaccountably wanders from the encampment. When he returns three days later, he argues against Gawain's proposed siege and leads a foray which inexplicably routs the giants. Glimpsing the knights, they flee their stronghold, leaving Tristram and company as the surprised liberators of the ladies. This episode concludes the Arthurian section of Frere's work; Cantos III and IV describe the giants attacking a monastery because they detest the sound of the friars' bells. After bombarding the monastery with stones, the giants abruptly cease for no apparent reason. The work ends by returning us neatly to the beginning of Canto I. As the monks survey the desolation and wonder why their attackers withdrew, we learn that the giants have rushed away to capture the ladies whose disappearance will draw Arthur's knights away from their Christmas feast.

This circular device does more than represent a harness maker's faulty notion of beginning *in medias res*, for we do not merely plunge into the middle of a tale in traditional epic fashion, return to the past, work our way back to the middle, and then move on. Frere in a sense indicates that the work cannot end, and that somehow it never quite gets under way, for the end is the beginning. When we arrive back at the beginning, moreover, we become aware that little has happened, much as when Tristram leads his reconnaissance party towards the giants' fortress, but becomes lost in the darkness and arrives back at his starting point. Though he subsequently routs the giants, chance rather than logic or action accounts for the measure of success. Frere thus superficially invites his readers to see little point in the tale, but at the same time, the disorganised and digressive narrative structure of the Whistlecrafts, as well as the chaotic actions of the characters, imply that Frere is concerned with the need for order, organisation, and leadership.

For the Arthurian elements of his comedy Frere shows little specific indebtedness to medieval literature, although even before the 1816 publication of the *Morte Darthur* he probably knew Malory through his friendship with George Ellis. Frere's story follows Arthurian literature only in the familiar romance motif of the knights' quest initiated at a feast by a distressed damsel's plea for assistance. While the story line is freely innovative, however, Frere's characterisation is fairly traditional, except that his colloquial language and wry view of human nature render his Arthurian characters overtly comic. Though Arthur, who, conventionally, represents civilising justice, remains undeveloped, his court comes alive in fuller detail, and in a comic vein natural to the low vision of the harness makers. The aristocratic society is earthy and animated, rather like the vivacious 'scullery tribe' who prepare their Christmas feast below stairs. The knights' 'manners were refin'd and perfect—saving / Some modern graces, which they could not catch, / As spitting through the teeth' (I, x). These polished fellows, 'a manly, generous generation', remain 'prepar'd, on proper provocation, / To give the lie, pull noses, stab and kick; / And for that very reason, it is said, / They were so very courteous and well-bred' (I, xi).

For all the comedy of this boisterous setting, Frere permits some of the subtler drama underlying the traditional Arthurian legends to surface fleetingly. He suggests, for example, Launcelot's concealed tensions: 'As if some secret recollection shook / His inward heart with unacknowledged pain' (I, xv). Even this seemingly sensitive view of Launcelot hints of irony, however, for the Whistlecrafts use a fictitious source, 'Morgan's Chronicle', as their 'authority' for Launcelot's character (I, xii–xiv). Tristram acquires more overtly satiric and more ambiguous colouring than Launcelot. Frere does nothing with the medieval tradition of the lover who unwittingly consumes the fateful love potion with Iseult, but he does build on the general view of Tristram's craftiness and manifold talents, which he would have encountered in Scott's edition of *Sir Tristrem*. But Frere's Tristram is a prodigal, mirthful, sportive figure—'Somewhat more learned than became a Knight, / It was reported he could read and write' (I, xxii). He easily entertains courtiers with his ready wit, tales, and songs. Setting out for battle with his falcon, spaniel, and horde of jests, he remains enigmatic. Most perplexing is his temporarily abandoning the quest for the captured ladies: 'That morning Tristram happen'd to secede: / . . . some suspected / He went lest his advice should be neglected' (II, xix). During his absence he pursues a strange red bird, an incident which calls to mind medieval romance motifs of knights pursuing magical beasts into supernatural adventures. Here, however, Tristram's hunt proves to be only a whimsical diversion from the serious business at hand, and Frere emphasises the quirky unpredictability of the knight. The supernatural bird, which in medieval romance would have heralded marvels, only teases Tristram's perverse desire for mastery (II, xxii). The point seems to be that the plebeian minds of our harness makers conceive not of heroes, but of all too human figures whose vanity and pettiness prompt them to subordinate important missions to self-aggrandising or trivial concerns. Even their battle heroics become comic, as when Tristram decapitates a giant so quickly that the trunk stands bewildered for a time before it falls beside its head. Similar puzzlement plagues both the participants and the narrators when they analyse the heroics: 'The Giants ran away—they knew not why— / Sir Tristram gained the point—he knew not how— / He could account for it no more than I' (II, xl).

Frere's purposes for describing such battlefield shenanigans may have been quite specific and topical. His contemporaries read *The Monks and the Giants*, especially the behaviour of Tristram and Gawain at the siege, as a satire of British conduct of the Peninsular campaigns against Napoleon (1808–13). The failure of Sir John Moore's expedition against the French had somewhat discredited Frere, who at the time had served as Envoy and Plenipotentiary to the Spanish Central Junta.[17] Although Frere denied any political invective and suggested that he abandoned the poem because readers wrongly persisted in reading it as political satire,[18] it obliquely criticises the lack of discipline and organisation in the Spanish and Portuguese expeditions—just the sort of issue that Frere had addressed as a principal contributor (along with George Ellis) to the brilliant satiric political journal, the *Anti-Jacobin* (1797–98). For readers today, however, the topical satire is virtually lost.

Ultimately *The Monks and the Giants* achieves little, which is not really surprising when we know that Frere divided his leisure time between composing verses and playing backgammon. The poem to some extent burlesques heroic pretensions as well as mundane Whistlecraft minds unable to conceive of greatness. Its principal target is the human personality, with its egotism, triviality, and instability. But not even the author claimed much significance for the work. He explained that he abandoned his 'mere *jeu d'esprit*', although he had projected another episode and written further verses, because 'to persevere in a nonsensical work merely for the sake of the good judges of nonsense' was scarcely worthwhile.[19] The major interest of the work today lies not in its matter but in its manner: Frere's sprightly style, colloquial ease, lilting pace, ingenious comic rhymes, and engaging juxtaposition of serious and comic elements. Its greatest importance is that it reintroduced into English the use of an *ottava rima* stanza (which had been used occasionally in the Renaissance by such poets as Wyatt, Spenser, and Drayton) for a long poem in the spirit of the Italian serio-comic romances of Pulci, Berni, and Boiardo. Apparently Frere's work enjoyed only minor success. Although the publisher John Murray issued three editions in quick succession, the poem did not sell well, and remainder copies were long available. But one reader was much influenced by the style, and to Frere must go substantial credit for inspiring many of the stylistic felicities of Byron's *Beppo* and *Don Juan*.

As an Arthurian work, *The Monks and the Giants* contributed little to the revival of Arthurian tradition in nineteenth-century England. The best that may be said is that the poem avoids the melodramatic excesses of Thelwall, uses Arthurian figures in a new episode which is not wholly incompatible with traditional depictions, and amuses its readers without making Arthurian matter itself ridiculous.

v. Thomas Love Peacock, *The Misfortunes of Elphin* (1829)

A more consistently successful satiric use of Arthurian material is Thomas Love Peacock's prose romance *The Misfortunes of Elphin*, which like *The Monks and the Giants* focuses not on a polished chivalric society or on tales drawn from romances such as Malory's, but on the more primitive, earthy society first associated with the Celtic, supernatural Arthur. The work is one of Peacock's most distinguished brief romance-novels. Most often remembered as a critic of Romanticism (despite his friendship with Shelley), Peacock had married a Welsh woman and studied the Welsh language and literature. Written with this background, *The Misfortunes of Elphin* creates the aura of early Welsh tales while at the same time offering the neoclassical satire so pronounced in his other novels. The product is a curious mixture: nostalgic descriptions of Welsh settings and romanticised glimpses of young love and heroism combined with unsentimental views of rugged medieval life. These disparate elements harmonise in a satire of human foibles limited to no particular age or place.

Peacock had referred superficially to Arthurian matter in two early poems, but they scarcely foreshadowed the more substantial treatment of Celtic legend in his prose. In the verse, published by the Juvenile Library, Arthurian characters introduce lessons on grammar and history. 'Sir Hornbook: or, Childe Launcelot's Expedition, A Grammatico-Allegorical Ballad' (1814) presents rudimentary lessons in grammar and syntax through the motif of the chivalric quest. It is difficult to imagine that any child could be inspired by Childe Launcelot's mission: guided by Sir Hornbook past Sir Substantive, the lady Adjective, Sir Pronoun, and Sir Verb, he arrives before the Muses' gates, where he is left to wander in the sacred bowers of Etymology. 'The Round Table; or, King Arthur's Feast' (1817) is rather more interesting (though perhaps not for children) in that it exhibits the irony characteristic of Peacock's prose works and hints at the usefulness of legend for contemporary satire. Peacock's preface describes his innovation in using the myth of Arthur's expected reappearance as a premise for listing English monarchs. Merlin, to lessen his king's tedium as he awaits return to England, conjures up a banquet for the rulers who succeeded Arthur. Peacock depicts them through amusing satiric details—Henry VIII's wives dine with axes suspended above their heads; Catholic James II insists that everyone eat Roman macaroni. This sprightly irreverence also marks the introduction of Arthur: 'King Arthur sat down by the lonely sea-coast, / As thin as a lath, and as pale as a ghost.' Although the poem begins with Arthur (smoking a pipe) inquiring 'when shall the fates re-establish my reign, / And spread my round-table in Britain again?', Peacock's history lesson, like his grammar lesson, did nothing to re-establish Arthur's literary reign. But Peacock saw greater possibilities in the Arthurian legend than his juvenile poems realised, and in 1816 he began a work which uses the material to criticise contemporary society pointedly. In *Calidore*, a prose satire never completed and published only after his death, Peacock invents an account of Arthur's life between the battle of Camlan and his promised return to England. Unlike traditional conceptions of Avalon, Peacock's reunites the King with his knights, Merlin, and 'his dear queen Guenever, and her dear friend Sir Launcelot' on an island already inhabited by the boisterous pagan deities, led by Bacchus, who were displaced by the medieval Christianity associated with Arthurian chivalry. The courtiers enthusiastically take up the Bacchanalian existence. Because Arthur occasionally wonders if the time is ripe for his return to England, Merlin magically dispatches a youth to nineteenth-century Wales to assess the situation. In a manner reminiscent of *Gulliver's Travels*, the bewildering and comic experiences of this naif criticise the more 'civilised' society, until the fragment abruptly breaks off.

Peacock's more ambitious and extended treatment of Arthurian legend in the comic romance *The Misfortunes of Elphin* achieves vitality not only from developing the satiric potential merely hinted at in 'King Arthur's Feast' and the fragment of *Calidore*, but also from following medieval tradition more skilfully than do these earlier whimsical pieces. He draws not from the relatively sophisticated romances, available even in the Welsh—(in *Gereint*, *Owein*, and *Peredur*)—but from primitive and mythic poems, tales, and pseudo-history. His use of Celtic materials was resourceful and even daring, for at the time he wrote, nearly a decade before Lady Charlotte Guest's distinguished translations called the *Mabinogion*, these seemingly naive, unpolished works were considered to be rustic curiosities scarcely worthy of serious literary interest. Peacock vividly evokes the spirit of this early literature, with its disarming sense of wonder, its love of exaggeration, and its relish for playing with language and sound. His accomplishment results from serious study of medieval materials and respectful delight in their vigour. Even so, he departs from the tradition seen in the early Welsh material in two significant ways: He reduces the role of supernatural occurrences and portents and omits the magical powers of individual characters so important in Welsh tales, and he includes material familiar from Latin chronicle accounts (such as Arthur's triumphant return from the battle of Badon Hill) but foreign to Welsh story. As in the early *Culhwch and Olwen* and *The Dream of Rhonabwy*, both included in Lady Guest's *Mabinogion*, Arthur is not the central character, but a presence who by the end of the work redresses wrongs and restores order. Even as Peacock pieces his plot from motifs and incidents traditional in Welsh lore and literature, he stamps everything with his own characteristic play with language (especially inflated diction and neologisms), neoclassical satire, and irony.

The plot traces several 'misfortunes' of Elphin, a Celtic princeling. First, his province is almost totally inundated when the kingdom's protective embankment crumbles during a storm. This disaster occurs through the drunken negligence of Seithenyn ap Seithyn, keeper of the embankment. After escaping the flood, Elphin marries the daughter of Seithenyn (who has presumably drowned) and becomes a salmon fisher hard pressed to survive on the tiny remains of his kingdom. Another apparent misfortune befalls Elphin when a dream prophesying that he will find a great treasure in his salmon nets yields only an unknown infant in a basket. This child, Taliesin, eventually becomes the foremost of the Celtic bards. In his youth, he remedies Elphin's second serious misfortune, imprisonment by Maelgon for insisting that Angharad, Elphin's wife, is the fairest and chastest wife in the island of Britain. In order to effect the release of his foster father, Taliesin craftily seizes the son of Elphin's captor and asks King Arthur to persuade Maelgon to exchange prisoners. To win Arthur's support, Taliesin discovers the whereabouts of Gwenyvar, who has been abducted by King Melvas. An unexpected bonus of Taliesin's endeavour is his discovery that Seithenyn had actually survived the inundation many years before and continues to consume a flood of wine with unabated zeal. The novel concludes with all prisoners freed, Gwenyvar restored to Arthur, Taliesin betrothed to his beloved, and Seithenyn named second butler in charge of Arthur's wines.

This eventful plot (one of Peacock's best sustained narratives) grows from his direct contact with Wales and his reading such works as Richard Colt Hoare's translation of the 'Itinerary through Wales, and the Description of Wales' by Giraldus Cambrensis, a twelfth-century account of the history, customs, and topography of the region; Owen Jones' *Myvyrian Archaiology of Wales*, a large collection of Welsh literature and triads; Edward Davies' study, *The Mythology and Rites of the Druids*, which translates an account of Taliesin's birth; and *The Cambro-Britain*, a journal of Celtic studies published between 1819 and 1822. In addition, Peacock may also have known more esoteric works such as Edward Jones' *Bardic Museum* (1802), which condenses part of the *History of Taliesin*; T. J. L. Pritchard's *Land Beneath the Sea* (1824), and Percy Enderbie's *Cambria Triumphans* (1661; repr. 1810).[20]

This study of Celtic material provided the three traditional tales fused in Peacock's plot: The story of Seithenyn and the flooding of the land of Gwythno (the subject of a poem in the twelfth-century *Black Book of Carmarthen*), the birth and prophecies of Taliesin (familiar from many Celtic poems and tales and the twelfth-century *Book of Taliesin*), and the abduction of Arthur's queen by Melvas (told in the eleventh-century *Vita Gildae* by Caradoc of Llancarfan and also familiar in the abduction by Meleagant in the twelfth-century *Lancelot* of Chrétien de Troyes). In the process of conflating these three stories, Peacock records a great deal of Welsh folk heritage. He offers legendary explanations for land formations, describes in detail cultural phenomena such as Yule celebrations, and explores etymologies of Welsh terms. He also encapsulates such legends as the story of Merlin's hamper (which each night multiplies its contents a hundred-fold), alludes to such ballads as 'The Boy and the Mantle', and uses such motifs recurrent in Welsh tales as the mysterious arrival of an infant and the debate over whose wife is most chaste. He also includes in chapter epigraphs and in the narrative itself a number of the distinctive Welsh *Triads*, in which, Peacock says, the Welsh 'bound up all their knowledge, physical, traditional, and mythological' (p. 60). Thus Peacock refers to such pity lists as 'three principal cities of the isle of Britain', 'three foundations of intellect', 'three primary requisites of poetical genius', and 'three chaste kisses of the island of Britain'.

The Misfortunes of Elphin is consequently a delightful storehouse of miscellaneous Celtic literary and folk material, and Peacock took pride in its medieval authenticity. His friend Edward Strachey recalled: 'I heard him say that he had great difficulty in getting at the true story of Taliesin's birth . . . and he was proud of the fact that Welsh archaeologists treated his book as a serious and valuable addition to Welsh history.'[21] Peacock thus reflected—and advanced—the enthusiasm of antiquarians, historians, and editors of the Celtic revival, and *The Misfortunes of Elphin* was soon after publication said to be 'the most entertaining book, if not the best, that has yet been published on the ancient customs and traditions of Wales'.[22]

Though grounded in traditional material, however, Peacock's work is exceedingly individual and inventive. Perhaps the clearest illustration of his creative use of old material is to be seen in the songs which punctuate the narrative. Some of these are translations—though extremely loose—of authentic Celtic songs; all manifest a convincing bardic spirit derived from Peacock's acquaintance with medieval songs; but the best are Peacock's invention. He freely adapted Welsh originals which appeared in the *Myvyrian Archaiology of Wales* ('The Consolation of Elphin' matches its source more closely than the others). Clearly, however, the most memorable of the songs are Peacock's own, as in 'The War-Song of Dinas Vawr', which T. H. White was later to adapt: 'The mountain sheep are sweeter, / But the valley sheep are fatter; / We therefore deemed it meeter / To carry off the latter' (p. 89).

The energy, wit, and good cheer of Peacock's songs enliven the barbarism of his Celtic world. This Arthurian society is peopled by rough tribal chieftains who not only sing exuberantly in the mead halls, but once outside, snatch other men's cattle and wives with equal relish. For all Peacock's delight in the vigour and animation of this world, he never sentimentalises his characters. Arthur, for example, is not simply the national hero described in the chronicles, the only 'human hope against' the 'infidel Saxons' (p. 128), for Peacock always anchors his heroic suggestions to 'the mutability of all sublunary things' (p. 101). Thus this view of Arthur as a heroic saviour balances with Taliesin's prophetic awareness that 'notwithstanding the actual triumphs of Arthur', the struggle with the Saxons will culminate in his follower's 'being dispossessed of all the land of Britain, except the wild region of Wales'. This satiric echo of the generally disparaging English view of the region Peacock had found so beautiful precedes a more serious satiric thrust at human foibles: The forecast defeat is 'a result which political sagacity might have apprehended from [the Britons'] disunion' (p. 102).

Even the heroic Arthur himself remains susceptible to satire. Although he seems eager to regain his lost queen, he readily assuages his longing with great festivities. After Melvas decamps before Arthur can locate him and Gwenyvar, the 'king of the kings of Britain' is 'reduced to the alternative of making the best of his Christmas with the ladies, princes, and bards who crowded his court' (p. 109). Apparently this proves no unpalatable task, for he 'kept his Christmas so merrily, that the memory of it passed into a proverb: "As merry as Christmas in Caer Lleon" ' (p. 111). Arthur's relationship with his queen remains the subject of comic innuendo throughout the work. His cuckoldry becomes the topic of conversation over wine cups, and when Taliesin restores Gwenyvar to Arthur 'as pure as on the day King Melvas has carried her off', Modred's wife retorts, 'None here will doubt that' (p. 146). Such wry aspersions on Gwenyvar's fidelity suggest the sort of ironic undercutting which persistently tempers Peacock's portrayal of medieval men and women: he keeps us aware that great epochs are shaped by mere mortals. Gwenyvar at this point slaps Modred's sharp-tongued wife, reminding us of the ironically trivial cause for the ultimate destruction of Arthur's order in the original Welsh legends, for, as Peacock correctly says, 'This slap is recorded in the Bardic Triads as one of the Three Fatal Slaps of the Island of Britain. A terrible effect is ascribed to this small cause; for it is said to have been the basis of that enmity between Arthur and Modred, which terminated in the battle of Camlan, wherein all the flower of Britain perished on both sides' (p. 147).

No other Arthurian characters figure prominently in Peacock's narrative, although some—Gawain, Caradoc, and Tristram, for example—are briefly identified. Merlin, who as a bard is inferior to Taliesin, appears as 'Merddin Gwyllt, or Merlin the Wild, who was so deep in the secrets of nature, that he obtained the fame of a magician, to which he had at least as good a title as either Friar Bacon or Cornelius Agrippa' (p. 108). Like Arthur, Merlin furnishes possibilities for sly humour: in this primitive Christian society, he is thought to be 'secretly attached' to 'a mystical type of the doctrines and fortunes of Druidism' (p. 138). More than individual characters, however, the bustling court town of Caer Lleon, 'now the seat of the most illustrious sovereign that had yet held the sceptre of Britain' (p. 101), comes alive. Built by Romans, whose baths, temples, and amphitheatres still stand as emblems of 'the vicissitudes of empire' (p. 101), the city boasts 'streets . . . thronged with people, especially of the fighting order, of whom a greater number flocked about Arthur, than he always found it convenient to pay' (p. 106). These playful portrayals of Arthurian characters and setting and the pertly rueful references to human weaknesses shaping history account for only a fraction of the rich humour in *The Misfortunes of Elphin*. The most overt comedy is provided by the character Seithenyn ap Seithyn, and the most significant comic satire by Peacock's juxtaposing medieval and modern societies.

Seithenyn, the subject of several poems which made him well known in Welsh legend, is introduced in an epigraph drawn from a Welsh Triad naming 'The three immortal drunkards of the isle of Britain' (p. 10). As enamoured of wine as Falstaff is of sack, this riotous figure has been compared to Shakespeare's old knight as one of the great comic figures in English literature.[23] Drunkenly contorted 'logic' permeates Seithenyn's speeches. When Elphin warns that the embankment protecting the realm from the sea may soon collapse, Seithenyn's rebuttal illustrates Peacock's method of turning medieval comedy into serious satire of nineteenth-century issues: 'Every thing that is old must decay. That the embankment is old, I am free to confess; that it is somewhat rotten in parts, I will not altogether deny; that it is any the worse for that, I do most sturdily gainsay. It does its business well. . . . Our ancestors were wiser than we: they built it in their wisdom; and, if we should be so rash as to try to mend it, we should only mar it' (p. 15). He continues that 'there is nothing so dangerous as innovation', and 'this immortal work has stood for centuries, and will stand for centuries more, if we let it alone' (p. 16). The speech mockingly echoes the sentiments of conservative members of Parliament in Regency England who opposed the changes embodied in the Reform Bill of 1832 and praised the sanctity of the existing order.[24] Elsewhere Peacock's narrative voice criticises a wide range of topics, including nineteenth-century economic practices, pollution and the dehumanising aspects of industrialism, foolish literary tastes, and even the British convention of banal talk about the weather.

One reviewer deplored Peacock's method of satirising the present by comparing it to the earlier age: 'It is not for the genuine satirist, either directly or indirectly, to insinuate the superiority of half-barbaric states of existence, by partially adverting to the evils consequent on higher stages of civilisation.'[25] His specious premise notwithstanding, the reviewer failed to perceive that Peacock's satire does not criticise the present alone. Because he does not glamorise the relatively primitive age of Arthur, his satiric barbs graze its eccentricities and imperfections as well as those of the present. For all its comedy and good humour, the work shows knavery—selfishness, pride, and cruelty—to be the general condition of man, regardless of the historical period.

In fusing medieval and modern elements in his narrative, Peacock suggests the importance of interpreting the past meaningfully. His version of nineteenth-century attitudes towards the remains of Glastonbury Abbey indicates that we often misunderstand or misvalue former ages. On the one hand, dry, factual analysis can lead us to study the medieval world in isolation from our own, disregarding organic connections between the two: 'These ruins were overgrown with the finest ivy in England, till it was, not long since, pulled down by some Vandal, whom the Society of Antiquaries had sent down to make drawings of the walls, which he executed literally, by stripping them bare, that he might draw the walls, and nothing else.' Thus the student of the past may shear away some of its value for the present by looking only at the concrete or by preventing the accretions of intervening time from blending the old gracefully with the new. At the other extreme, sentimentalists—the 'musing moralist' who merely 'dreams of the days that are gone' and the 'sentimental cockney' who postures melodramatically—may distort the past (p. 116). Whereas the sketching 'Vandal' reads only stone, these two types mistakenly read their imaginations as the testimony of history.

In his own version of Arthurian story Peacock attempted to forge from tradition a new literature meaningful to a new age. His recasting of the traditional matter in so inventive and distinctive a form may be related to his critical theory expressed several years earlier in 'The Four Ages of Poetry' (1820). In the essay he describes the literary periods of antiquity in a sequence proceeding from an age of iron to gold, declining to silver, finally to brass. He then describes the literature of modern times, beginning with the poetry of the Middle Ages as the modern equivalent of the iron age. Medieval romances of 'Arthur and his knights of the round table' were barbaric (though somewhat enlightened by classical learning), superstitious, adventurous, and chivalric. The succeeding modern golden age he places in the days of Ariosto and Shakespeare. A rather full quotation may suggest how closely his description of the Renaissance achievement anticipates his own in *The Misfortunes of Elphin*: 'From these ingredients of the iron age of modern poetry, dispersed in the rhymes of minstrels and the songs of the troubadours, arose the golden age, in which the scattered materials were harmonised and blended about the time of the revival of learning; but with this peculiar difference, that Greek and Roman literature pervaded all the poetry of the golden age of modern poetry, and hence resulted a heterogeneous compound of all ages and nations in one picture; an infinite licence, which gave to the poet the free range of the whole field of imagination and memory.'[26] In his own Celtic tale, Peacock by comparing Gwenyvar to Helen of Troy, or Merlin to Friar Bacon, or by describing Phoenician and Carthaginian economic exploitation of the Britons, insistently keeps the present and the classical past, as well as the Middle Ages, purposefully in the mind of his reader. For he defines as the greatest literary works those which freely draw from the spirited, romantic, and at the same time barbaric ages, then colour this experience with the civility and grace of classical learning, and finally render this composite with imaginative licence and exuberant language.

In part his statement of what constitutes the golden age of modern poetry arises from his criticisms of Romantic verse, and especially of his contemporaries' efforts to evoke past ages. They were, by and large, "wallowing in the rubbish of departed ignorance, and raking up the ashes of dead savages to find gew-gaws and rattles for the grown babies of the age.' Robert Southey, for example, 'wades through ponderous volumes of travels and old chronicles, from which he carefully selects all that is false, useless, and absurd, as being essentially poetical; and when he has a commonplace book full of monstrosities, strings them into an epic' (p. 128). Thus Romantic poets, he wrote, produced 'a modern-antique compound of frippery and barbarism, in which the puling sentimentality of the present time is grafted on the misrepresented ruggedness of the past into a heterogeneous congeries of unamalgamating manners' (p. 129).

Peacock's rhetoric in 'The Four Ages of Poetry', which becomes increasingly strident in castigating his contemporaries in the modern age of brass, may be seen as ironic hyperbole; he perhaps intended to goad Shelley into stating his opposing critical theories, the result being *The Defence of Poetry*. But we can also see that Peacock's description of the poetry of the golden age presages his own treatment of Arthurian material. Composed of stone quarried from Welsh tradition, sculpted by a hand trained in classical learning and neoclassical satire, and polished to a brightness by the free play of imagination and language, *The Misfortunes of Elphin* stands alone in the Romantic period as a monument to the creative possibilities for Arthurian tradition in the contemporary world. Apparently the work was not especially popular; forty years after its publication, remaindered copies were still available. Yet by eschewing the sentimental view of medieval romances so soporific in the hands of Milman, for example, Peacock treated his age to a serio-comic, romantic-satiric, traditional-innovative, poetic-prose oddity which was Arthur's most artistically interesting reappearance in British literature of the first three decades of the nineteenth-century, and one which remains engaging even today.

vi. Reginald Heber, *Morte D'Arthur: A Fragment* (1830)

Despite the achievement of Peacock's romance, Arthur and the Round Table still waited to be restored to literary prominence in a serious artistic work. The best effort up to 1830 is Reginald Heber's *Morte D'Arthur*. This narrative of 159 Spenserian stanzas focuses on Lancelot and Guenevere, begins the story of Balin, and, in a brief song, compresses the legend of Tristram. Begun as early as 1810 and regretfully abandoned by the busy prelate by 1819, the fragment promised to bring together, perhaps on an epic scale, major stories from Malory. Heber, writing before the editions of Malory in 1816 and 1817, may have read the two early copies of the *Morte Darthur* included in the library of his half-brother, the noted book collector Richard Heber. He also gleaned material from George Ellis' account of a French *Lancelot* (giving the *enfance* of the knight) and abstract of the Auchinleck manuscript *Merlin*, both summarised in *Specimens of Early English Metrical Romances*. But in the main, Heber followed the *Morte Darthur* rather faithfully, while organising the material in a more straightforward chronology than Malory's episodic, digressive narrative. Most important, Heber, a composer of hymns and later Bishop of Calcutta, altered traditional material to raise the moral tone of Malory's work, especially by justifying the queen's love for Lancelot as an innocent relationship begun years before she comes to court. She marries Arthur without knowing that her lost love is the peerless Lancelot.

The narrative begins with Ganora (Heber's name for Guenevere, used in Ellis' introduction and Scott's *Marmion*), who has been raised as a village maid, sadly enduring her nuptial celebration. Although she still loves a forester whom she has not seen for seven years, she stoically determines to honour her marriage. Suddenly a beautiful white hind with bloodied haunches bursts into the great hall, pursued by a 'grisly troop of hell-hounds' with 'claws of molten brass, and eyes of flame', followed by a lovely lady incongruously brandishing a 'ruthless . . . spear' (I, xliii; a motif based on Malory, III, v). Even though the huntress declares the hind to be 'righteous prey' and Ganora's 'fiercest foe' (I, xlvii), the queen mercifully protects the beast. The hunting troop withdraws in a flurry, scattering traces of gore among a chastened wedding party. In Canto II the hind by night resumes her normal form as Morgue, Arthur's inimical sister. Significantly altering tradition, Heber traces her hostility toward Arthur to her youthful love affair with a squire. Chancing upon his sister and this low-born lover embracing, Arthur, 'impetuous to destroy' (II, xxv), had slain the youth. Morgue subsequently became a malevolent enchantress, 'the goblin leader of a goblin crew' (II, xxvii). Although Arthur's conflict with his sister's paramour may have been suggested by the fight between Arthur and Accolon in Malory (IV, x–xi), Arthur's rash slaughter, precipitating Morgue's conversion to sorcery, is Heber's invention. On the morning following Arthur's wedding, a new adventure begins when a beautiful lady seeks the knight who is destined to regain her lands from a usurper. This episode recounts the beginning of the tale of Balin, who as in Malory is released from Arthur's prison to attempt the quest after all the other knights fail to remove the lady's magical sword from its sheath. Unlike Malory's rash knight, who refuses to return the sword to the damsel and then uses it to kill the Lady of the Lake, Heber's Balin leaves court with the maiden; the fragment follows his adventures no further. In Canto III Ganora discovers in the 'Grail Chapel of the Round Table', in a mural representing great battles against the heathens, the image of her beloved forester beneath the arms and name of Lancelot. She then learns from court damsels that Lancelot, who has been absent from court since before she arrived, avoids amorous entanglements because he loves an unknown rustic maiden. At this point the narrative breaks off, as Ganora 'with her kerchief shrouding close her face, / Broke from th' unfinish'd tale and sadly left the place' (III, xlii).

In one sense Heber's tale is not quite unfinished, however, for he has clearly anticipated the desolation, familiar from Malory, caused by the love of Lancelot and Guenevere and by Modred's hostility toward Arthur. In the first canto the huntress pursuing the white hind prophesies the fall of Arthur's kingdom when she urges Ganora to slay the hind or withdraw from court: 'The battle's roar resounds for thee, and groans of mangled men!' (I, xlv). When Heber departs from Malory, his innovations usually prove less effective than the medieval source. The Bishop obviously eschews 'immorality' and ennobles his central characters, as when he legitimises the love of Ganora and Lancelot with their guiltless prior history. Less accountable than these contrived corrections of Malory's 'lapses' in moral sensibility is Heber's idiosyncratic treatment of the Grail. On the altar of the Round Table chapel, Ganora finds the sacred symbol:

'the three-times hallow'd Grayle / To Britain's realm awhile in mercy lent, / Till sin defil'd the land, and lust incontinent' (III, xv). Whereas these lines suggest that Heber might have used the Grail more symbolically later in his projected narrative to emphasise the society's decline, the prosaic quality of the physical Grail standing on daily display reduces the lofty mystical possibilities in Malory to a mundane and limited actuality.

Heber's representation of the Round Table becomes most engrossing when he captures the movement and vigour of the tourney, hunt, or battle. Arthur appears as a noble conqueror who shares with his knights the vigorous pleasures of 'swift steeds, keen dogs, sharp swords, and armour bright' (I, xxii). The portrait in the chapel mural of Merlin in battle (perhaps suggested by Ellis' *Specimens*) illustrates Heber's most spirited writing. Such compelling touches as Merlin's 'prophet frenzy', 'swart' visage, tangled hair, and 'portentous glare' (III, xxiv) at times redeem Heber's frequently stilted Spenserian stanzas, archaic and awkward language, sentimentality, and moral earnestness. Occasionally, however, his moralising abruptly intrudes upon the narrative, as when he interrupts a glimpse of Ganora's lovelonging to criticise woman's weakness for creature comforts. Although such moral messages mar the poem, Heber considered them important and intentionally made the second canto 'much fuller of moralisation than the former'.[27] Besides intruding so didactically, Heber also marred his poem by emulating epic style, as had his friend Milman, with elaborate similes and ornate references to Phoebus Apollo driving his fiery chariot or Aurora springing from Tithonus' bed.

Despite such stylistic overreaching, Heber must be credited for endowing his characters with a psychological complexity not found in earlier nineteenth-century British Arthurian works. Although he affirms Ganora's goodness to the point of tedium, he also portrays in her an interesting range of emotion, as in her subtly shifting attitudes toward Arthur and her conflicting feelings when she discovers Lancelot to be her forester. Arthur exhibits the greatest possibilities for psychological definition. A man of 'thoughtful eye / And brow that might not, even in mirth, abate / Its regal care and wonted majesty', he succumbs to a 'lover's ecstasy' but is somehow unsuited to love (I, viii); yet he is capable of friendship so deep that tears fall unbidden when he thinks of the absent Lancelot. Significantly too, his nobility blends with peevishness, as when he fails to achieve the blade which Balin subsequently draws forth: 'So Arthur back the charmed steel restor'd, / And turn'd with sullen scowl his eyes away' (II, xlvi).

Heber's characters, totally unlike the flat stereotypes of Thelwall or Milman, thus anticipate the modern psychological exploration of traditional and legendary figures which would soon prove so important in the works of Tennyson and Morris. At the same time that Heber's poem pointed the way towards more complex psychological dimensions and greater human interest, it also suggested the value of accommodating a realistic sense of personality with the supernatural elements of Arthurian legend. Whereas Thelwall offered impoverished characterisation overwhelmed by spectacular effects and grotesque monsters, Heber rather gracefully used the marvels of medieval romance. By interweaving

Malory's shape-shifters, magic hinds, and enchanted swords with the psychological complexities of his characters, he sustained two apparently antithetical qualities for which the *Morte Darthur* appealed to readers of the nineteenth-century—both the contemporaneity and the timelessness of living legend.

While Heber's work exerted no discernible influence on later nineteenth-century writers, we should recognise that despite the weaknesses of his own poem, he in some ways anticipated how subsequent writers would effectively revitalise Arthurian matter for their age. Besides illustrating both the value of following traditional story to allow archetypes to imbue a new poem with power, and the importance of realistically complex characterisation, Heber's poem by its major weakness, its failure to develop the symbolic nature of the material, pointed the way for more significant treatments. By missing the potential symbolic richness, Heber created nothing more than a good story, a readable work which lacks the substance necessary for real distinction.

Heber's one further foray into Arthuriana, *Fragments of The Masque of Gwendolen* (written 1816, published 1830), proved less successful. Unlike his *Morte D'Arthur*, the masque develops through dialogue and stage directions, thus precluding narrative passages which in the earlier work contained Heber's liveliest writing. Like his *Morte D'Arthur*, the masque remains unfinished. Whatever transitions and amplifications Heber might have added, however, the story of the loathly lady, which is told in the medieval ballad 'The Marriage of Sir Gawaine', published in Percy's *Reliques* (analogues include Chaucer's *Wife of Bath's Tale* and a fifteenth-century romance *The Weddynge of Sir Gawen and Dame Ragnell*), seems virtually complete. When Gwendolen rejects Merlin's marriage proposal, he makes her hideously ugly. Meanwhile, Arthur has angrily sworn that a miscreant knight must die unless he finds a champion who can tell the king what women most desire. Gawain acquires the secret from the now loathly Gwendolen: women most want mastery. After he saves the doomed knight Llewellin, Gwendolen requires Gawain to repay his debt by marrying her. Although he first swears to wed her and then leave the land forever, he finally agrees to remain with her, exhibiting the graciousness traditionally associated with Gawain in English romance. As he offers 'one kiss of peace' (p. 206), he crosses himself to counter the evil suggested by her grotesque countenance; Merlin's spell breaks instantly.

While this brief piece presents the opportunity for some interesting characterisation—as when the silver-haired Arthur rues his rash decree on Llewellin's fate—both character and dialogue remain lamentably melodramatic. The most intriguing aspect of the work is Heber's blending of elements from varied sources. In addition to the loathly lady motif drawn from the medieval ballad, elements come from Malory, the synopses of romances in Ellis' *Specimens*, and Heber's own imagination. Merlin's malevolence was probably suggested by Ellis' work, as was the association of the wizard with the name Gwendolen, whom Ellis cites as the magician's wife in the *Vita Merlini*, Geoffrey of Monmouth's twelfth-century account. As in Malory, Merlin is enchanted by a Lady of the Lake. Unlike Malory, however, Heber makes her a paramour who is jealous of Merlin's 'wanderings'. Despite this combination of traditional and innovative detail, the piece is only a curiosity. Regarding Heber's Arthurian works, we must concur with the judgment that led him to abandon the *Morte D'Arthur*: He 'had no time to take [it] up as any thing more than occasional amusement, and merely as such [it] cost . . . too much trouble and time.'[28]

vii. William Wordsworth, *The Egyptian Maid* (1835)

Heber's achievement in the *Morte D'Arthur* would today seem even less significant if William Wordsworth had carried out his early idea of writing a major work on the chivalric past of England, 'some British theme, some old / Romantic tale by Milton left unsung', with 'dire enchantments', 'warlike feats', and 'Christian meekness hallowing faithful loves' (*The Prelude*, 1850, I, 168–85). But his only Arthurian poem, *The Egyptian Maid; or, The Romance of the Water Lily*, begun in 1828 and published in 1835, is a relatively disappointing narrative. Wordsworth cited the 1816 Walker and Edwards' edition of Malory as the source for 'the names and persons' in the poem; 'for the rest the Author is answerable' (prefatory note). As he indicated, his story does not come from Arthurian legend, but it draws loosely upon at least three motifs or situations in Malory: the erratic and sometimes destructive machinations of Merlin; the dying damsel floating to Camelot in the tale of the Maid of Astolat; and the healing of Sir Urry by a momentarily sanctified Lancelot. Of Wordsworth's own invention is the tale of the Egyptian Maid sent by her father—a pagan conquered and converted to the true faith by Arthur—to wed a Christian knight.

The poem begins with Merlin's sighting the lady's ship, the Water Lily of the subtitle, which 'seemed to hang in air'. Unaccountably, his admiration for the craft suddenly changes to envy, and he conjures a storm which destroys the vessel. The Lady of the Lake (Nina, 'a gentle Sorceress') chastises Merlin for impeding this voyage of 'Christian service' and demands that Merlin convey the unconscious maiden to Arthur's court. At Caerleon the knights in succession touch the maiden, hoping that 'for the favoured One, the Flower may bloom / Once more' (ll. 255–6). Each fails, until Galahad, who has earlier glimpsed the lady in a prophetic vision, rouses her. The poem concludes with the pair marrying as angels sing a nuptial tune that memorialises the divine ordinance of these events.

From an Arthurian standpoint Wordsworth's poem is interesting for its allusions to traditional tales, but even more for its imaginative symbolic innovation. The traditional elements appear primarily in references to familiar situations. The brief portrait of Launcelot, for example, suggests the dramatic intensity of his conflicting loves and loyalties, and Guinevere's pleasure when he fails to restore the Egyptian Maid succinctly implies the very human dimensions of her love. Another passage ironically capsulizes the anguish of Tristram's legendary romance by suggesting his relief when he fails to awaken the lady and thereby escapes another amorous entanglement: 'the fair Izonda he had wooed / With love too true, a love with pangs too sharp, / From hope too distant, not to dread another' (ll. 292–4).

Wordsworth's Arthur here, as elsewhere in his verse, is traditionally noble and gracious. In a sonnet entitled 'Struggle of the Britons Against the Barbarians' (#10 of the *Ecclesiastical Sonnets*, 1st series), Wordsworth had celebrated the king's prowess and purity: wearing a 'towering casque' and 'bearing through the stormy field / Tne virgin sculptured on his Christian shield', Arthur easily daunts his foes. Wordsworth had also alluded to the invigorating myth of the once and future king, 'who, to upper light restored, / With that terrific sword / Which yet he brandishes for future war, / Shall lift his country's fame above the polar star!' (*Artegal and Elidure*). *The Egyptian Maid* depicts not so much Arthur's heroism as his magnanimity. When he hears the story of the capsized vessel, he immediately assumes responsibility for the lady's fate.

Arthur's response emphasises the puzzling aspects of Wordsworth's Merlin, who instigates the lady's danger. Elsewhere in Wordsworth's poetry Merlin is equally ambiguous. *Artegal and Elidure* includes the 'sage enchanter Merlin's subtle schemes' with the 'feats of Arthur and his knightly peers', and the sonnet 'With How Sad Steps, O Moon' alludes to Merlin's great powers of enchantment. But Wordsworth refers to the magician disparagingly in *The Prelude*, where he describes the 'anarchy and din, / Barbarian and infernal' at a St Bartholomew's Fair and includes bogus prophets or 'modern Merlins' among the tawdry sham he despises (VII, 713). Here his use of the name as a generic term for fortune tellers and astrologers parallels the practice of such cheap publications of the early nineteenth century as *Urania; or the Astrologers Chronicle and Mystical Magazine*, edited by 'Merlinus Anglicus, jun.'. In *The Egyptian Maid* Merlin's 'envious spleen' and 'freakish will' produce apparently gratuitous malice. The Merlin whom Wordsworth knew from Malory is likewise a puzzling figure whose prophecies sometimes lead to destruction. But most often in Malory Merlin's oracular powers and occasionally playful antics serve the important end of testing or instructing the knights. Wordsworth, by focusing on the malice of his Merlin, casts him in a new and important symbolic role.

In the conflict between the two supernatural figures, Merlin and Nina, and in the union of the Egyptian Maid and Sir Galahad Wordsworth may be seen to offer a highly imaginative version of the Grail story. Opposed by the old magic or supernatural of Merlin, and associated with the newly benevolent supernatural of Nina, the Egyptian Maid in effect personifies the Grail. Transported from a distant exotic land rich in hermetic associations, she is preserved—to usher in a new order—not by the touch of a flawed knight associated with human love such as Lancelot, who in Malory similarly heals Sir Urry, but by the stainless knight who achieves the Grail, Sir Galahad. His early dream of the Maiden parallels his anticipatory visions of the Grail in Malory, and as in the *Morte Darthur*, his sitting in the Siege Perilous demonstrates his sanctification for union with the sacred symbol.

Thus on one level Wordsworth may be said to reshape the Grail story in human but overtly symbolic terms. Despite its ostensible sentimentality and frequent verbal infelicities, the poem commands interest as an innovative recasting of Arthurian myth. Yet perhaps the overt sentiment and stylistic lapses constitute not narrative weakness but intentional irony. Remembering that Wordsworth's sense of humour revealed itself in 'a convulsive inclination to laughter about the mouth, a good deal at variance with the solemn, stately expression of the rest of his face,'[29] we may recognise in the poem some ludic elements in an ostensibly sober setting.

This play centres on the artist's difficulties in handling symbols and myth. Wordsworth's headnote emphasises that the poem concerns itself with art and symbols, and in this context the implications of the ship and maiden prove particularly teasing. By designating the poem as *The Romance of the Water Lily*, the subtitle focuses on the vessel, which Wordsworth identified as the starting point of the work. He gleaned the idea of a ship named the Water Lily—thus linked to a plant that had been his 'delight' from boyhood—from an offhand conversation with his nephew,[30] then joined to it the image of a 'beautiful work of ancient art' which he viewed in the British Museum. This sculpture of a 'Goddess appearing to rise out of the full-blown [lotus] flower' he reproduced in a carving on the prow of his vessel. Wordsworth associated the boat and its icon with the artistic imagination not only through the introductory reference to the Townley Marbles, but also through a simile comparing the motion of the bark to that of the moon, a recurring Romantic image for the imagination.

In the light of this concern with symbols and artistic creativity, Merlin cuts an extremely ironic figure. An artificer of legendary skill, he quickly proves to be something of a bungler, having great power but little finesse or purpose. He perversely destroys richly imaginative beauty and, until roused by Nina, hides from the fury of a storm he himself has devised, his invention seemingly having gone awry. On another level, we can see the poem demonstrating the difficulties of an artist's communicating through symbol, for the artificer Merlin quickly sinks the poet's most elaborately wrought symbol and then endeavours to rouse the poet's potentially allegorical heroine from unconsciousness. Furnished with contrivances such as clapping swans, obtrusive archaisms such as 'eftsoons', and sentimental phrasing, the poem may be seen as a burlesque of poetic uses of myth and symbol, much in the vein of humour of such a poem as 'The Idiot Boy', where Wordsworth overturns the supernatural and melodramatic conventions of the ballad in a mock heroic manner. But if Wordsworth intended similar play in *The Egyptian Maid*, his readers have rarely relished it. And although they have appreciated his using Arthurian material in felicitous images—as in his exquisite comparison of a fern at Grasmere to the 'Lady of the Mere, / Sole-sitting by the shores of old romance' (#4 of *Poems on the Naming of Places*)—readers have not appreciated the ingenuity of his treatment of the Grail story. The poem consequently did little to revitalise Arthurian legend.

By the end of the third decade of the nineteenth century, Arthurian legend had reappeared in English literature in a variety of works, which included an inept melodrama, partially effective burlesque and satire, and uneven failures in epic manner. It had been treated by writers as diverse as a political reformer, a whimsical dilettante, clergymen (all writing to fill leisure time), one of the most popular writers of the period, and, with comparatively slight results, the pre-eminent poet of the age. None of these works demonstrably influenced the Arthurian literature soon to follow in the Victorian period. Later writers were to be stirred not by the bland productions of their immediate forerunners, but by medieval works themselves—most especially by Malory. From this mine of legend, the pre-eminent poet of the next age, Tennyson, was to quarry abundant treasure.

3

Arthur Redux

British Literature of the Mid-Nineteenth Century

i. Alfred Tennyson, 'The Lady of Shalott' (1832); 'Sir Launcelot and Queen
Guinevere', 'Sir Galahad', 'Morte d'Arthur (1842)

Although John Leyden had predicted that Scott, the influential Wizard of the
North, would herald 'proud Arthur's march from Fairyland' (*Scenes of Infancy*),
it was actually the fledgling idol of a later day who more than any other
individual effected Arthur's return to literary prominence. When Alfred
Tennyson, recently a Cambridge student, with one volume of poetry already to
his credit, published 'The Lady of Shalott' in late 1832 (the year Scott died), he
began to focus the popular medievalism fostered by Scott's metrical romances
and novels more specifically on the literary potential of Arthuriana. In addition
to publishing this one poem, which attracted considerable attention from
reviewers, Tennyson circulated among enthusiastic university friends verses
written between 1830 and 1834 on 'Sir Launcelot and Queen Guinevere' and
'Sir Galahad'. Along with other unpublished lines of a projected Launcelot
narrative, these two works whetted the appetites of Tennyson's coterie for a
fuller treatment of the legend. After 1842, when the Launcelot and Galahad
poems were published with a superior revised version of 'The Lady of Shalott'
and with the 'Morte d'Arthur', an elegiac narrative on the passing of Arthur,
reviewers joined the poet's friends in anticipating a major Arthurian work.

Even if Tennyson had never fulfilled these expectations in the second half of
the century with his epic-scale *Idylls of the King*, the influence of the four brief
early poems would have guaranteed his prominence in any study of nineteenth-
century Arthurian tradition. The more ambitious Arthurian works of Thelwall,
Milman, Frere, Peacock, and Heber had drawn comparatively little critical
attention and exerted slight influence on later writers. (Tennyson himself, for
example, who later became friendly with Milman and who owned a copy of
Frere's burlesque, as well as collections of poetry by Scott and Wordsworth,
recorded no notice of the Arthurian poems written in the first thirty years of the
century.) In contrast, the young Victorian's early Arthurian works not only fired
enthusiasm in writers such as Morris and Swinburne, but also inspired drawings
and paintings representing Arthurian story. Even before Tennyson published
any of the *Idylls*, Moxon's 1857 illustrated edition of the Laureate's poetry
included six illustrations of Arthurian subjects: two, by Dante Gabriel Rossetti

and William Holman Hunt, of 'The Lady of Shalott'; two by Daniel Maclise of scenes in the 'Morte d'Arthur'; and two others by Rossetti, one of 'Sir Galahad' and another based on a four-line allusion to Arthur in 'The Palace of Art'. Most important, perhaps, Tennyson's uses of the legend helped direct readers' attention to the treasury of the *Morte Darthur*, encouraging, for instance, the Pre-Raphaelites' delight in Malory. It is hardly incidental that as college men, Edward Burne-Jones and William Morris revered both the early works of Tennyson and the *Morte Darthur*, or that Rossetti in 1856–57 moved from illustrating Tennyson (whom he listed in 1848 among 'the Immortals'[1]) to decorating the Oxford Union hall with the ill-fated murals based on episodes in Malory. Burne-Jones in 1854 was drawing designs for 'The Lady of Shalott' and soon afterwards was planning with Morris to found a chivalric order having Malory's Sir Galahad as its patron. The close connection between these artists' interest in Tennyson's poetry and their love of Malory is illustrated by Burne-Jones' directing a friend to prepare for their new order by studying Tennyson's 1842 poem: 'Learn Sir Galahad by heart.'[2]

Not all readers approved Tennyson's versions of Malory's material. Even so appreciative a reader as William Morris found this Galahad 'rather a mild youth.'[3] The harshest criticism questioned the contemporary relevance of the remote setting and culture: 'The miraculous legend of "Excalibur" does not come very near to us.'[4] J. W. Croker, one of the more acerbic reviewers of 'The Lady of Shalott', identified its relatively unfamiliar setting in a sarcastic footnote: 'The same Camelot, in Somersetshire, we presume, which is alluded to by Kent in *King Lear*—Goose! if I had thee upon Sarum plain, / I'd drive thee cackling home to Camelot.'[5] Such criticism notwithstanding, Tennyson in effect created a taste for Arthurian poetry unprecedented since the Middle Ages.[6] Although Croker confidently assumed that Camelot provided habitation more suitable for cackling geese than for intelligent readers of 1833, by 1854 another reviewer could deplore the excessive practicality of Englishmen which kept Arthurian legend unfamiliar: 'it is their own fault if they do not know the "Morte d'Arthur".'[7] Tennyson had, however, anticipated the difficulties posed by the unfamiliar material. When he referred in 'The Palace of Art' (1832) to Arthur in Avalon, he proposed to educate his readers with an explanatory footnote, as Scott had done when he alluded to Arthurian legend in *Marmion* (which Tennyson had imitated in a boyhood poem of some 6,000 lines).[8] His closest friend Arthur Henry Hallam goaded him toward greater artistic self-confidence: 'Don't be humbugged . . . you may put a note or two if you will, yet Milton did not to *Paradise Lost*.'[9] When Tennyson published his Arthurian poems of 1832 and 1842 with neither explanations nor apologies, they were the first significant examples since the Middle Ages of English *belles lettres* that were consistently Arthurian.

Yet 'The Lady of Shalott', the first of the four to be published, is only slenderly Arthurian. Examining the poem in the light of its sources suggests Tennyson's accomplishment in both exploiting traditional elements of the legend and drawing modern implications through innovative situation and detail. This matter of modernity or 'relevance' proved to be an especially sensitive problem for a young poet in a period when reviewers emphasised the writer's role as an ethical and moral guide. Interestingly, in this poem Tennyson uses Arthurian legend as a vehicle for making the same point that critics hostile to such subject matter often made: Art should reflect actual life, not dreamy, escapist conceptions fostered by aesthetic isolation. The lady of the poem weaves and sings in a remote tower until she sees the dynamic Lancelot riding past and then risks death by following him into the sphere of human involvements at Camelot. As Tennyson is said to have expressed his theme, 'The new-born love for something, for some one in the wide world from which she has been so long secluded, takes her out of the region of shadows into that of realities.'[10]

Beyond the names of Arthur, Lancelot, and Camelot, Tennyson's poem shares with Malory's version of the tale of Elaine, Lily Maid of Astolat, only the general situation of a lady's dying for love of Lancelot and floating to Camelot. Although Tennyson remarked that he had loved the *Morte Darthur* since he was 'little more than a boy' (*Memoir*, II, 128) and had probably read the edition in the Tennyson library some time in the 1820s, he said that he did not think he 'had ever heard of' Malory's Elaine when he wrote 'The Lady of Shalott', and doubted 'whether I should ever have put it in that shape if I had been then aware of the Maid of Astolat in *Mort Arthur*'.[11] He described his source for the poem as 'an Italian novelette, *Donna di Scalotta*', which his son later identified as a tale from 'the *Cento Novelle Antiche*, dated conjecturally before 1321' and edited in 1804 by G. Ferrarrio. This collection of tales was in fact well known and readily accessible in Italian, which Tennyson read, as well as through such English works as John Dunlop's *History of Fiction* (1814) and Thomas Roscoe's *Italian Novelists* (1825).[12] Comparing Tennyson's poem with the Italian story reveals that he invented all the engaging particulars—the island setting, the lady's weaving and singing, the mirror, the magic curse—which embody the poem's theme of the stultification of artistic isolation. Also unique to Tennyson's version is the idea that the lady falls in love with Lancelot from a distance and the two never meet—a point which emphasises the symbolic nature of the lady's actions. Tennyson thus achieved a new story rich in contemporary implications without creating any of the bizarre effects of the non-traditional Arthurian works produced earlier in the century.

The greatest appeal of the poem lies not in its reshaping of traditional story but in its stylistic effects—its vivid, picturesque setting and lyrical charm, especially in the memorable refrains contrasting the isolated Shalott with Camelot—and in its poignant evocation of the enigmatic relationship of art to life. Yet the poem implies a general view of the Round Table world which becomes increasingly significant and symbolic in Tennyson's later Arthurian idylls. For him Camelot comes to represent a society in which all human actions are meaningfully interrelated, as is suggested in 'The Lady of Shalott' when Lancelot unwittingly causes the lady to search for fuller life. Only through actively participating in this society, despite risks to inner vision or personal aesthetics, can an individual fulfil himself. Tennyson suggests this idea by showing the lady to be 'half sick' of mere 'shadows of the world' even before Lancelot's dynamic appeal draws her towards Camelot.

As Malory's romance and Tennyson's own *Idylls* reveal, Camelot never becomes an ideal society; nevertheless, man's chief responsibility is to join his fellows in improving society rather than withdrawing from it. Tennyson's revisions of 'The Lady of Shalott', especially changes in the final stanza, intensify this idea. In the earliest printed version, the inhabitants of Camelot seem rather obtuse and more interested in their personal safety than in the mysteries of the lady's fate. The improved conclusion suggests that the knights share a greater sensitivity to the common perils of existence and a sympathetic humaneness lacking in the earlier version. This concept, central to all Tennyson's Arthurian verse, that despite its imperfections Camelot represents human society to which all individuals must commit themselves, contrasts significantly with some later poets' conceptions of the Order. Whereas Tennyson in the *Idylls* in effect illustrates Scott's definition of chivalry as the use of individual freedom to defend the social order, Morris and Swinburne imply that the glory of chivalry lives in characters who follow independent visions. For such writers, Camelot—despite its aesthetically appealing pageantry—represents a repressive and hypocritical society which thwarts individuals, who should pursue personal fulfilment in their own appetites and values.

Allied with his idea of Camelot is Tennyson's conception of Arthur, first expressed not in 'The Lady of Shalott' but in a brief allusion in 'The Palace of Art', also published in 1832 and substantially revised for reissue in 1842. This poem, in which Tennyson meant to show that 'the Godlike life is with man and for man' (*Memoir*, I, 119), even more overtly than 'The Lady of Shalott' describes the emptiness of living in art or aesthetic idealism separated from human relationships. Among the art treasures of the palace King Arthur appears in an arras depicting his removal from human society to Avalon (a scene illustrated by Rossetti for Moxon's 1857 edition). Significantly, in the legend of the once and future king this withdrawal from the world follows Arthur's failure to establish a perfect order, but it also presages his return. Arthur's picture hangs in the Palace of Art with those of other men actively committed to improving human society—scientists, philosophers, statesmen, and lawgivers, and such artists as Milton and Dante, who (in words Byron applied to Dante) were 'brave and active citizens', 'agents' rather than mere 'writers'.[13]

Even though this view of Arthur and of Camelot—which remains consistent throughout the *Idylls*—contrasts significantly with the conceptions of such poets as Morris and Swinburne, their early enthusiasm for Tennyson's first Arthurian poems suggests that his works planted seeds for their own. Tennyson's hues and particularity of detail must have suggested to the Pre-Raphaelites the picturesqueness of the Arthurian world. Besides the lush imagery and atmospheric charm of 'The Lady of Shalott', Tennyson in his next Arthurian publications also provided the young Pre-Raphaelites with an exuberant portrayal of passionate love. The forty-five-line lyric of 'Sir Launcelot and Queen Guinevere', written at least partially in 1830, published in 1842, and subtitled 'A Fragment', zestfully paints an apparently amoral view of the affair. Although the opening lines imply that love involves both pleasure and pain, they also introduce the illicit relationship as part of nature's joy and freedom. After depicting an animated, melodious, shimmering bliss, however, the poem ends with irony centred in one ambiguous word: 'A man had given all other bliss / . . . / To waste his whole heart in one kiss / Upon her perfect lips' (ll. 42–5). Although waste may here mean 'expend', its more usual connotation fits the larger narrative framework within which Tennyson originally planned to set the poem.

This lyric, along with a dozen lines sung by Launcelot to his 'Life of the Life within my blood' (inviting her to 'Bathe with me in the fiery flood, / And mingle kisses, tears, and sighs'), was conceived as part of a fuller Lancelot ballad. The larger context of the legend would doubtless have qualified Tennyson's apparent praise of folly. The amorous frankness of the Launcelot and Guinevere lyric and the scrap of Launcelot's song had prompted Tennyson's Cambridge friend J. M. Kemble to caution humorously that it 'be kept as quiet as possible' 'for the sake of my future clerical views and Ælfred's and Sir L.'s character'.[14] But Kemble also sketched Tennyson's plan for the projected *Ballad of Sir Lancelot*, which reveals that the total work would treat not only the delights of passion but also the ideals flaunted by Lancelot's adultery:

> in the Spring, Queen Guinevere and Sir Lancelot ride through the forest green, fayre and amorous: And such a queen! such a knight! Merlin . . . meets them, and tells Sir L. that he's doing well for his fame to be riding about with a light o' love &c. Whereupon the knight, nowise backward in retort, tells him it is a shame such an old scandal to antiquity should be talking, since his own propensities are no secret. . . . Merlin, who tropically is Worldly Prudence, is of course miserably floored. So are the representatives of Worldly Force, who in the shape of three knights, sheathed, Sir, in trap from toe to toe, run at Sir L. and are most unceremoniously shot from their saddles like stones from a sling. But the Garde Joyeuse is now in sight; the knight I confess is singing but a loose song, when his own son Sir Galahad (the type of Chastity) passes by; he knows his father but does not speak to him, *blushes and rides on his way!*[15]

Kemble's synopsis is in some ways more important than the fragment of Lancelot ballad which was actually published, for it establishes that in the early 1830s Tennyson was already thinking of treating Arthurian legend in a substantial narrative that would be highly symbolic if not allegorical. Even though the fragment 'Sir Launcelot and Queen Guinevere' is a slight piece on its own, it is significant in nineteenth-century Arthurian tradition for two reasons: its pictorial and sensuous qualities doubtless influenced the Pre-Raphaelite fondness for Arthurian story, and its references to the inter-relationship of pleasure and pain, the riches and waste of passion, anticipated the psychological dimensions which Tennyson as well as Morris and Swinburne would later explore in medieval love stories.

But in another Arthurian poem published in 1842 (though written by 1834), the 84-line monologue 'Sir Galahad', Tennyson develops none of the possible psychological complexities of the speaker. He focuses almost entirely on the symbolic nature of the 'type of Chastity', who on earth eschews human passions for the 'Pure lilies of eternal peace' (l. 67). In so doing Tennyson was already crystallising the conflict he would later develop in 'The Holy Grail' between an ideal of social commitment embodied in Camelot and Arthur and a transcendent ideal vouchsafed to only the rare individual. Although the monologue remains psychologically flat, it expresses its ideal of purity in vigorous language and image, and Burne-Jones' enthusiasm for learning the poem 'by heart' probably derived as much from its rhythmic appeal as from its uplifting message.

In the fourth of his early Arthurian poems, the 'Morte d'Arthur', a narrative of 272 blank verse lines written in 1833–34 but first published in 1842, Tennyson used the symbolic value of Arthurian legend far more meaningfully than in the Galahad monologue. In the fall of the Round Table he discerned a myth precisely suited to embody his own era's intense concern with disruptive change. As the modern frame 'The Epic' implies (see chapter one), nineteenth-century Englishmen felt with good reason that they were seeing the end of an era essentially rooted in the social hierarchy, economy, and religion of the Middle Ages. Appropriately, medieval legend which recorded a comparable sense of social upheaval and decay provided Tennyson with a mythic representation for this contemporary concern.

While the sombre tone of the work and the symbolic details of the wasteland setting and declining year capture the frustrations and fears of the Victorian age, the 'Morte d'Arthur' also implicitly counters a sense of doom. When Tennyson's king describes his failure and departure from this world, he characterises the end also as a beginning: 'The old order changeth, yielding place to new, / And God fulfills himself in many ways' (ll. 240–1). By lifting contemporary concerns to the level of myth Tennyson reinforces this optimistic message in two particular ways. First, the apparent social collapse feared in the nineteenth century is related through the universality of myth to recurring patterns of failure and renewal. The story of Arthur's removal to Avalon calls up the legend of his return—here also associated with the concept of regeneration and a second coming implicit in Christianity. Second, Arthurian myth could also remind the nineteenth-century audience that the collapse seemingly imminent for their own society had been endured by past civilisations. More particularly, Britain and the glory of Arthur (as apologists for Tudor and Stuart monarchies had emphasised) had survived even the loss of Arthur. Moreover, the ideals of Camelot had endured in the myth itself, leaving the failures of the past not only as reminders that man may survive difficult transitions, but also as lessons of how to proceed and what to avoid.

Besides suggesting that contemporary crises were neither unique nor final, Tennyson's embodiment of current uncertainties in myth also objectified volatile issues. Through legend he could criticise or caution without pontificating. For example, when Bedivere twice hesitates to throw Excalibur into the water as Arthur directs, Tennyson dramatises and criticises values or perspectives prevalent in his own day. The first time, not knowing that it will summon aid for the king, Bedivere fails to cast away the sword because he is dazzled by the value of the jewelled hilt. Arthur reprimands the knight for his materialism, and within the context of chivalric ideals Tennyson pointedly rebukes the widespread materialism of his own age. The second time Bedivere tries to cast away Excalibur, he falters because of the sword's aesthetic charm. This response combines materialism with a reverence for symbol, for Bedivere imagines that the sword may one day remind men of the past glories of his order. His attitude raises the issue of how one can justify preserving history—or myth—in art. Like later generations whom Bedivere anticipates will revere the era Excalibur represents, Tennyson memorialises values of the past in the Arthurian legend. But his reviving the myth differs significantly from the exhibition of the sword that Bedivere envisions. To the knight, Excalibur as symbol will primarily stir a sense of loss. For Tennyson, in contrast, such a symbol—or the legend itself—retains value only if it proves useful. It not only must memorialise the past and stimulate sentiment, but also must effect necessary changes and new good—as when Excalibur summons the barge that will transport Arthur to Avalon.

Besides serving such symbolic or thematic ends, Bedivere also marks an advance in Tennyson's Arthurian characterisation. Vacillating between his own values and desires and his loyalty to the king, the knight shows greater emotional complexity than either the symbolic Lady of Shalott and Galahad, or the picturesque but relatively undeveloped lovers in 'Sir Launcelot and Queen Guinevere'. Within the mythic context, this credible psychology invests potentially remote abstractions with human interest not fully realised in Tennyson's three other early Arthurian works. The 'Morte d'Arthur' is simultaneously more derivative and more ambitious than these other poems. Derivative in that it follows Malory's romance very closely, it for precisely this reason achieves distinctive power by utilising the archetypal or symbolic value of traditional story. By adapting the story line of the medieval romance in a sustained narrative, Tennyson unearthed possibilities for communicating larger complexes of meaning than the brief lyric or monologue could convey.

Viewed together, the four poems Tennyson published in 1832 and 1842 anticipated in several ways his more developed craftsmanship and virtuosity in the *Idylls*. In the early works he sustained picturesque effects, explored the symbolic possibilities inherent in the legend, and amplified the range of emotion and attitude suggested in Malory's characters. He also investigated a variety of tones and forms with which he could treat legend, ranging from the buoyant lyrical description of 'Sir Launcelot and Queen Guinevere'; to the vigorous rhythms and imagery, and the possibilities of the monologue form, in 'Sir Galahad'; to the amplified narrative and elegiac tone of the 'Morte d'Arthur'. In the *Idylls* he would effectively use all of these variations in mood, tone, and form.

Beyond preparing himself in these ways to treat Arthurian legend more fully, Tennyson through the early poems not only created a rich awareness of Arthurian literature that invited other writers to the material, but also provided a standard by which they would be measured. Reviewers of subsequent Arthurian works by Bulwer-Lytton, Arnold, Morris, and Swinburne rarely failed to evaluate their poems in the light of Tennyson's. He had also stimulated keen anticipation that 'the literary resurrection of King Arthur and his knights, after so many centuries' entombment in the Avalon of forgetfulness', which was induced by the 'awakening trumpet sounded' in 'The Lady of Shalott', would culminate in the grand Arthurian work contemplated by Milton and Wordsworth.[16]

ii. Edward Bulwer-Lytton, *King Arthur* (1848)

The year before Tennyson began satisfying this hope by publishing four *Idylls of the King*, a reviewer lamented the failure of Edward Bulwer-Lytton's *King Arthur* to fulfil the epic promise of the material, 'the British subject which Milton resigned in despair to the feebleness of Bulwer, or—may it be hoped?—to the fullness of Tennyson's powers.' Most readers found that Bulwer, the popular novelist who in 1866 became Bulwer-Lytton, Lord Lytton, gave them more news of Arthur and less art than they could relish. This astonishing work, quite rightly described by another critic, Richard Garnett, as 'affected and artificial', would seem specifically calculated to test his judgement that Tennyson's resurrection of the Arthurian legend had proved 'the indestructibility of anything truly beautiful'.[17] Although Garnett referred to the legend's endurance through time, an even greater test of indestructibility was its incarnation in Bulwer's unrestrained mixture of Arthurian elements with Welsh lore, Norse mythology, classical material, Eskimos, and lost Etrurian tribes.

Of the major Arthurian works written after Tennyson published his 1832 and 1842 volumes, Bulwer's long narrative poem shows, simultaneously, the least awareness of recent trends in using traditional story and the greatest ambition in its scheme. Bulwer followed the practice of Renaissance and Enlightenment writers in freely inventing episodes without precedent or appropriateness, inserting Arthurian characters in stories and settings wildly foreign to them. His *King Arthur* also aims more patently than other Arthurian narratives of the nineteenth century to achieve epic stature. Despite a modest prefatory disclaimer that authors cannot appropriate to their own works the label 'epic', which 'a long succession of readers has alone the prerogative to confirm' (Preface to *King Arthur*, p. vi), Bulwer sought 'to construct from the elements of national romance, something approaching to the completeness of epic narrative' (p. v). The two key phrases of this description point up discrepancies between Bulwer's aim and his accomplishment. The discrepancies lie in the limited extent to which he used 'the elements of national romance' and the uneven proportions in which he mixed three elements—'the Probable, the Allegorical, and the Marvellous'—

which, according to him, as with Pope, constituted 'the completeness of epic narrative'. An extremely simplified and compressed synopsis of the intricate plot suggests both the slight role of Arthurian 'national romance' and the unwieldy preponderance of 'the Marvellous' in *King Arthur*.

The young king undertakes a three-fold quest to secure his realm against Saxon domination: he must bring to Caerleon a diamond sword possessed by the Lady of the Lake, the silver shield of Thor guarded by a dwarf, and a childlike guide dwelling with the Fate who spins the thread of life. (This combination of quests associated with Arthurian story, Norse mythology, and the Perseus legend reflects from the outset Bulwer's eclectic use of unrelated material.) After eluding some fairly conventional dangers, Arthur experiences the first of several incongruously nonmedieval adventures. In the 'Happy Valley' of an ancient Etrurian tribe Arthur falls in love with the princess Aegle. When he resumes his quest, she learns that he has been purposely directed into danger, and she plunges into a raging river to die with him. He survives, and after mourning her, takes up the quest and achieves the sword kept by the Lady of the Lake.

Meanwhile, Gawaine falls into comical mishaps, being pinched unmercifully by elves and nearly sacrificed to a pagan goddess. Lancelot falls in love with Genevra, a Saxon convert to Christianity. Arthur, after winning the sword, travels with Genevra's Norwegian crew to the North Pole. There he battles walruses, meets Gawaine (who has become the hero of a group of Eskimo pygmies), and wins the shield of Thor. Returning to Caerleon, which has been besieged by Saxons, Arthur discovers the third object of his quest in a fair damsel, Genevieve (who turns out to be Genevra's long-lost childhood companion). It seems she has guided Arthur through his adventures in the guise of a dove, which, strangely, has all along seemed to be his 'Platonic soul-mate'. Finally the examples of the selfless Christian convert Genevieve and the magnanimous Christian king induce the pagans to make peace. The poem ends promising marriages between Genevra and Lancelot and Genevieve and Arthur, as well as harmony among Saxons, Vandals, and Britons.

Obviously the story offers quite a bit more of the 'Marvellous' than of the Probable or Allegorical (yet perhaps much that would ordinarily be deemed improbable could seem likely to the adventurous Bulwer, who himself had some rather extraordinary experiences). Moreover, little in the work is recognisably Arthurian. Although the main characters remain fairly true to stock medieval conceptions, they are divorced from the stories most often associated with them and lack the richness of even the sometimes one-dimensional portraits of the Middle Ages. For example, Bulwer gives a version of Lancelot's *enfances* that follows the French *Lancelot* as recounted in both Ellis' *Specimens of Early English Metrical Romances* and a note, which Bulwer cites, in Ellis' edition of Gregory Lewis Way's translation of French *fabliaux*. But he avoids the tradition of Lancelot's guilty love for the queen. This knight, a spiritual twin of Arthur, shows none of the divided loyalties of Malory's character. In fact Bulwer elaborately exonerates Lancelot of the 'slander' heaped on him by writers over the centuries by not only giving both the king and his knight their own ladies, but also by explaining in a footnote how Lancelot's reputation became erroneously blackened: because the names Genevra and Genevieve had both been used in French romances to identify Guenevere, writers had mistaken two separate figures for one. This fastidious refinement considerably reduces the power of the traditional characters. It also seems peculiarly moralistic in the work of one who had ridiculed Tennyson's decorum by referring to him as 'school-miss Alfred'[18] and, later, labelled him 'a poet adapted to a mixed audience of school-girls and Oxford dons'. Despite his criticisms of Tennyson's transforming traditional characters—'I can scarcely understand how any *man* could reconcile himself to dwarf such mythical characters as Arthur, Lancelot and Merlin, into a whimpering old gentleman, a frenchified household traitor and a drivelling dotard'[19]—Bulwer actually strips much of the interest from his own Arthur.

He cited medieval precedent for his general treatment of Arthurian legend and characters, in that romances had surrounded 'the heroes of the fifth or sixth century with the chivalrous attributes of the thirteenth or fourteenth'. But he also stipulated that his king was 'neither the Arthur of the Mabinogion nor of Geoffrey of Monmouth' (Book I, note 7). He departed from this chronicle tradition specifically by limiting Arthur's power and showing magnanimity and humility, rather than prowess and courage, to be the essence of heroism. Bulwer's Arthur is not a conqueror; at best he can achieve only uneasy, temporary peace with the Saxons. The sword he draws from the stone proves 'Powerless to win, though potent to defend, / Its blade will shiver in a conqueror's clasp; / A weapon meeter for the herdsman's end / . . . / Some churl who seeks to guard humble hearth' (VII, xvii). While Bulwer recognised the discrepancy between his and the chronicle Arthur, he was only partly correct in claiming kinship between his character and 'the Arthur of Romance' (Preface, p. x). His priggishly pure king has no genuine model in medieval literature. Invariably prompt with humble, pious sentiments, he is wearisomely predictable and lacks the human inconsistencies abounding in the more interesting Arthur of medieval romance. The flatness of Arthur and the other characters derives largely from Bulwer's desire to model his work and his hero on the patterns of classical epic while at the same time illustrating a chivalric, Christian ethic. Unfortunately, the allusions and parallels to the *Aeneid* inadvertently emphasise the mannered style, sentimentality, and sterility of his work, making it an unintentional parody rather than an artful echo of the Virgilian model.

Significantly, the most successful portion of the work derives not from epic inspiration but from an Arthurian fabliau which combined three familiar medieval motifs. Bulwer comically describes Gawaine's adventure with a churlish host who requires the knight to sleep in his daughter's bedchamber, a motif seen in the Middle English *Carle of Carlyle*. This situation is joined to the motif of the Perilous Bed, which appears in a more serious context, associated with the Grail quest, in Chrétien's *Perceval* and Malory's story of Sir Bors (XI, iv), and in a rather parodic form in Chrétien's *Lancelot*. Whenever Bulwer's knight gets into the lady's bed, blades descend from the ceiling to wound him. After crouching watchfully in a corner throughout the night, Gawaine leaves with the daughter, who declares herself his wife. She soon proves fickle, however. Unlike her dog, who remains faithful to Gawaine, she unaccountably prefers to ride away with a churl. This last incident echoes the medieval motif of contrasting faithful dogs with faithless women, seen in the *Vengeance of Raguidel*, the Prose *Tristan*, and in Malory's account of Sir Dinas (IX, xxxix). Bulwer's version of Gawain's adventure closely follows the amalgamation of the three motifs in the twelfth-century *Chevalier à l'Epée*, collected in P. J. B. LeGrand's *Fabliaux*, translated from the French by Gregory Lewis Way in 1815.

In this episode—so closely derived from a medieval source—and in other sections which treat Gawaine in the humorous spirit of many medieval romances, we see Bulwer's talent for burlesque and satire. At times he achieves a sprightly rhyme, vivacious diction, and unrestrained comedy reminiscent of *Don Juan*, as when Gawaine tries to dissuade his captor from sacrificing him to the goddess Freya and finds that words, for once, fail him: 'Foiled in the weapons which he most had boasted, / He felt sound logic proved he should be roasted' (VIII, lxxiii). Such comic passages demonstrate that if he had used Arthurian material consistently in burlesque or satire, Bulwer might have created a piece still entertaining today. But while the witty passages move energetically, most of the 9,408 lines bog down in stilted language, exaggerated epic pretension, abruptly fluctuating tone, and sentimentality. Few works have been so bizarrely inventive and so trite at the same time.

The poem demonstrates how the antiquarian and literary historicism which stimulated the revival of Arthur could seriously encumber artistic conceptions. It becomes leaden with references to classical literature and history and to Welsh lore, frequently explained in footnotes. Just a sampling of the classical authorities cited includes Aeschylus, Apollodorus, Caesar, Cicero, Diodorus Siculus, Ennius, Herodotus, Lucan, Pliny, Plutarch, Strabo, Tacitus, and Virgil. For medieval material, Bulwer refers to recent studies such as Palgrave's *History of England* and Sharon Turner's *History of the Anglo-Saxons*, as well as to antiquarian and literary sources such as Richard Hoare's translation of Giraldus Cambrensis, the Welsh *Triads*, Layamon's *Brut*, Geoffrey of Monmouth's *Historia*, Charlotte Guest's *Mabinogion*, Southey's notes to the *Morte d'Arthur*, and Ellis' edition of Way's French *Fabliaux*. Impressive as this range of learning is, it often interferes with the poem's tone and atmosphere, theme and symbolism.

Aside from its attention to Welsh language, topography, literature, and legend; its use of supernatural elements reminiscent of Welsh tales; and most important, the story of Gawaine and the Perilous Bed, the ponderous *King Arthur* contains little of Arthurian significance. Yet Bulwer, whose medieval interests were reflected not only in his antiquarian footnotes but also in the home he Gothicised and filled with armour, remained fond of the poem and nettled by its poor reception. He prided himself that no 'previous romantic poem' resembled it 'in its main design, or in the character of its principal incidents' (Preface, p. ix), without recognising this inventiveness as the reason the poem was already dated when it appeared in 1848. Although as a novelist he proved uncommonly astute in discerning readers' changing tastes, as an Arthurian poet he produced a work as insignificant as the pieces of the earlier nineteenth century. In a few passages it rivals the comic achievement of Frere and Peacock; but mostly it rivals the ineptness of Thelwall and Milman. Bulwer admitted that he wrote the poem after it had been in his mind for twenty years, and it clearly seems of 1828 vintage. Unlike Tennyson, who likewise contemplated his Arthurian cycle for decades before he published, Bulwer failed to perceive how to modernise traditional story psychologically and symbolically. Even though satiric and comic lines or episodes glitter occasionally, *King Arthur* seems merely a large chunk of fool's gold among the genuine Arthurian treasures of the nineteenth century.

iii. Matthew Arnold, *Tristram and Iseult* (1852)

Four years after Bulwer's work appeared, Matthew Arnold published one of these treasures in *Tristram and Iseult*, a narrative poem on the most popular love story of the Western world from the twelfth to the fifteenth centuries. The legend's appeal became nearly as great in the nineteenth century, capturing the fancy of Tennyson (1872) and Swinburne (1882), of Pre-Raphaelite painters in the Oxford Union murals of 1857, and of a number of dramatists soon after the turn of the century. It had been incorporated into the Arthurian cycle at an early stage and had provided a model for the love of Lancelot and Guinevere; and it offered relatively reticent Victorians such as Arnold and Tennyson a sanctioned vehicle for depicting unbridled passion. The medium of legend allowed these poets to treat a highly charged subject allusively, camouflaging sexuality with medieval effects and the emblematic love potion, and distancing the raw story in time and place. Yet Arnold—and Tennyson after him—made little of the love potion itself, and while allowing tradition and stylisation to diminish the shocking elements of the subject somewhat, handled medieval characters in ways consistent with a contemporary sense of human mental processes and behaviour. At the risk of slighting his stylistic accomplishment, we may judge that Arnold's most interesting achievement lay in treating the legend in such a way that it seems medieval yet particularly modern, meaningful and arresting for his own day.

The poem primarily echoes the traditional story, but with sufficient flexibility in details of plot and character to create this sense of contemporaneity. Arnold actually followed no medieval version directly. He came upon the tale in the first article of a series on 'Les poèmes gallois et les romans de la Table-Ronde' by the antiquarian Théodore de la Villemarqué. The article, published in the *Revue de Paris* of 1841, briefly summarises the story in prose, including Tristram's early accomplishments, the love potion, the forced separation of the lovers occasionally interrupted by duplicitous meetings, Tristram's marriage to Iseult of Brittany, his efforts to forget sorrow by courting danger, his request that Iseult of Ireland come to heal his grievous wound, his wife's lie that his paramour refused to come, and his dying of 'chagrin' before Iseult of Ireland arrives.[20] From this account

Arnold took all but the deception of Iseult of Brittany. After he began the poem, he looked into the matter of sources or 'originals'. He found in Malory's *Morte Darthur* little beyond his concluding line, but used other details and background information from Southey's notes and preface to the 1817 edition. Besides noting what Arnold took directly from these sources and what he changed or omitted, we may profitably contrast his meanings and methods with those of the romance tradition in order to see how he, unlike Arthurian writers earlier in the nineteenth century, effectively modernised his material.

By staying close to established tradition, Arnold taps its universal implications, which resonate through the poem in the conflicting loyalties of Tristram and the debilitating effects of his passion. Arnold's changes in story and character are few but significant; they primarily increase the psychological realism of the figures and make the story seem more poignant because more common to human experience. These modern applications are emphasised by experimental narrative techniques: Arnold combines monologue with dialogue and descriptive-narrative passages; makes abrupt transitions, sometimes in the manner of stream-of-consciousness narration; uses flashbacks and dreams to suggest the workings of the mind; and closes each of the three sections of the poem with codas or tailpieces, imagistic scenes which symbolically comment on the events within the body of the work.

The first two sections of Arnold's poem focus on the last moments of Tristram's life. As he waits for Iseult of Ireland, he fitfully dreams of episodes in their past. She arrives just in time to speak with him briefly, then dies as he does. The third section of the poem describes the static existence of Tristram's wife, Iseult of Brittany, who lives on in relative isolation with their children.

This sketch suggests several of the limited but important changes Arnold makes in the traditional story. First, he avoids the two familiar versions of the knight's death—ignominious slaughter by King Mark, which emphasises the dishonourable character of the whole affair, and the story of the black and white sails drawn from the Theseus legend. Though La Villemarqué does not record the detail of the coloured sails, he incorporates this version in Iseult of Brittany's lie, following Thomas' twelfth-century Anglo-Norman fragment. There the spurned wife purposefully lies to Tristram that the ship which bears Iseult of Ireland to him has hoisted black sails, thus signalling that she has refused to come. Arnold later wrote that when he composed the poem, he was not familiar with the motif of the coloured sails, 'a beautiful way of ending, which I should perhaps have used, had I known of it'.[21] But his alternate version achieves two significant ends: It allows the lovers to speak one last time, and it distinguishes Iseult of Brittany from the mean-spirited, vengeful wife who in medieval story hastens Tristram's death. Both of these departures from the standard story heighten the complexity of the principal characters and the poignancy of their situation.

The final conversation permitted by Arnold's innovation reveals conflicting emotions hardly dramatised in the early romances. In Béroul's twelfth-century French *Roman de Tristan*, for example, each lover similarly demonstrates a concern for his personal hardships. Having freely delighted in each other in the

Forest of Morrois at the expense of all other comforts, they are reminded by King Mark's discovery of their hiding place of the agreeable life at court they have sacrificed for love (symbolically, this change of attitude is linked to the end of the love potion's effectiveness). Béroul's Tristan enumerates his own lost status and material comforts in eighteen lines; only afterwards does he think of the queen's deprivations—for which six lines suffice. Iseult shows similar self-concern when she repents. While these speeches in Béroul present a rather flat and unflattering sense of each character's concentration on personal grievances, the progression of sentiments in Arnold's dialogue shows each figure's regret coexisting with the tenderest feelings. Moreover, the pains of which his lovers complain are not external—not the loss of rank or wealth—but internal. The feelings of Arnold's lovers never reach the emotional pitch depicted later in the *Liebestod* of Wagner's operatic treatment of the story (1859), for Arnold purposefully keeps the complexities of the love within the realm of more normal human experience. He also controls emotion by counterpointing his lovers' dialogue with the affecting but objectifying images in the codas.

The second major change in the traditional circumstances of Tristram's death similarly enriches the medieval characterisations. Arnold's Iseult of Brittany, unlike the vindictive wife in La Villemarqué's synopsis or Thomas' fragment, acts magnanimously. This sympathetic portrait complements another of Arnold's changes in medieval story, the fact that Tristram and his wife have children. This alteration does not increase the sense of pathos so much as it subtly defines and complicates the plight of Tristram. Where the marriage appears in medieval romance—in Thomas' fragment and its derivatives, in the French Prose *Tristan*, and in Malory's *Morte Darthur*—it remains unconsummated because of Tristram's dominating passion. (In Eilhart von Oberge's *Tristrant*, it is finally consummated only after Tristram has visited his mistress following his wedding. This is the version followed in Dunlop's *History of Fiction*, from which Arnold drew a prefatory note for his second edition of *Tristram and Iseult*, but which he apparently did not consult before the poem was initially published.) In medieval romance, the knight's brief attempt at another existence remains a sterile alternative to his sterile affair. In contrast, Arnold's giving Tristram such an appealing wife and loved children anchors the knight's turmoil in the domestic realm and underscores the tragic insufficiency of such love to cure him. Arnold also enhances the portrait of Iseult of Ireland by omitting, for example, references to Brangain and to the ambiguous oath, which La Villemarqué mentions. Arnold thereby avoids calling up Iseult's murderous proclivities and her moral flexibility. While the queen is a less dramatic figure, perhaps, without these dimensions, Arnold's changes in characters and events do not vitiate the power of the traditional story so much as reinvest it in familiar experience.

Through other means Arnold captures the spirit and themes of medieval story in details that similarly enrich the human personalities and relate the story to the more recognisable modern world. Usually he does so by encapsulating essential bits of the legend in telling details, as when he draws on the entire background of Tristram's manifold excellences and talents in the single pregnant detail of his harp and hunting dress lying unused on the sick bed. La Villemarqué and Southey both mention Tristram's accomplishment as harper and hunter, and a catalogue of Tristram's talents is integral to the medieval story, necessary to intensify the waste when passion thwarts his potential. Gottfried von Strassburg, for example, who gives the fullest account of the love story in his thirteenth-century *Tristan*, for the purpose of such contrast also gives the fullest version of the knight's *enfances*, training, and early achievements. Arnold captures this sense of Tristram's squandered potential in a passage describing his participation in holy and nationalistic warfare. In a flashback a delirious dream of the past (an example of Arnold's experimental narrative techniques), Tristram recalls the failure of the highest forms of knightly activity to rouse him from sorrowful lethargy.

Elsewhere Arnold adapts another traditional element of the legend to more realistic and modern representation. Malory, like his source the French Prose *Tristan* (and the account in Dunlop's *History of Fiction*), includes an episode in which love so deprives Tristram of reason that he runs wild in the forest as a lunatic. Arnold re-embodies the significance of this emblematic hyperbole in his character's disorientation and frustration, and he suggests this mental and emotional instability through the disrupted, disjointed narrative technique, as well as through Tristram's fluctuating between lucidity and unconsciousness, dreams, and memories. Within these feverish dreams Arnold dramatises Tristram's past lack of reason and will. In the remembered campaign against Saxons and Romans, for instance, he found peace only in delusion, in the kind of 'lunacy' effected by the play of moonlight on a forest pool that for an instant seemed to picture the face of Iseult of Ireland.

Arnold treats the traditional symbol of Tristram's passion, the love potion, in similar fashion. Though in a flashback he describes the fatal drink mentioned by La Villemarqué and Southey's notes, the role of the magical potion recedes behind psychological effects. Arnold transfers the significance of the drink to fevers of the blood and fires of the brain. The possibility of emphasising human psychology rather than magic as the source of Tristram's debilitation is actually anticipated in medieval romance itself, when in Béroul the love potion nominally wears off but the lovers soon resume their affair, or when in both Gottfried and Malory the young couple obviously love before they quaff the potion. Arnold carefully subordinates the role of the drink by focusing on emotional and mental states.

All of Arnold's adaptations in character, plot, and emblem or symbol in one sense contract the possibilities of medieval tradition by bringing everything more definitely into the realm of ordinary human experience—Tristram's children, his conflicting attitudes when Iseult of Ireland finally arrives, his mental disorientation and frustration instead of lunacy. But at the same time, such changes expand the legend's usefulness in modern literature by centring the story in what is real and typical in the human personality and by shifting action from external to internal consequence.

A further innovation in Arnold's version is his use of a Breton bard to narrate the story long after Iseult of Ireland and Tristram have died. This device intensifies the sense of contemporaneity, for even though this narrator himself lived long ago, he shows us a poet applying the messages of a traditional story to his own time. This narrator emphasises that the lovers' death scene, described as a tableau, is an emblem from the distant past. Yet he discerns in their story parallels to the experiences of the present world, where deluding passion, whether love or another consuming aspiration, can vitiate all happiness. But equally destructive, he concludes, is the absence of passion, the incapacity to feel anything deeply. This is the peculiarly modern experience which he describes as 'the gradual furnace of the world' (III, 119). The narrator here obviously echoes Arnold's frequent observations on the emotional sterility of his own age. His note in a manuscript of *Tristram and Iseult* makes the point specifically: 'The misery of the present age is not in the intensity of men's suffering—but in their incapacity to suffer, enjoy, feel at all, wholly and profoundly.'[22] This emotional deprivation Arnold elsewhere linked to the spiritual and aesthetic impoverishment of the nineteenth century, or what he ungrammatically but emphatically termed its 'unpoetrylessness'.[23] Although the destructiveness of unrestrained passion is the most obvious theme of *Tristram and Iseult*, the poem also emphasises, obliquely, the importance of imagination and aesthetic creativity as means of objectifying and distancing painful actuality. This theme is most clearly focused in the Merlin story which concludes the work.

This coda is another of Arnold's significant innovations, for the tales of Tristram and the magician are nowhere significantly connected in medieval romance. Arnold himself indicated that, although he was especially fond of the tale of Vivian's enchanting Merlin, he had appended it as an afterthought and was uncertain of its effect.[24] But in illustrating the escape from the finite physical world of a besotted lover who, significantly, is also a master of fantasy, the Merlin story provides another standard for assessing Tristram's destiny. Here, as throughout the poem, Arnold contrasts the scene of escape with a vast landscape beyond. Merlin meets his fate in a small glen, insulated from the surrounding 'sea of leaf and bough' (III, 202). Recognising the singularity of the spot, he chooses to stop because 'No fairer resting-place a man could find' (210). He falls into a sleep so deep that it seems 'more like death' (214)—an image thematically and verbally related to Tristram's death, earlier misconstrued by the tapestry Huntsman as sleep. In this passage Arnold selectively draws from two different sources, a second article by La Villemarqué in an 1837 edition of the *Revue de Paris*, 'Visite au tombeau de Merlin', and Southey's notes on the Vulgate *Merlin* in the Preface to his Malory.[25] La Villemarqué suggests that Vivian induces Merlin's sleep as the first stage in her enchantment, while Southey's synopsis suggests that Merlin falls asleep fatigued by lovemaking. In contrast to both his sources, Arnold attributes the sleep neither to the fay nor even to natural fatigue. Rather, stating that 'a sleep / Fell upon Merlin' (213–14), the poet suggests operation of some power beyond human control.

Vivian *then* weaves a spell that confines him, but the responsibility lies with Merlin, who 'Forgot his craft, and his best wits took flight; / And he grew fond, and eager to obey / His mistress, use her empire as she may' (182–4).

Though called a 'false fay', Vivian appears as a phenomenon native to the realm of enchantment. The incident occurs in a 'fairy-haunted land' (153) where 'the spirit of the woods was in her face' (180). The circumstances of Merlin's enchantment seem more positive than negative. Whereas Tristram the lover reveals that life dominated by passion becomes painful in the actual world, we see Merlin settled in a resting place of unsurpassed beauty, a secure 'little plot of magic ground', a 'daisied circle' (220–1). As in the scene of Tristram and Iseult in a death tableau wondrous and beautiful to the Huntsman—himself preserved in an artefact—Merlin becomes suspended in a scene of magical and lasting beauty (in contrast to the prisons in La Villemarqué and Southey, where only the strength of the enclosing tower is emphasised). In Arnold's poem the transformation is not permanent, however, for it will persist only 'till the judgement-day' (222), that is, until eternal peace replaces the 'gradual furnace of the world'. Merlin's imprisonment affords an escape from the painful existence that he, as a lover like Tristram, can expect. In La Villemarqué's account and Southey's synopsis—as well as in Dunlop's *History of Fiction*—Vivian intends her lover no harm. She playfully weaves the spell without believing that it will immure him. She also returns to the enchanted prison to caress him and manifests great sorrow over his fate. Arnold, however, at this point follows the *Morte Darthur*—even borrows Malory's phrasing—to express Vivian's relief at escaping the kind of infatuation marking Merlin and Tristram. 'Passing weary of his love' (224), Vivian without regret delivers Merlin to an enchanted peace attained by Tristram only in a poet's fanciful reinterpretation of his death. At the same time, she frees herself from the sorrow attending both Iseults: 'she herself whither she will can rove' (223). Merlin's craft and wit are mastered by his passion. Even so, through enchantment of his own devising, he escapes from potential anguish into a calm, beautiful stasis.

In *Tristram and Iseult* Merlin represents an imagination that escapes ordinary passions by means of the peace, beauty, and permanence of art.[26] But, as the subject of legend told over centuries—by Breton dames, the widowed Iseult, the poem's narrator, and by Arnold—Merlin also serves the instructive purposes of didactic art. The characters in *Tristram and Iseult* illustrate varying degrees of success in using their imaginations to cope with the barrenness and 'unpoetry-lessness' of life. Those who remain most fully immersed in mundane experience are least able to derive lasting benefit from their imaginations. Iseult of Brittany employs her creativity as a story-teller only to escape from pain. The narrator, safely distanced from the unhappy experiences, shares them only vicariously. Yet his frustrated editorialising and spluttering against life in general suggest his failure to achieve control over his art or the life on which he comments. It is, finally, Arnold and his reading audience who can use art—and more specifically, Arthurian legend—not just as an escape or an anodyne, but as a fundamental remedy for the maladies of existence.

Through subtle craftsmanship and innovative use of the Tristram and Merlin legends, Arnold fashioned both a traditional caution against unrestrained passion and a modern injunction to keep alive imagination and aesthetic creativity as means of organising, interpreting, and coping with life. By using remote medieval legend simultaneously to distance and to embody these themes, he offered his age a paradigm of how to fulfil the second charge. Though Arnold remained fond of *Tristram and Iseult*, he was a bit uncertain about its effectiveness—as he was about his poetry in general. But he once observed that although he had 'less poetical sentiment than Tennyson', he was 'likely enough to have my turn'.[27] Happily for us, because they combined the traditional values of legends with modern ones, the Arthurian poems of both Arnold and Tennyson still enjoy their 'turn' today.

iv. Owen Meredith, 'Queen Guenevere', 'Elayne le Blanc', 'The Parting of Launcelot and Guenevere' (1855); Robert Stephen Hawker, *The Quest of the Sangraal* (1863); Thomas Westwood, *The Sword of Kingship* (1866) and *The Quest of the Sancgreall* (1868).

Considerably less interesting artistically than Arnold's poem are three brief pieces by 'Owen Meredith', Edward Robert Bulwer-Lytton, First Earl Lytton—son of the Edward Bulwer-Lytton who wrote *King Arthur*. Yet Meredith's experimentation with picturesque effects, point of view, and psychological amplification of the Arthurian material deserve some note. The longest of the three, 'The Parting of Launcelot and Guenevere', is most significant for possibly influencing—or at least, anticipating—Tennyson, who received a gift copy of the 1855 collection which contained Meredith's Arthurian poems, and who would in 1876 dedicate a drama to him.

The slightest piece, 'Queen Guenevere', in forty-seven lines describes the queen in picturesque detail. It is narrated in the first-person by an unidentified speaker, for whom this glimpse of the lovely queen constitutes an epiphany. (He recounts the moment in language strongly reminiscent of Keats' image of 'stout Cortez' discovering the Pacific.) The speaker's wonderment is reinforced by Meredith's end symbol, a peregrine falcon that has flown 'athwart strange lands . . . / To look into the great eyes of the Queen.' In 'Elayne le Blanc' Meredith probes the damsel's psychology. Though he does not use Tennyson's symbolic loom, mirror, and curse, the poem of nearly 300 lines would seem to amplify the situation in 'The Lady of Shalott'. Isolated, Elayne languishes because she has no knight. She pines for the romance of Arthur's court, which Launcelot embodies in the final lines, where Elayne sees him riding past in glittering armour.

If 'Elayne le Blanc' seems obviously influenced by Tennyson, the indebtedness may be reversed in the case of Meredith's longest Arthurian work, 'The Parting of Launcelot and Guenevere: A Fragment'. This poem derives from the beginning of Malory's Elaine of Astolat story, where the queen upbraids Launcelot for foregoing a tournament in order to stay behind with her, the episode Tennyson would use in 'Lancelot and Elaine'. Unlike Tennyson's idyll, Meredith's poem follows Malory by dating the episode some time after the Grail quest and by mentioning Arthur's wrath when the lovers remain behind. But his innovations in Malory's characters and situations in several ways anticipate Tennyson's treatment of the lovers in three of the earliest idylls, published only four years after Meredith's Arthurian poems appeared. Most significant, Meredith here elaborates the quarrels and tensions of the lovers, as Tennyson was soon to do in 'Lancelot and Elaine'. Meredith's Launcelot, like Tennyson's, is acutely aware that his love and knightly accomplishments have been blighted. And Meredith's queen grows increasingly remorseful and aware of her sins, as Tennyson's character would in 'Guinevere'. Besides these general conceptions of character and situation, Meredith's poems may also have suggested particulars to Tennyson, as in the detail of the happy lovers spending their days hawking, perhaps echoed in 'Merlin and Vivien'.

Owen Meredith's 'Elayne le Blanc' thus reflects the influence of Tennyson's early Arthurian verse, and in turn, his works, in their conception of the characters' psychology, anticipate the idylls. The extent to which Tennyson's Arthurian poems captured the nineteenth-century imagination registers in the host of subsequent treatments they stimulated. These ranged from flattering imitation, to vigorously independent versions (sometimes specifically identified by their authors as anti-Tennysonian), to satire and parody, most often directed against Tennyson's manner rather than his matter. Perhaps the best of those by relatively insignificant poets in the middle decades of the century is Robert Stephen Hawker's *Quest of the Sangraal*. In important ways Hawker does not 'follow' Tennyson: he used the Grail story five years before Tennyson did; his treatment of the Grail as a religious symbol differs extensively from Tennyson's; and his tone and style vary markedly from the Laureate's. Yet he may properly be seen as following Tennyson in that, although he had long been interested in Arthurian lore, he never wrote on the subject until 1863 (when he was sixty), several years after Tennyson's first group of *Idylls* had established the popular appeal of the material. Before this, Hawker, a zealous Cornish antiquarian who emulated the old ballads and embodied the folklore of his beloved region in a series of sprightly *Cornish Ballads*, had evoked Arthurian legend only indirectly in two brief poems by associating the names of Guenevere and Arthur with local customs. 'Queen Guennivar's Round' lustily contrasts 'old Cornwall's bounding daughters' with Greek nymphs and naiads, and 'King Arthur's Waes-Hael' (1860) commemorates a Cornish Yule custom in what may be described as a religious drinking-song. The success of Tennyson's first *Idylls*—which Hawker welcomed in a brief poem, 'To Alfred Tennyson' (1859), as the literary resurrection of Arthur in 'laurelled verse' which would enable the king to 'live, and die no more'—doubtless spurred Hawker to treat Arthurian story in a narrative poem, like Tennyson's written in blank verse and derived principally from Malory.

But Hawker's version of the Grail story offers quite a different sense of the legend than the Laureate would embody in his later idyll. Hawker had discussed Arthurian material—which he proprietarily described as 'Cornwall and King Arthur, *my* themes'—with Tennyson when he visited Hawker's Morwenstow vicarage in 1848, and 'lent him Books and MSS. about King Arthur, . . . which I perhaps shall never see again.'[28] Subsequently the eccentric vicar flattered himself that he had initiated Tennyson's interest in the material.[29] But even though he recommended that Tennyson compose a Grail idyll, Hawker doubted in 1862, the year before he proceeded with his own version, whether the Laureate was 'endowed with the necessary faculty to deal with it,' for he was insufficiently religious or mystical 'to win the Grace demanded in its Scribe.'[30] Apparently Tennyson shared this sentiment somewhat, for as early as 1859 he had hesitated to use the story, doubting 'whether such a subject could be handled in these days, without incurring a charge of irreverence.'[31] Hawker's *Quest of the Sangraal* reflects just the mystical conception he deemed impossible for Tennyson to handle. Himself entranced by romance, mysticism, and ritual (he converted to Catholicism on his deathbed), Hawker viewed the Grail as 'the Type of the Gospel, and the loss and recovery are emblems of the failure of our light and its Restoration.'[32] The poem begins with Arthur's knights exuberantly shouting, 'Ho! for the Sangraal.' Arthur briefly recounts the history of the Grail, brought to England by Joseph of Arimathea, then dispatches the eager questers. The work concludes with Merlin's conjuring for Arthur three visions which cryptically forecast Britain's future. (Hawker later explained what few readers might be expected to discern, that these visions represent, first, Arthur's wars, then Saxon and Norman conquests, and finally, the period 'from 1536 to 1863 with my notions of the Battle of Waterloo and the Armstrong Gun—Gas, Steam, Electric Telegraph.'[33])

Hawker's narrative follows the *Morte Darthur* in the general concept of the mystical symbol, as well as in the basic view of the characters—noble Arthur, pure Galahad, troubled Lancelot—but also draws heavily on his own imagination. For example, he reduces the number of Grail questers to four, Lancelot, Perceval, Tristram, and Galahad, each of whom is to seek the Grail throughout a quadrant of the earth. Most important, Hawker emphasises that this quest confirms the greatness of the Arthurian Order. The holy relic has withdrawn from England because of the wickedness of several generations, and its restoration will renew purity. Consequently Hawker's King Arthur fervently endorses the quest, remaining behind only because he must tend his flock (as would Tennyson's king, who, however, would also regard the quest as a misguided disruption of his Order). While the symbolism of Hawker's concluding prophetic visions remains obscure, even with his explanation, his symbolic interpretation of the Grail itself, which he based on extensive antiquarian reading, Hebrew lore, and recent medieval scholarship such as that of Francisque Michel and Théodore de la Villemarqué,[34] functions effectively throughout the poem. Also effective are the animated, even rugged, rhythm and diction, which give the work a continuing, if modest, charm. Perhaps the piece would have succeeded more fully if Hawker had completed the three further 'chants' he originally projected. But given his attitude toward the mystical symbol, it is difficult to envision how he could have followed the traditional story through to its sober conclusion, moving from the spiritual vigour and confidence expressed in his poem to the legendary failure of the Order. His idealisation of Arthur and the Grail quest, far more than the 'adverse Banker's Balance' that he later blamed, probably inhibited his proceeding with the narrative.[35]

Despite the limited scope of his poem, Hawker felt it surpassed Tennyson's treatment of the Grail, and he proudly pointed out that Longfellow concurred.[36] Perhaps this competitive spirit made him especially sensitive to what he perceived as the plagiarism of a still more minor poet, Thomas Westwood. In 1866 Westwood, better known as an angling authority than as a poet, published a brief narrative, 'The Sword of Kingship', based on the first book of Malory, which recounts Arthur's birth, childhood, drawing the sword from the stone, and coronation. His second Arthurian piece, in six books or chapters, he entitled *The Quest of the Sancgreal*, and although he followed Malory in making Galahad the Grail hero and invented a number of episodes himself, he also borrowed from Hawker. The vicar was piqued not only over the resemblance of Westwood's title to his own, but also over the echoes of his memorable opening line: Hawker's 'Ho! for the Sangraal! vanish'd Vase of Heaven!' recurs only slightly altered in Westwood's 'Ho! for the Sancgreall, blessed Blood of God!' But besides these points of resemblance to Hawker, Westwood's greatest debt was to Tennyson, for his blank verse patently imitates that of the early *Idylls*. Ironically, while this imitation gives Westwood's work its greatest distinction, it also renders the poem wholly inconsequential, for what Westwood accomplished would in the next year be surpassed by the Grail idyll of his stylistic model. By following Tennyson's lead in reshaping Arthurian material, Hawker and Westwood, through the inferiority of their Grail poems, emphasised the achievement of the *Idylls of the King*.

4

An Epic in 'the Fashion of the Day'

Idylls of the King

When in 1859 Tennyson finally published four new Arthurian poems as *Idylls of the King*, reviewers greeted them enthusiastically as the first parts of the long-awaited Arthurian epic.[1] From the early 1830s he had apparently contemplated a major work based on the legends, but the form it should take challenged him for some time. Between 1833 and 1840 he thought to cast it as an epic, but also, as a surviving sketch reveals, considered writing a five-act musical drama.[2] After John Sterling's hostile review of the 'Morte d'Arthur' (by which Tennyson may have been testing public reaction to the idea of an Arthurian epic), he remarked that 'a small vessel, built on fine lines, is likely to float further down the stream of Time than a big raft.'[3] Instead of a continuous narrative he chose to shape the legends into a series of idylls, each a contained, concentrated episode or picture in epic manner.

The choice of form proved fortuitous. Though each idyll narrates a discrete episode, they together portray the entire history of the Round Table. A number of devices unify the separate poems, particularly their settings throughout the year; they move from spring in the first hopeful narratives, through an increasingly ominous summer, to a desolate autumn in 'The Last Tournament', and finally to 'The Passing of Arthur' on the last day of the year. Other image patterns integrate the tales—references to music, animals, clothing, colour, songs and dreams—as do numerous echoes in phrasing and parallels between characters, motifs, and situations.

Except for the two Geraint idylls, based on a tale in the *Mabinogion*, Tennyson drew the episodes primarily from Malory's *Morte Darthur*. But his alterations in character, detail, plot sequence, and theme make this a highly independent cycle rather than merely an updated re-telling of medieval romance. The principal innovation is Tennyson's conception of Arthur himself, for the King is not the noble but flawed figure of medieval romance, but an idealised, highly symbolic figure. Tennyson had early explored the symbolic possibilities of Arthurian matter in notes, apparently for an epic, drafted about 1833, which suggest that he contemplated treating the material allegorically: 'K. A. Religious Faith'. 'Modred, the sceptical understanding'. 'The Round Table: liberal institutions'.[4] As they came to be written, however, the *Idylls* develop no formal allegory.

Tennyson commented on the persistent questions about his symbolism that 'they have taken my hobby, and ridden it too hard, and have explained some things too allegorically, although there is an allegorical or perhaps rather a parabolic drift in the poem.' He later was to define the general tenor of his symbolism in the epilogue 'To the Queen', which describes Arthur as 'Ideal manhood closed in real man,' and identifies the poem's central conflict as 'Sense at war with Soul.' Elsewhere he articulated the general symbolic pattern: 'The whole . . . is the dream of man coming into practical life and ruined by one sin. Birth is a mystery and death is a mystery, and in the midst lies the tableland of life, and its struggles and performances. It is not the history of one man or of one generation but of a whole cycle of generations.'[5] He frankly acknowledged his didactic aims: 'I tried in my "Idylls" to teach men . . . the need of the Ideal.'[6] Despite his explanations of the symbolism, the *Idylls* are susceptible of multiple, complex interpretations, as suggested by Tennyson's comparing poetry to 'shot-silk with many glancing colours. Every reader must find his own interpretation according to his ability.'[7]

Though his son said that Tennyson had the scheme of the *Idylls* in mind as early as 1855,[8] actual composition occupied four separate periods after the earliest piece, the narrative of Arthur's death written in 1833–34. When he began the *Idylls* in earnest, he wrote four poems on love stories associated with Arthurian legend. These tales offer striking contrasts between good and bad women, wholesome and debilitating love (later phrased 'Sense at war with Soul'). The earliest printing, an 1857 trial edition of only six copies, illustrated the principle of contrast in its title, *Enid and Nimuë: or, The True and the False*. In 1859 he published these two (Nimuë now changed to Vivien), with poems on the antithetical figures Elaine and Guinevere, as *The True and the False: Four Idylls of the King*. The next period of composition came in 1868–69, when Tennyson began to make clear the plan of the sequence. At this point he described the beginnings of the Order in 'The Coming of Arthur' and added 'The Holy Grail', thereby expanding the subject matter and emphasising the breakdown of the Round Table. He added 'Pelleas and Ettarre', a love story paralleling the initial four idylls, set in the context of the Order's fragmentation after the Grail quest. And he completed the frame by developing the earlier 'Morte d'Arthur' into 'The Passing of Arthur'. Between 1870 and 1872 Tennyson wrote two additional idylls, beginning with the optimistic 'Gareth and Lynette' to elaborate the possibilities suggested in 'The Coming of Arthur', interrupting it to write a sombre tale of dissolution, 'The Last Tournament', then finishing the Gareth story. Tennyson did not write the final idyll, 'Balin and Balan' until 1872–74, and it was published only in 1885. By dividing the Enid idyll into two parts in 1873, he achieved the twelve books anticipated in 'The Epic', his original frame for the 'Morte d'Arthur'.

i. 'The Coming of Arthur' (1869)

The first idyll in the final collection, 'The Coming of Arthur' was actually the seventh to be written. In it Tennyson recounts the beginning of Arthur's reign, adopting 'purposely archaic' language in order to connect the opening idyll with the closing one, which was first conceived as the 'Morte d'Arthur', to complete the frame for the other stories. Publication of 'The Coming of Arthur' made much clearer the lines of Tennyson's cycle, for while it emphasises the hopeful beginnings and positive achievements of Arthur's new order, it persistently hints of the impending decay which becomes increasingly apparent in the five love stories and the Grail story, all of which had been written by this time.

'The Coming of Arthur' illustrates two ways in which Tennyson purposefully manipulates his source material. First, he obviously selects, condenses, and reorganises Malory's much fuller and less straightforward narrative, not merely to give a more coherent and dramatically focused narrative, but to emphasise themes and reinterpret ideas. For example, Tennyson places Arthur's aid to Leodogran, which in Malory follows his defeating the British lords and kings who challenge his kingship, before the internecine warfare. Thus Tennyson provides evidence from the beginning of the tale that Arthur has sufficient prowess for leadership and also establishes the realm's need for civilising more than for simple political unity.

Tennyson also selects and deletes incidents to concentrate symbolic meanings, as when he retains from Malory many of Arthur's achievements but omits his amorous liaisons and his slaughter of all the children born on May Day. On one level, this treatment diminishes the interest in some characterisations, which are made to fit symbolic or even allegorical patterns. But while he flattens and allegorises characters, Tennyson also uses subtle details of action and imagery to convey a stylised but psychologically rich sense of the human personality, as in the two brief glimpses of Guinevere in this idyll.

In compressing and reorganising his source material for 'The Coming of Arthur', Tennyson gathered into only 437 blank verse lines—later expanded to 518—a great deal of the substance of three early books in Caxton's edition of the *Morte Darthur*, Book I on Arthur's birth and rise to power, Book III on his marriage, and Book V on his conflict with the Roman emperor Lucius. The subject of the idyll is literally how Arthur 'made a realm'. While Tennyson retains the main outlines of Malory's story, however, his focus is entirely different. He considerably minimises the significance of conquests and battles; for example, Malory's lengthy account of the conflict with the Romans is compressed into the half line 'and Arthur strove with Rome'. Instead of prowess and conquest, the source of unity and strength in Arthur's new order is his spiritual identity, as Bellicent's description of his coronation—which occurs *before* he subdues either the rebellious British kings or the Romans—makes clear. She recounts how he bound his knights to him through 'so strait vows' that they were dazed and shaken. These vows are much less specific than the Pentecostal oath which is the source in Malory: 'then the king . . . charged them never to do outrageousity nor murder, and always to flee treason; also, by no means to be cruel, but to give mercy unto him that asketh mercy, upon pain of forfeiture of their worship and lordship of King Arthur for evermore; and always to do ladies, damosels, and gentlewomen succour, upon pain of death.

Also, that no man take no battles in a wrongful quarrel for no law, nor for no world's goods' (III, xv). Tennyson's knights are bound simply to the King's 'own self', making Arthur the spiritual embodiment of all that the Order is to be.

To centre the King's power over his followers in his nature rather than in his achievements, Tennyson focuses not on events but on Leodogran's uncertainty, even after benefiting from Arthur's help, about whether he is truly king. Not that Tennyson sacrifices all action, but he considerably reduces its role and relates events of conquest in curiously static, symbolic passages. The most dynamic action passage, for example, the battle scene between Arthur and the British barons and kings who question his claim to the throne, occupies only thirty lines, most of which describe the setting, and the joyous victory seems patently emblematic: 'So like a painted battle the war stood / Silenced, the living quiet as the dead, / And in the heart of Arthur joy was lord.' Aside from this rather indirect way of directly narrating events, Tennyson conveys most of the action through innovative use of flashbacks and of story-within-story techniques, thus giving past events a similarly static and symbolic character. He begins well into Malory's story of Arthur, after his coronation, and describes the King's rise to power through stories told by Bedivere, Bellicent, and Bleys. Since these different versions of different moments in the past exist, as it were, simultaneously, side by side in the 'present', we are less concerned with them as a sequence of events than as symbols in which the central issues of the poem coalesce. The question is not how Arthur became king, but whether he is king. Tennyson's chief device for shifting attention from Arthur's practical achievements to his spiritual legitimacy is to centre the poem on Leodogran rather than on battles, dramatising the King's internal conflict over Arthur's identity.

In Malory, the issue of whether Arthur will wed Guinevere seems scarcely momentous. Coming after Arthur's claim has been established by the portent of the sword in the stone (which Tennyson omits) and several great battles, his marriage proposal is accepted eagerly by Leodegrance as 'the best tidings that ever I heard' (III, i). Tennyson, by tracing Leodogran's uncertainty about the King's identity, shifts the issue from 'prowess and noblesse', which have already been established by victory over Leodogran's foes, to Arthur's essential nature and identity.

In the first of the three narratives which Leodogran solicits to help him decide about Arthur's suit, Tennyson follows but considerably alters Malory's version of Arthur's birth. Putting it into the mouth of Bedivere, Tennyson cleanses the story of its raw passion and brutality. Although Uther still covets another man's wife, he does not fall ill with passion, or—disguised as her husband by Merlin's magic—ravish Igraine. Tennyson's Uther wins Igraine by force, but holy wedlock (somewhat marred by 'shameful swiftness') precedes Arthur's conception. After thus purging the conventional version of Arthur's birth of the elements most shocking to Victorian moral sensibilities, Tennyson offers two other accounts—entirely original to him—which emphasise that Arthur's 'coming' as king is something quite different from birth. (Significantly,

Tennyson had originally entitled his trial edition 'The Birth of Arthur', but he changed it much as he had changed the original title of the 'Morte d'Arthur' to 'The Passing of Arthur'.) It is also important that he resists using Malory's story of the sword in the stone, which gives public evidence of Arthur's claim to the throne. Tennyson keeps the 'facts' uncertain or debatable, for all three accounts give only the limited testimony of a single person. Moreover, Bedivere has his evidence from others; Bellicent, biased as Arthur's loving half-sister, is partially uncertain herself; and Bleys' testimony is filtered through Bellicent. (The name Bellicent itself should be mentioned as one of Tennyson's purposeful alterations. In Malory, the same figure is Margawse, on whom Arthur incestuously begets Mordred. To exonerate his king of such licentiousness, Tennyson altogether changes the identity of Gawain's and Modred's mother, using a name which appears in Ellis' *Specimens of Early English Metrical Romances* and in a footnote in Wright's edition of Malory.[9])

Minor alterations in Malory's story also keep alive ambiguities about Arthur's origins. According to Tennyson's Bedivere, Uther dies before Arthur's birth; thus the father cannot confirm Arthur's legitimacy, as he does in Malory. Similarly, Tennyson's prophet Bleys, Merlin's teacher, dies after divulging his secret to Bellicent, so he similarly cannot confirm the story, whereas in Malory Bleys lives throughout Arthur's reign, recording its chief events (I, xvii). These three characters who tell stories of Arthur's coming represent a progression in the kind of understanding necessary to comprehend the true nature of the King. Bedivere, significant as the first-made knight, repeats the testimony of brave warriors who have witnessed Arthur's kinship to Uther in prowess. Bellicent, who has loved her half-brother from childhood, has long perceived both his graciousness and his righteousness, and has intuitively felt he must be king. Bleys, in offering an ostensibly eyewitness account of Arthur's supernatural origins, speaks as the prophet, whose understanding depends upon intuitive and symbolic perceptions more than on the evidence of concrete actuality.

An important element of these three stories of Arthur's coming to kingship is Tennyson's deletion of the traditional role of magic in the story of Uther and Igraine; instead, he associates Arthur with a specifically Christian supernatural. Although in Malory's story of Arthur's birth, Merlin's magic, by enabling Uther to lie with Igraine, engenders a great national hero, it also allows a lustful king to ravish a virtuous wife after he has killed her husband. In Tennyson's version, Bedivere's account of Arthur's conception mentions no such ambiguous magic. But in the two stories told by Bellicent, figures and details clearly associated with the Christian supernatural consecrate Arthur's spiritual legitimacy as king. Although Bellicent hopes to persuade Leodegran to accept Arthur, she actually casts doubt on Bedivere's insistence that Arthur is Uther's son. Yet she recalls that at his coronation, a supernatural light shone through a stained-glass representation of the Crucifixion. The colours traditionally associated with Faith, Hope, and Charity irradiated Arthur, as well as his supernatural attendants—the Lady of the Lake (whom Tennyson identifies in a note as 'the Church'), who can 'walk the waters like our Lord', and three fair queens (whom

Tennyson elsewhere associates with the three theological virtues).

Although the validity of the three accounts of Arthur's coming to the throne cannot be ascertained, they chiefly shift attention from the issue of Arthur's parentage to his spiritual consecration. But as Merlin enigmatically suggests, 'truth is this to me, and that to thee; / And truth or clothed or naked let it be.' Merlin's riddling and the three conflicting stories thrust the problem of determining Arthur's legitimacy back on the puzzled Leodogran, who is then visited by a dream which suggests Arthur's spiritual rather than genealogical pedigree: rejected on earth as 'no son of Uther, and no king of ours,' he is 'crowned' in heaven. After all his uncertainty, Leodogran finally accepts this supernatural testimony and recognises Arthur as king. This, in effect, is the actual 'coming' of Arthur to the throne. It depends not on parentage or even dragon ships on fiery waves, but on other men's recognising the validity of Arthur's spiritual claim to the throne.

But even as Leodogran's accepting Arthur as king establishes the Order, it ironically links Arthur's coming to his passing, for his marriage to Guinevere is the beginning of the end. Tennyson sets up this irony in the opening lines of the poem, which focus on Guinevere. Throughout the idyll Arthur's coming is irrevocably linked to his fall by a variety of details, as when Arthur sadly reads the messages on the two sides of Excalibur's blade—'Take me,' and 'Cast me away'—or when Tennyson deliberately echoes a memorable phrase first published some twenty-seven years earlier in the 'Morte d'Arthur' and retained in the expanded version of 'The Passing of Arthur': 'The old order changeth, yielding place to new.' This line, already associated with Arthur's fall, gleams ironically in his declaration that the Round Table society will now replace Rome as 'The slowly-fading mistress of the world'.

The treatment of Guinevere also shows how Tennyson, for all his allegorising of Arthur, did not seriously diminish the human interest of his characters. Tennyson portrays her only slightly, through oblique glimpses—the detail of her 'drooping eyes' as she utters her marriage vow, and the earlier detail of her looking on the host of Arthur's knights and failing utterly to see the King. Whereas Malory overtly states Guinevere's threat to the Order when Merlin warns that 'Guenever was not wholesome for him to take to wife, for . . . Launcelot should love her, and she him again' (III, i), Tennyson makes her actions, as reflections of her psychological state, foreshadow tragedy. Such hints that Arthur's marriage marks both his coming and his passing appear in other Tennysonian innovations. For example, Lancelot is already established at Arthur's court as his best friend, and Modred's perfidy surfaces as he eavesdrops on Bellicent's story. Through such details Tennyson includes in the first idyll of the final series elements he had already elaborated in 'Guinevere' and 'The Passing of Arthur'. The opening book consequently contains the germ of all those which follow.

ii. 'Gareth and Lynette' (1872)

Having emphasised in 'The Coming of Arthur' that the King 'made a realm' less by dint of action than by the spiritual legitimacy of his claim to the throne, Tennyson in the next idyll of the finished sequence traces the development of qualities necessary in the King's followers. This version of Malory's story of the Fair Unknown, the untested youth who proves his worthiness, shows an apparently ordinary man spreading Arthur's civilising principles beyond the halls of Camelot. Published in 1872, 'Gareth and Lynette' was actually the next-to-last idyll completed, before Tennyson added 'Balin and Balan' and divided the original Geraint idyll into two to make twelve. Having already shown in the idylls written earlier the disintegration of the Order, Tennyson in this one went back to emphasise its originally bright possibilities.[10]

He very closely follows passages in Book VII of Malory's *Morte Darthur*, but alters several features of the tale to focus key ideas. He uses the story much earlier in his cycle than Malory does. This shift allows the tale to pick up threads from the coming of Arthur—who was himself a Fair Unknown—and to show an untainted youth spreading Arthur's ideals of justice throughout the realm. Tennyson also selects only the first part of the full story in Malory, subordinating the love element amplified in the *Morte Darthur*. He thereby highlights the virtues of humility, courtesy, and prowess shown by Gareth, and while referring to love in Lynette's gradual conversion and the final lines, he holds in abeyance the issue of love which becomes so destructive in the following idylls. Tennyson has Lynette, not her imprisoned sister, as in Malory, fall in love with Gareth, not so much to focus on their relationship as to provide evidence of Gareth's strength of character, which overcomes Lynette's initial repugnance at being championed by a kitchen boy. Finally, Tennyson rearranges details to create a fairly specific allegory out of elements that are less pointed and more folkloristic in Malory. These changes, more than the others, develop the perspective which Tennyson's story of the Fair Unknown establishes for evaluating the later idylls; it concentrates on contrasts between appearance and actuality and on the difficulty of interpreting symbols and evidence.

From the beginning of 'Gareth and Lynette' Tennyson seems to clarify ambiguities and resolve puzzles left tantalising in the *Morte Darthur*. Malory simply introduces the unknown as an attractive, sturdy youth whose background remains hidden from readers until after he has served a year in the kitchen and has actually undertaken his quest. At that point he reveals his identity to Lancelot and is knighted. But Arthur remains ignorant of the youth's identity and therefore presents a puzzle: why should he agree to give an unknown, untested boy so significant a mission? Following the familiar romance motif that the King refuses to dine at great festivals until some marvels occur, Malory's Arthur initially receives the youth at Camelot to gratify his taste for the unusual. This enthusiasm for adventure and the boy's fair appearance may justify his year at court, but the King's willingness to entrust a serious quest to an unproved quantity remains perplexing, as Lynette's shock suggests. The ambiguity of Arthur's choice is emphasised much later when the knights conquered by Gareth begin to accumulate at Camelot and the King declares: 'Jesu . . . I marvel what knight he is, and of what lineage he is come. He was with me a twelvemonth, and poorly and shamefully he was fostered' (VII, xxiii).

Before Tennyson's youth impresses Arthur by his demeanour, the poet carefully identifies Gareth to the reader as the King's worthy nephew, comparing him to Gawain, contrasting him with Modred, and establishing through his conversations with Bellicent his graciousness, sense of justice, and eagerness for knightly endeavours. This introduction, Tennyson's addition to Malory's story, effectively dispels the mystery of the unknown's parentage. Moreover, before King Arthur grants the unknown's desire for a quest, he has already learned from Bellicent of Gareth's noble blood and therefore assesses the youth on the basis of more than his promising appearance. The king's knowledge advances the poem's thematic concern with appearances and actualities, which is more specifically developed in the allegory Tennyson contributes to the tale, but Arthur's knowledge of Gareth's identity also ties in with concerns initiated in the preceding idyll.

In 'The Coming of Arthur' Leodogran first considers Arthur's genealogy gravely important, but later concentrates on his inherent fitness for kingship. Though Arthur's success in saving Leodogran's realm suggests that, family name aside, he is worthy, this fitness is less a matter of actions than of his essential nature. Similarly, 'Gareth and Lynette' establishes that much besides lineage is the essence of knighthood, as the contrast between Gareth and his brother Modred suggests. In a keen sense, Gareth, in spite of the heritage that Arthur knows, must earn his identity, and through more than physical prowess. He first cultivates humility and the ideal of service in his stint as kitchen boy. On the actual quest, moreover, courtesy becomes even more important than courage and prowess, for Lynette's taunts prove more difficult to quell than armed challenges. Through this narrative Tennyson shows how the spiritual qualities of the otherworldly Arthur (suggested by Bellicent's and Bleys' narratives) can be translated by mere men into actions in the ordinary world. For the first time, we follow the efforts of a knight of the Round Table to continue what Arthur has begun.

In the course of this quest, Tennyson condenses and simplifies Malory, by reducing, for example, the number of times Lynette refuses to dine with Gareth and the number of foes he must overcome. Tennyson's most significant alteration is to shape suggestive elements of medieval folklore into a specific allegory. By transforming Malory's Green Knight, Red Knight, Blue Knight, Black Knight, and Red Knight of the Red Laundes into the figures of Morning-Star, Noonday Sun, Evening-Star, and Death, Tennyson forged a not altogether successful allegory: Youth with his deeds challenges the cycle of ageing and death; or as the poet defined the allegory, 'the three loops of the river typify the three ages of life; and the guardians at the crossing the temptations of these ages.'[11] Whereas Malory's Gareth encounters the Black Knight first, and finally meets the generally demonic Red Knight of the Red Laundes, Tennyson builds up to the Black Knight, with his commonplace association with death. But Tennyson's allegory crashes abruptly with Gareth's exposing the figure of Death to be only 'a blooming boy'. Though Tennyson may be implying that the true knight conquers death and achieves a type of rebirth through the fame he wins and the good he effects in the world, the allegory may actually function as a kind of burlesque. Certainly the tone of much of the idyll is overtly comic— from young Gareth's striving after persuasive rhetorical effects when he addresses his mother, to Lynette's scorn of kitchen smells. In the allegory of Death, Tennyson shows how easily men can be deluded, for the blatant symbolism proves to be not emblematic truth but illusion. This revelation forces reinterpretation of other, less obvious symbols throughout the tale, and throughout the remaining idylls. It also focuses on an issue raised throughout 'Gareth and Lynette' and subsequent stories—the relationship between appearance and reality.

The issue crystallises when Gareth appears at court. As the Fair Unknown, he soon goes by a pseudonym, 'Sir Fairhands' (the Beaumains of Malory). This symbolic label simultaneously derides Gareth's scullery occupations and celebrates his potential prowess. Clearly Gareth is what he seems to be and is not what he seems. His fair countenance and open manner persuade many people of his excellence even before he proves himself by action. But he is obviously also an impostor among kitchen boys. While Gareth's nature remains unproved, the responsibility of interpreting, of discerning the essence beneath the accidents of dress, environment, and name, rests with the beholder. Sir Kay, like Lynette, deduces wrongly from the quite obvious. Lancelot, like Merlin, realises correctly that the apparent belies reality. Whereas Gareth's quest exposes the obvious symbol of Death to be actually a 'blooming boy', it also shows beneath the boyish surface of the protagonist a true knight.

But the relationship of symbol to truth and of appearance to reality proves much more complex with regard to the image of Camelot itself. When Gareth and his comrades approach the city, it seems less actual than symbolic—a floating image that appears and disappears in mist, 'a city of Enchanters' that is 'but all a vision'. Camelot's gate portrays the Lady of the Lake so 'realistically' that water seems to flow from her dress, yet the image also has overtly symbolic significance. The Lady's supernatural support of the Round Table is pictorially linked to its Christian foundations, as she spreads her arms 'like the cross' and bears on her breast 'the sacred fish'. As the youths gaze on the symbolic sculpture, these plastic images assume the semblance of living beings, 'began to move, seethe, twine and curl,' seemingly life more than symbol. When Gareth recoils from this confusion, Merlin explains that at Camelot 'there is nothing in it as it seems / Saving the King; though some there be that hold / The King a shadow, and the city real.'

These passages, in raising questions about the substantiality of Camelot as an embodiment of Arthur's ideals, call to mind a sketch Tennyson had made for an Arthurian epic as early as 1833. It describes Camelot as a sacred mount that

97

'rose from the deeps with gardens and bowers and palaces': 'The Mount was the most beautiful in the world. . . . But all underneath it was hollow, and the mountain trembled, . . . and there ran a prophecy that the mountain and the city on some wild morning would topple into the abyss and be no more.'[12] Merlin, the purveyor of wisdom couched in symbolic language that expresses and at the same time conceals truth, emphasises the responsibility of each man to discern the truth residing in symbols, and to determine whether Arthur or the threatened city be more real. All before Gareth is, in the 'Riddling of the Bards', 'Confusion, and illusion, and relation, / Elusion, and occasion, and evasion.'

Throughout the remaining idylls (all of which, except for 'Balin and Balan', were already written) Tennyson asks whether reality is the unreal king or the all-too-familiar city, which is supposed to represent the symbolic Arthur but ultimately reflects flawed human actualities. While 'Gareth and Lynette' shows an apparently unlikely youth actually expanding the civilisation illustrated by Arthur's judgements in the great hall, subsequent idylls show apparently noble reflections of the King eroding that civilisation from within Camelot itself.

iii and iv. 'The Marriage of Geraint' and 'Geraint and Enid' (1859)

The third and fourth idylls in the final sequence originally appeared as one, 'Enid', in the first gathering of four *Idylls of the King*, subtitled *The True and the False*, published in 1859. While the work functions in this original context to describe one of two true women contrasted with two false ones, in its final context of the Arthurian cycle the tale embodies many more concerns. It extends or recapitulates, in two episodes, the story of the Fair Unknown; it echoes the idea of knights' expanding Arthur's justice and civilisation beyond Camelot; it introduces a new theme merely hinted in 'The Coming of Arthur'— the disastrous effects of love on the Round Table; and it re-examines the problem of interpreting experience and understanding emblems and symbols. Unlike the other idylls, these two draw not from Malory but from a source only peripherally Arthurian, the Welsh *Mabinogion*. When he composed the Enid poem Tennyson had been studying Welsh language and lore. The old story permitted him to examine an issue prominent in the other three idylls published in 1859, the effects on society of disloyalty in marriage. 'Elaine' and 'Vivien' measured the results of the adultery examined in 'Guinevere'. The Welsh tale of the loyal wife wrongly suspected by her husband provided an additional dimension in offering an antithesis to Guinevere and Arthur, whose marriage remains centrally important to the life of the Round Table. In the final sequence of the *Idylls*, Geraint's story also extends the two preceding tales, which end with weddings, by following the knight's experience after his marriage.

Why in 1873 Tennyson divided 'Enid' into two idylls is not clear. It was much longer than any other, totalling 1818 lines, compared to the 1417 lines in the next longest, 'Lancelot and Elaine'. More important, the division brought the number of idylls up to twelve, the Virgilian and Miltonic number of epic completeness. Though Tennyson cautioned against viewing the *Idylls* as such, he had suggested the notion in 'The Epic'.[13] More important, however, the story, like its source in the *Mabinogion*, 'Geraint, Son of Erbin', naturally falls into two parts. Although Tennyson's introductory passage begins the second part of the story, his flashback technique returns the narrative to the earlier part, to what Geraint thinks back on as the halcyon days that will never come again. Here we follow Geraint righting wrongs and expanding the sphere of Arthurian justice far beyond the great hall of Camelot, much as Gareth does. Pursuing the discourteous knight Edyrn without his armour and heraldic devices, then entering the contest for the golden sparrow hawk in borrowed, rusted weapons and armour, Geraint in effect fights as a Fair Unknown. Like Gareth he creates his identity as he puts into practice the ideals of the Round Table Order. In sending Edyrn back to Camelot to be regenerated, Geraint admirably follows the pattern of civilising established in both 'The Coming of Arthur' and 'Gareth and Lynette', and this part of his story ends, as do the first two idylls, with the hero's marriage. Tennyson emphasises this sense of justice triumphant by making Edyrn's guilt, which remains uncertain in the *Mabinogion*, undisputed. 'The Marriage of Geraint' thus shows the hero's virtue to be an extension of Arthur's principles and shows his ventures to continue the process of 'making' the realm.

But by beginning the idyll with Geraint's fears about Enid's fidelity, Tennyson qualifies this sense of creation and progress. The brooding opening functions much as the details describing Guinevere's reaction to Arthur in the first idyll. Although marriage concludes both tales, the beginnings ironically caution that these unions pose dangers. The second part of the story, 'Geraint and Enid', develops this concern when we see the damaging effects not of too little love, as is suggested in Guinevere's unresponsiveness to Arthur, but of blind, excessive love. In this section Geraint is again tested as he tests Enid; and she in effect assumes the role of the Fair Unknown. Stripped of her courtly garb and attendants, she issues forth, anonymous and humbly dressed, on a quest which tests her modesty, fidelity, and courage. While the purpose of her endeavours, from her point of view, is simply to satisfy the inexplicable whims of her husband, the effect is to continue the process of civilising the realm.

To break from the hypocrisy he believes has infected Enid at court— specifically in the 'guilty love' of Lancelot and the queen—Geraint merely uses the lawlessness of outlying regions as an excuse for leaving Camelot. In the *Mabinogion* this is the real reason Geraint and Enid leave Arthur's court; only after the prince has restored order to his father's realm does he fall into the uxoriousness which generates his misunderstanding of Enid. In Tennyson's version, however, although Geraint does not focus on the needs of society, the various thefts and drunken violence illustrate the need for civilising control. The home of the Earl of Doorm epitomises this lawlessness, and in this setting Geraint is almost literally, and certainly figuratively, reborn as a knight. Thought to be on the point of death, he rises to reaffirm the values of the king he has fled. Having shown in the first part of the Geraint tale a parallel to the coming of Arthur and to Gareth's achievements, Tennyson in the second dramatises the dangerous conflicts between the responsibilities of the warrior hero and the appeal of love. Thus the tale explores the temptations of becoming a knight of the boudoir, which increasingly becomes an issue in the stories of Merlin, Pelleas, Tristram, and Lancelot.

Tennyson's chief innovation in the story is to link Geraint's suspicions about Enid to his suspicions about Guinevere and Lancelot, an association not made in the *Mabinogion*. Geraint reacts to unsupported rumour and misprizes his own treasure. Even though he returns to Camelot with his faith in Enid restored, he remains uneasy about the queen. The idyll therefore ends joyfully, with Geraint restored to Enid and to Arthur, but also ominously. Yet Tennyson carefully suggests that Guinevere does not fully betray the values and goals of the Order. After Geraint sends the brutish Edyrn to Camelot, 'sudden as a beast new-caged', Guinevere helps to civilise him. Her noble example influences him to abandon the 'wolf's' life. The beast imagery here picks up a pattern that Tennyson uses effectively throughout the *Idylls*, and shows the progress made since 'The Coming of Arthur', where military might rather than benevolent example was required to subdue men who behaved as beasts in Leodogran's realm. This passage also reveals that Guinevere is more than the vaguely reluctant queen mentioned in the opening idyll. Her positive influence over Edyrn, like her devotion to the good Enid, demonstrates her potential to fulfil Arthur's hope that the two 'reigning with one will in everything' might 'Have power on this dark land to lighten it, / And power on this dead world to make it live' ('The Coming of Arthur').

In the Geraint tales Tennyson also amplifies the difficulties of discerning between appearances and reality, so prominent a theme in the two preceding idylls. The issue arises in several of Tennyson's additions to the *Mabinogion*, such as passages focusing on Enid's clothing—her humble rags, the beautiful dress recovered from her more affluent past, the splendid attire provided at Camelot. These dresses, ironically, accrue significance as symbols of the insignificance of such symbols. Their meaning remains unclear to various characters; though Limours and Doorm, for example, read Enid's rags as testimony that Geraint loves her no longer, the old dress means something quite different to Enid and to Geraint. Moreover, changes of clothing from humble garb to royal finery, and back again, do not reflect changes in Enid's nature, any more than the rusty armour Geraint dons to fight Edyrn reflects his skill as a knight. Tennyson also suggests that language itself, which would seem to be man's best hope for clarifying meaning, is, after all, akin to the 'riddling of the bards' mentioned in the previous idylls. By having Enid utter her fears in words clearly misleading to Geraint—'O me, I fear that I am no true wife' (Tennyson's addition to his source)—he emphasises, as he did in the conflicting accounts of Arthur's origins in 'The Coming of Arthur', that man must 'hear' the spirit rather than the letter, must unriddle the riddles of existence which even seemingly clear language may obscure. The opening lines of 'Geraint and Enid' make the issue explicit. They lament that we 'forge a life-long trouble for ourselves, / By taking true for false, or false for true'. But even the apparently obvious import here is perplexing in the context of ambiguities raised by the tale. Guinevere, for example, proves to be both true and false as queen. While false as wife, she fulfils the role Arthur has envisioned for her by humanising Edyrn. The shadowy ground between extremes of true and false embodied in Guinevere lies at the heart of the next idyll, when as with Geraint and Edyrn, the negative force of her rumoured liaison with Lancelot counters her positive influence.

v. 'Balin and Balan' (1885)

The last of the idylls to be written (begun in 1872, published in 1885), 'Balin and Balan' functions in Tennyson, as in Malory, largely as a transition. Tennyson introduced it to keep the sombre tale of 'Merlin and Vivien' from coming into the sequence too early.[14] But in the *Idylls* the Balin story serves two further purposes: it foreshadows the Grail story, as it does in the *Morte Darthur*, and it develops the concern with Guinevere's adultery, an issue which has no place in Malory's version of the tale, where it precedes Arthur's marriage. (In the *Morte Darthur* the Balin section actually precedes all the episodes used in the *Idylls* except for Arthur's coronation.) By moving the episode to a later position and adding to it Guinevere's role in Balin's ordeal, Tennyson invests the tale with multiple meanings, significantly amplifies the symbolism of Balin's divided nature—reflected in the duplicating names, and uses the story not just to prophesy doom—as Malory does—but also to illustrate the actual process of dissolution already under way at Camelot.

Deterioration of the whole society is focused in Balin, a divided self in whom passion wars against reason, wrath against good will. Nicknamed 'the Savage', he is actually a 'noble savage' who desires to quell the beast within. But he cannot acquire self-restraint and humanity at the court, for despite its superficial decorum and civility, courtly customs have by this time become almost too ingenious, artificial to the point of hypocrisy. What passes for 'courtesy'—a concern since Sir Kay and Lynette provided examples of discourtesy in 'Gareth and Lynette'—is perhaps sham, and Balin is too naïve and too rash to interpret correctly.

In the preceding Geraint idylls, the court, especially as represented by the queen, could still civilise the beast in Edyrn, but the subtle discrepancies between ideals and actualities have now widened too much for the undiscerning Balin to fathom. Extending the animal imagery introduced in the opening idyll, where Arthur purges Leodogran's realm of men reared to act like beasts, the Balin story reverses the process of taming the beast illustrated also in the Geraint idylls. The court in fact contributes to Balin's wildness, for rumours about Camelot finally confirm rather than cure his savagery.

In Tennyson Balin's good faith is suggested by his long expiation, through three years of exile, for having attacked Arthur's thrall. In Malory's version, Balin is released after six months in Arthur's prison—a finite punishment rather than a prolonged effort to reform—when he pulls the Lady of the Lake's sword from its enchanted scabbard. He thereby demonstrates that he is 'a clean knight without villainy' and consecrated for her quest (II, i). By removing the supernatural element, Tennyson emphasises Balin's human effort to purify himself sufficiently to rejoin the Round Table. But as in the cases of Gareth and, especially, Geraint, this effort becomes less a matter of prowess than of interpreting actuality, of sorting shadow from substance. In this regard, an essential paradox underlies Balin's recognising the falseness at Camelot. He initially refuses to believe the 'truth' about Lancelot and Guinevere which his own eyes perceive, but then accepts as 'truth' the lies of Vivien (whom Tennyson adds to the story). This confusion again emphasises the difficulties in separating fact from fiction, for in this instance although Vivien's lie may capture some truth, Balin's self-delusion about the queen's purity intuitively also captures truth. Flawed though Lancelot and Guinevere may be, they remain essentially better than the slime suggested by the false Vivien. Balin founders in his attempts to distinguish appearance from reality largely because he confronts them with feeling unaided by reason. This inadequacy is pointed up by the absence of his brother Balan, who is in effect, as the echoic name suggests, an aspect of Balin himself—reason, control, and the human dimension that must supplant the bestial. Tennyson stresses this symbolic division of the self by making Balan not the younger brother found in Malory, but a twin who dies, as he was born, in the same moment as Balin.

The psychological problem of synthesising a divided nature obviously elaborates in overt terms the turmoil of such figures as Lancelot and Guinevere, who throughout the remaining idylls in the sequence (all composed before this one) reveal inner conflicts as their 'faith unfaithful' keeps them 'falsely true'. The symbolic tale of fratricide can also be seen as a kind of paradigm for all the conflicts which undermine the stability of Arthur's order, from Urien's opposing his brother Leodogran in the opening idyll; to the fratricide of the nameless brothers, one the king with the diamond crown, in 'Lancelot and Elaine'; to the clash between spiritual brothers (Arthur and Lancelot) and kinsmen (Arthur and Modred) in the final idyll.

The symbolic and ultimately fatal division within Balin also continues Tennyson's focus on individuals who create their own identities as they build Arthurian society. Balin's tale may be seen to reverse the motif of the Fair Unknown developed in the preceding idylls in the figures of Arthur, Gareth, Geraint, and even Enid. Balin sets out specifically to create a new identity as one of Arthur's knights. To do so, he adopts a heraldic device which proclaims his new nature before he has earned it; he exchanges the rude beast on his shield for a royal crown before he has subdued the animal within himself. When in his fury he allows the lawlessness of the land to overwhelm him, he sets aside the image of the queen's crown—a symbol now highly ironic as a mere shadow of a 'shadow of the King'. At this point he and Balan battle because his identity, rather than having been established by a successful quest, has been obliterated, and he has defaced the ambiguous heraldic symbol which he never earned.

Tennyson links Balin's unsuccessful quest for a new identity to the central quest in whch the entire Round Table redefines its nature and goals, the pursuit of the Holy Grail. Tennyson's treatment of Balin and his connection with the Grail story entirely reinterprets the Quest's significance in the Arthurian cycle. In Malory, this quest is a memorial to the failure of the worldly Order, showing that all men must pursue religious salvation. In the *Idylls*, in contrast, Tennyson specifically associates pursuit of the Grail with selfish delusions which disregard society's needs. The Grail quest becomes not so much a way to salvation as a threat to noble order. In 'Balin and Balan' Tennyson foreshadows this view of the Grail story by altering Malory's concept of Pellam and of the Dolorous Stroke.

The *Morte Darthur* justifies Balin's attack on Pellam's kinsman, which causes the conflict between Balin and Pellam: this Garlon has wounded an innocent man, who can be restored only by his attacker's blood. In Tennyson, Balin simply loses control because Garlon taunts him about Guinevere's impurity. Thus Tennyson reduces Balin's motivation to petty fury against gossip. Similarly but even more significantly, Tennyson diminishes the stature of Pellam, who in Malory is the legitimate kinsman of Joseph of Arimathea and 'the most worshipful man that lived in those days' (II, xvi). This holy Pellam, keeper of the Grail lance, Tennyson transforms into a seemingly insincere religious zealot who opposes Arthur's nobility with an unpleasantly extreme asceticism. (In contrast to Arthur, who remains magnanimously naïve about Guinevere, Pellam has set aside his faithful wife to avoid being 'polluted'.) These changes in Pellam and Balin's conflict with him remove Tennyson's tale from mystical associations with the Grail quest to the human sphere of petty self-concern. In Malory, Balin seizes the holy lance, wounds Pellam with the Dolorous Stroke, and simultaneously lays waste the land, causing 'great dole, tray and tene' (II, xvi). The action creates a compelling need for redemption represented by the Grail. In Tennyson, however, Balin does not wound Pellam or create an external wasteland. Instead, he defiles the holy symbol—which, though 'reputed to be red with sinless blood', may in the light of Pellam's suspect sincerity be bogus. Balin vaults on it from a window and later uses it to slay his own brother. The Dolorous Stroke in Tennyson becomes not the blow which supernaturally creates the wasteland, but the fratricidal stroke symbolic in human rather than religious terms. By removing from the tale many of its associations with the Grail, Tennyson emphasises that the wasteland in essence is not the supernaturally symbolic landscape, but the inner world or psychological experience of Balin. Like this episode which foreshadows it, Tennyson's Grail quest focuses attention on the need to perfect human society; consequently the Quest appears to be less a fulfilment of the Arthurian vision than—like Pellam's in this idyll—a misleading rival vision.

vi. 'Merlin and Vivien' (1859)

Originally appearing as 'Vivien' in the 1859 edition of four idylls, 'Merlin and Vivien' was written in 1856 and given its final title in 1870. In 1857 Tennyson had coupled it with 'Enid' in the trial edition of six copies, *Enid and Nimuë: The True and the False*, the earliest idylls to appear in print. The story of Merlin's enchantment appears very early in the *Morte Darthur*, following the episodes of Arthur's winning the crown, Balin's adventures, and Arthur's marriage. By making the story sixth of the final twelve idylls, Tennyson features the loss of Merlin as a more dramatic and consequential chapter in the decay of the Order and uses it more specifically to parallel the other disastrous loves. Though most of the tale is purely Tennyson's invention, his changes in what he did borrow from two brief medieval accounts are slight but significant. The spirit of the tale in Malory (IV, i) and in the Vulgate *Merlin*, which Tennyson doubtless knew from Southey's synopsis in the 1817 edition of Malory, differs markedly from that of the idyll. In the medieval story, Merlin is a rather predatory figure who ceaselessly pursues Nimuë—and always he 'lay about the lady to have her maidenhood'. Nimuë, a damsel of the lake, represents a benevolent supernatural; throughout the *Morte Darthur* she assists the King and his Order. Unable to elude Merlin and fearful 'because he was a devil's son', Nimuë finally encloses him under a rock. Though Merlin has foreseen this disaster and warned Arthur (in the Vulgate *Merlin* he tells Bleys), he neither restrains his passion nor amends his behaviour. The episode in Malory removes Merlin's magic and prophetic guidance early in the cycle, leaving Arthur and his knights to rise and fall on their own.

In Tennyson the tale, coming so much later and paralleling other amorous disasters, emphasises the forces undermining the Round Table (which in the *Morte Darthur* is still in the process of conquering, unifying, and creating long after Merlin disappears). Tennyson's departures from Malory and the Vulgate *Merlin* alter the themes of the tale significantly. First, Tennyson considerably purifies the character of his magician. Rumours that Merlin is a devil's son are here presented as malicious, envious gossip, and the magician appears to be singularly noble and altruistic. In refuting Vivien's charges of impurity at Camelot, he invariably offers humane, charitable versions of human conduct. Most important, his tales—all Tennyson's invention—counsel subordinating personal desires to the public weal. In this regard he embodies the altruistic ideals represented in the early idylls by Arthur, Gareth, and Geraint, which will be thwarted by the self-seeking in subsequent idylls. Vivien's conquest of Merlin depicts the mastery of selfless love by selfish passions, the defeat of the social ethic. In order to sharpen this symbolic conflict, Tennyson not only purifies the ambiguous medieval Merlin figure, but also replaces the innocuous Nimuë of Malory's tale with his own false, licentious Vivien. While the Viviane of the Vulgate *Merlin* is similarly seductive and false, she is also more appealing than Tennyson's villainess. She regrets that her enchantment succeeds (she expects it to fail), and she visits Merlin in his enchanted tower—'for afterwards there was never night nor day in which she was not there'. Tennyson's vixen

registers no such regret. In pronouncing Merlin a fool, however, she unconsciously judges herself (as the forest echo implies), for she has failed entirely
to profit from Merlin's didactic tales about the importance of subordinating
personal desires to social service, or 'use'.

Beyond transforming the characters of Merlin and Vivien and using the tale
later in the cycle, Tennyson changes the implications of the legend fairly
dramatically by linking it not only to the concern with Lancelot and Guinevere's
love but also to the suspicions of impurity raised by Vivien's gossip. The tale
becomes part of a larger pattern of mistrust and of decaying idealism which is
still more rumoured than real, perhaps, but fatally pervasive. By altering the
occasion for Merlin's enchantment by Vivien Tennyson makes his most
important implications about the Order's decline. In the medieval versions,
Merlin pursues Nimuë or Viviane, even though he foresees his personal
disaster, because he is obsessed by passion. In the idyll, Merlin flees a prophetic
glimpse of public, not personal, disaster; he is plagued by a vision of the
society's demise: 'An ever-moaning battle in the mist', 'death in all life and lying
in all love', and 'the high purpose broken by the worm'. Vivien pursues him and
eventually wears down his efforts to preserve and defend the good he discerns in
the mere mortals of Camelot. Reversing Malory's description that Nimuë is
'passing weary' of Merlin's passion, Tennyson shows Merlin 'weary' of the
falseness and spite manifested by Vivien.

While the narrative builds upon the comedy inherent in the January–May
romance, Tennyson highlights its tragic dimension by showing not a beguiled
old fool succumbing to passion, but a prophet fully aware of Vivien's perfidy
who yields to a crushing weariness generated by his recognising the widening
gap between the ideals of Arthur and the realities of men. Moreover, allusions to
the Fall of Man extend the significance of Merlin's capitulation, making it the
general pattern now predictable throughout the *Idylls*. Though Merlin
charitably likens Vivien's curiosity to Eve's, as the vice 'which ruined man /
Through woman the first hour', Tennyson shows her figuratively to be the
seductive serpent. Wearing a 'snake of gold' in her hair, itself an 'uncoiling'
braid, she literally slithers from her posture at Merlin's feet, coiling herself in a
serpentine *S* around the length of his body, where she 'clung like a snake'.
Finally she stands before Merlin 'stiff as a viper frozen', revealed to be 'the
bare-grinning skeleton of death'.

While these references to the Fall of Man emphasise the common condition of
mankind, the Merlin tale does more than simply point up the inevitability of
human flaws and, consequently, the Order's failure. First, the references to the
Fall and Merlin's full awareness of Vivien's perfidy underscore the element of
choice and of individual responsibility in such episodes. Second, the tale provides
an occasion for reaffirming the good at court, which we, as well as the characters
within the *Idylls*, may be forgetting. As Merlin explains away Vivien's examples
of baseness at court, he reveals that appearances are misleading, that in each case
purity exists where she and others see only pollution. Merlin's explanations
re-emphasise the importance of sorting shadow from substance. He not only

affirms the genuine worth of the King himself, but even asks us to reassess the rumoured guilt of Lancelot and Guinevere. Although Merlin never declares them innocent of adultery, he at least offers a generous explanation for their attraction—Guinevere initially mistook Lancelot for the King and innocently fixed her love on him. But the scene between the 'lovers' also causes us to re-examine assumptions based on rumour and appearances. In the preceding idyll Vivien admittedly lies about Lancelot and Guinevere, basing her account on her own perverted sense of human nature. In 'Merlin and Vivien' Tennyson shows an ambiguous relationship. Vivien's assumptions are challenged by the fact that as they ride away together, Lancelot and Guinevere—as she said they would—do concentrate on a hunting falcon. This detail at least allows the possibility that their meetings are not, as rumour suggests, merely love trysts.

Here, as in the preceding idyll depicting Pellam's court, Tennyson provides an alternative to Camelot in King Mark's Cornish court. Whatever its flaws, the Arthurian Order poses an arresting contrast to its alternatives. Though 'Merlin and Vivien' advances the sense of impending doom, throughout the idyll Tennyson stresses the Order's good features and positive possibilities. Although Vivien sees herself triumphant at the end—and by removing Merlin she has perhaps hastened the decline of Camelot—we at this point affirm the value of the Order by sharing the judgement of the forest echo that Vivien is the fool. For all its grimness, this idyll puts before us for one last time the possible innocence of Lancelot and Guinevere, insists on the innocence of many others who have been misjudged, and contrasts Arthur's court, with its flawed idealism, with a court flawed by having no ideals at all.

vii. 'Lancelot and Elaine' (1859)

'Lancelot and Elaine' (first published as 'Elaine' in *The True and the False*, 1859), Tennyson's version of Malory's Maid of Astolat story, finally confirms the guilt of Lancelot and Guinevere, which is openly acknowledged much earlier in the *Morte Darthur*. Various alterations and additions to Malory's story stress the Order's failure. One significant change is Tennyson's positioning of the story at this point in the Arthurian cycle. In the *Morte Darthur* the Maid of Astolat episode follows the quest for the Holy Grail. Although Lancelot has achieved limited success in the spiritual search and vowed to eschew further adultery, he almost immediately begins 'to resort unto Queen Guenever again, and forgat the promise and the perfection that he made in the quest' (XVIII, i). Gossip flourishes at court, Lancelot's efforts to suppress scandal offend Guenevere, and ensuing mis-understandings and jealousy culminate in the Elaine episode. While Tennyson's tale similarly reveals growing mistrust between the lovers, it also has a meaningful function as a prelude to the Grail quest. For instead of showing, as in Malory, that Lancelot returns to sin after the quest, Tennyson's tale fully demonstrates why the chief knight will not achieve the Grail.

Malory prefaces the Grail quest with the story of another, quite different Elaine (XI–XII). In this episode, Lancelot, unaware that he is destined to beget the Grail knight Galahad, is tricked by magic into lying with the daughter of Pelles. Although Lancelot himself will not fully achieve the Grail, he fathers the knight who will do so and thus demonstrates his worthiness. Tennyson similarly elevates Lancelot by alluding to the rumour that he fathered Galahad, but by not recounting the story of Pelles' daughter, Tennyson merely skims Malory's most complimentary detail and preserves Lancelot's dignity by omitting the rest. Preceding the Grail idyll with the Maid of Astolat story, Tennyson effectively shows the strain and destructiveness of Lancelot's love for the queen and illustrates the human frailties which will limit his achieving the Grail, while also poignantly emphasising the worthiness and potential which are squandered by his ignoble attachment.

The pervasiveness of such human weakness throughout the Order is emphasised by Tennyson's altering the character of Sir Gawain. In Malory's Maid of Astolat story, Gawaine embodies ideal courtesy to women, a role imposed on him early in the *Morte Darthur* after he accidentally slays a lady. He swears to 'be with all ladies, and to fight for their quarrels; and that ever he should be courteous' (III, viii). Yet Malory's knight manifests notable inconsistencies. In the same book where he vows unending courtesy, he also betrays his oath to advance Pelleas' suit and instead woos Ettarde for himself. Later, however, in the Maid of Astolat story (XVIII) he exhibits no such perfidy. Unlike Tennyson's knight, who seeks Lancelot unwillingly, Malory's Gawaine selflessly determines to find the wounded Lancelot and treats Elaine courteously. While the episodic nature of Malory's narrative permits many such inconsistencies, Tennyson eliminates them in order to build events and characterisation, tension and drama, unrelentingly towards the *Idylls'* climax. In 'Lancelot and Elaine' his first full portrait of Gawain establishes the duplicity and dishonour which mark the knight through the remaining idylls. Gawain's traits here are those revealed in Malory's Pelleas and Ettarde story, which Tennyson would himself use for a later idyll (ninth in the final series of twelve) to intensify the sense of decadence in the Arthurian society.

In 'Lancelot and Elaine' Gawain, wantonly flirting with the innocent Elaine, declares that if she 'will learn the courtesies of the court, / We two shall know each other'. He not only plays with the coarse innuendo that he will 'know' her in the Biblical sense of the word, but also calls into question the nature of courtesy, which becomes a major concern in this idyll. For Gawain the term seemingly signifies only superficial behaviour, more specifically, the ways of flirtation. Guinevere betrays a similar sense that courtesy involves little more than appearances. She directs Lancelot to keep Elaine (whom she assumes he now loves) away from Camelot, for she 'Would shun to break those bounds of courtesy / In which as Arthur's Queen I move and rule'. She fails to consider the more essential aspects of her role as 'Arthur's Queen', just as Lancelot fails to ponder the fundamental lack of courtesy fostered by his love for Guinevere. He too uses the term superficially when he tries, ineptly, to thwart Elaine's love with one 'discourtesy', leaving her without farewell. Through the character of Gawain Tennyson relates the concept of courtesy to much more than behaviour in flirtation and love. An antithesis of the paragon of courtesy to women which he traditionally represents, Tennyson's Gawain lacks integrity and fidelity to Arthur's ideals. Interested primarily in the festivities at court, he only reluctantly obeys Arthur's directive to find the wounded Lancelot, then lightly abandons his mission. When Arthur upbraids him, declaring 'Obedience is the courtesy due to kings', we are reminded that from 'Gareth and Lynette' on, the *Idylls* explore courtesy as a multifaceted embodiment of all that is noble and righteous.

Besides re-examining notions of courtesy embraced by the court, 'Lancelot and Elaine' also reworks the motif of the Fair Unknown to illustrate the society's decline; both Lancelot and Elaine may be said to reverse or pervert the role. Unlike young Arthur and Gareth, for example, who create names for themselves as they advance the ideals of the Order, Lancelot—to camouflage his duplicity and adultery—lays aside an identity already established by noble deeds. In the mimic battle (unlike the serious conflicts of the Unknowns Arthur, Gareth, and Geraint) his fighting with borrowed armour and Torre's blank shield wreaks confusion and destruction, principally because as the Unknown he fights his own kinsmen. This situation thereby echoes the fratricide of Balin and Balan, which likewise results from a flawed knight's setting aside his identifying shield.

Elaine similarly reverses the pattern of the Fair Unknown. Unlike Gareth, who comes to Camelot seeking creative opportunities, she wilfully pursues self-destruction. While Tennyson in the 1859 *Idylls* linked Elaine and Enid, his other female figure of the Fair Unknown, as two 'true' women, their situations contrast dramatically. Whereas Tennyson shows true Enid restoring her husband to the service of Arthurian ideals, this idyll focuses on the insufficiency of Elaine's virtuous love to redeem Lancelot. In reversing the motif of the Fair Unknown, Tennyson also reverses the pattern of clothing imagery associated with Enid. As Elaine plans her journey to Camelot, she asks her family, in a passage added by Tennyson to the source material, to deck her bed 'like the Queen's / For richness, and me also like the Queen / In all I have of rich'. The irony of her request abides in the fact that, as in the story of Balin, who takes a royal heraldic device before he earns it (by stifling the beast that properly identifies him on his shield), Elaine here assumes a guise inappropriate to her artlessness. Even more ironically, she aspires to a courtly image which by now rings hollow. Knowing what we know of the court, we prize the simplicity of Enid in her faded gown and of Elaine in her natural state.

Throughout the tale such incidents stress wasted potential, that which might have been if Lancelot could have loved wisely and well a maiden so aptly suited to him. Elaine's appropriateness for him is suggested by details linking the Lily Maid to the image of the 'spiritual lily', 'perfect-pure', haunting Lancelot's dream in 'Balin and Balan'. Though Guinevere in that idyll argues only for full-bodied love associated with the rose, Elaine would seem potentially to combine the attributes of both rose and lily, as her favour, the red sleeve embroidered with pearls, suggests. Tennyson considerably alters the character of Malory's Lily

Maid to underscore her purity. In the *Morte Darthur* when Lancelot refuses to marry Elaine, she unabashedly asks to be his paramour, an indelicacy which Tennyson avoids by having his Elaine ask merely to 'serve' and 'follow' him 'through the world'. Malory also focuses on Elaine's worldly, very physical love when she defends her passion even as the priest shrives her. While Tennyson offers an Elaine far less physical (though her blushes and swoons betray some physicality), he also reduces Malory's specific concern with conflicts between religion and sensuous love.

The idyll not only develops the role of earthly love in the fall of Camelot, but also re-examines notions of innocence earlier considered in Gareth, Enid, and Balin. From the simple innocence of Gareth and Enid, Tennyson moves to the more complicated 'innocence' of Balin. Though free of the tainting subtleties of the court, he is also brutish. Elaine's innocence, though very different from Balin's, likewise contains the seeds of its own destruction. An innocence too fond and foolish, it generates damaging self-delusion, as in her misreading and misuse of symbols. While she pores over her unnamed knight's shield, she fabricates an identity or personal history for him. Not content to imagine Lancelot's biography, however, she adds to the symbol of his identity an icon for herself. As she embroiders the elaborate cover for his shield (Tennyson's addition to the story), she inserts into Lancelot's heraldic device 'a yellow-throated nestling in the nest', an emblem of herself, whom Tennyson later compares to a 'helpless innocent bird'. Through her 'fantasy' or self-delusion, she weaves her own doom.

Tennyson relates the issue of fantasy and fancy to Arthur himself, focusing a continuously vexing concern: although fantasies may obviously destroy, they may also inspire, as when Balin, fancying the queen pure, temporarily quells the beast within. Though Guinevere judges Arthur to be something of a fool, 'Rapt in this fancy of his Table Round', the idylls consistently contrast the good and ill effects of Arthur's ideals. Ultimately the King, believing that his knights can achieve his goals, may be seen as the most innocent of all the characters. His trusting nature contrasts markedly with the greater worldly wisdom of Malory's king. In the *Morte Darthur* he is, for example, more aware of court gossip. Hearing rumours that Lancelot and Guinevere contrive to remain together instead of attending the tournament, Malory's king grows 'heavy and passing wroth' (XVIII, viii). Moreover, in Malory's Maid of Astolat episode, Arthur recognises Lancelot's ruse of anonymity. Having seen his knight travelling to the tournament, he knows throughout the joust that the hero is in fact Lancelot. Although Tennyson employs a certain dramatic irony in having Arthur liken the victorious unknown to his greatest knight, the King's ignorance more significantly emphasises both Arthur's naïve but noble trust and Lancelot's ignoble but pained duplicity.

The conflict between Lancelot's essential worthiness and this debasement is highlighted by two of Tennyson's artful additions to Malory's story, the diamond prize and Lancelot's closing soliloquy. The *Morte Darthur* names no specific prize at the Winchester tournament, though Tennyson probably gleaned the detail from a later passage, immediately following Elaine's death, where at a great joust for a diamond prize her brother Lavaine distinguishes himself (XVIII, xxi). Tennyson invents the ominous tale of the diamond crown, which links the prizes, accrued by Lancelot over nine long years, to fratricide, obviously characterising his betrayal of his spiritual brother Arthur. But the symbolic implications of the diamonds are even broader, for when Arthur first donned the crown, he 'in his heart / Heard murmurs, "Lo, thou likewise shalt be King".' The lines sombrely predict that he will be king only in the temporary and uneasy way that any mortal may be king.

When Guinevere contemptuously flings the diamonds into the river, a detail anticipated by Elaine's dreaming that a diamond slips through her fingers, she epitomises the waste so pronounced in the idyll. Recognising the ephemeral value, or worthlessness, of such a prize—and perhaps of such a love as the queen's—Lancelot utters an agonised yet nobly introspective soliloquy. These lines not only sum up the concerns of this episode, but, by showing Lancelot's remorse, also anticipate the concerns of the tale which came next in both its date of composition and its place in the final sequence of *Idylls*. When Lancelot exclaims that if he will not 'break / These bonds' that 'defame' him, God should 'send a sudden Angel down / To seize me by the hair and bear me far, / And fling me deep in that forgotten mere', he anticipates the spiritual chastisement that awaits him in 'The Holy Grail'. While 'Lancelot and Elaine' illustrates the tragedy of idolatrous worldly love, whether pure like Elaine's love for Lancelot, or passionate like his love for the queen, the next idyll shows the equally destructive effects of pursuing a spiritual emblem in ways inappropriate for most flawed men. Looking forward to 'The Holy Grail', Tennyson departs from Malory by having Galahad and Percivale, the Grail knights, bear away the body of pure Elaine.

viii. 'The Holy Grail' (1869)

Although at Cambridge in the early 1830s, Tennyson had mentally composed a poem on Lancelot's Grail quest—'in as good verse' as he ever wrote—he did not write an idyll on the subject, central to the Arthurian story since the thirteenth-century French Vulgate cycle, until 1869, when he added 'The Holy Grail' with three others to the original four idylls. Ten years earlier he had rejected Macaulay's suggestion (frequently echoed by the poet's wife Emily and even urged by Queen Victoria) that he use the legend, because he doubted 'whether such a subject could be handled in these days, without incurring a charge of irreverence. . . . The old writers *believed* in the Sangreal.'[15] When he finally undertook the idyll, both Hawker and Westwood had recently published their Grail poems, but Tennyson uses the story in a highly revisionist way. His treatment varies significantly not only from these two contemporary versions, but from all medieval versions as well.

From the late Middle Ages on, Galahad's achievement of the Grail quest had come to represent the *raison d'être* of the Arthurian Order. While Percivale's quest, originating with Chrétien de Troyes and receiving its fullest statement in Wolfram von Eschenbach, emphasises the personal accomplishment of the hero in redeeming the Wasteland, the Galahad quest, originating with the Vulgate cycle, shows both the failure of the Arthurian world and the way to perfection which redeemed its fall. The knights are called upon to find the Grail in order to take it away from a world not worthy of containing it. And instead of having the Grail hero reconcile the two worlds, as Wolfram's Parzival does, the Galahad quest, as seen in both the Vulgate cycle and Malory, shows the need for man to leave this world behind. Tennyson's version, in contrast, insists that whatever the symbolic value of the Grail, most men should pursue perfection and ultimately achieve grace by serving human society.

This is not to say that Tennyson discounted the mysticism and Christian supernatural of the legend. He once commented that the idyll 'expressed . . . my strong feeling as to the Reality of the Unseen',[16] and Galahad's exaltation clearly represents an ideal union with the transcendent. But the uniqueness of Galahad's purity results in his being translated alive to heaven (in Malory, he dies before his soul rises to the Celestial City). By suspending the laws of mortality Tennyson stresses Galahad's singularity and the impossibility of such experience for most men. Contrasted against this ideal of spiritual perfection, the knights who variously fail illustrate that man should properly devote himself to good work rather than to illusions promising premature bliss. As Tennyson pointedly explained his theme, 'religion in many turns from practical goodness to the quest after the supernatural and marvellous and selfish religious excitement. Few are those for whom the quest is a source of spiritual strength.'[17] As much as it is the healing force described by Percivale, the Grail is here, as Arthur says, 'a sign to maim this Order which I made.'

By several additions and alterations to the source material in the *Morte Darthur* Tennyson advances his themes. He compresses Malory's lengthy account, often telescoping several adventures into one.[18] Most important, he alters King Arthur and invents the character Ambrosius, both of whom express the ideal of 'practical goodness'. A third significant invention is his writing the story as Percivale's monologue, punctuated by Ambrosius' queries. Revealing Percivale's inconsistencies and uncertainties, this device demonstrates the unsuitability of this quest for most men and illustrates the human limitations that betray Arthur's ideal of service.

Tennyson's Arthur here exhibits a wisdom not revealed in preceding idylls. As a perceptive judge, he contrasts pointedly with Malory's king, who expresses little regard for the philosophical or religious issues of the quest. In the *Morte Darthur*, although Arthur is present when the veiled Grail appears at court, he does not vow to pursue it. While anticipating that many questers will not return, he shows no sense that the endeavour is inappropriate for most. He remains behind because, apparently, he does not incline towards so spiritual a goal, and we are aware of his essential inadequacy for the quest. He regrets Gawaine's vow, which prompts the others, because he loves the play, conquest, and fellowship of the Round Table: 'I have loved [these knights] as well as my life, wherefore it shall grieve me right sore, the departition of this fellowship: for I have had an old custom to have them in my fellowship' (XIII, vii). When the questers return, Arthur makes 'great joy' and scarcely notes the significance of their experiences; life at court resumes, little changed.

In contrast, Tennyson's king regards the quest as a serious threat to his philosophy of social commitment. Absent from Camelot—enforcing justice—when the Grail appears to Galahad, Arthur immediately recognises that the other knights are deluded. He objects to the quest because he desires to serve society: 'often, O my knights, / Your places being vacant at my side, / This chance of noble deeds will come and go / Unchallenged.' Arthur expresses his altruistic ideal of service in a humble metaphor that thoroughly revises notions of kingship depicted in medieval romance. He views a king not as a lofty figure, but as a servant or caretaker. When he sombrely welcomes the dispirited returning knights (not making 'joy' as in Malory), Arthur poignantly describes himself as a lowly labourer responsible for cultivating a small plot. By redefining kingship and chivalry as humble service, he exposes the egotistical motivation of many questers.

Tennyson's depiction of Arthur clarifies some of the 'riddling' of earlier idylls. From Leodogran's uncertainty about Arthur's origins, to Merlin's observation that some 'hold / The King a shadow, and the city real', ('Gareth and Lynette'), to Guinevere's description of the King 'Rapt in this fancy of his Table Round, / And swearing men to vows impossible' ('Lancelot and Elaine'), Arthur's pragmatism and role in the 'real' world remains uncertain. Here, however, while the knights pursue 'wandering fires', the King expresses his idealism in 'practical goodness'. To show the practicality of the King's 'vision' of service, Tennyson invents Ambrosius, the monk who elicits Percivale's recollections of the quest. Though this character did not appear in an early draft of the idyll, in subsequent prose drafts he acquired increasing importance. In the final version, Ambrosius, on a mundane and limited scale, practises Arthur's philosophy. Tennyson called attention to the commonplace—even comical—aspects of the monk by contrasting his 'babbling homely utterances' with 'the sweeping passages of blank verse'.[19] Far less dignified and imposing than the King, Ambrosius nonetheless serves his fellows in the Arthurian spirit. Whereas the questers feel that they must leave this world, Camelot, to pursue the other world, the Spiritual City, Ambrosius' monastery significantly houses both religious devotion and social commitment. Sworn to religious idealism associated with the Grail, the monastics remain oddly uninformed about the legend. Their 'old books' are 'mute' regarding this 'miracle', and Ambrosius asks if the Grail is 'the phantom of a cup that comes and goes'. While the legend remains unknown to the monk, the life of man does not, and he works in his 'little thorpe' like Arthur's labourer ploughing his small field, or in the monk's own metaphor, he knows his folk 'as well as ever shepherd knew his sheep'.

Ambrosius' naïve questions frequently betray a curiosity more worldly than spiritual. He asks, for example, if Percivale was driven from glamorous Camelot by 'earthly passion crost'. But his ironically linking Percivale's spiritual quest with failed earthly love is not inappropriate. To associate worldly and religious devotion, Tennyson adds a minor but significant detail to Malory's story of Percivale's sister, the mystic whose prayers summon the vision of the Grail. When her fervent (though chaste) love for a man was 'rudely blunted', she turned with equal fervour to religious devotion, apparently establishing a proper hierarchy of love. The Arthurian knights would seem on the surface to be repeating this pattern by pursuing the Grail, but just as their worldly love in the preceding idylls has proved flawed, their spiritual love here proves wanting. Tennyson's Gawain blatantly illustrates such corrupt love, both worldly and religious: in the last idyll, having made improper advances to Elaine, he here perverts the quest into a hedonistic dalliance with 'merry maidens'. Tennyson contrasts Gawain with a figure who combines human and religious love, Sir Bors. Patterned fairly faithfully on Malory's character, Tennyson's Bors— whose role, like Ambrosius', was considerably expanded in early prose drafts— demonstrates the selfless love conspicuously lacking in Gawain. Throughout the quest he longs not for his own success, but for the triumph of his kinsman Lancelot. Malory memorialises Bors' selflessness when he sees a pelican in a dry tree, a symbol of sterility, offering restorative liquid to its nestlings. Tennyson compresses this symbolism in Bors' heraldic device, the pelican fabled to rend its breast to feed its young. This selfless shedding of its own blood obviously associates Bors' emblem with the symbolic Grail, which Tennyson identifies as the cup Christ used at the Last Supper, and traditionally is also said to be the vessel in which Joseph of Arimathea collected Christ's redemptive blood. The pelican, like the Grail, thus is the emblem of Arthur's ideal of selfless service to others—earlier identified by Merlin as 'use' ('Merlin and Vivien'). Self-abnegation wins Bors a limited vision of the Grail, after which—unlike Percivale—he returns to human society.

Having Percivale tell the entire story of the idyll—a device used nowhere else in the *Idylls*—Tennyson achieves a number of interesting effects. This first-person testimony would seem designed to make the supernatural events believable, and in a sense Percivale's uneasiness between this world and the spiritual realm (in the monastery where Ambrosius comfortably combines the two) confirms the reality of his transcendent experience. Yet, having seen the Grail, he betrays an odd lack of understanding. His account mixes self-abnegation with pride; it balances devotion to spiritual goals with wistful delight in the glory that was Camelot— 'had you but known our mighty hall'. Though reflecting a purity almost sufficient for the transcendent sphere, Percivale also demonstrates the limited understanding which keeps men from achieving both Arthur's goals and those of the Grail quest. While early medieval versions of the Percivale story, such as Chrétien's—which Tennyson knew—depict him as a naïf who initially fails to understand but learns to act properly, Tennyson's knight, like Malory's, does not participate in this tradition. Instead, Tennyson's comparably naïve Ambrosius intuitively approaches the ideals symbolised by the Grail.

Another of Tennyson's inventions, the four zones of sculpture in Camelot's great hall, defines the issues of this episode by relating them to the beast imagery and the motif of the 'riddling of the Bards' seen in preceding idylls. The first three sculptures symbolically recapitulate the progress made in Arthur's reign: 'in the lowest beasts are slaying men, / And in the second men are slaying beasts, / And on the third are warriors, perfect men.' The fourth depicts the possibility of perfection: 'men with growing wings'. While Galahad may be said to have achieved this fourth state, none of the other knights can ascend directly to heaven. But the riddling nature of such plastic arts at Camelot requires a less literal interpretation of how man may acquire angelic wings. Arthur in his closing speech, with its metaphor of the ploughing hind, tells his remaining knights how they can grow wings. Though Camelot lies figuratively and literally in ruins, Arthur suggests that the Round Table may be restored through diligent labour—then the hinds may glory in transcendent visions. But hope dims when even so good a knight as Percivale withdraws from the Order because he has missed the point—'So spake the King: I knew not all he meant.'

ix. 'Pelleas and Ettarre' (1869)

After completing 'The Holy Grail' (in the autumn of 1868), Tennyson turned from the Order's collapse to its beginnings in 'The Coming of Arthur' (mostly written in February 1869).[20] He then immediately returned (writing in the spring of 1869) to the aftermath of the Grail quest in 'Pelleas and Ettarre'. The Pelleas episode, ninth in his series of twelve idylls, appears early in the *Morte Darthur*, and in order to make it thematically appropriate at so late a point in his cycle, Tennyson alters numerous details and changes the happy ending to tragedy. He had apparently contemplated using the story nearly ten years before he actually wrote 'Pelleas and Ettarre',[21] at about the time he had published the first four idylls; but not until he had written the Grail idyll had he established the necessary thematic context for such a radical reshaping of the Pelleas tale.

In the *Morte Darthur* the story appears in Book IV, which in recounting numerous adventures of Arthur's knights shows the excesses and inadequacies that will impede their fulfilling the Pentecostal oath sworn at the end of Book III. But the episode also shows an essentially good knight, though he has temporarily succumbed to foolish, debasing love, being rescued by the benevolent enchantress Nimuë. Pelleas subsequently becomes a worthy knight (mentioned later in the episode of the healing of Sir Urre). The Pelleas story, like others at this point in the *Morte Darthur*, shows the knights stumbling, but nonetheless creating and extending the Order. It ends happily, Pelleas rewarded with a lifelong mutual love.

Tennyson, in contrast, narrates the tale after the Grail quest has undermined the unity and ambitions of the Round Table, and this structural shift requires a tragic conclusion. But initially, the idyll seems to depict a new beginning. In

Malory, Pelleas is already an established knight when he encounters Ettard; Tennyson's Pelleas, however, is an untested youth of the second generation to become Arthurian knights—those who should 'fill the gap / Left by the Holy Quest'. He arrives at court as a Fair Unknown who would seem destined, like young Arthur in the idyll Tennyson had just completed and like Gareth in the idyll to be begun in the coming autumn, to help establish (or in this case, to re-establish) Arthur's Order. Yet Pelleas rapidly becomes a parody of the Fair Unknown. Much as Arthur in the opening idyll wins Excalibur and Guinevere or Gareth in the second idyll gains his armour and Lynette, Pelleas in the Tournament of Youth acquires a sword and a circlet for his 'Queen of Beauty'. But like the tournament, which at best imitates the worthy quests of Arthur and Gareth, these prizes have little genuine worth. When he first encounters ugly reality, Pelleas altogether loses the idealism necessary to regenerate the Order. Unlike Gareth, who withstands the taunts of a scornful lady and distinguishes appearance from reality by unmasking the disguised knights, finally earning his lady's love, Pelleas subjugates himself to win Ettarre's approval, and, having unmasked only one false knight—Gawain—wrongly assumes that all the Order must be equally base. Instead of establishing his own identity by expanding Arthur's Order, he finally proclaims that he has 'no name, no name', and will henceforth be 'a scourge . . . / To lash the treasons of the Table Round'. Whereas Gareth can emulate Arthur, Pelleas—because of the fallen world he confronts—cannot, though ironically he has dreamed that he will find a Guinevere, to whom he 'will be thine Arthur when we meet'. He plays Arthur's role only in loving a woman who betrays him. His recognising that he has been betrayed (while Arthur continues to trust) emphasises not only the increasing decadence of the society, in which Ettarre and Gawaine sin openly, but also the rapidity with which the new breed of Arthurian knight abandons idealism along with illusions.

Pelleas' tragedy extends far beyond his defeat in love to the total corruption of his world view. Recognising the falseness of Ettarre and Gawaine drives him to a wildness further intensified by his learning about Guinevere and Lancelot. Ironically, it is Percivale, having removed himself from worldly concerns, who with good intentions reveals this truth and contributes to the tragedy, much as he with good intentions has contributed to the Order's decline by participating in the Quest. Pelleas' disillusionment makes him suspect even the King, a notion so impossible to a first-generation Arthurian knight that Percivale can answer Pelleas' doubts only with amazed hyperbole: 'The King! . . . / Why then let men couple at once with wolves.'

Pelleas has come to reflect not the idealism and promise of Gareth so much as the troubled bestiality of Balin, whose tale—yet to be added—would follow those of Gareth and Geraint. While the beast imagery continuing in this idyll connects Pelleas with Balin, they differ significantly, and these differences, like those between Pelleas and Gareth, stress the gradual debasement of the Arthurian Order. Whereas Balin struggles long and hard against the beast in himself, Pelleas succumbs quickly to disillusionment and despair. Most important, Balin questions the purity of Guinevere, who calls herself but 'a shadow of the King'; Pelleas doubts the King himself, who embodies all the Order's ideals. Pelleas' hasty despair is also emphasised by a minor departure from Malory. In the *Morte Darthur*, after he sees the lovers in bed, Pelleas rides away from Ettard's pavilion for a half mile before deciding to kill them; then he falters in his purpose, repeating the half-mile ride before he again returns to slay them. Tennyson's Pelleas gets only as far as the castle bridge—once—before he returns to exact revenge. Though in both cases Pelleas cannot murder defenseless sleepers, Malory's knight agonises over the matter more intently than his counterpart in the *Idylls*.

Tennyson's Pelleas moves beyond the impetuosity of Balin, who falls victim to himself, to victimise others. Imagery associates the knight with the predatory Vivien, who seeks nothing less than destruction of the Order. Whereas Vivien had envisioned Camelot's being undermined by a little rat boring at the protective dyke, Pelleas now sees Camelot, infested within, as a 'black nest of rats'. And like the serpentine Vivien who annihilates Merlin with her magic, Pelleas, at the end of the idyll 'hissing' like a serpent, would kill Guinevere if he had his weapon. As in 'Merlin and Vivien' the serpent imagery calls up the Fall of Man. Early in the tale Pelleas awakens, like Milton's Adam, to find his dream of a mate reality. Yet the idyll's garden imagery testifies that this is no Eden, but the world after the Fall. When Pelleas, having come from 'waste islands', dreams in a lush forest and awakens to find Ettarre, her attentions quickly persuade him that in this 'happy world . . . all, meseems, / Are happy; I the happiest of them all'. But he learns that besides natural thorns, the rose here may conceal a devouring worm, and brambles invade the garden at Ettarre's castle. Unlike Guinevere's garden, in which red roses of passion co-exist with chaste lilies, Ettarre's is an overgrown jumble of only roses, red and white. When Pelleas finally sees Gawain and Ettarre sleeping together, he withdraws like 'a hand that pushes through the leaf / To find a nest and feels a snake'. When next we see Pelleas, in 'The Last Tournament', he has fled the garden of the fallen Arthurian world only to die in a swamp.

False ideas of love, as much as anything, have corrupted the Camelot Arthur would have restored to an Eden-like purity. Pelleas' ludicrous idealisation of an unworthy woman illustrates the artificiality of 'courtly' love. He not only chooses a base object for his esteem, but also accepts artifice as the way of love, viewing her rebuffs as 'the ways of ladies' and a 'trial of faith'. Though Tennyson's knight, to see his lady, submits to bondage (a situation so degrading that it stirs manly sentiments in even the feckless Gawain), he never experiences the extreme humiliation described by Malory, whose knight is tied beneath his horse's tail. But the idyll sketches an equally debasing psychological emasculation and bondage. Pelleas' tragedy could hardly be averted by a gentle enchantress such as Malory's Nimuë, for Tennyson's knight has become psychologically incapable of love. This change stems from his confused belief that love is worship. The episode thus restates concerns in preceding idylls with idolatrous love, whether innocent—like Geraint's, Balin's, and Elaine's, or guilty—like Lancelot's. Moreover, when Pelleas, simultaneously swearing to love Ettarre and to be a knight, exhibits the shining countenance 'of a priest of old / . . . Kindled by fire from heaven', he calls to mind the questers in the preceding tale who pursued the symbol rather than cultivating the qualities represented by the Grail.

So blinded, Pelleas cannot discern the substantial differences between Gawain and Ettarre on the one hand and Lancelot and Guinevere on the other. Though both liaisons are adulterous, the royal lovers in this idyll show great nobility, ignoring Ettarre's base innuendo and treating Pelleas compassionately. Since the embittered Pelleas now resembles Arthur even less than Ettarre and Gawain resemble Guinevere and Lancelot, the false parallel that he draws between the two love triangles will lead him—as the Red Knight in 'The Last Tournament', the next idyll in the sequence—to establish a grotesque parody of the Round Table. Sombre as the poem is (Tennyson thought it 'almost the saddest of the Idylls'[22]), it nevertheless shows some goodness or positive potential surviving in the Arthurian world. Besides the graciousness of Lancelot and Guinevere, vestiges of merit surface in Ettarre, who belatedly cherishes the worthiness in Pelleas which she has destroyed. But this conversion—psychological, not, as in Malory, supernatural—offers too little, too late. The Order's collapse is inevitable; like Modred, we know 'The time is hard at hand'.

x. 'The Last Tournament' (1871)

Tennyson's account of Tristram and Isolt—the only idyll to appear first in a periodical (*The Contemporary Review*, December 1871)—takes from Malory the knight's marriage to Isolt of Brittany, his winning tournaments at Arthur's court, and his murder by the vile King Mark (XIX, xi and XX, vi). But the Laureate radically alters the character of Tristram, whom Malory consistently couples with Lancelot as 'two the best knights that ever were in Arthur's days, and the best lovers' (X, v). Tennyson joins his allusive version of the love story to two situations he devised: Arthur's foray against the Red Knight, which derives its descriptive detail from Malory's Gareth story; and the final tournament at Camelot, which differs significantly from the last tournament in the *Morte Darthur*. These combined episodes, in one of Tennyson's most complex and artful poems, reveal that in love, on the tourney field, and in battle Arthur's knights have completely abandoned his principles.

Unlike Malory's Tristram, who is unfailingly courteous, Tennyson's knight is haughty and crude, roughly seizing his tournament prize with bloody hands, refusing to praise the ladies present, and declaring that prowess and practice—not purity—win victories. In the *Morte Darthur*, in contrast, Tristram performs so gallantly in tournaments that Lancelot more than once declines the prize in Tristram's favour (IX, xxxiii and X, lxxvi). Tennyson's 'last tournament' differs dramatically from the final tourney in the *Morte Darthur* (XIX, xiii), where Arthur presides but Lancelot does not joust because 'none of the dangerous

117

knights' participate. This tournament allows less experienced knights to demonstrate their prowess, two performing so nobly that they are made knights of the Round Table. Thus even at this late point in Malory's cycle, just before Arthur is induced to make war on Lancelot, the Order is still growing, still attracting able and worthy men.

In the idyll Tennyson heightens the sense of doom by removing Arthur from Camelot. When he was absent on a similar mission in 'The Holy Grail', his knights undertook a misguided but essentially idealistic quest. Here, however, the King's absence authorises only ignoble behaviour. A brooding Lancelot, presiding over the lists, becomes so disheartened by others' baseness and by his own dishonour that he cannot enforce the tournament rules. Moreover, Tennyson intensifies the decay through the symbolism of the Dead Innocent, most literally embodied by the babe whom Guinevere cannot sustain. (This figure— perhaps suggested by a story in Sharon Turner's *History of the Anglo-Saxons*[23]— is linked by the jewel and nestling imagery and by the tournament to Elaine, similarly unable to survive in the Arthurian world.)

But the idyll shows other innocents being destroyed by the decadence of Camelot. One such figure is Dagonet the Fool. In the *Morte Darthur* the antics of Dagonet, the sketchy original for Tennyson's more fully developed character, reveal knights' flaws, as when Tristram, deranged by love, dumps the Fool into a well (IX, xviii), or when the cowardly Mark flees the armed Fool, evoking a chorus of laughter from Arthur's knights (X, xii). Dagonet's jests highlight others' weakness, even though he never judges them overtly. But Camelot prizes him for his mirth: 'for King Arthur loved him passing well, and made him knight with his own hands'. In Tennyson Gawain has jocularly made Dagonet a 'mock-knight', but he is less a sportive figure than the traditional wise fool, an innocent who intuitively perceives true values. He is a mock-knight in the sense that his mockery exposes the extent to which the actual knights have mocked the King's principles. Recognising their betrayal of Arthur destroys the Fool's innocence, and although Malory's Dagonet 'at every tournament . . . began to make King Arthur to laugh', this tournament idyll concludes with the Fool sobbing to his King, 'I shall never make thee smile again'.

Tennyson's Dagonet seems also to draw from Malory's Sir Dinadan, a companion to Sir Tristram who is regarded as 'the best bourder', 'the merriest knight . . . and the maddest talker' (X, lvi). In the *Morte Darthur* this joker provides a measurement of others' worthiness—'For Dinadan had such a custom that he loved all good knights that were valiant, and he hated all those that were destroyers of good knights' (X, xxv)—and he frequently ridicules the flawed chivalry practised by Arthurian knights, especially their excesses in love—'I marvel of Sir Tristram and more other lovers, what aileth them to be so mad and so sotted upon women' (X, lvi).

A similar critic of knights, especially of Tristram as a lover, Tennyson's Dagonet stresses the superiority of Arthur's idealism by contrasting the 'harmony' of Arthur's music with the cacophony of Tristram's. Though in medieval tradition he is the greatest harper, Tennyson's knight 'twangled' on his harp. Dagonet speaks of the 'broken music' of Tristram's adultery, which, unlike the music of Orpheus, leads towards hell. The Fool's criticism of Tristram's musical distortion picks up an image pattern recurring throughout the *Idylls*, from 'Gareth and Lynette', where Camelot—less important as a place than as a symbol—is said to be a city 'built / To music, therefore never built at all. / And therefore built for ever.' Disharmony increases in subsequent idylls, notably in 'Balin and Balan' (begun the year after 'The Last Tournament' was published), where Balin for a time feels 'his being move / In music with his Order, and the King', but he finally distorts the 'wholesome music of the wood' by screaming like a 'Wood-devil'.

Tristram's songs in 'The Last Tournament' reveal his failure to participate in Arthur's harmony: his is an independent, 'solo', vision, and following it he breaks vows made not only to Arthur but to both his Isolts. His songs celebrating 'free love', described by images of impermanence, testify that the lack of principle he revealed in the tournament permeates his love relationships as well. His abandonment of standards in order to gratify his desire for Mark's wife—no love potion exonerates them here—also prepares him to violate that relationship when he meets Isolt of Brittany. Such unprincipled self-indulgence yields an uneasy alliance in which jealousy and hatred for Mark fuel the lovers' passion. While Tristram uses the adultery of Lancelot and Guinevere to woo his uncle's queen (historically, the originally non-Arthurian Tristram story may have provided the pattern for the Lancelot-Guinevere story), Tennyson uses Tristram's affair to comment on the ignobility of Lancelot's. The parallels allow the poet to show the perfidy of Lancelot and the queen to be the most damaging crime at Camelot because it influences others. But at the same time, this oblique method of commenting on Lancelot and Guinevere also maintains their dignity by keeping their crime offstage, allowing Tennyson in the following idyll to treat them sympathetically and to depict a conversion in Guinevere we could never accept in the base Isolt. Tristram's infidelity in love, like his renegade behaviour in the tourney, demonstrates his inability to fulfil the Arthurian ideals which he now dismisses as 'inviolable vows, / Which flesh and blood perforce would violate'. Tristram thus espouses the lawlessness of 'Mark's way' which literally destroys him.

As in the last tournament and Tristram's love, so in Arthur's campaign against the Red Knight failure to maintain principles debases a worthy endeavour. The episode carries out the theme of dead innocence associated with the tournament. It shows Arthur setting out with the 'new-made' knights who should revitalise the Order after the Grail quest. Their foe is the knight who failed in a similar role in the preceding idyll, Pelleas. Loss of innocence led him to establish a rival Order more villainous than the alternative courts of Pellam and Mark depicted in earlier idylls. Whereas those two societies obviously differed from Camelot, the Red Knight's by its open pollution comments on the state of Arthur's realm. Tennyson's description of the Red Knight and his domain draws on Malory's descriptions of innocent Gareth's confrontation with the demonic Red Knight of the Red Laundes (Tennyson apparently interrupted work on his Gareth tale to compose 'The Last Tournament').[24] Here Malory's details such as dead knights hanging from trees create a horror appropriate to Pelleas' death: drunk, he falls from his horse into the swamp. But more horrifying is the death of innocence in the conquering Arthurian knights, who 'trampled out his face from being known, / And sank his head in mire', and in the process 'slimed themselves'. In battle they abandon all principles of honourable conduct, as Tristram abandoned the rules of tournament and of love. Unable to hear the King 'for their own cries' (a parallel to Tristram's solo harping), they pervert their noble mission into a 'massacre' of men and women.

Bitingly, Tennyson declares that after the massacre 'all the ways were safe from shore to shore', but Arthur now perceives that his men 'reel back into the beast' he thought to vanquish. This idyll culminates the process of unmaking the realm which Arthur had so purposely 'made' in 'The Coming of Arthur'. The failure of his hope is linked to revived scepticism about his origins which functions so prominently in the opening idyll, where the realm is 'made' largely because Leodogran and the knights accept Arthur's spiritual legitimacy as King. Expressing these renewed doubts about Arthur's origin, Tristram demonstrates the failure of faith which has prevented the Round Table from reflecting the perfection of the King: 'Dropt down from heaven? washed up from out the deep? / They failed to trace him through the flesh and blood / Of our old kings.' Gone forever are the days when, believing in the King despite his uncertain origins, 'every knight / Believed himself a greater than himself', and Tristram dismisses the greatness of the Order as but 'the wholesome madness of an hour'.

Having shown the failure of chivalric principles in love, tournaments, and righteous battles against evil, and most important, the failure of faith in the King himself, the idyll builds to the gravest death of innocence—the King's disillusionment. Arthur will no longer smile at Dagonet because, like the Fool's, his own comic or hopeful spirit has been extinguished: 'In the heart of Arthur,' formerly the most innocent figure at Camelot, 'pain was lord.'

xi. 'Guinevere' (1859)

'Guinevere', published in 1859 with the first group of *Idylls*, dramatises a portion of Malory's conclusion, the queen's withdrawing to a nunnery. In the *Morte Darthur* her repentance, which turns Lancelot likewise to a religious life, comes after the final battle between Arthur and Mordred. It thus stands as the necessary corrective to the human passions and frailties which ruin the Order, demonstrating that one must move beyond this world to achieve salvation. As 'The Holy Grail' makes clear, however, the *Idylls* stress the importance of creating a more perfect Order here on earth. By placing the queen's conversion before the final battle, Tennyson uses the tale not to show the ultimate insignificance of worldly endeavours, but to confirm the worth of the Arthurian vision undermined by her improper values and actions.

As he initially planned an Arthurian cycle, years before he wrote 'Guinevere', Tennyson may have thought to follow Malory's closing sequence of events. In 'The Epic' his fictive poet Everard Hall had used the 'Morte d'Arthur', which later became the kernel of 'The Passing of Arthur', as the eleventh in his twelve-book Arthurian epic. While some readers subsequently anticipated that the Laureate's cycle would end with a twelfth idyll depicting Arthur's return to this world,[25] it is more likely that if he ever thought to follow the King's passing with another idyll, Malory's account of Lancelot and Guinevere would have provided the pattern. Tennyson could hardly have located Arthur's mythic second coming in any period of English history, nor would the present or future have provided a more auspicious setting; as the narrator's dream in 'The Epic' suggested, Arthur's returning as 'a modern gentleman / Of stateliest port' scarcely satisfied the mythic vision.

More important, however, Tennyson's thematic conception required a new ordering of Malory's closing events. Whereas the *Morte Darthur* shows Arthur's human imperfections as well as his prowess, the *Idylls* depict the perfect hero—not the King 'Of Geoffrey's book, or him of Malleor's', who like his age 'hovered between war and wantonness', but 'Ideal manhood closed in real man' ('To the Queen', a dedicatory postscript added to the *Idylls* in 1873). The *Morte Darthur* increasingly features Lancelot as its hero, and therefore concludes fittingly with Guinevere's conversion precipitating Lancelot's salvation. Tennyson's cycle must finally focus on the ideal figure whom the Order has failed. In 'Guinevere' the queen's remorse appropriately directs attention from the various fallen knights to the King himself.

Tennyson's rearrangement of episodes may have been suggested by Geoffrey of Monmouth's *Historia*, where Guinevere flees to a nunnery when she learns that Mordred, who has usurped the throne and married her, has rallied his troops to fight the King again (XI, i). What Tennyson derives from Malory he alters significantly. Most important, he intensifies the lovers' sense of guilt, making his queen's psychomachia more consequential than the military encounters featured in the *Morte Darthur*. Until their religious conversions after Arthur's death, Malory's lovers persistently deny their adultery, even though the narrative consistently reveals it. Although Malory's Lancelot recognises his culpability during the Grail quest and again when his healing of Sir Urre demonstrates the potential he has wasted, the queen never—until after Arthur dies and her world collapses—reveals a sense of guilt. Remorse exerts little pressure, and Malory's lovers separate only because circumstances force them to part: Lancelot kills a dozen conspirators outside the queen's chamber, rescues her from the fire to which Arthur (not very reluctantly) has consigned her, and by inadvertently slaying Gareth and Gaheris makes their brother Gawaine push Arthur into war. After this, Lancelot and Guinevere live together at Joyous Gard, seemingly troubled less by conscience than by Arthur's extended siege. Lancelot repeatedly seeks reconciliation and at the Pope's instigation restores Guinevere to the King.

Tennyson, in contrast, focuses on Guinevere's internal conflict. For years she has agonised over her infidelity. Early in their affair—when the queen was still poised, as in a symbolic tableau, between Enid, 'her best' and Vivien, 'the wiliest and the worst'—Modred failed to find any evidence against her; yet she developed an abiding sense of guilt. Finally conscience prevails, and even before Arthur learns of her infidelity she determines to part with Lancelot. The tryst exposed by Modred is to be their last. Tennyson's remorseful lovers, unlike Malory's pair, entertain no thought of quelling rumour to resume life at Arthur's court.

The progress of rumour has become an important measure of the Order's dissolution. Not only has gossip allowed knights such as Tristram to justify treachery, but in passing from the lips of corrupt liars such as Vivien in 'Balin and Balan' and 'Merlin and Vivien' to the mouths of pure figures remote from court like Percivale in 'Pelleas and Ettarre' and the innocent novice in this idyll, rumours show that the contagion has spread to all levels throughout the realm. Guinevere's choosing to go to Almesbury before Arthur condemns her or the battles begin demonstrates her moral recognition of her insidious influence.

Her inner conflict shows throughout her conversation with the naïve novice—Tennyson's creation—and in her interview with Arthur—likewise Tennyson's invention. (Malory shows Guinevere speaking at Amesbury only to Lancelot, whom she inspires to make religious expiation.) Besides dramatising Guinevere's turmoil and changing attitude towards the King, their final conversation allows Arthur to describe, formally, the Order's principles and goals, which the idylls have illustrated mostly through examples of their antitheses. Although the Pentecostal oath in the *Morte Darthur* rather specifically defines the standards of the Order before the Grail quest, the vows sworn by Tennyson's knights bind them to the King himself. Consequently a problem central to most idylls is the individual's responsibility to esteem the King and practise his principles. As chief of those who have failed to do so, the queen has 'spoilt the purpose' of his life, which in 'The Coming of Arthur' the King associated with his marriage. Other reminiscences of the opening idyll demonstrate that the Order has collapsed because others, like the Queen, have failed to understand and prize the King. In 'The Coming of Arthur', Leodogran was puzzled by supernatural explanations of Arthur's origins. By the time Guinevere retreats to the convent, folk throughout the realm believe Arthur's kingship was sanctified by such supernatural portents as fairies freely dispensing wine in the cellars of Camelot. Arthur has been passing into a fiction in the popular imagination and folk history even as his actual Order has become a parody of itself.

The novice's 'prattle' about Camelot provides a public gloss on Guinevere's recollected private history. The social implications of her pursuit of pleasure recapitulate the concerns of preceding idylls, and the tension between public responsibility and private desires coalesces most forcefully in the King's judgement of his queen. Tennyson's characterization of Arthur in this speech has drawn the most biting criticism directed at the *Idylls*. Readers such as Swinburne have denounced the King as a complaisant cuckold, a prig, the basest exemplar of Victorian morality sitting in judgement.[26] But Arthur here fulfils his own image of kingship, expressed at the end of 'The Holy Grail' in the metaphor of the labourer at the plough. He first attends to public responsibilities, and only then indulges his private vision, in this instance his hope of reunion with Guinevere in heaven. Yet Arthur is man as well as symbol, a point made by Tennyson's final addition to the frequently revised *Idylls*[27]—the line affirming that Arthur's 'ideal manhood' is 'closed in real man'. From his humanity grow both bitterness towards the faithless wife and continuing love for her. This tenderness distinguishes him from Malory's Arthur, who is 'sorrier for my good knights' loss than for the loss of my fair queen; for queens I might have enow, but such a fellowship of good knights shall never be together in no company' (XX, ix). Even though Tennyson's King consistently puts social good before his own desires, his confession 'Let no man dream but that I love thee still' poignantly affirms the humanity of his idealism.

Tennyson's changes in the character of Guinevere prove as significant as these alterations of Arthur. Depicted only sketchily in the *Morte Darthur* and other medieval romance, where she is most notable for jealousy and duplicity, Guinevere in the idyll is a complex, human figure. Tennyson suggested her baseness in the preceding idyll by underlining the parallel between her and Isolt. But even as we share Arthur's judgement of her, Guinevere earns our sympathy. Actually her sin allows Arthur to achieve a measured success even as his Order fails, for Guinevere, the person closest to the King and most important to his success, has formerly dismissed him as 'cold, / High, self-contained, and passionless'. But in their final conversation she learns to evaluate his 'highness' more properly, realising, 'Ah my God, / What might I not have made of thy fair world, / Had I but loved thy highest creature here? / . . . We needs must love the highest when we see it.'

Thus the Order's collapse brings Arthur's greatest personal triumph in that his nobility finally wins appropriate esteem from the one who has most under-valued him. Contrasts between this scene, with Guinevere flinging herself at Arthur's feet to expiate her guilt, and that with Vivien cringing at Merlin's feet in order to ensnare him illuminate Arthur's victory here. Merlin capitulates to Vivien less because of passion than because Camelot's failings have wearied him. Arthur, while loving Guinevere despite her infidelity and fully recognising his Order's failure, wins an ethical victory. Consequently the interview ends not as in 'Merlin and Vivien', with evil vanquishing Merlin by the magic of Vivien's 'waving hands', but with the King triumphing by forgiving the queen and 'waving . . . hands that blest'. Like Ettarre's belatedly recognising Pelleas' worth, Guinevere's proper perception comes too late to avert tragedy. But her change nevertheless demonstrates that even the most recreant can finally embrace the values of the King. His redemptive love for her remains as the corrective to all the wrong loving in previous idylls. While the public challenge on the battlefield awaits, in the personal relationship Arthur has won at last. The poem fittingly ends—unlike the preceding several idylls that drearily depict destruction—with Guinevere attaining dignity as an Abbess and, ultimately, achieving grace 'where beyond these voices there is peace'.

xii. 'The Passing of Arthur' (1869)

More than half of what in 1869 became 'The Passing of Arthur' (ll. 170–440) Tennyson had published in 1842 as the 'Morte d'Arthur'. This poem, in point of time the first of the idylls written (to which Tennyson added 169 introductory and 69 concluding lines, otherwise revising little after its initial publication), may be said to have shaped his Arthurian saga, for during the nearly forty years of composition Tennyson worked towards an end already defined. Yet in the final sequence the idyll substantially refocuses all that has come before. The preceding poems have been building to a tragic crescendo. Tennyson said that he composed the last poem in order of time, 'Balin and Balan', in order to keep 'Merlin and Vivien' from coming in too soon, a remark which demonstrates the care with which he structured and paced the sequence, slowly intensifying the tragedy. In 'The Passing of Arthur' the elegiac tone, the wasteland setting and slaughter of the 'last weird battle in the west', Bedivere's desolation, and the three queens' lamentation establish the tragic sense one has come to expect at this point. But balancing the Order's collapse and finally becoming the central focus of the idyll is a stately and surprisingly joyful glimpse of the mythic hero's return home. Tennyson suggests this positive end to all the failure, waste, and destruction through numerous details and symbols and through additions and changes to Malory's account of the final battle. The reassessment of Arthur's role forced by this conclusion adds a new mythic dimension to the *Idylls* as a whole.

In the poem Arthur first appears to be spiritually defeated. He bemoans the absence of God in man— 'I found Him in the shining of the stars, / . . . But in His ways with men I find Him not.' And he judges all his work vain—'all my realm / Reels back into the beast, and is no more.' However the Biblical echo in his bitter complaint links the Order's collapse and the King's impending departure from the world to the Crucifixion, which seemed tragic to a limited perspective but was actually triumphant. Though Arthur cries, 'My God, thou hast forgotten me in my death', he immediately afterward recaptures his faith: 'I pass but shall not die.' Bedivere similarly connects Arthur's sojourn in this world with Christ's by comparing the high tide of the Round Table to the days when 'the light . . . led / The holy Elders with the gift of myrrh'. By creating parallels between Arthur's endeavours in this world and Christ's, Tennyson revises our sense of the King's mission and, therefore, of his success. In establishing the Order and pronouncing his ideals, Arthur—like the labourer he described ploughing his appointed field—has performed his duties in this world. This was the proper equivalent of the Grail quest, directed not away from this world, but towards it. While Arthur's followers achieve his perfection no more fully than Christ's followers could emulate the Son of God, the King has provided man with appropriate patterns (and we must remember the successes of Gareth, Geraint, Enid, Dagonet, even, belatedly, of Ettarre and Guinevere). Consequently, the idyll concludes with Arthur victorious.

Tennyson's version here differs signally from Malory's where the King is specifically said to die. The *Morte Darthur* also recounts the legend that Arthur was 'led away in a ship wherein were three queens' and cites the myth of his second coming, '*Rex quondam Rexque futurus*'. Even so, Malory unlike Tennyson casts doubt on the legend: 'I will not say it shall be so, but rather I will say, here in this world he changed his life.' Malory's Bedivere, moreover, mourns at the 'new graven' tomb he recognises to be Arthur's. Tennyson, in contrast, from 'The Coming of Arthur' stresses the mystic elements surrounding Arthur, especially his mysterious origins. Merlin has riddled that his passing will be as enigmatic as his coming: 'From the great deep to the great deep he goes' ('The Coming of Arthur'). Though Bedivere now recalls this phrase, the idyll finally shows the King arriving at a 'fair city' 'beyond the limit of the world', much as Galahad in 'The Holy Grail' passes to 'the spiritual city'. What Bedivere faintly hears suggests the hero's triumphant return to his natural home after completing his quest: 'It seemed there came . . . / Sounds, as if some fair city were one voice / Around the king returning from his wars.' Coupled with the associations with Christ, this greeting—which Tennyson described in a note as a 'triumph of welcome given to him who has proved himself "more than conqueror" '[28]—commemorates the return to the spiritual realm of an ideal hero who has fought his battles and carried his message in the world of man.

Tennyson establishes the King's victory by changing considerably Malory's account of the fight between Arthur and Modred. In the *Morte Darthur* the King surveys the mass slaughter and sees that he has won the battle. On his side remain Bedivere and Lucan, whereas Mordred stands alone. At this point Malory's Arthur refuses to let well enough alone, despite his knights' warning, 'if ye leave off now this wicked day of destiny is past' (XXI, iv). In killing Mordred he sustains his death wound, appropriately a blow to the head, the traditional seat of pride. (Tennyson ameliorates this detail by focusing the blow on Arthur's helmet, 'which many a heathen sword / Had beaten thin'.) The mutual slaughter is the climax of the ancient enmity stemming from Arthur's incestuous paternity, and the King's inadequacy is further suggested by wide popular support of Mordred, because 'with Arthur was none other life but war and strife' (XXI, i). Tennyson, sustaining his idealization of Arthur, omits these elements. As in 'Guinevere', the King specifically denies any kinship to Modred. Moreover, Arthur describes the killing as his final service to society, his 'one last act of kinghood'. Executing Modred is the last of many instances, such as his campaigns against bandits in 'The Holy Grail' and the Red Knight in 'The Last Tournament', in which Arthur dispenses justice to society. Because Modred here is not associated with any particular wrong— Tennyson does not mention Malory's story that Mordred usurps the throne and seizes Guinevere—the knight stands for a general, almost motiveless evil opposing Arthur's goodness. Similarly, Tennyson avoids identifying this battle as an aftermath of the conflict with Lancelot (he alludes once to 'Lancelot's war'), for that challenge to Arthur was resolved as a victory of sorts by Guinevere's conversion in the preceding idyll.

Tennyson also suggests that this battle is an almost cosmic confrontation between good and evil through the details of the wasteland setting and the 'deathwhite mist' enshrouding the battlefield—both of which are his additions to Malory. The mist creates chaos; 'confusion' falls even on Arthur, knight slays friend as well as foe, and the fallen 'Looked up for heaven, and only saw the mist'. This is an Armageddon—as Tennyson suggested by comparing his lines to *Revelation* (XVI, 21).[29] The fitness of Arthur's passing into the spiritual realm at the end of this cataclysmic battle is confirmed by Tennyson's version of the King's prophetic dream. In the *Morte Darthur* Gawaine has fallen in an earlier battle with Mordred. In a dream the dead knight warns the King not to fight until Lancelot joins his forces. Gawaine thus tells the King how to avoid death, but Arthur's pride and wrath render the warning useless. After the dream he inadvertently signals battle to begin by drawing his sword to slay an adder. Malory's emphasis on chance and the King's carelessness disappear in Tennyson's version and the two battles against Mordred become one cataclysmic encounter; moreover, the dream of Gawain functions quite differently in the *Idylls*. Tennyson's dead knight tells Arthur not how to avoid death, but why he should desire his predicted passing from this world. Gawain describes the restless afterlife, being 'blown along a wandering wind', awaiting men like himself who have pursued 'hollow' worldly delights. He then testifies that for the King, in contrast, 'there is an isle of rest', the Avillion Arthur describes as a paradise 'where falls not hail, or rain, or any snow, / Nor ever wind blows loudly'.

Though Arthur fittingly passes beyond the flux of this world, Arthurian order and idealism survive the challenge of Modred's chaotic evil. Tennyson makes this point through Bedivere, the first-made and last-surviving Arthurian knight. His function parallels Ambrosius' in 'The Holy Grail', where though great knights failed to practise the Arthurian ideal of serving society, the pedestrian monk serves his fellow man. In 'The Passing of Arthur' Bedivere similarly carries on something of the Arthurian Order (though like Percivale narrating 'The Holy Grail' he does not understand all he sees or says). He perpetuates its ideals by recounting its history. In this sense Bedivere carries out Arthur's dictum that man must adapt to change, 'Lest one good custom should corrupt the world'. From Malory Tennyson took some of Arthur's parting words to Bedivere: 'Comfort thyself: what comfort is in me?' But in the *Morte Darthur* when the King continues, 'do as well as thou mayest, for in me is no trust for to trust in' (XXI, v), he acknowledges his inability to console Bedivere. In Tennyson, on the other hand, Arthur recalls the example of his own life and then directs Bedivere to pray for others, instructing the knight to find resources for a useful life within himself. Finally Bedivere not only handles his grief but serves his fellow man by telling Arthur's story to 'new faces, other minds'. He thus preserves the Arthurian message, much as he had hoped that Excalibur would if he saved it from the mere. He had envisioned that the sword would in 'the aftertime' remind men of the glory that was Camelot, 'winning reverence', 'honour', and 'fame' for Arthur. But

126

Excalibur, like the Grail and like the King, must be removed from this world. Arthurian principles must survive not in talismanic symbols but in real men, and Bedivere ultimately assumes the role of perpetuating Arthur's ideals.

Having shown throughout the *Idylls* 'the temporary triumph of evil, the confusion of moral order, closing in the great "Battle of the West" ',[30] Tennyson concludes with a sombre but highly hopeful message quite different from Malory's closing concern with individual religious salvation: An ideal, Christ-like Arthur brought his message to the world. Though its one manifestation—Camelot—failed, the values once enunciated may be enacted by other men in a new day—as the 'old order changeth', 'God fulfils himself in many ways'. To seal this highly independent version of Arthurian myth, Tennyson closes with images of renewal not found in Malory's account, where Bedivere weeps through the night after Arthur's craft vanishes in the darkness: Straining to see the barge, Tennyson's Bedivere watches the King 'vanish into light. / And the new sun rose bringing the new year.'

Tennyson's disclaimer that the poem is a series of idylls rather than an epic notwithstanding, most reviewers of the day hailed them as such and through the years of composition called for more poems to complete the scheme. W. E. Gladstone, who was to become Prime Minister a decade later, described the aspects of Arthurian romance which would lend themselves to epic treatment: 'It is national: it is Christian. It is also human in the largest and deepest sense; and, therefore, though highly national, it is universal.'[31] The religious implications of the idylls are apparent. Equally conspicuous to Victorian readers were the topical and nationalistic concerns—for example, the interest in civilising remote regions and expanding the empire; the desire to preserve traditions in periods of rapid change; alarm over increasing materialism and sensuality; and (a reaction against Romanticism) awareness of the social consequences of private actions. A dedication to Prince Albert (1862) and the epilogue 'To the Queen' (1873) heightened readers' awareness of the work's contemporaneity (the epilogue refers rather specifically to unrest in the Canadian corner of the Empire). Some readers objected to this adulteration of medieval matter—Swinburne, for example, acerbically criticised the 'Morte d'Albert'—but the popularity of the *Idylls* remained unabated from the first edition of four, which sold 10,000 copies within a week, to the eleventh edition in 1889, which was the first to contain all twelve idylls.

Though constantly busy with other projects, Tennyson remained engaged by the Arthurian cycle throughout his life, from his days at Cambridge to the last year of his life, when he added to the epilogue the last-written line, which appeared only posthumously. In his later years he considered writing a drama on the Tristram story, for he felt that the requirements of his cycle had kept him from realising its full power.[32] While Aubrey de Vere overstated when he wrote in *Alfred Tennyson* (1893) that 'Great Arthur's legend he alone dared tell', Tennyson was indeed alone among poets since the Middle Ages in writing an Arthuriad that encompassed the entire traditional cycle. It is fitting that Tennyson summarised his own life in Arthurian metaphor in the poem which he termed his 'literary history'.[33] In 1852 he had used the pseudonym 'Merlin' for some political verse, and when in 1889 he surveyed his artistic career in 'Merlin and the Gleam', he again used the sage as his mask, depicting himself as the aged, imaginative magician, idealistically pursuing 'the gleam' even unto 'the land's / Last limit'.

Perhaps it is no exaggeration to say that even if no other nineteenth-century poet besides Tennyson had read Malory's *Morte Darthur*, the *Idylls* would have generated a significant Arthurian revival, as other writers imitated, parodied, and reacted against the work. Carlyle once twitted Tennyson's preoccupation with old subject matter, saying that the Laureate was 'sitting on a dung-heap among innumerable dead dogs'.[34] That preoccupation fertilised a remarkable flowering of new Arthuriana.

The most ambitious work of a major English poet, and a most carefully crafted poem by a master craftsman, *Idylls of the King* has great artistic appeal apart from any consideration of its significance as a restatement of myth. But as a reshaping of Arthurian material, it is especially important. Tennyson used the legend not to provide nostalgic romance (though like Scott and Heber he offers this in some degree), or to celebrate the monarchy (though like Renaissance writers and Milman he indirectly praises current monarchs), or to diagnose contemporary ills (though like Frere and Peacock he offers this too).

Although over the years critics have castigated the work's artificiality, inept story-telling, remoteness from the Middle Ages, and conversely, remoteness from its own age, it endures as one of the major long poems in English largely because it achieves a meaningful mythic dimension. It creates the history of a society that is at once psychologically realistic and mythic, simultaneously old, timeless, and distinctly modern. By raising Arthur from the level of the national hero of the chronicles and the often ambiguous figurehead of romance to make him exemplify man's highest hopes and possibilities, Tennyson redefined the King and the meaning of his story, giving the western world a new myth artfully forged from the old.

5

The Pre-Raphaelites

Morris and Swinburne

Interest in the Arthurian legend appears to have arisen independently among the young artists and writers who belonged to or were associated with the Pre-Raphaelite movement. D. G. Rossetti had discovered Malory some time before Morris and Burne-Jones first met him, and later, with some older colleagues, contributed woodcut illustrations to the Arthurian poems in Edward Moxon's 1857 edition of Tennyson's poems. Morris and Burne-Jones, while undergraduates at Oxford, spent much time reading and discussing the copy of *Le Morte Darthur* which Morris had bought for them both, because the impecunious Burne-Jones could not afford it. Swinburne, meanwhile, had become familiar with the story of Tristram and Iseult in childhood, and indeed claimed that in so far as a child could understand it, the story had been his delight before he was ten years old. Their fascination with the Arthurian legend was of course part of the wider interest in the Middle Ages which these young men shared, and which was becoming an important trend in the mid-nineteenth century. But though D. G. Rossetti was well read in medieval Italian literature and Morris in English and French, both found Malory a more fruitful source of subjects for new creative work than other medieval writers, just as the imagination of other artists and authors was fired by various aspects of the Arthurian legend very much more than by any other medieval romance or topic. It was to *Le Morte Darthur* that Rossetti and his friends naturally turned for subjects for the decoration of the Oxford Union, in their corporate endeavour in the Long Vacation of 1857. By 1858, it was possible for Richard Garnett, reviewing Morris's poem, 'The Defence of Guenevere' in *The Literary Gazette*,[1] to remark that the Pre-Raphaelite poets and painters had 'made the Arthurian cyclus their own', and for another critic to assert that 'pre-Raffaelitism' had taken *Morte d'Arthur* under its special protection.[2]

The Pre-Raphaelites' enthusiasm for the past was comprehensive: it included not merely the literature, the art and the architecture, but also the crafts, the social structures and to some extent the religious practices of the Middle Ages. Out of it they constructed an image of medieval times that was of course highly selective and romanticised, but not necessarily the worse for that. The Arthurian legend offered them a symbolic system for the poignant and dramatic presentation of those inward dramas of the soul which in their view were the stuff of poetry and of art. It allowed truth to nature in the depiction of scene and background to be combined with the stylisation appropriate to the age of chivalry. Their attraction to the Middle Ages was neither mere escapism nor simply nostalgia because it was closely connected with their active need to find a mythology—or mythologies—to give outward form to inner experience. While other myths also provided them with symbols, Arthurian legend offered greater possibilities than other stories for the expression of the human passions. What could not be directly treated in a modern setting could be presented as a tragic occurrence in remoter, perhaps more primitive times: the story of Tristram, for example, gave Swinburne more freedom to write about illicit love than a contemporary story would have afforded him. Overwhelming passion and its moments of ecstasy and torment, as well as relationships condemned by society, could thus find expression; and at the same time the writer or artist could use the story as a medium for the expression of his own inner experience. The subjectivity no longer acceptable to contemporary literary taste could be avoided through the use of symbolism, as the Arthurian legend provided an outlet for introspective tendencies.

Though the image of the Middle Ages which the Pre-Raphaelites created was in some respects a romanticised one, their Arthurian world was one in which suffering was acknowledged and confronted, not ignored or magically dispelled. Their shared vision enabled them to interpret Malory with a consistency of tone and value, expressed through pictorial detail of an equal consistency, and to construct an imaginary world that was self-contained and autonomous. It has sometimes been suggested that Morris's 'Defence of Guenevere' poems are little more than a series of vividly realised pictures strung together, but in fact the verbal pictures also provide a psychological counterpart to the events of the poems. Morris's imagery suggests a desolate and frightening, at times almost surrealistic world in which inner experience takes on concrete form. In 'King Arthur's Tomb', for example, as the Queen is waiting for Launcelot's last visit after Arthur's death, and looking back over her past life, Morris says that beyond her window, 'the grey downs bare / Grew into lumps of sin to Guenevere'. Here and in his other Arthurian poems, Morris depicts a world which knows depths of suffering undreamed of in most other Arthurian texts of the nineteenth century. His vision is a sombre one, but its subtlety seems to have been little appreciated. It does not depend upon a facile correspondence between emotion and atmospheric effects; it does not idealise the Middle Ages, though emblematic images often give a romantic surface patterning. For although the Pre-Raphaelites, and perhaps Morris most of all, could see in the Middle Ages much that they felt to be attractive and even to be desired in modern life, the Arthurian legends did not furnish for them a fantasy that could be re-worked into an ideal dream-world.

The shared experience of the Arthurian legend, the extraordinary homogeneity which is perhaps the most striking aspect of the Pre-Raphaelites' embodiment of it, whether in painting or in poetry, may perhaps be attributed to no small extent to Tennyson's influence. Tennyson's poetic techniques indicated ways in which Arthurian themes could be given pictorial settings, either in poetry or in painting, as well as ways in which some aspects of the medieval world could be conceptualised and imaginatively reconstructed in art and literature. When Rossetti, together with Millais, Holman Hunt and Maclise, undertook to provide the woodblock illustrations for Moxon's 1857 edition of Tennyson's poems, Rossetti commented that he had undertaken the work of illustration because it was possible in doing it 'to allegorise on one's own hook . . . without killing, for oneself and everyone, a distinct idea of the poet's'.[3] It was the influence of Rossetti's pictures, however, even more than Tennyson's poems, that affected William Morris. Rossetti had illustrated 'The Lady of Shalott', 'Sir Galahad' and 'Morte D'Arthur', as well as offering an Arthurian subject, 'King Arthur and the Weeping Queens', as an illustration for 'The Palace of Art'. His 'Sir Galahad at the Ruined Chapel', like his earlier water-colour of 'Arthur's Tomb: the Last Meeting of Launcelot and Guenevere' (1855), gives an indication of the interchange of ideas between Rossetti and Morris. The latter's poems, 'King Arthur's Tomb' and 'Sir Galahad, A Christmas Mystery', are close in spirit and visual imagery to Rossetti's illustrations, while Morris's poem, 'The Defence of Guenevere', may be seen as the inspiration of Rossetti's 'Launcelot in the Queen's Chamber'.

Generally speaking, however, Tennyson's influence on the artists of his time was enormous: he had 'invented a new poetry' which suggested not only subjects that they were eager to paint, but also a way of looking at them and representing them that was consonant with current artistic theory. Later, his moral attitude to some aspects of the Arthurian stories also had its effect, which could be counter-productive, but which could not be ignored.

The stories of Tristram and Iseult, of the Grail quest and of Lancelot and Guenevere were those which held the strongest appeal for the Pre-Raphaelites, partly because they lent themselves most readily to a psychological approach, and partly because they allowed artist or writer to focus on a moment of dramatic confrontation or discovery. Though Malory's straightforward narrative usually formed the basis of their reinterpretation, the symbolical use of detail gives a new resonance to the stories. It is frequently a dark, mysterious world that the Pre-Raphaelites depict, and the dim interiors of the pictures often suggest the nature of the inner experience with which they are concerned. Though it is beyond the scope of this chapter to discuss Pre-Raphaelite art in any detail, something may perhaps be said about the way in which it gives expression to Arthurian themes, for the sake of comparison with the literary treatments of the same period. The close relationship mentioned earlier between D. G. Rossetti's watercolour, 'Arthur's Tomb', and Morris's poem on the same subject is significant; the cramped, tormented arrangement of the figures of the lovers expresses the mental anguish of their farewell, with Arthur's rigid effigy between them as Launcelot strives to draw close to Guenevere. Morris's poem captures the same mood of frustration and torment. It is the most despairing or the saddest moment that is usually chosen: Guenevere or Iseult alone in mournful contemplation as depicted by Morris, for example, or Rossetti's 'Arthur and the Weeping Queens'. The figures often give a strong sense of arrested movement; the world to which they belong is constrained and oppressive. It has its own richness and beauty, but often the scene is disordered and suggests distress. Holman Hunt's 'Lady of Shalott' is entangled in her thread within the strange circle of her loom, in a scene where the shadow and confusion seem to mirror her state of mind. Rossetti's Tristram and Iseult drink the love-potion together in the darkness of the ship's cabin, not on the deck, in the sunshine. The scene symbolises the constricting power of the passion from which there can be no escape; they are isolated and imprisoned by the experience. In the moment of actual or psychological turmoil in which the figures in these pictures are so often frozen, their inner tension is implied. The Grail pictures of Burne-Jones or of Arthur Hughes not only convey through the contrast of darkness and light the metaphorical darkness and confusion of the world, but something of the fear and anguish of the lonely quest. Rocks, trees and brambles press in upon the knights as they approach the Grail vision, but there is often in these pictures a different kind of arrested movement, a passive steady attention to mysteries incomprehensible to the uninitiated, and which perhaps can never be more than suggested in art or literature.

The Arthurian legend was a major source of inspiration for Burne-Jones throughout his life. In book illustration as well as in full-scale pictures, in his designs for the great Grail tapestries manufactured for Morris and Co. at Merton Abbey, as in his designs for Henry Irving's production of J. Comyns Carr's *King Arthur* in 1895 (discussed in Chapter 7), for example, Burne-Jones returned again and again to Arthurian themes. The world of the Grail Quest was for him holy ground; 'It is such a sacred land to me that nothing in the world touches it in comparison', his wife records him as saying.[4] While Irving took a different view, Burne-Jones wished 'to keep all the highest things secret and remote from people; if they wanted to look they should go a hard journey to see', and he found it deeply painful to see the story of Arthur made into a trivial spectacle in the theatre. The intensity of his imaginative experience of the Grail myth is suggested by his comments on Wagner's *Parsifal*, which he heard in the Albert Hall in 1884: he claimed that Wagner 'made sounds that are really and truly . . . the very sounds that were to be heard in the Sangraal Chapel. I recognised them in a moment.'[5] Burne-Jones seems to have been less interested in the theme of romantic love than many of his contemporaries, but he found in the story of the Grail Quest, which he first encountered at an impressionable age, an unending source of symbolic meaning.

Other artists associated with Rossetti continued to paint Arthurian pictures in the decades following the Oxford Union venture. Arthur Hughes, for example, in such pictures as 'Enid and Geraint' and 'The Birth of Sir Tristram' of 1862, 'Sir Galahad' (1870) and 'The Lady of Shalott' (1873) and Frederick Sandys's 'Morgan le Fay' (1864) as well as Ford Madox Brown's strange 'Death of Sir Tristram' (1864) show the extent of the appeal of Arthurian topics to painters in the second half of the century.

Aubrey Beardsley may also be mentioned here, as the distinguished illustrator of the edition of Malory's *Le Morte Darthur* of 1893. He began as a Pre-Raphaelite and gradually developed his own very individual style while he was working on the illustrations for this book. His interpretation of the Arthurian scenes and figures stems from a quite different vision from that of the older Pre-Raphaelites. His decorative patterning and the very stylised nature of his designs suggest that he did not share the imaginative experience of Malory of Rossetti, Morris and Burne-Jones: his illustrations are not 'felt'. Indeed, though they capture the mystery and strangeness which we associate with many of the stories, he makes no attempt to depict powerful emotions or to suggest states of mind; his figures belong to a dream-world in which joy and sorrow have no place. His is a valid form of illustration, but his knights and ladies are marionettes rather than live actors, in a timeless, non-naturalistic setting. Beardsley's Camelot bears no resemblance to Malory's, but his vision is a beautiful and a positive one, and in the modernity which it finally attains, indicates changing attitudes to Arthurian legend at the end of the century.

The moral earnestness of painters such as Burne-Jones naturally inspired the choice and treatment of subjects. Such earnestness, shared by many in the mid-nineteenth century, led to a preference for poetry that aimed at enlarging the sympathies of its readers by concerning itself with characters and situations that drew forth an emotional response. This demand encouraged the writing of narrative poetry and dramatic monologue, while it discouraged more subjective poetry, now suspect because it was thought to result from unhealthy intro-spection. The search for subjects that could be treated with objectivity and that would enlarge the reader's sympathies was complicated by the concern about the ethical and religious value and tone of subject-matter and treatment, since poetry was not seen simply as an art-form, but in a much broader moral context. The Arthurian legend, though it admirably provided material that could enlarge the sympathies, could also be seen as having in it undesirable elements from a moral point of view. On the one hand it was possible for Charlotte Yonge in *The Heir of Redclyffe* to recommend Malory's *Le Morte Darthur* as a splendid book for young people, her high Anglican piety not offended, presumably, by the 'murder, hate, . . . and sin' which Caxton identifies as the evil aspects of Arthurian society. On the other hand, J. M. Ludlow, reviewing Tennyson's *Idylls* in *Macmillan's Magazine* in November 1859, although he admits the beauty of Tennyson's treatment of the story of Guenevere, complains that 'one cannot but regret that time and genius should be spent upon so "revolting" a subject'.[6] Tennyson is demonstrating the 'self-punishing power of guilty love', indeed, but he has a higher lesson to teach as well, because he is a Christian poet. Ludlow is concerned with the moral aspects of the *Idylls*, both as to subject-matter and treatment. Though poetry should enlarge the sympathies, not all critics would have accepted that sympathy for sinners should be included.

The preference, until the later decades of the century, for poetry that dealt with the more common and familiar aspects of life often lent itself to triviality. However, the developing interest in psychology (indicated by, among other things, the popularity of such pseudo-sciences as phrenology and mesmerism) and a gradual broadening of attitudes led to a greater readiness on the part of reviewers and readers to encounter more complex and less conventional characters and situations, such as the poetry of Robert Browning continued to offer them. The influence of Browning on other writers was also of great significance: his Dramatic Monologues suggested to the young William Morris the possibility of a psychological approach to the Arthurian themes, and enabled him to see that the exploration of states of mind and emotion might be an appropriate task for poetry. The reader of Malory's *Le Morte Darthur* must deduce what he can about the workings of the protagonists' minds from their words and actions: it was scarcely possible for the medieval writer to see his characters as individuals whose idiosyncrasies and inmost thoughts and motives it was his business to delineate. Traditional tales do not call for detailed individual characterisation; their protagonists are necessarily types. But for the nineteenth-century writer, or artist, it was possible to stop the story, as it were, and to take a given moment or incident or situation and explore the thoughts and emotions of the participants in it. Morris, meditating on Guenevere and Galahad, could investigate what might have been going on in their minds, and give expression to it in poetry or painting. Morris's 'The Defence of Guenevere' laid him open to censure by presenting the Queen as defiant, finally triumphant and uncondemned, but it also made it apparent that the story could be treated in different ways, and that the Arthurian legend could extend as well as enlarge the reader's sympathies. Though stern moral disapproval might be the immediate reaction to the sinful Queen, her pleading suggested that other responses might also be appropriate, whatever the final verdict might be. In the same way, the Pre-Raphaelite fascination with the Grail legend, finding expression in the art of Burne-Jones and others, and in the poems of Morris, pointed the way to a deeper understanding of a certain kind of religious experience. Such experience might not be shared by many, but it could be better understood and evaluated by those who did not share it, through the mediation of Pre-Raphaelite art. The reader's sympathies are both enlarged and extended by Morris's 'Sir Galahad', confronting the demands of his religious vocation in solitariness and deprivation. The possibility of analysing and dramatising the Arthurian stories from a psychological point of view was one of the great discoveries of the nineteenth-century writers on these themes. They detected a lack in the medieval versions of the stories, and were quick to supply what was felt to be a deficiency in characterisation.

On another matter which concerned the Pre-Raphaelites' absorption with Arthurian legend, critical opinion was divided in the eighteen-fifties. Should the subjects of poetry be drawn from the past, or from contemporary life? Charles Kingsley in a review of Arnold's poems of 1853 gives both points of view. He first paraphrases the argument of those who claim that topics from the past are preferable: ' "No," they say, "a living poetry is impossible, henceforth; and all that the singer can do, unless he chooses to degrade his powers, by setting to rhyme the spiritual dyspepsia of an unhealthy and nerveless time, is to betake himself to the greater dead; to reproduce, as well as he can, their thoughts; perhaps to awaken men to admire—to make them imitate is now hopeless—the noble deeds of their forefathers." ' However, Kingsley sees the 'elements of poetry' all around us 'if we could but see them; there will be for ever. There is poetry in Australian emigrations, Britannia-tubular bridges, Solent steam-reviews . . .'[7] Like Kingsley, many critics believed that poetry should reflect the age, and wanted to see a great national poem on a noble theme from a poet who could be considered as a worthy successor to Milton and Wordsworth. Such a poem would be the embodiment of the Victorian national ideal, the distillation of the spirit of the age, and might at the same time be both a celebration of Victorian achievement and an inspiration for the future. Though Tennyson's *Idylls* no doubt came closest to accomplishing this in some respects, pride in achievement and hope for the future are not their predominating characteristics.

The revival of interest in the figure of Arthur did not ultimately lead to the great national epic that the age felt it should have, but it made it increasingly possible for 'living poetry' with its roots firmly embedded in the past, to provide a medium for the expression of contemporary thought. As it became increasingly apparent that the Arthurian legend was more than legend, was in fact the great national fount of myth and symbol, poets became increasingly able to draw on it more extensively. Poets and artists found that it could easily be used figuratively, could be related to modern problems, and so could be directly relevant to contemporary society rather than merely romantic or escapist.

It has been suggested that Rossetti, Morris, Burne-Jones and others of the Pre-Raphaelites found in the Arthurian legend subjects which allowed them to give expression to, and indeed also to analyse, states of mind and emotion. Their work did not always conform with the preconceptions about art and poetry of their contemporaries, partly because the imaginary world which they shared could not be an idealised one, concerned as it was less with the ecstasies of passionate love than with more complex and often more painful states of mind that were equally inherent in the traditional stories. Although they did not treat the subjects allegorically, through their subtle use of symbolic imagery and their poignant evocations of thought and emotion, they expanded the horizons of the nineteenth-century mind both through their art and through their poetry.

i. Morris, *The Defence of Guenevere and Other Poems* (1858); Du Maurier, *A Legend of Camelot* (1866)

Although Morris's introduction to Malory did not come until he was an undergraduate at Oxford, his interest in the Middle Ages originated in early childhood and prepared the soil for his later devotion to *Le Morte Darthur* and other medieval literature. He is said to have read all Scott's Waverley Novels by the age of seven; as a small boy he used to ride through Epping Forest in a little suit of armour. His interest in medieval architecture dates at least from his school-boy years at Marlborough, when he was able on holidays to make expeditions into the neighbouring countryside to look at churches. Thus, when he and Burne-Jones discovered Malory, it gave a new dimension to his interest in the past. It is not surprising that a boy whose imaginative life was so encouraged and fostered should have later made use of Arthurian themes for the expression of his more adult fantasies, but perhaps the most interesting thing is that despite his devotion to and close familiarity with Malory, he wrote only six Arthurian poems, of which 'The Defence of Guenevere', 'King Arthur's Tomb' and 'Sir Galahad: a Christmas Mystery' are the most important, published in 1858 when he was twenty-four. He never returned to Arthurian topics in any later writing.

'My work is the embodiment of dreams in one form or another', wrote Morris to his friend Cormell Price in 1856, and this early formulation was to hold good in one way or another throughout his life. But the 'embodiment of dreams' suggests the need to create imaginary worlds, and it seems likely that the Arthurian theme imposed its own conditions on Morris and forced him to move into territory where he could give his imagination a freer rein. Morris's Arthurian poems probably come closer than any other nineteenth-century interpretation to the spirit of Malory, although he makes some minor changes in the stories that he uses as basis for his own work. In his poems he attempts to enter into the experiences and events that Malory records, to examine crucial moments within the story from the point of view of the protagonists, and so to suggest how Guenevere might have reacted to a public accusation of adultery, what the thoughts of Launcelot and Guenevere might have been just before and during their last meeting, and how Galahad felt about his commitment to the Grail quest. The poems are close to Malory in their uncritical acceptance of the lovers' situation, and avant-garde in their uncensorious treatment of the relationship. The influence of Browning is apparent in the psychological approach, the influence of Rossetti in the sharply realised visual detail, and in both respects Morris is, as it were, supplying Malory's deficiencies. Morris's protagonists are seen against a background which is often stylised and symbolic with its towers and gardens, bright heraldic colours and flowers, and its Pre-Raphaelite figures with their long throats and flowing hair. Morris's medieval world is not Malory's: his medieval settings re-create the Middle Ages, yet relate to *Le Morte Darthur* more closely than the poems of Arnold, Swinburne and Tennyson do. Morris's poems thus supplement Malory, providing new insights into the traditional stories, without completely re-interpreting them, or using them freely as myths. Morris takes a particular point in the narrative and explores it in psychological terms, and his identification with the protagonists gave his interpretations an authenticity that reviewers found lacking in the Arthurian poems of Bulwer Lytton and Tennyson. As they speak or meditate, Morris's characters evoke their past lives, and their memories build up images of the life of Camelot or Glastonbury. For all its beauty, Morris's medieval world is no Earthly Paradise: the characters are caught in a moment of suffering or weakness: Guenevere confronts death, or the realisation of her guilt, or a final separation from Launcelot; Galahad speaks in a moment of self-pitying despair, Launcelot in sleepless confusion or in incredulous horror at Guenevere's rejection of him. The reader sees an unexpected aspect of the familiar, heroic figure.

At the same time, there is a strong sense that the poems mean more than they seem to say. Each one involves the topic of choice or vocation, or a static moment before a change of state. It seems probable that the topics and incidents that he chose had a special importance and a symbolic significance for Morris, only apparent upon close examination of the poems in the context of his life at the period when he was writing them.

May Morris records her father as saying—of course many years after the publication of *The Defence of Guenevere* poems—that the best way to retell an old romance was to 'read it through, then shut the book and write it out again as a new story for yourself', and these Arthurian poems suggest that this is, at least in part, what Morris has done.

In the first poem, 'The Defence of Guenevere', Morris presents a scene, not to be found in Malory, in which Gawain is Guenevere's accuser, and she defends herself against his accusation, unstated in the poem. Malory portrays Guenevere as a woman both petulant and querulous, yet capable of unselfish courage and noble feeling, a character who through dialogue and action, emerges from the last books of the story as increasingly vivid and credible, and whose maddening capriciousness enhances the reader's sense of her appeal, for her beauty must indeed be great to retain Launcelot's devotion to her despite her cruelty to him. Morris gives Guenevere the spirit with which Malory had endowed her, but it takes a different form, as she justifies her past life with desperate but queenly eloquence. Cancelling an earlier, explanatory opening, Morris plunges into the scene without introduction:

> *But knowing now that they would have her speak,*
> *She threw her wet hair backward from her brow,*
> *Her hand close to her mouth touching her cheek*

The complex mixture of defiance, shame and contempt for the listening lords leads in to her first attempt to gain their sympathy by recounting the choice that she had been forced to make, in ignorance, long before, between Arthur and Launcelot. In symbolical terms, she describes how she first found herself obliged to choose, not simply between Arthur and Launcelot, but between two ways of life, one way apparently sterile and deadening, the other enriching. At the moment of choice, she did not realise that the first was the way of salvation, the second of damnation. She tells her hearers how, when she was 'quite alone and very weak', indeed actually confronting death, 'A great God's angel' had stood at the foot of her bed holding on wands two 'choosing cloths', one 'blue, / wavy and long', the other 'cut short and red'. 'Heaven's colour, the blue', she decides; but the blue cloth symbolises not heaven, but hell. Appealing to the sympathy of her audience, she continues:

> *Perhaps you then would roll upon your bed,*
>
> *And cry to all good men that loved you well*
> *'Ah Christ! if only I had known, known, known.'*

She returns to the story of Launcelot's coming to court at Christmas, his splendour suggested by the acclaim of heralds and the pealing of bells, after she had been 'bought / By Arthur's great name and his little love'. The court listens in silence as she describes the slow but irresistible growth of her love for Launcelot, in terms of the cycle of the year, and through an image of gradual slipping down a path into the sea. The moment of final yielding to temptation takes place in a 'quiet garden walled round every way', like the enclosed gardens of medieval romance carrying suggestions of the Garden of Eden, but also symbolising inner experience.

Morris, in making Guenevere repudiate Gawain's accusation, makes her an enigmatic figure. 'God knows I speak truth, saying that you lie' she declares to Gawain, asserting that she could not weep if she were evil enough to be guilty. Morris's imaginative insight represents her as caught up in a tumult of emotions, well aware of her status as a great queen, but also of her position as an accused woman facing a terrible death, isolated and to all appearances guilty, with no defence but her beauty. She is brought to bay at last, with no champion to rescue her, and the impassioned courage of her confrontation of her enemies contrasts with the weakness which had caused her to yield to Launcelot's love. She appeals to Gawain's sympathy and better feelings, she attempts to frighten him with the threat that she will haunt him. Undaunted by his turning away, she returns to her story with renewed determination: 'See me hew down your proofs'. She reminds her listeners of what had happened to Mellyagraunce after he had dared to accuse her of adultery with one of her wounded knights in his castle after he had carried her off. In a dramatic evocation of the scene, she recalls how she had been chained by the waist to the stake to be burnt, and how Launcelot had fought Mellyagraunce, until suddenly Launcelot had struck the sword from his antagonist's hand:

> *Caught it, and swung it; that was all the fight*
>
> *Except a spout of blood on the hot land;*
> *For it was hottest summer; and I know*
> *I wonder'd how the fire, while I should stand,*
>
> *And burn, against the heat, would quiver so,*
> *Yards above my head; thus these matters went.*

The startlingly vivid recollection reminds her hearers of what they have in mind to do to the Queen. The pictorial imagery, moving from blood to fire, increases the psychological realism by suggesting the horror of the experience as well as its potential, in the Queen's eyes, as a means of shocking her accusers into revulsion against the act of burning her.

She pauses to remind the audience of her beauty, which they would destroy, and that the truth of what she has said may be seen in her face. She moves on to the attack of Mordred and Agravaine, when she and Launcelot were alone together, and repudiates the suggestion that she and her lover were other than innocent, for 'When a queen says with gentle queenly sound: / "O true as steel come now and talk with me"'", what good knight would refuse? Though Guenevere speaks of the moment of terror when the bawling and stone-throwing of Mordred and his party began, she does not mention Launcelot's heroic fight against his enemies, and Morris does not allow her or Launcelot the noble words that Malory gives them in that tense, dramatic scene. Instead she admits to her own weakness and fear:

> *The stones they threw up rattled o'er my head,*
> *And made me dizzier; till within a while*
>
> *My maids were all about me, and my head*
> *On Launcelot's breast was being soothed away*
> *From its white chattering.*

In the end, her defence proves nothing, for there is only her word against Gawain's and no other character speaks but the Queen. She insists again:

> *God knows I speak truth, saying that you lie!*
> *All I have said is truth, by Christ's dear tears.*

Her tale is done, but at that moment, her knight Launcelot appears 'at need'. Does she truly believe throughout her defence that she is innocent, or does she merely assert it in the hope that her beauty will persuade her hearers to agree? The uncertainty adds to the subtlety of the portrayal.

Morris has altered the story as he found it in Malory at this point, where after Mordred's attack, Arthur is obliged to condemn Guenevere to the stake:

> So then there was made great ordinance in this heat, that the queen must be judged to the death. And the law was such in those days that whatsomever they were, of what estate or degree, if they were found guilty of treason, there should be none other remedy but death; and either the men or the taking with the deed should be causer of their hasty judgment. And right so was it ordained for Queen Guenever, by cause Sir Mordred was escaped sore wounded, and the death of thirteen knights of the Round Table. These proofs and experiences caused King Arthur to command the queen to the fire there to be brent. Then spake Sir Gawaine and said: My lord Arthur, I would counsel you not to be over-hasty, but that ye would put it in respite, this judgment of my lady the queen, for many causes. (XX, vii)

It is in fact Gawaine's continuing speech (in which he tries to restrain Arthur) that is Guenevere's defence in Malory: 'For I dare say, said Sir Gawaine, my lady, your queen, is to you both good and true.' Morris knew Malory so well that it is very unlikely that he was confused about the details and events at this crucial point in the story.

His changes allowed Guenevere to tell her own story, in making her own defence, and to appear in her queenly splendour; but there are other elements in Morris's version that are less easy to account for, for example the introduction of the strange choosing-cloths, and Guenevere's own emphasis on her beauty.

The phrase 'choosing-cloths' seems to have been coined by Morris himself: the visual image that lies behind the term is that of banners. Guenevere's choice is between the long wavy pennon which in medieval heraldry was assigned to a young knight, and the short pennon of a proven warrior. Morris and Burne-Jones were both at this time reading Froissart,[8] and their edition contained many illustrations of scenes in which just such banners were depicted. Burne-Jones had a sketch-book devoted solely to these two types of banners; and Morris often mentions banners in his early poems. He also, as the choosing-cloths indicate, had a keen sense of medieval colour-symbolism: blue is conventionally indeed 'heaven's colour', as also the colour of true and faithful love, while red often symbolises passion. His interest in heraldry would probably have suggested to him the appropriateness of the blue and red choosing-cloths as devices for Launcelot and Arthur; blue for the long and faithful love of Launcelot, red for the royal standard of Arthur, whose 'little love' had originally caused him to marry Guenevere against the advice of Merlin. Her choice of the 'heaven' of Launcelot's love threatens final damnation for her, while she rejects the choice that would have made life hell but promised heaven after it.

The invention of the choosing-cloths emphasises the originality of Morris's treatment of his material, and points to the inner significance of the poem. For Guenevere has no choice in Malory: her role is almost entirely passive; in Morris's poem, she must make a choice which is not only significant and frightening, but also very difficult and conclusive—'Now choose one cloth for ever'. The addition of this episode seems to suggest that it had a special importance for Morris. He had had to make significant choices himself in the years in which he was absorbing Malory, and the *Defence of Guenevere* poems were written at that stage in his life when he had finally decided to abandon his long-standing intention of entering into Holy Orders, to the acute disappointment of his family. Such an intention can hardly have been set aside without inner conflict and a sense of guilt, while to go against the fondest wishes of a Victorian mother was no easy undertaking, as a letter of explanation written in November 1855 suggests.[9] Not only did Morris give up what had always been thought of as his vocation when he joined Street to begin training as an architect in 1856, but he was to stoop still lower (in terms of upper middle-class assumptions) in later abandoning this profession, under D. G. Rossetti's influence, at the end of 1856 in the hopes of becoming a painter. Morris's biographer remarks upon the adverse reaction of Morris's family, adding that 'It had always been taken for granted that he was to enter the Church. . . . To be a painter was barely respectable . . . Mrs Morris at first hardly credited the project announced to her.' On Morris himself, he continues, 'the resolution had an unsettling, and for a time, almost a disastrous effect'; for the two years during which he was trying to become a painter, he was moody and irritable, brooded much by himself, 'and lost for the time a good deal of his old sweetness'.[10]

The close identification with Guenevere in the poem, which enabled him to produce her 'defence', is in itself surprising in a young man in his early twenties, and can perhaps be seen as relating to his own dilemma when confronted with the choice between the commitment made in ignorance of its implications, and now seen as life-denying, and the alternative which allows fuller scope for growth and fulfilment. It is not difficult to see that Guenevere may have symbolised the creative side of his nature, allowed to find expression in liberating union with the practical, represented by Launcelot, the 'mighty man of his hands' as Malory constantly describes him. Unconventional and unacceptable in terms of contemporary attitudes, such a union calls forth the 'defence' of William Morris, too, as his creativity seeks a means of expression through art and rejects the choice, made in ignorance, of a career in the Church.

Thus in 'The Defence of Guenevere' Morris makes use of an Arthurian theme to give expression to inner conflict, and to express what contemporary literary conventions would otherwise have found too subjective. Its unconventionality as regards moral attitudes, indicated by Morris's implicit championing of the adulterous queen, contrasts with Tennyson's censorious attitude to her, as well as with Ludlow's, quoted earlier, but as in other respects, the poem is closer in its tolerance and sympathy to Malory's presentation.

In the next poem in the volume, 'King Arthur's Tomb', Morris again slightly alters the details of the episode as described by Malory, in order to recount the last meeting of Launcelot and Guenevere. The poem can be closely related to D. G. Rosetti's earlier painting on the same subject, but Morris again adopts a psychological approach, imagining the states of mind of Launcelot and Guenevere as they draw near to each other for the last time.

D. G. Rossetti had already made the lovers' last meeting more dramatic by depicting it actually at Arthur's tomb, instead of simply in the cloister at Amesbury, and Morris follows this pattern. He breaks away from Malory's treatment of the episode by including no counterpart to the formal, dignified dialogue of the lovers when they first meet, or to Guenevere's final taunts when she urges Launcelot to 'go to thy realm, and there take thee a wife, and live with her in joy and bliss'.[11] The scene in 'King Arthur's Tomb' is less moving than in *Le Morte Darthur*, but Swinburne is right in his praise of the poem for the different kind of excellence that it achieves: 'But where among other and older poets of his time and country, is one comparable for perception and expression of tragic truth, of subtle and noble, terrible and piteous things? where a touch of passion at once so broad and so sure? The figures here given have the blood and breath, the shape and step of life; they can move and suffer; their repentance is as real as their desire; their shame lies as deep as their love . . . The retrospective vision of Launcelot and Guenevere is as passionate and profound as life.'[12]

The poem begins with Launcelot's long journey through a hot August day and night, and the thoughts that absorb him as his horse plods wearily on.

Through the dusty heat of the day and the dim moonlight he muses on the beginning of his love for Guenevere. By means of stylised, emblematic images, Morris conveys a sense of their relationship, of Launcelot's worship and the distance that separates him from Guenevere. The intensity of his passionate devotion is augmented by the sense of frustration, by his yearning for contact— to kiss her feet, to touch her hand against his lips, to let her head rest against his breast, in 'the old garden life'. His memories capture the Pre-Raphaelite vision of the Middle Ages, in terms of the bright colours of medieval manuscripts, red and blue and gold, and the images of saints and lilies, of swaying arras and daisied meadows. They also evoke a portrait of Guenevere, young, beautiful and queenly, as Launcelot first knew her, which makes more poignant and more dramatic the change in her and her rejection of him when they meet at last.

As Launcelot approaches Glastonbury where he is to meet Guenevere, the poem turns to her. Her longing for him is equal to his for her, but a sense of guilt and sin has overwhelmed her with the coming of dawn. Colour fades from the poem: 'yet a blight / Had settled on her, all her robes were black', and in the morning twilight as she had lain waiting for day, 'the grey downs bare / Grew into lumps of sin to Guenevere'. She confronts death, judgement and hell, but at the same time she is aware of her beauty, for she is beautiful even as Christ and his Mother. When the lovers meet later at the tomb, Launcelot is confused and horrified by her rejection of him; her words do not express grief at the war that their love has brought about, or at the death of Arthur and his knights, but a tormenting sense of guilt and fear of hell for him as well as for herself. She is making a supreme effort to save him by rejecting him. Swinburne comments on this part of the poem: 'Again, when Guenevere has maddened herself and him with wild words of reproach and remorse, abhorrence and attraction, her sharp and sudden memory of old sights and sounds and splendid irrevocable days finds word and form not less noble and faithful to fact and life. The first word of Arthur bidding her cherish the knight "whom all the land called his banner, sword, and shield"; the long first pressure of Launcelot's lips on her hand; . . . the solitary sound of birds singing in her gardens, while in the lists the noise went on of spears and shouts telling which knight of them all rode here or there; the crying of ladies' names as men and horses clashed one against another; . . . the agony of anger and horror which gives edge and venom to her memory—all these points and phases of passion are alike truly and nobly rendered.'[13] Guenevere's memories of times past complement Launcelot's in giving a sense not of the 'old garden life', but of the more active public life of chivalry which formed the background to their love.

In changing the point of view to accommodate a psychological exploration of the Queen's state of mind, Morris presents in the end a more sombre impression of the spiritual condition of the lovers than does Malory with his confident assertion of their final salvation. Guenevere's last taunting words to Launcelot, evoking an image of him in hell, 'curl'd Body and face and limbs in agony', may seem at first sight medieval, but is totally alien to Malory.

Moving as the poem is to the modern reader—for despite its carelessness of composition it is in many ways successful—it is difficult now to recover a sense of the romance that its subject held for the nineteenth-century reader who invested the idea of love with a passionate intensity almost beyond the power of the present-day imagination to comprehend. Morris and his contemporaries found in medieval tales of love an excitement which they endeavoured to recapture in their own work, and which may be related to the fascination felt by nineteenth-century scholars for the concept of 'courtly love' which they believed to be a feature of medieval society and literature. Though more fantasy than fact, it was an idea that suited their age, because it made it possible to romanticise illicit love-affairs and to find ways in which they could be regarded as acceptable to morality and religion. Walter Pater, discussing Morris's *Defence of Guenevere* volume, speaks of the close relationship in the Middle Ages between religion and sensuous love. Religious feeling expressed itself through the 'idolatry of the cloister', in worship of the Virgin Mary, while the 'imaginative loves' of the Provencal poets took the form of a rival religion with a rival 'cultus'. Worship of an idealised and idolised lady was an essential feature of each. The Provencal poets learnt from religion the art of 'directing towards an imaginary object sentiments whose natural direction is towards objects of sense' and the form of love which they evolved was to be defined by 'the absence of the beloved, choosing to be without hope, protesting against all lower uses of love, barren, extravagant, antinomian. It is the love which is incompatible with marriage, for the chevalier who never comes, of the serf for the chatelaine, the rose for the nightingale . . .'[14] Pater suggests that Morris has learned the secret of this love, too, and given it expression in his Arthurian poems. Though Pater's conception of love in the Middle Ages does not quite seem to describe the relationship of Malory's Launcelot and Guenevere—for when Sir Launcelot was found in the Queen's chamber, for example, Malory says that 'whether they were abed or at other manner of disports, me list not hereof make no mention, for love that time was not as is nowadays'[15]—Pater reads 'King Arthur's Tomb' in this light, as the expression of a frenzied, forever unappeased longing and devotion. He claims that Morris has 'diffused through "King Arthur's Tomb" the maddening white glare of the sun, and tyranny of the moon, not tender and far-off, but close down—the sorcerer's moon, large and feverish. The colouring is intricate and delirious, as of "scarlet lilies". The influence of summer is like a poison in one's blood, with a sudden bewildering sickening of life and all things.' For the nineteenth century, such poetry seems to have been heady stuff. But Pater's attitude to medieval love helps to explain the great imaginative appeal of the love-stories within the Arthurian legend for his contemporaries.

Like 'The Defence of Guenevere', 'King Arthur's Tomb' seems to be about more than the traditional 'sin they said we did', as Guenevere terms it. Walter Pater, in the review just quoted, says very perceptively of the Arthurian poems: 'What is characteristic in them is the strange suggestion of a deliberate choice between Christ and a rival lover.' It seems probable that, metaphorically speaking, this is what the poems are really about, only it is the choice that Morris is finding himself making in actual life between the Church and art. It is perhaps significant that Guenevere sees herself under two aspects: on the one hand, through the eyes of those who judge by conventional standards; but at the same time in a different light, as beautiful in the way that Christ and his Mother are beautiful, that is to say beautiful in a spiritual sense. This assurance of the special nature of her beauty seems to point to her symbolic significance: as a symbol for the creative imagination she is necessarily beautiful; but the world cares nothing for the union of the creative imagination with the practical, and despises and rejects art. The poem may thus suggest Morris's doubts about his role as artist, and about his ability to realise his creative potential in practical terms; at the same time it expresses uncertainty about the consequences and moral justification of the course he had chosen.

The theme of vocation is dominant in the next poem in the volume, 'Sir Galahad, A Christmas Mystery', which presents the figure of Galahad in an unconventional light. Of Tennyson's Galahad Morris had once said, according to Mackail,[16] that he was 'rather a mild youth'; now the figure becomes a young man unable to accept the isolation and frustration that his vocation imposes, and the poem begins and ends in sadness. Images of desolation, night and wintry weather match Galahad's mood of depression, alone in a chapel in the forest, as he reflects on his stultifyingly lonely and unending quest. The intensity of Rossetti's grief-stricken gaze in 'The Woodspurge' of 1856 is paralleled in Galahad's contemplation of the detail of his surroundings in the chapel. The first-person narration, the de-romanticised Galahad, 'heartless and stupid' as he compares his life with the lives of others, suggest Morris's close identification with the protagonist. Galahad is obsessed with thoughts of the satisfaction others find in fantasies or in the actuality of sexual love—Palomydes with his passion for Iseult, his own father Launcelot with Guenevere—and he imagines the comments that ordinary people will make one day when he is found dead in his armour in the snow: 'Ah! poor chaste body!' He muses bitterly on the lovers that he had seen exchanging last farewell kisses before the Quest for the Sangreal began, and then, suddenly, he has a vision of 'One sitting on the altar as a throne, / Whose face no man could say he did not know'. Christ speaks reassuringly to him of his love and of his constant presence and care of him, telling him that indeed earthly love is happy but asking 'would you for a little time be glad / To make me sorry long day after day?' The vision ends, and angels and saints enter, to arm Galahad to finish the quest, for he must join Bors and Percival and board the wondrous ship. The vision has brought reassurance and peace to Galahad, but when he is armed, Bors and Percival and his sister enter to give news of the outside world: 'poor merry Dinadan' is dead, Lionel and Gauwaine have returned from the quest shamed, Lavaine is feared dead—'everywhere / The knights come foil'd from the great quest, in vain; / In vain they struggle for the vision fair'.

The tone of the despairing lines which end the poem, overpowering the brightness of the vision, suggests that the quest had a personal significance for Morris. Though moments of vision might bring temporary reassurance, they give way to hopelessness once more in this unhappy poem. In earlier days

Galahad had been a particularly significant figure for Morris, as is apparent from his earlier thoughts of founding an Order named after him. His new enthusiasm for art, together with the natural consequences of growing up, as well as disappointment with the religious climate of Oxford in the 1850s, caused Morris to abandon the idea. Though he probably grew out of his youthful piety when he decided to give up his intention of being ordained, the 'dialogue of the soul with itself' which constitutes a large part of his Galahad poem suggests that the process of change was not altogether an easy or a painless one.

The fourth Arthurian poem, in which Galahad also plays an important part, is 'The Chapel in Lyonness'. This strange poem is in a different mode, its atmosphere stylised, dreamlike and unreal beside the sharply realistic detail and naturalistic musing and dialogue which figure in 'Sir Galahad'. There are three speakers in 'The Chapel in Lyonness', Sir Ozana le Cure Hardy (a very minor figure in Malory), Sir Galahad and Sir Bors, and though each speaks in turn, as if to a listener, there is no interchange between them. Sir Ozana lies in a trance in the chapel, with the truncheon of a spear deep in his breast, 'Though no man any blood could spy'. His life is a living death, as he lies watched by Galahad 'all day long and every day'. Galahad speaks of how he sang to Ozana, but his singing 'moved him not'; and then of how he left the chapel and returned with a wild rose which he laid across Ozana's mouth, who then suddenly smiled, moved and drew out a golden tress of hair. Next Bors enters and hears Ozana's murmur, 'There comes no sleep nor any love', and sees Galahad stoop and kiss him: then at last Ozana is released from suffering and he shivers with delight, longing to die and join his beloved. He admits that 'his life went wrong', and soon after, beginning to fathom the mystery, he dies. The last lines of the poem suggest that Galahad sees a vision of Ozana reunited with his beloved in bliss.

Again, the underlying pattern seems to be of conflict, in this case between body and soul, or between the higher and the lower nature. Ozana is—in appropriately medieval terms—wounded by love, and held in a long trance-like living death, preceded by madness, from which Galahad could not release him. All Galahad's spiritual songs prevent Ozana from being able either to live or to die; it is only when he thinks of Launcelot and breaks off his song that the rose can work its greater magic. As the symbol of earthly love, it suggests the acknowledgement and acceptance of love, and enables Ozana to move and to take his love-token and be released, into a final fulfilment and understanding which can only be achieved beyond the Chapel, with its implications of dedication to the celibate life. It is a rose, not a lily that Galahad brings to Ozana from the garden, implying love rather than renunciation; just as it is a golden tress that Ozana presses to his heart, not the hair-shirt of asceticism. So in this poem Morris makes use of Arthurian characters, taking Ozana, who is little more than a name in Malory, as the central figure, and setting the scene in a little chapel from the Grail story, to create an atmosphere totally dissimilar from anything in *Le Morte Darthur*, but quintessentially Pre-Raphaelite. The poem is not a psychological interpretation of a well-known Arthurian episode but the product of Morris's creative imagination, and expressive through its symbolism of his own frustrations and conflicts.

Thus in these Arthurian poems, as in two others, 'Near Avalon' and 'A Good Knight in Prison', which refer to Guenevere and Launcelot but do not make use of Arthurian themes, Morris is not concerned with the great contemporary topics that find expression in much nineteenth-century Arthurian literature—the problems of the loveless marriage and love outside marriage—but with the externalisation and resolving of his own tensions and doubts. He neither glorifies romantic love nor explicitly censures adultery; indeed in his first two poems, Launcelot's and Guenevere's love becomes the symbol of a different kind of union which need not, indeed cannot be judged in terms of conventional morality, for 'The Defence of Guenevere' is a defence of the creative vocation and its source of inspiration. Assurance gives place to doubt in 'Arthur's Tomb', while the Galahad poems approach the problem of vocation from another angle.

The undercurrent of bitter frustration which plays so important a part in all the poems arises not merely from Morris's need in his early twenties for an outlet for his enormous creative energies, but also from a consciously or unconsciously suppressed desire for sexual satisfaction, too. The poems are full of sexual imagery, but the secondary symbols of hair, lips and hands predominate. The lips of lovers strain to meet, hands reach out for brief and tenuous contact, insentient tresses link Launcelot and Guenevere, Ozana and his love. The stylised or emblematic nature of much of the imagery distracts attention from its physicality, as for example in these lines:

> *And she would let me wind*
> *Her hair around my neck, so that it fell*
> *Upon my red robe, strange in the twilight*
> *With many unnamed colours, till the bell*
> *Of her mouth on my cheek sent a delight*
> *Through all my ways of being . . .*

Here, the red robe, the twilight and the bell-image give an impression of the setting, and so mask the sensuous feeling with which the lines are really concerned. This sensuousness, absent in Malory, together with the psychological approach which Morris adopted in the first three of his Arthurian poems is one of the main innovations that he brought to Arthurian legend in the nineteenth century. In addition, his powerful evocation of the Arthurian world, brilliant in its colour, haunting in its images, and alive with passion, can still capture the imagination. In giving the old stories a private and personal, rather than a merely public and general meaning, he made the symbolic potential of the traditional material more accessible to later writers. That he wrote no more Arthurian poems after 1858 perhaps suggests that when the difficult period with which the subjects were associated was left behind, he had no wish to revisit Camelot.

Morris's poems lack Malory's cosmic optimism: the cold breath of Calvinism which seems to have given a new exclusiveness to heaven in the nineteenth century can be felt even here, threatening eternal punishment to those who have sinned. Nor could Morris share Malory's predominant interest in the institution of the Round Table itself, or in the code of chivalry and the noble ideal on which the institution was based. But as with many other nineteenth-century writers, that aspect of the story with which Malory was perhaps least concerned proved the most fruitful point of entry for Morris. While Malory is little concerned with love, except as a potentially disruptive force in society, for Morris the love of Launcelot and Guenevere was of wider symbolic significance, and led him to the psychological realism which would have been impossible for a medieval writer.

Morris's *Defence of Guenevere* volume was the first Pre-Raphaelite poetry to appear, and the immediate reaction to it on the part of reviewers and the public was not at all favourable. Very few copies were sold. The difficulty of the poems was a major objection, and one which was not raised against his later poetry, from *Jason* onwards. Though some reviewers recognised Morris's poetic power, and acclaimed it heartily, sometimes in looking back to *The Defence of Guenevere* volume when considering later works, they were almost unanimous in preferring the more lucid and readily intelligible *Earthly Paradise* to his earlier poems.

The first review, in *The Spectator* for February 1858, testifies to the philistinism and lack of taste of the reviewer rather than to the quality of the poems: 'the author has introduced into his poems touches . . . of real coarseness and immorality. To our taste, the style is as bad as bad can be . . . He combines the mawkish simplicity of the Cockney school with the prosaic baldness of the worst passages of Tennyson.'[17] The writer ends by complaining about the deep-seated faults of affectation and bad taste, though affectation was a charge frequently levelled against these poems by reviewers unsympathetic to 'Pre-Raphaelitism'. Others complained of the carelessness of Morris's writing, a criticism for which there was perhaps more justification.

It is significant that the hostile criticism tended to come from the less well-known critics. Those who recognised the power behind the poems and perceived Morris's poetic gifts were of course his friends, Rossetti and Swinburne, but also Browning (who, though much older, may perhaps be included, since Morris had made his acquaintance on joining Rossetti's circle in London), as well as Ruskin and Walter Pater. They were, not surprisingly, less discouraged by the difficulty and obscurity of the poems than other readers. Indeed, Browning expressed a preference for Morris's 'first sprightly runnings' as against his later verse, in a letter of 1870.[18] Walter Pater, in his unsigned review of the first volume of *The Earthly Paradise* (previously quoted, p. 143) described 'The Defence of Guenevere' as 'a thing tormented and awry with passion, like the body of Guenevere defending herself from the charge of adultery, and the accent falls in strange, unwonted places with the force of a great cry'. He goes on to comment obliquely on the earlier poems in noting the change of manner apparent in *The Life and Death of Jason* of 1867: 'Here there is no delirium or illusion, no experiences of mere soul while the body and the bodily senses sleep or wake with convulsed intensity at the prompting of imaginative love.'

Another significant aspect of the comments which greeted *The Defence of Guenevere* volume is the attention paid to Morris's capacity for reproducing 'the tone of thought and feeling of a past age'. Richard Garnett in *The Literary Gazette* commented that 'the rough chivalry of the middle ages appears as it were transfigured, and shining with a saintly halo of inexpressible loveliness'.[19] Some critics found fidelity to nature in the poems, and several found Morris's treatment of Arthurian themes superior to Tennyson's, because Tennyson wrote as a modern, while Morris entered into the mind of medieval man. J. H. Shorthouse, contrasting Morris with Tennyson in 1859, describes 'The Defence of Guenevere' as 'the most wonderful reproduction of the tone of thought and feeling of a past age that has ever been achieved'.[20] He suggests that, if the Arthurian Romances are ever to be 'worthily rewritten in modern poetry, it will be as he [Morris] has done it, and not otherwise'. Garnett's view is similar: 'Tennyson's "Sir Galahad" is Tennyson himself in an enthusiastic and devotional mood; Mr Morris's is the actual champion, just as he lived and moved and had his being some twelve hundred years ago. Tennyson is the orator who makes a speech for another; Mr Morris the reporter who writes down what another man says.' It is with the Arthurian poems that these writers are most concerned: the Froissartian poems in *The Defence of Guenevere and Other Poems* seem on the whole to have made less impact on the critics, suggesting that there was by this time a context within which Arthurian literature was read, and that expectations as to what form new versions should take had already begun to take shape.

Within this period and closely related to the poems of Tennyson and Morris, as well as to the whole Pre-Raphaelite vision of the Arthurian world, appeared George du Maurier's parodic *A Legend of Camelot*. It was first published in *Punch* in the spring of 1866, in five instalments, combining verse and woodcut illustrations, and was reprinted as a book with coloured illustrations more than thirty years later in 1898. In both verses and pictures, du Maurier parodied what he considered as the absurdities within Tennyson's and Morris's Arthurian poems, as well as a number of distinctive features of Pre-Raphaelite art. The result is a comprehensive and amusing attack, though du Maurier was unable to sustain his impetus throughout the *Legend*.

The poem makes fun of both the subject-matter and the form of such poems as 'The Lady of Shalott' and Morris's *Defence of Guenevere* poems. Its absurdly named heroine 'Tall Braunighrindas' 'left her tower, and wandered down' to Camelot, where she encountered Sir Galahad and Sir Launcelot, seeking some quest to undertake, 'Or burden bear, or trouble make'. Du Maurier draws attention to the type-image of the Pre-Raphaelite woman in both his pictorial and verbal descriptions of Braunighrindas, whose immense head of hair reaches to her feet, and whose characteristic attitudes parody the familiar portraits of Rossetti's women:

'*She thrust her chin towards Galahad*' . . .
'*And folks did ask her in the street*
"*How fared it with her long pale feet?*"
O miserie!
And blinkt, as though 'twere hard to bear
The red-heat of her blazing hair!
O miserie!'

Sir Galahad has Braunighrindas's hair woven into a cloak for her by a nearby weaver, since she is very scantily clad, but at this point the poem begins to lose impetus. A Jewish old-clothes trader appears, offers five shekels for her and her hair, and is apparently killed on the spot by Gauwaine. Echoes of Tennyson, 'The bold Sir Launcelot mused a bit', and of Morris's more mannered archaisms follow as Braunighrindas meets another damsel called Fiddle-le-Strynges-le-Fay; and they eventually find that both are married to Gauwaine. So 'having walkt a little space / They . . . chanted loud a wondrous plaint'. In the end, both drown, though not as gracefully in du Maurier's illustration as Ophelia does in the well-known picture by Millais that is here mocked.

Despite the weakness of the verse and illustrations in the later part of *A Legend of Camelot*, it continues to hit its target with some justness and considerable ingenuity. Though du Maurier may well have been prompted by the appearance of Edward Moxon's edition of Tennyson's poems with its illustrations by D. G. Rossetti and others in 1858 as Leonée Ormond has suggested,[21] his scope is very much wider than restriction of the parody to this one work would allow. In mocking them, it helps to define some aspects of the mid-century treatment of Arthurian themes.

ii. Swinburne: *Tristram of Lyonnesse and Other Poems* (1882); *The Tale of Balen* (1896)

Swinburne, as has already been indicated, was early fascinated by the Arthurian legend, and seems to have written a poem on the theme of Tristram while still a schoolboy. Later, at Oxford, he came under the influence of William Morris, and his earliest attempts at Arthurian poems to survive, 'Queen Yseult', 'Lancelot' and 'Joyeuse Garde' are full of echoes of Morris's *Defence of Guenevere* poems. Queen Yseult is a Pre-Raphaelite beauty:

And no gems the maiden had,
But with tresses golden-glad
Was her perfect body clad.[22]

Again and again phrases reminiscent of Morris occur—'her dear face', 'hot and bitter drouth', 'the happy garden land'—and there is, if anything, even more flowing, glowing golden hair, more locks and tresses and deep streams of dropping hair than anywhere else in the work of the Pre-Raphaelites. The form of the story that Swinburne tells is certainly a strange one: Yseult comes to collect Tristram on a winter night and carries him on her back through the snow, with bare feet, so that no-one will know that they have been together. Many stanzas are given to Tristram's bridal night with Yseult of Brittany, 'sleeping in her maidenhood', in which the full poignance of the situation of both characters is brought out. 'Lancelot', too, is in form and cadence strongly reminiscent of Morris's early poems, in particular of 'Sir Galahad: A Christmas Mystery'.

> *Always sate I, watching her*
> *By her carven gilded chair,*
> *Full of wonder and great fear*
> *If one long lock of her hair*
> *In the soft wind sink or stir,*
> *Fallen to her knee.*

The poem, which deals allusively with the conflict in Lancelot's soul as a result of his love for Guenevere, which holds him back in the quest for the Grail, ends inconclusively. In 'Joyeuse Garde' Swinburne attempts something different, an evocation of the situation and atmosphere at Joyeuse Garde, from the point of view of Yseult. It suggests a preliminary sketch for *Tristram of Lyonnesse*.

It was not until the publication of Tennyson's 'The Holy Grail' in 1869 that Swinburne set to work in earnest on the theme of Tristram and Iseult. He wrote to Rossetti: 'I fell tooth and nail upon "Tristram and Iseult" and wrote an overture of the poem projected, all yesterday. My first attempt at a poetic narrative may not be as good as "Gudrun", but if it doesn't lick the Morte d'Albert, I hope I may not die without extreme unction.'[23] It was not Tennyson's version of the story of Tristram in 'The Last Tournament', since it was not published until 1871, that prompted him to return to the theme in the first instance; but the enthusiasm with which he began upon the project did not result in its early completion, for the poem did not appear until 1882.

By 1869, Swinburne no longer associated himself with the Pre-Raphaelites as far as his work was concerned, and had freed himself from Morris's early influence. He adopted a new mode, modelling his verse, as he explained in the letter to D. G. Rossetti quoted above, 'not after the Chaucerian cadence of Jason, but after my own scheme of movement and modulation in Anactoria, which I consider original in structure and combination'. He studied the medieval versions of the story as related by Thomas, Béroul and Malory, though he seems not to have made direct use of Eilhart or Gottfried. Sir Walter Scott's edition of the Middle English 'Sir Tristrem' was a primary source. Though the author claimed that Wagner was a major influence (as Stoddard Martin points out in his study of Wagner's influence on English literature[24]) it is very unlikely that Swinburne could have known his music at all when he wrote 'Queen Yseult'; as also that he could have known *Tristan und Isolde*, except perhaps as piano music, when he wrote his *Tristram*. Martin further maintains that Swinburne's aesthetic was derived from Shelley and the Romantic tradition rather than from Wagner, and adds that though his poetry 'has moments of clear contact with Wagner—in favoured images such as the sea, themes such as the association of love with death, style which was equally passionate and prolonged, and subjects from the rediscovered body of partially pagan north European myths', they are coincidental rather than the result of direct influence, and indeed are characteristics shared with other contemporary writers.

Swinburne's intention, as he expressed it in the Dedicatory Epistle to the poem, was to present his story straightforwardly, 'as it was known to the age of Dante . . . mainly through a succession of dramatic scenes or pictures with descriptive settings or backgrounds'. This dignified aim may be contrasted with some of Swinburne's other comments: he intended, he said, to show Guenevere, long afterwards at Camelot, in 'a tête-a-tête with Iseult, when they exchange confidences about their husbands and lovers'; and in his letter to Rossetti of February 1870, he said that he hoped 'to make the copulative passages of the poem more warm . . . than anything my chaste Muse has yet attempted'. Their warmth, in the end, though rather tepid by present-day standards, caused Watts-Dunton some nervousness about the poem's reception, and *Tristram of Lyonnesse* was published with a padding of miscellaneous verse accompanying it to deaden the impact.

The old story enabled Swinburne to analyse the lovers' experience and its implications, to discuss at least indirectly the problem of such situations, and to give expression to the emotional intensity of frustrated sexual desire. The retelling of the legend gave him a freedom less available to the nineteenth-century novelist of contemporary life, and the romanticised world of the Middle Ages provided the ideal setting. Critics complained of the incongruity of allowing Tristram, the medieval knight, to express modern sentiments, but that the poem should have some sort of contemporary relevance, since its theme is Love, was obviously a large part of its point. There is, in fact, very little in the work that suggests the Middle Ages.

His story enabled Swinburne to create a setting in which natural imagery could provide the symbols of both emotion and sexual experience. He begins with the voyage, with 'the fair ship stoutly sailing' (as does Wagner) to take Iseult to her bridegroom King Mark in Cornwall, only summarising briefly, in introducing Tristram, the earlier part of the traditional story which deals with his birth and upbringing, and the adventures which take him to Iseult's home in Ireland. Swinburne is not much interested in Tristram as paragon of chivalry and courtesy, but only in the experience of passionate love. On the other hand, he does not immediately introduce the love-potion as Wagner does, because he has other things to do first. He creates a glitteringly beautiful, idealised picture of ship, sea and sky as a setting for Iseult's beauty, which, blended with the splendour of the morning, suggests her innocence and youth. She is still childlike, 'as if a rose's blood Beat in the live heart of a lily-bud' (Vol. IV, p. 34). She questions Tristram about Arthur's court, and hears the old story of Morgause and Arthur, of the terrible consequences of their love: 'Blind to him blind his sister brought forth seed', followed by the prophecy of the doom to come from 'the sin they knew not'. In Tristram and Iseult alone on the ship, against an elemental background, and far from the dark world of past sin and future retribution, Swinburne creates an image of high romance to offset the other aspects of the unhappy story—its deception, frustration and despair—and to glorify the power of irresistible passion.

The poem is in many ways a late offshoot of the Romantic tradition, and Swinburne's admiration for Shelley is very much apparent in his adoption of some aspects of his techniques. Like Shelley in 'Epipsychidion', Swinburne through natural images and the suggestion of scene and atmospheric conditions builds up an erotic atmosphere and suggests intense emotional experience. When Shelley imagines his beloved,

> The glory of her being, issuing hence,
> Stains the dead, blank, cold air with a warm shade
> Of unentangled intermixture, made
> By Love, of light and motion: one intense
> Diffusion, one serene Omnipresence,
> Whose flowing outlines mingle in their flowing,
> Around her cheeks and utmost fingers glowing
> With the unintermitted blood, which there
> Quivers, (as in a fleece of snow-like air
> The crimson pulse of living morning quiver,)
> Continuously prolonged, and ending never,
> Till they are lost, and in that Beauty furled
> Which penetrates and clasps and fills the world.

Swinburne's description of Iseult in the early morning is even more sensuous and suggestive:

> And her heart sprang in Iseult, and she drew
> With all her spirit and life the sunrise through
> . . . . . .
> And as the august great blossom of the dawn
> Burst, and the full sun scarce from sea withdrawn
> Seemed on the fiery water a flower afloat,
> So as a fire the mighty morning smote
> Throughout her, and incensed with the influent hour
> Her whole soul's one great mystical red flower
> Burst, and the bud of her sweet spirit broke
> Rose-fashion, and the strong spring at a stroke
> Thrilled, and was cloven, and from the full sheath came
> The whole rose of the woman red as flame.

(Vol. IV, p. 46)

After this, Swinburne's later 'copulative passages' come as rather an anticlimax.

Childhood is left behind with Iseult's experience of the sunrise, but before the love-potion is consumed, Swinburne changes the mood of ecstasy by once again introducing the threat of evil. He returns to Merlin's sinister origins and to Mordred and Agravane, and images of the Waste Land remind the reader of the wider context of the lovers' story. Then a squall strikes the ship, and Tristram goes to the help of the crew; when the danger is past, he is thirsty and Iseult fetches the love-draught. They drink

> *And all their life changed in them, for they quaffed*
> *Death.*   (Vol. IV, p. 56)

Shuddering with terror, not knowing what they have done, they are drawn together until 'their four lips became one burning mouth'. (Vol. IV, p. 57)

The poem is not simply about the experience of ungovernable passion, unacceptable to society, but about the cruelty of life, of the chance happening that leads to inescapable disaster or entanglement. It further enabled Swinburne to raise questions about guilt and responsibility; as well as about death and judgement, which were still controversial topics even towards the end of the century. Through it he was able to romanticise and idealise a situation with which much nineteenth-century literature is concerned, the mismatch, the meeting that comes too late, the life-long commitment that can bring no happiness. Here it is presented in its most powerful imaginative form, for both Tristram and Iseult are entirely guiltless and unaware of the possible implications of their action. Though there is a hint of the story of the Fall in the 'serpentine desire' that Tristram feels, he could not know that what he did would be disastrous. Swinburne's dramatic presentation of this moment, fraught with horrified realisation, brings out the psychological significance of the experience. Both the lovers have only just emerged from childhood; the ship and their voyage represent the state of transition from childhood to adulthood when, alone together, both are vulnerable and defenceless. They are the victims not only of a natural experience, but also of the well-meant intentions of their elders to arrange their lives for them. The symbol of the love-draught, like Eve's apple, is resonant with the hidden implications of a perpetually re-enacted natural experience. That Swinburne follows the earlier versions of the story that make the draught the sole cause of their love (instead of as in Thomas's version, allowing them to fall in love before they drink it) enhances their innocence and the dramatic quality of the episode, though, through the natural imagery of sun and flower, he has already linked them symbolically in an innocent organic union.

The compelling force of their love is the subject of the next section, which deals with the arrival at King Mark's court and the wedding night. Swinburne manages the substitution of Brangwain for Iseult with considerable delicacy, while not losing any of the ironies inherent in the situation. He makes Mark, awaiting the arrival of Iseult, a convincing figure of latent passion:

> *and his face was as the face of one*
> *Long time athirst and hungering for the sun . . .*
> *A swart lean man but kinglike, still of guise,*
> *With black streaked beard and cold unquiet eyes*
> *Close-mouthed, gaunt-cheeked, wan as a morning moon*
>
> (Vol. IV, pp. 59–60)

In due course,

> *Soft like a bride came Brangwain to King Mark,*
> *And to the queen came Tristram.* (p. 61)

But when Mark wakes he sees Iseult and

> *all that strange hair shed*
> *Across the tissued pillows, fold on fold,*
> *Innumerable, incomparable, all gold . . .*
> *so shone its flowering crown above*
> *The brows enwound with that imperial wreath,*
> *And framed with fragrant radiance round the face beneath*
> *And the king marvelled . . . and said out of his heart*
> *'What have I done of good for God to bless*
> *That all this he should give me, tress on tress . . .'* (p. 61)

The superbly Pre-Raphaelite picture is underlaid by the irony that it is only Iseult's hair that has been 'given' him. To the modern reader, unshocked by the situation, it is a successfully handled episode which avoids the unromantic explicitness of the medieval versions without bowdlerising, but it is scarcely as sensational now as it must have been meant to be. Swinburne reserved his greatest powers of erotic suggestion for later passages, such as the lovers' meetings in the forest bower, where with natural imagery as earlier in the poem, he builds up an impression of feverish love-making; as Tristram embraces Iseult, she is merged with flower images as he

> *strained her to him till all her faint breath sank*
> *And her bright limbs palpitated and shrank*
> *And rose and fluctuated as flowers in rain*
> *That bends them and they tremble and rise again*
> *And heave and straighten and quiver all through with bliss*
> *And turn afresh their mouths as for a kiss . . .* (p. 70)

The sea-imagery, used thematically throughout the poem, ends the idyllic episode with equal voluptuousness:

> *Her lips for love's sake bade love's will be done*
> *And all the sea lay subject to the sun.* (p. 72)

So, as in the Haidée episode in Byron's *Don Juan*, a sense of joy and fulfilment in a beautiful world is created; but the bower in which the lovers lie together summer-long, reminiscent of Keats' vision of Cupid and Psyche, suggests the extent of the fantasy that is being created. Juan and Haidée have to eat; she becomes pregnant, and her furious father tears the lovers apart: Byron makes sure that realism surrounds his idyll of young love. Swinburne's lovers here, however, as later in Joyous Gard, are lotus-eaters upon whom reality never impinges. They want nothing but love, they do nothing but make love without weariness or satiety. Their bower, far away from court and castle, almost out of time, emphasises the self-enclosed, sterile nature of their love, excessive and disproportioned as it is. The fantasy of the all-sufficiency of love has something regressive about it, for, denied the creative complementariness of adult love, Tristram and Iseult together inhabit and can only find satisfaction in a womb-like, isolated world of their own. It is, however, a fantasy in which we the more eagerly indulge because of the attraction of its other aspects: the fantasy of the first love that retains its intensity and faithfulness through life, in an equal balance of devotion.

Tristram's banishment at the end of this episode leads to his exile in Brittany, where the King's daughter is also called Iseult. She, too, is young, virginal and doomed to love him; the intensity of her passion for him is significant, for her frustration when Tristram marries her and is unable to consummate the marriage, is an important theme in the poem. Swinburne makes a convincing study of Iseult's patient expectation turning to bitterness and eventually poisoning her love and her nature. Tristram's inability to fulfil his obligation to his bride directs attention to another significant aspect of the story. There is a deeper level of meaning, as Anne Wilson has pointed out in *Traditional Romance and Tale*, in her very interesting discussion in Freudian terms of the implications of the story. She suggests that 'The story of Tristan appears to be the story of the eternal sadness associated with the hero's having to renounce his maternal first love. Indeed, he has been unable to renounce the sexual side of his love for her in his mind and therefore embarks on a search for her which can never be satisfied in his lifetime.'[25] Anne Wilson draws attention, in an earlier discussion, to the fact that there are three Iseults, the first a mother-figure to whom Tristram goes for healing of a wound in his thigh. He later arranges a marriage between King Mark, a father-figure, and Queen Iseult's daughter Iseult because he cannot dissociate Iseult the daughter from Iseult the mother, so that for him, she is taboo. In his mind he possesses Iseult, though she belongs to another man; he cannot consummate his marriage with the third Iseult, because of his association of her with the first. Such an interpretation makes sense of some very puzzling aspects of the story (particularly in the earlier episodes which Swinburne did not include in his version), suggests an additional reason for what we feel to be the power of the story, and indicates why it is this story which was so important to Swinburne (whose psychological make-up remained unhappy throughout his life) rather than, for example, the story of Lancelot and Guenevere, or of the Grail.

Though one may see, at the deepest level, and beneath conscious intention, such a meaning as giving power to the story, like other symbolic stories it can provide a medium for other meanings, too, and for the deliberate discussion of serious issues. In 'Iseult at Tintagel', which is the climax of the poem, Iseult of Ireland, separated from the now-banished Tristram, is considering her own situation and the degree of guilt to be ascribed to her. Alone on a night of storm, she meditates on the paradox of her sinful love, and weighs her love for God against her guilty love for Tristram, the purity of Christ against her own uncleanness. Can love of such intensity for a mere mortal be itself acceptable to God, and is repentance possible? she asks herself. She does not blame fate or God for the love that came from drinking the love-draught; rather she claims that she has chosen to love Tristram more than God. The conflict in her mind, as she struggles to renounce Tristram so that he will not be damned, is echoed by the fierce storm outside:

> And swordlike was the sound of the iron wind,
> And as a breaking battle was the sea. (p. 97)

The scene rises to a climax as she pleads with God for mercy, and implores Christ to have pity on their sufferings, and the storm becomes more fearful:

> And as man's anguish clamouring cried the wind
> And as God's anger answering rang the sea. (p. 101)

As she prays to bear the weight of all their guilt, Tristram's as well as hers, the storm begins to die down. The intensity of the scene is increased by the irony that at the very moment that Iseult offers herself for Tristram's redemption, he has married Iseult in Brittany, and by the contrast of the harsh and merciless anger of God with the faithful love of Tristram's hound at her side.

Though Swinburne makes use of rather obvious devices such as the storm and the faithful hound to intensify the effect of this section, it contrasts well with the earlier ones and brings into the poem serious matters for consideration which give it a metaphysical dimension that it would otherwise have lacked. To the modern reader the topics under discussion may seem rather academic, but for many of Swinburne's contemporaries they were highly relevant to their own lives. Iseult takes her spiritual situation seriously, and her debate raises her love from the level of mere carnal desire to that of noble and self-sacrificing devotion. Swinburne suggests, not that love of such irresistible force must be morally justifiable, but that love so prepared to sacrifice itself for the sake of another must be a sufficient atonement. In this respect, he is perhaps closer to the medieval trust in the mercy of God, through which in Malory Guenevere and Lancelot are finally saved, than is Tennyson, whose moral indignation is so apparent in both his Tristram and his Lancelot and Guenevere stories. Iseult is so far a Victorian as to see herself as 'unclean till the day I die', but the 'fallen woman' aspect of her story is not stressed.

The poet was reproved by a reviewer for making Tristram talk like a modern young man, instead of like a medieval knight, an accusation which left Swinburne unrepentant, since it had never been his intention to produce a medieval pastiche. The whole argument about responsibility, guilt and atonement presents an interesting example of how Swinburne modernised his story, and attempted to give it new meaning and relevance for his own age. For— contrary perhaps to expectations—anxiety about guilt and future punishment does not feature in the medieval versions of the story, and in *Tristram of Lyonnesse* it is an addition of the nineteenth-century author to meet the tastes of his contemporaries. He further updates the story by stressing Tristram's guilt in terms of a breach of the Ten Commandments instead of a breach of chivalry, or a betrayal of loyalty.

At the very end of the poem, however, Swinburne suggests that the lovers have won forgiveness and peace, for Tristram has put himself in the hands of God. The ending, taken from Thomas's version, is dramatically managed in a way that intensifies the total meaning of the poem. As Iseult of Ireland draws near to the coast of Brittany in the white-sailed ship, Iseult of the White Hands declares to Tristram that the sails are black, and grief kills him before Queen Iseult can land and reach him. We have seen the sweet and loving nature of Iseult of Brittany embittered by the humiliation and frustration of Tristram's refusal to consummate their marriage and his desertion of her; as a consequence, she cannot resist the temptation to revenge herself by deceiving him and thwarting her rival, in the full knowledge of what she is doing. With dreadful irony, as she deceives Tristram at the last, she says to herself, 'I am death'. Iseult of Ireland comes too late, but her identification with Tristram, in death as in life, is proved at once, when 'she felt his death upon her', and 'their four lips became one silent mouth'. The hatred of Iseult of Brittany has hastened Tristram's death, but the love of Iseult of Ireland unites them in death, in a passage reminiscent of Shelley's *Adonais*:

> *nor might now*
> *Fear and desire bid soar their souls or bow.*
> *Lift up their hearts or break them, dread nor disbelief*
> *Touch them with shadowy cold or fiery sting . . .*
> *And round the sleep that fell around them then*
> *Earth lies not wrapped, nor records wrought of men . . .*
> *But all time long the might of all the main*
> *Spread round them as round earth soft heaven is spread,*
> *And peace more strong than death round all the dead.* (pp. 165–6)

They are made one with nature, 'And over them, while death and life shall be, The light and sound and darkness of the sea'. (p. 168)

Swinburne's poem is a fine re-creation of the old story, very much more than a mere re-telling of the tale, for it releases from it new meanings. Charles Williams, writing of Arthurian matters, says that, of nineteenth-century writers, Swinburne 'gets nearest to the tone of Myth'.[26] Swinburne's skilful handling of his source material eliminates what for the modern reader might be considered irrelevant detail, and so is able to focus attention on the main theme, the topic of romantic love and the subsidiary topic of sexual fulfilment. The medieval versions of the story are much concerned with the 'enfances' of Tristram, with his noble origins, his upbringing, his courtly and chivalric accomplishments and adventures, and in the depiction of the heroic society to which he belonged. Though the medieval audience was deeply interested in stories of the power of love, their interest was of a different kind from that of the modern reader, just as the experience of love had a different context, social and spiritual. For Swinburne's contemporaries, the psychological aspects were of greater importance because of their greater awareness of the complexity of the individual's response to experience. Swinburne's treatment of the story eliminates many of the incidents by which medieval authors gave a sense of what was going on in the minds of their protagonists, in order to explore in greater detail through dialogue and soliloquy, their thoughts and emotions, and to give a sense of inner experience through atmospheric imagery, as when, before his battle with his namesake's enemy, Tristram bathes in the sea. Here, images of sea and sun keep the love-theme in the reader's mind:

> but with a cry of love that rang
> As from a trumpet golden mouthed, he sprang,
> As toward a mother's where his head might rest
> Her child rejoicing, toward the strong sea's breast . . .
> . . . and against the tide
> Struck strongly forth with amorous arms made wide
> To take the bright breast of the wave to his
> And on his lips the sharp sweet minute's kiss
> Given of the wave's lip for a breath's space curled
> And pure as at the daydawn of the world. (p. 144)

Here sea-images, earlier in the poem used to suggest Iseult, help to indicate Tristram's longing for her, while the whole episode suggests his virility. At the same time, bride and mother images overlap significantly.

Such a passage would have been impossible for a medieval author. The medieval sources suggested Tristram's manly powers through the details of his upbringing, and through his various martial exploits; the intensity of his love is indicated by his becoming mad. Swinburne is careful to eliminate unromantic as well as extraneous details from his version: the intriguing and plotting of the jealous courtiers, for example, and Tristram's unappealing disguises. By doing so, he focuses attention on the two main characters; even Mark and Brangain play a very minor part. Swinburne thus achieves and maintains a quintessentially romantic tone.

The setting for the medieval versions of the story is a recognisably medieval world, where battles, hunting, feasting and courtly entertainments of various kinds take place. The world of the lovers in Swinburne literally suffers a sea-change, with striking effect and immensely increased symbolic power. The image of the sea dominates the poem as the scene of or background to the action, but also as a symbol for Iseult, as sundering flood and sea of life, as echo of inner conflict and symbol of fluctuating emotion. It not only unifies the poem, but it also gathers up and gives expression to all the romanticism associated with the story: the wild yearning, the overwhelming passion, the calm joy of the moments of fulfilment, the agony of separation, the longing for the ship bearing Iseult at the end. The poem thus establishes its own imaginary world. Perfectly synthesised in imagery and feeling, it draws together past and present in a form that is highly wrought and richly varied.

Though the poem is little read at the present time, the twentieth-century verdict on *Tristram of Lyonnesse* rates it fairly highly. Its reception when it first came out was mixed: the *Saturday Review* thought the story 'better let alone by poets', barbarous and unsuitable for modern treatment, and the poetry sometimes obscure, rhetorical and 'effusively erotic'.[27] The *Spectator* complained that Swinburne's treatment of the subject is not pleasant; he 'paints the sensual appetite with a redundancy and excess that excite disgust'.[28] William Morris 'made two or three attempts to read it' but failed, though 'it certainly did seem very fine.' But he felt that Swinburne's work was founded on literature, not on nature, and so could not 'take serious hold on people'.[29] George Meredith was more enthusiastic in recommending Swinburne to a possible future reviewer—this was in 1873, however, long before *Tristram* appeared—saying: 'Take him at his best he is by far the best—finest poet; truest artist—of the young lot—when he refrains from pointing a hand at the genitals.'[30] F. W. H. Myers writing on Swinburne in the *Nineteenth Century* in January 1893, found in *Tristram* something more than erotic effusions: the poem gives expression to 'the strict materialistic synthesis clad in its most splendid colouring, and its most inexorable scorn of men'.[31] And he asserts that 'Mr Swinburne has presented with singular fire' the resolve 'that even if there be no moral purpose already in the world, man shall put it there'. He did not complain, as other reviewers did, of the tale's expansiveness, but though this was an accusation levelled against it by Oliver Elton in a chapter in his *Modern Studies* (1907),[32] Elton described it as a true romance, in which time is abolished, and the active world a far-off murmur, its subject 'not so much the long-canonised lovers as Love itself'.

Reviewers on the whole tended to prefer the *Tale of Balen*, as a greater poem and better done, and morally unprovocative. Elton liked 'the gusty airs and thrilling scents of his own countryside' which Swinburne captures in his poem. He evidently felt more at ease with its 'proud and manly march', and that 'vigour of the Northern blood, wild-hearted and strong-headed, which befits a teller of tales in rhyme' and saw in it a 'sudden resurrection of lyric Power'.[33] To the modern reader, it comes as an anticlimax, both in form and content, after the strange splendours of *Tristram*.

The story itself, in Malory's version, which Swinburne used, is long, and its complexities hard to follow. Swinburne makes the narrative more straightforward and logical, partly because he gives a sharper focus to the character of Balen. The poem tells how Balen, a knight from the North country, comes to Arthur's court and is insulted there as an outsider by a knight of the court. A fight ensues, the knight is killed, and Balen imprisoned by Arthur for six months. On his release, still under a cloud, he is able to free a damsel from a sword which no other knight can remove from her girdle, and insists on keeping the sword as his lawful prize, despite warnings of impending doom from both her and Merlin. Now he is known as the knight of the two swords and sets out to vindicate his reputation. He overcomes the King of Wales, Arthur's old enemy, slays the evil Garlon and inflicts the dolorous blow on King Pellam with the customary disastrous consequences of creating a Waste Land. Eventually he reaches a castle where he has to fight the champion who guards the island, and exchanges his battered shield for a better one, so that each knight fights an unknown antagonist. Only when they both remove their helmets, being each wounded to death, does each recognise the other as his beloved brother.

Swinburne depicts Balen as a fearless and strongwilled young man, passionately desirous of recognition, who has been jeered at for his North-country origins and scorned by the court. He is obstinate and foolhardy, and the explicit motivation that Swinburne attributes to him leads him from one violent and disastrous encounter to another, heedless of all attempts to save him. There is no attempt to suggest a specific symbolic meaning for the story: it simply presents the working out of the tragic pattern to its end. Unlike *Tristram of Lyonnesse*, it involves no moral problems, and has no particular contemporary relevance. Like Arnold's *Sohrab and Rustum*, it fits into the pattern of family tragedy, poignantly suggesting that literally, or more frequently figuratively, in real life we may destroy those whom we love most through ignorance or folly. Perhaps at a deeper unconscious level of meaning the story is about self-destruction, a conflict within the individual that cannot be resolved. The names of the brothers, Balen and Balan, are so similar as to suggest not two personalities but two aspects of the same person. Born of one womb, dying at the same time, they are identified in birth and death. Balen, in insisting on possessing two swords, is in a sense doubly aggressive, and perhaps represents the overdeveloped, emotionally wilful, aggressive aspect of personality. Almost all his encounters lead to death, for he either deliberately kills or brings about the death of all who cross his path, male or female. His encounter with Pellam destroys the castle and lays waste the land as well as killing the king. He will not give up the sword; he cannot stop destroying, until finally his alter ego Balan is destroyed too. Balan would represent the underdeveloped, stable, protective aspect of personality.

Swinburne's version is rich and effective though too protracted. The action takes place against the background of the passing year, moving from the hopes and promise of spring, to winter, when

> *Aloud and dark as hell or hate*
> *Round Balen's head the wind of fate*
> *Blew storm and cloud from death's wide gate.*

The form is unfortunate. Jogging four-stressed lines in nine-line stanzas, very insistently rhymed, create a trivialising, almost parodic effect. In trying to use a more medieval form, it seems, Swinburne has unintentionally produced a stanza which reminds the reader of Chaucer's 'Sir Thopas'. However, the story is swift-moving, and although unduly weighted with nature-imagery, is not too remote from Malory. The poem gives the modern reader a sense of the medieval world as the nineteenth century saw it, and it presents the scenes of battle with unusual energy. It manages the magic skilfully: Merlin's appearances, and Garlon's invisibility have some credibility in the context which Swinburne creates for them. Perhaps most successful of all is the way in which he synthesises realism and romance, the fairytale and the tragic elements. The mocking of Balen at the beginning motivates his later actions; his eventual coming forward to deliver the maiden from the sword moves the story into the genre of fairy- or folk-tale, for he is the chosen hero, unrecognised and so far despised, whose chance to prove himself has come. A happy ending ought to ensue from this motif, but the realism of Balen's over-reaction to earlier taunts sweeps the story on to its tragic conclusion.

When all is said and done, however, the claim of the poem to recognition depends very much more on the power of the motifs in the source-material than on anything else. It keeps the story alive and suggests the richness still to be found in the Arthurian legend, but it lacks poetic distinction and fails to draw a new, contemporary significance from the traditional matter.

Swinburne, writing in 1872, entered the controversy mentioned earlier on the appropriate subject matter for poetry, and his comments are particularly interesting in relation to his Arthurian poems: 'It is but lost labour that the champions on one side summon us to renounce the present and all its works, and return to bathe our spirits in the purer air and living springs of the past. . . . Art knows nothing of time. . . . To the question "can these bones live?" there is but one answer; if the spirit and breath of art be breathed upon them indeed . . .' He continues, 'the muse is omnipresent and eternal, and forsakes neither Athens nor Jerusalem, Camelot nor Troy, Argonaut nor Crusader, to dwell as she does with equal goodwill among modern appliances in London and New York'.[34] Art knows nothing of time in *Tristram of Lyonesse*, and what for many readers must be the dry bones of the medieval versions of the story are triumphantly brought to new life in Swinburne's vibrant re-interpretation. Like William Morris, but liberated from his constricting influence, Swinburne found new forms for the old stories and gave them a new validity. Like the Pre-Raphaelite painters in another medium, he gave expression to the vision of romantic love characteristic of his time, and by so doing, charted for later periods an important aspect of human experience.

6

Arthur's 'Return' in the New World

American Literature of the Nineteenth and Early Twentieth Centuries

Though less pervasive than the medievalism in nineteenth-century English architecture, art, and letters, medievalism in America was perhaps more striking because of its obvious self-consciousness and purposeful invention. In a landscape devoid of authentic medieval structures or ruins, Gothic buildings—which began to appear as early as the first decade of the century and flourished by the 1830s[1]—brought something entirely new, because 'old', to the face of America. In one sense this emulation of European architectural trends demonstrated the callow state of the building arts in a callow nation. More significantly, however, it also illustrated the young culture's desire to participate in the sophisticated and diverse heritage of western civilisation.

The historical vacuum of the New World turned writers in various ways to European and English material even as they developed an independent and uniquely American literature. Washington Irving, for example (whose brother-in-law built a castle on the Hudson), explained in 1819 that he found in European material, 'mouldering stone' and 'ruined castle', the 'accumulated treasures of age' by which one could 'escape . . . from the commonplace realities of the present' into 'the shadowy grandeurs of the past' ('The Author's Account of Himself', *The Sketch Book of Geoffrey Crayon*). The aesthetic appeal of romance attracted America no less than industrial England, and like Irving, Nathaniel Hawthorne identified 'the difficulty of writing a romance about a country where there is no shadow, no antiquity, no mystery, no picturesque and gloomy wrong, nor anything but a commonplace prosperity' (Preface to *The Marble Faun*, 1860). James Fenimore Cooper (who added battlements to his New York farmhouse) lamented the 'poverty of materials' in America (*Notions of the Americans*, 1828) even as he created an autochthonous literature by wedding native matter to the traditional conventions of romance. His hero of the American frontier, originated in the Leather-Stocking Tales, may be regarded as the knight of medieval romance transplanted to America.

Medievalism in general, and romance in particular, reached nineteenth-century American writers through such widely-read works as Bishop Hurd's *Letters on Chivalry and Romance* (1762), Percy's *Reliques of Ancient English Poetry* (1765–94), George Ellis' *Specimens of Early English Metrical Romances* (1805), the poems and novels of Moore, Byron, Disraeli, Burns, Bulwer-Lytton, and Macpherson, as well as numerous editions of Froissart and Malory.

The major source of American notions of medieval culture was the amazingly popular Walter Scott; in the single decade from 1813 to 1823 American presses printed over five million copies of his Waverley novels. His medievalism sometimes elicited satire, however, as in Washington Irving's *Bracebridge Hall; or, the Humorists* (1822). Written after Irving visited Scott at Abbotsford in 1817 (when the Baronet read to him from 'the old Romance of Arthur'[2]), the work subjects to gentle irony the antiquarianism of a country Squire, who is modelled—like Peacock's Mr Chainmail in *Crochet Castle*—on Scott. The Squire lives in a past of falconry and heraldry. He shares these enthusiasms with the neighbourhood parson, who pores over old tomes that exert 'as intoxicating an effect' on antiquarian bibliophiles 'as the adventures of the heroes of the Round Table' would have 'on all true knights'. Beneath the comedy of such remoteness from contemporary currents, however, Irving reveals the dignity of the Squire's medieval ideals. When he sends his son off to the army, he presents him a biography of the Chevalier Bayard (the fifteenth-century knight reputed to be 'sans peur et sans reproche'). In the volume the Squire inscribes Sir Ector's inspiring eulogy for Lancelot recorded in the final pages of the *Morte Darthur*.

Scott's medievalism, while hardly—as Mark Twain charged—a cause of the Civil War, especially influenced concepts of chivalry in the American South. Early in the century, Southern novelists sometimes satirised popular attempts to practise romanticised notions of knighthood, and they often expressed their criticisms through Arthurian allusions.[3] John Pendleton Kennedy, for example, printed on the title page of his 1832 novel *Swallow Barn*—which may be said to have begun the mode of the 'plantation novel'—part of Caxton's preface to the *Morte Darthur*. He warned that, as romance, the work about to be read should be taken lightly: 'And, for to pass the time, this book shall be pleasant to read in. But for to give faith and believe that all is true that is contained therein, ye be at your own liberty.' The novel laughs at youth's foolish chivalric idealism, and Kennedy twists an echo of Malory into a judgement on the silly courtly wooers of his own day: Malory's purposely naïve pose—'whether they were abed or at other manner of disports, me list not hereof make no mention, for love that time was not as is nowadays' (XX, iii)—becomes 'love, in those days, was not that tame, docile, obedient minion that it is now'. In a similar vein, John Esten Cooke used Arthurian references in his account of *The Youth of Jefferson: Or a Chronicle of College Scrapes* (1854) to criticise exaggerated modern idealisations of women, which one character reasons will promote women's rights. He praises Galahad for having merely loved woman as 'an earthly consoler', rather than adoring her 'as god'.

After the Civil War Southern novelists rarely viewed chivalry with amusement, for knighthood came to epitomise spiritual and religious ideals associated with the defeated Confederacy.[4] They alluded to medieval legend to glorify their fallen leaders and vanished way of life. A novel by Cooke, *Mohun: or, the Last Days of Lee and His Paladins* (1869), illustrates this point and also suggests the importance of Tennyson in familiarising American writers with Arthurian story.

When a Southern colonel contemplates life after the Confederacy's collapse, he describes himself in terms of Tennyson's Bedivere in the 'Morte d'Arthur' (1842) and 'The Passing of Arthur' (1869): 'Jackson dead at Chancellorsville— Stuart at Yellow Tavern—thenceforth I seemed to have lost my support, to grope and totter in darkness, without a guide! These two kings of battle had gone down in the storm, and, like the Knight of Arthur, I looked around me, with vacant and inquiring eyes, asking whither I was now to direct my steps, and what work I should work in the coming years.' Tennyson's influence on Southern novelists continued to the turn of the century, as Thomas Nelson Page's *Gordon Keith* (1903) suggests. Here the idealistic hero moves listeners by reading aloud from the *Idylls*: 'He made you live in Arthur's court, because he lived there himself.'⁵ In his biography of the greatest Southern hero, *Robert E. Lee, Man and Soldier* (1911), Page also refers to Arthurian legend to describe the Confederacy's chivalric ideals: He compares General Lee to 'the mystic White Knight of the Round Table', to 'Launcelot brave' and 'Galahad clean'.

Like these novelists, Sidney Lanier employed Arthurian legend to express Southern chivalric ideals in his popularisation of Malory, *The Boy's King Arthur* (1880; he also wrote a *Boy's Mabinogion*, 1881). Lanier saw Arthurian romance as a means of inspiriting the defeated South by describing chivalry not as a militant way of life but as a philosophical idealism. As he wrote after the war, 'The days of chivalry are not gone, they are only spiritualized . . . the knight of the 19th century fights, not with trenchant sword, but with trenchant soul.'⁶ To mould 'trenchant souls', Lanier retold Malory's stories about heroism, gallantry, and purity, especially emphasising conduct on the tournament and battle grounds and on the Grail quest. He carefully excised all references to passion and adultery in the Launcelot story (although the narrative remarks that Tristram and Isolde love each other), with the result that much of the action involving Launcelot and Guenever seems unmotivated. Lanier underscored his inspirational purposes by inserting a didactic message (reminiscent of Caxton's preface) in the closing account of Launcelot's death. It exhorts readers to view Arthur's and Launcelot's deaths as warnings, and to follow 'those gracious knightly deeds, that is to say, to dread God, and to love righteousness, faithfully and courageously to serve your sovereign prince; and the more that God hath given you the triumphal honour, the meeker ye ought to be, ever fearing the unstableness of this deceitful world'. Besides the stories from Malory, Lanier in an introduction briefly narrated sections of Geoffrey of Monmouth, Layamon, and the *Queste del Saint Graal*. Although he is one of America's more distinguished nineteenth-century poets, Lanier remains most widely known for *The Boy's King Arthur*.

Another important version of Malory had appeared in 1858, Thomas Bulfinch's *The Age of Chivalry, or Legends of King Arthur* (followed in 1862 by a companion volume of French romances, *Legends of Charlemagne*). Besides tales from the *Morte Darthur* such as Guenevere and the Poisoned Apple, Lancelot as Knight of the Cart, and Elaine of Astolat—Bulfinch printed a number of stories from other sources. These include the tale of Tristram's death involving the coloured sails, from Thomas's fragment (retold in such works as John Dunlop's *History of Fiction*); Gawain's marriage to the loathly lady from the ballad 'The Marriage of Sir Gawain' and the romance 'Weddynge of Sir Gawen and Dame Ragnell'; the Perceval story taken from 'Peredur' in the *Mabinogion*; and a story of Caradoc beheading a stranger with whom he agrees to exchange blows (an analogue of *Gawain and the Green Knight*) from the First Continuation of Chrétien's *Perceval*. Besides making available versions of Arthurian tales other than Malory's, Bulfinch's collection became significant in two ways: As a companion to his volume on classical mythology, it indicated the importance that Arthurian material had achieved in America as a body of mythology and 'a treasure-house of poetical material' (Preface): furthermore, it established this eminence before publication of Tennyson's first *Idylls*, which appeared the following year. (Tennyson's library included a copy of Bulfinch's *Legends of King Arthur*.[7])

Even so, during the first half of the century when English poets such as Scott, Wordsworth, and Frere wrote Arthurian works, few American poets used the material. Chief among those who did is Ralph Waldo Emerson. His earliest poetic reference to Arthur appears in a comic song he wrote when he was a student, for a Harvard literary club calling itself 'The Knights of the Square Table' (1819): 'The Knights of King Arthur of chivalrous fame / When the world echoed wide to each champion's name / Yet equalled not Harvard's fraternity fair / But the *Round* Table yields to the fame of the Square.'[8] His journals, notebooks, and early lectures refer to Arthur more seriously as a great hero and a grand literary subject, and reveal Emerson's familiarity with Arthurian material in Geoffrey of Monmouth, Layamon, Malory, Sharon Turner, Joseph Warton, George Ellis, Joseph Ritson, and Robert Southey. Emerson alluded to Arthurian material for purposes quite different from those he attributed to medieval writers. In an 1835 lecture contrasting medieval romance with Greek allegorical 'fable', Emerson observed that 'the whole object' of romance was 'amusement by the incidents of the story itself' rather than 'the discovery of a hidden sense'. He added, however, that although romance aimed to entertain, it 'has often (I may say, always) a moral in spite of itself'.[9] In a later journal entry, he noted that because Tennyson in the first *Idylls* succeeded in extracting meaning—'hidden sense'—from the distant legends and was able to 'universalise his fable', the Laureate had created the long-awaited 'national poem of Arthur' and equalled the work of Homer, Aristophanes, and Dante.[10]

In five poems where Merlin represents the ideal poet, Emerson altogether avoids telling 'incidents of the story' for the sake of 'amusement' and uses Arthurian allusions didactically. 'Politics' merely cites Merlin as a figure of wisdom, whereas 'The Harp' calls up the story of Merlin's enchantment— 'Merlin paying the pain of sin, / Pent in a dungeon made of air.' A pair of poems, 'Merlin I' and 'Merlin II' (1846), depict two aspects of the ideal poet. In the first, Merlin represents the powerful, 'kingly bard' whose spontaneous song 'can make the wild blood start / In its mystic springs', because he smites 'the chords rudely and hard'. The companion poem describes a poet's ordered, controlled capacity for 'subtle rhymes'.

'Merlin's Song' likewise uses Merlin as the ideal bard, counselling mankind to exercise charity and humility. This poem reveals Emerson's acquaintance with Welsh bardic tradition. The speaker who passes on Merlin's wisdom addresses the reader as 'Cyndyllan's son', exhorting him to contemplate his mortality and to eschew concern with material goods. The phrase alludes to an ancient Welsh hero who became a medieval symbol of mutability. His story grew familiar from a series of medieval Welsh elegiac stanzas in which Heledd, Cynddylan's sister, mourns the loss of her family, especially her favourite brother and his great hall. Emerson quotes translations of some elegiac Cynddylan verses in his 1835 lecture, 'Permanent Traits of the English National Genius'. These Welsh verses (collected in the *Red Book of Hergest*) were associated with a similar series attributed in Emerson's day to Llywarch Hen, and he knew them from William Owen's 1792 translation *The Heroic Elegies and Other Pieces of Llywarc-Hen*.[11]

Emerson's acquaintance with such a tradition attests the significance of Welsh legend in transmitting Arthurian story to nineteenth-century writers. While Malory remained the most widely available and familiar source, Emerson—like Peacock and Tennyson, for example—was obviously engaged by the Welsh material. Emerson's indebtedness to Welsh poetry for his conception of Merlin suggests also the origins of an intriguing poem, never published, contained in an early notebook. 'Arthur's Dream' (1821) describes Arthur's brooding vision of giant figures with 'mantled brows' digging 'black and ample' graves which turn out to be their own.[12] The poem would seem to have been suggested by the Welsh 'Stanzas of the Graves' (in the *Black Book of Carmarthen*), a series of seventy-three stanzas referring to the graves of great heroes. These verses, which appear in the *Myvyrian Archaiology of Wales* (1801), are important because they contain what may be the earliest literary reference to Arthur, and the declaration that 'the grave of Arthur will not be known' suggests the legend of his mythic survival. These 'Stanzas of the Graves' (which mention the Cynddylan cited in Emerson's 'Merlin's Song') describe graves in open country like the 'dusky plain' in 'Arthur's Dream' and may have suggested to Emerson the details of 'blood red robes' and giant figures.

More difficult to trace to a medieval source is Emerson's notebook sketch of Arthur as a Grail hero. The king follows two white kids through an enchanted forest in Cornwall to a cave with the Grail sculpted above its entrance. After Arthur disappears into the cave and enters the fabulous palace of the Lady of the Lake, 'long and sorrowfully did the champions of the Round Table bewail the absence of their king'.[13] The French *Perlesvaus*—unlike other medieval narratives—depicts Arthur seeking the Grail, but its details differ considerably from Emerson's. He has fused several motifs familiar from Welsh tradition, such as the white beasts which lead a knight into a supernatural adventure, the enchanted forest, and fairy music. 'Arthur's Dream' and the prose Grail sketch suggest Emerson's unrealised potential as an Arthurian poet, for unlike his Merlin poems, they create scenes of richly evocative imagery and detail which could have been developed as intriguing new episodes in the old legend.

Emerson's contemporary James Russell Lowell wrote one slenderly Arthurian poem, 'The Vision of Sir Launfal' (1848). Lowell, who entitled a collection of literary essays *The Round Table*, had in 1843 written a medieval narrative, 'A Legend of Brittany', which, while not Arthurian, names its villain, a Knight Templar, Modred. Lowell lectured on metrical romances and ballads, wrote about 'romans d'avantures' and lays, and maintained an interest in medieval romance throughout his lifetime. In 1872, for example, he preferred the 'simpleness' of the Anglo-Norman romance *Fergus* (edited by Françisque Michel in 1841 and by E. Martin in 1872) to the artifice of Tennyson's *Idylls*.[14]

'The Vision of Sir Launfal' is only tangentially Arthurian, in that it employs the Grail quest motif elaborated, as Lowell's introductory note specifies, in Book XVII of the *Morte Darthur* and in Tennyson's 'exquisite' poem 'Sir Galahad' (published six years before Lowell's 'Launfal'). Although in medieval romance Launfal belongs to the Round Table, Lowell depicts him in a time after Arthur's reign. The Grail quest of Lowell's knight actually takes place within a dream. Intending to set out on the following morning to seek the Grail, he sleeps among the rushes on the floor and has a 'vision true'. The dream depicts two scenes. The first shows Launfal, a maiden knight, proudly setting forth on his quest and disdainfully tossing a coin to a leper, from whom he inwardly recoils. The second shows Launfal, now an 'old, bent man, worn out and frail', returning unsuccessful from his quest, to an ancestral castle now locked against him. When Launfal humbly shares his last crust of bread and a drink of spring water, the leper who receives his kindness is transformed into Christ. Launfal at this point awakens, having learned from his vision that the Grail symbolises charity, and that it is to be found at home if one willingly shares all he has. The poem anticipates Tennyson's Grail idyll in that serving one's fellows proves to be man's proper quest. But Lowell couches the message in terms reminiscent of English Romanticism: Nature's bounty, bestowed freely on all, contrasts with human pride and materialism.

Lowell probably derived the name of his hero from Thomas Chestre's mid-fourteenth-century verse romance *Sir Launfal*, which had appeared in Joseph Ritson's *Ancient English Metrical Romances* (1802) and Joseph Halliwell's *Illustrations of the Fairy Mythology of A Midsummer Night's Dream* (1845). Lowell also knew Chestre's probable sources, the *Lai de Lanval* by Marie de France, whom Lowell rated among the best medieval writers,[15] and *Graelant*, at that time attributed to Marie. While these works describe the knight's liaison with a fairy mistress rather than a Grail quest, they emphasise Launfal's largesse, the virtue which Lowell's knight acquires. Chestre's romance suggests the pattern of events in Lowell's poem in that the hero is reduced to poverty, then a beneficent supernatural figure restores his fortune, and later he shares his wealth with the disadvantaged—in one instance he provides a feast to fifty poor people.

The poem draws upon traditional Grail stories relatively little, except in using the convention of prophetic dreams or visions which permit questers to glimpse the Grail. Lowell had long esteemed the Perceval legend, however, and his essays especially commend Wolfram's *Parzival*. In 1839 Lowell had announced an intention to change his name to Perceval Lowell, but soon afterwards instead began signing letters with the pen name 'Hugh Perceval'.[16] He had in his library a copy of the *Roman du Saint-Graal*, edited in 1841 by Françisque Michel, whose introduction provides information on Joseph of Arimathea mentioned in Lowell's prefatory note to the poem.[17]

Lowell had criticised medieval Arthurian romance for being 'a procession of armor and plumes, mere spectacle, not vision'—a charge related to his later criticism of Tennyson's *Idylls*. He compared the idylls to 'modern-medieval pictures', which defraud the audience by 'masquerade'; only the costumes are 'genuine'.[18] Despite Launfal's golden spurs and gilded mail and his castle's rush-strewn floor and clanging drawbridge, Lowell's poem provides little medieval costume and quite overtly emphasises 'vision'—in this case messages about the beauties of Nature and the essence of true charity. 'The Vision of Sir Launfal' contributes little to Arthurian tradition. Its strengths lie primarily in lovely but sentimental descriptions of Nature and in numerous pithy pronouncements about charity that remain favourite pieces for schoolroom recitation: 'Not what we give, but what we share, / For the gift without the giver is bare.'

Tennyson's impress on late nineteenth-century Arthurian poetry is as marked in America as in England. Two Arthurian pieces by the minor poet Harry Lyman Koopman (1888) vividly demonstrate this influence. 'The Death of Guinevere' specifically continues the 'Guinevere' of the *Idylls*. Tennyson's novice, now become abbess herself, describes how Guinevere died smiling a greeting to Arthur in heaven. Koopman's sonnet 'My Galahad' actually begins by quoting from Tennyson's 'Holy Grail'—Koopman alters only the last word of Arthur's admonition to Galahad, 'God make thee good as thou art beautiful'. Oscar Fay Adams' *Post-Laureate Idylls* (1886; second series 1906) reveal Tennyson's influence in a quite different way, for while they imitate his manner, they considerably alter his matter. In fairly good Tennysonian blank verse they offer a pastiche of lines from the *Idylls* but tell original stories and introduce characters not in Tennyson's narratives. For example, Adams adds to Tennyson's version of Tristram's death Isolt of Brittany hiding behind a curtain with another woman (Maid Marian, bringing in the Robin Hood legends), who was Tristram's earlier love. Adams also plays with Malory by attributing Sir Ector's eulogy for Lancelot to Sir Bors, because Ector is crying into his handkerchief; and Adams parodies Lowell by writing a 'Vision of Sir Lionel'. Interesting though they may be, these pieces are hardly distinguished. Walt Whitman—who praised Tennyson's *Idylls* as his best work[19]—may have spoken for at least the better American poets of the period when he judged in 'Song of the Exposition' (1871, 1881) that Arthur had 'vanish'd with all his knights, Merlin and Lancelot and Galahad, all gone, dissolv'd utterly like an exhalation' and 'dirged by Tennyson's sweet sad rhyme'. But the poem also declares that the 'lessons of our New World' are 'not to create only, or found only, / But to bring perhaps from afar what is already founded, / To give it our own identity'. Mark Twain was to give a distinctively American identity to Arthurian legend.

i. Mark Twain, *A Connecticut Yankee in King Arthur's Court* (1889)

Mark Twain, in his enduring satire aimed partly at the vogue for Arthuriana, *A Connecticut Yankee in King Arthur's Court*, reacts not only against Tennyson's *Idylls*, but also against more vapid romanticisations of the material, such as Madison J. Cawein's narrative poem *Accolon of Gaul*, published like Twain's novel in 1889. Cawein responded to the great popularity of Arthurian material by looking for new stories to develop. While he alluded to the familiar tale of Merlin's enchantment by Viviane and borrowed from the Tristram legend the motif of a sword between sleeping lovers, Cawein narrated Malory's less familiar story of Accolon, lover of Morgane the Fay (IV, vi–xiv). As in the *Morte Darthur*, the enchantress steals Excalibur and arms Accolon to fight the king. Cawein's poem demonstrated that many Arthurian tales remained to be explored in modern literature. But his flat characterisation and predictable melodrama, overwhelmed by extravagant descriptions, represented precisely the insipid romance that Twain found so irrelevant to modern times.

In his novel, Twain (Samuel Langhorne Clemens), who had already debunked romanticised views of the English Renaissance in *1601* (1880), uses the now familiar literary device of time travel to satirise society through the evaluations of a character from another civilisation and age. The device had been used in nineteenth-century English Arthurian literature only in Peacock's fragment *Calidore*, in which a youth from Arthur's company in Avalon travels by Merlin's magic to nineteenth-century England, where his observations satirise contemporary matters ranging from paper currency to winebibbing clerics. Twain reverses this process by having a nineteenth-century American, Hank Morgan, the head superintendent in a Connecticut arms factory, travel back in time to Arthur's sixth-century court. Once there, Hank uses modern science and technology to displace Merlin as chief magician. He becomes the 'Boss' and for ten years works to turn Arthur's realm into a copy of modern America, with newspapers, telephone and telegraph, steamboats and bicycles, a military academy and Sunday schools. After the final battle between Mordred and Arthur, Hank declares the land a republic with himself as its head. But the traditonal forces oppose him, and though the Boss with a handful of youths defeats 25,000 knights, Merlin casts him into an enchanted sleep. In the modern introduction, he has awakened from this sleep in nineteenth-century England. Unlike Peacock's *Calidore*, which criticises only the society being inspected by the naïve visitor, *Connecticut Yankee* satirises not only the medieval world—and contemporary literary treatments of it—but also the modern world of the protagonist and the author.

Twain's concern is with human nature in all ages. In a draft for his preface, he identified the subject as laws and customs from 'several Christian countries and various Christian centuries'.[20] Because such social practices existed in 'far later times, it is safe to consider that it is no libel upon the sixth century to suppose them to have been in practice in that day also'. He used such varied sources as histories of the French Revolution and of slavery in the American South. His

Arthurian material, however, comes directly from Malory. He may have been acquainted with the *Morte Darthur* from a copy of Sidney Lanier's abridgement, *The Boy's King Arthur*, published shortly before the Twain household ordered it in 1880. But his Arthurian interest was particularly stimulated in 1884, when his friend George Washington Cable gave him a copy of Malory. Twain and Cable, then touring together to give joint readings from their works, began playing with Malory's story and style. Twain took to addressing the travelling manager of the tour as 'Sir Sagramore le Desirous', and wrote to his wife that 'we have all used the quaint language of the book in talk in the cars and hotels'. Though Twain was generally hostile to romanticism, he frankly revered some aspects of the *Morte Darthur*. In his 1885 speech memorialising President Ulysses S. Grant, he quoted extensively from Ector's noble eulogy for Launcelot, and in the next year he described his intentions for *Connecticut Yankee*: 'I shall leave unsmirched & unbelittled the great and beautiful *characters* drawn by the master hand of old Malory', and 'should grieve indeed' if the climactic incidents 'should lose their pathos & their tears through my handling'.

The work as it finally evolved, however, subjects Malory's matter and manner to broad comedy and pointed satire. Twain's lengthy quotations from the *Morte Darthur*—all taken from Sir Edward Strachey's version of the Globe edition (one of the issues after 1869, when Strachey included a name index used by Twain)—reveal his comic and parodic techniques. Although Twain condensed some passages, the quotations are reproduced virtually verbatim, except for two bowdlerisations: 'So god me help' becomes 'truly', and 'clave him to the navel' becomes 'clave him to the middle'. The first extended quotation is presented 'straight', as a passage describing Launcelot's exploits which the narrator (presumably Twain) reads in the *Morte Darthur* (VI, xi) just before he meets the Yankee who has written the fantastic account of his life at Arthur's court.

From this point, however, Twain either attributes the passages from Malory to characters whose personalities heighten the comedy or quotes them as newspaper accounts, humorous anachronisms in the sixth century. For example, Merlin, a pompous windbag, narrates the story of Arthur's receiving Excalibur from the Lady of the Lake (*Morte Darthur*, I, xxiii). He puts everyone to sleep because he has told the tale so many times before. Two tales appear as newspaper columns. One describes a tournament (*Morte Darthur*, VII, xxviii); the other, purporting to be the earliest example of 'war correspondence', tells the story of Arthur's killing Mordred (*Morte Darthur*, XXI, iv). The baldest comedy develops in two stories put into the mouth of the damosel Alisande, 'Sandy', the chatterbox for whom Hank undertakes a quest and then, according to chivalric custom, eventually marries. Coming from Sandy, these two stories, one reciting the adventures of Gawaine and Uwaine (*Morte Darthur*, IV, xvi–xviii), and the other the adventures of Sir Marhaus (IV, xxiv–xxv), seem to be inane chatter. Hank's interjections and questions, by contrasting his acid sarcasm and breezy colloquialism with Sandy's (Malory's) romanticism and archaism, heighten the comedy. Besides quoting these passages, Twain also uses numerous details, situations, and names from Malory, as when he refers to

Guenever's interest in Launcelot or the legend of Gawaine's strength daily waxing and waning, when he summarises the denouement of the *Morte Darthur* (XX – XXI), or ludicrously composes a baseball team of Arthur's foes named throughout the *Morte Darthur*.

The borrowings from Malory satirise not only the improbable content of medieval romance, but also its style, its repetition and stilted language. As Hank evaluates Sandy's storytelling: 'these archaics are a little *too* simple; the vocabulary is too limited, and so, by consequence, descriptions suffer in the matter of variety; they run too much to level Saharas of fact, and not enough to picturesque detail; this throws about them a certain air of the monotonous; in fact the fights are all alike. . . . You can't tell one fight from another nor who whipped who; and as a *picture*, of living, raging, roaring battle, sho! why, it's pale and noiseless—just ghosts scuffling in a fog.' This last image, recalling the fog in Tennyson's description of the 'last weird battle in the west', points out that Twain was burlesquing not only medieval romance but also nineteenth-century idealisations of Arthurian matter.

Material in his notebooks demonstrates that Twain had Tennyson much in mind as he worked on the novel. He once planned an episode showing Hank in a bardic competition with contestants reciting poems by Tennyson—'Break, Break, Break', 'The Fair Maid of Astolat', and 'some exploit of Launcelot . . . from Idyls'. In the earliest version of the novel to be made public, a selection read by Twain to a gathering of the Military Service Institute in late 1886, he had Launcelot, on a quest, discover a 'college of princesses', parodying Tennyson's 1847 poem, *The Princess*, with its medieval university for women. Daniel Beard's illustrations for *Connecticut Yankee* also satirise the poet of the *Idylls*, whose portraits provided models for Merlin. In the final version of the novel, Twain echoes 'The Lady of Shalott' by referring to Sandy 'when she went down to Camelot', and more strikingly, echoes the *Idylls*. When Hank assesses his power at Camelot—'I was no shadow of a king; I was the substance, the king himself was the shadow'—he recalls Merlin's comments regarding Arthur's substance, 'Some there be that hold / The King a shadow, and the city real' ('Gareth and Lynette').

Beneath the obvious fun of literary parody and burlesque, Twain's principal intention in the novel was to condemn economic and social servitude and the repression of rigid class systems. His depiction of the downtrodden masses sometimes descends to melodrama, as when a young mother hangs for stealing to feed the infant she clasps to her breast on the gallows. But he effectively contrasts the essentially foolish, idle, and destructive nobility, who seem at times to be lovable children playing games, with the much abused peasantry. This attack on monarchy and aristocracy was the element of the work most vigorously emphasised by early publicity and reviews. Brochures soliciting advance subscriptions for the book appealed to American pride in the superiority of their democracy over the decadent English class system by describing the novel as 'a book that appeals to all true Americans'. The publisher said the work aimed 'to show that true nobility is inherent, not inherited; that birth confers no rights not sustained by nature'. Playing up the 'satire on English nobility and royalty', Twain insisted in an excessively vigorous letter to his London publisher, Andrew Chatto, that if necessary he would seek another publisher and pay publishing costs from his own pocket to insure that no word of his text be altered to lessen its sting for English readers. 'The book was not written for America, it was written for England. So many Englishmen have done their sincerest best to teach us something for our betterment, that it seems to me high time that some of us should . . . pry up the English nation to a little higher level of manhood in turn.' This sarcasm expressed American annoyance—especially Twain's—at such English attitudes as those of Matthew Arnold, who remarked the cultural impoverishment of America and had cited Twain as an example of rude and childish Yankee humour. (Arnold had recently criticised Twain's favourite, Ulysses Grant, for abusing *shall* and *will*. In an early draft of *Connecticut Yankee* Twain had in turn allowed the crude American to instruct the English Sandy in this grammatical refinement.)

While advance publicity chauvinistically played up the work's attack on the aristocracy, however, this is but one object of Twain's satire. Another major target is organised religion, and the superstition and conformity it fosters. Twain directed his publisher not to mention this subject in the advertising, because he wanted 'to catch the reader unwarned, & modify his views if I can'. Other topics for satire include contemporary issues ranging from protective tariffs to the spoils system in political appointments. Thus, though the work burlesques romanticised views of the Middle Ages and exposes medieval barbarism, the principal targets are dark aspects of human nature which are limited to no particular age or culture—greed, hypocrisy, sham, superstition, brutality. As the work progresses, moreover, it becomes increasingly apparent that contemporary culture—American perhaps more than British—is the primary subject. Referring frequently to the social injustices of pre-Revolutionary France, Twain overtly attacks not only slavery but the no less real servitude of workers in modern factories. (One of Beard's illustrations pointedly juxtaposes three pictures: a medieval king with a chained serf, a modern slave owner with a bound Black, and a wealthy capitalist with a factory worker.) Although the novel ostensibly celebrates the ingenuity and creativity of modern science and technology, it increasingly reveals that apparent advances have also heightened man's destructive capabilities. All Hank Morgan's creative endeavours end in mass slaughter, extinguishing the modern culture he has wrought. Ironically, the destructiveness of modern inventions resides not only in gunpowder and electricity, but also in modern capitalism. Twain traces the fall of Camelot, and ultimately of Hank's 'modern' society, to Launcelot's manipulations of the economy. When his great profits anger the other knights of the Round Table Stock Exchange, they tell Arthur of Guenever's adultery and, as in Malory, calamity ensues.

Twain underscored the barbarism which associates modern man with his medieval antecedents by linking his nineteenth-century Yankee to the evil

Morgan le Fay. Though in early versions of the narrative Twain named his protagonist Peters, Robert Smith, and Hank Smith, by 1887 he purposefully changed the name to Morgan. By echoing the name of the enchantress, he suggests that despite the humanity that the Boss exhibits throughout the narrative, his scientific resourcefulness should finally be seen in the same context as the machinations of the evil magician. Hank, whom Twain described as 'a perfect ignoramus', by the end of the story has subordinated all finer impulses to egotism, hunger for power, and destructiveness. Though he speaks in humanitarian terms, he kills without compunction. His powers quite literally turn men into weapons: armoured knights who are electrocuted by his fence kill the friends who attempt to rescue them, and the 25,000 corpses imprison the Boss and his few remaining followers. Grotesquely, the putrefaction of decaying bodies will finally kill all survivors of the fray.

Apparently Twain had initially envisioned using medieval material for a happy farce rather than so dark a satire. He described the germ of the novel in an 1883 notebook entry: 'Dream of being a knight errant in armor in the middle ages. Have the notions & habits of thought of the present day mixed with the necessities of that. No pockets in the armor. . . . Can't scratch. Cold in the head—can't blow—can't get at handkerchief, can't use iron sleeve. . . . Always getting struck by lightning. Fall down, can't get up.' While this sketch ultimately developed into a delightful comic chapter on Hank's difficulties with his suit of armour, such geniality diminishes throughout *Connecticut Yankee*. For many readers, especially for English reviewers, the combination of farce, frontier humour, and grim irony with a starkly unromantic picture of Arthur and his court seemed grave iconoclasm after the *Idylls of the King*. One English reviewer commented, 'A book . . . that tries to deface our moral and literary currency by bruising and soiling the image of King Arthur, as left to us by legend and consecrated by poetry, is a very unworthy production of the great humorist's pen.'[21] Another declared that 'an attack on the ideals associated with King Arthur is a coarse pandering to that passion for irreverence which is at the basis of a great deal of Yankee wit'. Such readers were particularly sensitive to Twain's portrayal of Arthur, who initially appears as a moral child. But the novel actually reveals the king's essential nobility. In contrast to Hank, who merely speaks humanely, Arthur without any consciousness of caste or personal danger tenderly carries a peasant child dying of smallpox.

Critics also objected to Twain's treatment of the Grail quest, which Hank describes in typically bumptious terms: 'The boys all took a flier at the Holy Grail now and then. It was a several-years' cruise. They always put in the long absence snooping around, in the most conscientious way, though none of them had any idea where the Holy Grail really was, and I don't think any of them actually expected to find it, or would have known what to do with it if he *had* run across it. . . . Every year expeditions went out holy grailing and next year relief expeditions went out to hunt for *them*. There was worlds of reputation in it, but no money.' This prompted the reviewer for the *Pall Mall Gazette* to inveigh against Twain's vulgarisation of 'the symbol—in the old romance—of individual effort to arrive at perfection in personal life, to attain to high, unselfish, irreproachable conduct'.

Actually Twain's satire goads men towards precisely such goals. He prods with laughter, which he elsewhere described as the 'one really effective weapon' that can blow a 'colossal humbug' 'to rags and atoms at a blast' (*The Mysterious Stranger*). Although Twain had originally declared that he had no intention of ever publishing *Connecticut Yankee*, 'or any other book', and would lazily pursue it for himself, writing three chapters a year for the next thirty years, financial need prompted him to publish it only five years after he recorded the first farcical sketch in his notebook. But one may speculate that even without financial exigencies, his brooding over such matters as 'the thing in man which makes him cruel to a slave' would have compelled him to vent his thoughts in print. As he wrote to his friend and literary adviser William Dean Howells, he was generally satisfied with the *Connecticut Yankee*, but he recognised that he could never fully express the things that 'burn in me', for 'they would require a library—& a pen warmed-up in hell'. Such sentiments emphasise that even though critics of the day consistently contrasted Twain's work with Tennyson's Arthurian story, he no less than the Laureate used the legends to illustrate the evil in man and to teach 'the need of the Ideal'.

Like the *Idylls*, *A Connecticut Yankee in King Arthur's Court* spawned a number of imitations and adaptations, but they generally copied only the comedy and ignored Twain's serious purposes. The most popular adaptations have been movies, beginning with a silent film in 1921 (with Harry C. Myers as the Yankee) and sound versions in 1931 (with Will Rogers) and in 1949 (a musical with Bing Crosby). In 1927 Richard Rogers and Lorenz Hart staged a musical version which ran for more than 400 performances, and in 1943 they staged a new version with the Yankee an officer in the Navy. In recent years the American public has endured an animated cartoon of the 'Connecticut Rabbit in King Arthur's Court' and a Walt Disney film originally entitled 'Unidentified Flying Oddball' (1979, starring Denis Dugan as a NASA engineer and Kenneth More as King Arthur), re-released on television as 'The Spaceman in King Arthur's Court' (1982). At best these films and plays may be described as trivial parodies of a far superior satire.

ii. Richard Hovey, *Launcelot and Guenevere: A Poem in Dramas* (1891–1907)

While advertisements for *A Connecticut Yankee in King Arthur's Court* proudly proclaimed 'it will be to English nobility and royalty what Don Quixote was to ancient chivalry', the poet Richard Hovey soon began publishing serious verse dramas in which he intended that 'all trace of the Don Quixote flavor . . . be eliminated' from Arthurian story.[22] Like England, America in the last two decades of the nineteenth century and first three of the twentieth produced a large number of Arthurian dramas. Many of these American works were written

174

for limited and local audiences—as school and camp plays, exercises in drama classes, and radio broadcasts—and few were actually published. The plays of Richard Hovey deserve mention less for their accomplishment than for his grand conception.

Best known for three volumes of *Songs from Vagabondia* (1894–1901), written in collaboration with Bliss Carman, and for his translations of Maurice Maeterlinck, Hovey viewed Sidney Lanier as a spiritual mentor and once received a laurel crown from Lanier's widow. He intended his greatest work to be an ambitious series of Arthurian dramas, three trilogies collectively entitled *Launcelot and Guenevere: A Poem in Dramas*. Of the nine plays planned, only four were completed when Hovey died in 1900 at the age of thirty-five. Three years before he published the first dramas, he had alluded to Arthurian story in a sonnet, 'Launcelot and Gawaine' (written 1888, published 1898), which cites Launcelot as a paragon of fidelity and Gawaine as an emblem of inconstancy. A decade later he echoed this view of Gawaine in another sonnet, 'The Last Love of Gawaine' (written 1898, published 1908). These slight pieces suggest that for Hovey the greatest interest in Arthurian material lay in the psychological dimensions inherent in the characters' situations.

In the dramatic cycle, each trilogy was to begin with a musical masque that highlighted the supernatural content of the legends and suggested themes of a succeeding tragedy and of a third drama which in some way resolved the conflicts elaborated in the tragedy. The introductory masque, *The Quest of Merlin* (1891), shows the magician in Avalon seeking prophetic advice about Arthur's marriage. He learns that the union will bring disaster to the realm. But the masque ends with soliloquies by three stars—representing Arthur, Launcelot, and Guenevere. They suggest that for each of the three characters, apparent defeat will lead to some higher reward.

Although the notes written by Hovey's widow suggest his general indebtedness to Arthurian tradition, principally to Malory, they also emphasise his innovations. This masque joins to Arthurian material figures from classical and Northern mythology and fairy lore, creating a mixture more competently written but no less incongruous than John Thelwall's *Fairy of the Lake*. At Mount Hecla Merlin questions the 'Norns', then passes magically to Avalon, where he meets Pan, Bacchus, and Aphrodite, with various Sylphs, Naiads, and Dryads, as well as the Valkyrs, Mab, Puck, Oberon, and a good measure of Christian angels. Hovey's 'Schema and Commentary' for the series, written in 1898, claims that *The Quest of Merlin* 'symbolically . . . suggests the *philosophical* drift' of the whole poem of nine plays; its meaning, however, remains obscure. In terms of Arthurian story, the masque is most interesting for its view of the harmonious relationship between Merlin and Nimue, his prophetic guide as well as his beloved.

When Hovey treats Arthurian story without supernatural embellishment, following his intention to focus on 'the psychological problem' illustrated by the Launcelot and Guenevere story, he succeeds rather better. This central problem is the conflict between individual and social values: 'Launcelot and Guenevere are

175

placed in a position where they must either sacrifice the existing order of things to themselves or themselves to the existing order of things' ('Commentary'). *The Marriage of Guenevere: A Tragedy* (1891) combines accounts of Arthur's marriage and of his conflict with Rome to show the intricate connections between private and public matters. This issue is first suggested when Arthur must choose whether to undertake two missions to ensure the public welfare or hasten to his wedding. Though in this instance he dispatches Launcelot to handle one matter and postpones the other for a day, this play and the next one show Arthur approximating the Tennysonian ideal of social responsibility, acting as king before husband. (Ironically, Hovey preferred the Arthurian works of Swinburne, who celebrates individualism, to those of Tennyson, whose Arthur, he felt, lacked human and tragic appeal.[23]) Launcelot and Guenevere, on the other hand, in this drama put personal fulfilment before public commitments. To Hovey their tragedy lies in 'Love overthrowing friendship as well as more general social obligations' ('Commentary'). Actions of less central characters also develop this theme. Morgause, for example, tries to exact personal revenge on Arthur by allying herself with Roman spies to unsettle his rule.

Although Hovey draws primarily from Malory, he features several situations from other sources. Most notably he develops the role of Galehault found in the Vulgate Prose *Lancelot* (edited 1867–77), where the knight arranges the meeting between Lancelot and Guenevere which initiates their love affair. (Dante commemorated this role of Galehault as a dignified Pandarus in the *Inferno*, where Paolo and Francesca are enticed to kiss by the Lancelot romance which becomes their own 'Galeotto'.)

In a striking innovation to traditional story, Hovey partially justifies the relationship of Launcelot and Guenevere by asserting that they fell in love two years before her marriage, when Launcelot, exhausted and starving, was rescued by Guenevere and her fool Dagonet. (Hovey also invents Dagonet's service to Guenevere before she marries Arthur.) From that moment, Launcelot has loved her and dedicated his glorious achievements to this unknown 'Lady of the Hills'. (This extenuating circumstance calls to mind Reginald Heber's excusing of the lovers with a prior association.) Hovey similarly romanticises the traditional story by depicting Guenevere as the virgin 'bride' of her spiritual mate Launcelot. To this end, Hovey borrows from the Tristram legend the motif of the sword placed between a sleeping couple. Arthur, sensitive to his bride's trepidation on her wedding night, places Excalibur between them, then rushes away early the next morning to quell Mark's uprising. Although Hovey's inventions generally romanticise traditional material, his details sometimes challenge late Victorian decorum. Galehault, encouraging Launcelot to declare his love, introduces an element of sexuality in a heretofore abstract relationship: 'Can / You calmly think that even your friend of friends, / Lacking her heart, should call her body his, / Should sting that throat with kisses and—?' A scene in the next drama in the sequence shows the Emperor Lucius, who has captured the queen as she travels to Rome, forcibly kissing her. Guenevere, revolted to the point of inarticulateness, repulses him: 'Ah!—Oh! . . . oh! . . . thou hast dared—thou . . . Gah!' Tepid in contrast to the open sexuality in Malory, even this limited frankness is surprising in Hovey's plays, for they otherwise react against the vogue for realism recently initiated by continental dramatists. In an essay, 'The Passing of Realism', which appeared in 1895, between publication of *The Marriage of Guenevere* and his next Arthurian drama, Hovey defended the importance of realism but noted its deficiencies in beauty: 'Art having forgotten the earth too long, needed to sprawl upon it for a while for refreshment. It is a good thing as a phase, tho in itself something unpleasant. It is an attitude of fatigue and fatigue is usually un-beautiful.' He continued, 'We must have the real; but we must portray it as . . . the process of the ideal, not as a meaningless and empty husk.'[24] Throughout his dramas he pursues realism in his characters' states of mind, but he also strives for idealising, beautifying effects. These in turn diminish the power of his characterisation.

Although *The Marriage of Guenevere* ends with Arthur staunchly defending Launcelot and Guenevere against Morgause's charges of adultery, the next play in the series, *The Birth of Galahad: A Romantic Drama* (1898) begins by showing the public and private difficulties produced by their love. Hovey departs from tradition by having Guenevere bear Launcelot's child, Galahad. Although *The Birth of Galahad* emphasises the moral and ethical problems created by the love affair, the birth of the Grail knight consecrates the lovers' union. To harmonise this innovation with the traditional story that Elaine, daughter of Pelles, bears Launcelot's son, Hovey introduces Ylen, Guenevere's life-long friend. She protects the lovers by pretending that Galahad is her son. (This situation may owe something to Hovey's personal circumstances. His liaison with an older, married woman—later his wife—had in 1892 produced a son, who was discreetly left in the care of a foster mother.)

Hovey's second major innovation in *The Birth of Galahad*, continuing the story of the preceding play, intertwines the fortunes of Launcelot and Guenevere with Arthur's war against Rome. Here the Romans, nearly defeated by Arthur, intercept Guenevere's letter notifying Launcelot of Galahad's birth. They later capture the queen en route to Rome. With the letter and the queen, the Emperor Lucius tries to blackmail Launcelot into betraying Arthur. This dilemma intensifies the conflict between Launcelot's loyalties to Arthur and to the queen. Both fidelities survive, however, when Launcelot kills Lucius and the Britons capture Rome. Thus the play partly resolves the tragedy of *The Marriage of Guenevere*. It shows, in Hovey's words, 'Love still supreme, but seeking and partly finding a way to be loyal to friendship and the State, too.' His principal inventions—Guenevere's plight as the mother who must conceal her love child and Launcelot's dilemma over how to save Guenevere from Lucius without betraying Arthur—expand the possibilities for complex psychological explorations. But Hovey's style vitiates the potential power of such situations. Striving for Shakespearian effects, he achieves only melodrama.

The fourth play completed by Hovey, like *The Quest of Merlin* an operatic masque which blends classical, medieval, and Christian supernatural, presents a muddled, vaguely Shelleyan aesthetic mysticism. *Taliesin: A Masque* (1899) relates the quest for poetic inspiration—represented by Taliesin, the bard who seeks to fill Merlin's now vacant place at Camelot—to the quest for spiritual perfection represented by Percival, a youth who has just been knighted. Hovey takes the Taliesin figure from Welsh tales (especially the account in Charlotte Guest's *Mabinogion*), which associate him with Elphin, whose land has been inundated by the sea. Hovey's young, untested Percival derives from the legend found in Chrétien de Troyes, Wolfram von Eschenbach, and the Welsh tale 'Peredur' in the *Mabinogion*. (Hovey gives Guenevere a brother named Peredure.) But Hovey also draws on Tennyson in that Percival has left Camelot because he is 'heartsore with the scandals of the court'.

With Taliesin, Percival arrives at the Graal Chapel of King Evelac, the King of Sarras from the Vulgate *Estoire del Saint Graal* (edited in 1861–63 by F. J. Furnivall for the Roxburgh Club and even earlier, in 1841, by Françisque Michel. Evelac's story is also narrated briefly in the *Morte Darthur*, XIV, iii–iv). Percival partially glimpses the Grail, and Taliesin hears from a host of supernatural figures—including Apollo, the nine Muses, and 'the Seven Angels who see God continually'—a fuzzy philosophy about love and art. Throughout the play the significance of the Grail remains unclear. Nimuë symbolises artistic inspiration, especially in a scene doubtless titillating but difficult to stage at the century's end. Her clothing seems 'to melt away into draperies of light', becoming a mist that dissipates, 'leaving the goddess manifest in her beauty'. Although a contemporary critic described the masque as 'a poet's poem', its aesthetic doctrine remains vague.

Fragments of the remaining five dramas, published posthumously in 1907, and the sketch he made in 1898 indicate that Hovey intended to treat the stories of the Grail (showing the failure of attempts to renounce love through religious devotion), the Maid of Astolat (depicting the 'gradual reconquest of love over religion'), the death of Arthur ('essential conflict made objective and settled with the sword'), and, finally, the king's passage to Avalon (showing a 'true harmonic solution'). In the last speech of the nine plays—which was actually the first passage of the series to be written (1889)—Launcelot observes that 'now mine eyes look out / At peace upon a peaceful universe. / . . . our sins are but God's thunderclouds, / That hide the glorious sun a little while; / And afterwards the fields bring forth their fruit.'

Hovey's dramas command attention chiefly for their overall conception, as ambitious as Tennyson's plan for the *Idylls* had been, of a series of full-length dramas recounting much of the Arthurian cycle. Despite some indebtedness to details and attitudes found in Tennyson, however, Hovey's work diverges from the Laureate's in its primary theme. Tennyson stressed the importance of the individual's commitment to society. Hovey recognised the threat to the public well-being posed by personal desires, yet he urged society to accommodate individual freedom. In adumbrating such 'modern' themes, the dramas promise more interest for twentieth-century readers than they sustain. Early passages indicate, for example, that the plays will explore the issue of women's limited roles in society. Guenevere was, for Hovey's day, in many ways the 'new woman'. But when the queen begins to love Launcelot, her desire for greater freedom and greater responsibility quickly vanishes. Finally, Hovey's dramas remain significant for their possible influence on the Arthurian works of Edwin Arlington Robinson.

Between Hovey's dramas and Robinson's works, continuing interest in Arthurian story produced several brief and generally undistinguished poems by writers who achieved popularity or critical acclaim for their non-Arthurian verse. Sara Teasdale, whose later lyrics explore emotions with great delicacy, creates in 'Guenevere' (1911) a competent monologue, uttered at Amesbury, that attributes the queen's loss of everything to only one 'night and day' of love. A slighter lyric in the same collection depicts Iseult of Ireland's pain but confirms that she would exchange places with 'no woman born'. James Whitcomb Riley, whose reputation as an Indiana dialect poet and folksy humorist makes him a rather unlikely Arthurian, likewise wrote an Almesbury monologue, 'Guenevere' (1913). Edgar Lee Masters, justly noted for his con-centrated psychological analysis in *The Spoon River Anthology*, failed to exercise this special talent when treating Arthurian characters in two ballad-like poems (1916) that closely follow Malory. The 'Ballad of Launcelot and Elaine' narrates the knight's encounter with Pelles' daughter, and 'The Death of Sir Launcelot' only slightly alters Malory's account of the deathbed vision.

In 1921 Edna St Vincent Millay published 'Elaine', a lyric in which Elaine of Astolat poignantly implores Lancelot to visit her, and in an untitled sonnet cited Isolde and Guinevere as women who risked disaster for love. The most incon-gruous among these short Arthurian works by poets of some reputation are two published by Vachel Lindsay in 1923. Best known for poems that exploit noise and action rather than subtlety, Lindsay becomes oppressively didactic with his Arthurian references. 'Galahad, Knight Who Perished', which invokes the ideal of male chastity, is 'dedicated to all Crusaders against the International and Interstate Traffic in Young Girls'. 'King Arthur's Men Have Come Again', which he wrote 'while a field-worker in the Anti-Saloon League of Illinois', cites Arthur, Cromwell, and Abraham Lincoln as righteous conquerors. Measured against such trivial poems, the three major Arthurian poems by Edwin Arlington Robinson seem striking indeed.

iii. Edwin Arlington Robinson, *Merlin* (1917); *Lancelot* (1920); *Tristram* (1927)

Robinson's long poems remain the most distinguished Arthurian works yet produced in America. Although he took the framework of his stories from Malory, he echoed and artfully reshaped materials from the Vulgate *Merlin* (probably known through a modern synopsis), Arnold, Morris, Tennyson, Swinburne, Wagner, and even Hovey.[25] But Robinson took his people from life, and every aspect of the works unfolds through character. Actions which Malory details Robinson reveals obliquely through characters' reactions; psychological revelation replaces narrative, and dialogue conveys plot, theme, even symbolism. Poised as he was between reticent Victorians and symbolic modernists, Robinson realistically probed the psychological complexities inherent in the legendary characters' situations to a degree unsurpassed by Arthurian writers either before or since. Although he wrote in blank verse (often metrically strained), Robinson may be said to treat the legends in the manner of a realistic novelist. Remembering that with the exception of comedy and satire—as in the works of Thomas Love Peacock and Mark Twain, and in the twentieth century, James Branch Cabell and John Erskine—Arthurian lore had since Malory remained the province of poets and verse dramatists, we may better recognise Robinson's achievement by viewing him (in Vachel Lindsay's terms) as a 'novelist distilled into a poet'.

Publication of the poems spanned a decade, even though Robinson conceived them as a trilogy and wrote the first two in relatively quick succession. At the time he began *Lancelot*, in 1917, he already had *Tristram* fermenting 'in pickle'.[26] Both *Lancelot* and *Tristram* remained in pickle for years, however, because *Merlin* proved unsuccessful commercially. But if the vogue for long poems on legendary subject matter seemed to his wary publishers to have been exhausted, Robinson's treatment proved otherwise. When it appeared a decade after *Merlin*, *Tristram* (1927) quickly became a great financial and critical success. Featured as the Literary Guild's Book of the Month, it went through many reprintings in the first year (sources variously report from twelve to twenty) and won Robinson his third Pulitzer Prize.

But the contemporary significance of the poems at first eluded some critics. Because Robinson's earlier poetry had concentrated so thoroughly on modern men and women in complex contemporary situations, his using medieval matter initially surprised reviewers. One, discussing *Lancelot*, commented that although Robinson had 'expanded' reality in his previous verse, he had 'suddenly put about it, on the outer edge, a ring of white vision, figuring it with the stars of a vague and remote legend'.[27] But as Robinson treats it, the legend remains neither starry nor remote. His creating multi-dimensional, intricate characters and subordinating the events so much emphasised in medieval romance reflect his preference, expressed in 1895, for 'the romance of the commonplace—without any guns or swords or cavaliers to speak of'.[28] His first long Arthurian piece derived from Malory ('devoured' by Robinson at the age of seventeen[29]) depicts Lancelot escaping from the queen's chamber and rescuing her from the flames amid a good deal of slaughter, without swords or cavaliers. He reveals the events by having Gawaine and Bedivere discuss their feelings about them. And although Lamorak appears as a stalwart man of action, 'of oak and iron', we see him engaged only in discourse. Robinson is able to tell his story in this oblique way, often through relatively minor characters, only because the legends had become so well known. Within the familiar, his purposeful alterations of incidents, details, and characters achieve new emphases.

Robinson distills the 'commonplace', or the universal in human experience, by removing the magical and mystical. Only five years before T. S. Eliot was to emphasise the contemporary relevance of mythic aspects, Robinson stripped away potions, enchantments, and the two features most popular later in the twentieth century, the magic of Merlin and the mystical associations of the Grail. Robinson's pruning exposes the timeless, and therefore timely, applicability of the legend to a world involved in the 'Great War'. Countering reviewers' dismay over the medieval subject matter, he insisted that *Merlin*, published in the year the United States entered World War I, and *Lancelot*, published two years after the armistice, depicted the contemporary chaos and impending collapse of western civilisation: the poems 'were suggested by the world war—Camelot representing in a way the going of a world that is now pretty much gone'. Even more pointedly, Lancelot in the poems 'may be taken as a rather distant symbol of Germany, though the reader will do well not to make too much of this'.[30]

Merlin, dramatising the eve of Camelot's fall when Arthur confronts the adultery of Lancelot and Guinevere, analyses how individuals destroy civilisations: Lancelot 'makes war / Of love'; Arthur, 'being bitten to the soul / By love and hate . . . / Makes war of madness'; Gawaine, avenging his brothers, 'makes war of hate'; Modred 'makes war of his ambition'—'And somewhere in the middle of all this / There's a squeezed world that elbows for attention.' Even though Bedivere, an idealistic supporter of the king and state, refuses to believe that 'the world, / Now rocking', can 'go down in sound and blood / And ashes and sick ruin, . . . for the sake / Of three men and a woman', the wise fool Dagonet recognises that because of individual actions, the entire world has become 'a disease without a doctor'.

Robinson's Dagonet, who astutely judges the situation at Camelot, owes a good deal to Tennyson's character. His recognition that 'If you see what's around us every day, / You need no other showing to go mad', destroys his mirth. Like the Fool in 'The Last Tournament', who sobs at Arthur's feet that he will never again make the king smile, Robinson's Dagonet, incapable of singing to cheer his king, falls to his knees and weeps 'for what he knew'.

At the end of the poem Dagonet contemplates Camelot's inevitable collapse with Merlin, whose story Robinson derives from no medieval source. Instead of disappearing permanently, long before the end of Arthur's reign, Robinson's Merlin willingly leaves Camelot to live with Vivian for ten years in Broceliande. After this private bliss, he returns to Camelot when the king discovers the queen's betrayal. Having counselled Arthur to suppress personal anguish and to mind his kingdom, Merlin returns to Broceliande, only to discover that since the chaos of the public world has impinged on his privacy—Lancelot's situation reminding him that personal fulfilment may thwart social good—this limited realm of unlimited self-gratification no longer contents him. Returning to Camelot, he recognises that by now events have rendered his advice pointless. So he wanders away with Dagonet.

Robinson strips from the Merlin and Vivian story the magic of medieval versions and Arnold's and Tennyson's reshapings. Both Vivian and Merlin refute rumours of their supernatural heritage. She weaves no magic spell to imprison him, and Merlin himself possesses no magical powers. He merely has intuition and insight superior to other men's. Vivian is neither the vile seductress of the

Idylls nor the unwilling object of Merlin's lust, as in Malory. She may owe something to Arnold's conception in the final coda to *Tristram and Iseult*, but before Merlin's return from Camelot, she never grows 'weary' of his love. Of the possible influences, she probably owes most to the Vivien of the Vulgate *Merlin*. There the fay heartily loves the magician, weaves her spell in order to keep him with her always, and then remains with him in his captivity. (Although the Vulgate *Merlin* was not readily accessible, except in Southey's summary in the 1817 edition of Malory, Robinson read a synopsis of it in Stephen Humphreys Gurteen's *The Arthurian Epic*, published in 1895, a copy of which he borrowed the year before *Merlin* appeared.[31]) Despite some general affinities with this medieval figure, however, Robinson's character is unique in her complexity and immense appeal. She engages Merlin with her intellect, wit, and variety. Her effect on him is equally complex.

When Merlin first enters Vivian's domain through gates which ten years later she wistfully closes behind him, he wonders whether they admit him to hell or heaven, whether the gatekeeper be a devil or St Peter. Echoing the medieval tales of his enchantment, both Merlin and Vivian metaphorically refer to his sojourn as imprisonment, but he elects to live in her spacious domain and remains free to leave at will. Her forest and well-provisioned castle contrast vividly with Merlin's narrow place beneath a rock in Malory, his tower in the Vulgate *Merlin*, his 'daisied circle' in Arnold, or the oak tree in Tennyson. Robinson contrasts Merlin's 'prison' with these prisons by recasting the oak image from the *Idylls* when Merlin declares his independence from Vivian. Sitting with her beneath an oak where she has previously 'spoiled' his 'noble thoughts' with love play, he discusses his resolve to leave Broceliande. Though residents of Camelot view Broceliande as Merlin's tomb and regard his return as a resurrection, the forest is for a time his prelapsarian Eden and his Paradise. With Vivian Merlin sybaritically enjoys all sensuous pleasures—flowers, exotic food and wine, music; even 'wise books of every lore of every land' here merely satisfy his appetite for intellectual pleasure instead of serving mankind. Reciprocal love with Vivian, who provides both physical and intellectual companionship, completes his private fulfilment.

Although some critics have judged that the poem does not integrate Merlin's love story with the plight at Arthur's court, Merlin's situation actually dramatises the source of social disintegration in Camelot—the gratification of individual desires sought by Lancelot and Guinevere, Arthur, Gawaine, and Modred. In using the tale to parallel and suggest the central problems at Camelot, Robinson recalls Tennyson's method of developing the central story through a series of parallel tales. Robinson makes this point especially through imagery which links Merlin's actions to the condition of Camelot, as when the sage quaffs a special wine on his first night in Broceliande: 'With a hand that shook / Like Arthur's kingdom, Merlin slowly raised / A golden cup.' A vision which comes to him before he consummates his relationship with Vivian and again before he leaves doomed Camelot similarly joins the two situations: He sees 'a crumbling sky / Of black and crimson, with a crimson cloud / That held a far off town of many towers. / All swayed and shaken, till at last they fell, / And there was nothing but a crimson cloud / That crumbled into nothing.'

Once Merlin confronts the social chaos wrought by individual appetites at Camelot and becomes unable to resume his life of pleasure in Broceliande, he brings into his Eden a disruptive Tree of Knowledge, a recognition of the public ramifications of private choices which Vivian tauntingly calls his 'new insistence upon sin'. Robinson plays against the Fall of Man imagery of Tennyson's 'Merlin and Vivien' to create a sympathetic, human Vivian and themes different from the Laureate's. Like Tennyson, Robinson associates Vivian with serpents; she boasts 'I'm cruel and I'm cold, and I like snakes'. Tennyson's villainess, who stands before Merlin 'stiff as a viper frozen' just before she imprisons him, proves to be more serpent than Eve in the re-enactment of the Fall. In contrast, Robinson's Vivian, like Eve, shares the responsibility and also the anguish of their loss of Eden. When Merlin considers leaving Broceliande, she asks, 'Why do you look at me as at a snake / All coiled to spring at you and strike you dead? / I am not going to spring at you, or bite you; / I'm going home.' And she bitterly but pathetically supposes that Merlin has now judged Broceliande an insufficient 'refuge / Where two disheartened sinners may forget / A world that has today no place for them'.

The division wrought within Merlin by public responsibilities competing with personal desires is reflected in his physical metamorphosis. At Vivian's insistence he shaves his beard (they jokingly compare him to Samson) and dons the sprightly clothes of a lover, acquiring an appearance ill suited to his return to Camelot. And when he comes back to Vivian, he wears a mien inappropriate to a gay lover. This spiritual division also re-echoes in the two figures named Blaise—one the 'learnedest of hermits' and Merlin's 'confessor' (like the Blaise in the Vulgate version who baptises Merlin), the other the gate keeper who unlocks for Merlin the garden of love.

During his stay in Broceliande, both he and Vivian believe that through love they can escape the force of Time. In a sense Merlin's initiation into love humanises him by drawing him from the timelessness of his special insights; as he remarks to Vivian, 'I have not lived in Time until to-day'. But by living only in isolation, making the world outside a vacuum, the lovers attempt to transcend the flux of human affairs. Vivian judges that 'we are out of Time. . . . We have this place, / And you must hold us in it or we die.' As the realists at Camelot like Lamorak recognise, however, 'every woman mewing' (he specifically means Guinevere) 'shall some day be a handful of small ashes'. After Merlin sees his accomplishments, and Arthur's, collapsing at Camelot, he takes back to Broceliande a discomfiting 'cold angel' that he soon recognises is 'Change'. But Robinson does not depict Change and Time as agents of only destruction and loss. Early in the poem Lamorak unwittingly forecasts a positive change to be wrought by time—Guinevere's repentance. He wrongly declares that argument will not transform what by nature is a 'slippery queen' into a 'nun who counts and burns / Herself to nothing with her beads and candles'. Time can effect precisely such a change. Moreover, changes toppling Camelot may achieve good results. Robinson anticipated that he would be viewed as 'an evangelist of ruin', but he admonished a friend not to call the ending 'sad': 'There is nothing especially sad about the end of kings and the redemption of the world, and that is what Merlin seems to be driving at.'[32]

Robinson expresses hope in a muted echo of Tennyson's optimistic statement that 'The old order changeth, yielding place to new, / And God fulfils himself in many ways.' Robinson's Merlin, having rejected personally gratifying isolation in Broceliande and anticipating the fall of Camelot, affirms that 'in the end / Are more beginnings, Dagonet, than men / Shall name or know today'. As they turn away from Camelot, Merlin, now 'king', and the wise Fool, his devoted subject, suggest the beginning of a newer order. They in a sense fulfil Dagonet's ironic prescription uttered earlier to Bedivere: 'When all men are like you and me, my lord, / When all are rational or rickety, / There may be no more war.'

By combining the traditional story of Lancelot and Guinevere, Arthur and Modred with a new tale of Merlin and Vivian, Robinson effectively treats the perennial clash between the needs of society and the desires of individuals. Most important, the poem vividly portrays the psychological turbulence and the intricate relationships of the individuals involved in the old story. The work shows not only Merlin's complexity as he attempts to be both lover and public figure, but also others' contradictory reactions to him. Robinson deftly depicts the subtleties of interpersonal relationships not only in the intense moments when society teeters on the brink of extinction or queens and knights face death, but also in mundane situations, as when Merlin dines with Vivian on his first night in Broceliande. He puzzles over the ticklish matter of how he can properly balance his attentions to the lady and to the food she has specially prepared for him: When she chides him for neglecting her for the victuals, he counters, 'and if I did not eat, / Your sending out of ships and caravans / To get whatever 'tis that's in this thing / Would be a sorrow for you all your days'. In such familiar and comic moments, as well as in the tragic, Robinson's language is often memorable, either for its commonplace aptness (for Vivian, Merlin makes 'other men / As ordinary as arithmetic') or for its drama (like Guinevere's, Vivian's 'beauty and her grace / Made passing trash of empires').

Robinson's *Lancelot*, begun as soon as he had finished *Merlin*, records the dissolution of Arthur's order so ominously anticipated by the earlier poem. Here Robinson closely follows the events of Malory's Books XX and XXI: Modred's ruse exposes the lovers in the queen's chamber; Lancelot rescues Guinevere from the fire; Arthur besieges Joyous Gard and, at Gawaine's insistence, pursues Lancelot in France; Arthur and Modred die on Salisbury Plain; and Lancelot bids farewell to Guinevere at Almesbury. As in *Merlin*, Robinson describes these events through the characters' soliloquies and dialogue. Again he subordinates what happens to the characters' attitudes and feelings that both cause the events and result from them. Developing the psychological dimensions suggested by Morris' *Defence of Guenevere* and Tennyson's *Idylls* (both of which Robinson much admired) and, less effectively, by Hovey's

Marriage of Guinevere (which Robinson did not like but consulted when he wrote *Lancelot*[33]), the poem depicts more complex characters in Lancelot and Guinevere than appear in previous Arthurian works.

He redefines Lancelot subtly but significantly by altering the source of the knight's inner conflict. The two objects of his divided loyalty become not Guinevere and Arthur but Guinevere and the 'Light' which he partially perceived on his Quest. In Malory's version of the legend, Lancelot's limited achievement of the Grail troubles him for a time, as does his healing Sir Urre, by reminding him of the perfection he could have attained had he not loved the queen. But soon afterwards 'Sir Launcelot began to resort unto Queen Guenever again, and forgat the promise and the perfection that he made in the quest' (XVIII, i). In Malory's account of the climactic events which here concern Robinson, Launcelot sorrows not so much for his failure in the Grail quest as for his betrayal of Arthur and the Round Table. Even more emphatically in Tennyson's *Idylls*, which commend serving society rather than questing for the Grail, Lancelot's anguish arises from a 'faith unfaithful' that requires him to betray either Guinevere or the king. For Robinson's protagonist, however, the compelling conflict lies between the queen and the 'Light'. Lancelot clearly regrets that he has brought Arthur's 'fame and honor to the dust', but from the beginning of the poem he wrestles with a compulsion to leave Guinevere in order to pursue the symbolic Light.

Significantly, Robinson minimises the traditional mystical and religious associations of the Grail, as he had deleted magic and the supernatural from the Merlin story. The word *Grail* occurs only once in the poem. Instead, Robinson uses the terms *Light* and *Gleam* (perhaps suggested by Tennyson's 1889 poem 'Merlin and the Gleam') to symbolise moral and ethical virtue, or what he once described as 'a spiritual realisation of Things and their significance'.[34]

Robinson had used the image in a brief Arthurian poem 'Siege Perilous' (1916), written the year before *Merlin*, which succinctly depicts Galahad's venture in the consecrated seat. The verse associates the 'Light' with the traditional Grail: 'There fell one day upon his eyes a light / Ethereal, and he heard no more men speaking; / He saw their shaken heads, but no long sight / Was his but for the end that he went seeking.' But Robinson modernised the motif with an unsettling suggestion that achieving a vision of the Grail merely begins the arduous task of following the Light: 'The end he sought was not the end; the crown / He won shall unto many still be given. / Moreover, there was reason here to frown: / No fury thundered, no flame fell from heaven.' As early as 1897, in the non-Arthurian 'Octave VIII' Robinson had used the related image of 'compensate spirit-gleams / Of Wisdom [that] shaft the darkness here and there, / Like scattered lamps', which anticipates imagery in *Merlin*, where the Grail is 'a Light wherein men saw themselves / In one another as they might become— / Or so they dreamed'. In *Lancelot*, Robinson's Light echoes these earlier images and signifies moral and ethical rectitude more than anything traditionally mystical or religious.

Guinevere, a competing 'glory of white and gold', consistently clouds 'with an insidious gleam / Of earth' the Gleam 'that was not of earth'. She therefore makes

Lancelot 'a thing of night', and he suspends his intended pursuit of the Gleam for one last night with her, thereby falling into Modred's trap. (On this point Robinson follows Tennyson by saying the tryst in the queen's bedroom is to be their last, but here Lancelot rather than Guinevere determines that they must part.) Lancelot's tragedy transcends his personal betrayal of Arthur, for it originates in his inability to turn from Camelot to a new order: 'God, what a rain of ashes falls on him./ Who sees the new and cannot leave the old!'

Instead of resolving Lancelot's ambivalence by having him 'die a holy man' as in Malory (Tennyson's phrase), Robinson has his hero finally choose, at Guinevere's insistence, to follow the Light. Earlier, when Lancelot restores Guinevere to Arthur, he does so partly to end the slaughter of combat; his poem vividly expands the anti-war sentiments expressed in *Merlin*. But the Light provides greater motivation. After Lancelot renounces Guinevere, however, her appeal lingers. When he arrives from France too late to help Arthur against Modred, he searches her out at Amesbury. Robinson's penitent queen, like Malory's, refuses to come away with Lancelot. (This scene neatly balances the poignant scene at Joyous Gard in which Guinevere begs her lover not to return her to the king.) But unlike Malory's knight, Robinson's Lancelot does not emulate the queen's withdrawal into the religious life. Instead, he rides alone after the Light. He sees a fleeting vision of Galahad 'in a mist of gold', then nothing—until 'in the darkness came the Light'. Lancelot's glory lies not in religious retreat, but in his stoically renouncing a corrupting self-indulgence and seeking a new order. As he earlier observed (in words especially pointed in the context of World War I), the proper course is not to grieve over Camelot's fall, but to go on in new directions: 'A played-out world, / Although that world be ours, had best be dead.' Robinson implied this theme when he declared 'the most significant line' in *Merlin* and *Lancelot* to be Gawaine's remark that 'The world has paid enough / For Camelot'.[35]

As the rival to Lancelot's selfless vision of Light, Guinevere like Vivian in *Merlin* represents the great appeal of love and individual happiness. When Lancelot contemplates leaving her, she stands before him as 'his inventory of the world / That he must lose'. Anticipating the end of the world they have known, she urges not the renunciation Lancelot envisions, but intense indulgence in rapidly vanishing delight: 'Why not before it goes . . . / Have yet one morsel more of life together, / Before death sweeps the table?' Though she reveals 'malice' and 'fury', this acidity ultimately emphasises her vulnerability and poignant desire for happiness. Robinson rather diffidently referred to his efforts to create richly complex female characters: He ironically described Merlin, who dotes on Vivian's mixture of 'guile' and 'graciousness', as a 'suffragist'. Of Lancelot's queen he wrote, 'I don't know whether I deserve a crown or a foolscap for trying to make Guinevere interesting—a fact that hasn't to my knowledge been accomplished heretofore—but she must have had a way with her or there wouldn't have been such an everlasting amount of fuss made over her.'[36]

When Guinevere contemplates returning to Arthur from Joyous Gard, she herself marvels that there is so much 'fuss'—'I wonder / Why the King cared!' But her dignity and pathos when she reviews her situation as a possession sold by her father for a crown, or when she struggles against Lancelot's resolve to return her to Arthur, effectively demonstrate her legendary appeal. She arouses greatest sympathy when she challenges Lancelot's renunciation of love to follow the Light: 'Where does history tell you / The Lord himself would seem in so great haste / As you for your perfection?' Yet her strengths foreshadow the capacity for selfless control revealed when she undertakes religious expiation and directs Lancelot to resume his quest: 'We are going by two roads to the same end.'

Robinson's Gawaine, like Lancelot and Guinevere, finally attains the stoic self-control which the poem depicts as humanity's best hope in the face of chaos. He begins as the traditionally 'light' Gawaine, who returns from the Grail quest 'so soon / That we had hardly missed him', the man who, 'if the stars went out, would only laugh'. But he changes radically. First he learns to hate without reserve when Lancelot unwittingly kills his brothers; then he achieves a capacity to place humanity's needs before his own. He initially taunts Lancelot for being 'too vaporous to be sharing / The carnal feast of life'. He soon recognises, however, that Lancelot's 'carnal' appetite wrestles with his 'vaporous' idealism so vigorously that his heart is 'pulled . . . half out of him by the roots'. Having learned much about human turmoil since the opening scene, Gawaine finally jeers only at selfishness that thwarts general human happiness. Robinson records this metamorphosis in small dramatic details: In the first scene Gawaine flippantly insists that a brooding Lancelot take his hand, a gesture of the lightest form of friendship. Before he dies, he repentantly takes Lancelot's hand in a gesture of genuine love. Though his actions follow those narrated by Malory, Robinson's Gawaine stands unprecedented in Arthurian literature as a vividly realised psychological study.

Like Gawaine, Arthur experiences a harrowing personal loss, but unlike his nephew he never achieves a broad humanistic vision. Flawed, as in Malory, by having two illegitimate sons and wilfully marrying Guinevere despite Merlin's prophecy, he falters when he tries to combine the desires of the man with the responsibilities of the king. Bedivere describes Arthur's pathos when he discovers Guinevere's infidelity: 'Now you may hear him in the corridor, / Like a sick landlord shuffling to the light / For one last look-out on his mortgaged hills.' But at times Arthur stoically recognises the inevitable, as when he observes that Gawaine's vengeance and Modred's ambition 'will make of my Round Table . . . a thing of wreck / And yesterday—a furniture forgotten'. Arthur dies on Salisbury Plain without heroic fanfare and with only passing mention of unfounded 'tales told of a ship'.

Robinson initially included in *Lancelot* a scene showing Modred planning with Agravaine and Colgrevance to trap Lancelot and Guinevere. Thinking that the publishers considered the poem too long, however, he removed the 164 lines (published in 1929 as *Modred: A Fragment*). Deleting the scene proved fortunate, for Modred, who never appears in the poem, remains horrifying as a disembodied force of evil. Gawaine, characteristically ironic, introduces this view: 'God made him as He made the crocodile, / To prove He was omnipotent. Having done so, / And seeing then that Camelot, of all places / Ripe for annihilation, most required him, / He put him there at once.' As the brutal embodiment of selfishness, Modred also becomes its scourge, 'the Almighty's instrument / Of a world's overthrow'.

Despite such artful innovations as the symbolic 'Light' and the rich characterisations of Lancelot, Guinevere, and Gawaine, *Lancelot* exerted what Robinson termed 'a refrigerating effect on the critics', partly because they thought the many nineteenth-century reinterpretations had exhausted Arthurian material.[37] But in using traditional story as the context for realistic psychological portrayals, he may be said to have taken the 'old-fashioned way to be new' (Robert Frost's description of Robinson).

Of his three long Arthurian poems, *Tristram* (1927) most vividly demonstrates the power of what might just as properly be termed Robinson's 'new-fashioned way to be old'. The Tristram story had long teased him. He had conceived the poem as early as 1917, along with the first two Arthurian pieces. Although he suspended work on the Tristram tale after *Lancelot* elicited poor reviews and sales, in 1925 he acknowledged that 'our old friend Tristram, whom I have been fighting off for some five years, got me finally by the throat and refused to let go'.[38] This old friend's insistence produced a modern version of the legend which elaborates the human relationships, especially by expanding the role of Isolt of Brittany. It also extends two themes introduced by *Merlin* and *Lancelot*: through love one may conquer time, and through stoic fortitude and self-control one may conquer adversity. Although Robinson wrote that the poem 'adapted' the 'merest outline of the old legend',[39] it intricately combines invention with echoes of a number of medieval and modern versions of the tale.

Robinson knew Wagner's *Tristan und Isolde* intimately and loved it so much that during one improvident period he spent money earmarked for much-needed trousers on opera tickets.[40] Like Wagner, Robinson depicts the central love story in three principal scenes. As in the opera, the climactic scene shows the lovers' deaths. But Robinson chooses for his first two scenes episodes less extraordinary than the moments Wagner features. Whereas Wagner depicts the heroine's deciding not to kill Tristram for having slain her uncle, and then the lovers' quaffing the love potion, Robinson dramatises Isolt's wedding night, when Tristram betrays his passion and Mark banishes him, and, second, the lovers' idyllic summer at Joyous Gard.

In each of his three episodes, Robinson makes important changes in the story found in medieval and modern versions. Most obviously, he omits the love potion altogether. Wagner had already 'modernised' the story by making the potion symbol rather than cause of the passion. Nevertheless, 'the fool potion' seemed 'silly' even in the powerful opera. Robinson wanted to show 'what might have happened to human beings in those circumstances, without their wits and wills having been taken away by some impossible . . . concoction'. The philtre was 'wholly superfluous', because 'men and women can make trouble enough for themselves'.[41] While Robinson makes the love evolve solely from emotional affinities, he draws upon the legend metaphorically, as he had in *Merlin*, where characters describe Merlin's sojourn in Broceliande as imprisonment. On Isolt's wedding night, for example, Tristram suffers from 'an abject ineptitude / That like a drug had held him'. And when the lovers meet at Joyous Gard, Isolt's love 'sings' through him 'like a wild wine'. Robinson similarly alludes metaphorically to other medieval motifs, as when he calls up Gottfried's depiction (also recounted in Joseph Bédier's version, published in 1900) of the sleeping lovers separated by a sword: Robinson's Isolt refuses to accept 'the sword that must for ever be between us'.

Despite the barriers which separate Tristram and Isolt, they achieve what Robinson's Vivian had desired—through love they transcend time. Unlike Vivian, they do not seek this transcendence outside the human sphere of flux, although they find fulfilment only at Joyous Gard out of Mark's reach. Whereas they initially remain too much bound by convention to seize their desires, Tristram observes that 'Time had saved for him / The flower that he had not the wit to seize'. Once awakened to their passion, the lovers can destroy all chronological sense of time, for 'when two loves like ours / Wear down the wall of time dividing them, / Two oceans come together and flow over / Time and his evil work'. They triumph over time by replacing duration with intensity: 'Time is not life. For many . . . / Living is mostly for a time not dying— / . . . Whatever / It is that fills life high and full, till fate / Itself may do no more, it is not time. / Years are not life.' Such love as theirs reaches a kind of infinity: 'There is a love that will outshine the stars.'

Describing the love of Tristram and Isolt, Robinson achieves a sensuousness and lyricism rare in his poetry and reminiscent of Swinburne. While writing *Tristram*, Robinson had consulted 'Swinburne's melodious poem' with the aim of avoiding 'possible collisions'.[42] Robinson's poem absorbed much from Swinburne's exaltation of love as a means of transcending time and death. It also echoes at least one specific episode, Tristram's joyful swim in the ocean, as well as Swinburne's imagery and language. One suspects, for example, the influence of Swinburne's description of four lips becoming 'one burning mouth' in Robinson's 'Isolt . . . / Muffled his mouth with hers in a long kiss, / Blending in their catastrophe two fires / That made one fire'. Robinson acknowledged that 'the key and color' of *Tristram* differed from those of *Merlin* and *Lancelot*, and might lead readers to think he was 'a little tired of hearing too much about my New England reticence'.[43] But his lyricism, while perhaps suggested by Swinburne, never becomes extravagant or intensely sensuous. If anything, the 'key and color' of the poem would seem to develop inevitably from the subject matter.

The lovers' bliss ends when Mark abducts Isolt from Joyous Gard. This Mark initially follows the pattern of duplicity and brutality provided in the *Morte Darthur*. Like Malory's Cornish king, he goes to prison for forging papal documents threatening Tristram. But Robinson's Mark finally learns from Isolt's 'white face' that he cannot thwart the lovers' union or in any meaningful way vanquish his rival. Somewhat like the magnanimous king in Wagner (and in Wagner's source, Gottfried), Robinson's Mark finally treats the lovers generously.

189

He allows Tristram access to the failing queen. While the lovers are taking a fond farewell, Mark's feeble-minded, reptilian nephew Andred stabs Tristram in the back. Isolt dies with him. The *Morte Darthur* depicts a similarly vile Andred who plots against Tristram (VIII, xxxii; XIX, xi). In Malory, however, Mark kills Tristram. Again, Robinson's version resembles Wagner's, in which Melot, the spying kinsman of a just King Mark, murders Tristram. (J. Comyns Carr's 1906 drama *Tristan and Iseult*, in which Andred stabs the hero, may also have influenced Robinson, but there Mark instigates the murder.)

Robinson emphasised his serious effort to devise an appropriate death for the lovers: 'Yesterday I killed T. and I. in an experimental sort of way.' After three tries, he had 'almost as hard a time in making them stay dead as they had in dying. This may sound irreverent, but you know how important it is that important people . . . should have a proper taking-off.'[44] The death he finally chose eliminates the romance motif of the black and white sails and also exonerates Mark, who murders Tristram in Tennyson as in Malory. This change permits Mark to become enlightened and ennobled by his suffering. At the end he sympathetically comments on the limitations of Tristram's and Isolt's love. Their intensity, by its very nature, vitiates most other pleasures in life and makes death an escape from pain: 'There was no more for them—and this is peace.'

Isolt of Brittany learns even more than Mark from the lovers' experience. She not only loves deeply, but also survives loss of love by exercising stoic fortitude and self-control. In doing so, she elucidates a theme finally more important than the idea that love transcends time. To emphasise the significance of self-control and fortitude, Robinson expands the wife's role far beyond that found in medieval versions. In three major episodes her experience frames and divides the love story of her husband and her rival. Throughout these scenes—when she awaits Tristram's return to Brittany before their marriage, when she anxiously expects him to go to the Queen of Cornwall, and when she learns of his death— she combines genuine love with a controlled acceptance of adversity. Arnold's poem, which similarly expanded the wife's role and made her more sympathetic than the spiteful prototype in Thomas' fragment, doubtless influenced this sympathetic portrait. Yet Robinson departs from Arnold by allowing his character to develop an understanding and wisdom not apparent in Arnold's naïve character. Arnold's Iseult of Brittany remains an innocent victim of thwarted love. Her life proves so barren—despite her children—that each day becomes its predecessor's 'exact repeated effigy'. In contrast, Robinson's character attains a wisdom that enables her, like his Lancelot, to accept loss and turn constructively to a new life.

Although Isolt of Brittany longs for fulfilling love, she learns to accept actuality without losing the capacity to dream of more. At the beginning of the poem her father gently counsels her not to hope Tristram will return to Brittany, as the knight has lightly promised, and advises her to prefer 'comfort and expediency' to the consuming passion Tristram and his queen will come to know. Howel hopes that his daughter will 'Be wise enough not to ask more of life / Than to be life'. She, however, achieves a wisdom more vital than Howel's ideal of moderating desire. Robinson describes this wisdom in imagery which forecasts new beginnings: 'wisdom . . . like a dawn that comes up slowly / Out of an unknown ocean'. Such understanding enables her to recognise that dreams fail, but leaves her free to dream: 'I am not one / Who must have everything', she recognises, 'yet I must have / My dreams if I must live'.

Robinson's three Arthurian poems describe vain struggles against chaos and loss. Nevertheless, like Arnold he saw that artistic interpretations of the legends provide some relief from the unhappiness they depict. He once commented, for example, that while 'the whole western world is going to be blown to pieces, asphyxiated, and starved', watching a performance of Wagner's *Tristan* allowed him 'for a few hours' to fancy 'that our so-called civilisation might not be going after all—though of course it is'.[45] Beyond aesthetic relief, he—again like Arnold—used the legends to illustrate the fortitude which constitutes man's defence against chaos. When Mark's hatred moderates to compassion, when the lovers' anguish yields to peace, and most especially, when Isolt of Brittany's pain becomes equanimity, Robinson offers the affirmation he required in his own works generally: though 'a trifle solemn in my verses, . . . I intend that there shall always be at least a suggestion of something wiser than hatred and something better than despair'.[46]

Tristram offers a corrective to the problems developed in Robinson's two earlier Arthurian narratives, amplifying the stoic resourcefulness finally achieved by Merlin and Lancelot when they leave Camelot. Although the Tristram story precedes the other two in the chronology of events, anticipations of Camelot's fall link the poem to its predecessors and create a sense of their simultaneity. King Howel, for example, mentions rumours that Modred will overthrow Arthur. Tristram goes to be made a knight of 'the Round Table— / So long the symbol of a world in order, / Soon to be overthrown by love and fate / And loyalty forsworn'. Through imagery Robinson associates Tristram's experience with the fate of Camelot, for Isolt of Ireland sees him 'more as a thunder-stricken tower of life / Brought down by fire, than as a stricken man / Brought down by fate'. Also, by having Lancelot and Guinevere arrange the lovers' sojourn at Joyous Gard, and—more of an innovation—by bringing Morgan and Gawaine into their story, Robinson further connects the Tristram story with the fate of the Arthurian world. Queen Morgan (lacking the magic powers of Malory's 'fay') shelters Tristram after Mark banishes him, an episode perhaps suggested by the *Morte Darthur*, where she briefly holds him captive (IX, xl). Morgan represents a crass, self-serving love predicated on 'comfort and expediency' and antithetical to the love of Tristram and Isolt. Gawaine here appears as the light, golden-tongued figure of Welsh story and medieval romance. He derives in part from Tennyson's character, who tries to seduce Elaine of Astolat and abandons his mission for Arthur in 'Lancelot and Elaine'. Not so knavish as Tennyson's character, however, he ceases his suit when he understands Isolt of Brittany's innocence and fidelity to Tristram. Moreover, Gawaine betrays his commission by reporting Mark's imprisonment only to assuage Isolt's fears for her husband.

In his innovative reshaping of traditional story Robinson employed some haunting dramatic imagery, especially the ocean waves which repeat to Tristram the name 'Isolt', and sound to Isolt of Brittany the name 'Tristram'. As an image of eternal flux, the sea effectively symbolises both the lovers' relationship to time and infinity and Isolt of Brittany's resolute acceptance of change. Even more evocative are the frequent references to white birds, the gulls associated with Isolt of Brittany and with the lovers. The image concludes the poem solemnly, simultaneously suggesting eternity and dynamic change: 'And there was nothing alive but white birds flying, / Flying, and always flying, and still flying, / And the white sunlight flashing on the sea.'

Robinson characteristically expected little response to his Arthurian works. He acknowledged that 'a long poem nowadays is at best a getting down on one's knees to invite disaster', and declared that *Merlin* and *Lancelot* 'will never be read until people are made to read them'.[47] Whatever the weaknesses of his verse and the merits of his characterisation, Robinson's chief accomplishment in treating Arthurian story is that he stripped from the tales all hints of heroic grandeur and idealisation but still depicted the situations and characters nobly. His works amplify the dignity of the material merely by showing its human consequence.

The prose fiction written in the early decades of the twentieth century rarely achieved this feat. The novels of Warwick Deeping, for example, treat Arthurian story as romance, undercutting much of the realism attained by Robinson's poems. In *Uther and Igraine* (1902, new edition 1928) Deeping's characters initially promise to be fairly interesting and human, but he increasingly magnifies their virtues and vices until they become types. He also simulates a historical realism by depicting Arthur's world not as the chivalrous court of the late Middle Ages as found in Malory (followed by Tennyson and most nineteenth-century poets), but as the more appropriately rugged tribal society of the sixth century. Yet even this seeming realism soon yields romance, for the world of Deeping's novels depicts Roman elegance more than the crude realities of Saxon invasions and Briton resistance.

Uther and Igraine begins, however, as a competent and relatively interesting historical romance which creates a new love story for Arthur's parents. Igraine, a spirited novice who finds her passion for life and beauty far stronger than her piety, is rescued from marauding Saxons by a young knight who calls himself 'Pelleas'. Although he loves her, he leaves her because he assumes she has already taken holy vows. He is actually Uther Pendragon and soon becomes king. Igraine sets out to find her knight. She tries vainly to avoid marrying Gorlois, who has conceived a fanatical passion for her. Having reached the point at which Malory takes up Igraine's story, Deeping thoroughly alters the account in the *Morte Darthur* (I, i). Merlin, foreseeing a great destiny for Igraine but apparently not understanding its particulars, magically makes Gorlois resemble her beloved Pelleas. The episode thus reverses the traditional situation in which

Merlin makes Uther look like Gorlois so that the king can lie with the Duke's wife. Igraine follows the disguised Gorlois into a forest, where a priest marries them. After enduring the hateful marriage for a time, she flees. By Merlin's wiser intervention, Uther finds her, but honour forbids their union while Gorlois lives. Gorlois captures Igraine and determines to break her spirit by beating and starving her. Finally Uther discovers this treachery, Mark and Tristan help rescue Igraine (another unlikely twist in Arthurian story), and Uther kills Gorlois. As destiny and literary tradition require, the lovers are united.

At the outset Igraine appears as an intriguing, spirited heroine, a 'golden falcon of a woman', 'an untamable thing'. But Deeping's romantic excess reaches its peak when she dons a suit of armour and rides about the countryside for several months, rescuing a shepherdess from ravishment and, finally, tilting with Gorlois for her freedom.

Beyond the main situation in which Uther must kill Gorlois in order to marry Igraine, nothing in the tale follows traditional story. Deeping uses names familiar from medieval romance for wholly new situations: Gorlois jousts with 'the Green Knight' and Igraine has a maid named Isolde. Merlin wears capacious black velvet robes and many rings, and the villainess is a hussy named Morgan la Blanche.

In *The Man Who Went Back* (1940), Deeping uses the situation of Mark Twain's *Connecticut Yankee*, but without intentional humour. As the result of an automobile accident, a twentieth-century Englishman returns to the time of Aurelius Ambrosius. He becomes a 'dux bellorum' and fights the Saxons. As in *Uther and Igraine*, Deeping's version of sixth-century society is highly unrealistic. Other prose writers of the early twentieth century followed Twain's lead far more successfully by emulating not his plot situation, but his comic and satiric attitude. Besides the more significant works of James Branch Cabell and John Erskine, two brief comic pieces—one an episode in a novel, the other a short story—deserve mention.

The silly, romantic Arthurian 'dramas' written in the first decades of the century for school and camp groups may have suggested to Booth Tarkington the beginning of his humorous novel *Penrod* (1914), about a twelve-year-old who hurries from one misadventure to another. In his initial appearance, the youth seethes over his 'destiny . . . to declaim the loathsome sentiments of a character named . . . the Child of Sir Lancelot' in Mrs Lora Rewbush's 'Children's Pageant of the Table Round'. Himself the author of an earthier romance 'Harold Ramores: The Roadagent, or Wild Life Among the Rocky Mts.', Penrod detests Mrs Rewbush's saccharin speeches on chivalry. Irksome beyond endurance, however, is the 'medieval' costume devised by his mother and sister from old silk hose, a dress bodice, and red flannel underwear. He 'looked like nothing ever remotely imagined by Sir Thomas Malory or Alfred Tennyson;—for that matter, he looked like nothing ever before seen on earth'. He preserves his male pride by hiding this costume under a pair of overalls, themselves hidden beneath his 'medieval' golf cape. When he convulses the

audience by doffing his cape, and at the same time twists the arm of his rival—
the pageant's Child Sir Galahad—during their speech on charity, Tarkington
comically reveals how far from *The Boy's King Arthur* a modern youth's
experience could be.

Heywood Broun's short story 'The Fifty-first Dragon' (1921) similarly jests
with chivalric notions without using a traditional Arthurian story or traditional
conceptions of Arthurian characters. Gawaine le Coeur-Hardy (Sir Osanna's
epithet in Malory), the least promising youth at knight school, lacks spirit. To
cure this deficiency, the idealistic Head Master trains Gawaine to slay dragons
with a battle axe. To give the timid boy courage, he assigns Gawaine a 'magic
word' (although the young knight would have much preferred a cap to make
himself invisible). After forty-nine successes, Gawain swaggers proudly. But
on the fiftieth encounter he becomes so unsettled by a clever old dragon that
he temporarily forgets his talismanic word. After he slays the dragon without
first saying *Rumplesnitz*, he recognises that the word exercises no magic.
Gawaine confronts his mortality, loses confidence, and becomes a tasty morsel
for his fifty-first dragon. Defeat notwithstanding, he becomes a legendary hero
for the knight school, the stories about him growing grander as time passes.
Broun's tale playfully debunks hero worship by exposing the commonplace
reality behind heroic legend.

iv. James Branch Cabell, *Jurgen: A Comedy of Justice* (1919)

James Branch Cabell's romance novel *Jurgen*, an early version of which
appeared in *The Smart Set* (1918), remains one of the most unusual and sophisticated satiric uses of Arthurian material. Today the work is primarily remembered for having stirred controversy with its abundant sexual euphemisms.
These prompted the New York Society for the Suppression of Vice in January
1920 to seize the printer's plates and all copies of the novel—already in its third
edition—from the editor's offices. During the nearly two years which elapsed
before the trial, a number of important writers and critics (including Arthurians
Edwin Arlington Robinson and John Erskine) protested the censorship. By the
time the judge directed the jury to drop the obscenity charges against the
publishers, notoriety had assured good sales when the novel was again released
in October 1922. But the legal battle over the book's sexual frankness, while
generating an immediate audience, doubtless limited its long-term appeal, for it
emphasised an aspect of the novel which soon seemed dated. Subsequent
generations, increasingly accustomed to more graphic erotica, have generally
failed to discover the other, genuine charms of Cabell's highly imaginative ironic
romance.

Jurgen is perhaps the most significant work in Cabell's ambitious eighteen-
volume series of novels, tales, and poems collectively entitled *The Biography of
the Life of Manuel*. The collection traces the history of Manuel, the thirteenth-

century 'Redeemer of Poictesme' (Cabell's imaginary French province) and his descendants, who eventually reside in twentieth-century Virginia. *Jurgen* narrates the fantastic adventures of a thirteenth-century pawnbroker as he is magically reinvested with youth; enjoys amorous liaisons with Guenevere, the Persian goddess Anaïtis, and Helen of Troy; then visits Hell and Heaven; and finally returns to the realities of middle-aged domesticity with a shrewish wife.

In the Arthurian episode Jurgen frees captive Guenevere from the troll king Thragnar. Returning the young princess to her father, Jurgen introduces himself as the 'Duke of Logreus' and asks to marry her. However, she has already been promised to King Arthur. As her father Gogyrvan Gawr of Cameliard (a name drawn from the Welsh Triads[48]) observes sarcastically, 'a king takes precedence of a duke'. (Such sarcasm is the dominant tone of the book.) In pragmatically choosing a king for his son-in-law and subverting the chivalric principle that a knight marries the damsel he has saved, Gogyrvan illustrates the novel's method of satirically contrasting chivalric ideals with human actualities. Guenevere's father similarly undercuts the chivalric ideal of female chastity by advising Jurgen to take his pleasure with her before she marries. He thus encourages nightly trysts between the young lovers which end only when she is escorted by Lancelot (as in Tennyson) to her wedding. The frank but euphemistic sexuality of this episode patently challenges chivalric notions long associated with Arthurian story. But Cabell achieves subtle effects beyond the obvious satire. Guenevere's father is hardly an unprincipled pander. As he suggests that Jurgen fulfil his desire for Guenevere, Gogyrvan memorably illustrates the fleeting nature of youth, beauty, and happiness. Cabell's satiric debunking of chivalric ideals here blends a jocular *carpe diem* pragmatism with a melancholy sense of the transience of human happiness.

Such a complex perspective persists throughout the satire. Cabell humorously undercuts many aspects of the chivalric order, as when Jurgen unheroically prefers to watch—rather than to fight—tournaments, or when he wryly observes the inanity of idealising obviously imperfect women. At times the humour derives from Cabell's ironic versions of medieval motifs. In one instance, for example, Jurgen beseeches a lady to help him win his beloved, and when she agrees, declares that she is the one he woos. This motif, seen in Malory's tale of Pelleas and Ettarde, here acquires added humour when the lady automatically assumes they will marry, but Jurgen hastily argues that 'there is no need to bother a priest about our private affairs'.

Jurgen remains breezily and sarcastically aware of how often human behaviour falls short of lofty chivalric ideals: 'These men who considered that all you possessed was loaned you to devote to the service of your God, your King and every woman who crossed your path, could hardly be behaving rationally. To talk of serving God sounded as sonorously and as inspiritingly as a drum: yes, and a drum had nothing but air in it.' Merlin, who 'created this Chivalry', also describes the obvious discrepancy between ideals and human shortcomings when he forecasts—and commiserates—Guenevere's destiny 'to enter queen-hood and become a symbol': 'She will now be worshipped as a revelation of

Heaven's splendour, and being flesh and blood, she will not like it.'

Cabell later used Merlin to express similar ideas in *Something About Eve* (1927). In this romance, which focuses on the fantastic adventures of a modern Virginian descended from Manuel and Jurgen, Merlin Ambrosius (the name as found in Geoffrey of Monmouth) describes how he created chivalry. Arthur and his knights were 'toys' which Merlin transformed from a 'gaping, smooth-chinned boy' and 'shaggy followers' by fostering the 'beautiful notion' that man was 'Heaven's heir'. This fiction yielded 'eminently picturesque' results, but the order rapidly decayed as the knights 'forgot the very pretty notion' which Merlin had given them 'to play with'. At this point the wizard gives a uniquely Cabellian reinterpretation of his enchantment by Nimuë. Here she is an enticing child whom Merlin allows to immure him only so long as he delights to dally with her. The account, with its loving Nimuë and hawthorne bush, follows that in the Vulgate cycle rather than Malory's version. Like the Arthurian episode in *Jurgen*, this one shows chivalric ideals failing because of human weaknesses, especially sexual self-indulgence.

In a letter addressed 'To Sir Galahad of the Siege Perilous' (in *Ladies and Gentlemen: A Parcel of Reconsiderations*, 1934), Cabell reverted to this concern with human weaknesses. In breezy conversational style the epistle recounts Malory's version of the Grail quest (referring also to Tennyson's early poem 'Sir Galahad'). It concludes that although men approve Galahad's ideals, they cannot live them. Galahad exhibits 'a supernal holiness which, at the bottom of our human hearts, we do not really like or quite trust'.

Even though he emphasised such contrasts between mythic ideals and human realities, Cabell implies in *Jurgen* that a society's myths have value precisely insofar as they do not reflect human limitations. They enrich man because they embody values that remain unattainable. When near the conclusion of the work Jurgen is offered a second liaison with Guenevere, he refuses because he has come to see the vanity of pursuing lost youth and perfect happiness. But he has also achieved something more positive than the loss of romantic illusions. He comes to see Guenevere as more than just a fleshly woman whom he has momentarily desired. He recognises her as a symbol of Faith. Cabell alludes to the traditional story sufficiently to remind us that as a woman, Guenevere is far from ideal; her indiscretions result in Lancelot's becoming a monk and Arthur's retreating to Avalon. But as Guenevere points out, her beauty has symbolic value as a 'surety, as to the power and kindliness of [men's] great Father'. Though Jurgen himself never attains the faith necessary for such an ennobling vision, it is with significantly wistful regret that he recognises he is 'not altogether sure' he is 'Heaven's vicar upon earth'. He thereby forces us to re-evaluate his earlier scorn for the 'foolish' Arthurian chivalry, which saw life as 'a high-hearted journeying homeward' to God.

In *Jurgen* Cabell effectively dramatises the three attitudes possible to man which he said underlay all of the *Biography of the Life of Manuel*—the chivalric, the gallant, and the poetic. Chivalry, flourishing in Guenevere's Arthurian world, idealistically views each man as God's vicar, and life as an opportunity for him to approach perfection. As Jurgen's awareness of the foolishness, brutality, and conspicuous adultery of this world reveals, recognising the discrepancies between ideals and actualities can produce disillusionment, or a form of 'gallantry' which is sceptical, hedonistic, even libertine.[49] Throughout most of the novel Jurgen reflects this attitude of gallantry. He observes the farcical elements of high-minded chivalry and seeks momentary pleasures in casual liaisons. By the end of *Jurgen*, the gallant pawnbroker—who is also a poet—approaches Cabell's third and most desirable attitude, the poetic. From this perspective one discerns the limitations and inequities of human existence, yet also recognises the importance of imaginative visions, which, though unattainable, ennoble man as he seeks to create the ideal or permanent.[50] At the same time pragmatic and somewhat idealistic, the tutored Jurgen finally seeks union not with idealised mythic figures such as Guenevere, but with his imperfect human wife, scolding Lisa. Yet even as he seems to settle for this flawed reality, he discerns certain charms about Lisa that he—as a sceptical gallant—failed to see earlier. In blending satire directed against all sorts of human foolishness with mythic emblems of human ideals, Cabell himself illustrates precisely this 'poetic' attitude.

Cabell's references to Arthurian lore show no specific indebtedness to particular medieval works. Instead he uses the general tradition that had by now become part of English and American consciousness. (James P. Cover, with whom Cabell discussed his sources, in a volume of *Notes on Jurgen* cites no specific indebtedness for the Arthurian material, remarking only that the legend had become familiar mainly through Malory and Tennyson.[51]) Though Cabell later read actual medieval romances, he first knew the stories as they were popularised in Charles Henry Hanson's *Stories of the Days of King Arthur* (1887). This childhood favourite had helped establish Cabell's sense of chivalry, which he early associated with General Robert E. Lee and the Confederacy.[52] Cabell's method was to embellish his versions of old story with what may appear to be specific allusions but are actually his own innovations. For example, he introduced *Jurgen* with what looks like a quotation from Middle English, but proves to be Cabell imitating Chaucer. He delighted in citing bogus authorities and fictitious sources, and he confessed—or boasted—to a scholar who proposed to study his works, that he could never remember his sources, or even distinguish what he borrowed from what he originated.[53]

Among his additions to Arthurian legend is his history of Excalibur, here called Caliburn as in Geoffrey of Monmouth and Layamon. Jurgen takes the sword from Thragnar, Guenevere's abductor, and then brandishes it (usually as a sexual gesture) throughout the Arthurian episode. Once Jurgen is bested by words, however, he discards the sword in favour of language, which he thinks to be a more potent weapon. Later, the Lady of the Lake gives Caliburn to King Arthur, 'who with its aid rose to be hailed as one of the Nine Worthies of the World', winning 'eternal fame with that which Jurgen flung away'. The Lady of the Lake also illustrates Cabell's zany but purposeful violation of Arthurian tradition. Following tradition, he identifies her as Lancelot's foster mother, but he calls her Anaïtis, a variant of Anahita, a Persian fertility goddess. Beyond her connection with Lancelot, Cabell does not associate his Anaïtis with Arthurian tradition. Though he tentatively identified this sorceress in his notes as Morgaine la Fée or Nimuë,[54] Cabell adopted the name Anaïtis (an anagram for *insatia*, an apt characterisation of her sexual appetite), so that in succeeding Guenevere as Jurgen's mistress, she could transport him to another place, time, and mythos.

By having Jurgen travel from Arthurian England to the realms of Anaïtis and Helen of Troy, to Hell and Heaven, and back again to his thirteenth-century Poictesme, Cabell creates a farce more confusing and less unified than that in Twain's satiric narrative of time travel. While obviously following the lead of Twain, whom he celebrated in *Jurgen* as one of three eminent American writers plagued by obtuse critics, Cabell, unlike Twain, complicated his romance with erudite, and often comically fraudulent, allusions to disparate literatures, philosophies, and myths. (His mingling Arthurian legend with classical and other mythologies recalls Peacock's method of punctuating Welsh lore with classical references. Cabell's work is both more fantastic and less cheerful in its comedy than *The Misfortunes of Elphin*.) Cabell's combining mythologies offended some otherwise friendly readers. One who read the unpublished manuscript objected to having 'all mythology and all legend hustling together. . . . nothing is served except confusion by mixing them up'.[55]

The confusion notwithstanding, Cabell's mythic mixture expresses an important theme. For while *Jurgen*, like *A Connecticut Yankee in King Arthur's Court*, satirises the idealism and actual practices of both the Arthurian and modern worlds, it goes beyond satire to emphasise the value of myth-making as man's means of embodying visions which can help him at least in part to reshape reality closer to his ideals. Though many readers may be baffled by Cabell's allusiveness, eclecticism, and private myth-making, and some may be annoyed by his inveterate fondness for anagrams and other word play, *Jurgen*, often outrageously comic, deserves to be more widely read.

v. John Erskine, *Galahad: Enough of His Life to Explain His Reputation* (1926); *Tristan and Isolde: Restoring Palamede* (1932)

John Erskine's two Arthurian novels follow medieval legends more closely than Cabell's work. If less surprising and less clever than *Jurgen*, they nevertheless offer some amusing satire. In an essay on 'Malory's Le Morte D'Arthur' (1928) Erskine finds the distinction of Malory's work in 'the dramatic vigor of the incidents, as over against the psychological interpretation which is the charm of most other versions'.[56] Like the 'other versions', his two novels turn on character more than on incident.

Galahad (1926) fulfils the promise of the subtitle and 'explains' Galahad's 'reputation' by detailing Lancelot's relationships with Guinevere and two

Elaines, depicting through them the chivalric world which the youth, 'an absolutely new kind of man', rejects. Incorporating a few Tennysonian elements, such as Lancelot's having escorted Guinevere to her wedding, Erskine generally follows Malory. But he alters stories in order to analyse love and chivalry with a thoroughly twentieth-century irony.

Erskine's version of the story of Elaine, daughter of Pelles (*Morte Darthur*, XI–XII) deletes all the supernatural elements found in Malory: Elaine expresses no interest in conceiving a Grail knight; she wants only to ensnare Lancelot by having his child. She gets him into bed not by enchantment, but by her wiles and physical appeal. After Guinevere's jealousy drives him mad, he recovers and lives with Elaine for some time. Erskine restores Lancelot to Guinevere by combining Malory's Mador and Meliagrance stories (XVIII and XIX). When Meliagrance accuses the queen of treason (trysting with Lancelot), Bors brings Lancelot back to court to defend her in the lists. Erskine invents an account of Galahad's initiation at Camelot, mostly under the maternal tutelage of Guinevere, then ends by adapting the Maid of Astolat story (*Morte Darthur*, XVIII). Lancelot does not go to the Winchester tournament to stifle rumour about his adultery, nor does he there sustain wounds that require Elaine's nursing. Erskine's changes in this last tale make it parallel more closely the initial encounter between Lancelot and the other Elaine. This paralleling of the two Elaine stories heightens both the intensity and the comedy of Guinevere's jealousy. Hearing that Lancelot has worn a lady's red sleeve in the jousts, she assumes that he has returned to Galahad's mother. Her confusion is resolved only when she views the body of the Elaine who has died floating to Camelot; she recognises with amazement that 'There were two of them'.

As with the first Elaine's seducing Lancelot, Erskine consistently avoids the supernatural; events derive from human motivations. The first chapter announces that the novel will not perpetuate legend or fable, but will 'tell the story as it happened in our world, to people like ourselves or only a little better—the story, that is, as it was before poets . . . used it as a language for remote and mystical things'. Though concerned with Galahad, the novel virtually ignores the Grail story, except for mentioning in the final chapter that Galahad 'is devoting himself . . . to the search for the holiest treasure in the world'. Instead, the novel depicts the confused, often contradictory efforts of men and women to find 'treasure in the world' through chivalric activity and love.

Erskine's depictions of love and chivalry analyse the characters' various value systems—abstract, humanistic, and relativistic. Principles of the Arthurian Order are shown to be both idealistic and pragmatic, grand and petty, enriching and limiting. The chief problem at Camelot is not that it is corrupt; this is not the fallen world of Tennyson's later idylls. It is simply the imperfect world of men and women. Since Arthur and Lancelot have civilised the realm and wrought order from chaos, people do not quite know what they should be doing with their time. The knights could fight dragons, but no one has seen any. The dilemma forces them to reassess what endeavours are worthwhile.

Galahad's mother repeatedly criticises the wastefulness of jousting and battling. She insists that knights should seek personal fulfilment closer to home, 'no matter what the Court would say'. Quick to discard standards of decorum in order to achieve her desires—for example, her night with Lancelot—she endorses a practical, relativistic system of values. When Lancelot and Galahad describe knighthood as a commitment to the public weal rather than to personal fulfilment, their chivalry seems, in contrast to her philosophy, highly idealistic. Yet Guinevere criticises chivalry from a precisely antithetical view, holding chivalric traditions too earthbound, too much concerned with expedience rather than ideals. She unsettles young Galahad's enthusiasm for Arthurian chivalry, for instance, by challenging his belief that victory establishes right.

Lancelot would seem to confirm her criticism that chivalry is essentially pragmatic when he caustically points out that her 'sophistry' will render Galahad impotent: 'Imagine some one needing his help in danger . . . and he'll be debating which side of the quarrel is more righteous!' But Lancelot's sarcasm further implies that the practical aspects of chivalry arise from consistent, not relative values: 'If he sees a man strike a woman, I suppose you'll want him to ascertain, before he interferes, whether the woman doesn't deserve a beating!'

Guinevere, however, rejects chivalric idealism as too commonplace. She seeks higher—though undefined—goals. Her affair with Lancelot began because she aspired to do something grand. But because women had few opportunities for achievement, she tried to realise her ambitions through a man. Giving up hope of 'making something' of Arthur, she expected Lancelot to 'act out [her] vision'. Yet she finally deems him, like the king, too much limited to pedestrian tasks. His quests have dwindled to insignificant investigations of complaints that the hay sent to Camelot's stables is substandard.

When Galahad appears, a naïve and relatively unformed creature, Arthur hopes through him to rejuvenate the old ways of the Order, 'before there were too many women'. But Guinevere seizes the opportunity to create a thoroughly new kind of man, so devoted to 'beautiful conduct' that, as Lancelot tells her, he is 'looking for a kind of goodness which belongs in heaven'. Under her tutelage Galahad develops an unpleasantly rigid code devoid of compassion for human frailty. The work's greatest irony is that Guinevere, on one level capable of inspiring Galahad's lofty idealism, and on another level given to adultery and inconsistent jealousy, is the author of the moral code which finally forces Galahad to reject her. On the other hand, Arthur, who has known about her affair for many years, recognises that the adulterous lovers have 'larger hearts and more generous thoughts' than Galahad. Unlike Galahad's abstract idealism, Arthur's humanism fulfils Guinevere's prescription to leave this world 'more beautiful, with more in it to respond to'.

Erskine illustrates these controversies about human values largely through a sexist dialectic, in which Arthur and Lancelot argue for balance, conservatism, practicality, and humaneness, while Elaine and Guinevere—for all their charms—scheme, manipulate, criticise chivalric achievements, and indulge too much in 'ideas' and 'talk'. The ongoing battle between the sexes finally seems to be the truest test of chivalry as a value system that is both pragmatic and idealistic. Having for many years suffered sorely at the hands of Guinevere and Elaine, Lancelot at the end of the novel withdraws to a monastery, ashamed that Arthur has known all along of his betrayal. Yet he is no tragic figure. Significantly, he does not undergo the spiritual conversion of Malory's Lancelot to achieve salvation. He is merely a sane, humane man who seems heroic because, as his final words imply, he tolerates human imperfection: 'can't a man be in a way of grace and still ask questions?'

While animated by scattered passages of genuine comedy and imbued with an often salubrious irony, Erskine's novel too often lapses into undistinguished dialogue. But the experiences of his self-effacing and intelligent Arthur, his long-suffering but resilient Lancelot, and the charming vixens who afflict them offer a creative, frequently entertaining modern use of Arthurian legend.

Perhaps a slightly better novel but one less interesting for its Arthurian elements is Erskine's *Tristan and Isolde: Restoring Palamede* (1932). It refocuses the love story by making Palamede, the Saracen who loves Isolde, the protagonist. As in *Galahad*, much of the book's irony and humour arises from the conflict between a naïve young man's conception of chivalry and the realities of men and women. As a youth, Palamede absorbs from his slave, a captured Crusader, a highly romanticised vision of chivalry. Discontent with the peaceful but comparatively pedestrian life around him—where 'love is earthly and selfish'—he seeks the 'wise and beautiful [chivalric] way of life', said to have been invented by Merlin (an idea advanced by Cabell in *Something About Eve* five years earlier). Though to him Isolde would seem to inspire love that is 'a disinterested kind of worship', he soon finds that the life around her belies courtly and Christian ideals. King Mark is crude and cowardly; Tristan faithless; and—as he finally discovers— even Isolde is too fleshly to rest content with being worshipped. After he matures sufficiently to admit that he, too, desires Isolde as much as he worships her, Palamede returns to his homeland.

Although Erskine focuses on Palamede, the hero of several French and Italian medieval romances, to an extent unprecedented in the *Morte Darthur*, he basically follows Malory's version of the Tristan story. He amplifies such situations as Mark's and Tristan's rivalry for Segwarides' wife, Tristan's involvement with Faranom's daughter, and his marriage to Isolde of Brittany. Expanding these episodes to explore their psychological intricacies, Erskine deletes supernatural material, notably Palamede's pursuit of the Questing Beast. Most important, he specifically discounts the legendary love potion: 'The minstrels made much of a magic draught which Brangain, according to them, poured in the cup when Isolde was crossing the sea to marry King Mark. . . . The minstrels were always singing about magic drinks! No, the doom of these lovers came upon them . . . under the open sky, in the glade by the sea. They were what they were, and they were young.'

Erskine expands the role of Brangain—whom he makes Isolde's nearly identical cousin—considerably beyond its importance in medieval romance. As Palamede becomes the hero of the tale, she becomes its heroine and his obvious match. Here, as in Gottfried von Strassburg and Béroul (Malory does not use the story), Brangain replaces Mark's bride in the wedding bed. Erskine also embellishes the story with many additional details. For instance, in medieval versions, Brangain is tied to a tree in the forest and Palamede rescues her. In Malory, jealous women at court are trying to get rid of the queen's favourite. In Gottfried and Béroul, Isolde wants to kill Brangain to keep her affair with Tristan secret. In Erskine, Mark's gardeners tie Brangain to an oak to renew the land by reviving a Druidical fertility rite. The episode thus plays with the idea of the waste land needing renewal and develops the novel's satire of chivalric society. On close inspection it proves far more primitive than the graceful culture Palamede has left behind.

When Erskine refers directly to Arthurian tradition, he generally treats it whimsically and sarcastically, as when the slave Jaafar recounted Merlin's enchantment by Nimuë to the boy Palamede: 'What Merlin was doing in the forest was never explicitly revealed, but he went on nothing but errands of mercy, and if he met anyone on the road, it was always a distressed damsel, and she was always beautiful. In every case but one, she was also good. Palamede noticed the high average.' Palamede's slave also comically sanitised Malory's tale of Uther and Igraine: 'Merlin did something to Uther, by way of magic, and the next time he met Ygraine she saw that he was what she needed and unconsciously had yearned for, and they were happy ever after, beginning immediately.' 'At the moment when Uther, through this science of Merlin's, attained bliss, Ygraine was the wife of the Duke of Cornwall, but Jaafar hastened lightly over that aspect of the story.'

Similar depictions debunk romance heroes and supply ironically drawn, but psychologically realistic, characters. Unlike Erskine's Galahad, who becomes an unpleasantly ascetic contrast to the flawed humanity of Camelot, Palamede as he loses his naïve illusions becomes increasingly engaging and dignified. Brangain is similarly appealing—a spirited, good humoured, and interesting woman much more attractive than the wilful females in *Galahad*. In focusing on these two figures, the conclusion of *Tristan and Isolde* departs from medieval versions of the story. Palamede deals Tristan his death wound, then escorts Isolde to his deathbed. The Saracen afterward sets out for his homeland, with Brangain quickly following him. Presumably they live happily in the culture Palamede earlier rejected for a chivalric myth, achieving a quiet wisdom, gentleness, humour, and love that is 'earthly and selfish'—but mutually fulfilling.

While such an articulate and ironic retelling of legend is inherently interesting and amusing, Erskine rather quickly exhausts the appeal of his central situation, the naïf's disenchantment, and the tale rapidly becomes predictable. Besides stripping away the heroic and mythic elements to review traditional story in the light of human realities, the novel also illustrates a way of expanding the familiar material by featuring characters who figure only minimally in early versions. On the whole, however, Erskine's two Arthurian novels have only minor significance today. They fall short of the genuine achievements of Robinson's artful poems and Twain's influential satire. Even so, they—like the host of less successful poems and dramas of the late nineteenth and early twentieth centuries—demonstrate that Arthur had found a home in America.

7

Dramatic New Developments

Early Twentieth-Century British Literature

Henry Irving's production of J. Comyns Carr's *King Arthur* at the Lyceum on January 12th, 1895 seems to have started a new trend in Arthurian literature: it was followed by a very large number of plays, of varying quality, in the next three decades, and most of those writers who were attracted to Arthurian themes preferred to give them dramatic form. J. C. Carr's *King Arthur* was a box office success, its first night attended by royalty, and it ran for more than a hundred performances, but most of the plays which followed it were either chamber dramas or never intended for performance.

The end of the nineteenth century was a period of rapid and significant development in the drama. Pinero, Oscar Wilde, Barrie and Shaw were writing, and after some years when there had been such a dearth of good plays that the English theatre had even had to rely to a large extent on French plays, there was something of a renaissance. The interest in psychological studies, already apparent in the novel and in poetry, also found expression in the drama; and audiences were more prepared to encounter previously less acceptable subjects such as illicit love, madness, and social problems of various kinds. A new skill in handling character, situation and dialogue is apparent in many of the plays of the last decade of the nineteenth century, and in many of the Arthurian plays, though J. C. Carr's *King Arthur*, it must be admitted, is not one of them. The demand for realism was offset by a lingering relish for melodrama and romance, and a liking for costume plays in contrast to those with modern settings. The Arthurian legend provided subjects rich in psychological interest, affording clashes of personality which could be treated with varying degrees of seriousness or melodrama, and an opportunity for romance to find expression in both text and scenic effects.

Henry Irving, always on the look-out for suitable material, had long wanted a play on King Arthur so that he could play the part of the 'spotless king' (according to his biographer, Percy Fitzgerald), and indeed one had been written for him by W. G. Wills, but it was found to be unsatisfactory, and J. C. Carr was asked to 'lick it into shape'. Unable to make anything of it, he offered to write another and 'somewhat to the surprise of the public, he who had been art-critic, manager of Grosvenor and New Galleries, dramatist and designer of dresses, etc. for the Lyceum, now came forward as a poet; and a very respectable poet he proved to be, with harmonious, mellifluous lines, effective from a stage point of view'.[1] Irving considered the play languid and 'lacking in ginger', but thought its construction sound. Carr said that he went to Malory for the basis of the play, but he made very considerable adjustments to Malory's narrative, and the style is flat and banal. Irving had other resources to draw on to enliven the production, however, and Sir Arthur Sullivan was persuaded to compose music for it, and to conduct. Sir Edward Burne-Jones, who had never done anything of the kind before, and disliked the theatre but wished to oblige Irving, designed the costumes and sets. He 'supplied some exquisite combinations or arrangements of colour, which were certainly new to stage-land' and when later Irving was knighted, 'there was to be the unprecedented incident of no fewer than *three* knights—a musician, a painter and an actor—combining their talents in a single play'.[2] The play resembles a masque, with striking scenic effects: the Prologue was set beside 'The Magic Mere', with a Chorus of Lake Spirits singing; while swimming maidens imported from *Rheingold* contrived to find Excalibur 'most skilfully'. Visions—of Guinevere, of the Holy Grail—appeared and faded, peals of thunder and flashes of lightning accompanied the machinations of the villainous Morgan and Mordred, and threatened the lovers' meeting in the forest glade, and at the end, as the stage darkened, Arthur was borne away in the barge, with the three queens bending over his body, while a final chorus chanted:

> *Arise, and sleep no more;*
> *Greet the dawn, the night is o'er,*
> *England's sword is in the sea!*[3]

Clement Scott, who reviewed the production,[4] suggests in his enthusiastic but also critical account of the play something of the appeal of its theme for his contemporaries. He says that it has been long awaited: 'At last "King Arthur" is to be acted at the Lyceum; at last Henry Irving is to be the "half-divine" ruler and founder of the Table Round!' Everyone, it seems, had his own ideas of how it ought to be done—'The poets, and the sentimentalists, and the aesthetes, pestered poor Mr Irving with their ideas on "King Arthur".' Everyone comes to the theatre with their minds 'saturated with and steeped in the Tennysonian version of the legend'. Scott later indicates the contemporary concept of Arthur's character: 'He is a warrior, but still he is a demi-god. A halo of light should be about his head. His face should be one of transcendent majesty . . .' Scott was disappointed that Arthur was presented in a tight-fitting suit of black armour, undraped in any way, which made him 'a man unromantic, unheroic, unideal', and robbed him of the air of dignity and distinction that he should have had. (Fortunately the appeal of Ellen Terry as Guinevere was, by contrast, enhanced by the priceless costume which had been designed for her; the audience found her 'tender and lovely', 'touching and pathetic'.)

In addition to the scenic effects, the 'lawless passion', the moral conflicts and the poignant emotions were the play's great attractions. Lancelot is presented as 'a deeply religious man, tormented with an unholy love'; saintly-minded and stainless, he longs to go in quest of the Grail, and Scott comments on the 'rare dramatic skill' with which Carr 'has designed the mental complication'. In this version of the story, Lancelot and Guinevere do not reveal their love for each other until the time of the Grail Quest, and the compression of the narrative brings all the events close together. Guinevere's Maying does not end in the attack of Meliagaunt, but allows a Midsummer Night's Dream-like episode in the woodland glades in which Lancelot and Guinevere meet and make love, apparently for the first time: 'we do not remember a more beautiful love passage than that between Mr Forbes Robertson and Miss Ellen Terry, when the dear waist had been clasped at last by the eager, yet reluctant arms. In an instant the saint disappears in the lover; the obedient slave becomes the all-conquering master. The floodgates of reticence and reserve have been broken down, and out pours the full torrent of pent-up devotion. But it is only momentary. . . .' (p. 378). Lest it should be thought that the author was responsible for the rapture apparently experienced by the audience in watching the scene, it is instructive to refer to the text:

> Guin.   *Nay, scold me not.*
> *There's nothing haunts me when I have thee near.*
> *Love shuts the door on all things save itself,*
> *On all that's past, on all that is to come*
> *When thou art by! Tell me, 'tis so with thee?*
> Lan.   *Ay, sweet, 'tis so.*
> Guin.   *Ah, say it once again!*
> *I could not live, Lancelot, if in thy heart*
> *There lurked the tiniest little ache or pain*
> *Love might not cure.*
> Lan.   *Thou knowest all my heart;*
> *And in my love, which knows no law but love,*
> *The future and the past are drowning straws*
> *Caught in the full tide of our present joy,*
> *That neither ebbs nor flows.*[5]

'They part in tears, but with chastened hearts', and meanwhile 'the poor blind, trusting King' knows nothing. But the secret is soon revealed, through the letter which Elaine of Astolat, dying of love for Lancelot, clasps in her hand when her barge floats down to Camelot. The pathos of this scene is rapidly succeeded by the dramatic contrast of Guinevere's confession of her guilt, and Arthur's attempted vengeance—he rushes at Lancelot, who is standing near, but Excalibur drops from his palsied hand, while his anguish over his prostrate wife is 'infinitely pathetic'. Guinevere is next seen in prison with Dagonet the fool; Mordred ascends the throne and proposes to burn her at the stake, but Arthur, presumed dead, reappears to save her. He and Mordred fight, and Mordred escapes, but Arthur is mortally wounded and dies with the repentant Guinevere at his feet.

The play appealed to Sarah Bernhardt, and she had it translated into French with the intention of playing the part of Lancelot, though she was never to do so. It was as successful when Irving took it to the United States as it had been in London. It undoubtedly gave audiences what they wanted from the story of Arthur and from the theatre at the time.

But not all critics were as warm in their praise as Clement Scott, whose approval was even expressed for Mr Comyns Carr's 'most creditable and scholarly work'. Another writer in the *Saturday Review*[6] assessed the text in terms with which the modern reader is likely to have some sympathy: 'Mr. Comyns Carr is frankly a jobber and nothing else . . . And all the time, whilst the voice, the gesture, the emotion expressed, are those of the hero-king, the talk is the talk of an angry and jealous coster-monger, exalted by the abject submission of the other parties to a transport of magnanimity in refraining from reviling his wife and punching her lover's head. . . . As to Miss Ellen Terry, it was the old story, a born actress of real women's parts condemned to figure as a mere artist's model in costume plays. . . . It is pathetic to see Miss Terry snatching at some fleeting touch of nature in her part' and passing on to 'the next length of arid sham-feminine twaddle in blank verse, which she pumps out in little rhythmic strokes in a desperate and all too obvious effort to make music of it'. The author of this vigorous criticism was G. B. Shaw.

Tennyson's *Idylls* not only created a very widespread interest in the Arthurian legend, but also revealed the dramatic potential of the stories from many different aspects. The stories of King Arthur, of Lancelot and Guenevere, and of Elaine of Astolat had the greatest appeal for dramatists for obvious reasons; later, the story of Tristram and Iseult became the dominant theme, as writers broke away from—or perhaps reacted against—the influence of Tennyson. There were, however, some plays which took less familiar or less romantic topics as their basis, and of these, Henry Newbolt's *Mordred: A Tragedy* is the most distinguished and the most interesting. This was published in 1895, but it appears never to have been staged. A poetic drama in five acts, its theme is the relationship between Mordred and his father, Arthur, and the implications of Arthur's guilt in begetting him form the rest of the story. It shows both originality and ingenuity, is well constructed, and is not without literary merit.

The drama opens at the height of Arthur's fame, when the ideals of the Round Table are everywhere upheld, and justice and peace have been success-fully established throughout the kingdom. At this point, Mordred comes to the court and asks for knighthood, which Arthur grants him, not knowing who he really is. Guinevere and Lancelot have only just realised their love for each other, and though they shortly afterwards declare it, each nobly strives to keep it under control. Then Agravaine and Mordred meet, and Mordred astounds his brother by revealing his true parentage. Now the Round Table begins to encounter difficulties: Pelleas bursts in to complain that Gawain has, under pretext of helping him, seduced his beloved. Arthur, like a wise and patient headmaster summoning trouble-makers to his study, calls for Mordred after seeing the guilty Gawain, and explains that Gawain must be banished. Mordred defends his half-brother and begins to use his secret weapon: he hints to Arthur, though without naming Morgance, that he knows of Arthur's youthful sin of incest. As he explains later to Agravaine:

> *I told enough; beneath my visor's helm*
> *The King hath seen the face of buried sin*
> *Glaring with dreadful eyes.*   (p. 48)

Soon the court is filled with rumours of Arthur's corruption, and in consequence Lancelot tries to persuade Guinevere to flee with him. Before the court, Arthur has to give judgement in the case of Pelleas and Gawain, but he evades the issue to save his own face. He exonerates Gawain on the grounds that he is a true knight who has declared his innocence; Arthur insists that among the ideals of the Round Table is the principle that one man's word against another's is enough. Thus he can, if need be, deal with Mordred's accusation in the same way.

Shortly afterwards, Lancelot makes an assignation with Guinevere; he will ride with the King's hunting-party and then secretly return at night. Arthur, later in the day, is distressed at the news of Tristram's and Iseult's betrayal of Mark, and their flight to Joyous Gard, and then to hear of the death of Lamorak by treachery, but this is followed by worse news: Mordred reports Lancelot's return to Camelot, and denounces him. Arthur starts back for the court, but by the time of his arrival, Guinevere has found sanctuary at Amesbury; Mordred, however, plans with Gawain to bring Arthur and Guinevere together so that the King can forgive her. If he refuses to do so, Mordred will reveal his father's guilt. When the King and Queen meet, Arthur is generous to her, but grieved and amazed to learn that she had never loved him. Guinevere, no longer the guilt-stricken, remorseful and defiled creature of some of the contemporary versions of the story, reproaches her husband not only for his sin with Morgance, but also with the injustice of his treatment of Pelleas and Gawain. Only then does Arthur understand who Mordred is—he had been told that the product of his misdeed had died in infancy. Now it is the turn of Guinevere to be generous: she expresses her loyalty to her husband and her readiness to help him.

The next scenes lead up to the Last Battle. Mordred finds the ideals of the Round Table, with the obligations which its vows imply, intolerably constricting; he sees himself as the victim of 'tyranny'. Arthur declares that Constantine shall succeed him, and at last the opposition between father and son breaks out into open conflict, and Mordred dies at Arthur's hand, pleading for 'life! One year of life—untyrannised!' The drama ends with the departure of the dying Arthur on the ship.

Newbolt has taken Malory as the basis of his poetic drama, but with many modifications. He emphasises the essential goodness and generosity of the principal characters: Lancelot and Guinevere struggle to resist temptation, and Guinevere speaks warmly, when Lancelot declares his love, of Arthur's goodness to her:

> *he has kept for me*
> *In sacred dedication, the one gift*
> *that none can offer twice, the crown of love,*
> *The undivided faith of body and soul* (p. 19)

and so she will not leave her husband for Lancelot, even though Arthur's integrity is being questioned. Arthur has long since completely forgotten and as it were lived down his youthful misdemeanour, and after many years devoted to establishing and maintaining a noble ideal he is caught unawares by Mordred's insinuations, and the accusation of a sin that seems out of character with the man as everyone knows him. He is the embodiment of the Victorian father-figure, upright, demanding, middle-aged—in a sense, inhuman, except that he has feet of clay. Mordred, the 'difficult' son, detests both what he sees as his father's hypocrisy, and like a misfit in a public school, the ethos of the Round Table.

> *Life's not a mummer's dance, that we should walk it*
> *Stiffly composed and following one by one*
> *The same set figure: 'tis most orderly*
> *When ordered least . . .* (p. 23)

he declares impatiently. He is no melodramatic villain, as is Comyns Carr's Mordred, but rather the son who has been wronged: in his last confrontation with his father he asserts: 'I have more right / To take thy life than thou could'st ever claim / To give me mine!' (p. 121). Throughout the drama he shows restraint and even a capacity to appreciate the nobility of others. He is reluctant to oppose Lancelot, 'out of all to cross the one / Most knightly and most noble' (p. 49).

Newbolt places as an epigraph to the work a quotation from Hegel, translated by Walter Pater, which suggests the conception of tragedy underlying *Mordred*: 'In genuine tragedy . . . they must be powers both alike moral and justifiable, which from this side and from that come into collision. Two opposed Rights come forth: the one breaks itself to pieces against the other: in this way both alike suffer loss: while both alike are justified, the one towards the other: not as if this were right, that other wrong.' Arthur and Mordred are thus to be seen as 'two opposed Rights', each to be accorded some sympathy. Adultery fades into the background, while the love of Lancelot and Guinevere is seen as romantic, unfortunate, but not degradingly sinful. Indeed Guinevere is represented as a high-principled, dignified woman who has suffered patiently and endeavours to resist temptation when it comes.

The drama lacks passion, but the situations and relationships hold the reader's attention. The plot is intriguing and the scenes well varied; Newbolt does not attempt much historical realism, but there is realism of another kind in the strained relationships between the protagonists. Without the fire of William Morris's interpretations of Arthurian situations, or the moral fervour of Tennyson's *Idylls*, it yet gives a sense of the characters as real people struggling with intractable moral problems. And with psychological problems, too:

209

Newbolt has sensitively and seriously considered the implications of the Arthur-Morgause episode in a dignified and sustained poetic drama. It makes a fascinating contrast with J. Comyns Carr's vapid though very successful play of the same year.

Two years later in 1897, F. B. Money Coutts published, under the title of *King Arthur*, 'A Trilogy of Lyrical Dramas founded on The Morte D'Arthur of Sir Thomas Malory', consisting of 'Merlin', 'Launcelot' and 'Guinevere'. They are of little literary value, partly because of the unfortunate form that Coutts adopted for them, but worth noticing for two reasons. The first is that in his Introduction, Coutts made some interesting comments on his subject, and the second, that obviously dissatisfied with his work, he tried again, and in 1907 published a much improved version of the trilogy, with the addition of another little play to precede the others, 'Uther Pendragon'. In the first version, unlike Newbolt, Coutts found Mordred's origins as given by Malory distasteful, and so represented him as the legitimate son of Morgan le Fay: 'By this means the taint of his parenthood is removed, and, while he retains his personality, his actions are guided by one who has the powers of darkness for her allies.' His conception of the figure of Arthur is also very different from the popular one: for Coutts, the King is a pathetic figure, 'a dog-like attendant on a Providence that betrays him'.[7] But despite this, Coutts recognises the story of Arthur as 'our one great English Legend' and sees it as an allegory of the eternal conflict between the spiritual and sensuous part of man's nature. Thus King Arthur represents the spiritual, Guinevere the sensuous, while Launcelot is the emblem of mankind itself. In a narrower sense, he continues, it is an allegory of 'the life of a nation; or rather, of all nations'.[8]

After this impressive interpretation, the reader is surprised to encounter an absurdly operatic style, at times reminiscent of pantomime, which makes even the sacred mysteries of the Grail sound ridiculous:

> *This is the mystical cup,*
> *All worshipful knights would see;*
> *For they that achieve it sup*
> *With the Prophet of Galilee!*[9]

Equally unfortunate is the expression of Arthur's distress when he discovers Guinevere's guilt:

> *If your swoon is sweet with some fairyland sweven,*
> *Dream on! Never wake to this wild, wild world!*
> *For the stars by your sin have been blotted from heaven,*
> *The moon disempearled!*[10]

Guinevere recovers and is led out, while Arthur follows 'wistfully'. The revised version, *The Romance of King Arthur*, is a less banal, though still a sentimental, vulgar re-telling of incidents from Malory, whose phrases Coutts here and there incorporates. Guinevere pines for a lover; she is 'weary to death of Arthur's devotion to Religion, Chivalry and the State'. Meanwhile Morgan plots rather obtrusively for the overthrow of Arthur and his kingdom. Coutts has tried to update Malory by tightening up the plot and embroidering the solemn moments, as for example at the death of Launcelot:

> *Therewith came*
> *Six knights in purple mantles, and they staunched*
> *His blood and softly bore him to a hall*
> *Of porphyry, in the Castle; in the midst*
> *An altar, shrouded with white linen, stood*
> *Whereon was set a cup of emerald hue*
> *That inly smouldered as with ruby fire. . . .*[11]

As in Comyns Carr's *King Arthur*, the passion for surface realism and scenic effect almost obliterates meaning, but some of Coutts' contemporaries admired it.

Some other works reveal aspects of general interest. John Davidson's 'A Ballad of Lancelot' (later renamed 'The Last Ballad') was published in 1899.[12] This is an attractive, though undistinguished poem on the theme of the madness of Lancelot, set in 'Lyonnesse, The wave-worn kingdom of romance'. It has touches of Pre-Raphaelite charm without the underlying strength of the Pre-Raphaelite vision at its best. Lancelot has torn himself away from Guinevere, and serves his king in every strenuous, lonely quest that he can undertake, but is haunted by his longing for the queen, and decides to go and see her once more before he dies:

> *'Once ere I die' he said, and turned*
> *Westward his faded silken sails.*

Arthur keeps court, 'a glittering rout' and Lancelot's heart fails him when he sees it, so he forbears his soul's desire, and turns away. In Lyonnesse, he rushes, mad, into the forest in anguish of mind, seeing 'Her love and my love, noxious lust!'; and believing that they are both 'dupes of their senses', is overcome with revulsion. He meets Galahad and they recognise each other; Galahad sets off on his Quest and Lancelot longs to go too, but he fights for 'a vision of the cup—In vain' because the vision of the Queen obsesses him. Nevertheless, his love for the Queen and her goodness saves him:

> *He saw her like a goddess sit*
> *Enthroned upon the noonday sun*

and the power and purity of his worship for her redeem him:

> *His love, in utter woe annealed,*
> *Escaped the furnace, sweet and clear—*
> *His love that on the world had sealed*
> *The look, the soul of Guinevere.*

211

This rather discursive narrative poem in ballad form, though it lacks intensity, makes a new approach to the theme of the love of Lancelot and Guinevere. It is only with the experience of Lancelot that it is concerned, and not with the dramatic situation of the lovers. The treatment of passion is interesting, in that it is Lancelot's inner revulsion against what he feels to be the grosser aspects of his love that motivates his actions, while the sublimation of his love and the devotion to a 'good woman' save him. Davidson rejects the ambiguity generally found in contemporary treatments of the theme: the glamorisation of the irresistible but illicit love which is at the same time censured, sternly renounced and deeply repented. But in avoiding the subject of adultery for visionary flights of fancy, Davidson weakens the story; and not even the theme of madness, which seems to have interested a number of other authors at this time, can offset the poem's prevailing romanticism.

Poignant death-scenes become a feature of many of the Arthurian works of the turn of the century. The stories of Tristram and Iseult, as of Lancelot and Guenevere, offer opportunity for the development of what aroused interest as peculiarly heart-rending episodes. In particular, the love-death theme, immortalised by Wagner in 1859 in *Tristan und Isolde*, seems to have taken hold of the popular imagination. Laurence Binyon's poem 'Tristram's End', written in 1897, is an example of this. After an introductory section, the second part of the poem takes the form of dialogue between Tristram and Isoult in alternating eight-line stanzas, as Tristram, stricken to death, is at last re-united with Isoult. The pathos of the scene is enhanced by the contrasting emotions of the lovers: Tristram declares

> *Isoult, Isoult, thy kiss!*
> *To sorrow though I was made*
> *I die in bliss, in bliss*

and Isoult answers:

> *Tristram, my heart must break.*
> *O leave me not in the grave*
> *Of the dark world! Me too take!*
> *Save me, O Tristram, save!*[13]

Their end is as romantic as their love, the sadness of it softened by the last meeting, in contrast with the starker original version of the story which allows Iseult to arrive only after the death of her lover. Isoult of Brittany is conceived as a less jealous figure than in most other versions; she wakes in the night, feels anxious about her husband, goes to his room, and there finds both lovers dead. She is filled with remorse, and declares that she loved Tristram not enough. Then she has the lovers dressed in wedding clothes and sent back together to Mark in Cornwall. The poem as a whole, though not without charm and some depth of feeling, is little more than a watered-down version of Arnold's *Tristram and Iseult*.

Graham Hill's play *Guinevere* of 1906 takes us back to the genre of Comyns Carr's *King Arthur* of the previous decade. Hill sensationalises the story, and picks out those elements in it most capable of being made melodramatic. The action moves at a sharp pace. In the first scene, villains plot, the arrival of Guinevere as bride is awaited, and complaints about Arthur's icy virtue are elaborately aired. In the next scene, Launcelot and Guinevere find themselves in love—she had fallen in love with him earlier, when she first saw him—and overcome with rapture, the 'lovers disappear into the forest'. The next act introduces the poisoned apple motif, here presented as a device of Vivien's to discredit Guinevere. The theme of patriotic duty is also introduced, as Arthur reminds his consort that

> We, too, my Queen,
> We two belong, by right, to England first[14]

and that she, too, is 'part of life's appointed work'. But suspicions are being sown in Arthur's mind, while Agravaine and Mordred plot to seize the throne at once and make Vivien queen, and Launcelot determines to go overseas, for ever, to avoid further temptation. Indeed, he comes to say goodbye but while he and Guinevere are conversing about their common sense of duty and exchanging prayers and last goodbyes, uproar breaks out, the door is beaten down, and Arthur enters with his knights. He reproaches the lovers, who seem to be falsely accused on this particular occasion, but he refuses to listen. His attention is however distracted by the arrival of a messenger announcing a joint attack by Mordred and King Mark of Cornwall. The last act takes place in the convent to which Guinevere has retreated, and where she is seen in terrible suspense about the outcome of the battle, but soon a page arrives with the news that Arthur and Mordred are both dead. He is promptly followed by Launcelot, dying from wounds, and Guinevere's expressions of love for him evoke horrified comments from the nuns who witness the scene. The love-death theme satisfactorily rounds off the tale of woe, as declaring 'in life / In death, we are together still', Launcelot dies, and Guinevere falls dead over his body.

This blank verse drama is only interesting for what it suggests about contemporary tastes, and the idea of what a play should be. It is certainly full of incident, and some fine feelings, but as G. B. Shaw said of Comyns Carr, Hill was 'frankly a jobber', whose version of the story does little more than testify to the extent of the current interest in the Arthurian legend.

The extent to which the Arthurian legends had become popular in the early years of this century is further demonstrated by such works as Arthur Dillon's *King Arthur Pendragon* (1906), as well as Ernest Rhys's *Gwenevere: A Lyric Play* (1905), and *Enid* and *The Masque of the Grail* (1908). Dillon's is a rather precious blank verse play; based on Malory and the verse of Dr Sebastian Evans, or so the author states. The large cast includes Merlin and Nimuë (the latter in the act of imprisoning Merlin in a tree in the first scene), and also Tristan and Isolde. The play treats the traditional stories very freely, but has little literary or dramatic merit. Ernest Rhys's *Gwenevere*, which was performed at the Coronet Theatre in 1905, is based on the Welsh legends, on which he had written distinguished critical works, and the French romances, but in it Galahad is confronted with what seems a modern moral dilemma. Is he to follow the Quest to share the glorious achievements of his companions, or to stay at home, giving up youth and even life itself to care for the stricken Pelleas in the Castle of Carbonek? Through the renunciation that he chooses, he finally achieves the Grail. *Enid* and *The Masque of the Grail* were both performed at the Court Theatre in 1908, with music by Vincent Thomas. Rhys in a preface to *Enid* comments on the unfavourable contemporary attitude to romance, blaming 'Mr Shaw, the great anti-romantic of our time', for helping to put it out of fashion.

From this point onwards, the theme of Tristram and Iseult becomes dominant in Arthurian literature in a number of dramatic treatments. It is plot and situation rather than the analysis of character or of the experience of over-whelming love that the writers are most interested in, and the story allows considerable scope for variation and for dramatic treatment. The love-potion and the act of falling in love, the jealous husband, the implications of there being two Iseults, the motif of the white and black sails, and the final love-death, were all elements that could be developed in different ways to increase the effectiveness of the work. The first of the dramas on the theme is by J. Comyns Carr; his *Tristram and Iseult* of 1906 was intended for performance. As with his earlier *King Arthur*, although his extensive theatrical experience enabled Carr to produce a well-constructed and dramatic piece, the quality of the writing does not come up to the demands of the subject.

The version is notable, however, in that it makes considerable use of the earlier incidents of the story which most previous writers passed over. Tristram is in Ireland to be healed—by Iseult, rather than by her mother—and in addition to slaying Moraunt, he has saved Iseult from an unwelcome match. Comyns Carr includes the incident of the fragment of the sword which reveals Tristram's identity in this well-managed first act. The drinking of the love-draught is complicated by the suggestion that it is really poison meant for Mark, which adds excitement to the moment when Tristram boldly drains the cup; and the mixed motives of the protagonists and the inherent ironies of the situation increase its interest. But what follows is disappointing: the lovers can only express their sensations in terms of flowery visions which fail to create the necessary impression of dawning passion and of the frightening alternation of joy and horror. In the next act, Comyns Carr's taste for elaborate sets is apparent, as Iseult waits for her lover near her forest bower, which appears to have a turret, seen through trees, with a stream flowing into a pool, surrounded by banks and rocky mounds. Iseult seems to have managed to defer the consummation of her marriage by insisting on keeping a lonely nightly vigil in her bower out of grief at the death of her uncle, Moraunt: unlike Swinburne, all the dramatists avoid the substitution of Brangane for Iseult on her wedding night. Iseult comes to Tristram, but they suspect that they are spied upon, and their rapturous love-making is enhanced by the knowledge that at any moment they may be taken by Mark and his courtiers. The love-death fantasy is played with throughout the scene, as the lovers speak of their experience: the love-potion had

> *freed two prisoned souls*
> *That else were bound for ever. It was life.*
> *Aye, life, not death, thou gavest us to drink!*
> *What else is life but love.*[15]

Tristram comments 'We thought 'twas death we drank, and so it was',[16] though later he asserts that 'death and life are one! and Life and Love!'[17] 'Then, Death, come quickly!' replies Iseult, and soon Mark appears, with his companion Andred, who stabs Tristram in the back and leaves him to die in the arms of Iseult. The prompt dispatch of Tristram on the stage makes a dramatic incident, contrasting with the tender scenes which precede it, and also with what follows. Iseult dies beside Tristram in a final tableau, while a vision (also seen earlier in the play by Iseult) of Iseult of the White Hands appears: she is, as it were, that aspect of Iseult that has the power of healing. The sail-motif also appears in the final moments, as the ship of death appears to carry away the lovers, for 'For all Love's wounds there is no cure but Death!' It is a sentimental, trivialising version of the story, though constructed with some technical competence.

T. H. Lee, whose *Marriage of Iseult and Other Plays* was published in 1909, refers in his preface to the earlier treatments of both Wagner and J. Comyns Carr, and asserts that the story is not suitable for a full-length drama, because it needs swift natural movement and not expanded treatment. His play is therefore a tragedy in two scenes, and it contains only four characters. It is noteworthy for the extreme view that it takes of Iseult's situation as the wife of Mark, and the remarkably forthright terms in which she defines it: 'For she that does not love her husband is / A strumpet', and marriage, if not based on mutual love, is 'licensed harlotry'. Indeed, she goes further, and insists that in taking her to Mark, Tristram is committing rape; that with Mark, she will be an adulteress. The drama is also unusual in its handling of the love-draught motif: Iseult on the ship fills two goblets with wine from a large flask, and then adds drops from a smaller flask, apparently with the intention of poisoning both Tristram and herself. Brangane sees this, pours away the wine, and substitutes the love-potion; all of this is unknown to Iseult, who tells Tristram that the wine is poisoned as they both drink. In the second aubade-like scene in which the lovers speak much of honour, and assert that their love is no sin, Iseult says that since a miracle 'did hap' when first they drank, she will try another drink, and each drinks in turn from a goblet. This 'truly is / The love-draught!—Now I know how 'tis I am / But one with thee', Iseult exclaims, and they both die, just as

Mark enters. He is given one of the most memorably unhappy lines in Arthurian drama. 'O, God! My God!—I'm crushed!' he says when he sees what has happened, and exits sobbing. Even apart from such sublime infelicities, the effect of the play as a whole is very unconvincing and melodramatic: the compression of the story so as to eliminate all but the basic essentials of the plot does not succeed in producing an artistically satisfying result. The attempt to intensify the poignancy of Iseult's situation by references to strumpets is more strident than moving. But this play looks forward to Hardy's *Famous Tragedy of the Queen of Cornwall* where a somewhat similar compression, achieved through stylisation and techniques reminiscent of Greek tragedy, succeeds in achieving an austere power.

In 1913, Martha Kinross's *Tristram and Isoult*, a three-act play in blank verse, appeared. This handles the traditional story freely, like most of the other plays on the same topic, but is remarkable for the very feminist tone which pervades it. It opens in Camelot, where Guinevere and Isoult are watching a joust, and exchanging confidences. Guinevere laments her marriage and her present situation, Isoult says that Tristram first fell in love with her while he was being healed of his wound. Tristram is already married to Isoult of Brittany, but Isoult of Cornwall has followed him to Camelot, accompanied by Brangane. The theme of patriotism, which comes first in Tristram's life, is introduced, for Tristram has to hurry away to defend Cornwall against invaders. In the second act, at Tintagil, the battle has been won, and the jealous Mark, returning from it, taunts Isoult with her love for Tristram and tries to get his revenge by making her afraid. In a curiously violent scene, he tries to throw her over the parapet of the castle on to the rocks, and they struggle desperately together.

> *Isoult!*
> *Shall I not break thy body's vase and spill*
> *Its royal wine ere he may drink again?*[18]

says Mark, and he gloats over the idea of making 'this flesh a bleeding pulp'. But though Tristram later expresses his contempt for Mark, who has long been dependent on him for the defence of his kingdom, Mark finds strength enough to stab him. In the next act, Tristram is dying in Brittany, tended by his wife, here represented as a paragon of kindness and understanding. She has herself sent for Isoult of Cornwall, who soon arrives, and a touching dialogue takes place between the two Isoults. Queen Isoult regrets that between them, she and Tristram have brought such sorrow upon Isoult of Brittany. After this, exclaiming rather grandly 'Come thou, my sea', Tristram dies, and Isoult poisons herself. The ending is thus more realistic than the usual love-death where Iseult (or Guinevere) instantly expires from sorrow. Isoult's death is a deliberate and defiant act of courage, melodramatic though it of course is, and typical of the militant feminism of the play as a whole.

Though this play has no great literary merit, it gives an unusual variation on the theme by presenting it from a woman's point of view. Like the play by T. H. Lee previously discussed, it also indicates how through their Arthurian subject-matter, these little plays express for their age different responses to marital relationships, to moral problems, and to society. Both suggest changing attitudes and in each there is a hint of a more modern tone. Such love as that of Tristram and Iseult no longer needs to be justified; it asserts its right to recognition, and its pre-eminence over duty. The new generation preferred the defiance of Iseult to the repentance of Guinevere.

The *Tristan and Iseult* (1917) of the Decadent poet Arthur Symons is interesting as an example of Symbolist drama, and is a play still worth reading. It contrasts strikingly with J. Comyns Carr's *King Arthur* of 1895, indicating the changes that had taken place in the theatre since the turn of the century. For in his *Tristan and Iseult*, Symons was attempting to achieve something very different from the lavish spectacle and realistic effects of Henry Irving's production. He aimed at offering his audience, through ecstatic identification with the lovers, a quasi-religious experience. The play was inspired by Wagner's *Tristan und Isolde*, which Symons heard shortly before he began to write his own version, but he had come under the spell of Wagner on a visit to Bayreuth some years earlier.[19] Thus he seems to have hoped to achieve something of the effect of opera through the synthesis of words, stylised movement, and appropriate sets. It was also his ambition to have the work performed in Rome, where Wagner had died, with Eleanora Duse—to whom the work was dedicated—as Iseult, though this was never realised.

The play begins in Ireland with the earlier episodes of the story to supply the motivation for Iseult's antagonism to Tristan, which later changes dramatically to bewildered love. It allows the story to start in a low key, with a domestic scene which includes the Queen, Iseult's mother, and Iseult of the White Hands as well as Iseult of Ireland. Much happens within it, nevertheless, for Meriadoc, the son of Morold, wishes to marry Iseult; Tristram is proved to be the slayer of Morold when the sword is pieced together, at the point when he has just arrived to claim Iseult for King Mark; and Iseult of Brittany restrains the angry passions that spring up at the discovery of Tristram's guilt, so that he is eventually forgiven by the Queen. Iseult bitterly resents being the subject of a political match, for Mark is already an old man, and refuses to accept that being a queen herself will be any consolation. She sweeps out contemptuously with Brangaene to

> *talk of being queens,*
> *Not in this market, where they bid for us.*[20]

Later on the ship for Cornwall, she reverts to her unfortunate plight:

> *My mother sold me, Tristan bought me, Mark*
> *Pays down the price and takes me.* (p. 37)

Meriadoc, accompanying her, suggests the assassination of Tristan. Already we are a long way from the flowery visions and romantic fantasies of the earlier Tristan plays. The two Iseults have been quite sharply differentiated, and Iseult of Ireland in particular emerges as an individual, whose plight is portrayed with considerable sympathy.

Eventually Iseult decides to make up her quarrel with Tristan and to seal their accord with a drink. The drinking of the potion is led up to in so matter-of-fact a manner that its effect is the more striking. It is almost literally a waking to love, for they both feel that they have slept and suddenly wakened, and both express bewildered astonishment:

> '*Tristan!*'
> '*Iseult! O, is it life or death. . . ?*' (p. 48)

Iseult's reaction changes to fear, and she crouches down on the seat,

> *O what is love, and why is love so bitter*
> *After the blinding sweetness of a moment?*
> *I am afraid, I am afraid of love,*
> *This is some death that has got hold of me . . .* (p. 51)

Tristan is firmly resolute, but scarcely comforting:

> *Fear not, Iseult; this thing must be endured.*
> *We have not sought it, it must be endured.*

The impact of the love-draught is convincingly suggested through what is for the most part very natural-sounding though pedestrian dialogue. Symons, moreover, succeeds in suggesting a deepening of the relationship between them as they discuss their predicament in the next act. As they argue about and try to analyse their experience of love, it takes on an almost blasphemously sacramental quality: Iseult says, 'Tristan, this is my body and my blood, And they are yours' (p. 73). But their love is not sublimated or over-spiritualised: the anguished intensity of her emotion is suggested in Iseult's later words to Tristan: 'Tristan, take hold of me and hold me fast, And hurt my fingers between both your hands' (p. 74).

An additional strength of the play lies in the relationship between Mark and Tristan. Mark, though he is old and stern, is not caricatured as a jealous husband. Like Newbolt's Arthur, he is more like a patient headmaster, restrained and dignified. When he comes upon the lovers his first words to Iseult are:

> *Queen, I have come to take you to your throne,*
> *My kingdom cannot spare you.* (p. 76)

He reproaches Tristan for his ingratitude in a scene that has a depth and subtlety of feeling unsurpassed in any other version, and Tristan, overcome

218

with shame, is unable to reply. Iseult has to answer for him, with a naïve directness that suggests how young she is:

> *My lord, you see that Tristan cannot speak,*
> *You see that Tristan is too honourable*
> *To speak the truth.* (p. 78)

Mark, however, insists on an answer from Tristan himself: 'stand up before me, Tristan. Answer me' (p. 79), and Tristan admits that he has wronged Mark, and is banished. The disparity in age intensifies the effectiveness of the situation: Mark is a father-figure for Tristan, their rivalry in love misplaced and inappropriate, a feature of the relationship that is developed at the end of the drama.

In the final act, Tristan has been wounded by Meriadoc with a poisoned dagger, and lies dying, watched by Iseult of Brittany, here portrayed with some sympathy as they await the arrival of the ship. When her maid tells her that Tristan has been calling for her, she is not deceived, but sadly reflects on her situation:

> *Iseult is coming in the ship: he lives*
> *Until the ship is here. She will come in*
> *And take my husband, who was never hers,*
> *Out of my arms. I have not stolen her name;*
> *It is my own poor name. I have not stolen*
> *Her love from this proud queen: it still is hers,*
> *He is all hers, but he is also mine.*
> *Why should she come, being so rich, to me*
> *Who am so poor?* (p. 90)

Tristan's delirium adds to the realism of the death-bed scene, and to its pathos:

> *Iseult,*
> *Where are you gone? You were here by my bed,*
> *You would have healed me: some one thrust you back.*
> *What are these white hands that I see, there, there*
> *Thrusting you back until you fade away?*
> *I cannot see you any longer. Who*
> *Is this pale woman with the angry eyes?*

(Looking at Iseult) *You are beautiful and yet I do not know you.*

Iseult of Brittany: *I am not angry, but you kill my heart.*
> *Do you not know me, Tristan?* (pp. 100–1)

Though she is 'not angry', in a moment of uncontrollable jealousy she declares that the approaching sail is black, and Tristan falls back dead. As she is overcome with hysterical weeping, Iseult of Cornwall comes in, and she confesses to her rival:

> *Too late, too late! I told him that the sail*
> *Was black. I killed him. It was I who killed him.* (p. 106)

But with calm dignity Iseult of Cornwall exonerates her:

> *Comfort yourself, Iseult of Brittany,*
> *And hide your head and weep, if you will weep,*
> *Because it had to be, and leave me here.*
> *You have done nothing in this mighty death.* (p. 106)

Queen Iseult's death almost immediately afterwards beside Tristan's body strains credulity in a play of so much psychological realism, but is dramatically effective. It is followed by the entry of Mark, who on discovering the lovers dead, is told by Brangaene the whole story of the love-potion and its consequences. His final speech ends the drama in a spirit of generosity:

> *Had I but known! Tristan, had I but known!*
> *Had my son Tristan but had faith in me*
> *And told me all the truth, then had I given*
> *Iseult, whom I have loved, to be his wife.*
> *But now has all this woe come to an end*
> *In sorrow, and because we were all blind.*
> *The woman whom I loved, and my one friend,*
> *Lie here, and I am living still. . . .* (p. 109)

Mark's nobility, and the tragic consequences of human blindness as well as of the painful situation in which 'father' and 'son' are rivals for the love of the same woman, give depth and power to Symons' work. Though, insofar as he was influenced by Arnold and the Pre-Raphaelites, Symons' treatment of the legend of Tristram and Iseult was a traditional one, his Symbolist approach results in a poetically distinguished drama.

Laurence Binyon's *Arthur: A Tragedy* of 1923 returns to the now almost worked-out vein of the story of Arthur, Lancelot and Guenevere. Interest had moved away from this part of the legend to the story of Tristram and Iseult, as the large number of poems and in particular dramas of the previous decade indicate, before taking new directions with the publication of T. S. Eliot's *The Waste Land*. Binyon's *Arthur* is a moving and very competent treatment of his subject, indeed it is the best of the dramas which deal with the last part of the *Morte Darthur* and have Arthur as protagonist. Binyon dedicated his play to Sir John and Lady Martin Harvey, for whom he had agreed to write it, and he mentions in his dedication his debt to them for their help in its construction. 'Memory goes back to the June day, now long ago, when first I undertook to write for you a play out of Malory's pages on a theme long pondered by you both.' He goes on to recall days spent in the interchange of ideas 'in thinking out and talking over crucial situations; in rejecting and recasting; in the search for essential structure'. The result of all this is that the play is very much better structured than most, if not all the others on Arthurian themes, but as the work of a poet, it has also much greater literary value than J. Comyns Carr's theatrical but banal productions. *Arthur* was, moreover, conceived as a full scale drama, and was performed with a very large cast at the Old Vic in 1923; though austere and much less spectacular, it does not seem to have been the popular success that Henry Irving's production of *King Arthur* at the Lyceum had been.

Binyon's text, though based on Malory, differs in its narrative outline at many points, but *Le Morte Darthur* is very ingeniously adapted to give a great variety of different kinds of dramatic scenes. The play opens with a vigorous scene at Astolat, in which Elaine declares her love for Launcelot, Lavaine begs his father to allow him to follow Launcelot, and Torre angrily asserts that Launcelot is the Queen's paramour and rages at what he sees as his deliberate trifling with Elaine's feelings. This imaginatively free handling of the source-material provides motivation for the plot, as well as dramatic tension, yet follows Malory closely in suggesting Launcelot's charisma. The next scene turns to Arthur, portrayed sympathetically as an anxious but trusting monarch, in whose mind a suspicion of some as yet indefinable treachery has begun to be sown, and Bedivere suggests that the envy and ambition of Mordred may be at the root of it, though Arthur, insisting that he never wronged him, is incredulous. Launcelot now returns, and is welcomed by the court after the long absence during which Elaine had nursed him; he had been suffering from a severe wound in the side, caused by an unlucky shot from a hunter. The scene allows of many changes of mood, however: when Launcelot and Guenevere are at last alone, Launcelot voices his suspicions of Mordred's enmity towards him, and of the danger that they are in, but Guenevere in a lyrical passage remembers their past happiness and hopes for happiness to come—'Why should we not take what there is of joy, So little as there is, so little?'[21] Launcelot tries to break away from her and to renounce temptation, but Guenevere reproaches him with weariness of her and suggests that he has transferred his affections to a younger woman, then rushes out mad with jealousy. Binyon's closeness to Malory in this scene gives it a realism that the more romantic passages of some of the earlier dramas on the theme very markedly lack. We see Launcelot and Guenevere as mature and complex personalities whose love brings them more anguish than joy. This scene is followed by the death of Elaine, but here, Binyon is much less successful in creating a moving episode: the scene is in rather flat prose, Elaine's 'ghostly father' is changed for her actual father, and her concern to get the letter written and delivered promptly distracts attention from the pathos of her dying for love, and her assertion that she does no offence in loving an earthly man. Instead of Malory's 'Why should I leave such thoughts? Am I not an earthly woman? . . . For sweet Lord Jesu, said the fair maiden, I take Thee to record, on Thee I was never great offencer against Thy laws; but that I loved this noble knight, Sir Launcelot, out of measure, and of myself, good Lord, I might not withstand the fervent love wherefore I have my death',[22] we are given the contents of her letter, a very commonplace affair.

The fourth scene opens with the malevolent plotting of Mordred and Agravaine, who hope to discredit Launcelot, get him banished, and seize their opportunity to gain power. Then follows a feast presided over by Guenevere, with Arthur and Launcelot absent—a very uneasy social occasion to begin with, becoming more and more tense and acrimonious as Mordred provokes Guenevere by mentioning again and again the red sleeve that he has seen Launcelot wearing as his token. Instead of the poisoned apple of earlier versions Mordred's poisonous insinuations made with feigned innocence, and his odiously offensive manner—

> *I ask your pardon if I spoke amiss,*
> *I marvel that a sleeve, a mere red sleeve—* (p. 57)

cause the party to break up in violent antagonism between Launcelot's and Mordred's factions. Agravaine declares, when the Queen has left, that her guilty face has betrayed her:

> *you know it by her eye*
> *And cheek of flame that spoke clear as a trumpet*
> *'Launcelot is mine! None else shall have his love*
> *While I have breath and can deceive the King.'* (p. 58)

As Guenevere savagely reproaches Launcelot immediately afterwards with his falsehood to her, the barge appears with the body of Elaine, and all is explained. But though Arthur is present and hears the letter, he realises that the atmosphere is highly charged and with un-Arthurian perspicacity asks himself 'Why that clamour / And then the silence when I came among them?' (p. 66). It is a good touch which adds to the tension and to the realism of the situation.

The story moves on to the meeting of Launcelot and Guenevere which ends in the attack of Mordred and his party. Launcelot has come to say goodbye for ever, as in Graham Hill's *Guinevere*, but before they can even think of being, in Malory's words, 'abed or at any other manner of disports', the lovers are attacked; as in Malory, a furious fight follows, and the enemy are routed. Ironically, however, at the very moment when they were about to part for ever, it becomes impossible for Launcelot to go, leaving Guenevere at the mercy of Mordred's unbounded malice and treachery. Guenevere urges him to go; Launcelot determines to tell everything to the King, but Mordred is there first, covered in blood and fiercely denouncing the Queen and Launcelot. In an effective contrast, Arthur when at last he is alone sees that it is dawn and remembers his first meeting with Guenevere:

> *Dawn. Is it dawn so soon?*
> *The birds sang soft so when I wooed her, soft*
> *And thrilling with low pipe. Smell of the grass,*
> *Dew, and her face, wonderful, coming towards me . . .* (p. 84)

He prays, but rises determined that justice must be done, Guenevere punished, and Gareth and Gaheris sent to arrest her.

Binyon ingeniously rearranges the details of the narrative so that Launcelot, in the act of carrying Guenevere to safety in Joyous Gard, encounters Gareth and Gaheris as they carry out this duty, and kills them without recognising them, in so doing incurring Gawain's unending hatred. A messenger reports the incident:

> Someone cried
> '*Look where the Queen is taken to her death!*'
> ...   .
> *And sudden like a lion burst on us*
> *Sir Launcelot. . . . I know not whence he came*
> *Out of the mist; his sword flashed in his hand,*
> *But not so terrible as his eyes. They flamed.*
> *You would have thought that when he saw the Queen*
> *His very reason rushed right out of him.*
>
> ...   .
>   *He was mad,*
> *Blood-mad he seemed; he knew not what he did,*
> *He struck so sudden. . . .*   (p. 89)

The next scene takes place at the siege of Joyous Gard; Launcelot comes to parley with Arthur, refusing both to fight him and to hand over Guenevere to justice on the accusation of Mordred. A tremendous storm conveniently breaks out, while at the same time Gawain attacks Launcelot and fierce fighting ensues in the murk and confusion of the darkened stage. As it abates, Arthur and Launcelot confront each other alone, and Launcelot makes a frank confession to Arthur:

> Oh, my King,
> *Had we but met before, thus, face to face!*
> *Arthur, you trusted me; and though I guard*
> *Your Queen from death, I have not failed you since.*
>   *I*
> *Have done you wrong that nothing can undo. . . .*
>   *Since first my eyes*
> *Saw Guenevere, I loved her.*   (p. 108)

He asks Arthur to pardon her, but it is impossible: 'A man may pardon, but the King may not. /The King is justice, or no more a King' (p. 109). At this point a bishop arrives and insists that Guenevere shall be restored to Arthur, and that he shall be reconciled with Launcelot. Peace is made, Launcelot finally departs, and Arthur and Guenevere find themselves 'stript As trees after the tempest' of all passion; Guenevere renounces the world and retires to Amesbury. Arthur

223

visits her there some time later—a long time later, it seems—before the Last Battle, from which he knows that he will not return; each seems like a ghost of their former selves, and each is able to speak with detachment now of their former lives, to see where they were at fault, and to ask forgiveness. Arthur realises his insufficiency as a husband, Guenevere grieves for the 'unending desolation' that resulted from her sin, as a result of which 'the young men / Have fallen in their blood'. Arthur laments to see 'the realm, / I dreamed to make one flawless crystal, cracked / To fragments; and the loss, the waste'. He recognises his own blindness and weakness; but the scene ends with his prophecy for the future:

> A seed is sown in Britain, Guenevere;
> And whether men wait for a hundred years
> Or for a thousand, they shall find it flower
> In youth unborn. (p. 122)

The play ends with the message that love alone can change the hearts of men, love is what the world needs, as chanting voices herald a vision of the barge carrying Arthur to Avalon with the three sorrowing Queens.

Binyon's *Arthur* is a nobly conceived and well structured play in which the interplay of character leads to psychological realism. It is fast-moving and its action well motivated; Binyon avoids the archaic and in so doing achieves a greater contemporary relevance. Despite the alterations he made in the narrative for the sake of increased dramatic power and compactness, he clearly had a keen sense of Malory's meaning in *Le Morte Darthur*, as his study of Arthur suggests. Like other dramatic writers on the same theme, he made Arthur the true hero of the tragedy, rather than Launcelot. His Launcelot is a noble and high-minded figure, but he never assumes the stature of Malory's Launcelot. It seems to have been impossible for later writers to recapture the glory of Launcelot's chivalric and martial prowess, and in any case he was tainted for the Victorians by his passion for the Queen so that nothing could quite restore his medieval splendour. Tennyson's Arthur seems to have created a prototype from which it was difficult to get away, and which made it impossible to shift the emphasis back in the direction of Launcelot.

Though the play does not make any specifically contemporary comments, it is impossible to read it to the end without seeing in it some oblique references to the First World War which had made so great an impact upon Binyon's generation. In Guenevere's references to the young men who have died, and in the hope for a better future, there is a suggestion of a parallel to the twentieth-century experience of the terrible destruction which resulted from political folly and blindness, and the hope that the 'war to end war' would lead to a better world. The convent at Amesbury becomes a dressing-station for the battle casualties, if further proof were needed of what Binyon has in mind, and the final emphasis on the love that suffices seems pointless unless it is applied in the wider context of national and indeed international relationships. For a more direct and symbolic application of Arthurian themes to the experiences of the 1914–18 war, however, readers had to wait for the publication of David Jones's *In Parenthesis* in 1937.

Though he did not live to complete it, Binyon attempted another Arthurian work, *The Madness of Merlin*, the first part of which, edited by Gordon Bottomley, appeared in 1947. The two further parts which were to have followed exist only in fragmentary notes. Gordon Bottomley in his preface states that Binyon intended to treat the Merlin theme for its own sake, not merely as an episode in a larger story, and that he meant it to be about the 'ardours and agonies, and doubts and dilemmas of our contemporary life, by reference to the timeless factor common to all generations'.[23] Binyon took the outline of the story from Geoffrey of Monmouth; in it, like both Launcelot and Tristram at different points in *Le Morte Darthur*, Merlin goes mad from distress of mind and takes to the woods, where he lives like an animal. Several times over he is found and brought back to court, but escapes again to solitude; his later prophecies are the product of his period of madness in the forest. Binyon made clear in a letter to Bottomley written in 1942 that he had special meanings to convey through the poem: 'the theme of it is Merlin's discovery . . . that he needs the experience of love and suffering to be complete . . . I want to illustrate the way things always turn out differently from what one expects, and the results of excessive idealism'. The poem was to have as leitmotiv, 'the habit of mankind to put discoveries to bad uses'.[24] It is easy to see that Binyon is trying to make symbolic use of the story, but it would appear that he did not live to work out precisely what he wanted to do with it. What survives of his attempt to give form to his conception has some moving passages in it, as Merlin expresses his bewilderment at his and the general human predicament—'Many are the dark paths in the hearts of men, / And who, save God, can follow into their darkness?' He questions the justice of God, who makes 'one shapely and strong, / And the other crooked and halting from his birth' (p. 46). He searches for 'The invisible innermost secret reality', and experiences a terrible vision of darkness and emptiness, while at another moment he has a sense of 'chains of words, frozen words' which 'bury laughter, bury joy', yet at the same time he feels 'ensnared by the wild flesh' (pp. 52–7). Though the ideas are not fully worked out and what there is of the poem is rather unstructured, it is an interesting experiment. Furthermore, it can be seen as relating to a new trend in the twentieth century, the fascination with the figure of Merlin, which together with the Waste Land and Grail Quest motifs, have gradually come to dominate modern Arthurian literature.

While other writers analysed the psychology of Arthurian characters or the moral condition of the protagonists, or found in the legends new symbolic meanings for their contemporaries, John Masefield seems to have been attracted to the Arthurian legend mainly as a source of material for dramatic action or racy narrative poems. His verse play, *Tristan and Isolt*, was written for performance at the Oxford Playhouse in 1923, and later performed by the Lena Ashwell players at the Century Theatre, Bayswater in 1927. Though it is quite well constructed, its verse is flat and it never succeeds in communicating either passion or a sense of the tragic. It merely indicates the continuing appeal of its subject. As later in his Arthurian poems, Masefield manipulates his sources with great freedom, combining elements from the Welsh Triads and from Gottfried, and taking the Welsh forms of the names for his characters. But these diverse materials are awkwardly blended, and throughout the play, the tone is constantly shifting in an uncomfortable mixture of fantasy and realism.

The main focus of the play is on the difficulties with which the lovers are beset. Its outline covers Tristan's life from his early youth, before he has even seen Isolt, to his death, though it follows no traditional narrative pattern. Tristan and Isolt love before they have even drunk the potion. Their love is sealed before they leave Ireland by drinking the 'magical wine' meant for Isolt's wedding night, and this love is consummated on the same night, when they are together on board ship. Marc and Isolt are married immediately upon her arrival and immediately Kai and Bedwyr, played as middle-aged scheming enemies of the lovers, become suspicious and set to work to trap them. Masefield introduces a contrasting comic element by means of a swineherd and his family, in an episode adapted from the Triads. The close relationship between Hog with his wife Sowkin, and Marc with his court is also perhaps intended to indicate a primitive society in which king and peasant can make easy contact. These rustic interludes are, however, clumsy and jarring, though they usefully give a sense of the passing of time in the main action.

Masefield, unlike other playwrights, includes a scene in which Tristan and Isolt persuade Brangwen to go to the marriage bed in place of her mistress. Its realistic tone is at variance with much else in the play, but in itself it is well done. Masefield dramatises Gottfried's more indirect account: 'They begged and implored Brangane till they brought her to the point where she promised to do the deed. But she promised to do it most reluctantly.' In the play, Brangwen is well differentiated from Isolt, and there is an authentic touch in the dialogue as she tries to resist her mistress's pressure: 'O hush, madam, hush! the very thought is such shame'.[25] Tristan appears to overcome her reluctance eventually by devising a means of preserving her virginity by putting a sleeping draught in the cup of 'magical wine', some of which still remains for the wedding night despite the lovers' earlier quaffing of it. But before the wine can be carried to Marc and Brangwen in the marriage bed, Tristan and Isolt drink of it yet again, as Isolt says:

> *My mother asked that the bride and her groom should drink*
> *This wine, on their marriage night. Pledge your love, husband* (p. 45)

and Tristan replies, 'To our love, sweet wife'. After this, Brangwen drinks with the unsuspecting Marc, but drops the gold cup because she is shaking so much, and only the 'bitter brown ooze' of the drug which Tristan had added is left for the king, who at once falls asleep.

The motif of drinking is again introduced, though Masefield does not make much of its symbolic potential, when Isolt's faithfulness is to be assayed by the drinking of 'the water of test', after she has been accused of admitting Tristan to her chamber. Kai assures her that 'None but the guilty are poisoned by it', upon which Isolt pleasantly enquires, 'Have all you innocents drunk it?' As she is about to drink it, Tristan returns and dashes the cup to the floor in the nick of time: its contents are immediately seen to be corrosive. At this point, the lovers leave together for the forest bower, where they are later discovered by Marc, sleeping with the sword laid between them. He leaves his glove as a token of his presence, and his generosity and mercy in sparing them so deeply impress Isolt when she wakes that she insists on abandoning Tristan and returning to her husband. War has come, however, and Marc is later killed in battle, while Tristan, deserted by his beloved, goes mad.

Masefield makes some strange alterations to the traditional narrative at this point: Isolt's repentance causes her to continue to reject Tristan even after the death of Marc, as well as before she hears news of his fate. A strange capriciousness and cruelty direct her actions, and the magical wine, so potent in most re-tellings of the story, seems to have lost its efficacy at this point in Masefield's play. Isolt even instructs her servants to pursue Tristan from the court, adding that 'The man who kills that outlaw shall be rewarded'. Eventually, however, she is united with the dying Tristan in the forest as he sings a version of Gottfried's

> *Isot ma drue, Isot mamie*
> *en vus ma mort, en vus ma vie*[26]

He then dies, and she stabs herself. There is no Isolt of the White Hands, no episode of the black and white sails in Masefield's version.

It seems possible that, in constructing his new version of the story, Masefield saw the relationship of the lovers as resembling that of Cathy and Heathcliff in *Wuthering Heights*. Isolt's perverse cruelty to Tristan is reminiscent of Cathy's treatment of Heathcliff; she speaks of herself as the cruel killer of her lover, as Heathcliff accuses Cathy of being his murderer. There seem to be verbal echoes between the two works, and, though it is obviously a romantic common-place, there may be a more direct correspondence between the passages in which Cathy and Isolt look forward to life after death. But, though it is built on the traditional idea of the all-consuming romantic passion between the doomed lovers, and has a touch of dramatic power, Masefield's play fails to achieve poetic distinction and tragic force because it lacks direction.

His *Midsummer Night and Other Tales in Verse* (1928) is a collection of twenty-two poems most of which are based on Malory and the Welsh tradition, supplemented here and there by motifs from classical mythology. The poems do not follow the usual narrative sequence, or attempt to cover the whole story of

Arthur; instead Masefield has freely selected from, adapted and supplemented traditional material. He combines poems of a sentimental nature with more vigorous narratives which often include battles and fierce hand-to-hand encounters. But he is not interested in chivalry; his Arthur is not the embodiment of courtliness and prowess, as in Malory, but as Margaret Reid[27] describes him, a 'real fighting pirate king'. In consequence he is a much diminished figure, and the story of Gwenivere's unfaithfulness, the treachery of Modred, and the downfall of the Round Table is told with pathos rather than with a sense of the tragedy of the destruction of a noble ideal and institution. Yet a romantic glow suffuses the cyle: the individual stories are often placed in natural settings as rich with birds and flowers as a medieval tapestry, though the general effect is not in any way medieval. Masefield tells the sad story with narrative competence and many realistic touches, but seldom succeeds in raising it above the level of the trivial, or in releasing the intrinsic power of the traditional stories.

Masefield seems to have found the traditional account of the begetting of Arthur morally unacceptable, and his cycle begins with a different version of his own devising. The young Uther asks her father for the hand of the unmarried Ygraine—each has fallen in love at first sight with the other. He is refused, but disguises himself, enters her castle at night, and carries her off. A hermit marries them and Arthur is conceived on their only night together: the angry father overtakes and kills Uther the next day and takes Ygraine back to Tintagel. Here she weaves a tapestry of her sad story while she awaits the birth of her child, or sits by the shore until:

> Often a dark-eyed deer with fawn at heel,
> Would shyly nuzzle her to share her meal,
> And robin redbreasts percht upon her hand.[28]

The story is sentimentalised and elaborated with the addition of the weaving-motif and the natural imagery. Masefield, curiously enough, supplies at the end of the cycle in 'The Old Tale of the Begetting' a second unbowdlerised version of the story as Malory tells it, beginning by way of justification:

> The men of old, who made the tale for us,
> Declare that Uther begat Arthur thus:—   (p. 156)

In this form, the story is succinct, realistic and bitter, and as a result, much more effective than the earlier version.

Masefield at several points introduces supernatural elements into the story of Arthur: in the second poem of the cycle, 'The Birth of Arthur', Ygraine takes her baby to Pendragon Ledge at moonrise where he is visited by wraithlike forms of kings and queens who offer him spiritual gifts and obscurely prophesy his future. Masefield, however, is not interested in the traditional story of Arthur's upbringing, and entirely omits the dramatic story of the sword in the stone with its powerful psychological undertones. In 'Badon Hill' and 'The

228

Sailing of Hell Race', Arthur's prowess as war-leader and sea-captain is established, and Masefield is in his element. In the second of these poems in particular, realistic details of the voyage combine with the supernatural in a manner reminiscent of Coleridge's *The Ancient Mariner*, as Arthur visits the three kingdoms of hell. On his return, he is greeted by princess Gwenivere, who arrives in a remarkably dashing manner, driving a 'bright chariot . . . all aflame with gold':

> *Two stallions dragged that chariot like a spate,*
> *White stallions lovely as the leaping pard . . .*
> *Urged by a green-clad woman, who, elate,*
> *With streaming red-gold hair . . .*
> *Croucht watchful . . .* (p. 64)

Here as elsewhere in the cycle Masefield makes use of vivid pictorial images, reminding one of the Pre-Raphaelites.

Later, in a strange poem deriving from classical sources, 'Arthur and his Ring', the young Arthur slips the precious ring given to him by Gwenivere on to the finger of a statue of Venus, and the goddess then comes to life and takes this as an offer of marriage, which she accepts. The story seems to have been devised to explain how the worship of the old Roman deities came to be displaced by Christianity; here again Masefield introduces an apocryphal story into the cycle, together with a supernatural element and a classical atmosphere.

In the poem entitled 'Midsummer Night' round which all the rest are grouped, the supernatural is dominant again, and the theme of Arthur's eventual return is introduced. The twentieth-century protagonist comes upon King Arthur's door in a hillside on the downs. Far within, Arthur and all his company sit motionless at a banquet, from which they waken briefly each midsummer night. The main characters are each permitted to speak, and in turn they confess their responsibility for the final downfall of the Round Table, each ridden with a sense of guilt. 'I was the cause of the disastrous end' claims Arthur first, while Gwenivere, the next to speak, says that she 'destroyed the realm', and Lancelot then asserts that he 'dealt the land the blow / From which the griefs began'. Gwenivere's sister, who is also the wife of Modred, follows, confessing to her poisonous hate, but Modred in a malignant and contemptuous tirade, proudly asserts that it was he who brought about the catastrophe:

> *Not you, with your begettings, father mine,*
> *Not you, my red-gold Queen, adultress proud . . .*
> *You were but nerves; I, Modred, was the spine.*
>
> *You were poor puppets in a master's game;*
> *I, Modred, was the cause of what befell.*
> *I, Modred, Arthur's bastard, schemed and planned;*
> *I, with my single hand,*
> *Gave but a touch, and, lo, the troubles came;*
> *And royalty was ended in the land.* (pp. 82–3)

When their hour is up the figures turn to stone, but the poem ends with the hope of Arthur's return 'To purge the blot and make the broken whole . . . And build the lasting beauty left unbuilt / Because of all the follies of our guilt' (p. 85).

Masefield's story lacks the Christian context by means of which the tragedy is seen in the light of eternity: Malory's Guenevere and Launcelot, for example, have no need to confess their guilt each midsummer night, for their sins are expiated and their forgiveness assured. In Masefield, Arthur's guilt is here seen as the guilt of the older generation of modern society, responsible for the holocaust of the First World War and its aftermath.

Masefield is at his best in such poems as 'The Fight on the Wall' which follows 'Midsummer Night', in which with great vigour he recounts Lancelot's fight against Modred, Agravaine and their party, when they trap him with the queen. Nevertheless the story is both oddly altered and vulgarised: Queen Gwenivere goes through the town alone at night, 'through the unbuilt quarter, / Past heaps of brick and slate' to an assignation with Lancelot. She is followed by Modred, who watching her, says malevolently to himself, like the villain of a nineteenth-century melodrama:

> *You think it safe. It isn't . . .*
> *Go on, my dear.* (p. 89)

When Modred and his followers later shout their challenge to him to come out, Lancelot exclaims with a flat banality:

> *This filthy crying*
> *Is more than I can stand.* (p. 95)

Vigorous though Masefield's action is, it lacks the dignity and power of Malory's more tersely narrated scene, with its moving verbal exchanges between Launcelot and Guenevere. Malory's Guenevere is every inch a queen in the moment of greatest danger; but the face of Masefield's Gwenivere is white as paper as she comments flatly:

> *This of tonight will be a story*
> *Not matched agen.* (p. 105)

Realism weakens rather than enhances Masefield's treatment of this incident.

A number of separate poems are devoted to the ending of the story: after Arthur's death, Gwenivere becomes the Abbess at Amesbury but continues to love Lancelot despite her vows. She is summoned to his deathbed but arrives too late. The 'best knight of the world', so nobly lamented by Ector in Malory, diminished by the realism of Gwenivere's last sight of him:

> *Now he lay dead; old, old, with silver hair.*
> *I had not ever thought of him as old . . .* (pp. 148–9)

Gwenivere asserts that her love still burns within her, and that in itself it will atone for their sins, but it is a less satisfying and more sentimental ending to the great love story than the anguished renunciation of *Le Morte Darthur*.

In 'The Old Tale of the Breaking of the Links', drawn, he claims, from French poets, Masefield begins with a dramatic scene in which Gwenivere is summoned to the hall for judgement after Modred's accusation, and in which she answers the charge brought against her with a biting irony and spirit reminiscent of Morris's 'Defence of Guenevere'. The comparison shows that Masefield is less interested in Gwenivere's situation and 'defence', however, than in the ensuing fight when Lancelot and his followers burst in and lay about them to rescue the Queen. But the poem ends dramatically and with an appropriately symbolical touch as, on their way to Joyous Gard when the fight is over, Lancelot and Gwenivere 'set their tired horses to the east', and before them 'A darkness was upon the face of things: / To that they rode' (p. 171).

The ballad form, constantly varied, provides the basis for Masefield's cycle. He does not attempt to imitate the medieval ballad, but the form is often admirably suited to fast-moving narrative which can accommodate both realistic detail and magic. The romantic world of the sad love story, of glorious conquest in battle, of vast supernatural horrors encountered and overcome, of homely incident and of freely adapted classical story contributes images and associations and echoes which give a certain amount of surface richness to the poems. Masefield emphasises the poignance of the human situations, but his protagonists, depicted without much psychological depth, lack heroic stature. His poems derive from the earlier dream-world of Coleridge and Keats, and are closer to the nineteenth-century ballad, in atmosphere as well as in form, than to other contemporary treatments of Arthurian themes.

As well as his play, Masefield wrote two poems on Tristan and Isolt, and again we have a very different treatment from that of other writers. The first poem, 'The Love Gift', ingeniously applies the folk-tale motif of the unwanted gift to the situation of King Marc, the lovers and Brangwen, and relates Marc's suffering to other aspects of human misery. Masefield tells the story of how a forest-goddess rewarded Marc for the protection he had afforded her by offering him the choice of Wisdom, Power or Immortality, gifts which may be given away but not shared. He chooses the latter, given to him in the form of a golden quince, which he bestows upon his beloved Isolt. She does not want immortality for herself alone and gives it to Tristan, but for the same reason he hands it on to Brangwen. She, anguished by her love for Marc (for she, as well, has 'drunk the dram') unwittingly gives it to him, and he at once realises that Isolt has betrayed him. Grief-stricken, he wanders out and encounters a little boy weeping because his mother is dying. Marc takes the golden fruit to the mother and she is saved; but now he is aware of a deeper sorrow even than his own, the sum of all human grief, 'The pitiful child's crying of the race / For comfort of a soul no longer there'.

The second poem, 'Tristan's Singing', begins with the madness of Tristan, deserted by Isolt, as in Masefield's earlier play. Joy returns to him with a vision of the beauty and vitality of nature, culminating in an encounter with Nature herself. 'What are you, fiery beast or goddess?' he asks, and she tells him the 'tale of Changing, never young nor old'. In the second part of the poem, in the ruins of the forest bower, he sings the song he has learnt, of 'Nature and Desire, And of Eternity and Time long past' and like Orpheus, draws all creatures to him. Even Isolt in her palace hears it, takes horse, and gallops to him. Eventually in a strange apotheosis, the lovers become one in spirit, and they flee

> *Laughing aloft and singing and away*
> *Into some summer knowing no decay.*

Their mortal remains are entombed by Marc and become a shrine for lovers.

Like the 'Midsummer Night' poems, these two Tristan poems are successful in their way, but they lack power and symbolic resonance. There is something fortuitous about the meaning that ultimately emerges from them.

Hardy's short verse play on the theme of Tristram and Iseult, *The Famous Tragedy of the Queen of Cornwall*, had been in his mind, it seems, since 1870 when he first visited Tintagel with Emma Gifford, later to be his first wife, but he did not begin to write it until 1916, and it was only finished in 1923, shortly before its first performance. By the time that he finally completed the play, he was an old man of 83, apparently working under pressure to produce the work for local performance by the Hardy Players. (It was also later performed in London.) Despite its unpromising limitations, the play has considerable power. Hardy decided to observe the unities of time and place: its twenty-four short scenes are concerned with such a sequence of events as could actually take place within the time needed for performance, about one hour. The whole action takes place in the hall of the castle of Tintagel. Hardy has to some extent taken Greek drama as his model, and there is a chorus of the Shades of Dead Old Cornishmen and Dead Cornishwomen who comment on the action all through. A mannered, archaic diction prevails, as in the first words of the Chanters:

> *Tristram a captive of King Mark,*
> *Racked was the Queen with qualm and cark,*
> *Till reached her hand a written line,*
> *That quickened her to deft design.*

The reader's first impression is of a strange experiment undoubtedly by a great writer, but very much restricted by the limitations imposed upon it by the necessities of amateur performance and the dramatic mode he has chosen to adopt.

Nevertheless the play is surprisingly effective, for the situation with which it starts is explosive, and the assembling of the four protagonists, Mark, Tristram and the two Iseults within the four walls of the castle, endeavouring to avoid or to confront each other in the full strength of their passions, makes for suspense and good drama. Hardy deals only with the end of the story: it is assumed that the audience or reader knows enough of what has gone before to understand the situation. Mark has just returned from a voyage to find that his queen has also just come back from a voyage of her own. Queen Iseult had been sent for by Tristram, reported near to death, and had gone to Brittany to see him. Before she could land, news came that he was already dead, and so she returned to Cornwall without seeing him. However, the news was false; he has recovered, and disguised as an old harper has come to Mark's court, closely followed by his wife, Iseult of Brittany. Soon Mark, through the treacherous cunning of Andret, and his own jealous suspicion, discovers the presence of Tristram and stabs him to death. Then Queen Iseult enters, stabs Mark when she sees what has happened, and leaps to her death on the rocks below from the castle ramparts. Iseult of the White Hands, who has earlier reproached Tristram for his infidelity, re-enters to find her husband, her rival and King Mark all dead, and returns to Brittany.

There is nothing romantic about Hardy's treatment of the story. Tristram and Queen Iseult have six very brief encounters, in which Iseult expresses her bitterness that she should have to share Tristram with his wife, and in which Tristram sings his melancholy songs to her. Their moments together are inevitably few, for Tristram's presence is soon discovered; and moreover, Hardy allows equal prominence to Iseult of Brittany's upbraiding of her husband. The lovers are unable to escape from the ever-tightening ring of hostility, treachery and the force of destiny that encloses them, and the claustrophobic atmosphere thus built up allows them no time for romantic speeches. Hardy also creates a sense of growing tension between the lovers themselves as a result of Queen Iseult's jealousy of Tristram's wife, as well as of the anxieties and hopelessness of their situation. Despite the mannered dialogue, a harshly realistic impression is achieved.

To this, the insistence of Iseult of the White Hands contributes. It has been suggested that she is portrayed sympathetically, and that Hardy sounds a note of contrition in her final words.[29] But Iseult, however deeply wronged by Tristram, is nevertheless childish, impatient and uncomprehending in her complaints to her husband:

> *But you don't mean you'll live away from me,*
> *Leave me, and henceforth be unknown to me,*
> *O you don't surely? I could not help coming;*
> *Don't send me away—do not, do not, do so!*

Queen Iseult on overhearing this comments:

> *She has no claim to importune like that,*

and Tristram baldly tells his wife:

> *Thou canst not haunt another woman's house!*

Iseult's position is indeed unenviable but here she is making a very undignified scene, which elicits sympathy neither from her hearers nor from the reader. If Hardy was indeed thinking of his first wife, Emma, here, she was unfortunate in being so commemorated.

One might ask what Hardy had in mind, apart from the immediate purpose of providing an experimental play on a local legend for performance by amateur actors in a very simple setting. Why did he choose the very end of the story, and condense it so rigorously? Did the reduction of the romantic element, the dramatically tragic deaths of the lovers and of Mark have deeper implications? Since he chose to make the play end in this way, why did he not carry the action further, and include Iseult of Brittany in the final catastrophe? That the play related to his own experience in one respect is apparent from its dedication: 'In affectionate remembrance of those with whom I formerly spent many hours at the scene of the tradition, who have now all passed away save one', and a comment of his in a letter to Sydney Cockerell in 1916, after visiting Tintagel. He remarked that it revived memories of his visit with Emma in 1872, 'with an Iseult of my own, and of course she was mixed in the vision of the other'.[30] Hardy's selectivity and handling of the story, taking and emphasising the ultimate frustration, the injured innocence of Iseult of Brittany, and the violent retribution that ends the lives of the other protagonists, may perhaps have related in some way to his own experience. The interpretation is worlds away from the romantic, overwhelming love of most of the earlier versions of the story, with their more sympathetic portrayal of character. Though it is powerful, Hardy's play lacks tragic depth, lacks even pathos, as the death-bed scenes of earlier writers do not, but it makes an impressively different and more dramatic ending to the story than do most others.

This is the last major treatment of the story in the form of serious drama. The romantic potential of the legend was by this time exhausted, but by compressing the story so as to bring out the full bitterness of the situation of the protagonists as they reach a final confrontation, and through a strange blend of psychological realism and stylisation, Hardy achieves a characteristically sombre but striking reinterpretation.

8

'The Waste Land' and After

i. T. S. Eliot: *The Waste Land*

The publication in 1922 of T. S. Eliot's *The Waste Land* gave a new direction to Arthurian literature, a movement away from the dominant themes of the nineteenth century, romantic love and, to a lesser extent, patriotic feeling. Though the image of the Waste Land corresponded with Eliot's pessimistic outlook upon the modern world, it did much more than direct attention to the loss of moral and spiritual health and to contemporary decadence. In emphasising spiritual poverty, the image pointed directly towards that other aspect of the Arthurian myth which had a somewhat limited appeal for nineteenth-century writers, the Grail quest, conceived of as the means for achieving spiritual renewal in an evil time. It is thus with the more positive aspects of the Grail story that Charles Williams, for example, is concerned in the next two decades, and his *Taliessin through Logres* (1938) and *The Region of the Summer Stars* (1944) are among the most distinguished and serious treatments of Arthurian material in the twentieth century. Both T. S. Eliot and Charles Williams (as did some other contemporary writers) recognised the potential of the Arthurian stories as myth, and these writers were each able to penetrate beneath the surface narrative level of their source material to discover in it new meaning for their age. Charles Williams even drew attention to the limitations of earlier treatments in a review of April 1944, in which, referring to Hawker, Morris, Tennyson and Swinburne, he says that none of these poets 'had the full capacity of the mythical imagination'. Of Tennyson, Williams says that 'he was really writing (and very properly) a modern moral story, as he said he was. He could not—he did not try to—get the Myth.'[1] Though many nineteenth-century and early twentieth-century writers were well aware of the importance of myth, they seem to have found difficulty in seeing the Arthurian stories other than as material for simple re-telling, or as the basis for allegory. The striking change of attitude in the twentieth century naturally resulted from a combination of circumstances, but the most important single literary cause was the publication of Jessie Weston's *From Ritual to Romance* in 1920. Something of its influence is suggested by T. S. Eliot's 'Notes on the Waste Land' in which he says that 'Not only the title, but the plan and a good deal of the incidental symbolism of the poem were suggested by Miss Jessie L. Weston's book on the Grail legend: . . . . Indeed, so deeply am I indebted, Miss Weston's book will elucidate the difficulties of the poem much better than my notes can do; and I recommend it (apart from the great interest of the book itself) to any who think such elucidation of the poem worth the trouble.' Later, he regretted having sent so many enquirers off on a wild goose chase after Tarot cards and the Holy Grail, but the fact remains that *The Waste Land* does really to some extent owe its origin to Jessie Weston's theories.

From *Ritual to Romance* not only provided source-material for Eliot's poem, but also more indirectly, was one of the means by which the Grail myth acquired pre-eminence among Arthurian stories in the first half of the century. Jessie Weston's book gave a new authenticity to the Grail stories, by moving them into the field of anthropological studies. A medievalist with a special interest in Arthurian literature, she applied Sir James Frazer's approach in *The Golden Bough* to the Grail stories, interpreting them as survivals of ancient vegetation rites: 'The Grail Story is not . . . the product of imagination, literary or popular. At its root lies the record, more or less distorted, of an ancient Ritual, having for its ultimate object the initiation into the secret of life, physical and spiritual.'[2] Whether her theories are correct or not is unimportant beside the fact that her interpretation of the stories enabled the symbolic images around which they are organised to take on new connotations, while at the same time it drew attention to the element of myth underlying them. The images which had previously been associated mainly with the Christian tradition now acquired a new range of meanings, without necessarily losing their Christian values. By finding parallels in other literatures, Miss Weston traced the symbols of cup and lance back to the pre-Christian era, and declared that in the vegetation rites of various cults, they were originally sexual symbols. Thus the Lance was not simply the spear that had pierced Christ's side, the Grail not simply the cup of the Last Supper, which had afterwards held Christ's blood, but they were also 'sex symbols of immemorial antiquity and world-wide diffusion, the Lance, or Spear, representing the Male, the Cup, or Vase, the Female, reproductive energy'.[3] The theory is mainly speculation and few scholars would now maintain it, but it enabled a much wider range of interpretations to attach itself to the Grail legend, as *The Waste Land* demonstrates. Hitherto the story of the Grail, mediated by Malory or Wolfram, had been seen simply as medieval romance or as religious propaganda; now it took on fresh resonance as emanating from the dark abyss of time. The chivalry and romance could now be stripped away from the story, leaving the myth of the Waste Land and the Fisher King as symbols that could be used freely in new contexts. Though Eliot himself said that the plan and much of the incidental symbolism of his poem were suggested by Jessie Weston, the freedom with which he took and interpreted such symbols as he needed was such that in reading the poem it is difficult to see its relation to the Grail legend at all. Yet without *From Ritual to Romance* there would probably have been no such poem, for Eliot would have been unlikely to have taken either plan or symbolism from any other Arthurian source.

The Grail story is of course not the only myth to be woven into the texture of *The Waste Land*. Eliot's allusive poetic method involved an enormously wide range of reference, drawing extensively upon biblical and classical material as well as upon many different literatures. One of his most firmly held convictions appears to have been that a sense of the past is essential for the poet, to enable him to have some sort of historical perspective. In *Tradition and the Individual Talent* he remarks that 'the historical sense involves a perception, not only of the pastness of the past, but of its presence; the historical sense compels a man to write not merely with his own generation in his bones, but with a feeling that the whole of the literature of Europe from Homer and within it the whole of the literature of his own country has a simultaneous existence and composes a simultaneous order. This historical sense, which is a sense of the timeless as well as of the temporal and of the timeless and of the temporal together, is what makes a writer traditional. And it is at the same time what makes a writer most acutely conscious of his place in time, of his contemporaneity.'[4]

This historical sense includes for Eliot, as it did for James Joyce and David Jones later, Arthurian legend as part of that recognition of the 'timeless and the temporal' which yet allows an author to write of and for his age. For all three authors, as Eliot later says that it should be, the conscious present is an awareness of the past, which the poet must 'develop or procure'. Elsewhere, he maintained that 'something must be imported from the past to give our matter shape'. Mediated by Jessie Weston, the Grail story thus makes its contribution to the most influential poem so far of the twentieth century.

Eliot wrote dismissively of *The Waste Land* later: 'Various critics have done me the honour to interpret the poem in terms of criticism of the contemporary world, have considered it, indeed, as an important bit of social criticism. To me it was only the relief of a personal and wholly insignificant grouse against life; it is just a piece of rhythmical grumbling.'[5] Even if the poem is not to be regarded as 'an important bit of social criticism', it is concerned with 'life', which must be based on limited personal experience, and its 'rhythmical grumbling' conveys both general implications and a profound sense of both the horror and the potential glory of 'life'. The central theme of man's need for rebirth is one of timeless significance for which the symbolism of the Grail is an excellent vehicle. The Waste Land, though it includes twentieth-century London, 'the unreal city', is also much more than that, a state of mind rather than simply a place. Though it ends positively, with the hope of 'the peace that passes understanding', the poem is mainly concerned with the analysis of the condition of the Waste Land, what is wrong with 'life' rather than with a hopeful vision of the healing and redemption to be brought about by a quest successfully undertaken and fulfilled. Writing at a time when he was almost crushed by ill-health and financial anxieties, as well as by marital problems, Eliot could use allusions to the ancient myth to give expression to his personal distress and despondency through this myth while at the same time analysing the sickness of his society, in terms as relevant now as they were in the 1920s.

Though it has been argued that to interpret *The Waste Land* in terms of the Grail myth is to impose upon it a reductive scheme,[6] the effect is only reductive if one attempts to force a limiting correlation between the poem and the Grail legend in its entirety. In taking as much of the legend as he needed and using it allusively, Eliot made it easier for later writers such as David Jones to use Arthurian material in a similarly free manner. From the Grail legend he took only two major images, the Waste Land and the Fisher King. Though the Grail chapel appears in the last section, there is no quest, no hero, no Grail city or castle, no lance or cup. It is the devastation, rather than the means of revitalisation, with which the poem is concerned. The theme of the poem fundamentally runs counter to the underlying vegetation myth which Jessie Weston sees, and which suggests that the land, laid waste by the sickness of its ruler, waiting for deliverance and regeneration, will experience in the rising of the waters (foretold by the Tarot pack) the restoration of its fertility. For in *The Waste Land* there is at times too much water; and water is often associated with mechanical, joyless and unwanted sexual activity, that threatens rather than enhances life. Eliot sees a connection, not between sex and life, but between sex and death, sometimes in a literal sense, constantly in a metaphorical sense. The water images which recur again and again in 'The Fire Sermon' are associated not with refreshment and regeneration but rather with lust; the dull canal and the polluted river offer less hope of spiritual growth than does the parched, waiting landscape of 'What the Thunder Said'. The allusion to *Tristan und Isolde* in the first section, 'Oed' und leer das Meer'—'desolate and empty the sea'—immediately associates water with sex and implies that it may be death-bringing rather than otherwise, and this is reinforced by the clairvoyante's reading of the Tarot cards, 'Fear death by water'. If, as Jessie Weston postulates, the cards were originally used to predict the return of the life-bringing water (a somewhat improbable hypothesis) the mortal danger of which they now warn indicates Eliot's ironically different attitude to sexuality.

In the second section of the poem, scenes from both upper- and lower-class life suggest that fertility and wealth bring only spiritual sterility. Though 'ITS TIME', no-one has time for vision or for the quest. The Fisher King can only fish in the dull canal 'On a winter evening round behind the gashouse' where rats creep, dragging their slimy bellies through the vegetation, in strong contrast to Jessie Weston's regal concept. In *From Ritual to Romance* the Fisher King is seen as the essential centre of the whole cult, a being semi-divine, semi-human, standing between his people and his land, and the unseen forces which control their destiny; but in *The Waste Land* he has dwindled to an insignificant figure against a sordid background. His presence is again suggested in 'What the Thunder Said': the barren and rocky landscape affords him no ease, for 'Here one can neither stand nor lie nor sit.' Only in the last lines of the poem is there a change: the Fisher King sits upon the shore fishing, with the arid plain behind him. No Grail knight comes to heal him and to bring life to the land, but he appears to be not entirely helpless: 'Shall I at least set my lands in order?' he asks. There is hope; something can be done, some positive action taken, even in the Waste Land. The transference from the dull canal to the shore strengthens this sense, too. The empty chapel in the decayed hole among the mountains, long forgotten and deserted, offers no vision of the Grail; the old sources of spiritual strength have lost their validity and power, but the boat remains, diminished form of the Grail ship. An image of the human heart, it responds gaily and obediently 'to controlling hands', in harmony with the thunder's message, 'Give. Sympathise. Control.' Just as Jessie Weston sees the Grail story as originating in widespread and pre-Christian cults, so Eliot suggests that the hope of renewal may be found, not in outgrown forms of traditional religion, but in unfamiliar and unexpected places.

In *From Ritual to Romance*, Jessie Weston asserted that 'The Grail is a living force . . . it will rise to the surface again, and become once more a theme of vital inspiration.' The Grail myth was indeed a source of vital inspiration for Eliot, as later for J. Cowper Powys, Charles Williams and David Jones. Though Eliot's sombre vision stopped short of Miss Weston's later confident prediction: 'The Grail Quest was actually possible then, it is actually possible today', Charles Williams later showed how such a spiritual quest is in a sense still possible. Though Eliot's attention is directed primarily towards the Waste Land, the myth of the Grail becomes, in his great poem, an instrument of exploration, making possible an analysis of his own experience, at the same time that it illuminates our understanding of our own society. His 'rhythmical grumbling' is none the less valuable for being personal; indeed, Eliot himself later asserted that it was from 'acute personal reminiscence' that a poem drew its power. The despair and horror that he experienced so intensely in his contemplation of his own life and of the modern world nevertheless needed to find expression through myth in order to be set free from time and place and to communicate the timeless moral and spiritual insights of the poet to us at this very time and place.

ii. Some Minor Writers on the Grail Theme: A. E. Waite, Arthur Machen and Charles Williams in *'War in Heaven'*.

Eliot's sophisticated, cosmopolitan, immensely influential 'Arthurian' poem suggested how the symbolism of the Grail story could be used freely, allusively, yet without losing any of its traditional resonance in the work of the modern writer. *The Waste Land* remains essentially a secular poem, however, despite its concern with the spiritual condition of twentieth-century society. But while Jessie Weston was formulating her anthropological theory about the nature and origins of the Grail, its significance as a religious object and symbol seems to have increased towards the end of the nineteenth century and to have retained its meaningfulness for several decades. The decline in orthodox religious belief had created a climate in which such fringe movements as theosophy and occultism in its various forms could flourish, along with spiritualism and psychical research, and such figures as H. P. Blavatsky and Annie Besant attracted large numbers of followers. The interest in all sorts of paranormal experience was manifested in the continuing experimentation with mesmerism and animal magnetism, while hypnotism and homeopathic medicine offered unconventional modes of healing. All testified to the widespread desire for greater understanding of the mind and its powers, and in particular for understanding of the powers of the mind over the body. One of the results of the search for new forms of religious experience was a revival of interest in mysticism, and William James's *Varieties of Religious Experience* (1902), Friedrich von Hugel's *The Mystical Element of Religion* (1908 ff.) and Evelyn Underhill's *Mysticism* (1911) indicate the extent of this development. An influential figure in the world of occultism and other cults was A. E. Waite, described in his own time as 'a leading authority on the Higher Mysticism and Sacramental Religion', and author of two vast books relating to the Grail story. Waite saw connections between the Grail symbolism and some aspects of Freemasonry, as well as with the Tarot pack, though he disagreed fundamentally with Jessie Weston's interpretation of the origins of the legend. Mutual interest in the occult led to a brief association between Waite and the poet W. B. Yeats; and both Evelyn Underhill and Charles Williams were at some time members of the Hermetic Order of the Golden Dawn, an occult society which Waite founded, in collaboration with others, some time before 1900. Though Williams withdrew long before any of his own writing on the theme of the Grail was published, the influence of Waite can often be seen in his work, for example in a rather similar interest in the occult, in the value that he attaches to the Grail symbolism, and in his emphasis on the powers of the mind.

The first of Waite's books, *The Hidden Church of the Holy Graal*, appeared in 1909, and in it he declares that he is concerned with the 'hidden life' of those who have 'taken their place within the sanctuary of the mystic life' (p. vii). He sees 'Graal mysticism' as part of the 'unified Mystic Rite', thus asserting that the symbol of the Grail may have significance for the modern Christian. That the Grail legend was more than simply a subject of intellectual enquiry for Waite may be seen from the volume of poems that he published in 1921, *The Book of the Holy Graal*. It contains eighteen sections consisting of blank verse poems, each followed by a short lyric, and in these latter he used a variety of different forms. The poems are about his own personal mystical experience, in which Grail symbolism plays a large part, and tell of the spiritual love of the writer (referred to as Quaestor Dei) for 'Beata Mea', or Eva, who is in a sense a Grail-bearer. This love can only be fulfilled in spiritual union. The poems are very characteristic of their period, and not particularly distinguished, but they demonstrate the extent to which Grail symbolism was acquiring a new currency. Indeed, Waite himself remarks towards the end of the volume, 'Old stories now are preface to a new/Romance of soul . . .', and he also comments that the Holy Graal is still present in the world, as once it was in Arthur's days. Waite's interest in the Grail legend seems to have been life-long, for his last work, *The Holy Graal: its Legends and Symbolism*, appeared as late as 1933.

Different kinds of interest in the Grail converged in the early years of the twentieth century, so much so that Waite could assume that 'there is no scholar now living in England whose conditional sympathy at least I may not expect to command from the beginning', in writing his first book. Archaeological studies were involved too: the *Occult Review* of 1907 alleged that the Holy Grail had been discovered at Glastonbury, indicating that its identity as archaeological object and as mystic symbol overlapped. As a powerful spiritual symbol which was thought to bring together in its origins both pagan and Christian traditions, it offered a mythology which could be reshaped and which not only attracted orthodox Christians but provided a focus for mystical experience of unorthodox kinds.

Even before the publication of *The Waste Land* in 1922, Arthur Machen had used the image of the Grail in a modern setting in his prose narrative, *The Great Return* (1915). Instead of attempting to retell the story of the Quest, or to give new life to the familiar characters associated with it, he takes the Grail as a still active spiritual reality both in *The Great Return*, and, though in a quite different way, in *The Secret Glory* of 1922. He was already known for his story of *The Angels of Mons* (1915), in which he had described the appearance of a host of angels to some of the British troops at the battle of Mons in the First World War, a phenomenon which was believed by the credulous to have actually occurred. In *The Great Return*, somewhat similarly, Machen describes the incursion of the divine into the everyday modern world, in what purports to be a true account of strange events in an actual Welsh village. In a personal, anecdotal way, Machen tells of the return of the Grail to Llantrisant, resulting in a sick girl's visionary experience and miraculous healing, and other out of the ordinary occurrences. 'All this, of course, may have been altogether in the natural order . . . But as to the "phenomena", . . . Well, what do we know? . . . did the people "see" and "hear" what they expected to see and hear?' he asks.[7] He leaves the reader with the possibility that it may all have been caused by collective hallucination and telepathic communication; but what is of special interest here is the symbolic form in which the experience is expressed.

In *The Secret Glory*, Grail-imagery features in a different way. The book appears to be veiled autobiography, the story of a sensitive boy at a public school, whose suffering of brutal punishment and bullying is contrasted with his inner mystical experience. His father takes him as a child to a remote Welsh farmhouse, where he is shown the ravishingly beautiful Graal vessel, still preserved there by an old farmer. As he looks at the Graal he has visions, and from then on he walks 'in a strange light; he had been admitted into worlds undreamed of', and he has become aware of 'the inexpressible radiance of the invisible world'. The Graal vision has nothing to do with the ordinary everyday religious observances of school life. Its meaning is communicated in terms of nature-mysticism, in some fine descriptive passages. Yet, though his mystical experiences set the boy apart from his schoolfellows, the intensity of his inner life does not prevent him from turning upon his persecutors and effectively routing them with unexpected savagery. As in some later works which bring the Grail into the modern world, there is, as well as the mystical, a morbid and sadistic element, which here as elsewhere is expressed in surprisingly violent terms. The introduction of such symbolism into stories of contemporary life, however, makes them more striking and more worthy of notice than the often vapid little playlets popular in the early years of the century, which do no more than dramatise some part of the Arthurian story in a pseudo-medieval setting.

Charles Williams's *War in Heaven* (1930),[8] like John Cowper Powys's much greater *A Glastonbury Romance* which appeared two years later, is also based on the Grail legend, and both novels take as their theme the unending conflict between the powers of good and evil in the universe. In *War in Heaven*, good ultimately triumphs, and its power and splendour can be known in everyday life through mystical experience. The novel is Arthurian only in so far as it is based on the story of the Grail; the vessel itself is the central image, and three major characters are seen as representing Galahad, Percival and Bors. The setting is twentieth century, and there is no attempt to follow the traditional Grail story closely, but the analysis of the type of Galahad, represented here by an elderly Archdeacon, adds something new to modern treatments of the Arthurian theme. He is a Galahad de-romanticised, but through him Williams suggests that selflessness and spiritual insight may be found in unlikely places and among ordinary people.

The novel also asserts the power of prayer, and maintains the reality of psychic forces both for good and for evil, suggesting the insidiousness of evil in its efforts to gain power over the minds of the innocent and to pervert them to its purposes. In contrast with early versions of the story, this re-telling reveals its modernity in its emphasis on the strength and ubiquity of the powers of evil. The Grail is the immediate object of the struggle. It is the symbol of the goodness which those of evil intent wish to corrupt and to destroy; indeed, the wholesale, world-wide destruction of all that is good is the ultimate lust of those whose minds and wills are possessed by evil. Using the Grail as symbol in this way, Charles Williams adds a new element to the tradition by making some of the participants in the quest actively evil. Those who seek the Grail unworthily are not merely inadequate or sinful, as are Gawain, Lancelot and others in the earlier versions, but diabolically and vilely evil, and positively shown as such: the novel suggests some of the forms that such evil can take. The Grail is not simply a spiritual reality to be experienced in visions, but an actual object upon which men can set their hands, and which they can possess, if only temporarily. Its significance, however, corresponds with that of the medieval Grail: it is the means by which men can have knowledge of the divine; and its power, its holiness and its beauty capture the imagination and draw forth the same longing as they do in earlier treatments of the Grail quest.

As with his poetry, it is from the medieval legends that Charles Williams takes his theme, though the influence of A. E. Waite directs his interpretation of them. He alludes to Jessie Weston's *From Ritual to Romance* in the novel, but only in a disparaging way, and he obviously did not accept her belief that the origins of the Grail story were to be found in pagan rites. Nevertheless the Grail is seen in the novel as a source of renewal and increased vitality for the Waste Land. Williams suggests that, though the Grail has left this world, never to return, the spiritual power for which it stands can still be tapped, and that the vision of it can occur in everyday life. The initiation of one of the characters, a young child, into the 'holy mysteries', and his contact with spiritual reality, also apprehended by a number of other characters at the moment of the Grail's departure, indicate that the quest and vision are something that ordinary people can share, each according to his individual capacity.

The plot of *War in Heaven* concerns the attempts of a retired publisher, Mr Gregory Persimmons, and an explorer and antiquarian, Sir Giles Tumulty, to get possession of an ancient chalice which they believe to be the Grail vessel. It has long belonged to the parish of an elderly Archdeacon. He accidentally discovers its true but hitherto unsuspected identity at the point when it is stolen from him by Persimmons, who with Tumulty wishes to possess the chalice to pervert its power and to destroy it through the practice of black magic. They also attempt to gain power over a small child so as to make of him a 'pure and entire oblation' to the powers of evil, aided by some sinister and mysterious characters, a young Greek and an old Jew, in a seedy part of London. The Archdeacon is assisted in his efforts to get back the chalice by a junior member of Persimmons's firm, Kenneth Mornington, and by a Roman Catholic Duke, and an exciting series of events ensues. The Grail is wrested from the evil characters, but then regained by them, and used in very powerful occult rites, which lead to the death of Mornington, while the Duke and the Archdeacon are both forced temporarily to submit to the evil wills of their antagonists. But at the climax of the story another character appears, Prester John, who is—among other things—the Bearer and Keeper of the Grail. (The association of Prester John, a fabulous medieval monarch of Asia, who as both priest and king ruled vast dominions in the Far East, with the Grail story is probably due to the influence of A. E. Waite, who connects the two in his *Hidden Church of the Holy Graal*.) In Williams's novel, Prester John keeps guard over the innocent and is the channel of spiritual power. When, through his aid, the evil characters are overpowered, the Archdeacon, the innocent and those who have been trying to keep the Grail out of the hands of its enemies see Prester John celebrating the holy mysteries in the parish church, and experience a final transcendent vision in which priest and Grail disappear for ever from this world.

The conflict between good and evil in this novel is mainly represented through the opposition between prayer on the one hand, and black magic on the other. Though the Grail is a channel for spiritual power and 'an accidental storehouse of power that could be used' (p. 141), it is vulnerable to the fierce onslaughts of the forces of evil, concentrated upon it and upon the innocent through occult rites. Williams makes very apparent the loathesomeness of evil by representing the squalor and ugliness of its devotees and its habitations, the intensity of its energies and concentrated will-power, its utter ruthlessness. The magical rites through which the evil characters seek to accomplish their purposes have an authenticity which appears to originate in part at least, in Williams's own interest and experience of the occult as a member of the Order of the Golden Dawn, and from his study of magic and witchcraft. He effectively suggests the workings of the black magic which destroys Mornington at the climax of the novel:

> Kenneth had reeled to one of the white lines and was stumbling blindly, now forward, now backward, drawing deep choking breaths. The Greek had thrust his face out, and as the Duke saw it in the full light he gave a little gasp of dismay. For the face that he saw looked at him from a great distance and yet was itself that distance. It was white and staring and sick with a horrible sickness; he shut his eyes before this evil. All the gorgeous colours and pomps of sin of which he had been so often warned had disappeared; the war between good and evil existed no longer, for the thing beneath the Graal was not fighting but vomiting. (pp. 216–7)

Through the 'good' characters, the proposition is made that though evil and pain are displeasing to God, he permits them (p. 181); but though the novel makes very apparent the vileness of evil, it accepts it as existing within the divine plan. Unlike John Cowper Powys in *A Glastonbury Romance*, Charles Williams is neither concerned with the problem of pain nor outraged at the actuality of human suffering. *War in Heaven* is an expression of Williams's assured faith in ultimate goodness. In taking the Grail as the embodiment and symbol of the good, he shows how men may come by a variety of different approaches to a realisation of its meaning. The study of antiquity and of folk-lore may lead some to the Grail, as may 'exalted poetry and the high romantic tradition in literature', while the Archdeacon's mode of approach is through religious experience. The value of literature is asserted, for those who have come to knowledge through it find that the literary tradition is a living light which shines in the mind and has made the idea of the Grail familiar; indeed its familiarity, says Williams, has 'created for it a kind of potentiality' (p. 101). Like Powys later, Williams suggests that the power of human thought, accumulating through the ages, is to some extent responsible for the real power of the Grail. The symbol and the ideal that it represents have indeed an influence over men's minds, standing as they do for the higher aspirations and the spiritual yearnings of mankind, for the 'other', the 'devotion to something afar', the fleeting vision of beauty and perfection. To deny the significance and reality of the Grail, Williams says in a perceptive comment, would be to deny our own past.

The experience of the Grail varies, as does the means by which we come to knowledge of it, and Williams well represents the ecstasy of vision in terms of light, delightful sound, and the sense of joy. As the Archdeacon contemplates it,

> His spirit felt its own unreasonable gaiety opening into a wider joy; its dance became a more vital but therefore a vaster thing. Faintly again he heard the sound of music . . . from some non-spatial, non-temporal, non-personal existence. It was music, but not yet music . . . sound produced, not by things, but in the nature of

things. He looked, and looked again, and felt himself part of a moving river flowing towards some narrow channel on a ripple of which the Graal was as a gleam of supernatural light. (p. 117)

Williams conveys a sense of the splendour and the mystery of the Grail vision. For Kenneth Mornington, it is also the 'thing from which the awful romances sprang, and the symbolism of a thousand tales'. Contemplating it, he sees 'the chivalry of England riding on its quest . . . a grave young God communicating to a rapt companionship the mysterious symbol of unity', as the 'liturgical and romantic names' associated with the Grail stories and the names of their makers 'rose . . . gleamed and flamed about the Divine hero, and their readers, too—he also, least of all these' (p. 136). Williams perhaps more than any other writer makes explicit the fascination that the legend has exercised for the imagination throughout its long existence. Though there is sometimes, as in C. S. Lewis's writing on the Arthurian as on other themes, a slightly obtrusive religiosity, Williams on the whole succeeds in communicating a sense of the numinous and of contact with spiritual reality without seeming to indoctrinate.

Though it is in various ways a clumsy book, *War in Heaven* holds the reader's interest, for the action is fast moving. The scenes are varied and suspense is built up effectively. The impingement of the supernatural world upon the world of ordinary everyday experience is well managed for the most part, but the introduction of the figure of Prester John as a kind of *deus ex machina* is a not entirely satisfactory means of bringing about the defeat of the forces of evil. The characters are merely types, and most of them very wooden at that, only capable of carrying on Williams's psychomachia in a mechanical way, but the story does not require more elaborate characterisation. The dialogue is rather dated, though it can be agreeably humorous at times. *War in Heaven* can only rank as a minor work, but nevertheless it deserves serious consideration as a successful re-telling of the Grail story which demonstrates how it can still provide a symbol system for the modern writer who wishes to write of some of the deeper realities of life in his own time.

iii. Charles Williams, *Taliessin Through Logres* and *The Region of the Summer Stars*; C. S. Lewis, *That Hideous Strength*.

Charles Williams's cycle, written over the course of many years but probably never quite finished, was the work by which he wished to be remembered. *Taliessin through Logres* appeared in 1938 and was followed in 1944 by *The Region of the Summer Stars*, but the latter is not a sequel to the first: its eight poems, though written later, must be interpolated within the earlier work to maintain the narrative sequence. The order in which the poems should be read was suggested after Williams's death by his friend C. S. Lewis in *Arthurian Torso*,[9] and it is followed here when they are discussed in detail.

Charles Williams's poems, strange and difficult though they are, probably constitute the most original and extended poetic treatment of Arthurian material in the twentieth century. Williams believed that the myth of the Grail was the most important of the Arthurian stories: 'No invention can come near it; no fabulous imagination excel it; it is the central matter of the Matter of Britain'.[10] He considered that it had never been treated adequately in English verse, for Tennyson's version of the Quest was no more than an episode, and within this, the quest itself was only for the elect. Williams's own treatment of the story aims at and succeeds in bringing out the power and the universality of the myth, and in making it live again. His Arthurian poems give expression to his mystical sense of man's spiritual potential. The poems deserve to be better known, reaching as they do beyond T. S. Eliot's sombre vision of the Waste Land to a more positive and optimistic final position. Williams's poetic cycle is not about sin but about joy, about the possibility of a comprehensive fulfilment of individual potential in 'love, laughter, intelligence and prayer'; his version of the Grail story leads away from the stumblings and failures of western civilisation throughout its history, towards future achievement both in and out of this world.

The distinction of these poems lies partly in their breadth of vision. They are neither moralistic nor didactic. Instead of glorifying asceticism or puritanism, they require acceptance of the body and its needs, recommend tolerance and develop in all its complexity Williams's concept of love. There is a place for sexuality, a rôle for the normal and indeed for the commonplace in his imaginary world; while a pervasive generosity of spirit adds to the joyousness, the freshness and the energy of his re-handling of the Grail themes.

At the same time, he avoids both romanticism and pseudo-medievalism, placing the Arthurian theme in the larger context of western civilisation and deepening it by embedding it in the symbolism of the Byzantine empire, chosen for its complexity as a poetic image, and since made familiar to the modern reader by Yeats.[11] Williams's Grail-world stretches from Byzantium and beyond to the furthest reaches of Logres (Britain) and ultimately to Carbonek, the Grail-city. The Empire stands for all Creation; Unfallen Man; a proper social order; and the true physical body, as Williams himself explained. To this must be added the traditional associations of Byzantium with rich and splendid ceremonial, and the outward expression of a spiritual awareness and ideal. The use of such symbolism has the advantage that it can carry a wider range of meaning than the more localised symbolic settings of the medieval Grail stories could do, enabling Williams to avoid what Joseph Campbell in *The Masks of God: Creative Mythology* calls 'that sacerdotal fairyland of nuns, angelic voices, forest chapels, and consecrations'[12] characteristic of, for example, the *Queste del Saint Graal*. The poems are difficult largely because of this symbolism, but their richness and vitality as well as their depth of meaning, reward the patient reader. Williams further extends the range and power of the myth by another significant set of images, of the human body, pictorially illustrated in the end papers of *Taliessin* as a recumbent female form. Each province of the empire corresponds with a part of the body: Logres is the brain of the empire and Camelot (London) its mouth; the face looks towards Carbonek, the Grail city. Gaul is represented by the breasts of the figure, symbolising, as C. S. Lewis comments, traditional organisation, scholastic debates and doctrines, and theology. The hands correspond with Italy, where the Pope celebrating Mass performs a manual act; the navel with Byzantium itself—the centre; the genitals with Jerusalem. Caucasia is the 'rounded bottom of the Emperor's glory', 'the fool's shame', ridiculous yet of fundamental importance, 'not so much a particular part of the body as the whole body, or even the whole man, seen from a particular point of view'.[13] The idea of such symbolism, Anne Ridler comments in *The Image of the City* (p. xxv), may have been suggested by A. E. Waite's *The Secret Doctrine in Israel* (1913). This study of the Jewish mystical *Zohar* has as frontispiece a diagram of the Sephirotic Tree (alluded to in Williams's poem 'The Death of Palomides' in *Taliessin*) laid out upon the figure of a man, with the different properties related to different parts of the body. Whatever its origin, however, Williams's body imagery gives precise organic form to a large number of concepts, suggesting at the same time the interdependence and indeed unity of body and spirit.

Williams's version of the Grail story is the more impressive for being neither personal and subjective, nor focused on the ills of a corrupt society. The large scope and objectivity of these poems results in a far-reaching vision of divine purpose working itself out, yet demanding the co-operation of man, according to each one's individual gifts and capacities. It is within the long continuum of the history of western civilisation that the events of the story are enacted, so that its implications for twentieth-century society are set in perspective and the symbol of the Grail takes on a timeless significance. Like earlier versions of the story, the work gives expression to that sense of yearning and striving characteristic of our culture, yet without nostalgia; but it is concerned not so much with individual adventures as with states of being and states of mind, with growth of insight both moral and spiritual. Its meaning emerges gradually as the traditional story unfolds itself in a new way, challenging conventional attitudes and values. Though the Grail and those few who attain it cannot remain in this world, the realisation of its splendour is within the capacity of many, and that realisation is an experience of enlightenment which may take many different forms. Indirectly, even Guenevere can experience its power and be changed by it; an aspect of the poem's meaning is that the Grail's purposes involve and make use of the sinful as well as the virtuous. So that, although few can attain the ultimate vision, and the world can never be both permanently and comprehensively ameliorated by the power of the Grail, the general movement is towards acceptance of human frailty and towards optimism, rather than to élitism or despair. It is thus close in spirit (though not explicitly so) to the medieval versions of the Arthurian legend which see—as Malory does—the destruction of the Round Table and the death of Arthur as tragic indeed, but only relatively so, for beyond the failures and suffering of this life is the hope and joy of heaven. Nevertheless, it is not simply concerned either with the after-life or with the mystical experience attainable only by the devotee, for the joy and beauty and power represented by the Grail are immanent and domesticated in everyday life and apparent in the activities of ordinary human beings.

Much of the experience with which these poems are concerned is mediated through the figure of Taliessin himself, and through him Williams considers the function of the poet. Taliessin is Arthur's court poet, but at the same time he is the poet throughout the ages, whose task is to discern and to transmit truth and understanding. At the beginning of the cycle, he is the poet sprung from the Druids, taught first in Byzantium, and then in the course of the Middle Ages, in the schools of Gaul. As also for Dante, Virgil is Taliessin's guide and master in the arts of poetry. As the cycle progresses, so does Taliessin's knowledge of truth and his awareness of his rôle, until in the final poem, 'Taliessin at Lancelot's Mass', he sees the unity of experience symbolised by the gathering of 'all the dead lords of the Table' for the Mass, and by their relation to the supreme Unity. As he comes to understand the paradox of his own condition, 'manacled by the web, in the web made free', his whole being is transformed into joy, and 'that which was once Taliessin rides to the barrows of Wales / up the vales of the Wye', an apotheosis which brings him full circle with his beginning. His final vision at Lancelot's Mass can no longer be expressed in words, yet throughout the cycle, the Grail quest has been seen and interpreted, partly through his songs, but also through discussion with other witnesses of the events. It is also the poet's function to interpret to his ordinary unnamed, unlearned contemporaries the meanings of what he perceives, in terms that they can understand, even though such knowledge cannot always be communicated in literal language, or through straightforward explanation.

The relationship of the poet to his society, and his role as interpreter of hidden meaning, is thus an important theme within the cycle, as well as an effective means of moving the reader through the events with which it is concerned. The device both focuses attention, and at the same time provides a point of view, but it is not the only point of view. Palomides, the unchristened Saracen knight, speaks for himself in three poems widely spaced within the cycle. His experience is alien, his understanding clouded until just before his death, and he offers a different approach to the Round Table and its ideals, as to the group at the court of King Mark, from that of those already within the society. Similarly, Bors always speaks in his own person, putting forward the point of view of the good man, active in the everyday world, assessing the new developments to which Arthur's rule has given rise. Speaking privately, as it were, to his wife Elayne, his words indicate the depth, the joy and beauty of their relationship, the shared love from which love flows to others, making an implicit contrast with the sterile love of Lancelot and Guinevere, and of Palomides for Iseult.

The effect of the mode of narration implied by the different voices within the cycle, to which must be added that of the author as persona, as distinct from Taliessin, is to distance most of the familiar figures of the Arthurian world. Inevitably, the story is little concerned with Arthur and Guinevere, who are virtually outside the traditional Grail story. They are figures in the background who do not need to be fully realised. Lancelot might be expected to play a larger part, because of his active participation in the Grail quest in the medieval versions, but Williams is mainly concerned with his role as the agent of the divine purpose, in begetting Galahad. For Galahad's birth is brought about by 'holy enchantment' and an act of 'substitution' and one of its more significant implications is that 'the greater derives for ever from the lesser'. Lancelot's purely human viewpoint makes him interpet his act as unforgivable disloyalty to his love for the Queen, because he cannot know of the 'deliberate action of spiritual powers'. Only through the literal substitution of King Pelles's daughter for Guinevere at the appropriate moment can the greater good come into being. This idea of 'substitution', particularly in a metaphorical sense, is crucial to Williams's thought, finding its supreme example, of course, in the Crucifixion.

Though many of the major characters in the Arthurian story are distanced in Williams's version, stylised and diminished because of his symbolic purpose, they are not abstractions. Many are familiar, but there are others unnamed, too, and together they give richness and life to the cycle. Because of its time-span, it does not need to rely upon a sharply realised setting to give concreteness to the haunting imaginary world that it creates. Castle and palace-yard are as timeless, both as real and symbolic places, as is the cave where Palomides takes refuge with the beast for company. Most of the imagery is figurative, giving the cycle resonance without limiting it to a specific historical period, thus avoiding archaism.

In taking the Grail legend as the medium for his insights into certain 'states or principles of experience', Williams takes the traditional narrative itself as the basis of his sequence of poems, rather than merely drawing upon the legend for motifs and images. The effect is therefore to involve the reader's interest in the working out of the story as it builds to its climax in the coming of Galahad, and as the characters fulfil their individual destinies. The differing experiences of a wide range of characters, whether familiar or otherwise, contrast or complement each other as they converge towards the climax, and help to define its meaning. The last section transmutes the sadness of the destruction of the Round Table and the death of its members into the solemn splendour of the final transcendent apprehension of ineffable joy.

Unlike many mystical writers, Williams does not make use of the language of sexual love to communicate his perception of the nature of spiritual experience, but the cycle is not therefore lacking either in sensuousness or in passionate feeling. The poetic power of his images and the vigour of his verse combine to communicate both emotion and spiritual meaning, as in Galahad's last voyage which ends in the longed-for fulfilment of his quest:

> Through the sea of omnipotent fact rushed Galahad.
> He glowed white; he leaned against the wind
> down the curved road among the topless waters.
> He sang Judica te, Deus; the wind,
> driven by doves' wings along the arm-taut keel,
> sang against itself Judica te, Deus.

The passage suggests exhilaration and energy by means of the traditional images of the speeding ship and the doves; the sea image gives the incident a philosophical context, while the nature of Galahad is defined by his song 'Be thou my judge, O Lord, for I have walked innocently'. As the wind takes up the song, the concepts of man and nature as being alike part of God's creation and purpose, and of their essential unity are suggested; and beneath these lies the deeper meaning of the final journey to the Grail city, with its promise of fulfilment in spiritual union with the divine.

The separate poems within the sequence are remarkably varied in many ways, not least in poetic form. Many are stanzaic, the form varying between three- and eight-line stanzas. The quatrain recurs most frequently, but even within it, there is considerable variety in the use of rhyme and rhythm. 'The Coming of Palomides' is unique in that it is in rhyming couplets, with four stresses to a line, creating a jaunty and naïve effect, and thus differentiating the unchristened Saracen knight from other figures. He changes his tune later, in the course of his story. Many other poems, and particularly those concerned with the most significant events within the story, are in freer forms which can accommodate dialogue that is often vigorous and naturalistic, though sometimes mannered. These poems are interwoven with much internal rhyme, effective in patterning and unifying the verse and drawing attention to detail, but sometimes over insistent. One hears the cadences of Hopkins here, both in the sprung rhythm and in the word-clusters of which Williams is also fond. The texture of the verse is as rich, subtle and ingenious as the imagery within it, and as the meanings which ultimately emerge.

The Poems: an Interpretation.

The cycle begins with 'Prelude' in which Williams suggests the relationship of Logres to the spiritual city of Byzantium; Logres is Britain, though not yet the historical Britain, regarded as a province of the Empire, and the time (as Williams explains in his preface to *The Region of the Summer Stars*) is, historically, 'after the conversion of the Empire to Christianity but during the expectation of the Return of Our Lord'.

To preserve a logical narrative sequence, 'The Calling of Taliessin' from *The Region* should follow, because it tells of Taliessin's upbringing among the Welsh tribes, and of his meeting with Merlin and Brisen, who represent 'Time and space, duration and extension', and are both children of Nimuë, who is nature, or all the vast processes of nature. 'They are sent to set up in Logres a kingdom which shall be like the holy kingdom of Pelles at Carbonek', C. S. Lewis explains.[14] It is to be a kingdom of complete and balanced humanity, and they send the pagan poet on to Byzantium so that his understanding can be deepened by 'the exposition of grace'. A little later, in 'Taliessin's Return to Logres', he comes back, now uniting in himself both the old pagan and the higher spiritual experience of 'operative Providence' that he has gained from his interview with the Emperor. The condition of expectation which the poem builds up leads into the long 'Vision of the Empire', to which Taliessin as the king's poet is to give expression, suggesting the poet's function both as seer and as man of action.

'The organic body sang together': in 'The Vision of the Empire' the image of the human body as symbol of spiritual well-being, of harmony, tolerance and acceptance in an unfallen world is also introduced and explored. (At the same time the image of the body denotes historical process: 'The milk rises in the breasts of Gaul', where Taliessin has drunk in 'the schools', the seat of learning in the Middle Ages.) But all is not well in the Empire, and at this point, Williams shows how the Fall destroys the state of well-being. His concept of the Fall defines it as an 'alteration in knowledge'. Adam and Eve, living in a world entirely good, could only gain knowledge of good and evil by knowing good *as* evil, first of all in the form of shame, by experiencing as evil their bodies which were good. In consequence, throughout the Empire all is turned to evil:

> *A brainless form, as of the Emperor*
> *walks, indecent hands hidden under the cope . . .*

> *Inarticulate always on an inarticulate sea*
> *beyond P'o-lu the headless Emperor moves,*
> *the octopuses round him; lost are the Roman hands,*
> *lost are the substantial instruments of being.*

The holy has been changed into mindless evil, associated with the degradation of hell, or P'o-lu, with its clutching octopus tentacles, which prevent the proper functions of the human hands. But there is a return to vitality and spiritual activity as the section ends. The moment has come for the Calling of Arthur, and, in the poem of that name, this is presented not in terms of the traditional 'sword in the stone' moment of recognition of the awaited hero, but as a complex development and coming together of active forces, out of a primitive and savage pre-Arthurian state, which has been almost entirely indifferent to moral values. Ordinary people with vision are already putting things to rights, however:

> *Bors is up; his wife Elayne behind him*
> *mends the farms, gets food from Gaul . . .*
> *Lancelot hastens, coming with wagons and ships.*

Camelot, the embodiment of spiritual value, is asking to be built, for Christ is the City, and Camelot as the city is potentially the City of God. It is to supersede the wild world from which Merlin, 'Wolfish . . . black with hair, bleak with hunger, defiled / from a bed in the dung of cattle', comes. After the 'candles of new Camelot' have shone out and the new order has been established, the king is crowned and Merlin sees into the future to the coming of Percivale, signifying further spiritual growth. It is a peak of achievement, of insight, of harmony between divine purpose and human will, but, in 'The Crowning of Arthur', the achievement is already threatened.

> *Driving back that azure a sea rose black;*
> *On a fess of argent rode a red moon.*
> *The Queen Morgause leaned from a casement;*
> *her forehead's moon swallowed the fires,*
> *it was crimson on the bright-banded sable of Lamorack.*

Though this is followed by Merlin's vision of the glory of Logres, by Taliessin's vision of 'wildness formalised' and by the coming of Guinevere in all her beauty, 'in beleaguered Sophia they sang of the dolorous blow'.[15] The new order is threatened not by the old barbarism but by ungoverned passion. The symbolic images of Taliessin's vision of harmony and order dissolve in

> *molten metals and kindling colours pouring*
> *into the pyre; at the zenith lion and dragon*
> *rose, clawed, twisted, screamed;*
> *Taliessin beheld a god lie in his tomb.*

Worse still, there is uncertainty at the very heart of the new order as Arthur contemplates his city: 'the king made for the kingdom, or the kingdom made for the king?' There should be no doubt in his mind that the first half of the question is its own answer, yet Arthur's conception of his role is in conflict with Merlin's perception, inspired by the wisdom of Saint Sophia. As in the medieval versions of the Grail story, Arthur is a marginal figure: he lacks the vision of his poet. Unwittingly, he brings about the destruction of all that Camelot might have stood for, through his incestuous union with Morgause. But in the final sections of *Taliessin through Logres*, though his identity is further eclipsed at his death, as he is united with King Pelles:

> *the two kings were one, by exchange of death and healing.*

In 'Lancelot's Mass' the identification is shown as complete: they are 'singly seen in the Mass, owning the double Crown, / going to the altar Pelles, and Arthur moving down'. Williams further moves away from tradition by suggesting that Arthur is 'saved' by Guinevere:

> *Out of the queen's substitution the wounded and dead king*
> *entered into salvation to serve the holy Thing.*

252

'Substitution' is a word which for Williams carried a special significance. He interpreted St Paul's injunction 'Bear ye one another's burdens' in a metaphorical sense, as implying that in ordinary life it was possible for one person to bear the burden of another, for example by offering to take his burden of grief or anxiety or guilt and bear it for him, and for the sufferer to transfer his psychological burden to another. Here, the lines evoke a comparison between Guinevere and Alcestis, who gave her life for her husband, and imply that in some sense Guinevere gave herself for Arthur's salvation. His identification with Pelles, while it deprives him of his status as the national hero who will come again, shows Arthur finally as both made whole and spiritually strengthened.

The rôle of the poet Taliessin is meanwhile developed as the cycle progresses. In the wars he is a captain of horse, actively engaged, but he must wait with a 'passion of patience' until the moment for action comes. In 'Mount Badon', he is associated with Virgil, through whom comes inspiration and the means of expression for the Logos. Through the 'grand art' of poetry the 'thudding hammer of Thor' is mastered. In the powerfully beautiful 'Taliessin's Song of the Unicorn', the poet is like the unicorn of medieval legend. The 'quick panting unicorn' will come only to a girl, but the ordinary girl 'cannot like such a snorting alien love' and has the beast killed and its head set up over the bed where she gladly gives herself to the ironically named 'true man' who sets her free from it. 'Yet if any, having the cunning to call the grand beast' should dare to experience its impact, she could, sharing in the suffering of Christ and the Virgin Mary, release an undreamed-of power of spiritual song. Williams suggests a strange identification between the girl and Christ crucified, in which she is pinned to 'a background of dark bark, where the wood becomes one giant tree'. Pierced through hands and heart, she

> *should be called the Mother of the Unicorn's Voice . . .*
> *her son the new sound that goes*
> *surrounding the City's reach, the sound of enskied*
> *shouldering shapes . . .*
> *in her paramour's song, by intellectual nuptials enclosed.*

The unicorn, here representing the poet, is also traditionally a symbol of Christ; the images of virgin and poet interchange with Christ and the Virgin Mary to suggest new channels for the Word to flow in, and new sources of power. Here, the suffering that love entails is accepted, indeed sought, and its potential realised through intellectual union. The effect of the final vision is the more intense for its contrast with the uncomprehending destruction of the poet's power, through ignorance and selfishness, in the first part of the poem.

In 'Taliessin in the School of the Poets', Taliessin is at Camelot, where he sees his fellow poets preoccupied with their own personal sorrows and love affairs, and professionally, with poetic technique. Here he directs attention to the poet's duty to deal with more important matters, and to give form to the vision of spiritual beauty and of the underlying harmony and symmetry, represented by

253

the human body and by the idea of Byzantium. But he is not understood, though

> *in a harsh voice he cried*
> *of the stemming and staling of great verse,*
> *of poetry plunged in the void.*

Instead,

> *Breathless explorers of the image,*
> *innocent, lucent-eyed,*
> *the young poets studied precision.*

'Substitution' again provides the key to the interpretation of the next poem, 'Taliessin on the Death of Virgil'. Virgil, as pagan poet, cannot be saved without faith: 'Others he saved: himself he could not save'. As a pagan,

> *this was the truth of his Charon's ferrying—*
> *everlastingly plucked from and sucked from and plucked to*
> *and sucked to a grave.*

But in the second part of the poem, all those who have been or will yet be nourished by his poetry rush to 'close with his fall', and save him through their faith: he is 'fathered of his friends'.

In succeeding poems, the Arthurian world struggles towards the moment of Galahad's birth through the diverse experience of its various characters. The Saracen Palomides, brought up in the Islamic faith which denies the Incarnation, knows 'the measurement of man / that Euclid and Archimedes showed', but does not accept the 'Gospels trigonometrical' which 'measured the height of God-in-man' when he kneels to Mark at his court in Cornwall. He is fired with desire for Iseult when he sees the beauty of her bare arm, which he perceives symbolically in terms of an equilateral triangle. The triangle represents perfection, suggesting 'unions metaphysical', but as Palomides praises Iseult's beauty, suddenly her arm becomes 'empty of glory', and he breaks off his song as a quiver of anger replaces the vision conjured up by the unbroken lines of the triangle. The vision fades because there is division 'between / the queen's identity and the queen'; and Palomides now becomes aware of the presence of the questing beast. The vision of the perfect figure becomes three disconnected lines, then diminishes to three points, as Tristram murmurs by Iseult's head. We are left only with the death-bringing 'eternal triangle' of Iseult, Tristram and Mark, and Palomides with his unlawful and frustrated desire for Iseult. Because he cannot 'measure the height of God-in-man', Palomides cannot maintain the first moment of his vision of Iseult's beauty, which would have allowed him to love her without carnal desire.

Forms of evil assert themselves more powerfully in 'Lamorack and the Queen of Orkney', which follows. Now 'Logres' convulsed theme' is working itself out not only in the coming birth of Mordred, but in the deaths of Balin and Balan.

The vision of evil, like Yeats's in 'Leda and the Swan', encompasses the web of future doom and the coming destruction of the Round Table and Camelot. But meanwhile Bors and Elayne continue the work begun before the coming of Arthur. Earlier in the cycle, in 'Bors to Elayne: the Fish of Broceliande', Bors has a gift for Elayne, a fish that he has plucked from a stream that flowed to the sea, an unnamable undefined gift that merges bodily and spiritual joy. It symbolises, as well as 'the happy flesh', the *ichthys* or diagram of a fish used as a secret sign by the early Christians in the catacombs, which represents Christ, in the form of a 'diagram over the happy dead / who flashed in living will through the liquid wish'. Their union of body and spirit, of male and female, in an active partnership of service, constitutes an exemplary norm beside the sterile triangular relationships of Mark, Iseult and Tristram, and of Arthur seated between Guinevere and Morgause. Elayne is the active means of the extension of Christ's kingdom, the 'sole figure of the organic salvation of the good' as she stands with 'the bread of love' in her hand, the 'lightness of law' in her head. But as the new social order is established, Arthur's misguided ideas of progress lead to the striking of dragon-stamped coins, enthusiastically acclaimed by Kay and the Archbishop, though feared by Taliessin and Bors, for 'Compact is becoming contract; man only earns and pays'. Arthur is limited and mistaken, as earthly rulers must often be, in his understanding of the needs of the kingdom, as Taliessin's song implies:

More than the voice is the vision, the kingdom than the king.

Thus he cannot bring salvation to Logres.

As Taliessin sings this, however, Percivale comes, bringing hope of spiritual renewal; though characteristically the perceptions of those who await his entrance and who attend the ensuing Mass are restricted by their own limitations. The lords talked of their fights, 'the king in the elevation beheld and loved himself crowned', while 'Lancelot's gaze at the Host found only a ghost of the Queen'. Percivale's coming now brings with it new spiritual awareness, new freedom, and new impetus to the power of love which directly prepares the way for the coming of Galahad. In 'The Ascent of the Spear', this new understanding, mediated through Taliessin, is suggested in the incident of the girl set in the stocks for 'taking a stick to a sneering bastard slut, a Mongol ape' who had insulted her in a wrangle in the hall. The girl's pride is reproached by Taliessin; she is moved to repudiate her own pride and intolerance, and to confess, 'I was wrong from beginning—'. 'But not to an end', replies Taliessin: the stumble retrieved leads on to the hope of ultimate triumph. For Williams a good character is one who has *become* good. So in the ordinary affairs of life, the way is prepared for the higher vision. In the next poem, 'The Sister of Percivale', Taliessin is engaged in the making of 'ambiguous verse' and the poem itself suggests the complexity of experience and its inevitable ambiguities. A slave, her back scarred from beatings, is drawing water from the well, but her eyes reflect 'distant Byzantium', while the poet simultaneously sees the 'curved bottom of the world', and is puzzled by the problem of reconciling contraries and perceiving the relationships of disparate things. At the sound of a trumpet, Percivale's sister—here named Blanchefleur, though elsewhere sometimes Dindrane—arrives and Taliessin sees her standing between her brothers, Percivale and Lamorack, with their incongruously contrary natures. In the sources, Perceval's sister, towards the end of the Grail story, gives her life to save a lady who can only live if she is given the blood of 'a maid and a clene virgin in will and in work, and a king's daughter'.[16] As he greets her, Taliessin perceives the relationship between the scarred back of the slave and the lovely face of Blanchefleur—that they are two sides, or two complementary expressions of the same thing. Blanchefleur's coming is a 'transit of Venus', a reconciliation of contraries. As C. S. Lewis has pointed out in *Arthurian Torso* (p. 193), while other modern myths depict a dialectical world, Williams paints a co-inherent world.

At this point, four poems from the later *Region of the Summer Stars* carry on the narrative thread of the cycle. 'Taliessin in the Rose Garden', 'The Departure of Dindrane', 'The Founding of the Company' and 'The Queen's Servant' precede the events of 'The Son of Lancelot' and the five following poems in *Taliessin*.

In 'Taliessin in the Rose Garden', the only poem which has Guinevere as its main subject, Taliessin sees the Queen, both as she was intended to be and as she now is, and related to this, the cosmic significance of all women. The vision is expressed in terms of the zodiacal signs, which relate to bodily functions and so to the 'diversities of gifts' of which St Paul speaks.[17] Taliessin sees that Guinevere might and should have been Arthur's counterpart, the symbol of the sensuous, of matter, in harmonious union with the shaping intellect. He begs her to fulfil her function:

> Let the queen's majesty, the feminine headship of Logres,
> deign to exhibit the glory to the women of Logres;
> each to one vision, but the queen for all.

But the queen implicitly rejects this role; looking slyly for Lancelot, talking and laughing, refusing to understand.

> Has my lord dallied with poetry among the roses?

she asks Taliessin, but his deeper insight tells him that 'women's flesh lives the quest of the Grail', and 'Women's travel / holds in the natural the image of the supernatural'; their hands welcome, make beautiful, or pray. Guinevere's refusal of her role will, Taliessin sees, lead only to war and bloodshed, to the suffering which all must share, and which is ultimately one with the suffering of the Wounded King and of Christ himself. In this poem, Guinevere is a great queen, a woman of both charm and beauty glimpsed in her majesty, but like Arthur unable to live up to the demands of her calling. Williams suggests both her earthly splendour and her human frailty, while at the same time he indicates their implications in the wider context of spiritual reality.

'The Departure of Dindrane' carries on the theme of responsibility and vocation. Guinevere will not assume her proper function, while Dindrane departs for the convent where she is to fulfil her vocation in total dedication, and later to be responsible for the upbringing of Galahad. At the same time, a slave, after seven years' servitude, is approaching the moment when she may choose either to be sent back to her own country, or to be given a dowry and suitably married, or to commit herself to the service of the household for ever. As she waits for Dindrane's party to muster and set off, the slave sees 'love and a live heart lie in Dindrane / and all circumstance of bondage blessed in her body'. She understands in a moment of vision that order and discipline are one with beauty:

> The hazel of the cattle-goad, of the measuring rod,
> Of the slave's discipline, of Logres' highway, of Merlin's
> wand of magic, of her lord's line of verse,
> of the octave of song, of the footpace under the altar,
> straight and strong, was in Dindrane's bare arm,
> fair measure in the body of the body's deeds.

At once, in her heart, 'servitude and freedom were one and interchangeable'. In this understanding, she chooses to remain in Taliessin's household; like Dindrane, she commits herself to a servitude which is another form of freedom. At the same time the poem vividly evokes the scene between Dindrane and Taliessin, as these two who deeply love each other go their separate ways to fulfil their different vocations.

The Round Table has no significant place, as such, in Williams's cycle; instead the company that forms about Taliessin, as the king's poet, is all-important. Its members are not Grail knights, but constitute something more like a lay order 'of the commons', of minds adult in love and dedicated to love, but without formal vows. At the lowest level, it is a community which includes all those from the humblest to Dindrane herself before her going to Almesbury, who have a shared spiritual experience and faith. At a higher level the company also manifests, for each other, the love that leads to substitution, 'dying each other's life, living each other's death'. Few only among them attain the third level, to which Taliessin's own experience 'in the large vision of verse' bears testimony, of higher spiritual awareness. Taliessin, at a moment when he 'ached with belated verse', when 'his heart waited / for his voice, and again his voice for his dumb heart', challenged by Dinadan, is reluctant to accept that he is master of this unformulated company. But Dinadan points out that Taliessin is a catcher of souls. The King's poet must admit that he has a special rôle, though he should also see its inherent absurdity: God has no absolute need of an agent. Thinking himself the less, he must be 'their single bond'. So this company, small though it is, a mere 'remnant', retains the vision that Logres has lost.

C. S. Lewis saw in this poem strong autobiographical elements: Williams himself attracted such a 'company'. The fact strengthens the contemporary relevance of the cycle: in a world in which spiritual values are rapidly being lost, it is still possible for small groups of like-minded people, here and there, to maintain their vision.

'The Queen's Servant' is a strange and indeed, in C. S. Lewis's words, a daring poem, dealing with another aspect of the liberation which the spiritual life affords, though paradoxically 'Freedom . . . is the final task of servitude'. The slave must first unclothe herself in shining nakedness before she can be re-clothed with the richness and splendour of perfect liberty, and before she can be dismissed from the household, to serve the queen.

The appropriate point has now been reached in the sequence of events for the birth of Galahad, to which a long section is devoted. In its title, 'The Son of Lancelot', attention is directed rather to the significant fact that Lancelot fathered him than, in the first instance, to Galahad himself. The irony of the situation which leads to 'the begetting of a saint upon a virgin by a sinner who supposed himself to be with someone else's wife', in Joseph Campbell's words,[18] is one that suited Williams's purpose, for it suggests the working out of the divine purpose both by means of and in spite of human sinfulness. Lancelot is, in Malory's version 'the best knight of the world' and a man of spiritual potential, as the episode of the Healing of Sir Urry makes clear. As in that story (not included by Williams) Lancelot is a channel for divine grace, so he is also in the begetting of Galahad, though C. S. Lewis points out that Lancelot is one of Williams's few expressions of the dangers of concupiscence. Galahad's birth is an aspect of 'love's means to love': it occurs at a time of utmost need, when barbarism seems triumphant, when 'Over Europe and beyond Camelot the wolves ranged', when even the noble is endangered or dehumanised, as in Lancelot's subsequent madness. The rampant forces of evil, of destruction, are symbolised by the wolf, the 'fierce figure / of universal consumption'. Lancelot, in a 'delirium of lycanthropy' has become half-man, half-beast; Merlin assumes the form of a wolf to take the new-born Galahad from his place of birth to Almesbury, where Blanchefleur (otherwise Dindrane) will rear him. So what appears to be evil may be the instrument of good, as 'warm on a wolf's back, the High Prince rode into Logres'. The section ends with Lancelot's recovery, at Easter, while the King's whole household sing in praise of love.

Between Galahad's birth and his coming to Camelot there is only the section 'Palomides before his Christening', but the experience which the Saracen knight recounts appropriately fills the space with its suggestion of long years in the wilderness. Of this poem Williams himself wrote: 'Romantic love and social order have both become blank. All that there is is hardness and itch and scratchings on the rock. Dinadan realises that loss may be a greater possession than having: and Palomides, incapable of believing believingly, believes unbelievingly.' Without the means of grace, he struggles to overcome the questing beast which, for him, had come between 'the queen's meaning' and queen Iseult. He had assumed that the victory would be easy, and that he could then consent to be christened and come to the Table on his own terms, 'But things went wrong'. The cave to which he eventually comes, and where he remains long after, represents an inner state of sterility, degradation, delusion, fear and blindness. No victory over the beast that lurks in the cave is possible: only at last, the perception that there is a path over the mountain to Caerleon, and that 'the sky had turned round', enables Palomides, now 'dull, un-dimensioned', to escape and to ride at last to Dinadan and, sponsored by him, seek christening.

With 'The Coming of Galahad' the climax of the cycle is reached and its meaning more fully disclosed. The Grail has appeared in the hall, and all have had what food they liked best as the first consequence of its coming. In ceremony and in the creation of a Rite, the coming of the High Prince is celebrated. He will be laid in the king's bed, and take the place of Arthur and Guinevere in Camelot now.[19]

Outside, Taliessin, who has gone alone from the hall to the outer yards of the castle, looks up from the lowest point to where the procession winds upwards to the king's bed, where Galahad is to lie. As he stands looking up and singing to his harp among the jakes and latrines, he is encountered by Gareth, the king's scavenger, 'for cause of obedience set to the worst work'. Gareth comments on and asks the meaning of Galahad's coming, and Taliessin explains the splendour and implications of the event. Tonight Gareth is 'nothing', tomorrow he will be a prince again; he too has seen from among the slaves at the hall's door 'a mystery . . . a cup . . . as of the Grail itself'. But meanwhile he must accept, as all must,

> question and digestion, rejection and election,
> winged shapes of the Grail's officers . . .
>
> > . . . Sir,
> without this alley-way how can man prefer?
> and without preference can the Grail's grace be stored?

The coming of Galahad emphasises man's freedom to choose between good and evil, between what will nourish his nature and what will not, and the food now provided is 'meats of love, laughter, intelligence and prayer'. The section ends with Taliessin's final song, contrasting with the children's song he had sung before, as he celebrates this moment of glory with a song about the cosmic dance of the heavenly bodies.

Now Merlin's tasks are performed, and as 'time's foster-child', Galahad sits in the perilous chair, so Merlin goes to his appointed end. Palomides dies, accepting at last what he had always known, but which had been meaningless while he had lusted after earthly satisfactions, that 'The Lord created all things by means of his Blessing'. The time has now come for Galahad to enter Carbonek, healing the wounded king and achieving the Grail; it is at the same time the moment at which Logres must cease to be identified with Britain, when all that it represents will now only be found in the spiritual city of Carbonek. But first Galahad seeks reconciliation with his father, who is blind to the truth of the divine necessity by which he had been betrayed by Merlin and Brisen, and who knows only that he has been false to Guinevere. Galahad asks Lancelot to forgive his existence, to forgive 'the means of grace and the hope of glory'. Bors on behalf of Lancelot assents, and prays that his children assent, and 'through God join with me in bidding their birth', a striking insight, which at once recognises both our resistance to the demands of the divine and the moments when existence itself is torment. C. S. Lewis draws attention to the importance of this poem for an understanding of Williams's thought: it suggests that the state of holiness causes immense suffering not only to the saints, but to those who are closely connected with them. The saints by their very nature inflict suffering on the world: 'Who can seek the Grail without damaging the Round Table?'[20]

By contrast, 'The Meditation of Mordred' which follows suggests the cynicism and vulgar depravity of what is going on in Mordred's mind at this time, 'the king's son gone whoring with fantasy'. His ambition is to emulate the Emperor of P'o-lu, and his idea of paradise is a state of inertia. But the cycle moves on and in 'The Last Voyage', the Grail knights are speeding towards the city of Sarras on the ship of Solomon. The poem in celebrating the apotheosis of Galahad contrasts strikingly with 'The Meditation of Mordred' in the joy and vitality, the sense of 'strenuous liberty' that it creates. Here, the intellectual and the sensuous aspects of life are reconciled, power is matched to purpose and passion to peace.

As the ship sails on, however, many significant events happen simultaneously: Arthur dies, Mordred is overthrown, Pelles is healed, Logres is withdrawn to Carbonek, and what had been Logres becomes Britain. In 'The Prayers of the Pope' which follows, Williams suggests the condition of the world after the Grail has left it, in a sombre picture of

> *Savage growths, moods infinitely multiplied*
> *across the bleak plains, under rains and snows*
> *of myths bitter to bondage*

with 'children starved in sieges, prostituted women, / men made slaves or crucified'. C. S. Lewis comments on the recurring patterns observable in history which this illustrates[21]: 'Every Logres fails to receive the Grail and sinks into a mere Britain: Israel, Athens, medieval Christendom, the Reformation, the Counter-Reformation, the Enlightenment.' Through the Pope's vision, Williams symbolically includes both the remoter past of European history, and the more immediate past of twentieth-century war-torn Europe, and merges them into the imaginary world of the poem.

'Taliessin at Lancelot's Mass' ends the cycle somewhat as Malory ended *Le Morte Darthur*, in that Arthur has died, and Lancelot and Guinevere have 'taken them to perfection'. All the dead lords of the Table are present in the spirit as Lancelot celebrates Mass, and the stanzas ring with the triumphant music of spiritual consummation and unending joy. Taliessin's life ends: 'that which had been Taliessin made joy to a Joy unknown', and the Company is dispersed. But as with Malory, the finale leaves a sense that this is not really the end; Malory's bishop sees the angels 'heave up Sir Launcelot unto heaven' and sees the gates of heaven open for him. We are left with the assurance that his death is not the end for Launcelot. Williams's Company is broken up, their leaders and the lords of the Round Table are dead, but as the vision fades we are left with the sense that they are together still—elsewhere. This final poem sums up many of Williams's most characteristic ideas. The idea of substitution, of voluntarily bearing one another's burdens; the idea of the service that is perfect freedom; the equality, as 'each in turn [is] lordliest and least'; and the joy that the life of the Company brings, are all present in the poem.

For many modern readers, religious poetry is not attractive, yet the power of Williams's vision compels attention, as does the remarkable vitality and energy of the verse in which it is communicated. The variety, the subtlety and the pervasive joyousness of the cycle reward the reader who is prepared to take the trouble to interpret Williams's mythology. The Grail story takes on enhanced significance in *Taliessin through Logres* and *The Region of the Summer Stars*, which, while they recognise the ever-present desolation of the Waste Land, also assert the possibility of countering its evil with 'love, laughter, intelligence and prayer'.

That *Taliessin through Logres* and *The Region of the Summer Stars* were long in gestation is apparent from four poems inserted into a volume entitled *Three Plays*, published in 1931. These four poems had in fact been published previously, and are quite unconnected with the plays. They are all songs of Taliessin, the first Taliessin's 'Song of Logres', the second his 'Song of Byzantium', and these are followed by his songs 'Of the King's Crowning' and 'Of the Setting of Galahad in the King's Bed'. Thus together they already suggest the outline of the major work that was to follow some years later, the need of Logres, its relationship with Byzantium, the promise for the future, and its fulfilment in the coming of Galahad. Many of the concepts that these poems contain will be familiar to the reader of the later poems, as also the images. These four songs are, however, strikingly different in form from the later poems: each has a distinctive metrical pattern, and the rhythms are reminiscent of the rhythms of Kipling. All are divided into regular and rather insistently rhyming stanzas, very different from the subtle and intricate patterns of sound characteristic of Williams's later poems.

Charles Williams and C. S. Lewis belonged to the same small Oxford circle during the Second World War. When Williams died in 1945, he left un-finished a prose study of the history of the Arthurian legend, which was to have been entitled *The Figure of Arthur* (quoted in the previous section), the first two chapters of which he had read aloud to C. S. Lewis, while some further chapters had also been completed. To these, C. S. Lewis added six further chapters, explaining that he was adding 'to Williams's history of the legend an account of the last poet who has contributed to it—namely,

Williams himself'. It is these two separate works that make up *Arthurian Torso*, the very existence of which suggests the close and sympathetic intellectual relationship between the two men. It is therefore not surprising that C. S. Lewis's *That Hideous Strength* follows on, as it were, from Charles Williams's Grail poems, in particular in taking the idea of Logres as key to its meaning. Logres stands for the spiritual ideal, the ideal of excellence, which is always in conflict with the secular, self-seeking Britain. Logres is the peculiarly English form of the spiritual ideal, but other nations, too, have their own visions of excellence, making use of their own appropriate ideal or mythology.

That Hideous Strength,[22] first published in 1945, is the third of a trilogy but the only one of the novels to make use of Arthurian material. It is in many ways similar to Charles Williams's novel, *War in Heaven*, discussed earlier, though its allusions to a totalitarian regime and its methods give it a political dimension that Williams's novel lacks. In this allegorical story, 'Britain' is asserting itself, making use of science and sociology by means of the ironically named organisation N.I.C.E., the National Institute of Co-ordinated Experiments at Belbury, of which the aims are the reconditioning of the human race, so as to make man a really efficient animal. There are no lengths to which its members are not prepared to go, but the naïve, such as the book's 'hero', the young sociologist Mark Studdock, whose ambition is always to be a member of the progressive element and in the inner ring, are easily flattered and seduced into lending themselves to evil. NICE's programme is predictable: sterilisation of the unfit, liquidation of backward races, selective breeding; then real education, at first psychological, but later involving biochemical conditioning and direct manipulation of the brain, leading to a new type of man. Mark soon finds that there is no turning back: NICE has its own police, and intimidation and the liquidation of colleagues who have attempted to extricate themselves make it impossible for him to yield to the half-hearted promptings of his enfeebled better nature.

That Hideous Strength is also of interest because in it Merlin plays a significant part, as NICE attempts to harness his power for evil purposes. The place where Merlin is entombed, until the time of his next return to earth, is reputed to be on a small plot of land belonging to Bracton College in Edgestow University, which the college is very ready to sell in order to overcome financial problems. It is expected that on his return, Merlin will make use of black magic, which can be harnessed and exploited for the further enslavement of mankind. Merlin's power is needed by NICE to supplement that which is derived from modern science and technology. The institution believes that his magic is the last survival of something older and different (Ch. 9, Section 5), a potency deriving from the interaction of mind and matter, going back to a much earlier era, and that it is a primitive psychic power which knows nothing of either rationality or morality. Belbury is wrong, however: Merlin's magic does not go against nature, but for him 'every operation on Nature is a kind of personal contact' (Ch. 13, Section 4). It is not surprising, therefore, that the directors of Belbury are imposed upon when they think they have captured

Merlin, and do not recognise him when, later, he is among them, for they cannot distinguish truth from falsehood. As the evil powers are extended, establishing themselves in the Edgestow area so that ordinary people's lives are violently disrupted and they are driven out of their homes by brutal gangs of workmen looking for the tomb with bulldozers and so forth, a very small community is opposed to them. This community is directed by Ransom, 'hero' of the other volumes of the trilogy, alias Mr Fisher King, who is also the Pendragon, directly descended from a line going back to the sixth century, when Logres first came into existence. Round him gather those who are not on the side of evil, and to him, very much against her will, is drawn Mark's wife, Jane, neglected by her husband who is now completely committed to NICE. Jane has disturbing dreams, a sort of second-sight, which shows her something of what is going on under the power of NICE, and through these experiences, at first meaningless to her, the Logres community is eventually able to find Merlin, whose beneficent powers are ultimately instrumental in destroying NICE. When the evil is at last totally eradicated, Merlin departs for ever to another sphere, and Ransom, or Mr Fisher King, is able to return to Perelandra, where he will be healed of his wound, and join King Arthur in the third heaven, Aphallin.

The battle between good and evil, represented to some extent through Arthurian mythology, is at the same time also an overtly Christian fable. Jane, while within the Logres community, has what is described as a religious experience. She is expected to join, and to take vows of obedience though not knowing what she is to join or obey. She is eventually prepared to offer obedience to Mr Fisher King, who replies 'It is enough for the present . . . This is the courtesy of Deep Heaven: that when you mean well, He always takes you to have meant better than you knew. It will not be enough for always. He is very jealous. He will have you for no one but Himself in the end.' There is thus a vein of didacticism in the novel, reminiscent of some of Lewis's other writing.

It is perhaps unfortunate that Lewis should have chosen to emphasise the latent power of Merlin in his one 'Arthurian' book, in that it helps to push modern versions of the legend a little further in the direction of the morbid and sinister occult aspects which appear to predominate in some twentieth-century narratives, and so inevitably towards degeneration, away from the more serious idealising potential of the stories. *That Hideous Strength*, more-over, demonstrates the truth that it is much easier to make evil interesting than to make good attractive. Lewis is at his best in describing the college meeting at which the ruthless schemers, who have carefully thought out their plan of attack, very quickly get their own way, and overcome the opposition by choosing their time and skilfully manipulating the situation. The process of Mark's seduction as he is overcome by his desire to count for something and to be in on what is going on, carries conviction. The social interchanges within the rather unpleasant collegiate society of Bracton and the sinister NICE establishment are well managed, suggesting how Mark is drawn deeper and deeper in by flattery alternating with cold-shouldering and threatening. There are some good characterisations such as the nonentity Curry, who believes that he has a say in what is going on, but is actually being used all the time. Curry likes to think that he knows everyone and everything, and knowing nothing, complacently sells the pass. In such a story, all the characters are necessarily types, but 'Fairy' Hardcastle, the brutally sadistic, repulsively masculine woman who is chief of police, is imaginatively conceived, her hearty vulgarity increasing her entirely credible vileness.

Lewis is less successful with the depiction of the virtuous characters and their lives in beleaguered Logres: the bones of the allegory stick out too insistently, and the characters are placed in a cosy provincial setting which now seems very dated, while the horror of Belbury, the NICE establishment, is much less so. The homeliness of the dialogue of the Logres community jars, and Mr Fisher King alternates uncomfortably for the reader between omniscient splendour and ordinary humanity. There is also an unattractive male chauvinism which comes out when Lewis is concerned with the unfortunate Jane, whose main fault seems to be lack of obedience to her husband. (That obedience is 'an erotic necessity' does not make it much better.)

The moment of victory over the powers of evil, presented in elaborate images of light, warmth, colour, joy and harmony—and indeed even sexual activity—does not quite satisfy: the homeliness and humour are awkwardly mixed in with the supernatural manifestations. On the other hand, the episode in which Belbury and all who are beyond redemption there are destroyed is in itself somewhat sadistic. Lewis describes the final cataclysm, when the dinner guests are trampled and killed by the wild animals from the vivisection unit and menagerie, as well as by Mr Fisher King's bear, with an unpleasant zest, and the three most powerful men who survive this bloodbath finally kill each other or themselves in an unnecessarily extended episode. Allegorically it may be appropriate that animality should destroy the last remnants of such human beings, and that such evil should be self-destructive, but it is too vividly realised: it is hard to know how to respond to it. Lewis shows an ambivalence towards violence here, which remains to trouble the mind, though he tries to offset the scenes of retribution by an equally lively and concrete representation of spiritual joy showing itself in physical well-being and happiness.

As a study of how quickly men can be persuaded along the path of evil in the cause of a perverted ideal, and easily come to accept the use of scientific knowledge and technology for evil ends, *That Hideous Strength* is not without significance for our time. It legitimately brings Arthurian motifs into a new modern context, while emphasising the importance of all that is best in our national traditions of justice and humanity. Lewis suggests that education must play a major part in keeping alive the spirit of discipline and the great tradition from which personal responsibility can draw strength, and it is upon personal responsibility that our freedom depends. He has valuable things to say through the medium of such motifs as the figure of Merlin and the Fisher King, and his novel extends the range of meanings of which the Arthurian symbol-system has been capable in the twentieth century.

iv. Arthurian Themes in the Work of David Jones and in James Joyce's *Finnegans Wake*.

David Jones, who was both writer and artist, found the Arthurian legends a rich source of symbol and imagery through which to give expression to his experience of life in the trenches in the First World War. In the preface to his first book, *In Parenthesis* (1937), he wrote, 'I think the day by day in the Waste Land, the sudden violences and the long stillnesses, the sharp contours and unformed voids of that mysterious existence, profoundly affected the imaginations of those who suffered it. It was a place of enchantment. It is perhaps best described in Malory, book iv, chapter 15—that landscape spoke "with a grimly voice".' David Jones has produced no new retellings of the Arthurian stories, but to all three of his major works, Malory and the Welsh versions contribute a substantial amount of thematic imagery.

David Jones, though he grew up in London, was the son of a Welshman, and in consequence the Welsh medieval Arthurian texts had a special interest for him. His childhood familiarity with Malory was later reinforced when he was working with the remarkable and versatile artist and sculptor Eric Gill, who used to read *Le Morte Darthur* aloud to his family. Jones's passionate devotion to the Celtic past furnished him with a source of symbols through which he could communicate to the general reader not only something of his own and other men's experience of trench warfare, but also his deepest convictions about life and religion. The image of the Waste Land is a structural feature in both his first and his last works, and Grail imagery, linked to his Roman Catholic faith, pervades his writing, while at the same time the figure of Arthur and the concept of brothers-in-arms plays a very much larger part in his work than in that of other contemporary writers who use Arthurian themes. Though—like Eliot and Joyce—he is freely allusive in his method of using his material, the effect is very different, because he finds in the myth different aspects of meaning, and he uses it to very different ends. In a note to his later work, *The Anathemata*,[23] he comments on the particular bias that interest in the stories has usually taken in the past: 'Owing to the success of the later Launcelot-Guenevere theme as a romance motif, the earlier, more basic and more political theme in the "most pyteuous tale of the morte Arthure saunz gwerdon" has been some what overshadowed', and he goes on to suggest that there are elements of genuine historicity in the Mordred theme. David Jones has a closer understanding of Malory's purpose and a greater interest in the political aspects of *Le Morte Darthur* than other contemporary writers who have handled Arthurian themes. He is even less interested than Malory in the 'romantic' aspects of the material, but the comradeship of the Round Table provides an analogy for the comradeship of the trenches. He mentions in the Preface to *In Parenthesis* the extent to which, in the war, he lived with a consciousness of the past, of the very remote and the more intermediate and trivial past, and speaking of *Le Morte Darthur* he says, 'the similarity between "then" and "now" was not far from my mind'. It has been suggested that he appreciated Malory most for the sense of martial endeavour, the feeling of men doing things, good or bad, to the uttermost. What Caxton commended in Malory as expressed in his Preface to *Le Morte Darthur* may also be found in *In Parenthesis*: 'noble acts, feats of arms of chivalry, prowess, hardiness, humanity, love, courtesy and very gentleness'. The fear and horror and misery of the daily experience of trench warfare belong to a man's world without privacy and without romance: the world of Arthur's divided and hard-pressed kingdom in its last days is likewise one that cannot allow itself the luxury of introspection or the leisured indulgence of love. 'The greatest mortal war that ever was' that in Arthur's time destroyed 'the fairest fellow-ship of noble knights that ever held Christian king together',[24] provides a close imaginative analogy for David Jones's own experience of the wanton destruction and waste of modern war; 'and but we avoid wisely there is but death', in Malory's words.

In *In Parenthesis*,[25] the experiences of John Ball, the central figure representing Jones himself but also 'everyman', are seen in the context of and in terms of Arthurian myth. 'In King Pellam's Launde', John Ball is on guard, while close by are his comrades in arms,

> Dai de la Cote male taile,
> Watcyn, Wastebottom, and the rest,
> his friends.

> these sit in the wilderness, pent like lousy
> rodents all the day long; appointed scape-beasts come
> to the waste-lands, to grope; to stumble at the margin
> of familiar things—at the place of separation. (p. 70)

Dai de la Cote male taile presently sees his own experience as part of all the campaigns of the past:

> My fathers were with the Black Prinse of Wales
> at the passion of
> the blind Bohemian king.
> They served in these fields,
> it is in the histories that you can read it, Corporal—boys
> Gower, they were—it is writ down—yes.

> Wot about Methuselum, Taffy?
> I was with Abel when his brother found him,
> under the green tree.
> I built a shit-house for Artaxerxes.
> I was the spear in Balin's hand
> that made waste King Pellam's land. (p. 79)

Arthurian characters have their present-day equivalents: Agravain, the evil counsellor, appears as the type of the 'secondary, urging influence', prompting others to evil courses that are not of their own devising.

Though the experience of the soldiers in the trenches is presented as a continuation of an ancient tradition, David Jones sees beyond the more superficial aspects of similarity. The Arthurian legend makes possible a literal comparison between past and present, but at the same time it lends itself to metaphorical interpretations. John Ball and his friends are themselves participating in a Grail quest, enduring an initiation rite, and the question that would bring deliverance, the question that should be asked about the whole meaning of it all, has not been asked:

> You ought to ask: Why,
> what is this,
> what's the meaning of this.
>
> Because you don't ask,
> although the spear-shaft
> drips,
> there's neither steading—not a roof-tree.[26]   (p. 84)

All David Jones's writing is based on the conviction that myth is essential to poetry; whether the question 'What is poetry?' is taken to mean 'What is the nature of poetry?' or 'What is the material of poetry?' in each case the answer is myth.[27] But the poet is born into a given historical situation and so is inevitably limited by that situation as to what he can use as his materials. The range of choice, not only of poetic form but also of subject-matter, is dictated by the age. The poet, like the artist (and David Jones was both) is a sign-maker who must make signs for his age, for the nature of man demands not only the utile, but also the sacramental. It is from myths that poet and artist must make signs, but the validity and the availability of the traditional images that are to be thus used may be limited by the impoverishment of the culture within which the poet or artist is working. On these ideas rests David Jones's belief that the traditions, cultural or historical, must be kept alive, that the images must be kept current and the myths preserved for poet and artist to be able to fulfil their function, and for both individual and community to draw, from literature and art, a sense of identity. 'To conserve, to develop, to bring together, to make significant for the present what the past holds, without dilution or any deleting, but rather by understanding and transubstantiating the material, this is the function of genuine myth, neither pedantic nor popularising, not indifferent to scholarship, nor antiquarian, but saying always: "of these thou hast given me have I lost none".'[28] The myth of Arthur presents some difficulty to the modern reader, as Jones realises, for its availability has diminished; but he writes in the belief that the reader will *respond* to it, even though he may not fully recognise each allusion.

The myth of Arthur, for David Jones, is not a collection of romantic tales and medieval fantasies as it was for the Pre-Raphaelites but, whether it contains much or no historical truth, it is something that is yet of considerable significance as part of our traditional cultural heritage. 'We must be careful with our rejections', he said, if we are not to suffer impoverishment and trivialisation. Elsewhere he asserts the importance of the myth in a different way when he says that in writing *The Anathemata* he was 'trying to make a shape out of the very things out of which oneself is made'. James Joyce's use of the Tristram story in *Finnegans Wake* makes the same point indirectly: Tristram's love for Iseult is so much a part of Earwicker's unconscious mental processes that it is the means by which, dreaming, he conceptualises his own sexual desires.

David Jones's treatment of the myth of Arthur is not, however, either narrowly nationalistic or subjective. Rather it is historical, even archaeological in a metaphorical sense, concerned with what the traditional stories have meant to generation after generation of Britons. He directs his attention to the struggle and conflict, suffering and endurance, recurring again and again throughout history and making the past at one with the present and future, in a unity that is at once a source of inspiration and consolation. The tumult and torment of life in the twentieth-century, he suggests, give a deeper understanding of Malory than was possible before. Thus we are enabled to realise the symbolic potential of the myth of Arthur to an extent impossible in the nineteenth century, but also impossible in the Middle Ages and for Malory himself. Limited by his historical situation, Malory only partially appreciated 'the inwardness of the astonishing material at his disposal'.[29] It is a perceptive comment, which indicates the new range of meanings available to the modern mind resulting from different historical perspectives. In David Jones's own work, 'inwardness' is well served by Arthurian material; the Grail episodes in particular furnish images through which inner experience, individual or shared, can be suggested or explored.

The historical perspective into which the myth of Arthur is woven was for David Jones a most important feature of his complex poetic vision. In commenting on James Joyce he attributed his potency to his ability to communicate a sense of 'a whole unbroken past', but despite his admiration for Joyce, his own method of giving form to the past was entirely different. Whereas in Joyce, as in an English parish church, different historical periods come together under one roof in no particular order, David Jones sees history in strata, layer upon layer, in which the events of the past are past and yet potentially present as they continue to live in tradition and myth. The myth of Arthur, as it embodies the recurring patterns of human life, brings past and present into close conjunction: the desolation of the Waste Land, the approach to the Chapel Perilous, the question unasked when it should be asked, are, *mutatis mutandis*, as much a part of present experience as of past. But although David Jones represents the past in terms of strata, and sees it as providing analogies for and as impinging upon the present, he also sees time as transcended by the sacramental. Just as in the Christian religion, the ceremony of the Mass transcends time; so the Grail quest, renewed again and again in human lives, is the symbol of the meeting of an historical reality with the timeless and eternal. The tale of Balin and Balan, however, belongs in the strata of everyday experience; as brother unwittingly kills brother again and again throughout history, the story may now be seen as a symbol of the carnage of the First World War.

The cultural significance of Arthurian myth and of poetry as its embodiment is further indicated in David Jones's assertion that poetry is propaganda. 'Poetry is to be diagnosed as "dangerous" because it evokes and recalls, is a kind of *anamnesis* of, i.e. is an effective recalling of, something loved. In that sense it is inevitably "propaganda"', because it creates and perpetuates awareness of our national and individual identity. Poets are 'the most skilled artists and remembrancers & conservators of the things of the Island' and so upon them devolves the task of guarding the 'signa' and keeping alive the living past of Britain. But their task is made the more difficult by a cultural phenomenon which he calls 'the Break' which, occurring in the nineteenth century, cut men off from the old cultural traditions, made the meaning of the signs no longer readily accessible, and so deprived them of their power. This gap in continuity the poets must do their best to bridge, as Jones himself strove to do. However, though he did himself succeed to a considerable extent in giving force and currency to the symbols of the Christian tradition in both his writing and his art, it seems unlikely that anything can now restore them to their former power and resonance. With Arthurian myth it may be different, for whereas the readily accessible meaning of such Christian symbols as the Lamb of God or even the Cross itself has weakened, new interperetations and approaches such as Jessie Weston's have given increased range and power to such Arthurian themes as the Grail myth. The images of the Waste Land, of the Grail quest, and of the freeing of the waters have become meaningful as a result of the anthropological approach, and also perhaps more widely known.

Throughout his work David Jones makes use of 'signs' from the myth of Arthur: even in some of the 'fragments' in *The Sleeping Lord*, as for example 'The Fatigue' which has as its subject the Roman troops garrisoned in Syria Palaestina at the time of Christ's crucifixion, he uses Arthurian symbols. In 'The Fatigue', Christ on the cross is also the Hanged Man of the Tarot pack, and, in David Jones's note 'The figure associated with the wasted lands and the freeing of the waters, known to romance literature as Percival . . . in the Welsh deposits called Peredur', who is also called 'chief physician' in that tradition. In *Balaam's Ass*, a fragment begun in the late 1930s and which, like *In Parenthesis*, has for its subject the 1914–18 war, Grail imagery, Camelot and Broceliande are mentioned, and Christ is compared to Peredur, who left his mother to 'go for a soldier'.

The interweaving of myths and of traditions is a distinctive characteristic of all David Jones's work, which increases the resonance of some aspects of the Arthurian material on which he draws. The figure of Arthur is the most striking example of this, and as a result he assumes an importance which he has had for few, if any major writers other than Tennyson in post-medieval times. It is not so much with Arthur as reigning monarch, however, that David Jones is concerned, but with the Arthur of popular tradition, the once and future king or Sleeping Lord who may one day wake and come again. As living king he is indeed the embodiment of order and of past greatness, but by a process of gradual identification with Christ, he becomes increasingly the figure of the saviour and the channel of power, thus transcending altogether Malory's concept of the king. In David Jones's last work, *The Sleeping Lord and Other Fragments*, as the sleeping hero who will come again, he is identified with Wales, now seen as the Waste Land as well. The symbolic meanings coalesce as he becomes also Christ, the wounded king and the Grail-hero himself; by his resurrection alone the waters will be freed and the land renewed. His wounds represent the industrial exploitation of Wales, his sleep perhaps the dormant potentiality of its living Christian culture.

> *Is the Usk a drain for his gleaming tears*
> *who weeps for the land*
> > *who dreams his bitter dream*
> *for the folk of the land*
> *does Tawe clog for his sorrows*
> *do the parallel dark-seam drainers*
> > *mingle his anguish-stream*
> *with the scored valleys' tilted refuse.*
> *Does his freight of woe*
> > *flood South by East*
> *on Sirhywi and Ebwy*
> > *is it southly bourn*
> *on double Rhondda's fall to Taff?*[30]

In 'The Sleeping Lord' as in the preceding work in the volume, 'The Hunt', Jones's sources are Celtic rather than Malorian. 'The Hunt' refers to Arthur's hunt of the boar Trwyth recounted in the native Welsh early medieval prose-tale, 'Culhwch ac Olwen', but it is also to be seen as a type of the other-world voyage attributed to Arthur in Welsh tradition, and of the Harrowing of Hell, again suggesting an analogy between Arthur and Christ.

Though the Waste Land provides an appropriate symbol for the death and destruction brought about by war and by industrial exploitation, not only actually but also psychologically, David Jones suggests that there is at least some hope of healing, redemption and new life by firmly linking the Grail myth to living Christian belief. He is thus able to project an end to the Grail quest, instead of drawing attention only to its urgency. The Cross is the central fact, the enduring reality in human life, transcending time. The complex unity of human experience is suggested by the conjunction of fertility rite and Christian truth in the Grail, the horror of modern war with the Roman soldier's obedience to authority and Mordred's treachery. Instead of rejecting the Celtic tradition of Arthur's heroic exploits, David Jones gives it symbolic significance within the pattern of suffering, sacrifice and the hope of redemption, with the vision of which his work ended.

Some other aspects of David Jones's mode of treating the Arthurian themes also call for comment. In explaining in his Preface the meaning of the title *The Anathemata*, he emphasises that the work is about things: 'the devoted things', the votive offerings. It is about 'the blessed things that have taken on what is cursed and the profane things that somehow are redeemed; . . . things . . . that partake of the extra-utile and of the gratuitous; things that are the signs of something other, together with those signs that not only have the nature of a sign, but are themselves, under some mode, what they signify. Things set up, lifted up, or in whatever manner made over to the gods.' The declaration draws attention to an important characteristic of his writing: myth-maker though he is, his writing nevertheless has a concrete pictorial quality. Though it is the symbolic meaning of his Arthurian materials that is of primary importance, it is through the accumulation of subsidiary details that the symbolic meaning is built up. Though the total effect is not very visual, the detail is. In *The Anathemata*, for example, he progresses towards the culminating vision of the crucifixion in the last section, which is headed 'Sherthursdaye and Venus Day', referring to a passage in Malory's version of the Grail story. In this, Galahad has a vision of Christ who says to him 'This is . . . the holy dish wherein I ate the lamb on Sher-Thursday'.[31] Through this brief reference, David Jones evokes not only the Grail myth in its entirety, with all its traditional associations, but by alluding to the concrete objects of the 'holy dish' and 'the lamb', brings together the everyday and the sacramental, suggesting a whole range of symbolic meanings. In this last section of *The Anathemata*, Christ is also the Welsh Grail knight Peredur, 'vagrant-born, earth-fostered', who is now ready to put on 'his *man's* lorica', 'his *caligae*' and 'his two-edged gladius'. The passage places Christ in the context both of Rome and of Celtic legend, and at the same time suggests the medieval image of Christ as knight. It evokes a pictorial image of the ritual of arming, to be seen as part of a long biblical, classical and medieval tradition. As a reference to putting on the armour of God, it has complex symbolic significance, and the 'two-edged sword' raises further biblical echoes.

David Jones's perceptive comment on Malory's treatment of the Grail story incidentally throws light on his own techniques of composition: in the Grail episode in *Le Morte Darthur*, 'As in the world of dreams the objects are natural and sharply defined, but their juxtaposition is of the mind and of the imagination.'[32] In his own work the objects are often both natural and sharply defined, but he does not make use of the narrative structures of his source material to order them. The 'juxtaposition of the objects' recombines them in new mythic patterns; though they may allude to the Arthurian stories, they never follow them. The structure of the work, as in *The Anathemata*, may be sequential, but the rich surface texture brings together images of all kinds without regard for chronology. More perhaps than any other modern Arthurian writer, David Jones had a sense of how archetypal patterns and myths work; the 'signs' never, in his writing, even when they are obscure, leave the reader

271

oppressed by a sense of mythological lumber. The unifying power of his poetic imagination as it brings the 'fragments' into meaningful conjunction, releases their hidden significance. But the question of the validity and availability of the images must nevertheless remain: for many readers, Arthurian references are as obscure as biblical or classical ones, and no amount of annotation can bring them to life. Only if there is a revival of interest in our cultural heritage in English and other languages can the 'signs' so precious to David Jones be easily interpreted by more than a small number of specialist readers.

James Joyce's *Finnegans Wake* (1939), of which a section appeared in 1928 as *Anna Livia Plurabelle: fragment of Work in Progress*, takes up the theme of Tristram and Iseult again. Joyce's own comment on *Finnegans Wake* in a letter written while he was working on the book is a significant one: 'Perhaps I shall survive and perhaps the raving madness I write will survive and perhaps it is very funny. One thing is sure, however. Je suis bien triste.'[33] To the unprepared or impatient reader *Finnegans Wake* is raving madness; for the reader who will take the trouble to enter its dreamworld it is often very funny. Its puns, its portmanteau words, its irreverence together with its wide-ranging allusions and evocative power, work by an amazing combination of music-hall comedy with poetic techniques. But it soon becomes apparent that the comedy is only the surface texture of a serious and sometimes even sombre view of life. Sadness—rather than tragedy or pathos—underlies it; the sadness of frustration and of growing old, accepted but there none the less. The mixture is characteristic of much great literature: of Chaucer, of Shakespeare, of Dickens; and *Finnegans Wake* is great literature.

Edmund Wilson described James Joyce as 'the great poet of a new phase of the human consciousness';[34] it is, however, only through old myth that Joyce is able to enter this new phase and to present his findings. In the drowsing, dreaming mind which is the subject of *Finnegans Wake*, the myth of Tristram and Iseult is the main embodiment of the erotic fantasies of the protagonist. Joyce does not make use of any other Arthurian material; the Tristram story has a special appropriateness, of course, because of its Irish associations. The Tristram theme, introduced on the very first page of the novel, runs right through it, but even though the story as such plays a minimal part in the whole, Joyce's use of it suggests the vitality and flexibility of the Arthurian legend as a source of symbolic imagery.

Finnegans Wake is much more than the dream experience of one man. The name of the protagonist, H. C. Earwicker, stands for 'Here Comes Everybody', we are told, and not only is he to be regarded as representative of all humanity, but all human experience from the beginning of time, in a sense, flows through his unconscious mind. At the same time, the book is an allegory of the fall of man and the resurrection, as Joyce cryptically indicates by obscure references to St Paul's Epistle to the Romans, Chap. XI, v. 32: 'For God has consigned all men to disobedience, that he may have mercy upon us all.' The title is derived from a popular song about the apparently fatal fall from a ladder of Finnegan, a drunken Irish hod-carrier, who comes to life again on hearing the word 'whiskey'; and his fall is symbolic of Lucifer's and of Adam's fall, of Humpty-Dumpty's, of all falls in life or literature or popular tradition throughout time. Finnegan thus typifies all heroes and all ordinary mortals too, including Humphrey Chimpden Earwicker whose uneasy dreams he haunts.

Earwicker is a middle-aged man of Scandinavian descent, in some ways an outsider, who keeps a pub in Dublin. His wife is called Ann (or Anna Livia) and they have a daughter, Isabel, and twin sons Kevin (or Shaun) and Jerry (or Shem). After drinking too much, Earwicker in bed with his wife on the Saturday night with which the book is solely concerned, has a constant succession of vivid and often troubled dreams. Erotic fantasies mingle with the other workings of his unconscious mind, accompanied by insistent guilt-feelings. His wife has lost her former romantic appeal for him, and in his dream-world, his feelings are transferred to his daughter; in his confused unconscious he is not Earwicker but Tristram, and she is not Isabel but Iseult. Thus his incestuous desire for his daughter, released from waking control, is not only expressed but also made manageable by the transference of identity which the myth affords. In his dreams, Isabel/Iseult both is and is not his daughter: 'She is so pretty, truth to tell, wildwood's eyes and primarose hair, quietly, all the woods so wild, in mauves of moss and daphne-dews, how all so still she lay, neath of the whitethorn, child of tree, like some losthappy leaf, like blowing flower stilled as fain would she anon, for soon again 'twill be, win me, woo me, wed me, ah weary me! deeply, now evencalm lay sleeping' (p. 556).[35] Here Isabel is imagined both as a baby asleep in her cot, and as the desirable Iseult, in images which evoke the medieval lyric 'I sing of a maiden', as Earwicker's paternal love merges with erotic and perhaps even religious feeling.

In Earwicker's dream-world in which actuality blends with fantasy and one image runs into another he is Tristram, by a natural association of ideas. His pub is near the suburb of Chapelizod, said to be the birthplace of Iseult, and the local legend provides a natural outlet for his imagination, allowing him to see himself as the attractive young man that he most certainly is not any longer: 'Sir Tristram, violer d'amores, fr'over the short sea, had passencore rearrived from North Armorica on this side the scraggy isthmus of Europe Minor to wielder-fight his penisolate war . . .' (p. 3). But his dreams all derive from the family situation, from the complex of often conflicting emotions that accompany the relationships of husband and wife, parent and child. Earwicker's protective instincts and his ambitions for his children, his imaginative identification with both his daughter and his sons weave new potential relationships in his dreams. As often in dreams, the sense of time is dissolved, and as a result the pattern of relationships can shift to make Earwicker as young as his children. He is at the same time the ageing overweight publican and the 'spry young spark' Tristram, paradoxically both conscience-stricken and boldly defiant.

Here, as in other modern versions, the Tristram myth expresses a longing not only for sexual gratification, but for romance. A complex desire for imaginative and emotional satisfaction is suggested, not through the poetic images of earlier writers, however, but in terms of the everyday experience of Earwicker. At the same time, in the ebb and flow of thought and impulse, contempt for convention and authority is intermingled with the longing, unacknowledged by his conscious mind, for identification with the beloved child. Absorbed into Earwicker's irreverent imagination and placed in a twentieth-century Irish setting, the Tristram myth is shorn of both its traditional romantic quality and of its solemnity, but though it loses its dignity it does not lose its seriousness or its power.

Joyce does not give the reader the story of Tristram in its entirety, even in the form of allusions; he assumes that it is common knowledge. There is no drinking of the love-potion, for example, for it is only the situation that is of significance here: Tristram's unlawful desire for Iseult, implicitly forbidden by Mark, who must be seen as in a sense the embodiment of Earwicker's conscience or super-ego. As Earwicker's liberated imagination plays with the theme, it is through the squawks of the sea-gulls that his fantasies are expressed, removing them even further from his own conscious thought-processes, but at the same time mocking restraint and propriety:

> —Three quarks for Muster Mark!
> Sure he hasn't got much of a bark
> And sure any he has it's all beside the mark.
> But O, Wreneagle Almighty, wouldn't un be a sky of a lark
> To see that old buzzard whooping about for uns shirt in the dark
> And he hunting round for uns speckled trousers around by Palmerstown
>   Park?
> Hohohoho, moulty Mark!
> You're the rummest old rooster ever flopped out of a Noah's ark
> And you think you're cock of the wark.
> Fowls, up! Tristy's the spry young spark
> That'll tread her and wed her and bed her and red her
> Without ever winking the tail of a feather
> And that's how that chap's going to make his money and mark!
> Overhoved, shrillgleescreaming. That song sang seaswans. The

winging ones. Seahawk, seagull, curlew and plover, kestrel and capercallzie. All the birds of the sea they trolled out rightbold when they smacked the big kuss of Trustan with Usolde. (p. 383)

Joyce here reverses the medieval convention, which represented birds as human beings, to make his human beings birds. Then, as it often does in dreams, the scene changes and Tristram and Iseult are making love on board ship, gleefully observed by the 'four master waves of Erin', who are also, among other things, four old men and the four evangelists, and who constitute a recurrent chorus in the novel:

> And so there they were, with their palms in their hands, like the
> pulchrum's proculs, spraining their ears, luistening and listening to

274

the oceans of kissening, with their eyes glistening, all the four, when he was kiddling and cuddling and bunnyhugging scrumptious his colleen bawn and dinkum belle, an oscar sister, on the fifteen inch loveseat, behind the chieftainess stewardesses cubin, the hero, of Gaelic champion, the onliest one of her choice, her bleaueyedeal of a girl's friend, neither bigugly nor smallnice, meaning pretty much everything to her then, with his sinister dexterity, light and rufthandling, vicemversem her ragbags et assaucyetiams, fore and aft, on and offsides, the brueburnt sexfutter, handson and huntsem, that was palpably wrong and bulbubly improper, and cuddling her and kissing her, tootyfay charmaunt, in her ensemble of maidenna blue, with an overdress of net, tickled with goldies, Isolamisola, and whisping and lisping her about Trisolanisans, how one was whips for one was two and two was lips for one was three, and dissimulating themself, with his poghue like Arrah-na-poghue. . . . (p. 384)

Tristram has become the hero and champion of legend, yet at the same time he is like a modern film-star, a handsome, sunburnt six-footer, enjoying himself with enormous guilt-spiced zest behind the stewardess's cabin, in a twentieth-century setting. In reducing the episode to the dream of a rather lustful middle-aged publican, Joyce divests it of the poignant charm characteristic of the earlier versions, and yet still retains its power to suggest an important aspect of experience. Earwicker's turbulent desires, his natural wish to recapture his youth and to re-experience his youthful amatory pleasures, leads to the wish-fulfilment typical of dreams. But the vulgar and sensual 'cuddling and bunny-hugging scrumptious' in which he indulges not only have a sort of innocence, but are raised from the commonplace and lifted out of the realms of everyday experience as they are associated with the Tristram story, to become part of the universal dream of romantic love. The boundaries of the myth are extended, as through dream it becomes literally, as it were, the experience of Everyman.

The Tristram theme in *Finnegans Wake* thus canalises the unacceptable fantasy which Earwicker's unconscious mind throws up, sweeping his desires away from the real Isabel of the waking world towards the dream image of Iseult. Later on, his dream turns again to his son Kevin (now both Shaun and Jaun) who is preaching a sermon in St Bride's Academy, at which his sister Isabel is a pupil. In this dream she is Izzy, Sissy, Tizzy, poor Isley, at the same time sister and beloved, courted by the now adult Kevin, who is preaching because his name identifies him with St Kevin, and courting because his name identifies him with Don Juan. Earwicker in partially identifying with his son still expresses through the dream his attraction to his daughter, but in a yet more distanced way. Finally, towards the end of the novel, his dream shifts his attention back to his wife. As Isabel has been for him the young Iseult, Mark's Iseult, Anna is identified with Iseult's mother, the Queen Iseult who in the medieval versions of the story healed Tristram of his otherwise incurable wound. Now, as one of the boys has a nightmare, Anna goes to him; when the child is quietened and Anna returns to bed, Earwicker makes love to her, a deglamourised Tristram now, at 'half past quick in the morning . . . nine hundred and dirty too not out, at all times long past conquering cock of the morgans.' This unattractive pair, the portly Earwicker and Anna with her 'haggish expression, peaky nose', nevertheless seem to find more than merely physical satisfaction in their energetic if unromantic love-making after all: 'O I you O you me! Well, we all unite thoughtfully in rendering gratias, well, between loves repassed . . .' as they become 'Humperfelt and Anunska, wedded now evermore' (p. 584–5). For all the sadness of lost youth and beauty that Earwicker's dreams express, *Finnegans Wake* ends with acceptance and rueful gratitude for what can still be enjoyed. Then Earwicker slips back into childhood as he sinks to sleep again, with the nursery-rhyme echoes of 'Humbo, lock your kekkle up! Anny, blow your wickle out! . . . And you may go rightoway back to your Aunty Dilluvia, Humprey, after that!' (p. 585).

Anna is now much more than Humphrey's antediluvian wife, though of course she is that too. In the course of his dreams she has been identified with Eve, with Isis, with Iseult; his shifting images of her have made her also the temptress. She is, however, identified with the river Liffey, and with the river of time as well, and she represents both the life-giving and the love-bearing principle in the universe. She is a 'great mother', source of comfort and health, as Earwicker drifts back, from the actuality of his love-making in the time-bound waking world, to the timeless world of his imagination in which he is a child again. *Finnegans Wake* ends with a broken and unended sentence: A way a lone a last a loved a long the', leading back to the very beginning of the book, which started in the middle of a sentence. Thus Joyce suggests the unity, the continuity of human experience, 'eterne in mutabilitie' in Spenser's phrase, flowing on for ever as the river Liffey flows into the sea, 'riverrun, past Eve and Adam's, from swerve of shore to bend of bay'.

In *Finnegans Wake* Joyce moves away from naturalism into myth, in order to suggest the workings of the unconscious mind. The strange phantasmagoria, deriving partly from Earwicker's waking preoccupations, but drawing upon a vast range of literature and several languages with which the lowly protagonist could not possibly be acquainted, is at the same time brilliantly faithful to dream psychology, yet transcends normal experience in its poetic richness. The tumult of ever-shifting, merging sense-impressions, images and half-formulated concepts dazzles or maddens the reader with its unending stream of free associations, puns and multiple meanings. One of its structuring features is the opposition of contraries—of youth and age, male and female, day and night, for example—and this suggests both the everchanging attitudes and focus of the individual mind, and the ambiguities and conflicts inevitable in family relationships. For some of the inevitable complexities of these, the Tristram theme provides a perfect medium. The earlier forms of the story, with the triple image of Iseult as mother, unlawful beloved and virgin wife, and the father/son relationship of Mark and Tristram, provided Joyce with material well suited to his allusive technique.

As Eliot uses images associated with the Grail story in *The Waste Land* to comment on twentieth-century society and to indicate states of mind, so Joyce uses the Tristram story with equal freedom to communicate new poetic and psychological insights. In *Finnegans Wake* the Tristram theme is of course only one myth among many and it does not structure the book in the way that Waste Land imagery structures Eliot's poem, or the story of Odysseus underlies *Ulysses*. Its function is to objectify and at the same time to allow the reader to interpret what is going on below the level of consciousness in the mind of the protagonist. Joyce's technique, however, permits new meanings to emerge from the Tristram myth because it is not seen in isolation but as overlapping with or merging into other myths; and from these methods new aspects of, for example, Iseult appear. He adds to our recognition of the power and range of myth by deliberately using it to suggest only what is going on below the level of conscious control. Though *Finnegans Wake* cannot be regarded as an Arthurian text, it increases our awareness of the depths of symbolic meaning inherent in Arthurian myths, and their continuing importance for the modern writer.

Similarly Ezra Pound, in *Section: Rock Drill—85–95 de los cantares* (1955) makes use of Arthurian material (mainly drawn from Layamon's *Brut*) to communicate through reference to Merlin, Stonehenge, Uther and other related elements in the legends, his sense of the loss of tradition that time has brought about in Britain. As Christine Brooke-Rose has pointed out,[36] Pound takes what he wants from Layamon and telescopes historical periods and the events of the narrative. He identifies with Uther, Merlin and other legendary or historical figures to suggest complex ideas of loss, both cultural and personal, and even ideas of the poet's function and relation to tradition. The Arthurian theme does not structure either the section as a whole or even Canto 91, in which alone it appears, in the way that it does *The Waste Land*, but it is used figuratively in a not dissimilar and though very limited, still significant way.

v. John Cowper Powys, *A Glastonbury Romance* and *Porius*

In *A Glastonbury Romance* (1932), John Cowper Powys takes the Grail legend as the basis of a very long contemporary novel, set in Glastonbury. In this strange and complex book, both the local tradition and the literary tradition are used structurally and thematically. Powys's purpose in the novel, stated in his preface to the 1955 edition, was to 'convey a jumbled-up and squeezed together epitome of life's various dimensions', an intention which this remarkable book very successfully accomplishes. Powys is no less concerned with the religious dimension than any other, and through the symbol of the Grail he represents the ultimate mystery, though without conventional piety of any kind. The Grail, indeed, is for Powys the Celtic rather than the Christian symbol. The theme of the interaction of the spiritual with the human and mundane shifts the emphasis from the Waste Land to the more positive aspects of the story. The novel is centred on the lives of the inhabitants of Glastonbury because of its legendary connections with the tradition of the coming of the Grail to Britain, and as in other novels, Powys suggests that human lives (and indeed other forms of life as well) constantly interrelate with both good and evil cosmic powers, to which his characters are variously sensitive. To quote his own words, he explores 'the effect of a particular legend, a special myth, a unique tradition, from the remotest past in human history, upon a particular spot on the surface of this planet together with its crowd of inhabitants of every age and of every type of character . . . Its heroine is the Grail. Its hero is the Life poured into the Grail. Its message is that no one Receptacle of Life can contain or explain what the world offers us.' Powys was drawn to the story of the Grail by 'the unholy elements in both its history and its mystery; in other words the unquestionable fact that it was much older than Christianity itself' (xii–xiii).[37] Like some other modern writers, Powys was attracted also by the figure of Merlin, and insists that he was untouched by 'any pathetic neophytish craving to copy some pure-hearted Sir Galahad' himself. Thus his work looks forward to the later twentieth-century fascination with the figure of Merlin.

Though the title claims the book for the genre of romance, it is both more and less than romance in the true sense of the word. *A Glastonbury Romance* has many of the characteristics of a realistic novel, presenting a broad cross-section of society in early twentieth-century Glastonbury. Its comprehensiveness, its detailed presentation of everyday life and its enormous range of well-differentiated characters (there are nearly fifty) almost invite comparison with *Middlemarch*. Furthermore, the motif of the quest, which forms the underlying structure of romance, and might be expected to play a particularly important part in this work, is only incidental, and presented in a fragmentary way. The treatment of the subject, instead of tending towards idealisation, has in it a strong element of satire. But the work is a romance in the sense that Powys apparently really did believe in the vague supernatural powers he invoked, so that the story is basically a fantasy to which the sympathetic reader will bring a willing suspension of disbelief. It also represents an addition to the corpus of Grail-stories, an updating of the medieval genre, a re-telling in twentieth-century terms of the old legend. The story has become a part, Powys says, of the poetry of our race, and he carries it on into the mid-twentieth century.

The novel begins with the funeral of Canon Crow, followed by the reading of his will, at which the large party of relatives discover to their dismay that his considerable fortune has been left to Mr Geard, an evangelical lay-preacher known as 'Bloody Johnny' because of his habit of constantly referring to the blood of Christ. Mr Geard has endeared himself to the Canon by caring for him in his declining years. After the funeral, Philip Crow, a grandson who had expected to benefit from the will, returns to Glastonbury (also the home-town of Mr Geard) where he has a thriving business. His young cousin Mary Crow is companion to a Glastonbury lady, while another cousin, John, who has fallen in love with Mary on the day of the funeral, and who has no established occupation or home, also moves to the town in the hope of finding work there. He is taken on as his assistant by Mr Geard, who proposes to use his legacy to put Glastonbury on the map, by organising a Religious Fair, a non-denominational Glastonbury revival, and then to build a more substantial shrine there for the 'holy spring'. 'I shall make of that Blood a living Fountain on Chalice Hill, to which all the nations of the earth shall come for healing' (p. 455) says Mr Geard. At the surface level, the story is about the conflicts which ensue between those who support Mr Geard, soon after elected mayor, and Philip Crow, whose more entrepreneurial schemes include a plan for lighting and exploiting the caves of Wookey Hole as both a tourist attraction and a tin mine; and the conflict between Philip Crow the capitalist and Dave Spear the communist and his adherents. The wide range of characters, from the Marquis of P——— downwards, includes the professional classes represented by the doctor, the lawyer, the vicar Mat Dekker and his son Sam, and extends to Mother Legge who discreetly runs a brothel, and Mad Bet the local idiot. All in a sense are seekers—after power or money or love or spiritual fulfilment, or lesser kinds of gratification. Some believe in the Grail legend, others do not, but all of them, credulous or sceptical, atheists or orthodox Christians, are shown as being at the mercy of real cosmic powers of which at best they are only fitfully, partially and dimly aware, and these powers include the Grail itself.

The Grail is thus represented as at the same time an aspect of the spiritual powers which continuously interact with and influence life on earth, and an important element in local legend—so much so that it can still draw crowds of pilgrims and visitors from all over Europe to visit Glastonbury—a tourist attraction as well as a spiritual reality. Powys within the novel says of Glastonbury: 'There are only about a dozen reservoirs of world-magic on the whole surface of the globe—Jerusalem, . . . Rome . . . Mecca . . . Lhassa—and of these Glastonbury has the largest residue of unused power. Generations of mankind, aeons of past races, have—by their concentrated will—made Glastonbury miraculous' (p. 285). Glastonbury has other associations with Arthurian legend, however, and Powys rather schematically concentrates in and around the town all the main Arthurian events. The tomb of Joseph of Arimathea and the grave of Arthur are both at Glastonbury; one of the hills known as Chalice Hill is said to be the probable site of Carbonek the Grail city; Arthur threw away his sword Excalibur from Pomparlès bridge nearby, while the neighbouring Mark Moor Court is presented as the scene of Merlin's last appearance on earth, on his final visit to King Mark. In addition, there is a small ruin considered by some characters to be the chantry where Lancelot died. Ancient names persist at Glastonbury, too: ironically the district where Mother Legge keeps her brothel is called Camelot.

Arthurian legend thus survives in the local tradition of the Glastonbury of the novel. Powys also creates many analogies between the lives of the Arthurian characters, drawing particularly upon Malory, and the lives of his characters, though the identifications are not fixed and constant but continually shifting. He sees the incidents of the Arthurian story as being re-enacted in the lives of the inhabitants of Glastonbury. Thus, there is a point in the story when Sam, the rather good-for-nothing son of the vicar, has a religious experience reminiscent both of Percival's self-wounding and of King Pelles' wound; later renouncing all sexual experience in his devotion to Christ, he resembles Galahad, while in a sense his widowed father is Launcelot, in love with another man's wife. Sam has a vision of the Grail and a sensation as of being wounded by a spear while in a small black coal barge on the river, in an episode which recalls the traditional Grail story. Mr Geard is a Merlin-figure, the worker of white magic, and when he spends a night at Mark Moor Court his close imaginative identification with Merlin is complemented by the suggestion that the daughter of the Marquis of P. is Nimuë. To some extent the characters themselves see each other in Arthurian rôles: they see Will Hoylake, the Marquis's illegitimate son, and Persephone the wife of the communist Dave Spear, as Tristram and Iseult. For Owen Evans, the Welsh antiquary, Mad Bet is the Grail messenger, though later his wife Cordelia fulfils that function. Glastonbury itself, moreover, contains within itself both the Waste Land and the Urbs Beata of the traditional story.

Such identifications, however, do not exclude similar ones with classical mythology. Persephone is carried off to the underworld by Philip Crow in what is overtly a reference to the Greek myth, and there are several other comparable instances. The effect is to suggest the recurrence throughout the ages of such experience, which reinforces the idea that the Grail story is in some sense continuous, or being constantly re-enacted in the lives of ordinary people. Thus the Grail legend develops from mere local tradition and superstition to the dimensions of myth, meaningful for all ages.

Through the Grail legend Powys communicates his ideas both about spiritual reality and about the powers of the human mind. Both also involve the problem of pain, with which, here as elsewhere, he is deeply concerned. A number of characters in the novel represent different attitudes or modes of approach to this problem. But behind the everyday encounters and interactions of Glastonbury life, there is a cosmic power which exerts a constant influence on human and also on subhuman life, which Powys names the First Cause. The First Cause has a double nature, made up of both good and evil, each aspect of which has an independent will, so that they are in constant conflict. Existence, indeed, is essentially the product of the struggle between good and evil. The First Cause consists of a 'mingling of abominable cruelty with magnanimous consideration' (p. 373), and both its aspects possess the energy of sex, but one is creative, the other destructive. As one is good and the other evil, so one loves and the other hates. There is no creative energy, however, that is not composed of good and evil, and the conflict between them can never end, because it is the condition of existence itself. Life is a 'war-to-the-death', says Powys, between the Spirits of Good and Evil which encounter each other everywhere, 'in every crevice of consciousness and on every plane of being' (p. 349). It is, however, with the evil aspect of the First Cause and the cruelty of its will and energy that he is most deeply concerned. He insists that it is a living Person that dominates life and death, an arbitrary and wilful personality, and that in consequence, Personality, not love, is the secret of the universe. This is the 'mystery of mysteries': but Powys goes no further towards defining the nature of this Personality. Into it, however, are to be subsumed all other gods and spiritual powers that have been known to man from the earliest times. Mat Dekker's God, the God of orthodox Christianity, as well as the sun and the moon and Christ himself, are all only partial aspects of partial expressions of the First Cause. Nevertheless, within Powys's scheme of things Christ is a significant figure, though he is variously understood—or misunderstood—by different characters in the book. Christ is, above all else, the martyred God-Man who represents the suffering of all creation, an intermediary, and the personification of that aspect of the First Cause that is love; but in no way is he able to triumph finally, permanently or totally over the evil aspect of the First Cause. Though he can be close to and can make contact with human beings, they are liable to misinterpret and distort his meaning. Christ's power is a living reality, capable of being exploited by those who can become channels for it, but nevertheless Powys does not attach much importance to Christianity.

The traditional symbol of the Grail as a source of spiritual power is defined in various ways at different points in the book; understanding of it varies with the perceptions of those who seek to define it. Far older than Christianity, it is a many-named Mystery handed down through the ages through psychic channels, originating in the First Cause, but becoming a more independent entity in the course of time. Its relationship to time is important, for it is something that can break through the laws of nature, or ordinary cause and effect, a thing of power of which the power is actually increased by the fact that people have believed and do believe in it. That it has been associated with the blood of Christ, as the vessel legendarily reputed to have contained it, has increased its power, because of the belief attracted to it in Christian times. Thus it is a meeting point between the human and the divine: 'the desire of the generations mingling like water with the Blood of Christ, and caught in a fragment of Substance that is beyond Matter. It is a little nucleus of Eternity, dropped somehow from outer space upon one particular spot!', as Mr Geard defines it (pp. 457–8). It is a means of purification and redemption, intensifying at the same time love and indeed eroticism; it is a thing of magic rather than a religious object, and perhaps also to be regarded as a fertility symbol.

The Grail, as a source of power that can be harnessed, is a fount of goodness that can be opposed to the enormous and intolerable suffering in the world, brought about by the evil aspect of the First Cause. It is primarily through the character of Owen Evans that this theme is developed in the novel: he has a streak of sadism in his nature which makes him constantly vulnerable to the powers of evil. We see him striving over and over again to resist this impulse; though at times he yields to the extent of descending to the cellar (Avernus) of the second-hand bookshop, to look with self-loathing at a certain unspeakable book, and indulge the fantasies which his tormented mind longs to dwell on. When the Pageant sponsored by Mr Geard takes place, it includes within the Arthurian story a Glastonbury Passion Play, modelled on the Oberammergau

Play, and Mr Evans seeks to exorcise the vein of cruelty and evil in himself by playing the part of Christ, even to the extent of being fastened to the cross for the crucifixion scene. In this episode, he experiences imaginatively all the pain of men and animals throughout eternity, and is at the same time himself the torturer. The victims accuse him, and suggest that for him there can be no forgiveness, for he as torturer had continued to inflict the pain 'knowing what it meant' (p. 614). His experience combines that of Christ's suffering, representative of 'every victim', but beyond that, he is forced to identify himself with man's guilt as the inflicter of pain, with 'man the cruel', the channel of evil. Even this terrible experience which ends with his collapse, does not set him free from the horror which haunts him, however. It is only at the end of the book, when he is about to yield to intolerable temptation by conniving at a pointless and cold-blooded murder, that he is finally freed from his obsession by the love and patience of his wife Cordelia. When the evil is at last driven out of him, as it were, he is left prematurely aged and almost imbecile by the experience.

The problem of pain is examined in other ways through the character of Mr Geard, who has the strange gift of being able to identify completely with the suffering of others, but also to dispel it through the spiritual power for which he is a channel. So complete is his identification with others at times, that when Owen Evans in hospital recovering from his 'crucifixion' gives Geard a full account of his experience, which had culminated in his losing consciousness, Geard himself faints. Elsewhere, however, because for him Christ is a source of power to be exploited, a 'super-Merlin', he can even actually or apparently— Powys leaves us in some uncertainty about what 'really' happens in the novel at this point—cure cancer and bring the dead to life. This power of Geard's suggests that, in however limited a way, man has a means of opposing the suffering that derives from the evil aspect of the First Cause operating in the world. The argument is carried a stage further through Sam Dekker, who also believes that he is in contact with Christ, and who has a vision of the Grail. Mr Geard works miracles by means of the spiritual powers inherent in the Grail, but he does it 'casually, carelessly, almost indifferently; as if he had discovered that the whole Grail Quest were a mere by-product of some vast planetary reservoir of an unknown force' (p. 1000). Sam, on the other hand, has only the most ordinary of human powers, because he is actually opposing the good aspect of the First Cause, and is a 'mad perverter of Christ's secret' (p. 551) in forcing himself to act against the grain, by turning from his mistress (also the mother of his child) to a state of celibacy. He is to some extent like Geard, able to identify with pain, though he is not able to do much to alleviate it, and through him Powys raises the question, to what extent ought we to identify with the suffering of others? Sam's vision of the Grail gives him new insight into pain, forcing him to utter a cry, 'the final desperate cry of humanity to the crushing, torturing universe that had given it birth' (p. 940). Earlier, through this character, Powys asks at what point is it necessary to harden one's heart and cease to think of the pain of others? How far ought we to share suffering? The unsatisfactory conclusion is that there comes a point when 'to live at all we *must* forget'

(p. 932). That this is nevertheless the right conclusion is supported by the incident in which Sam visits a half-starved family who are half-starved because the miserly, bed-ridden husband will not allow his wife to buy food with the money they are given, which he insists on stowing under his mattress. Their suffering is unnecessary, crazy because deliberately chosen and self-inflicted, and should not evoke deep sympathy. John Crow, too, is capable of an equally sensitive awareness of pain in knowing that he is depriving Miss Drew of the companionship of Mary, whom he has just married secretly. 'What a thing— that not one perfect day can be enjoyed by anyone without hearing something groan or moan!' he reflects (p. 643). Waiting for Mary to come to him in the evening for their first night together, his mind is 'beating . . . against the blood-stained wedge of the world's pain, and he could not give himself up with absolute assent to his good hour' (p. 643). As he rages against the cruelty of the universe that inflicts such suffering, Mary comes out: Miss Drew has at last overcome her selfish desire to keep her companion with her, and has generously made her come. John's sympathy in this case, too, can be seen as somewhat excessive. The general tenor of the book is to suggest that joy in the beauty of living things and in the very experience of being alive is an appropriate response, and need not be restrained or stifled by the deliberate contemplation of suffering, or repudiated through asceticism.

In *A Glastonbury Romance* it is through the power of thought that men reach understanding and acquire spiritual power, not simply through given moments of revelation. Indeed, Powys says, the heightened consciousness of any living organism can cause a ripple in the creative silence of the First Cause (p. 21). The moments of high perception that lead to insight and the power that can ensue come from the interaction of mind and body, and it is at the meeting point of mind and matter that the soul exists. Through the power of thought, Mr Geard is able to make contact with divine power, and in his experience in the haunted chamber at Mark Moor Court, in overcoming fear he reaches a new understanding of what thought means. 'It is a live thing. It creates; it destroys; it begets. . . .' (p. 457). Thoughts 'can live and grow and generate, independently of the person in whose being they originated.' It is in this way that the power of the Grail has grown, in part at least, as a result of the thoughts of human beings through the ages.

It may be noted that somewhat similar attitudes to the problem of suffering and to the availability of spiritual power are expressed in the writings of John Cowper Powys and of Charles Williams through their use of the Grail story. The Arthurian legend is no longer merely a source of romantic material, as in earlier decades, of which the rich psychological interest may be used to draw attention to contemporary problems. Instead, these writers in their different ways widen the range of possible meanings inherent in the legend, so as to confront the mysteries of human existence. While Powys sees identification with the suffering of a fellow human being as a means by which healing power may be channelled to him, Williams writing a little later suggests that suffering may be voluntarily taken from the sufferer and endured for him by another person.

In *A Glastonbury Romance*, as in other novels, Powys depicts the natural world with a richness of sensuous detail to which the characters, or many of them, respond sensitively, whether consciously or not. Such a presentation demands a similar response to every aspect of experience, whether of the natural world or of human relationships, on the part of the reader, too. It also suggests a need to cultivate a psychic sensitivity to spiritual forces operating in this world. To describe Powys's thought as no more than a perversion of orthodox Christian doctrine is, however, to devalue both its spiritual and its moral power and to deny the strength and appeal of his very positive, if idiosyncratic, philosophy. For Powys, the mystic life demands the avoidance of two mortal sins, cruelty and possession. Cruelty necessarily entails suffering; the possessive instinct is the negation of love. But, though love is seen as something that may help to offset the power of evil, it is not much emphasised in the novel. Mat Dekker claims that it may have an importance beyond the world we know (p. 203), but it is rarely to be seen unmixed with selfishness and the desire to possess, and it is very little romanticised, though several pairs of lovers make their appearance in the novel.

Powys shows little interest in social theories or structures in *A Glastonbury Romance*, though the opposition between capitalism and communism plays a not insignificant part in it. Both the capitalist Philip Crow and the communist Dave Spear, representing extreme points of view, are somewhat repellent characters. There is no attempt to establish an order corresponding to the Round Table at Glastonbury, probably because such an élitist organisation would be anachronistic. Dave Spear, however, sets up a Russian-type commune, while Mr Geard's vision involves almost the whole community in the carrying out of his purpose, and all the inhabitants of Glastonbury gather for the presentation of the pageant. Though in general Powys regarded communism with approval, in *A Glastonbury Romance* the general impression one gains is that life is too complex, too multi-dimensional, for its problems to be much alleviated by any political programme.

Though it makes extensive use of the Grail legend in a variety of ways, the novel does not closely follow the traditional patterns. It derives its dynamic quality largely from the conflict and tension which arise from the opposing forces of good and evil within the First Cause. Working upon the world of matter and upon the human mind, they constitute a cosmic psychomachia. The book is further patterned by a series of oppositions, for example between Philip Crow, the greedy capitalist businessman, whose energies are all directed towards modernisation, scientific methods and the destruction of as much of Glastonbury's ancient heritage as opportunity affords, and Mr Geard. Mr Geard's ambition is to harness spiritual power and to work new miracles for the benefit of all mankind, while Crow wishes to make use of scientific power and technology for his own benefit. While Geard is able to identify with Christ, with whom he is in constant joyous communion, Philip Crow's attention is, by contrast, directed downwards, to the underworld of Wookey Hole with all its caves, and the tin mines which he intends to exploit. Like Owen Evans, whose secret life is carried on in both the dark places of his mind and in the cellar beneath the second-hand shop, Philip cannot turn his eyes upwards to Glastonbury tower, which represents the spiritual aspirations of the centuries.

The main patterning of *A Glastonbury Romance*, however, derives from the intricate interweaving of the lives of a very large number of Glastonbury people, and the great range of experience which this involves, from the highest moments of revelation and perception, to the humblest of bodily functions, a Rabelaisian mixture of the excremental with the sacramental. All aspects of life are potentially significant, and the life of animals, of plants and even of inanimate objects such as stones has a vibrance of its own which interacts with the human, as with the divine-diabolical First Cause.

Though the Arthurian legend is in one sense the inspiration of the book, and the characters and some of the events of the medieval versions are frequently alluded to, yet it is the meaning of the Grail as something timeless, as a real source of power, not merely a symbol in an old story, that is important for Powys, together with his belief in its effect on the lives of later generations. He has no need to retell the legend, nor to find exact and fixed equivalents for its characters among his characters, for *A Glastonbury Romance* is a novel which creates its own imaginary world of extraordinary power and conviction. It does not offer a retreat from reality into nostalgia or into a dream-world, but attempts to confront some of the serious and perpetual problems of human life.

Much later in his literary career, Powys wrote a second Arthurian novel, *Porius*, published in 1951. It is set in the Dark Ages, at the point when Roman rule has come to an end in Britain, and thus draws on the earlier, Celtic sources rather than on Malory. Powys said of the Dark Ages that they were his favourite of all ages. He presents this period as one that was highly civilised in its own way, on the basis of his own conviction that the world of learning was open to those who wished strongly enough to avail themselves of 'the uttermost wisdom of life'. In *Porius*, as in *A Glastonbury Romance*, Powys used Arthurian material as a means of communicating his deepest reflections on life. Though they are totally different in many ways, the two novels taken together constitute an astonishing tour-de-force, each making significant literal and symbolic use of the legends.

In a short prefatory introduction to the historical background to *Porius*, Powys draws an analogy between the period of which he is writing and the present day:

> As we contemplate this historic background to the autumn of the
> last year of the fifth century, it is impossible not to think of the
> background of human life from which today we watch the first half
> of the twentieth century dissolve into its second half. As the old
> gods were departing then, so the old gods are departing now. And
> as the future was dark with the terrifying possibilities of human

disaster then, so, today, are we confronted by the possibility of catastrophic world-events compared with which those that Arthur and his Counsellor and his Horsemen contended against seem, as the Hebrew poet said, 'a very little thing'. (p. xi)[38]

Porius is about our present power to create—or to destroy—our future. So, through his use of Arthurian material, Powys makes a unique comment on the predicament of modern man and suggests a positive approach to it; still less than his earlier Arthurian novel is *Porius* a mere retelling or dramatisation of traditional stories, even though it is set in an historical period.

The action of *Porius* takes place during one October week in the year A.D. 499 Although Arthur and Myrddin, Medrawd and Galahaut and some other traditional figures appear in the novel, they are all, with the exception of Myrddin, minor characters; nevertheless, they help to make a remote and almost unimaginable period more easy of access to the modern reader. Through Myrddin, Powys gave expression to some aspects of his nature mysticism, crucial to his meaning, as he could not have done without a figure traditionally associated with magical power.

Porius is the only son of Prince Einion, reigning prince of Edeyrnion in Wales, and of Princess Euronwy, cousin of the Emperor Arthur, when the Saxon invasions are beginning. He is a huge, immensely powerful, slow-moving young man, educated, thoughtful and sensitive. In the course of this long book, he decides to join with Arthur in attempting to repel the Saxons and he marries, but little else happens. Though the events—such as they are—all take place within one week, the most significant action is located within the minds of the characters. The traditional adventures and situations of Arthurian legend do not feature in this novel. Yet the period with which it is concerned is one of great significance: it is a time of revolutionary change, a time of painful transition from an old, familiar world-order to a new, unknown one.

Porius is himself partly of Roman descent, as is Arthur, but he is also kin to the forest people of Edeyrnion, the simple and primitive worshippers of the earth-goddess, and he is even kin, too, to the aboriginal giants of Cader Idris, of whom only two appear to survive when the story opens. The old matriarchal society, represented by the aged princesses, aunts of Prince Einion, known as the Modrybedd, or more familiarly as the Three Aunties, is also ending, thus intensifying the state of uncertainty which threatens the stability of the realm. But it is the wisdom of the old world, represented by the forest-people and particularly by Myrddin, that is needed for survival in the upheaval of the present.

It is Porius' belief that each individual creates his own future by the exercise of his free imagination:

It was the great Pelagius who have liberated him . . . But what was the real meaning of the growing exultation he had been feeling all that afternoon . . . ?

It came from Pelagius. He recognised *that* clearly enough: and now as he stared at the white foam on the river's surface he thought he knew just what it was! It was the idea that each solitary individual man had the power, from the very start of his conscious life, not so much by his will, for *that* was coerced by other wills, but by his free imagination, by the stories he told himself, to create his future. (pp. 40–1)

Elsewhere Porius says, 'Pelagius is right. Man's imagination and not God's will is what creates' (p. 141). He comes to the realisation that the human imagination must be free of all controlling systems of thought, must never be 'robbed of its power *to tell itself other stories*, and thus to create a different future' (p. 44). At a moment when he is intensely aware of human and animal suffering, Porius suddenly realises that to identify with such suffering is madness, for 'Moment by moment all that live recreate life and change this transitory reality!' (p. 48). It is determinism that imperils man's future, especially determinism in the form of belief in the will of an omniscient god. For 'The earth lasts and man lasts, and the animals and birds and fishes last, but gods and governments perish' (p. 277). Powys asserts the essential animality of man, and so his need to return to his roots, to identify with the earth through the deliberate cultivation of sensuous enjoyment and the spiritualising of bodily sensations, ideas which are communicated most notably through the figure of Myrddin.

Myrddin is a weird creature. He speaks in 'a low, hoarse, guttural whisper, like someone who had given up for long years the use of human speech'. His head is 'bare of everything but a crop of coal-black hair', his ears are 'the largest appendages of that kind that Porius had ever seen', while his eyes are unnaturally circular in shape and so close together that 'when they flashed with an interior light, . . . they created the illusion that they actually mingled with each other and became one, like the eye . . . of that monstrous Cyclops' (pp. 54–6). He is a 'troubled fungus-scented charnel-chilly mass of flesh and blood', seeming 'to reek of thousands upon thousands of earth-chasms full of the black leaf mould of the original planetary forests', but his voice can be a voice of awe-inspiring authority heard simultaneously at different levels of consciousness. Although he is a grotesque and repulsive figure, he is a medium for unseen forces stronger than himself. 'Nobody understands me but my animals and why should anyone understand me? *It were wiser not to!*' he says. 'Through my voice the Son of the Morning speaks, the god at whose word the heavens shiver and shake and all the angels hide their heads. Cronos is his name and he speaks through me; and my animals and my birds and my fishes hear his voice and rejoice; and the kings and the priests and the druids tremble! *He is the Future*, and all the blind leaders of the blind and all the false astronomers and false prophets and all the kings and emperors are sick because of him, and their hearts melt within them because of him' (p. 99–100). Myrddin is also the mouthpiece of the forest people of Edeyrnion, who—though they are weak and oppressed—through their endurance are identified with the power of the earth itself.

Myrddin prophesies the future deeds of Arthur: 'This simple Arthur . . . will clear the land of the fair heads for a generation . . . But back they must come and possess all our land . . . But our speech and our mountains and our mountain-farms we shall keep; and the Saeson themselves will be conquered by others . . .' (p. 100). The 'simple Arthur' is a mere mortal, while Myrddin has about him a titanic, enduring quality which seems to set him apart from human beings. At the very end of the novel, after he has been released by the efforts of Porius from imprisonment beneath the stone, Myrddin struggles to seal up forever the chasm in the cloven rock upon which he had been helplessly stretched, and as he does so, he groans forth an 'echoing, iron-jarring, primeval-metallic sound', the word 'Karchorodonta'. As he uttered the word 'he scowled up at the grey clouds with features contorted by a terrible and immortal defiance: "jagged" was the word, "jagged" the weapon, "jagged" the man's face!' (p. 680). Porius on the crag with Myrddin, 'fancied he could catch moving up to that mountain-top a vast, indescribable, multitudinous murmur, groping up, fumbling up, like a mist among mists, from all the forests and valleys of Ynys Prydein, the response of innumerable weak and terrified and unbeautiful and unconsidered and unprotected creatures, for whom this first-born and first-betrayed of the wily earth, this ancient accomplice of Time, this angulomeetis of subtle counsels, was still plotting a second Age of Gold' (p. 681). It is through this experience that Porius gains understanding, as he reflects: 'how absolutely alone in this chaos of things was every single soul, whether of insect or worm or reptile or fish or beast or bird or man or god. "There's nothing I can do," he said to himself, "but just accept this crazy loneliness in this unbounded chaos, and hope for the best among all the other crazy lonely selves!"' But 'such a chance-ruled chaos of souls, none of them without *some* fellow-feeling . . . is a better thing than a world of blind authority, a world ruled by one Caesar, or one God . . .' (p. 681). The words of the old aboriginal giants, 'endure to the end; enjoy to the end', are the book's final message, as Porius, Prometheus-like on his rock at the very end, abandons himself to sensuous contemplation.

Porius, this 'buggerly great book', as Powys himself called it, was also for him 'the Best Book of My Life', written in his old age, and expressive of his most deeply felt philosophy of life. It has a monumental quality, but also at the same time it manifests that delicate sensibility and minute awareness both of nature and of human and animal responses to it that is characteristic of Powys's work. It successfully communicates to the modern reader a sense of the archaic mind, and of a primitive world, while leaving one with an impression of the points of contact and of the community of mind between Dark Age and modern man. The deliberate anachronisms often enhance this, as when one of the old princesses says to herself: 'We think we're modern; we take our new-fangled civilization as something established forever; and then behold!—in a moment the wheel swings back, and we're the same old men and women we always were!' (p. 357).

The world which Powys conjures up is barbaric but not brutal—or rather, such brutality as there is, is played down instead of being emphasised (as it is in some later writers of Arthurian fictions set in the Dark Ages) for the sake of historical realism. The problem of pain is here, as earlier in *A Glastonbury Romance*, a serious concern, and Powys insists, not only that there is too much pain, but that the cruelty of the past must not be re-enacted. 'Too much pain, Prince Porius, too much pain, and not enough pleasure', says Myrddin (p. 408). Medrawd has his own answer to the problem: 'In life there's more pain than pleasure, more ugliness than beauty, more lies than truth, more misery than happiness, more cruelty than pity, more illusion than reality. So I have condemned life to die, and I have appointed war its executioner . . . I am come that the world should have death; and I am strong because death is more powerful than life, higher than life, larger than life, older than life, and deeper than life' (p. 570). This sinister, half-crazed, necrophiliac Medrawd is 'a lost soul, a soul in hell', and what he stands for in the novel is the complete negation and opposite of the life-principle symbolised by Myrddin. But although his activities in this book bear little relation to his traditional ones, he is one of the most convincingly evil Mordred-figures in modern literature.

Arthur, as has been said, plays only a minor part in this work, for such plot as there is demands little of him. He is, however, unlike some later twentieth-century presentations of the Romano-British Arthur, an impressive figure. He has the reputation, borne out by his words and deeds when he actually appears, of being 'the most courteous war-lord in the world' (p. 349). He is a superlative master of the art of war, a trained military technician, who is thrown into the highest good spirits by danger and conflict, but yet capable of the utmost tenderness both to human beings and to animals. He retains the capacity to become a national hero, unlike some other fifth-century Arthur figures in recent fiction, in a distinguished work which demonstrates the immense versatility of Arthurian legend as a source of symbols for our own age.

9

Arthurian Literature Since World War II

In recent decades writers have for the most part turned away from Malory's version of the Arthurian legend. They now base their works on earlier accounts and attempt to place Arthur in a Romano-British world. Some stories popular with earlier generations—especially those of Tristram and Iseult and, to a lesser extent, the Grail—have ceased to have much meaning. Nevertheless, Arthurian myths still remain a source of powerful symbolism. While idealism and love play a much diminished part, the destructive rivalry between closely associated men has acquired new significance. The theme of sexual rivalry often becomes linked to the struggle for power, political and military. Frequently this competition becomes more meaningful when the rivals are not equals. Whereas Malory directed attention primarily to Lancelot and Arthur, contemporary writers often focus on the relationship of Arthur and Mordred as father and son. Most often, rivalries within the Arthurian story symbolise—as in the earliest medieval accounts—conflicts between forces of good and evil, order and chaos.

Writers have cast their nets wide, of recent decades, to find new approaches, if not new meanings for the Arthurian stories, and the result has been an immense diversity. The new interest in the 'historical' Arthur, fostered by the work of historians of the Dark Ages such as John Morris and Leslie Alcock,[1] and of archaeologists and writers such as Geoffrey Ashe, has given us a very different national hero. No longer the idealised chivalric king, Arthur often becomes a rough, barbaric figure reflecting the brutality and savagery of the Dark Ages. Though Malory is still sometimes the source, and Arthur may be idealised, many writers explicitly intend to strip away what they see as the false trappings of chivalry and medieval romantic attitudes. Even when they acknowledge the symbolic potential of the stories, contemporary novelists often aim merely at straightforward historical interpretation. We now often have Arthur's story told by and from the viewpoint of a variety of different participants in it—Merlin, Bedivere, Kay or Lancelot, for example. We see Arthur through the eyes of one of his own contemporaries, often a hard-headed man of action, against what frequently purports to be a realistic background of life in the Dark Ages. Though the external circumstances may be well reconstructed, the difficulties of presenting the characters with psychological realism are often intractable.

British and American Arthurian literature published since World War II falls, roughly, into four identifiable categories. The first includes works still based primarily on Malory. The most significant and artistic of these—by T. H.

White and Thomas Berger—treat Arthurian legend comically and satirically. The remaining Arthurian literature reflects the influence of recent historical and archaeological research. But among these historically realistic works, attitudes towards the Arthurian order vary widely. A large number of writers have aimed solely at realistic character, setting and story, purging the legend of its supernatural elements and often of its heroism and idealism—in some instances, of its mythic dimension. These works tend increasingly towards an exaggerated naturalism, emphasising sex, violence and detailed carnage. Other recent novelists have wedded naturalistic descriptions to a consciousness of the nonrational workings of the mind. Through dreams, psychic phenomena, and narrative disjunction, they achieve heightened, often macabre and surrealistic effects. Most recently, especially in America, novelists have restored to psychologically realistic and historically credible stories the magic and supernatural of early Arthurian literature. They have also restored dignity and romance to Arthur and his world.

i

T. H. White's *The Once and Future King* (1958), despite its date of publication, can be seen as virtually the last of the Victorian versions, rather than the first of the modern. It was begun in the late 1930s and almost entirely completed in the early years of the Second World War, though it did not appear as a whole until much later. The first part, *The Sword in the Stone*, published in 1938, tells the story of Arthur's boyhood and growing up. It was followed by *The Witch in the Wood* (later *The Queen of Air and Darkness* in *The Once and Future King*) in 1939, and *The Ill-Made Knight* in 1940, though the final volume, *The Candle in the Wind*, seems not to have been finished until 1958, when all four parts were first published in one volume. A futher Arthurian work, *The Book of Merlyn*, discovered some years after White's death, was not published until 1977. Since some episodes in it virtually duplicate passages in the earlier books, and it provides an alternative ending to the whole, it seems probable that it was a draft from which White took some material for the edition of 1958, while rejecting the rest.

The Once and Future King is dated, argumentative and sometimes silly, but it will probably remain the most readable and the best known of Arthurian fictions published in the second half of this century. It has a popular appeal that greater works such as J. C. Powys's *A Glastonbury Romance* can never have, and also at times, imaginative and symbolic power. White's concern with the problem of war in the modern world gives it an underlying seriousness. It is more than a mere re-telling of the old stories, and its colloquial style and lively passages of dialogue make it readily accessible to the ordinary reader.

Like Malory through the ages, or Tennyson in the nineteenth century, T. H. White has made the story of Arthur available to a wide range of new readers. *The Once and Future King* has been of the greatest significance for the continuing interest in the Arthurian legend, particularly in the United States of America. Without it we should never have had *Camelot*, which has so successfully caught the popular imagination and kept the story alive, and which has in its turn added a new term to our political vocabulary.

In *The Sword in the Stone*, White describes the upbringing of Arthur, or the Wart, in the never-never land of a very pseudo-medieval past, on which he comments himself in *The Book of Merlyn*:[2] 'Fancy starting after William the Conqueror, and ending in the Wars of the Roses . . .' (p. 4). White's interest in the past, and knowledge of such medieval activities as hawking gives a sense of some of the actualities of life in the Middle Ages, but fantasy also plays a large part, accompanied by a rather juvenile vein of humour. The magic of Merlyn is domesticated and consequently trivialised, though it also serves a serious purpose. Merlyn, Arthur's tutor, allows his pupil by means of his magic to experience various different modes of being. As an ant, Arthur finds out what it is like to live in a totalitarian society; as a goose, he enjoys the contrast of life in a free, tolerant and unaggressive community. (These episodes also occur in *The Book of Merlyn*, though in them Arthur is an old man, not a boy.) The ants' way of life evokes Hitler's Germany, as White draws attention to the unquestioning acceptance of propaganda and compliance with orders that prevails among them. Arthur finds that he is unable to ask questions of the ants, because 'It was not only that their language had not got the words in which humans are interested—so that it would have been *impossible* to ask them whether they believed in Life, Liberty and the Pursuit of Happiness—but also that it was dangerous to ask questions at all. A question was a sign of insanity to them. Their life was not questionable: it was dictated.'[3] In *The Book of Merlyn*, White discusses at greater length and in a more abstract manner some different social patterns, and concludes that it is the totalitarian society that makes for war because of its lust for territorial expansion.

The second book, *The Queen of Air and Darkness*, takes up the story of Morgause and her sons, Gawain, Gareth, Agravaine and Gaheris. The queen is shown experimenting with magic in various unpleasant ways, while her sons in an effort to gain her love and get more attention for themselves, slaughter a noble and magnificent unicorn and drag home its mangled head as a present for her. By such psychological exploration of the upbringing and circumstances of his characters, White endeavours to prepare and account for the eventual downfall of the Round Table, the institution of which is still some way in the future. Arthur is now king, but still continuing his education with the help of Merlyn, who questions his belligerent attitudes and the value of chivalry: 'Look at the barns burnt, and dead men's legs sticking out of ponds, and horses with swelled bellies by the roadside, and mills falling down . . . That is chivalry nowadays. . . . And then you talk about a battle being fun' (p. 229). In spite of these images, the brutality of medieval warfare is distanced, its impact reduced to that of chapters in a school history book, in comparison with the descriptions of conflict to be found in more recent works such as Peter Vansittart's *Lancelot* (1978). Merlyn, whose life moves backwards in time from the twentieth century to the age in which Arthur is living, speaks from his experience of the sophisticated warfare of modern times, arguing that there is no excuse for war, for 'Wrongs have to be redressed by reason, not by force' (p. 238). Arthur struggles towards a more enlightened attitude, and meditates the founding of the Round Table, in order to 'harness Might so that it works for Right', only to come upon the problem of how he is to deal with those who are too wicked or too stupid to accept the principle. Kay's suggestion that those who will not comply with the ideals of the Order must be forced to do so at sword-point if need be is answered by Merlyn's 'hindsight': 'There was just such a man when I was young—an Austrian who invented a new way of life . . . He tried to impose his reformation by the sword' (p. 274). Merlyn's teaching gradually has its effect upon Arthur, but the old magician becomes increasingly confused and forgetful, and he is unable to prevent Arthur from succumbing to the power of Morgause. So Mordred is begotten. White comments: 'it seems, in tragedy, that innocence is not enough' (p. 323).

Lancelot is introduced in the third book, *The Ill-Made Knight*, as a man whose apparent obsession with chivalry and military adventure conceals a lasting sense of religious vocation. For Lancelot, White explains, 'God was a real person'; in consequence, he was involved in an 'Eternal Quadrangle' (p. 510). Lancelot's honour is one aspect of an integrity which includes chastity as well as loyalty to Arthur and Guenever. He is outraged by Elaine's seduction of him 'on that terrible evening' when 'he broke his taboo'. 'Before it, he had thought himself a man of God. Since then, he had been a swindle' (p. 540), 'for he put a higher value on chastity than is fashionable in our century. He believed, like the man in Lord Tennyson, that people could only have the strength of ten on account of their hearts being pure'. A sense of the working out of the great purpose which necessitates the birth of Galahad, of which Lancelot is the instrument, so central to such versions as that of Charles Williams, is absent from White's, although White's Lancelot is more innocent than Williams's. There is thus nothing to compensate for the horror that Lancelot experiences at the way in which he has been used. The significance of Galahad's birth is similarly minimised, so that, as with Mordred, his existence appears only as the inglorious consequence of a cruel mistake. Lancelot's love for Guenever is not consummated until after he has lost his virginity through the trickery of Elaine. His relationship with the Queen is thereby made to seem less reprehensible, but at the cost of presenting Elaine as a vulgar and almost repulsive figure.

Throughout *The Once and Future King*, even in *The Ill-Made Knight*, Arthur remains the focus of attention. White makes explicit Arthur's problems, presenting him as man rather than king. Like Merlyn, he is both a projection of some aspects of White himself, and a mouthpiece for his political opinions, the means by which the author conducts his argument and searches for solutions. Arthur's attempt to establish Right by Might fails, and he is unable to canalise the aggressive instincts of those who enjoy fighting, so that they fight for justice, because they run out of things to fight for. So the quest of the Grail is undertaken to provide a means by which the might of the Round Table can work for God. White deals with this episode by directing his reader back to Malory for a full account, since 'That way of telling the story can only be done once', and then giving a series of reports of their adventures from those who return from the Quest. Arthur and Guenever listen in silence, 'finding it difficult to talk about spiritual matters', as the knights in very matter-of-fact manner speak of the mysterious events. The other knights' resentment of Galahad, sourly described by Gawaine as a vegetarian and teetotaller who makes believe he is a virgin, and equally disliked by Aglovale for his 'insufferable self-confidence', suggests most people's total incomprehension of what the spiritual quest is all about. When Lancelot at last returns, wearing next his skin 'a horrible shirt of hair', and completely changed by his experience, he too is met by incomprehension, though he gives a superbly vivid account of his adventures. From this point White follows Malory's narrative more closely: Meliagraunce (presented as a cockney knight) abducts Guenever, and Lancelot heals Sir Urre.

White's blend of realism and romance is particularly effective in his portrayal of Lancelot and Guenever as middle-aged lovers; and by emphasising their maturity, he deliberately illustrates for the modern reader Malory's assertion that love in King Arthur's time was more stable and enduring, for then 'Men and women coude love togydirs seven yerys, . . . and than was love, trouthe and faythefulnes'. 'These people', says White, 'had struggled for a quarter of a century to reach their understanding, and now their Indian summer was before them' (p. 539). 'Lovers were not recruited then among the juveniles and adolescents: they were seasoned people, who knew what they were about. In those days people loved each other for their lives . . .' (p. 559). Arthur is old and weary by the end of the book, but Guenever has aged appropriately, too, so that though she is still beautiful, her hair is grey.

In the last book, Mordred, 'confused between the loves and hatreds of his frightful home' (p. 553), shows his enmity. Arthur has never revealed the story of his son's birth, out of consideration both for Mordred and for Lancelot and Guenever, though he later confesses it to them in a scene which makes him appear as an ineffectual, ordinary man rather than as a king. Here as elsewhere, the stature of the main figures is inevitably diminished by the naturalistic dialogue, which cannot rise to the height of the great moments in Malory.

As Arthur prepares for the last battle, White returns to the questions with which he has been concerned throughout the book. Arthur 'had been taught by Merlyn to believe that man was perfectible: that he was on the whole more decent than beastly: that good was worth trying: that there was no such thing as original sin' (p. 666). All his efforts had ended only in total warfare, total hatred, 'the most modern of hostilities'. The old king ponders the unanswerable questions: is man only a machine in an insensate universe? What was Right, what was Wrong? Here, White's characteristic nineteen-thirtyish liberal pacifism is put into the mouth of Arthur, as he concludes that wars are fought about nothing, and that the sole hope for the future can only lie in culture, and the establishment of a new Round Table. Arthur sends his young page, Tom

Malory, away from the coming battle to ensure that the story is preserved for the edification of posterity.

It seems to have been only after the publication of the early parts of his story that White decided to incorporate his ideas about war into his work. It was then that the idea of taking Arthur back to the animals, as he does in *The Book of Merlyn*, appears to have occurred to him. 'I have suddenly discovered', he wrote to his former tutor at Cambridge, 'that . . . the central theme of Morte d'Arthur is to find an antidote to war.'⁴ So, in this book, Arthur in his old age, before the Last Battle, meets Merlyn once more, underground in a badger's sett where he is greeted by a group of friendly animals and discusses with them the problems of man's aggressive nature. There is too much argument, relieved only occasionally by more attractive passages: Arthur's vision of England in the moonlight, for example, which gives him a sense of 'the beauty of humans . . . instead of their horribleness' (pp. 108–11). Arthur at this point becomes England, the true symbol of the nation, before he returns to the world for the last battle against Mordred the Führer.

In *The Book of Merlyn*, White tried out a different ending from that with which *The Once and Future King* concludes. After Arthur's death, he suggests, Guenever took the veil though 'she never cared for God', so as to make it easier for Lancelot to forsake the world himself. When Lancelot dies, White quotes Sir Ector's lament for him directly from Malory, describing it as 'one of the most touching pieces of prose in the language'. Finally, the book ends, as it begins, with reference to other versions of the legend. In the first chapter, White had referred to Nennius and Geoffrey of Monmouth, and to other writers, through to 'Victoria's lord' and Aubrey Beardsley, ending with 'poor old White'. ('Who is this Wight?' asks King Arthur on hearing the list of authors.) The last pages go on to deal with the legends that have grown up about Arthur's coming again and mention, with White's characteristic facetiousness, the work of Dr Sebastian Evans and Jessie Weston among others, but finally, like Malory, White speaks of himself again. 'Here ends the book of the Onetime King . . . Pray for Thomas Malory, Knight, and his humble disciple, who now voluntarily lays aside his books to fight for his kind.'

The Book of Merlyn is sentimental and polemical, and it does not complement *The Once and Future King*, nor finish the story more satisfactorily. Its interest lies in the way in which it enables the reader to follow more closely the process by which White made Arthurian legend a medium for new meaning, of particular relevance to the period in which he was writing.

The cleverness of T. H. White makes two American treatments of the Tristram story seem very bland in contrast. *Tristram of Lyonnesse: The Story of an Immortal Love* (1949), an expansive treatment by Ruth Collier Sharpe, modifies the legend to fit the formulae of historical romance. Sharpe moderates the usual agonies of the lovers and finally wrenches Arthurian tradition by contriving a happy ending. While it mainly follows Malory's story, *Tristram of Lyonnesse* includes episodes and details from Gottfried von Strassburg not found in most subsequent treatments, as when Tristram slays a dragon in Ireland, thus heightening the unrealistic aspects of the novel. Like Warwick Deeping, Sharpe makes no attempt to create an authentic historical setting. Her characters exchange visits, consume great quantities of tea, and sip sherry before dinner in the manner of Englishmen at eighteenth- or nineteenth-century country house parties. (Tristram himself confesses to a fondness for curries.)

Changes in plot and character diminish the intensity of traditional situations, so that the legend becomes merely a flowery love story fleshed out by extraneous characters and episodes, lacking in emotional depth and psychological interest.

Only four years later, the American novelist Dorothy James Roberts created a far more readable, straightforward, and spare account of the Tristram legend, *The Enchanted Cup* (1953). Her major achievement is supplying credible motivations that account for traditional elements of the story: most notably, she convincingly suggests the political enmities and alliances which make the young lovers' union impossible.

Roberts departs significantly from Malory by expanding the story of Yseult of Brittany, who loves Tristram from their adolescence at Hoël's court, and by emphasising the lovers' moral growth. After living happily at Launcelot's Joyous Gard, they voluntarily return to Cornwall to alleviate Mark's loneliness, for they recognise their responsibilities to this 'shattered victim' of their love. In Lyonesse they live 'in love and peace' for only a brief time before Mark stabs Tristram in the back. While not artistically significant, *The Enchanted Cup* develops the very human problems and political realities underlying the Tristram legend.

A short and rather trivial work, but with some similarities to T. H. White's book both in tone and in its blend of past and present, is the British writer, Naomi Mitchison's *To the Chapel Perilous* (1955). Two reporters working for the *Camelot Chronicle* and the *Northern Pict* are supposed to be following up the Grail story. They discover that there are many Grails: Galahad's sacred vessel, Morgause's cauldron, and Bor's Grail associated with fertility, to mention only a few, though no serious meaning emerges from the symbolic image. The events of the story take place in a facetiously presented Arthurian world, but some depth of feeling becomes apparent as it draws to its tragic conclusion.

In 1958–59 American novelist John Steinbeck undertook what he initially termed a 'translation' of Malory's *Morte Darthur* into a readily accessible modern idiom. Steinbeck had long been fascinated by the Arthurian saga. As early as 1935 he had used Arthurian motifs in *Tortilla Flat*, a comic short novel about paisanos in twentieth-century Monterey, California. To the house he inherited, a generous idler named Danny attracts a growing band of comrades. The theme underlying their episodic adventures (principally petty thefts of food and wine) is that selfish individuals can become a unit by sharing an altruistic vision. In his preface Steinbeck elucidated the Arthurian pattern of

Tortilla Flat: 'When you speak of Danny's house you are understood to mean a unit of which the parts are men, from which came sweetness and joy, philanthropy and, in the end, a mystic sorrow. For Danny's house was not unlike the Round Table, and Danny's friends were not unlike the knights of it. And this is the story of how that group came into being, of how it flourished and grew to be an organization beautiful and wise. This story deals with the adventuring of Danny's friends, with the good they did, with their thoughts and their endeavors. In the end, this story tells how the talisman was lost and how the group disintegrated.'

Steinbeck's chapter headings whimsically imitate those in Caxton's edition of Malory: 'How Danny, home from the wars, found himself an heir, and how he swore to protect the helpless.' The narrative comically mixes Arthurian motifs, as when Danny, the Arthur figure, like Malory's Lancelot and Tristram, for a time runs mad in the forest while his fellows consider him to be in love. Finally, drunk and belligerent Danny brandishes a table leg—his equivalent of Excalibur—and rushes to his death challenging a mythic foe, 'The Enemy who is worthy of Danny'. At his death the fellowship disbands.

When Steinbeck later returned to Arthurian story, to recount the legend as it appears in the recently published version of the Winchester manuscript, he apparently intended simply to retell Malory. Published in 1976 as *The Acts of King Arthur and His Noble Knights*, the work includes versions of what the Winchester manuscript, edited by Eugène Vinaver (1954), calls the tales of Arthur and Lancelot (corresponding to sections of Caxton's first six books). Steinbeck's changes in the stories of Merlin, Balin, and Accolon are essentially minor. They generally explain character motivations or reactions that Malory merely implies. Sometimes Steinbeck also simplifies the narrative, for example, describing battle scenes more lucidly and concisely.

If Steinbeck had continued to 'translate' with so few changes, little would distinguish the work from other abridged versions in modern language. But finally the novelist superseded the translator. Describing Malory's romance as 'the first and one of the greatest novels' in English, Steinbeck wrote that like Malory, he would reshape traditional material into his own novel. The last two sections Steinbeck completed (he skipped Winchester's second book, the tale of Arthur and Lucius) completely rework Malory's tales of Gawain, Ewein, and Marhault and of Sir Launcelot. In these largely original stories Steinbeck considerably embellishes characters, invents episodes, and creates humorous dialogues.

'Gawain, Ewain, and Marhalt' features amusing relationships between the three knights and the ladies with whom they swear to quest for adventure throughout the year. Egotistical Gawain can scarcely believe that his lovely young damsel proves so indifferent to his charms. Marhaus, travelling with a lady of middle age, experiences the delights of courtship and the boredom of domestic routine. Ewain has the most surprising and useful experience of all, for his aged lady subjects him to a rigorous programme of training in knightly skills. At the end of the year the knights return to Camelot, each preparing the version of his adventures he wants 'repeated down the ages'.

In 'The Noble Tale of Sir Lancelot of the Lake', Steinbeck's Arthur and Guinevere, concerned that their inactive knights are losing their sense of purpose and nobility, contrive for the idle young Lyonel to accompany Lancelot on a quest. Lancelot's dignity quickly converts the irresponsible scapegrace. The tale includes an amusing portrait of Sir Kay grumbling about his difficulties in running the royal household, for Lancelot keeps sending back prisoners who 'strip the king's larders bare'. Steinbeck concludes with Lancelot and Guinevere recognising their fateful mutual love.

Having treated less than one-fifth of Malory's *Morte Darthur*, Steinbeck abandoned the project, apparently working on it only briefly again in 1965. Published after his death, the volume includes letters recording his great enthusiasm for the work and testifying that he read and travelled widely to prepare for it. Doubtless the project faltered because of its ambitious nature. If he had devoted comparable space to the remaining tales. Steinbeck's complete version would have run to more than 1600 pages. Even more significantly, his conception had changed so radically as he proceeded that the first five books contrast jarringly with the last two in spirit, tone, and purpose. To continue would probably have required him to rewrite those opening chapters almost entirely—a formidable task.

Steinbeck's letters illuminate his interest in Arthurian material. Though he cites the story's parallels to contemporary concerns (as political protest, for example), he repeatedly focuses on its importance as myth: 'So many scholars have spent so much time trying to establish whether Arthur existed at all that they have lost track of the single truth that he exists over and over.' Moreover, 'Arthur is not a character. . . . Perhaps the large symbol figures can't be characters.' Yet Steinbeck like his contemporaries stressed credible psychological motivation and the sense that the legendary characters were human beings. He judged that Guinevere, for example, has been too often treated ineptly because 'she has always been the symbol when in fact she must have been a dame'. In its incomplete state, Steinbeck's work never resolves this ambivalence between symbolic and realistic conceptions of character and story. In the first five books, symbolic meanings resonate in Arthur's efforts to create order from chaos. In the last two books, the lifelike qualities of the 'dames' and men overshadow the mythic elements.

Two years after Steinbeck's fragments were published—but twenty years after they were penned—another American novelist much more successfully communicated the symbolic power of the legend through comically human characters and conversation. Thomas Berger's *Arthur Rex: A Legendary Novel* (1978) is the most significant Arthurian work produced in America since Edwin Arlington Robinson's poems. It not only recounts a large portion of the *Morte Darthur*, but also includes material from Geoffrey of Monmouth; from *Sir Gawain and the Green Knight* and the ballad and romance accounts of Gawain's marriage to the loathly lady; from the standard Perceval Grail story; and from the Tristram story as found in the early versions synthesised by Jospeh Bédier. Berger also alludes to more recent Arthurian writers, as when his Merlin echoes T. H. White's wizard, teaching young Arthur about water and air. One also suspects the influence of writers less central in Arthurian tradition such as John Hookham Frere, who anticipated Berger's depiction of a giant decapitated so quickly that he does not realise his condition until he tries to walk. Berger narrates all the legends comically, adding abundant sexual humour and combining archaisms with modern colloquial speech. But even as he emphasises the ridiculous elements in the old tales, their heroic, chivalric idealism remains undiminished by his irony. The meeting of Arthur and Guinevere illustrates Berger's narrative technique of comically undercutting idealisations while at the same time preserving their value. Arthur determines to marry for practical reasons. After the debacle with Margawse, he wants a wife to help him remain chaste. Leodegrance's daughter is a convenient and politically astute alliance. Guinevere immediately hates him, because his hunting falcon kills her canary. She is typically adolescent, with pimples on her face and jam on her dress. These realities notwithstanding, Arthur perceives her as a glory 'all golden and white' (perhaps an echo of Robinson's *Lancelot*) and loves her 'faithfully all his life long'. Initially Arthur is rather pompous, but he defines his problem with disarming candour: 'how to be righteous without being sanctimonious'. He also defines chivalry, as 'a code for . . . knightly behavior, in which justice is conditioned by generosity, valor shaped by courtesy'. 'The vulgar advantage is declined. Dignity is preserved, even in a foe,' and 'Graciousness is sought.'

Berger's account of Sir Gawaine and the Green Knight similarly raises serious ethical and philosophical concerns even as it amplifies the sexual comedy in the medieval original. Gawaine faces temptations in a Bower of Bliss that could be conceived only by the wryest twentieth-century Acrasia. In this humorous context Gawaine and his host debate the value of absolute freedom. To the young knight 'absolute liberty is the freedom to be depraved'. To Bercilak, absolute freedom is 'the only situation in which principles may be put to the proof'.

Gawaine becomes chaste because he loves Elaine of Astolat, who as in Malory loves Launcelot. Here Elaine saves Launcelot not from a tournament wound, but from malnutrition with which he punishes himself for loving Guinevere. Berger's account of Launcelot is a complex mixture of invention and details drawn not only from Malory but also from Chrétien's *Chevalier de la charette*, as in the motif of the sword bridge. Like the other tales in *Arthur Rex*, this account of the Meliagrant story ends in wry satire. Inspired by the nobility of Sir Launcelot, Meliagrant reforms his wicked ways. But his first altruistic action wins scant reward: the beggar whom he aids in turn robs and shoots him.

Berger's Tristram story likewise plays with several medieval sources while expressing the human turmoil beneath both the comedy of his version and the glamour of the old ones. To the details which appear in Bédier's reconstruction of the medieval prototype Berger characteristically adds his own amusing touches. For all this, the tale becomes especially touching when Tristram returns from Brittany to show his brother-in-law his queen's beauty. He finds a haggard, aged creature with 'white hair and yellowed skin', but he loves her more than ever.

Some of Berger's finest comedy and frankest idealism merge in his treatment of the Grail story, which includes the stories of both Perceval and Galahad. Here, as in Steinbeck's work, Arthur originates the quest because he fears that, lacking employment, his men are growing lax. Since it seems heretical 'to long for the devilish only to defeat it', Arthur looks for a positive quest for good to 'hone' his men's virtue.

Berger uses the Percival story found in Chrétien and Wolfram, though as in Malory he is the son of Pellinore. Berger's tale of Percival's being raised as a girl (drawn from the Achilles legend as much as from the Arthurian story) borders on farce. The youth learns to sew and crochet and wears dresses after he has grown to six feet and sports a moustache. He fights monsters and villains who invade his home, only to be told by his mother that these ordinary occurrences in no way reveal in him unusual prowess or bravery.

For all the comedy of Percival's adventures and misadventures, his purity for a time renews the Arthurian ideals. When Arthur knights him, contact with the pure youth (whom Arthur forgetfully calls Purnival, Percinell, Purslaine, and Pimpernel) restores the sharpness of Excalibur. Percival also discovers Galahad, who like himself has been isolated at home away from knightly activities. Galahad quickly demonstrates his natural superiority to even the great Percival, but at sixteen he is clearly dying, for God 'doth allow perfection only to him who is already dying'.

Instead of rising to the Celestial City, Galahad joins the other great Arthurian knights at Camlin. In battle he unknowingly kills Launcelot, the father he reveres, before he himself dies. This detail is one of many alterations of Malory's closing episodes by which Berger heightens the pathos of the conclusion. Mordred and his conspirator Morgan la Fay have become mere parodies of inept evil, and calamity originates not so much in evil as in accident and human ignorance and limitation. The fall of Camelot is tragic because 'it was unique in happening not by wicked design, but rather by the helpless accidents of fine men who meant well and who loved one another dearly.'

Although Berger consistently exposes the ordinary human beings behind the legends, he also insists that they are great and noble precisely because they are so human. He also defends the importance of myth: 'all men of that time lived and died by legend (and without it the world hath become a mean place).' Like T. H. White before him, Berger manages to satirise and laugh at traditional story without denigrating it, and *Arthur Rex* remains far more genial than Twain's *Connecticut Yankee*. The novel's often delightful combination of wit and wisdom can best be enjoyed by savouring Berger's play with details and allusion in individual episodes. As the last of the twentieth-century versions based mainly on Malory, *Arthur Rex* skilfully transmits the dignity of medieval story through a highly ironic modern consciousness.

Another important American novelist used Arthurian legend not as the basis of his story but, like James Joyce in *Finnegans Wake*, as a recurring motif that on a mythic level elucidates the story of his twentieth-century characters. In *Lancelot* (1977) Walker Percy weaves Arthurian motifs through the story of a contemporary Louisiana lawyer. Lancelot Andrewes Lamar, as his boyhood friend used to tell him, was named less for the seventeenth-century Anglican divine than for 'Lancelot du Lac, King Ban of Benwick's son'. Confronting his wife's adultery becomes, in Lance's mind, a quest for the 'Unholy Grail', and it culminates in his murdering her lover, then starting a fire that kills her and two others. In a mental institution a year after the crime, Lance unfolds the story to his friend, now a priest-psychiatrist named Father John, whom he earlier dubbed 'Percival'. Percy purposely garbles the parallels to Arthurian story to reveal Lance's distortions, his inability to make meaningful connections between events in his world and those in Arthurian legend.

At times Lance can ironically acknowledge his contrast with his heroic namesake: He was 'discharged from the army not bloody and victorious and battered by Sir Turquine but with persistent diarrhoea'. But he fails to see himself as the impotent alcoholic he has become. Like a parody of a Round Table knight championing the downtrodden and establishing a new order, he has participated in the crusade for Civil Rights ostentatiously but only superficially. Though he recognises the realities of the 'new South'—where his black servants' son can attend private school and escape to M.I.T. as a scientific wizard—Lance himself lives very much in the past. For example, he squelches Ku Klux Klan threats against his servants through the 'good ol' boy' network rather than by principled heroics. Equally outdated and artificial is his view of women, especially of his wife Margot, who needs a vocation, not a pedestal. And though he prizes Margot's intense sexuality, he at one point remarks that 'the sight of a lustful woman was as incredible as a fire-breathing dragon turning up at' the modern equivalent of the Round Table, 'the Rotary Club'. Unable to see that he cannot reshape the world by withdrawing from it, Lance never properly evaluates himself or achieves his quest. Yet by showing us sin—not only that of others, but his own—he partially achieves his goal of proving the existence of good by showing its opposite.

Like T. S. Eliot and James Joyce, Walker Percy has ingeniously used Arthurian motifs to illuminate the modern condition. The allusions not only suggest the moral sterility of the contemporary world but also imply the inadequacy of Southern chivalry for ordering and enriching life today. But through the figure of Percival (the name perhaps relating him to the novelist himself), Percy uses the Grail symbolism to posit hope for renewal.

Almost all of the works discussed in the following pages demonstrate the new trend in Arthurian literature, for with only a few exceptions, they are set in late fifth- or early sixth-century Britain, in the aftermath of the Roman withdrawal. In these novels, we are presented with an astonishing range of Arthur-figures. In Martin Borowsky's *The Queen's Knight* (1956), for example, Arthur is Mordred's puppet, a straw-king, fat and pink, with little piggish eyes and sparse hair. Elsewhere he is a capable soldier with an established reputation, an accursed man outlawed because of his incest, a leader capable of great cruelty as well as kindness, a warrior who can never actually be king because the Britons hate authority, as well as—more traditionally—an idealised, charismatic figure.

Similarly, the chivalric background with which we are familiar from Malory's *Le Morte Darthur* is often replaced by sordidly realistic settings, and in such works as Edward P. Frankland's *The Bear of Britain* (1944) we are given 'the real Arthur' undisguised by the 'incredible medieval fantasies' which have deluded us for so long, against a background of 'Mud, filth, broken bones, the reek of spilled ale and unwashed clothing'. The historical rather than the romantic approach also allows authors more freedom in presenting other characters, frequently with moral squalor to match the barbarous outward circumstances of their lives. Guenevere, for example, is not simply unfaithful, she becomes promiscuous, or a former prostitute. Mordred assumes a variety of different guises and is often presented sympathetically. Galahad, of course, seldom appears.

In *The Great Captains* (1956), Henry Treece endeavours to re-create a primitive society in a remote age. We see Artos as a half-savage tribesman, who when he first appears is under a curse because he has broken the tribe's taboo in committing incest with his sister. He is, however, of the oldest and most precious royal blood, and his innate superiority is shown by his immense strength. The motif of the sword in the stone is introduced in naturalistic rather than magical terms to demonstrate his unique power. Primitive tribal customs suggest a different world: Treece, unlike most other writers who have placed Arthur in the late fifth century, does not represent his characters as in all respects like ourselves. He does, nevertheless, allow them to develop: Artos who progresses from young tribesman to Artorius the *dux bellorum*, eventually becomes an old despot.

Treece shows Artos as warrior and leader, building up supremacy through a series of great battles, while at the same time suggesting how small the numbers involved must have been, and how unromantic such battles were. It is the horror rather than the glory of war that is emphasised, through descriptions of fierce encounters, fearful wounds and savage reprisals. Artos's ambition is to 'bring back Rome': and he eventually becomes Artorius, the *dux bellorum*, and studies Roman law and customs so as to make his rule more just and civilised. But in bringing back the customs of Rome he does not restore only the most civilised. He makes use of the old amphitheatre to punish the wife with whom he has made a hand-fast tribal marriage, when he finds that she has been unfaithful to him with Medrawt. She is forced to confront a savage bull, and is soon gored to death, in a scene which (like many others in the book) leaves us in no doubt as to the barbarity of the times.

The novel brings the story of Artorius to a close in an ingenious though nightmare ending. On a golden afternoon, three old men are seen in a garden, playing with a little girl. They are Artorius and Bedwyr, and the long-crazed Medrawt. The child—saved from death by Artorius in one of his campaigns—plays at kings and queens with him when suddenly, perhaps reminded of his old rivalry, Medrawt stabs him in the neck in a sudden burst of frenzy.

Treece's reconstruction and handling of the story are very plausible, and the familiar motifs of Arthurian legend—the sword in the stone, the founding of the Round Table, the doomed marriage, even the story of Tristram and Iseult—are given a new slant which still allows them to retain some of their resonance. Perhaps inevitably, *The Great Captains* lacks symbolic depth, despite the narrative skill of its author.

Rosemary Sutcliff's *Sword at Sunset* (1963) is also set in post-Roman Britain, but while allowing Artos to tell his own story, presents him as an idealised figure. It is a well told, romantic tale which achieves a certain dignity and restraint, as well as some intensity of feeling. Fifth-century Britain is shown as comparatively civilised, in strong contrast to the background depicted in the work of a number of other writers. Rosemary Sutcliff in a foreword perceptively draws attention to a significant structure underlying the traditional stories of Arthur, which she has adopted for her own version. The themes of sin and retribution constitute one element of this, while the concept of the brotherhood broken by the adulterous love of his closest friend for Arthur's wife provides the other part of the pattern. The motif of the Sacred King whose divine right it is to die for the life of his people is also introduced. Thus this version emphasises the importance of human relationships and moral values. Like Henry Treece's *The Great Captains*, it too has an ingeniously different ending: Artos wounded and horribly disfigured, voluntarily leaves his kingdom in the hands of Constantine, to seek healing in the Isle of Avalon.

One of the most successful Romano-British Arthurian romances is Mary Stewart's *The Crystal Cave* (1970). It begins the story of Merlin, which is completed in the two volumes that follow. Geoffrey of Monmouth is the source upon which she has based her account, but she has freely adapted it and invented details to suit the needs of a complex narrative. The characters are depicted in terms of modern psychology and moral attitudes, and set against the background of a romanticised fifth-century Romano-British society. Magic is introduced under the naturalistic guise of psychic phenomena or even ESP: Merlin's gift of sight permits visions, but in trances of piercing agony. He does not perform conjuring tricks. His powers are derived from the application of exceptional intelligence.

The book begins with the childhood of Merlin, the bastard son of Niniane and Ambrosius. He discovers his gift of vision in the crystal cave of a hermit who teaches him many things, including the art of healing, as he grows to be 'prince, poet, prophet and engineer'. Merlin tells the story of his life and of the patterns of destiny that work themselves out ultimately in the conception of Arthur.

The second volume, *The Hollow Hills* (1973) is concerned with Arthur's boyhood, though in a manner very different from that of T. H. White in *The Sword in the Stone*. Arthur's birth and upbringing are related by Merlin himself, and it is Merlin who finds the sword of the Emperor Maximus, made by Weland Smith, in a deserted temple of Mithras. It is this sword which will ultimately convince Arthur's rivals that he is the rightful king.

Arthur, when he is first seen, is a high-spirited nine year old, a fearless rider, a boy who creates an impression of 'blazing but controlled vitality'. His personality 'gathers legend as a drip-stone gathers lime' even while he is a child. When he claims the sword of the rightful king and leader, he makes clear by his noble and authoritative bearing that he is the chosen one. The scene is solemn and impressive, the darkness filled with mystery and vision as Arthur takes the great sword. A new era begins in the spiritual as well as the temporal sphere, for the carved sword on the old Mithraic altar crumbles until it has become only a hilt, a cross, beneath the inscription: TO HIM UNCONQUERED.

The Last Enchantment, which completes the trilogy, was not published until 1979, though presumably it was conceived much earlier. Merlin is still the narrator, but Mary Stewart invents new characters and changes the rôles of others. The story is put together from many sources: Malory, Nennius, the *Vita Merlini*, Chrétien's *Lancelot* and the *Anglo-Saxon Chronicle*. The action begins shortly before the birth of Arthur's bastard son, Mordred, who is smuggled away by Morgause. Lot, now Morgause's husband, orders the massacre of the babies that is designed to dispose of Mordred too, and causes the evil deed to be attributed to Arthur.

Camelot is eventually built, and Arthur married to Guinevere, but Mary Stewart makes Bedwyr instead of Lancelot the queen's lover, merely hinting at her unfaithfulness to Arthur. 'Tossed between desire and faith', Bedwyr nobly resists his passion. Arthur knows; he recognises the loneliness of Guinevere's position and the demands made on him that prevent him from giving her companionship. 'I am a king, and my life is a king's', he says; and then ignores the situation.

In this volume Mary Stewart depicts an ageing Merlin, who suffers from madness caused by poison administered to him by Morgause. When he at last recovers, he begins to teach his art to a gifted boy, Ninian, who has begged to be allowed to become his disciple. Ninian, however, is a girl in disguise—Nimuë, in fact. Merlin knows that he will be betrayed by a woman, but he is powerless to resist the charm of his new pupil, and becomes infatuated with her. In accordance with the traditional story, he is in due course imprisoned underground, a fate brought about with ingenious realism in this version. He eventually makes his escape, and at this point the trilogy ends, with Arthur still a young man, at the height of his power.

Mary Stewart's trilogy, in idealising Arthur and making him a romantic hero, belongs to the older tradition of Arthurian literature, though in placing him in a fifth-century setting she takes advantage of recent scholarly research. She presents Arthur as a strong, competent and just king. His England is idealised, too: the brutalities which some other writers stress do not appear in these books. The tone is thus very different from that of some other recent Arthurian versions, but probably contributes to the success of these romances on both sides of the Atlantic.

Victor Canning's Arthurian trilogy *The Crimson Chalice* (1976–78) was originally published as three separate works, and like Mary Stewart's novels, it places Arthur in his 'historical' setting. In a postscript to the first volume, Canning naïvely says that he has not attempted to follow strictly the lines of the accepted Arthurian legend because he thinks it bears little relation to the truth. *The Crimson Chalice* trivialises the story of Arthur by removing from it all the most powerful motifs, relationships and situations. The traditional account of Arthur's conception and birth, his upbringing and his later demonstration both of his right to the throne and of his fitness to lead are set aside. Though there is much factual detail about the circumstances of life in the fifth century, credibility is often strained both by Canning's attempts to recreate the historical background and by his substituted version of the events of the story. Canning's inability to appreciate the imaginative power of the Arthurian stories has produced a dismally debased and vulgarised version.

In John Gloag's *Artorius Rex* (1977), we have the story of Arthur told from yet another angle, in a strongly Romano-British background. The narrator is the seventy-four year old Caius Geladius, who looks back to a time when Britain was almost sinking back into barbarism. Like Catherine Christian's *The Pendragon* (discussed next), this is a soldier's account, and a very unromantic one at that. Caius Geladius comments on the crude habits of the Britons, offensive to his more refined Roman ways. He shows us an Artorius who falls disastrously in love with Gwinfreda, the daughter of a Saxon king, a very tough, horse-riding lady whose blatant sexuality rewards her with five children and the narrator's comment that she is 'just another of Cleopatra's many imitators'. Merlin is a fallible adviser to Artorius in this version, and Artorius never becomes king because the Britons will not submit to authority. Altogether it is an inglorious tale.

Catherine Christian's *The Pendragon*[5] (first published in 1978 under the title of *The Sword and the Flame*) is also set in the 'real historical world of the Dark Ages', but succeeds in idealising Arthur and what he stands for. The traditions of Roman civilisation and rule still linger on in Britain, and Roman discipline helps to withstand the Saxon inroads. Arthur whose story is told from boyhood to death, embodies a vision of Britain's rôle and destiny, as he asserts: 'I believe we are the only people . . . who can guard the true wisdom for the world, while the chaos of great changes shakes all nations round about us . . . Poor and small this island may be. But in it we must somehow keep a light burning—a rushlight that will re-kindle the lamps of the world when the great storm of these times has passed away.' (p. 156.)

Like Mary Stewart, Catherine Christian follows a trend that becomes more marked with the publication of some other contemporary Arthurian novels, in telling the story from the point of view of a minor character in the earlier tradition. Now, instead of Merlin's story, we have the story according to Bedivere. He is Arthur's life-long companion, and a professional soldier. Thus the emphasis falls upon the military aspects of Arthur's career, making it a tale of hard-fought campaigns in the Romano-British world, with no chivalric romance. The story is very competently told, with the customary modern psychological realism, and much historical detail. Catherine Christian handles the familiar episodes with considerable freedom, makes them plausible, and ingeniously shows them in a new light, but her version lacks the imaginative power of Mary Stewart's. Arthur becomes an inspiring and successful war leader, driving back the Saxons, endeavouring to stabilise the country and to establish justice and peace. His knights are a band of loyal Companions. The story of Medraut is effectively intertwined with Arthur's; as a child, he has been perverted by Morgause, who has encouraged him to believe that he is the unacknowledged son of Arthur. He is a hypocritical and sinister figure who insinuates himself as a youth into Arthur's favour, and becomes indispensable as a brilliant administrator responsible for the smooth running of the kingdom. Arthur even contemplates making him his heir, but is persuaded to pass him over in favour of Lancelot's unworldly and saintly son, Peredur. Medraut conceals his mortification and anger, and gathers to himself a group of like-minded youths. He is a homosexual, and he corrupts his young friends and alienates them from Arthur. Thus, like the figure of Mordred in other recent Arthurian fictions, he plays a prominent part in the story. The theme of Lancelot's and Guinevere's love fades into the background in consequence. Guinevere as a young girl had been dedicated to the Moon Goddess, whose initiation rites frequently caused sterility.

The Grail quest, as seen through Bedivere's eyes, is a disastrous distraction, the consequence of mere delusion, which disperses the Companions upon whose solidarity the security of the realm depends. Medraut through his cunning sees to it that Peredur shall find the responsibility of being Arthur's heir too much for him, so that he retreats 'from his true heritage into a dream-world that laid Britain waste'. Peredur's vision at Pentecost is not seen by all, but the Grail-message, given by Peredur's sister, persuades the knights to embark upon what Bedivere sees as a wild goose chase, when the whole story is reported to him afterwards in his distant province. The Grail quest thus makes Britain more vulnerable to attack, when Medraut goes overseas and raises a force to challenge Arthur's authority.

In making this a soldier's account of Arthur's story, Catherine Christian finds an ingenious solution to the problem of the magic. The episode of the drawing of the sword, for example, which marks Arthur's calling, is presented as a tale told with great verve by a skilled storyteller, a simple uneducated man who claims to have been present, and whose story seems to lose nothing in the telling: 'But what I seen, I seen, and I speak according. There *was* magic in what happened. The Lord Arthur's Excalibur's no ordinary weapon, and you can take that from me.' (p. 167.) Similarly, the reporting of the Grail episodes allows a note of scepticism to creep in, implying that though men say this is what they saw, it seems incredible to anyone who was not there. Christian's *The Pendragon* is a competent, straightforward retelling of the legends, but no new meanings emerge for the modern reader.

The Parsival tales by the American novelist Richard Monaco paint a far cruder picture of the military realities of life in the Arthurian world. *Parsival: Or a Knight's Tale* (1977) initially follows rather closely the incidents in Wolfram's *Parzival*. Monaco shows the naïf, raised away from the world of courts and battle, encountering 'godlike' knights and setting out to become one of them. The novel exploits the humour of Wolfram's situations—the foolish boy's literalness and naïveté in matters of social etiquette, love, and politics—with a distinctly modern relish for sexual explicitness and coarse language. When the youth callously kills the Red Knight in order to get his suit of armour, for example, Monaco heightens the comedy in the boy's ignorance of how to remove the armour: the only part of the equipment he can open is the codpiece.

Monaco removes from the story all romance and surface nobility. The mud and gore of the external environment reflect the interior condition of most characters. The other traditional Grail knight, Galahad, here leads raiding parties and cheats the mercenary Red Knight out of his pay. Gawain, who in Wolfram's narrative is the ideal knight and a counterpart in the courtly world to Parsival in the spiritual, here becomes a vile soldier who ravishes poor men's daughters as he steals their gold. By the end of the novel Gawain joins the force who track Parsival in hopes of finding the Grail, which they view only as a magical means to military and political power.

Chief among those who lust for temporal control achieved through force is Clinschor, patterned in some ways on Wolfram's villain. In the medieval narrative, however, Clinschor's role is much more limited. He imprisons men· and women in the Castle Marvelous until Gawain frees them. Monaco amplifies Clinschor into a diabolical enemy of the Arthurian order who is attempting to seize Arthur's realm as a first step in conquering the world and populating it with a pure race of supermen. In notes to the novel Monaco points out the relationship between his Clinschor and Adolf Hitler, and cites reports that Hitler's S.S. troops actually sought the Grail because its magical properties would facilitate his conquest of the world. Monaco develops this symbolism when Clinschor's knights, uniformed in menacing black and silver armour, impress men, women, and children to dig a huge pit which soon becomes their own mass grave.

In a world gone mad with war and the pervasive inhumanity it breeds, Arthur has grown tired and dispirited. Committed to withstand aggression, he has lost sight of more positive goals. Though he once believed in the Grail, he has failed to measure up to his youthful promise as one worthy to achieve it. Of all the Arthurian knights, only Parsival discovers the Grail, and he does so by rejecting the ethic of power that produces the horrors of war. *Parsival* concludes with the protagonist being seized in a drunken act of sex, by a blood-thirsty, anarchistic zealot and Gawain, whose mutilated face testifies gruesomely about battle. In these ignoble circumstances, however, Parsival achieves a measure of nobility by recognising that the power of the Grail resides in his own capacity for love and compassion. Similarly, Broaditch, the stalwart retainer who has searched for Parsival throughout the novel, having escaped Clinschor's death camp, selflessly turns back into danger to find his king.

Though marred by unnecessarily vulgar language and pruriently graphic descriptions of sex, Monaco's *Parsival* entertains the reader with young 'Parsi-fool's' comic escapades and sobers him with a grisly but arresting anatomy of brutality, authoritarianism, and war.

In *The Grail War* (1979) Monaco continues the story by recounting a second war initiated by Clinschor against Arthur's realm. Whereas *Parsival* derived much of its humour and thematic interest from echoes of Wolfram's medieval work, *The Grail War* virtually abandons Arthurian legend. The general situation may have been suggested by Geoffrey of Monmouth, who describes the unstable politics in England after Arthur's death, including civil war, foreign invasion, and—especially significant to Monaco's novel—the burning of a large part of the realm. The novel does not recount Arthur's death, but does distinguish it from traditional accounts: A year after Arthur dies, Lancelot, a loutish brute, remains at Camelot; and Modred, Arthur's illegitimate son by a servant, hopes through the machinations of his aunt Morgan la Fay to become king. Parsival's son Lohengrin (in Wolfram the heir of the Grail castle, and in Wagner the pure Swan Knight) here becomes a paid assassin and, for a time, Clinschor's pawn. In part he becomes villainous to rebel against the father who neglected him while seeking the Grail. All these Arthurian characters are unprincipled, violent, and unheroic.

The novel depicts the Arthurian world almost entirely in terms of mud, slop, stench, decay, and especially, faeces. Even so, *The Grail War* effectively conveys the pathos of Parsival's vain endeavour to maintain beauty and peace in a chaotic, generally vile world. He achieves great dignity, especially when he vanquishes Clinschor not by killing him, but by reducing him to gibbering impotence. As in *Parsival*, the hero realises that the power called the Grail resides in love and compassion. Consequently the object of his quest becomes not the holy vessel itself, but the son he has until now loved insufficiently.

This search provides the story for the third volume of Monaco's trilogy, *The Final Quest* (1980). Like *The Grail War* it derives little directly from Arthurian legend. Beginning at the end of the holocaust, it depicts futile lives in a waste land. As the Baron Howtlande ineffectively tries to unite the devasted British factions, the sorcerer Clinschor maniacally pursues the Grail. Yet several

Arthurian knights wrest personal victories from this chaos: Gawain rejects war and thus achieves spiritual health before he dies; Galahad discovers solace in tilling the soil. Monaco's trilogy culminates in a horrifying confrontation at the Grail Castle involving slaughter, cannibalism, and a nightmarish vision of industrialisation and murderous children. Even in this horror, Parsival celebrates life. He finds Lohengrin, now suffering from amnesia, and helps him purge the ghastly memories of war. In the trilogy Parsival's experiences become a very modern Grail story, purportedly dramatising the death and renewal of civilisation.

Peter Vansittart in his *Lancelot*[6] (1978) directly acknowledges his debt to John Morris's *The Age of Arthur*, and sets his novel in the period of upheaval immediately following the Roman withdrawal from Britain. Now we have the story according to Ker Maxim, later known as Lancelot, warrior and woman-iser, who here bears little resemblance to the conventional figure of Lancelot. The author takes for granted that the reader is conversant with the traditional story, however, and gives only a commentary on the familiar events, so as to make us see them in a different light.

The figure of Arthur is deprived of both romance and dignity. In the eyes of Lancelot, he is a barbarian, a man already battered and broken-toothed, who could have been mistaken for a gladiator. He is at ease only with 'the low-born, renegade, declassed—the Keis and Bedyrs' (p. 91). He is indifferent to the civilised life so prized by the Roman, indifferent to all comforts save those of the table. He is irreligious, promiscuous, sadistic—even said to have buried his captives alive. Gwenhever is no more attractive: she has been the inmate of a brothel, the favourite of Medraut, before her marriage to Artorius, and their relationship thereafter is rather that of master and slave than of man and wife. Not surprisingly, scenes of savage cruelty and bloodthirsty fighting figure prominently in the story of such characters, and pain becomes a recurrent topic.

This new interpretation goes further than most of those previously discussed in an attempt to recreate the Arthur of history and to place him in what may be supposed to be an authentic fifth-century situation. Idealism gives place to barbarism, romance to brutality; the Grail becomes a mere cauldron, and Gwenhever is last seen as a hideous, painted creature with missing teeth. Lancelot, however, as he records the deaths of Artorius and Medraut, recog-nises that 'Their stories can of course be told very differently—I am not impartial and do not wish to be.' In old age, he concedes 'what has disturbed me throughout, is the supposition that [Artorius] must have been rather more than I have described'. But to be certain of the truth is impossible, he con-tinues, for 'In telling stories we submit to matters beyond our control' (p. 170). Vansittart, despite his desire to return to and to represent the 'reality' from which Arthurian legend originated, in telling his story in terms of present-day notions of the age of Arthur, presents it in terms of the sexuality, sadism and violence which are often a feature of modern literature and other art forms. As a result, his version tells us more about our own late twentieth-century tastes and attitudes than about the fifth century.

Jim Hunter's novel, *Percival and the Presence of God*[7] (1978), is unusual in its serious treatment of the Grail quest. It is based on Chrétien's *Conte du Graal*, and concerned only with Percival, after his departure from home in search of Arthur's court, which he never succeeds in reaching. Again we have a familiar story in terms of the individual experience of a single character. Percival's is a solitary quest, though his first adventure is the raising of the siege of White-flower's castle, after which he becomes her lover, only continuing on his way after some months have passed. Although he has been brought up in the knightly code, he has a lively sense of spiritual reality and he is also haunted by his awareness of pain. His adventures bring him to the Fisher King, Henged, and to his castle, where Percival recalls the words of advice given to him by an old abbot, 'Wait; accept; keep silence', and in obedience to them refrains from asking the crucial question. During the feast that takes place there, the Fisher King, watched by the whole company, with Percival beside him, is attacked by intolerable pain as a procession enters the hall, a girl carrying a silver cup and a boy carrying a spear. Henged, still in agony, takes the spear-tip and holds it over the cup, while blood flows freely from it. As the bewildered Percival watches this strange spectacle, he mutters to himself the old abbot's teaching: 'receive, accept, let God's experience present itself in its own time' (p. 101). But this advice is terribly wrong. When, later, Percival rises and stumbles out of the hall, Henged gives a great cry, the blood is spilled, the door closes, and in the morning the castle is deserted and devoid of every living thing. Percival is unable to find Arthur, and his quest becomes a quest for Henged, in the hope of freeing him of his pain. He realises that if he had asked the questions—'(But even now I do not know *what* questions, what form)' (p. 137)—Henged would not now be suffering. In the end, Percival abandons his ambitions, lives a life of humble service to others, and is content to wait for the fulfilment of God's purpose for him.

One of the most striking features of this novel, which is set in a dream-world like that of William Morris's 'Sir Galahad', is the sense of isolation that it generates. The climax of the book, Percival's helpless and bewildered incapacity to ask the questions expected of him, is handled in such a way as to give the incident contemporary relevance. Not even to question why suffering is experienced is in a sense to condone it. Such acceptance allows the pain to be perpetuated, to be endlessly repeated, and perhaps we are meant to see an allusion to modern indifference here. The 'substitution'[8] of which Charles Williams speaks, whereby one person may bear the suffering of another for him, has no place in this story: Henged in his moment of torment 'accepted that there was no transference of his pain'. But though the scope of this Grail-novel is limited in several ways, Jim Hunter's original use of traditional material brings out its latent power.

*   *   *

The Dragon Lord (1979) by American novelist David Drake differs from most of the realistic and naturalistic works of the period by giving magic a prominent place in the story, but it details battle gear, military dress, and the choreography of combat with well-researched probability. Like most recent Arthurian fiction, it depicts Arthur as a battle chieftain ousting Saxons. But here 'the Leader' has a twisted foot that makes him terrified of becoming unhorsed in battle. He also has an egotistical obsession with becoming famous for the next thousand years. Arthur's warriors, 'the Companions', include mercenaries from many lands, disciplined to military precision by a coldly fierce Lancelot. The novel primarily traces the adventures of two such mercenaries, both remarkable warriors: Mael the Irishman and Starkad the Dane. In the course of the narrative Mael procures a dragon's head for Merlin to use in his magic; a good witch, Veleda, as a lover; and the shield and spear of Achilles.

Through a central metaphor the novel reveals the horror of uncontrolled power. Arthur orders Merlin to create a dragon that will 'kill and burn and waste the whole land from here to the seacoast. . . . to sear the Saxons until they either wade into the sea or beg me . . . for mercy!' Once he unleashes it against the Saxons, Merlin quickly loses control of the dragon and it turns against him. The impotent wizard changes himself into a willow tree to escape, an enchantment that will last until another magician releases him. Finally the benevolent witchcraft of Veleda and the prowess of Mael and Starkad vanquish the monster. As an adventure tale the novel has vitality; as an Arthurian story it primarily sustains the unflattering view of Arthur that grew common in the fiction of the seventies.

iii

Martyn Skinner's *Merlin or The Return of Arthur, A Satiric Epic* (1951) and his later *The Return of Arthur: A Poem of the Future* (1955) will be discussed here, with John Heath-Stubbs's *Artorius* (1973) as examples of the few poetic treatments of the Arthurian legend in the second half of the twentieth century.

Both Skinner's poems relate to the return of Arthur, and both are in the form of satiric epic, in the manner of Byron's *Don Juan*, with a similar stanza form. *Merlin* starts with Arthur in Avilion (or Avalon—Skinner uses both forms) whence he is recalled by Merlin. In order to prepare him for his return to earth, Merlin takes Arthur to Hell, described as a 'totalitarian technocracy', where he is shown a documentary film about the modern world, which sickens and horrifies him. The poem ends before he can return and fulfil his mission, so that in it Arthur is no more than a passive observer of the more unpleasant aspects of modern civilisation. *The Return of Arthur: A Poem of the Future* takes up the same theme and is really a continuation, though the verse is rather more flexible and ingenious. It depicts some aspects of English life about the year 2000, when Arthur accompanied by Merlin returns to a west country village, now in the grip of the only too familiar horrors of a totalitarian régime. Arthur intends to overthrow the régime with the help of Merlin and of some chosen members of the local population, including George Alban, a farmer. But the poem ends with the revolution still far in the future, for the author allows himself to be side-tracked into elaborately showing how George is separated from his wife and seduced by the forces of evil. Thus once again Arthur hardly enters upon the scene.

In spite of its different genre, this work has many similarities with C. S. Lewis's *That Hideous Strength*, both in the way in which it shows ordinary people becoming involved in the prevailing evil without realising it, and in the way in which it represents the régime. The poem, which was very highly praised when it first appeared, and which is indeed often clever and amusing can, however, hardly be classed as Arthurian literature, except in so far as it depends on the idea of Arthur's return in time of need.

John Heath-Stubbs's *Artorius*[9] takes the 'historical' Arthur as its subject. It is divided into twelve sections, each allotted to one of the signs of the zodiac. It is a rich and varied work: some sections are in alliterative verse, others in stanzaic form, or in prose, and there are also some dramatic passages. Much of it is parodic, and there are many literary allusions and echoes. The author comments on twentieth century life through the medium of the poem, as when Artorius descends to the Underworld and is shown a vision of the future (somewhat as in Martyn Skinner's poem) and of the 'horrors of history' that await his country:

> *Like a ship, offshore, with shattered masts,*
> *Battered and betrayed, the island of Britain,*
> *Through the thickening dusk of a third Dark Age,*
> *Drifted into dimness and a tedious decline,*
> *With two rival crews of contending rats.* (p. 42)

Artorius elects to return to the world and to live out the rest of his life, despite the sombre experience. Although Heath-Stubbs includes the main events of Arthur's story, they are only allowed to form a framework for the very diverse material that makes up the bulk of the work. Thus, after the Battle of Badon Hill when the hungry victors are slaughtering some sheep and preparing to roast them, they are astonished by 'an unexpected apparition'—

> *A fantastic figure, flailing its skinny arms,*
> *With a bristly beard blowing in the wind,*
> *And a patched cassock caught about his paunch.*
> *It was Cadoc, the holy man, who with a huddle of hermits,*
> *Woned in this wilderness, in wattle-built cabins,*
> *With Aves and orisons at the hours of office.*
> *His extreme squalor might be a scandal to the squeamish,*
> *But denoted, doubtless, to the faithful devotee*
> *He was set on the sanctified road towards Salem.*
> . . .   .

He rushed towards the army, rabid in his rage,
Banging his book, clanging his bell,
Clutching his candle, and cantillating his banns. (p. 12)

Though *Artorius* hardly qualifies as a serious treatment of the Arthurian themes, it is a work of some distinction which can be enjoyed for its wry comedy and its originality.

iv

Realism is of the essence of the novel, and much recent Arthurian fiction is as realistic as such stories permit. There is now, however, a marked trend in both fiction and cinema towards what has been labelled 'new neo-Gothic', implying fantasy-writing of an often bizarre kind: a combination of realism and the fantastic, of the natural and the supernatural, is becoming increasingly popular. The substitution of an imaginary world for the real one, or the incursion into the everyday world of happenings impossible by normal standards, makes it possible to look at reality from a different angle, to set aside ordinary expectations and to break free from conventional attitudes. This mode lends itself to the free expression of the unconscious in ways which have not previously been tolerated. The movement away from realism and into an imaginary world where the usual rules do not apply facilitates the inclusion of sexual fantasies, particularly those that are taboo. In some recent versions of Arthurian legend such as Robert Nye's *Merlin* and John Boorman's film *Excalibur*, for example, such incidents as the begetting of Arthur and of Mordred are treated with greater explicitness and in more detail than was acceptable before. The current interest in psychic phenomena and in the powers of the mind makes Merlin a more intriguing figure for the late twentieth century than most other Arthurian characters. We also see, in some recent versions of Arthurian story, that the reaction against both realism and idealism takes us into a realm of the imagination which is often grotesque and macabre. The new neo-Gothic creates its often surrealistic effects by unexpected conjunctions, discontinuities and merging, disregarding the everyday world's conventions of time and space. Traditional fairy-tales and myths are similarly being rewritten and redefined (as in Angela Carter's short story, *The Company of Wolves*, an up-dated version of Red Riding Hood), and it seems likely that the Arthurian legend may continue to provide material for quite new interpretations. Its supernatural and magical elements and its symbolic images suggest that it will go on being exploited in new ways.

In Robert Nye's *Merlin* (1978), the simultaneous movement away from both realism and idealism is clearly apparent. Nye claims that in this book he has 'stood the medieval world of chivalry on its head and . . . explored in a modern way the dark unconscious side of the Arthurian myth'. His approach to the story of Merlin owes much to Emma Jung's and Marie-Louise von Franz's *The Grail*

Legend[10] in which, by asserting that the unconscious mind is symbolically represented by the figure of Merlin, the authors suggest a new way in which Arthurian legend may be given contemporary relevance. The authors claim that Merlin's story offers a means of dealing with the conflict that arises between the conscious and the unconscious. Man has in the past, they maintain, struggled to identify himself with the good (and indeed the idealism generally predominant in Arthurian legend illustrates this), but now the greatest need is to recognise 'the dark instinctive side' of our nature, and instead of repressing it, to allow it freer play, and by so doing give life to the more archaic part of the self. The authors argue that such an opening up of the unconscious induces a broadening and deepening of consciousness, making possible a new and better orientation to life. It is such an opening up of the unconscious that Robert Nye has attempted in *Merlin*: the obscene fantasies, notably those attributed to Arthur, which constitute a considerable part of the book, are presumably intended to liberate the repressed unconscious of the reader from the 'clutches of consciousness'. But according to the authors of *The Grail Legend*, this liberation of the unconscious is only a part of what the figure of Merlin stands for: his 'painstaking attentiveness to the divine' during his forest years, by means of which he acquired wisdom and understanding, in the early stories concerned with him, is also of great significance. In Nye's book, however, in marked contrast to Mary Stewart's trilogy, this aspect of the figure of Merlin is entirely absent.

Nye's source for the thread of narrative upon which his book is strung is primarily Robert de Boron's *Merlin*, in which Merlin is said to be the son of a devil and of a virgin; thus he can represent the demonic side of sexuality. Nye maintains that the early stories also contain an element of sadism, apparent in Malory, and later in the work of Charles Williams and T. H. White, and this, of course, finds fuller expression in his own book.

The work is divided into four short books, the names of which (Black, White, Red, Gold) make the connection with alchemy, later reinforced by the traditional identification of Merlin with Mercurius, alluded to by the authors of *The Grail Legend*. The first book describes in detail the conception of Merlin, which he watches. The second is concerned with his birth and later with the conception of Arthur; the third with the boyhood of Arthur, educated by Merlin 'To KNOW, To DARE, To WILL, To keep SILENT'.[11] He is also instructed that 'Words in themselves are, then, good or evil, poisonous or wholesome', a useful dictum for the reader to apply to this 'feast of flesh and flagellation', as it is described by the publisher. For Merlin, Arthur is 'the creep', 'King creepy Arthur', who knows all along that Morgan is his half-sister, and in drug-induced hallucinations, indulges sadistic fantasies suggested by Merlin. Consequently, 'Mordred is the truth about King Arthur'. His later remorse for his incestuous fantasies and act makes 'The once and future cretin' virtually impotent, giving us yet another explanation for Guinevere's barrenness.

Reviewers have commented on the excellence of the 'theological dirty jokes' and on the 'erudite low comedy' of Nye's *Merlin*.[12] The literary allusions, to Malory, to Milton, Tennyson, Charles Williams, John Heath-Stubbs and others make this very learned pornography, but pornography it is. The book strikingly demonstrates the astonishing versatility and resilience of the Arthurian legend, however. Through an original treatment of traditional motifs, this book takes us deep into the midden of Nye's conscious unconscious; but, as he comments, if it seems a satirical attack, King Arthur can take it. Not even Nye can destroy his appeal.

Monty Python and the Holy Grail is briefly considered here because it has appeared in book form, first published in 1977. It consists of the film script, illustrated by stills, and like George du Maurier's *Legend of Camelot*, referred to in an earlier chapter, it parodies not only Arthurian story, but also some popular contemporary representations of it. A remote reminiscence of the Grail quest provides the slender thread of narrative, and Arthur, Galahad and Lancelot are the chief characters. Arthur's prowess is demonstrated in a tremendous fight with the indomitable Black Knight, and Galahad's purity is severely tried when he takes refuge in a castle inhabited by 'eightscore young blondes, all between sixteen and nineteen-and-a-half'. He is rescued, much against his will, by Lancelot, who more than lives up to his reputation for fighting when with fearless abandon he throws himself into a crowd of wedding guests and starts hacking and slashing. He courteously apologises afterwards: 'There you are you see . . . I just got excited again . . . I'm ever so sorry.' Though popular notions of Arthur and his knights are made fun of, it is the banal cinematic representations of chivalry that are most effectively parodied, with an accompaniment of 'Errol Flynn music' and scenes 'à la Seventh Seal', in which stereotyped misconceptions of the Middle Ages provide the humour. Kurasawa is not forgotten and recent historians of the age of Arthur contribute some sociological touches. There is something rather Gothic, rather medieval, about this absurd and amusing book: abandoning realism, perspective and logical progression, it is full of amazing feats, exaggerated horrors and 'bold bawdry', but as always, 'Arthur can take it'.

v

A final group of novels, most of them written in America in the late seventies, restore elements of magic and romance zealously purged by the realistic and naturalistic novelists of the period. While most of them place Arthur in the fifth-century tribal world, a few fantasy and science fiction works do not even attempt to describe a historically credible setting. All depict Arthur as the heroic figurehead in an idealistic order.

The situation in the fantasy *Excalibur* (1973) by American novelist Sanders Ann Laubenthal, derives from the legend—used by Robert Southey—of the Welsh prince Madoc, who is said to have established a twelfth-century settlement in North America, then disappeared while sailing back to Wales. Laubenthal locates Madoc's American civilization in Mobile, Alabama. Lest her setting seem ludicrous, Samuel Eliot Morison's *The European Discovery of North America* (1971) records that the town has a bronze tablet erected by the Daughters of the American Revolution 'in memory of Prince Madoc, a Welsh explorer, who landed on the shores of Mobile Bay in 1170 and left behind . . . the Welsh language.'

In twentieth-century Mobile, a Welsh archaeologist excavates for Madoc's lost community, Caer Mair, and discovers Excalibur. This Rhodri Meyrick is actually descended from Madoc—who was descended from Arthur—and is the current 'Pendragon'. Also visiting Silverthorn, a modern castle built over Caer Mair, is Morgan Cornwall, who turns out to be Morgan le Fay, the witch from Celtic lore. With the Tarot deck she conjures up Morgause, a manifestation of the force of evil. Morgause tries to persuade Morgan that the goddess Druan Gwen whom Morgan serves represents Darkness. But Morgan finally discerns that the mythic cauldron of Druan Gwen is but another emblem of the Grail, the powerful symbol of Light. Morgan therefore thwarts Morgause's plan to destroy the Grail with the magical Excalibur. Resistance to Morgause also comes from Cristant, a reincarnation of the last princess of Caer Mair.

Laubenthal's modern, fantastic dramatisation of the cosmic conflict between good and evil remains unconvincing and artistically trivial. However, the work offers an interesting pastiche of references to Celtic mythology—Bran the Blessed, Owein, the magic cauldron—and to Arthurian material. Laubenthal's characters—including the author of a dissertation offering 'An Interpretation of the Grail Quest in Malory'—frequently discuss *Le Morte Darthur* and Welsh lore. Consequently the novel may interest Arthurians who enjoy discovering familiar elements in an offbeat context.

Of the numerous American science fiction novels and stories that draw on Arthurian legend, one of the most competent is André Norton's *Merlin's Mirror* (1975). In focusing only on the Arthurian situation, Norton's work differs from most of the recent American science fiction, which uses Arthurian story only tangentially or in minor episodes, as do H. Warner Munn's two works associated with Merlin. Munn's *Merlin's Godson* (1976), for example, involves time travel from Arthurian Britain to America in the days of Hiawatha, and to the Lost Colony of Atlantis. The first part (originally published as 'King of the World's Edge' in 1939) includes a letter from a Roman Centurion under Arthur's command, written after he has fled England. It briefly recounts Arthur's wars with the Saxons, his marriage to Gwenhyvar, the Battle of Camlan, Myrddhin's securing the wounded king in enchanted sleep and then leading a remnant of Arthur's followers to found a new empire at the world's edge. Arthurian material constitutes less than one-tenth of the total work. Similarly, Munn's *Merlin's Ring* (1974) follows the exploits of Merlin's godson, Gwalchmai (not the Gawain of Arthurian story), as he journeys from Atlantis to Norseland, to the Far East, to France and the burning of Joan of Arc. A single episode is Arthurian; it describes Gwalchmai's finding Excalibur—with which Bedwyr rallied the Cymry to fight the Saxons after Arthur disappeared—and placing it in the hands of Arthur, asleep in Avalon.

Following traditional story much more closely than these works by Munn, Norton's *Merlin's Mirror* spins a fairly readable narrative out of the Merlin episodes in Geoffrey of Monmouth. In the vein of C. S. Lewis, Norton turns Arthurian material into a parable about the conflict between forces of good and evil. Merlin is the offspring not of an incubus, as in Geoffrey, but of a Sky Lord from the age of space travel. Before Merlin's time, an advanced civilisation arose when the good Sky Born mated with the people of earth. But the Sky Lords broke off these relations when they recognised man's propensity for violence, which was fanned by the wicked 'Dark Ones'. War erupted, the Sky Born withdrew, and man again became primitive. Generations later, Merlin is destined to restore peace through a mighty ruler, so that the Sky Ones may return.

Altering the traditional story of Uther and Igraine, Norton has Merlin merely create for Uther the illusion that he lies with the duchess of Cornwall in the guise of her husband. Actually, a Sky Lord engenders Arthur. Merlin intends to train the youth very carefully for the task of perfecting society, but in a significant variation on the traditional story of Merlin's enchantment, Nimuë shuts him within his cave for the first sixteen years of Arthur's life. By using a life-suspension system left behind by the space travellers, Merlin survives until the power of Nimuë's spell has weakened sufficiently for him to escape.

In the final battle between Arthur and Modred, Norton alters details from Malory. Combat begins when one of Modred's soldiers draws a sword against the apparition of a serpent conjured by Nimuë. After Modred's death, Merlin places the gravely wounded king not in a barge bound for Avalon, but in the life-suspension machine in his cave. The magician then steps into another. Thus preserved, the wizard and the king who 'was, is, will be' await the return of the Sky Born with their advanced medical arts. While Norton rather interestingly expands Geoffrey of Monmouth's story of the strange boy Merlin and effectively adapts traditional material to the formulae of science fiction, the book offers less to Arthurians than to sci-fi enthusiasts.

Three novels by Vera Chapman illustrate the return of romance, heroic idealisation, and unapologetic magic to Arthurian fiction. *The Green Knight* (1975) is based on the story of *Sir Gawain and the Green Knight*, claiming to be no more than a story, but it attempts to fill in some details omitted from the medieval poem, and in particular to suggest the motives of Morgan le Fay. The author also draws on the story of Sir Gawain and the Loathly Lady to bring the romance to a happy conclusion, but unfortunately it is entirely without the depth and power of the great medieval poem on which it is mainly based.

Vera Chapman's second Arthurian novel, *The King's Damosel* (1976), like *The Green Knight* creates a fuller story for a figure from medieval romance. Here the Lynett found in Malory's Gareth tale has grown to love the 'Beaumains' she originally scorned, but he marries her sister. When Lynett despairs, Merlin assures her that she has a great destiny. She undertakes the Quest with Lancelot, Perceval, and Bors. Alone of the four, she asks the necessary question at Carbonek, thereby healing the Grail King and receiving the holy vessel.

Lynett then returns to Arthur's court to serve as 'the King's Damosel'.

The last of Chapman's Arthurian series, *King Arthur's Daughter* (1976), describes a struggle for the throne after Arthur dies. The romance forecasts that although the Saxons will overrun the land Arthur had once united, the offspring of Lynett and Ambris will, through generations, disseminate Arthur's ideals and spirit among British stock. Chapman's novels, featuring improbable situations and sometimes insipid magic, are slight.

Like *The King's Damosel*, *Lionors* (1975), by American novelist Barbara Ferry Johnson, focuses on a character mentioned only briefly in Malory, a woman whom King Arthur loves called Lionors. As a result of its concentration on a single romantic episode at the expense of the legend's larger dimensions, it is a trivial work.

In *Firelord* (1980), American novelist Parke Godwin retells the full Arthurian story as the king's testament from his deathbed in Avalon. Despite the efforts of his monastic amanuensis to turn the events into heroic myth, Arthur insists that he record the human realities, for they were sufficiently heroic and profound: 'I want to write of us the way we were before some pedant petrifies us in an epic and substitutes his current ideal for ours. As for poets and bards, let one of *them* redecorate your life and you'll never be able to find any of it again.' As Arthur the narrator intends, Godwin's characters 'stride' through 'their world as it was'. Godwin achieves psychologically realistic characters and—using such sources as John Morris' *Age of Arthur* and Jean Markale's *King Arthur, King of Kings* (1976)—an aura of historical authenticity. But at the same time he freely combines figures, historical and legendary, who never coexisted: 'Assembled on one stage in one drama, they make a magnificent cast. It should have happened this way, it could have, and perhaps it did.' Godwin recognises that much of the power of the Arthurian tradition derives from its mythic aspects. He creates mythic effects with characters who, while seeming very human, become larger than life through the intensity and significance of their experiences. Moreover, Godwin invests the material with magical elements that refresh the sense of wonder intentionally removed from the legends by most twentieth-century writers.

Godwin vividly and effectively depicts the political intrigue and military conflicts in Britain, menaced from without by Saxons and from within by tribal jealousies. He balances these realistic adventures with a story of faerie. As a young warlord, Arthur is taken, under Merlin's direction, into the world of the Prydn, the dwarfish original human beings. Although they are harrassed by the 'tall folk' who consider them barbaric faeries, the Prydn know life and love as the proud and powerful cannot. From the Prydn Arthur learns 'To love, to care, to be small as well as great, gentle as well as strong. . . . To be a king . . . is to know how apart and lonely we are and still exist and *dare* to love in the face of that void.' Among the Prydn he marries Morgana and fathers Modred. At the insistence of Merlin, whom he finally judges to be his own 'genius', Arthur reluctantly returns to fulfil his destiny, to protect and unify Britain.

Godwin alters many details of traditional story. Lancelot, for example, who is never especially friendly with Arthur, marries Eleyne of Astolot. She combines the two Elaines in Malory, for she is the daughter of the Grail king (Godwin thus merges Malory's Pelles and Pellam) and the mother of Galahalt. But she is also an original—unattractively pious, humourless, and dull. The Grail she urges Lancelot to seek is finally discovered by Peredur (the Percival figure in the *Mabinogion*), who is here Guenevere's brother, a frail man who fights the Saxons but inclines toward the religious life. (Richard Hovey had previously given Guenevere a brother named Peredur, not associated with the Grail.) Having calculated the probable location of the Grail, Peredur fishes up from the bottom of a well a plain and totally uninspiring chalice which the church certifies to be the holy relic. To Arthur Peredur indirectly allows that the vessel may be bogus, but its symbolic significance is necessary: 'A sense of continuity. . . . Christ to Joseph to us. Something that won't change, that says we *are* His children no matter how we muck up the world. That's all I want.'

Godwin's novel is among the best recent reshapings of Arthurian material. It extends from Arthur's boyhood to his death, and includes many of the major traditional episodes, at least allusively. Its account of the Saxon wars—especially the battle of Mount Badon—and of the civil strife among Briton clans is fast-paced and gripping. It treats the human involvements, especially Arthur's relationship with Guenevere and his friendships with Bedivere, Trystan, and Gawain, with considerable complexity and sensitivity. Most of the narrative substitutes natural for supernatural details—a plain cup for the fabulous Grail; Arthur as Uther's bastard by Ygerna, but not through Merlin's enchantment. The Prydn, who speak a whimsical language conspicuously lacking the pronoun *I*, add a delightful, fresh element to the legend, while also providing a poignant tale of innocence persecuted by a 'sophisticated' combative culture. In sum, *Firelord* is a rich and wholly engrossing addition to Arthurian literature.

Sharan Newman's *Guinevere* (1981), a less ambitious American work, likewise sets a tale involving magic in a credible historical milieu. It invents a history for Guinevere (whose life before her marriage had not previously been treated by Arthurian writers) from the time of puberty to her wedding night. As the pampered daughter in an aristocratic family of Romano-Britons, she dwells in great luxury and fairytale safety while the Saxon wars rage around her. Sensitive to 'things that move freely upon and above the earth' like wild winds and flying geese, she lives most intensely in a world of magic, especially in a unique mental and emotional bond with the only living unicorn. This magical beast remains her companion until her wedding night, when in keeping with medieval mythology, her loss of virginity assures his death. But because of her special involvement with dreams and the fairy world, Guinevere remains unnaturally naïve about human relationships. Although she scarcely shares Arthur's zeal for reform, she recognises 'There is something very dear about him', and thinks 'I could learn to love him very much'. Her innocence and remoteness from the actual world make inevitable her disastrous impact on the Arthurian order.

Though the fantasy elements of Newman's romance, especially the relationship between Guinevere and her unicorn, may not appeal to all readers, the book depicts human interactions sensitively and treats Arthurian story and characters both naturally and wittily. Newman invents several appealing figures, such as Geraldus, always accompanied by a chorus of invisible singers (including a sultry fairy mistress), who are mistakenly regarded by everyone who cannot see or hear them as angels. Another interesting invention is Gaia, a stern hermitess who has renounced the love of Nennius, a seeker of rare manuscripts. Arthur is a disarming young man of great ability and personal charm. He woos Guinevere shyly and ineptly because he feels uncouth in her elegant, aristocratic environment. Most significantly, he eagerly envisions an ideal society, symbolised by a gleaming city of the arts to be built at Camelot.

The novel combines fantasy and whimsy with some moving, realistic characterisations and descriptions of the effects of war. Its characters also pronounce some entertaining evaluations of Arthurian legend, as when Guinevere's mother (referring to Merlin's prophecies to Vortigern in Geoffrey of Monmouth's *Historia*) comments on Merlin's reputation as a boy-prophet: 'Merlin was half out of his head when he spouted all that! . . . The poor lad had been dragged from his home, slandered as a devil's spawn and threatened with horrible death. Anyone would babble under those circumstances.' Though relatively slight, Newman's *Guinevere* adds a gracefully told and engaging tale to Arthurian legend.

In *Hawk of May* (1980), the first of her series of Arthurian fantasies, American novelist Gillian Bradshaw depicts the warrior society now so familiar from recent works. Into this generally realistic setting she weaves an original story of magic reminiscent of the early Celtic materials which supply her characters and background. Gwalchmai the Golden-Tongued narrates the story of his growth from a youth dismally inept as a warrior to the greatest fighter in Arthur's warband.

Bradshaw flavours her novel with Celtic, especially Irish, folklore and mythology, referring to the legends of CuChulainn, translating Celtic verse, and composing songs in the spirit of Welsh originals. Taliesin appears as the great prophetic bard. Arthur himself cuts an imposing figure as the chieftain who transcends other petty princelings by fighting for a dream—without one, he realises, war is pointless. A rather effective adventure tale, *Hawk of May* captures the symbolic significance of the Arthurian order as a force opposing chaos and evil, and it conjures a sense of mystery and magic inherent in the early Celtic versions of the Arthurian story.

Kingdom of Summer (1981) continues the story of Gwalchmai from the point of view of Rhys ap Sion, a stalwart young farmer who becomes the warrior's servant. A third novel by Bradshaw, *In Winter's Shadow*, is soon to be published.

It seems fitting to conclude this chapter by anticipating another new Arthurian work, for the legend's continuing appeal insures that still others will follow. Though a period of relative lack of interest in Arthurian story may follow the heavy flurry of new works published in the seventies—as the 1960s, for example, produced no significant new titles—this myth has clearly become the single most important mythical subject in British and American literature.

While classical mythology, dominant from the Middle Ages through the early nineteenth century, continues to inspire literary treatments, neither classical mythology as a whole nor any single story can rival Arthurian material in the number of new versions it has inspired since the mid-nineteenth century.

Obviously many of the Arthurian works written since 1800 are artistically uninteresting. A glance at the bibliography in this volume reveals that many have already fallen into deserved obscurity. Some which were popular at one time are virtually unread today. But Arthurian tradition doubtless remains vital partly because it can sustain works that are readily accessible and only temporarily popular. John Steinbeck observed that the legend survives because like 'all lasting and deep-seated folklore', it offers 'a mixture of profundity and childish nonsense'. He also observed that 'there is something in Malory that is longer-lived than T. H. White and more permanent than Alan Lerner or Mark Twain'. While the permanence of versions by White and Twain may remain debatable, the permanence of Arthurian myth in British and American literature does not.

Appendix I

Arthurian Editions Published between 1800 and 1850

Four pieces in Joseph Ritson's *Ancient English Metrical Romances* (1802), the romances of *Ywaine and Gawain, Launfal, Libeaus Desconus*, and passages on Arthurian exploits in the *Chronicle of England*.

Walter Scott's edition of *Sir Tristrem* (1804), the thirteenth-century metrical romance preserved in the Auchinleck manuscript which recounts the story of Tristram and Iseult; reprinted in 1806, 1811, 1819, 1833, and 1848.

Nennius' Latin chronicle, the *Historia Britonum* (1819), dating from about 800 and giving the earliest information about Arthur; with an English translation.

The Middle English stanzaic *Morte Arthur* (1819), written about 1400, containing the story of the maid of Astolat and the final episodes in the love of Lancelot and Guenevere and the collapse of Arthur's reign; edited by G. A. Panton for the Roxburghe Club.

The *Awntyrs off Arthure* (1822), the late fourteenth-century alliterative romance recounting Gawain's adventures as the champion of Guenevere; edited by David Laing for the Ancient Popular Poetry of Scotland.

Arthour and Merlin (1838), the late thirteenth-century metrical romance in the Auchinleck manuscript which follows Arthurian story from the death of Arthur's uncle Constans to the betrothal of Arthur and Guenevere; edited by W. D. Turnbull for the Abbotsford Club.

Charlotte Guest's translation of the Welsh *Mabinogion* (1838–49), including two tales in which Arthur figures.

Lancelot of the Laik (1839), the late fifteenth-century Scottish work which describes the achievements of Lancelot and Gawain; edited by J. Stevenson for the Maitland Club.

Sir Gawayne and the Green Knight, with ten other Gawain romances (1839), edited by Frederic Madden for the Bannatyne Club.

The Avowynge of King Arthur (1842), the early fifteenth-century romance tracing the adventures of Arthur, Gawain, Kay, and Baldwin; edited by J. Robson in *Three Early English Metrical Romances*.

J. A. Giles' edition of Geoffrey of Monmouth's Latin chronicle *Historia Regum Britanniae* (1844), written about 1136, which gives the earliest lengthy account of Arthur's conquests.

Two Arthurian romances, *Sir Perceval of Galles* and *Sir Degrevant*, (1844) from the Thornton manuscript, edited by James O. Halliwell in *Early English Metrical Romances* for the Camden Society.

Layamon's *Brut* (1847), the late twelfth-century alliterative verse chronicle which is the first English treatment of Arthurian story; edited by Madden for the Society of Antiquaries.

The alliterative *Morte Arthure* (1847), a fourteenth-century romance tracing events from Arthur's defiance of Rome to his death; edited by James O. Halliwell.

J. A. Giles' modern English translations of Nennius and Geoffrey of Monmouth (1848), published in *Six Old English Chronicles*.

Arthurian Literature Since 1800

A Chronological List

We are indebted in the first instance to C. S. Northup's and J. J. Parry's 'The Arthurian Legends: Modern Retellings of the Old Stories: an Annotated Bibliography' in the *Journal of English and Germanic Philology*, XLIII (April 1944) and to Paul A. Brown's 'The Arthurian Legends: Supplement to Northup and Parry's Annotated Bibliography (with further Supplement by John J. Parry)' in *JEGP*, XLIX (April 1950). Acknowledgement must also be made to Mary Wildman, whose 'Twentieth-Century Arthurian Literature—an annotated bibliography' in *Arthurian Literature I*, 1982, was particularly useful for the most recent works.

The bibliographies are compiled chronologically, to indicate the number of Arthurian texts published in each decade. We have, however, excluded from both (with some rare exceptions) certain classes of text, as not germane to our study of Arthurian literature. These are:

i. Poems etc. published only in periodicals, and obviously of an ephemeral nature.
ii. Translations
iii. Unpublished dramas
iv. Children's versions
v. Operas and films, though radio dramas have been included, since their medium is solely the spoken word.
vi. Texts based on Lohengrin.

A complete list of an author's Arthurian works is given in his first entry; shorter entries are given under the relevant date with a reference back to the date under which the main list can be found.

We have given brief descriptive notes on each item wherever possible, except in the case of works discussed in the text, to which reference should be made through the index.

There is no cross referencing between the two bibliographies, and authors whose first work has been published abroad are in most cases listed under their country of origin.

I. BRITISH AUTHORS

1800 **Thelwall, John** *The Fairy of the Lake: A Dramatic Romance in Three Acts*, in *Poems Chiefly Written in Retirement*. Hereford, 1801. An original story which includes the figures of Arthur, Guenevere and Tristram.

O'Hara, Kane *Tom Thumb, A Burletta, as it is now performed at the Theatres Royal, Drury-Lane, Covent Garden, and Hay-Market. Altered from Henry Fielding, Esq.* 1805.
Play originally produced in 1780; not printed until the revival of 1805.

1810 **Scott, Sir Walter** *The Bridal of Triermain: or The Vale of St John.* Edinburgh, 1813. Some portions under the title of 'The Vision of Triermain' had appeared in 'The Inferno of Altisodora' by Caleb Quotem in the *Edinburgh Annual Register*, Vol. II, pt. ii, 1809, publ. 1811.
The poem was made into a 'grand chivalric entertainment' under the name of *King Arthur and the Knights of the Round Table*, and was acted in London at the Drury Lane Theatre in December 1834.

Peacock, Thomas Love *Sir Hornbook; or Childe Launcelot's Expedition. A Grammatico-Allegorical Ballad.* London, 1814.

'The Round Table; or King Arthur's Feast', London, 1817.

The Misfortunes of Elphin (first published anonymously), London, 1829. A satirical novel.

Calidore. In *The Works of Thomas Love Peacock* VIII, London 1934. A novel satirising contemporary England, to which Arthur awaits his return.

Frere, John Hookham *The Monks and the Giants.* First publ. as *Prospectus and Specimen of an Intended National Work by William and Robert Whistlecraft*, London. The first two cantos were publ. in 1817, and the last two in 1818; all four reissued in 1821 with the present title.

Milman, Henry Hart *Samor, Lord of the Bright City: An Heroic Poem*, London 1818. A poem in twelve books in which Arthur plays a minor part.

325

1820 Hemans, Mrs Felicia 'Taliesin's Prophecy', in *Welsh Melodies*, London 1822.

Peacock, Thomas Love (1814) *The Misfortunes of Elphin*, 1829.

1830 Anonymous *Tom Thumb. A New Opera, to be performed at the Theatre of Politics, County Court House, Limerick*, 1830.
A short satire on contemporary Irish politics. Arthur and other characters from Fielding's Tom Thumb appear.

Tennyson, Alfred *Poems*, London, 1833.
Contains 'The Lady of Shalott' (much changed in the 1842 edition) and an Arthurian passage in 'The Palace of Art'.

Poems. 2 vols., London, 1842. Contains 'The Lady of Shalott' (much revised), 'Morte d'Arthur', 'Sir Galahad' and 'Sir Lancelot and Queen Guinevere'.

Idylls of the King, London 1859. Contains 'Enid', 'Vivien', 'Elaine' and 'Guinevere'.

The Holy Grail and Other Poems, London, 1870. Also Boston, 1870. (This volume, though dated 1869, was not published until Jan. 1870.)

The Works of Alfred Tennyson. 10 vols. London, 1870. Vol. IV contains the Dedication of the Idylls and 'The Coming of Arthur' and 'Geraint and Enid'. Vol. V contains 'Merlin and Vivien' and 'Lancelot and Elaine'. Vol. VI has 'The Holy Grail', 'Pelleas and Ettarre', 'Guinevere' and 'The Passing of Arthur'. The set was reissued in 1873 with an eleventh volume which contained 'Gareth and Lynette' and 'The Last Tournament'. In spite of the dates, this edition was the first in which some of the Idylls appeared under their present names. In Jan. 1870, Strahan & Co. issued the Arthurian poems separately as *Idylls of the King*.

'The Last Tournament', in *The Contemporary Review*, XIX (Dec. 1871).

Gareth and Lynette (and *The Last Tournament*), London 1872. The American edition, Boston 1872, contains *Gareth and Lynette* only.

'Balin and Balan' in *Tiresias and Other Poems*, London and New York, 1885.

The Poetical Works of Alfred Tennyson, London and New York, 1886. In this edition the *Idylls* were given their final form. Vol. VII contained the Dedication, 'The Coming of Arthur', 'Gareth and Lynette', 'The Marriage of Geraint' and 'Geraint and Enid'. Vol. VIII contained 'Balin and Balan', 'Merlin and Vivien', 'Lancelot and Elaine' and 'The Holy Grail'. Vol. IX contained 'Pelleas and Ettarre', 'The Last Tournament', 'Guinevere', 'The Passing of Arthur' and the Epilogue.

'Merlin and the Gleam' in *Demeter and Other Poems*, London and New York, 1889.

Anonymous   *King Arthur and the Knights of the Round Table: A New Grand Chivalric Entertainment in Three Acts*, London 1834. Based on Scott's *Bridal of Triermain*, and acted at the Drury Lane Theatre in Dec., 1834.

Wordsworth, William   *The Egyptian Maid: or The Romance of the Water Lily*. In *Yarrow Revisited, and Other Poems*, London 1835.

1840   **Heber, Reginald**   *Poetical Works*, London and Philadelphia 1841. Includes *Morte d'Arthur, A Fragment* and *Fragments of the Masque of Gwendolen*.

Riethmuller, Christopher J.   *Launcelot of the Lake, a Tragedy in Five Acts* (in verse). London 1843.

Horne, Richard Henry (Hengist)   'The Three Knights of Camelott'. In *Ballad Romances*, London 1846.

Lytton, Edward George Earle Lytton Bulwer-Lytton, First Baron   *King Arthur: An Epic Poem*. First published anonymously in 1848 in four instalments, immediately reissued by Colburn in two volumes. A second, revised edition was issued with the author's name on the title page in London in 1849. Also published in Leipzig in 1849.

The Fairy Bride: A Tale. A free rendering of 'Lanval'; in *Poetical and Dramatic Works* of 1853, though printed previously, possibly in 1849.

Tennyson, Alfred (1833)   *Poems*, 1842.

1850   **Watts, Alaric Alexander**   'The Home of Taliessin', in *Lyrics of the Heart, with Other Poems*, London 1851; Philadelphia 1853.
(Watts had earlier published a brief poem, 'The Lady and Merlin. A

327

Picture by (Stewart) Newton' in *The Gentleman's Magazine*, Feb. 1826, reprinted from *The Literary Magnet*. The poem is on Vivien's influence on Merlin.)

Arnold, Matthew   *Tristram and Iseult*, in *Empedocles on Etna and Other Poems by A*. London 1852.

Craik, Dinah Maria Mulock   *Avillion or the Happy Isles*, in *Avillion and Other Tales*, London 1853. A story about a dream in which the modern hero meets Galahad, Arthur and other Arthurian characters in Avillion.

'Meredith, Owen'   (Edward Robert Bulwer-Lytton, 1st Earl Bulwer-Lytton), 'Elayne le Blanc', 'The Parting of Launcelot and Guenevere' and 'Queen Guenevere' in *Clytemnestra and Other Poems*, London 1855.

Yonge, Charlotte M.   *The Story of Thomas Thumb*. Edinburgh 1856.

Morris, William   'The Chapel in Lyoness', in *The Oxford and Cambridge Magazine*, Sept. 1856.

Sir Galahad: A Christmas Mystery, London, 1858

The Defence of Guenevere and Other Poems, London 1858.

Collected Works, London 1910–15, contains fragments of 'The Maying of Queen Guenevere', 'Palomydes Quest' and 'In Arthur's House'; also a reference to an 'Iseult of Brittany'.

Swinburne, Algernon Charles   *Queen Yseult*. One canto printed in *Undergraduate Papers*, Dec. 1857. The remaining five were printed privately in 1918, and repr. in the Bonchurch Edition, 1925.

Tristram of Lyonesse, and Other Poems. London 1882.

The Tale of Balen. London 1896.

'King Ban: A Fragment'. In *Lady Maisie's Bairn and Other Poems*. London (privately printed) 1915. Repr. in *Posthumous Poems*, London 1917.

'Lancelot' and 'Joyeuse Garde' in *Poetical Works*, London 1925.

Anonymous   *Arthur's Knights: An Adventure from the Sangrale*. 1859.

Tennyson, Alfred (1833)   *Idylls of the King*, 1859.

1860 **Lang, Andrew** 'Sir Launcelot', in *St Andrews University Magazine*, March 1863. Repr. in J. B. Salmond (ed.) *Andrew Lang and St Andrews: A Centenary Anthology*, St Andrews 1944.

Brough, William *King Arthur, or the Days and Knights of the Round Table. A new and original Christmas Extravaganza in one act.* In Lacy's Acting Edition of Plays, Vol. 61. London 1864. A verse play acted at the Haymarket Theatre, Dec. 1863.

Hawker, Robert Stephen *The Quest of the Sangraal. Chant the First.* Exeter. Printed for the Author, 1864.

Cornish Ballads, Oxford and London 1869. Reprints the (unfinished) *Quest of the Sangraal* and includes 'Queen Guennivar's Round', which had previously appeared anonymously in *All the Year Round*, XII, Sept. 17, 1864.

Bruce, C. (Sir Charles), *The Story of Queen Guinevere and Sir Lancelot of the Lake, after the German of W. Hertz. With other poems.* London 1865. A very long poem in octosyllabic couplets.

Young, J. W. 'An Old Harrovian', *Lady Geraint Enid and other Productions*. London 1865. The title poem is intended to be humorous.

Westwood, Thomas *The Sword of Kingship. A Legend of the 'Morte d'Arthure'.* London 1866 (printed for private circulation).

The Quest of the Sancgreal, The Sword of Kingship, and Other Poems. London 1868.

Glennie, John Stuart Stuart *King Arthur or the Drama of the Revolution.* Vol. I, *Prologue and Overture*, London 1867; Vol. II, Play the First, *The Quest for Merlin*, 1870; *The Romance of the Youth of King Arthur*, 1880. The rest of the projected work never appeared. A philosophical treatment of the French Revolution under the form of Arthurian romance.

Morgan, Richard William *The Duke's Daughter: a Classic Tragedy.* London 1867.

Gordon, Adam Lindsay 'The Rhyme of Joyous Garde' in *Poems*, Oxford 1913. First published ?1868.

Simcox, George Augustus *Poems and Romances*, London 1869. Contains 'The Farewell of Ganore' and 'Gawain and the Lady of Avalon'.

329

1870 **Tennyson, Alfred** (1833) *The Holy Grail and Other Poems*, 1870; *The Works of Alfred Lord Tennyson*, 1870; 'The Last Tournament', 1871; *Gareth and Lynette*, 1872.

Anonymous 'Peredur or The Magic Basin' in *Some of the King's Idylls Unvarnished*, 1870.

Douglas, Christiana Jane *Arthur*. London 1870.

Hardy, Thomas 'When I set out for Lyonesse', 1870. In *Collected Poems*, London 1919.

The Famous Tragedy of the Queen of Cornwall at Tintagel in Lyonesse. A new version of an old story arranged as a play for mummers. In one act. London and New York, 1923.

Millard, Frederick *Tristram and Iseult*. Islesworth 1870. Privately printed.

Rossetti, Dante Gabriel *God's Graal*. An unfinished poem. See 'Rime Words for "God's Graal"' and 'Notes for "God's Graal"' in Paull F. Baum, *An Analytical List of Manuscripts in the Duke University Library*, Durham, N.C. 1931. Probably dates from 1871.

'How Sir Lancelot was made a Knight', a prose fragment, in *Works*. London 1911.

Gosse, Edmund Poem on the love of Lancelot and Guinevere in *On Viol and Flute*, London 1873. This poem was omitted from later editions of the work.

Jenkins, John 'The Grave of King Arthur' in *The Poetry of Wales*, London and Llanidloes, 1873. A short poem.

Dempster, Charlotte Louise *Iseulte*. London 1875.

Evans, Sebastian 'Arthur's Knighting' and 'The Eve of Morte Arthur' in *In the Studio: a Decade of Poems*. London 1875.

1880 **Hilton, B. H.** *Tristan*, 1882. Acted at the Liverpool Court Theatre, Sept. 1882.

Swinburne, Algernon (1857) *Tristram of Lyonesse, and Other Poems*, 1882.

Tennyson, Alfred (1833) 'Balin and Balan', 1885; *The Poetical Works of Alfred Tennyson*, 1886; 'Merlin and the Gleam', 1889.

Shorthouse, J. Henry *Sir Percival*. London 1886.

Fullarton, Ralph Macleod *Merlin: A Dramatic Poem*. Edinburgh 1889.

Henry, Richard *Lancelot the Lovely*. London 1889. A burlesque acted at the Avenue Theatre, London, April or May 1889.

Veitch, John *Merlin and Other Poems*. Edinburgh 1889.

1890 **Prince, Aelian** (pseud. for Carr, Francis), *Of Palomide, Famous Knight of King Arthur's Round Table*. London 1890. A long poem in blank verse.

Of Joyous Gard. London 1890.

Stevens, Stanley *Guinevere. Comic Opera*. Music by H. T. Pringuer. Acted at Kilburn Town Hall, March 19, 1890.

De Vere, Aubrey 'King Henry at the Tomb of King Arthur'. In *The Search after Proserpine and other Poems Classical and Meditative*. London 1892.

Macdonald, George 'The Sangreal: A part of the story omitted in the old romances', in *Poetical Works*, Vol. II, London 1893.

Binyon, Robert Laurence 'Tintagel'. In *Lyric Poems*, London 1894. Short poem.

The Death of Tristram. In *Odes*, London 1901. Repr. as *Tristram's End* in *Selected Poems*, New York 1922; and in *Collected Poems*, London 1931.

Arthur: A Tragedy. London and Boston 1923.

Menteath, Dora Stuart (Mrs G.F.S.), *Avalon: A Poetic Romance*. London 1894. Concerns a Victorian descendant of Mordred who achieves the elixir of life, but dies before he can drink it.

Carr, J. Comyns *King Arthur: A Drama in a Prologue and Four Acts.* Printed for private use only. London 1895. The trade edition, London 1895, is the same except for the title-page and the omission of one short passage from the last scene. Produced by Sir Henry Irving at the Lyceum Theatre, London, on Jan. 12, 1895; acted in the United States in the following year.

Tristram and Iseult: A Drama in Four Acts. London 1906. Acted at the Adelphi Theatre, with musical score by Christopher Wilson, in the same year.

Earle, Arthur W., and **E. Howley Sim** *King Arthur: An Examination of the Past.* A burlesque acted in James St., Buckingham Gate, May 16, 1895.

Newbolt, Sir Henry *Mordred: A Tragedy.* London 1895.

Croskey, Julian *Merlin: A Piratical Love Story.* London 1896.

Weston, Jessie L. 'Knights of King Arthur's Court'. In *The Rose-Tree of Hildesheim and Other Poems.* London 1896. Poems on Gawayne, Tristan, Lancelot and Perceval.

Swinburne, Algernon (1857) *The Tale of Balen*, 1896.

Coutts, Francis (Francis Burdett Thomas Coutts Nevill, Baron Latymer), *King Arthur: a trilogy of lyrical dramas founded on the Morte d'Arthur of Sir Thomas Malory, by F. B. Coutts.* (Privately printed, London 1897.)

The Romance of King Arthur. London 1907.

Rhys, Ernest 'The Story of Balin and Balan: From the *Morte d'Arthur*'. In *The Garden of Romance*, London and New York, 1897.

Welsh Ballads and Other Poems. London 1898. Contains five Arthurian poems.

Lays of the Round Table and Other Lyric Romances. London 1905.

Gwenevere: a Lyric Play. London 1905. Music by Vincent Thomas, first performed at the Coronet Theatre, London, in 1908.

Enid: a Lyric Play. London 1908. Music by Vincent Thomas, first performed at the Court Theatre, London, in 1908.

The Masque of the Grail. London 1908. Performed at the Court Theatre.

The Quest of the Grail: A Masque by E. Rhys, the Music by Vincent Thomas. London 1915.

The Leaf Burners and Other Poems. London, Toronto and New York, 1918. Includes three Arthurian poems.

Du Maurier, George *A Legend of Camelot*. New York and London, 1898. The title-poem appeared originally in *Punch*.

Wills, W. G. *King Arthur*. Not published in its entirety, but an outline, with extracts, appears in Freeman Wills' *W. G. Wills: Dramatist and Painter*. London 1898. Sir Henry Irving bought this play and asked J. Comyns Carr to revise it, but Carr wrote a new play instead.

Bidder, George *Merlin's Youth*. Westminster 1899. A long poem.

Davidson, John *The Last Ballad and Other Poems*. London and New York, 1899. Only the title-poem is Arthurian.

Sweetman, Elinor 'Pastoral of Galahad' and 'Pastoral of Lancelot' in *Pastorals and Other Poems*. London 1899.

1900 **Williams, Antonia** *Isolt: A New Telling*. London, published by the author, 1900. A drama. (There was another edition in 1915.)

Lounsbury, G. Constant *An Iseult Idyll and Other Poems*. London 1901.

Binyon, Robert Laurence (1894) *The Death of Tristram*, 1901.

Noel, Roden 'Tintadgel'. In *Collected Poems*. London 1902.

Leslie, Vera *Guinevere: Adapted from Tennyson's Poem*. Acted in London at the Court Theatre in June, 1903.

Lang, M. R. *Yseulte: A Dramatic Poem*. London 1905.

Hewlett, Maurice Published a number of works containing Arthurian allusions, between 1896 and 1912, but no primarily Arthurian works.

Steynor, Morley *Lancelot and Elaine: A Play in Five Acts.* London 1909, but performed at the Bijou Theatre, London, in April 1904.

Lancelot and Guenevere: A Play in a Prologue and Four Acts. London 1909, but performed at the Bijou Theatre in 1904 on the same occasion as *Lancelot and Elaine.*

Housman, Clemence *The Life of Sir Aglovale de Galis.* London 1905. A novel, repr. in 1954.

Cloriston, Henry *A Chapter from Malory (Book XXI, Chapter viii) retold in Spenserian Stanza.* London 1905.

Emma, Cyril *The Love Song of Tristram and Iseult.* London 1905.

Trevelyan, Robert C. *The Birth of Parsival: A Drama.* London and New York, 1905.

The New Parsifal: An Operatic Fable. London, printed for the author, 1914.

Both repr. in *Collected Works*, London 1939.

Rhys, Ernest (1897) *Lays of the Round Table and Other Lyric Romances,* 1905; *Gwenevere, a Lyric Play,* 1905; *Enid, a Lyric Play,* 1908; *The Masque of the Grail,* 1908.

Dillon, Arthur *King Arthur Pendragon.* London 1906. A drama in five Acts, with a comprehensive Arthurian cast.

Hill, Graham *Guinevere: A Tragedy in Three Acts.* London 1906. Acted at the Court Theatre, London, in October 1906.

Carr, J. Comyns (1895) *Tristram and Iseult,* 1906.

Edwards, Zachary *Avilion and Other Poems.* London 1907.

Chester, Norley (Emily Underdown), *Knights of the Grail, Lohengrin, Galahad.* London 1907.

Coutts, Francis (1897) *The Romance of King Arthur,* 1907.

Ellis, Thomas Evelyn (Eighth Baron Howard de Walden), *Lanval: A Drama in Four Acts.* London 1908. Blank verse.

Senior, Dorothy *The Clutch of Circumstance: or the Gates of Dawn.* London and New York, 1908. A novel.

Lee, Thomas Herbert *The Marriage of Iseult: A Tragedy in Two Scenes.* In *The Marriage of Iseult and Other Plays.* London 1909.

1910 **Baring, Maurice** *The Camelot Jousts.* In *Dead Letters.* First published in *The Morning Post*; repr. in book form, London and Boston, 1910. Imaginary letters written by Arthurian characters.

Hollins, Dorothea *The Quest: A Drama of Deliverance—In Seven Scenes and a Vision.* London 1910. In addition to King Arthur and Galahad, there are many non-Arthurian characters.

Manning, Frederic 'Tristram'. In *Poems.* London 1910.

Ankenbrand, Frank Jr. *Tristram and Iseult: A Play in Five Acts.* In *Collected Poems*, London and New York 1911. A play which claims to be based on Bédier's compilation of Tristram legends.

'Lancelot Speaks to Guenevere', Broadside No. 1, Philadelphia 1935. Short poem.

Boughton, Rutland and **Reginald R. Buckley** *Music-drama of the Future: Uther and Igraine, Choral Drama.* With essays by the collaborators, London 1911.

Boughton also composed the following Arthurian pieces:

The Chapel in Lyonesse (choral work) 1905.

The Birth of Arthur, 1908. Choral music-drama with words by Buckley, acted at Bournemouth in 1913.

The Round Table. Words by Buckley, rewritten by Boughton, 1914–16.

The Queen of Cornwall, based on Thomas Hardy's play, 1923–24.

The Lily Maid, an opera with words by Boughton, 1933–34.

Galahad, music drama with words by Boughton, 1943–44.

Avalon, music drama with words by Boughton, 1945–46.

Buckley also wrote *Arthur of Britain. Festival Drama.* London 1914. In addition to *The Birth of Arthur* and *The Round Table* (noted above under *Boughton*, it contained (Parts III and IV) *The Holy Grail* and *The Death of Arthur*.

Dawson, Coningsby *The Road to Avalon*. London and New York, 1911. An allegorical novel with Arthurian characters, in which the action only begins after the death of Arthur.

Doyle, Arthur Conan 'The Last of the Legions'. In *The Last Galley: Tales and Impressions*. London 1911. The only Arthurian content is a reference to Mordred as 'the wild chief of the Western Cymri'.

Field, Michael (Katherine Harris Bradley and Edith Emma Cooper), *Tristan de Leonois*. Bound in one volume with *The Accuser*. London 1911.

The Tragedy of Pardon. London 1911. A drama based on the story of Tristram.

Hearne, Isabel *Queen Herzeleid, or Sorrow-of-Heart, an Episode in the Boyhood of the Hero Parzival: Poetic Play in Three Acts*. London 1911.

Purnell, Charles William *The Modern Arthur and Other Poems*. London 1912.

Bell, Harold Idris 'From Tristan and Iseult' in *Poems from the Welsh*. Carnarvon 1913. (Translation of part of *Trystan ac Esyllt* by W. J. Gruffyd, Bangor Eisteddfod, 1902.)

Gillespy, Charlotte Ainsley *Guinevere or the Ladder of Love*. London 1913.

Glyn, Elinor *The Sequence 1905–1912*. London 1913. (Published in the United States as *Guinevere's Lover*.) A romance of high life in the early 20th century; Arthur becomes an elderly husband, Sir Humphrey, and Lancelot becomes Sir Hugh.

Howard, Newman 'A Ballad of Sir Kay (to E.D.H.)'. In *Collected Poems*. London 1913. The story of Kay and Lohot.

Kinross, Mrs Martha *Tristram and Isoult*. London 1913.

Sproston, S. *The Sword in the Stone: A Legend*. London 1914.

Trevelyan, Robert C. (1905) *The New Parsifal*, 1914.

Machen (formerly **Jones**), **Arthur** *The Great Return*. London 1915.

The Secret Glory. London and New York, 1922.

'Guinevere and Lancelot' in *Notes and Queries*, London 1926. Short story. The volume also contains an essay, 'The Holy Grail'.

Yeo, Margaret   *The Everlasting Quest (The Quest of the Grail)*. London 1915.

Rhys, Ernest (1897)   *The Quest of the Grail*, 1915; *The Leaf Burners and Other Poems*, 1918.

Symons, Arthur   *Tristan and Iseult*. London 1917. Repr. in *Collected Works*, London 1924.

'Iseult of Brittany' in *Cesare Borgia*. New York 1920.

'Merlin and Mark' in *Jezebel Mort and Other Poems*. London 1931.

Goodchild, John Arthur   *The Dream of a Scavenger: A Tale of Arthur in Plain English*. Retold from the Mabinogion and Modernised. Bath 1918.

Anonymous   *Lancelot and Guinevere: A Study in Three Scenes*. London 1919. A one-act play.

Brooks, Benjamin Gilbert   *Camelot* (Adventurers All Series, No. XXVI), Oxford 1919. A rather exotic blank-verse poem.

1920   **Keith, Chester**   *Queen's Knight*. London 1920.

Seymour, Alan   *Scenes from the Morte D'Arthur*. London 1920.

Levey, Sivori   *Sir Gareth's Quest. Adapted from Tennyson's 'Idylls of the King'. And arranged for costume representation*; and *Guinevere and Arthur. Adapted from Tennyson's 'Idylls of the King'* (The Pilgrimage Plays, Nos. 3 and 4) London 1920. In both plays the words of Tennyson are arranged for dramatic performance.

Paul, Evelyn   *The Romance of Tristram of Lyones and La Beale Isoude. Drawn out of the Celtic-French and Illuminated by Evelyn Paul.* London 1920. Part prose, part poetry; based on de Boron.

Waite, A. E.   *The Book of the Holy Graal*. London 1921. Poems.

Brumm, Charles *In Quest of the Holy Grail: A Hermit's War Lyrics. Selected from his Diary.* Revised edition, London 1921. Poems concerned with the search for peace among the nations, in terms of the Grail quest.

Eliot, T. S. *The Waste Land.* First published in *The Criterion,* I (1922). Repr. in *Poems 1909–1925.* London 1925.

Meyerstein, Edward H. W. 'In Merlin's Wood'. In *Poems.* Oxford 1922.

Thomas, Edward 'Isoud'. In *Cloud Castle and Other Papers.* London 1922.

Machen, Arthur (1915) *The Secret Glory,* 1922; 'Guinevere and Lancelot', 1926.

Berry, Charles Walter *King Arthur: a Poem.* London 1923. Poetic drama.

Rope, H. E. G. *The City of the Grail and Other Verses.* London 1923. The title poem is the only one with any Arthurian content.

Stevenson, Francis Seymour *Conflict and Quest.* London 1923. A long poem of which Canto IX is entitled 'A Castle of the Grail'.

Binyon, Robert Laurence (1894) *Arthur: A Tragedy,* 1923.

Hardy, Thomas (1870) *The Famous Tragedy of the Queen of Cornwall . . .,* 1923.

Galloway, C. F. J. *The Exploits of Lancelot: A Satire.* London 1924.

Philibin, An (John Hackett Pollock), *Tristram and Iseult: A Dramatic Poem.* Dublin 1924. A drama in one scene.

Williams, W. S. G. *Arthur is Arising.* London 1924.

Bond, Frederick Bligh *The Story of King Arthur and How He Saw the Sangreal: of his Institution of the Quest of the Holy Grail: and of the Promise of the Fulfilment of that Quest in the Latter Days.* Glastonbury Scripts, IX. 1925. A poem of forty-eight blank-verse stanzas. Privately printed.

De Beverley, Thomas (George Newcomen), *The Youth of Sir Arthour, The Quest of Sangreale, and Other Poems*. London 1925. Contains eight Arthurian poems.

King, Baragwanath *Arthur and Others in Cornwall*. London 1925. Contains only one Arthurian poem.

Hamilton, (Lord) Ernest William *Launcelot: A Romance of the Court of King Arthur*. London 1926. A novel.

Moore, George *Perronik the Fool*. London 1926. Grail story based on the Percival legend.

Boyd, Eric Forbes *Merlin's Hold*. London 1927.

James, Edwin Stanley 'Avalon'. In Grace Rhys (ed.), *A Celtic Anthology*. Edinburgh and New York, 1927. A short poem.

Macleod, Fiona (pseud. for William Sharp), 'Beyond the Blue Septentrions'. In *The Silence of Amor: Where the Forest Murmurs*. London 1927. Two legends of the polar stars which explain Arthur's association with the Great Bear.

Masefield, John *Tristan and Isolt*. London 1927. Verse drama.

Midsummer Night: A Verse Cycle. London 1928. Concerned with the legend that Arthur and his sleeping knights awake on midsummer night.

'The Love Gift' and 'Tristan's Singing' in *Minnie Maylow's Story and Other Tales and Scenes*. London 1931.

'Ballad of Sir Bors' in *Collected Poems*. London 1932.

'An Art Worker' in *Gautama the Enlightened and Other Verse*. London 1941. Contains some Arthurian lines.

Badon Parchments. London 1947. Fictional accounts of the Battle of Badon Hill.

'Tristan and Isolt' in *On the Hill*. London 1949. A poem which uses some motifs from the story of Romeo and Juliet, but with a happy ending.

Todhunter, John *Isolt of Ireland. A Legend in a Prologue and Three Acts*. London and Toronto, 1927.

Ormerod, James *Tristram's Tomb and Other Poems*. London 1928. The other poems include *Meliagraunce and Guenevere: Drama in Three Scenes* and *St Joseph of Arimathea: Drama in One Scene*.

Bailey, C. W. (in collaboration with N. S. Millican and G. R. Hammond) *King Arthur and the Knights of the Round Table*. In *The Quest of the Golden Fleece and Other Plays from Epic Poetry*. London and Edinburgh, 1929.

Bottomley, Gordon 'Merlin's Grave' in *Scenes and Plays*. London and New York, 1929. Poetic drama.

Glasscock, F. T. *The Symbolic Meaning of the Story of King Arthur*. Tintagel 1929. Retells the legends.

King Arthur: the Symbolic Story of King Arthur and the Knights of the Round Table and the Two-fold Quest. London 1931. A symbolic interpretation of Malory.

Mitchell, D. M. *Sir Tristram: A Tragedy in Four Acts*. London 1929.

Muir, Edwin 'Tristram Crazed', in *The New Adelphi*, 1929.

'Merlin' in *Collected Poems 1921–1951*, London 1952. Short poem, the source of the title of Mary Stewart's *The Crystal Cave* (q.v.)

Wright, S. Fowler *The Ballad of Elaine*. With decorations by Albert Wainwright. London 1929.

The Riding of Lancelot, London 1929. A poem.

Scenes from the Morte d'Arthur. Westminster ?1929.

1930 **Boss, Eleanor** *In Quest of the Holy Grail*. London and Edinburgh, 1930. Based on Tennyson.

Chesterton, Gilbert Keith *The Grave of Arthur*. Drawings by Celia Fiennes. London 1930. A poem.

Faraday, Wilfred Barnard *Pendragon*. London 1930. A novel.

Jones, F. H. *The Life and Death of King Arthur: A Play*. London 1930.

Newson, Ranald 'Balin and Balan, A Dramatic Poem' in *Poems*. London 1930.

Reynolds, Ernest Randolph *Tristram and Isoult*. Nottingham 1930.

Mephistopheles and the Golden Apples: A Fantastic Symphony in Seven Movements. Cambridge 1943. Includes an Interlude of Merlin at Tintagel, Merlin's Pantomime, an Interlude at Tintagel, and a song, 'Tristram and Iseult', sung by a siren at Tintagel.

Vere, D. B. *King Arthur: His Symbolic Story in Verse*. Tintagel 1930. Apparently connected with the fraternal order of 'The Fellowship of the Knights of the Round Table' which had its headquarters in King Arthur's Hall at Tintagel. See also Glasscock, F. T. (1929) for another text from a similar source.

Williams, Charles Walter Stansby *War in Heaven*, London 1930.

Three Plays, London 1931. Though the plays are not Arthurian, the volume contains four songs of Taliessin.

Taliessin through Logres, London 1938.

The Region of the Summer Stars, London 1944.

Masefield, John (1927) 'The Love Gift', 'Tristan's Singing', 1931; 'Ballad of Sir Bors', 1932.

Glasscock, F. T. (1929) *King Arthur: the Symbolic Story of King Arthur . . .*, 1931.

Powys, John Cowper *A Glastonbury Romance*, New York 1932; London 1933.

Maiden Castle, London 1937. Contains some Arthurian references.

Porius, London 1951.

Turnbull, E. Lucia, and **H. Dalwey Turnbull** *Through the Gates of Remembrance*. First Series. (A trilogy of plays centred round Glastonbury.) With illustrations by Marjorie Quennell. London 1933.

Kendon, Frank *Tristram*. London 1934. A narrative poem in nine sections.

Ryan, W. P. *King Arthur in Avalon*. London 1934. A one-act play.

Lindsay, Philip *The Little Wench*. London 1935. The 'little wench' is Guinevere; a novel about the love-life of Camelot.

Morgan, Charles *Sparkenbroke*. London 1936. A contemporary novel in which the hero, an author, in writing a new version of *Tristan and Isolde*, is writing of his own life.

Ankenbrand, Frank Jr (1911) 'Lancelot Speaks to Guenevere', 1935.

Padmore, E. S. *The Death of Arthur, The Story of the Holy Grail*. London 1936. Drama.

Jones, David *In Parenthesis*, London 1937.

The Anathemata, London 1952.

The Sleeping Lord, London 1974.

White, Terence Hanbury *The Sword in the Stone. With Decorations by the Author and End Papers by Robert Lawson*. London 1938.

The Witch in the Wood, with Decorations by the Author. London and New York, 1939.

The Ill-Made Knight. With Decorations by the Author. New York 1940.

The Once and Future King. London and New York, 1958.

The Book of Merlyn. Austin and London 1977.

Joyce, James Augustus Aloysius *Finnegans Wake*. London and New York, 1939.

1940   **Closs, Hannah Priebach** *Tristan*. London 1940. A novel.

White, T. H. (1938) *The Ill-Made Knight*, 1940.

Masefield, John (1927) 'An Art Worker', 1941; *Badon Parchments*, 1947; 'Tristan and Isolt', 1949.

Dane, Clemence (Winnifred Ashton), *The Saviours: Seven Plays on One Theme*. I. *Merlin*. II. *The Hope of Britain*. London 1942. Plays for radio, in all of which Merlin is the narrator. Arthur also appears in the seventh, *The Unknown Soldier*.

Bridie, James (Osborne Henry Mavor), *Plays for Plain People*. Includes *Lancelot, a Play in Two Acts* and *Holy Island, a Play in Three Acts*. London 1942. The second play was acted at the Arts Theatre in December 1942.

Cammell, Charles Richard 'The Return of Arthur', in *XXI Poems*. Edinburgh 1944.

Frankland, Edward *The Bear of Britain*. London 1944.

'Medraut and Gwenhwyfar' in *England Growing*. London 1944. An historical novel in which there is an episode about the relationship between Medraut and Gwenhwyfar.

Williams, Charles (1930) *The Region of the Summer Stars*, 1944.

Lewis, C. S. *That Hideous Strength. A Modern Fairy-tale for Grown-ups*. London 1945.

'Lancelot', in *Narrative Poems*, London 1969. Lancelot returns from the Grail Quest.

Baird, Edward *Brighid and the Dun Cow*. Birmingham 1946. Includes a prose fragment, 'They Went South by Way of Severn', about Myrddhin and the accession of Arthur.

Reed, Henry 'Tintagel', in *A Map of Verona and Other Poems*. London 1946. A poem in four parts on the story of Tristan and Iseult.

Fry, Christopher *Thor with Angels*. First acting edition published 1948. London 1969. The setting is the late sixth century; Merlin appears as a prophet long after Arthur's death.

1950 **Duggan, Arthur** *The Conscience of the King*. London 1951. An historical novel; the memoirs of Cerdic, in which Arthur makes a brief appearance.

Skinner, Martyn *Merlin or the Return of Arthur. A Satiric Epic*. London 1951.

The Return of Arthur. London 1955.

The Return of Arthur: a Poem of the Future. London 1966. Three parts in one volume.

Powys, John Cowper (1932) *Porius*, 1951.

Jones, David (1937) *The Anathemata*, 1952.

343

Costain, T. B. *The Silver Chalice*. London 1953. A retelling of the Grail legend but concerned only with the early Christians, in Palestine and elsewhere. Joseph of Arimathea, but no other Arthurian characters.

Smith, Arthur Saxon Dennett *Trystan Hag Ysolt: Verse*. London 1953. The Story of Tristan and Iseult in Cornish verse.

Mitchison, Naomi *To the Chapel Perilous*. London 1955.

Sheriff, R. C. *The Long Sunset*. London 1955. The setting is AD 410 but the atmosphere twentieth century.

Young, Francis Brett 'Hic Jacet Arthurus Rex Quondam Rexque Futurus' in *The Island*. London 1955. A poem.

Ditmas, E. M. R. *Gareth of Orkney*. London 1956. A straightforward retelling of Malory's 'Tale of Gareth'.

Treece, Henry *The Great Captains*. London 1956.

Wilbur, Richard 'Merlin Enthralled' in *Poems 1943–1956*. London 1957. A short poem.

Pomeroy, Florence M. *Tristan and Iseult: an Epic Poem in Twelve Books*. London 1958.

White, T. H. (1938) *The Once and Future King*, 1958.

Buchanan, Robert, D.D. *Fragments of the Table Round*. Glasgow ?1959.

Hill, Geoffrey 'Merlin'. In *For the Unfallen*, London 1959.

1960 **Priestley, J. B.** *The Thirty-first of June: a Tale of True Love, Enterprise and Progress in the Arthurian and Ad-Atomic Ages*. London 1961. Has a pseudo-medieval setting in the reign of King Arthur; otherwise not Arthurian.

Porteous, Frances *Knight of the Grail*. London 1962. An anthology of religious poetry, of which the title-poem is addressed to Galahad.

Sutcliff, Rosemary *Sword at Sunset*. London 1963. (Rosemary Sutcliff has also written a number of Arthurian novels for children, not listed here.)

344

Thompson, Francis (1859–1907), 'Epithalamium at the Marriage of Tristram and Isoude de les Blanches Mains', publ. in *The Lost Poems of Francis Thompson*, ed. Myrtle Pihlman Pope, Michigan 1966. According to the editor, based on an Old French work.

Turton, G. *Emperor Arthur*. London 1968. The story of Arthur told by Pelleas.

Peters, Elizabeth *The Camelot Caper*. London 1969. A thriller which revolves around Arthurian sites; not strictly Arthurian.

Lewis, C. S. (1945) 'Lancelot', 1969.

1970   **Stewart, Mary** *The Crystal Cave*. London 1970.

       The Hollow Hills. London 1973.

       The Last Enchantment. London 1978.

Taylor, Anna *Drustan the Wanderer: a Historical Novel Based on the Legend of Tristan and Yseult*. London 1971. Uses Malory's French sources and modern archaeological evidence.

Phillips, Douglas 'Merlin's Town' in *Beyond the Frontier*. London 1972. A poem about Carmarthen and the legend of Merlin's oak.

Ashe, Geoffrey *The Finger and the Moon*. London 1973. Part science fiction, part occult novel set in Glastonbury, but with little Arthurian content.

Heath-Stubbs, John *Artorius*. London 1974. A poem in twelve parts.

Arden, John, and **Margaretta D'Arcy** *The Island of the Mighty*. London 1974. A play which attempts to blend myth, history and modern political comment.

Jones, David (1937) *The Sleeping Lord*, 1974.

Viney, J. *Bright-helmed One*. London 1975. A story in three parts, told from the point of view of three different characters.

Canning, Victor *The Crimson Chalice*. London 1976.

      The Circle of the Gods. London 1977.

The Immortal Wound. London 1978.

All three republished as a trilogy, *The Crimson Chalice*, in one volume. London 1980.

Price, Anthony *Our Man in Camelot*. London 1975. A modern mystery story with an Arthurian thread running through it.

Hughes, Ian 'Marchlyn' in *Slate*. London 1977. A poem on the industrial exploitation of Wales, first published in the Anglo-Welsh review.

Chapman, Graham, and **Terry Jones, Terry Gilliam, Michael Palin, Eric Idle** and **John Cleese** *Monty Python and the Holy Grail*. London 1977. 'A first draft' for the film of the same name.

White, T. H. (1938) *The Book of Merlyn*, 1977.

Christian, Catherine *The Sword and the Flame*. London 1978. Republished as *The Pendragon*, London 1979.

Hunter, Jim *Percival and the Presence of God*. London 1978.

Nye, Robert *Merlin*. London 1978.

Smith, Ken *Tristan Crazy*. Newcastle-on-Tyne 1978. Ten poems on the theme of Tristan and Iseult.

Vansittart, Peter *Lancelot*. London 1978.

1980 **Norman, Diana** *King of the Last Days*. London 1981. A romance of the twelfth century, in which the monks of Glastonbury find Arthur's grave and try to send Excalibur (previously buried with him) to Henry II.

II. AMERICAN AUTHORS

1820 **Wilmer, Lambert A.** *Merlin*. In *North American* (Baltimore), 1 (Aug. 18 and 25, Sept. 1, 1827). Reissued immediately in pamphlet form by *The North American*. Repr. New York, 1941. A poetic drama of the life of Edgar Allan Poe, in which Merlin appears; otherwise not Arthurian.

1840 **Emerson, Ralph Waldo** 'Merlin I and II'. In *Poems*, Boston 1846. 'Merlin's Song'. In *May Day and Other Poems*, London 1867, Boston 1868. They also appear in *Poems*, Centenary edition of *Complete Works*, Vol. 9, Boston 1904.

Lowell, James Russell *The Vision of Sir Launfal*. Cambridge, Mass. 1848.

1870 **Hylton, John** *Arteloise. A Romance of King Arthur and the Knights of the Round Table*. Palmyra, N.J. 1877.

1880 **Young, W. W.** *Arthur Pendragon: A Play in Five Acts*. U.S. copyright April 8, 1880; acted at the Fifth Avenue Theater in New York in 1882, at the Park Theater in Brooklyn in Nov. 1888, and in Philadelphia.

Mitchell, S. Weir 'The Shriving of Guinevere', in *The Hill of Stones and Other Poems*, Boston 1882. Repr. in *Collected Poems*, New York 1896; and in *Selections*, London 1901. Christ, appearing as a white knight, challenges sinless courtiers to cast the first stone at Guinevere. *Collected Poems* also contains 'How Lancelot Came to the Nunnery in Search of the Queen', in which the author follows Malory.

Fawcett, Edgar *The New King Arthur: An Opera without Music*. New York and London, 1885.

Adams, Oscar Fay *Post-Laureate Idylls*. Boston 1886.

Post-Laureate Idylls, Second Series, in *Sicut Patribus and Other Verse* (privately printed) Boston 1906. Clever pastiche of lines from Tennyson, adding new episodes and characters.

Kobbé, Gustav *Merlin: An Opera in Three Acts*. Libretto by Siegfried Lépiner, music by Karl Goldmark; trans. by Gustav Kobbé. U.S. copyright Oct. 23, 1886. Performed at the Metropolitan Opera House, Jan. 1887.

Koopman, Harry L. 'The Death of Guinevere' and 'My Galahad', in *Orestes, a Dramatic Sketch and Other Poems*. Buffalo, New York 1888. Based on Tennyson.

Lathrop, George P.   *Elaine.* A play performed on May 14, 1888 at the Park Theater, Boston.

Cawein, Madison J.   *Accolon of Gaul with Other Poems.* Louisville, 1889. The title poem tells the story of Accolon, Morgane, and the theft of Excalibur.

Twain, Mark   (Samuel L. Clemens), *A Connecticut Yankee in King Arthur's Court.* New York and London, 1889. Some parts of the story were printed in *The Century,* XXXIX. Also published as *A Yankee at the Court of King Arthur,* London 1889.

1890   **Eytinge, Pearl**   *Vivien: A Play in Four Acts.* New York 1891.

Neilson, Frederick Brooke   *King Arthur and ye Knights of ye Table Rounde: or The Women in Gray, A Burlesque.* Philadelphia 1894. A burlesque written for performance by the Mask and Wig Club, University of Pennsylvania, 1894.

Miller, Emily C. H.   'From Avalon'. In *From Avalon and Other Poems,* Chicago 1896.

Hovey, Richard   'Launcelot and Gawaine', dated 1888, printed in *The Bookman* VI (Nov. 1897) and repr. in *Along the Trail: A Book of Lyrics,* Boston 1898.

'The Last Love of Gawaine', July 1898, in *The Bookman* VIII (Dec. 1898) and repr. in *To the End of the Trail,* New York 1908.

Launcelot and Guenevere: A Poem in Dramas (later printed as *The Quest of Merlin* and *The Marriage of Guenevere.*) New York and London 1891.

The Marriage of Guenevere: A Tragedy. Chicago 1895.

Taliesin. In *Poet-Lore* (1896), republished as *Taliesin: A Masque,* Boston 1899.

The Quest of Merlin: A Masque. Boston 1898.

The Birth of Galahad: A Romantic Drama. Boston 1898.

The Holy Grail and Other Fragments. Being the Uncompleted Parts of the Arthurian Dramas. New York 1907.

348

Babcock, William H. *Cian of the Chariots: A Romance of the Days of Arthur, Emperor of Britain, and his Knights of the Round Table; how they delivered London and overthrew the Saxons after the fall of Roman Britain.* Illus. by G. F. Barnes. Boston 1898.

Edwardson, E. *The Courteous Knight and Other Tales Borrowed from Spenser and Malory.* New York 1899.

Hall, John Leslie 'Cerdic and Arthur'. In *Old English Idyls*, Boston 1899. A poem imitative of Old English verse.

1900 Palfrey, Sara Hammond *King Arthur in Avalon and Other Poems.* Boston 1900.

Greenslet, Ferris *The Quest of the Holy Grail. An Interpretation and a Paraphrase of the Holy Legends . . . With Illustrations from the Frieze Decoration in the Boston Public Library by Edwin Austin Abbey, R.A.* Boston 1902. Galahad is the hero of adventures usually associated with Percival.

Pallen, Condé Benoist *The Death of Sir Launcelot and Other Poems.* Boston 1902. The title-poem was repr. in *Collected Poems*, New York 1916. Recounts the final events in Malory and ends with Launcelot's vision of the Celestial City.

Deeping, (George) Warwick *Uther and Igraine.* New York 1902; London 1928. A novel. Invents a new love story for Arthur's parents.

Love Among the Ruins, London and New York, 1904. A romance with an Arthurian atmosphere, but rather indefinite as to place and time.

The Man Who Went Back, London and New York, 1940. A novel about an Englishman who went back from the Second World War to the time of Gildas and Ambrosius and the Saxon invasions.

Lewis, Charlton M. *Gawayne and the Green Knight: A Fairy Tale.* New Haven 1903. A comic retelling in couplets which adds a sweetheart for Gawain.

Anspacher, Louis K. *Tristan and Isolde: A Tragedy.* New York 1904. Five act play in blank verse. Generally follows Wagner.

Baxter, Sylvester *The Legend of the Holy Grail as set forth in the Frieze painted by Edwin A. Abbey for the Boston Public Library.* Boston 1904.

Austin, Martha W. *Tristram and Isoult*. Boston 1905. A blank verse dramatic poem incorporating both traditional versions of Tristram's death.

Young, Stark *Guenevere: A Play in Five Acts*. New York 1906.

Conway, John William *Lancelot and Guinevere: A Drama in Five Acts*, 1907. U.S. copyright Dec. 12, 1903; printed copies deposited Dec. 7, 1907, but apparently it was not regularly published.

Mumford, Ethel W. *Merlin and Vivian: a Lyric Drama*. Music by Henry Kimball Hadley. New York 1907.

Newell, William W. *Isolt's Return. With Celtic designs by Marion L. Peabody*. Wayland, Mass., 1907. A poem.

Southworth, May E. *Galahad, Knight Errant*. Boston 1907. Repr. 1923.

Field, Eugene 'A Proper Trewe Idyll of Camelot'. In *A Little Book of Western Verse*. New York 1907. Repr. in *Poems*, New York 1910. Imitating Chaucerian language and using the Pied Piper motif, the poem criticises liquor and is set in Arthur's court.

Sterling, Sara H. *A Lady of King Arthur's Court: Being a Romance of the Holy Grail*. Pictured by Clara Elsene Peck. Philadelphia 1907; London 1909. A novel.

Hunt, Enid Leigh (Mrs D. E. Thornton), *The Advent of Arthur*. London and New York, 1908.

Jones, Thomas Samuel Jr. 'Joyous Garde' in *Interludes*, Clinton, New York 1908, and also in *Sonnets* and *The Rose Jar*, both of 1909. Jones wrote a number of Arthurian sonnets, all eventually published with the slightly longer 'Merlin's Cave' in *Shadow of the Perfect Rose* (collected poems), New York 1937.

Cram, Ralph A. *Excalibur: An Arthurian Drama*. Boston 1909. Written in 1893, as part of a trilogy which was never finished.

Hovey, Richard (1897) *The Holy Grail and Other Fragments*, 1907.

1910 **Taylor, Bert Leston** ('B.L.T.'), 'Bread Puddynge'. In *A Line-o'-Verse or Two*, Chicago ?1911. Repr. as Part II of the 2nd edition of *Motley Measures*, New York 1927.

Teasdale, Sara 'Guenevere' in *Helen of Troy and Other Poems*. New York and London, 1911. Reprinted in *Collected Poems*, New York 1937. 'At Tintagil' in *Dark of the Moon*, New York 1926, and in *Collected Poems*.

Yeames, Rev. James *Sir Gawain and the Green Knight: Play in Five Acts*. Detroit 1911. Based on Jessie Weston's version of *Gawain and the Green Knight*.

Carpenter, Rhys *The Tragedy of Etarre: A Poem*. New York 1912; London 1914. A dramatic poem in four acts and a prologue, from Book IV of Malory, with the innovation that Pelleas forgives Etarre and Gawaine.

Gould, Gerald 'Lancelot and Guinevere', in Burton E. Stevenson's *Home Book of Verse*. New York 1912. Short poem.

Heard, John Jr. *Tristram the Jester, A Play in Five Acts from the German of Ernest Hardt*. Boston 1913. This follows the original rather closely. A new version, keeping the general structure of the original version but with the third act greatly changed, later appeared in *Poet-Lore* XLIII (1936).

Merrington, Marguerite 'The Testing of Sir Gawayne: All Hallowe'en Play on the Arthurian Legend.' In *Festival Plays*, New York 1913.

Noyes, Alfred 'Riddles of Merlin', in *Collected Poems*, III. New York 1913.

Riley, James Whitcomb 'Guinevere', in *Complete Works* II, 146. Indianapolis 1913.

Tatum, Mrs Edith 'The Awakening of Iseult', in *Neale's Monthly*, II (Aug. 1913). Repr. in book form by Oglethorpe University Press, 1933. A prose story.

Tarkington, Booth. *Penrod*. New York 1914. A humorous novel about a boy in an Arthurian pageant.

Hooker, Brian *Morven and the Grail*. Oratorio, with music by Horatio Parker (Opus 79). Vocal score. Boston 1915. Written and composed for the Centenary Festival of the Handel and Haydn Society of Boston, April 1915.

Guthrie, Kenneth Sylvan   *Peronik the Innocent: or the Quest of the Golden Basin and the Diamond Lance*. Brooklyn 1915.

Dell, Floyd   *King Arthur's Socks: A Comedy*. In *Provincetown Plays, First Series*. New York 1916. Repr. in *King Arthur's Socks and Other Village Plays*, 1922. First produced in New York City by the Provincetown Players; a play of modern times about the love triangle involving a professor named Arthur, his wife Guenevere, and their friend Vivien.

Masters, Edgar Lee   *Songs and Satires*. New York 1916. Contains the 'Ballad of Launcelot and Elaine' and 'The Death of Launcelot'.

Reynolds, Marion Lee   *Geraint of Devon*. Boston 1916.

Graves, Alfred Percival   'The Coming of Sir Galahad and a Vision of the Grail', in *A Celtic Psaltery*. New York and London, 1917. A poem.

Robinson, Edwin Arlington   *Merlin: A Poem*. New York 1917. Repr. in *Collected Poems*, New York 1921, and in the enlarged edition of the *Poems* of 1937.

Lancelot: A Poem. Special edition of 450 copies for the Lyric Society, New York 1920. Repr. in *Collected Poems* of 1921 and 1937.

Tristram. New York 1927. Repr. in *Collected Poems* of 1937.

Modred: A Fragment. New York and New Haven 1929.

Lowe, Samuel E.   *In the Court of King Arthur*. Racine, Wis., 1918.

Cabell, James B.   *Jurgen. A Comedy of Justice*. New York 1919; London 1921.

'To Sir Galahad of the Siege Perilous' in *Ladies and Gentlemen: A Parcel of Reconsiderations*, New York 1934.

Tucker, Irwin St John   *The Sangreal: A Play in Four Acts*. Chicago 1919. Acted by the Cathedral Players of Chicago at St Luke's Parish House in Advent, 1922.

1920   **Chubb, Thomas Caldecott**   'Merlin', in *The White God and Other Poems*, New Haven 1920.

Robinson, Edwin Arlington (1917)   *Lancelot: A Poem*, 1920; *Tristram*, 1927; *Modred: A Fragment*, 1929.

Broun, Heywood 'The Fifty-first Dragon'. In Christopher Morley's *Modern Essays* (First Series). New York 1921. Repr. with drawings by Richard Decker in *The Golden Book*, XIII (May 1931), and in *Collected Edition of Heywood Broun*, New York 1941. A short story of Gawaine at the Knight-School.

McCloskey, George V. A. *The Flight of Guinevere and Other Poems*. New York 1921. Title poem in three parts records Arthur's disillusionment, Guinevere's renunciation, and Lancelot's sorrow. Second edition (1928) includes 'Nimue to Merlin', an invitation to join her in an 'embowered citadel'.

Millay, Edna St Vincent 'Elaine' in *Second April*, New York 1921. The first, untitled, sonnet in the volume alludes to Isolde and Guinevere.

Graff, Irvine *The Return of Arthur*. Boston 1922. A ballad in which Arthur returns as Lord Kitchener.

Marquis, Don (Robert Perry), *Sonnets to a Red-Haired Lady and Famous Love Affairs*. Garden City 1922. Contains a poem on Merlin.

'Tristram and Isolt', in Burton E. Stevenson's *Home Book of Modern Verse*. New York 1925.

'King O'Meara and Queen Guinevere', in *Sat. Eve. Post*, CCII, 37 (March 15th and 22nd, 1930).

O'Donnell, Charles L. 'Launcelot's Song', in *Cloister and Other Poems*. New York 1922; London 1923. A short poem.

Hayes, James Juvenal *Sir Kay, A Poem in the Old Style*. Sioux City, Iowa 1923.

Lindsay, (Nicholas) Vachel 'Galahad, Knight Who Perished' and 'King Arthur's Men Have Come Again', in *Collected Poems*. New York 1923.

Lyman, Dean Belden Jr. 'To Launcelot and the Rest', in *The Last Lutanist and Other Poems*. New Haven 1923.

Wodehouse, P. G. 'Sir Agravaine. A Blithesome and Knightly Tale. Throwing New Light upon the Mystery of Affinities.' Illustrated by J. H. Hammer. In *Chicago American*, July 8, 1923.

Auslander, Joseph 'Yseult' in *Sunrise Trumpets*. New York 1924.

Horton, Douglas *A Legend of the Grail. To Be Played or Read in the Season of Easter or Christmas*. Boston and Chicago 1925. Acted by the McKinley Mimes of the McKinley Memorial Presbyterian Church of Champaign, Illinois, on April 10, 1927.

Bishop, Farnham and Arthur Gilchrist Brodeur *The Altar of the Legion*. Illustrations by Henry Pitz. Boston 1926. A novel of Owain ap Urien and his Ravens, just after the death of Arthur. The introduction contains a poem, 'The Lost Land', which is slightly Arthurian.

Erskine, John *Galahad: Enough of His Life to Explain His Reputation*. Indianapolis 1926; London 1926. A novel.

Tristan and Isolde: Restoring Palamede. Indianapolis 1932 and London 1939.

Seven Tales from King Arthur's Court. Paintings by Dulac. In *American Weekly*, Feb. 4, 1940 to March 17, 1940.

Taft, Linwood *Galahad: A Pageant of the Holy Grail*. (Pageants with a Purpose) New York 1926.

Gerhardie, William 'Tristan and Isolde' in *Pretty Creatures*. New York and London, 1927. Short story; a modern love-affair between an American and an Austrian girl which makes frequent allusions to the Tristan story.

Bradley, Will *Launcelot and the Ladies*. New York 1927. Parallels a modern love story with the Launcelot-Guinevere-Elaine triangle; combines Malory's two Elaines.

Fields, Herbert, with Lorenz Hart and Richard Rogers *A Connecticut Yankee at King Arthur's Court*. Song and dance play in two acts with prologue and epilogue. Based on Mark Twain's novel. Acted in New York at the Vanderbilt Theater in Nov. 1927, and in Chicago at the Garrick Theater in March 1929. New version acted at Martin Beck Theater in New York, Nov. 1943.

Dalmon, Charles 'Camelot'. In *Twentieth-Century Poetry*, ed. J. Drinkwater, H. S. Canby and W. R. Benet. Cambridge, Mass. 1929. A short poem.

Royle, Edwin M. *Launcelot and Elaine*. New York 1929. A play in four acts and a prologue. Acted at the Greenwich Village Theatre in 1921 and at the McCarter Theatre in Princeton in March 1930.

1930 **Davis, Georgene** *The Round Table: A History Drawn from Unreliable Chronicles*. Rutland, Vermont 1930. A drama in two acts and an epilogue.

Furst, Clyde B. *Merlin*. New York 1930. A blank verse poem.

Hanemann, H. W. 'Ex-Caliber, or a Square Peg in a Round Table. Dr Collins takes a Good Look at King Arthur.' Section VIII in *The Facts of Life. A Book of Brighter Biography Executed in the Manner of some of our Best or Best-Known Writers, Scriveners, and Scribes*. New York 1930.

Hare, Amory (Mrs James Pemberton Hutchinson), *Tristram and Iseult: A Play*. With illustrations by Wharton Esherick. Gaylordsville, Conn., 1930.

Manley, William Ford *Sir Gawain and the Green Knight: adapted for radio*. (American School of the Air.) U.S. copyright, Feb. 9, 1931.

Parker, Dorothy 'Guinevere at her Fireside'. In *Deaths and Taxes*, New York 1931.

Erskine, John (1926) *Tristran and Isolde: Restoring Palamede*, 1932.

Kaplan, Freda and **Parker Wheatley** *King Arthur and his Knights of the Table Round*. Episode 1. A radio sketch. U.S. copyright Sept. 24, 1932.

Reed, Stanley Baird *Merlin, Maestro of Magic*. Episodes 1–9, a series of radio dramas. U.S. copyright July 15, 1932.

Taylor, David ('Dave'), *King Arthur and the Knights of the Round Table*. Episodes 1 and 2. A radio programme: American Radio Features Syndicate, Los Angeles. U.S. copyright, Nov. 7, 1933.

Butts, W. Marlin *The Youth of King Arthur: A Legendary Play in Five Scenes*. East Boston, Mass., 1935. A play for men or boys, originally produced at Camp Camelot, Foxboro, Mass.

Steinbeck, John *Tortilla Flat*. New York 1935. Not at first sight Arthurian, but the author likened the house and friends of his hero to the Round Table and its knights in his Preface to the work, and appears to have intended to follow an Arthurian theme.

The Acts of King Arthur and his Noble Knights, New York 1976. A modern English version of sections of the Winchester *Morte Darthur*.

Sheehan, Perley Poore *King Arthur: a Screen Play adapted . . . from the Arthurian Cycle of Legends in Le Morte d'Arthur, by Sir Thomas Malory.* Los Angeles 1936.

Ward, Christopher *Sir Galahad and Other Rimes. Pass-Keys to the Classics.* Illustrated by Richard Taylor. New York 1936. A number of burlesque poems.

Chase, Mary Ellen *Dawn in Lyonesse.* New York 1938. Relates the experiences of a twentieth-century waitress in Tintagil to the Tristan story.

A Candle at Night. In *Collier's*, May 9, 1942. Sequel to the above.

De Casseres, Benjamin *Sir Galahad: Knight of the Lidless Eye.* New York 1938.

1940 **Erskine, John** (1926) *Seven Tales from King Arthur's Court* (1940).

Fuller, John G. *A Connecticut Yankee in King Arthur's Court: A Comedy in Three Acts Based on Mark Twain's Book of the Same Title.* Boston and Los Angeles, 1941. The Yankee is an engineer just out of college, who travels back to Arthur's court.

Kennedy, Charles Rann *The Seventh Trumpet.* (A Repertory of Plays for a Company of Seven Players, VII.) New York 1942. Play of the Second World War, about 'The glorious recovery of (Glastonbury's) Holy Grail.' Acted at the Mansfield Theater, New York, Nov. 1941.

MacLeish, Archibald Fleming *The Destroyers.* New York 1942. A three-act play.

Chase, Mary Ellen (1938) *A Candle at Night*, 1942.

Percy, William Alexander 'The Green Bird Seeth Iseult' and 'A Brittany Idyll' in *Collected Poems*. New York 1943. A bird describes the drinking of the love-potion; in the 'idyll' a peasant girl compares herself to Iseult of Brittany awaiting her lover.

Foster, Harold R. 'Prince Valiant in the Days of King Arthur', in *Comic Weekly* of *Chicago Herald American*, *New York Journal American*, *Boston Herald*, and other papers. A comic strip in which Arthurian characters sometimes appear. Dates uncertain.

Toynbee, Philip   *Prothalamium.* New York 1947. 'A Cycle of the Holy Grail'.

Aycrigg, Ben   *In the Days of King Arthur.* Presented by Station WDBO, Orlando, Fla., May 1948. Arthur's battle with Accolon, taken from Malory.

Merlin the Magician. Presented by Station WDBO, Jan. 21, 1950. Morgan reveals the theft of Arthur's scabbard by Morgan le Fay.

The Pursuit of Morgan le Fay. Presented by Station WDBO, Jan. 27, 1950.

MacCormac, John   'The Enchanted Week-End'. In *From Unknown Worlds.* New York 1948. A novelette of modern times, introducing Merlin.

Tax, Ervin H.   *The Wraith of Gawain.* Prairie City, Ill., 1948. Long poem in eight books.

Sharpe, Ruth Collier   *Tristram of Lyonesse, The Story of an Immortal Love.* With illustrations from original paintings by Richard Sharpe. A novel. New York 1949. An expansive romantic novel in which Tristram and Ysolt of Ireland marry twice and finally achieve happiness.

1950   **Winters, Yvor**   'Sir Gawaine and the Green Knight' in *Collected Poems.* New York 1952. Short poem.

Roberts, Dorothy James   *The Enchanted Cup.* New York 1953.

Launcelot My Brother. New York 1954.

Kinsmen of the Grail. New York 1963.

The first of these novels is a straightforward retelling of the Tristram legend; the second is concerned with the end of the Round Table. All are based on Malory.

Garrett, Erwin Clarkson   *Arcturus and Other Verses.* Philadelphia 1954.

Borowsky, M.   *Queen's Knight.* New York 1955. A romance which represents Arthur as a country bumpkin in a vaguely medieval setting.

357

Pound, Ezra *Cantos*. No. XCI, first published in 1955, contains some Middle English references to Merlin.

Marshall, E. *Pagan King*. New York 1959. A Celtic Arthur tells his own story.

Wibberley, L. *Quest of Excalibur*. New York 1959. The ghost of King Arthur returns to England.

Roberts, Dorothy James (1953) *Kinsmen of the Grail*, 1963.

1960 **Seton, Anya** *Avalon*. Boston 1965. A novel with minimal Arthurian reference.

Saul, George Brandon 'The Fair Eselt: A Play'. In *Hound and Unicorn: Collected Verse—Lyrical, Narrative and Dramatic*. Philadelphia 1969.

1970 **Laubenthal, Sanders Anne** *Excalibur*. New York 1973. A fantasy novel depicting a descendant of the Welsh Prince Madoc who discovers Excalibur in 20th-century Mobile, Alabama.

Munn, H. Warner *Merlin's Ring*. New York 1974. Fantasy novel including an episode in which Gwalchmai restores Excalibur to Arthur, asleep in Avalon.

Merlin's Godson. New York 1976. Fantasy novel which reprints as Book I an episode, which first appeared in 1939, giving a Roman centurion's account of Arthur's marriage and the Battle of Camlan.

Chapman, Vera *The Green Knight*. New York and London 1975. A free retelling of *Sir Gawain and the Green Knight*, from the Lady's point of view.

King Arthur's Daughter. New York 1976.

The King's Damosel. New York 1976. All three novels were published in one volume as *The Three Damosels* in New York in 1978.

Johnson, Barbara Ferry *Lionors*. New York 1975. The story of Lionors, mother of Arthur's blind son, to the point where she buries the king in Avalon.

Norton, André *Merlin's Mirror*. New York 1975. Science fiction novel, telling an Arthurian story in the context of interplanetary communication.

Steinbeck, John (1935) *The Acts of King Arthur and his Noble Knights*, 1976.

Gloag, John *Artorius Rex*. New York 1977. Novel based on a Romano-British Arthur.

Percy, Walker *Lancelot*. New York 1977. A modern knight-errant in a quest after evil, using the motif of the Grail.

Monaco, Richard *Parsival, or a Knight's Tale*. New York 1977.

The Grail War, New York 1979.

The Final Quest. New York 1980. These novels together constitute a Parsival trilogy.

Berger, Thomas *Arthur Rex: A Legendary Novel*. New York 1978. A comic version of many stories in Malory, as well as other medieval accounts of Tristram, Percival and Gawain.

Drake, David *The Dragon Lord*. New York 1979. About two mercenaries in Arthur's band and a dragon which Merlin conjures to rout the Saxons.

Zelazny, Roger 'The Last Defender of Camelot', in a collection of short stories of the same name, New York 1979. Short story involving Merlin, Launcelot and Morgan le Fay in a science-fiction context.

1980   **Bradshaw, Gillian** *Hawk of May*. New York 1980. Set in the Dark Ages, a novel about Gwalchmai (Gawain) before he joins Arthur's band.

Kingdom of Summer. New York 1981. Continues Gawain's exploits in the war between Darkness and Light.

In Winter's Shadow. Forthcoming, New York. This will continue the series.

Godwin, Parke *Firelord*. New York 1980. Arthur reviews the legend as he lies on his deathbed.

359

Newman, Sharan *Guinevere*. New York 1981. The novel tells the story of Guinevere to her wedding night.

III. ARTHURIAN TEXTS FROM THE BRITISH COMMONWEALTH

Akhurst, William Mower *King Arthur, or Lancelot the Loose*, Melbourne 1868. 'A pantomimic extravaganza and burlesque in punning verse.'

Reade, John *The Prophecy of Merlin and Other Poems*, Montreal 1870.

Campbell, W. W. *Mordred. A Tragedy in Five Acts. Founded on the Arthurian Legend of Sir Thomas Malory.* In *Mordred and Hildebrand: A Book of Tragedies.* Ottawa 1895.

Taylor, T(homas) Hillhouse ('Toso Taylor'), *Parsifal: a Romantic 'Mystery' Drama.* Sydney 1906.

Bartlett, Gertrude (Mrs John W. C. Taylor), 'Ballade of Tristram's Last Harping'. In John W. Garvin's *Canadian Poets and Poetry*, New York 1916.

Collin, William Edwin *Monserrat and Other Poems.* Toronto 1930.

Brewer, George M. *The Holy Grail: A Whitsuntide Mystery of the Quest of the Soul. Founded on Ancient Legends derived from Various Sources.* Montreal 1933.

Badger, John D'Arcy *The Arthuriad*, Toronto 1972. Fifty-six sonnets on the return of Arthur; 'a major new contribution to ideology . . . a futurist radical-centrist interpretation of history and culture'.

AUTHOR-INDEX TO CHRONOLOGICAL LIST

References are to country and decade of publication.

A: United States of America
B: British Isles
C: British Commonwealth

Adams, Oscar Fay **A.1880**
Akhurst, William Mower **C.1860**
Ankenbrand, F. **B.1910**
Anonymous **B.1830, B.1850, B.1870, B.1910**
Anspacher, Louis K. **A.1900**
Arden, John and D'Arcy, Margaretta **B.1970**
Arnold, Matthew **B.1850**
Ashe, Geoffrey **B.1970**
Auslander, Joseph **A.1920**
Austin, Martha W. **A.1900**
Aycrigg, Ben **A.1940**
Babcock, William H. **A.1890**
Badger, John D'Arcy **C.1970**
Bailey, C. W. **B.1920**
Baird, Edward **B.1940**
Baring, Maurice **B.1910**
Bartlett, Gertrude (Mrs John W. C. Taylor) **C.1910**
Baxter, Sylvester **A.1900**
Bell, Harold Idris **B.1910**
Berger, Thomas **A.1970**
Berry, Charles Walter **B.1920**
Bidder, George **B.1890**
Binyon, Robert Laurence **B.1890**
Bishop, Farnham, and Brodeur, Arthur Gilchrist **A.1920**
Bond, Frederick Bligh **B.1920**
Borowsky, M. **A.1950**
Boss, Eleanor **B.1930**
Bottomley, Gordon **B.1920**
Boughton, Rutland, and Buckley, R. R. **B.1910**
Boyd, Eric Forbes **B.1920**
Bradley, Will **A.1920**
Bradshaw, Gillian **A.1980**
Brewer, George M. **C.1930**
Bridie, James (Osborne Henry Mavor) **B.1940**
Brooks, Benjamin Gilbert **B.1910**
Brough, William **B.1860**
Broun, Heywood **A.1920**
Bruce, C. (Sir Charles) **B.1860**
Brumm, Charles **B.1920**

Buchanan, Robert, D. D. **B.1950**
Butts, W. Marlin **A.1930**
Cabell, James B. **A.1910**
Cammell, Charles Richard **B.1940**
Campbell, W. W. **C.1890**
Canning, Victor **B.1970**
Carpenter, Rhys **A.1910**
Carr, Francis (Prince, Aelian) **B.1890**
Carr, J. Comyns **B.1890**
Cawein, Madison J. **A.1880**
Chapman, Graham (and Terry Jones, John Cleese et al.) **B.1970**
Chapman, Vera **A.1970**
Chase, Mary Ellen **A.1930**
Chester, Norley (Emily Underdown) **B.1900**
Chesterton, Gilbert Keith **B.1930**
Christian, Catherine **B.1970**
Chubb, Thomas Caldecott **A.1920**
Cloriston, Henry **B.1900**
Closs, Hannah Priebach **B.1940**
Collin, William Edwin **C.1930**
Conway, John William **A.1900**
Costain, T. B. **B.1950**
Coutts, Francis (Francis Burdett Coutts Nevill, Baron Latymer) **B.1890**
Craik, Dinah Maria Mulock **B.1850**
Cram, Ralph A. **A.1900**
Croskey, Julian **B.1890**
Dalmon, Charles **A.1920**
Dane, Clemence (Winnifred Ashton) **B.1940**
Davidson, John **B.1890**
Davis, Georgene **A.1930**
Dawson, Coningsby **B.1910**
De Beverley, Thomas (George Newcomen) **B.1920**
De Casseres, Benjamin **A.1930**
Deeping, (George) Warwick **A.1900**
Dell, Floyd **A.1910**
Dempster, Charlotte Louise **B.1870**
De Vere, Aubrey **B.1890**
Dillon, Arthur **B.1900**
Ditmas, E. M. R. **B.1950**
Douglas, Christiana Jane **B.1870**

Doyle, Arthur Conan **B.1910**
Drake, David **A.1970**
Duggan, Arthur **B.1950**
Du Maurier, George **B.1890**
Earle, Arthur W., and Sim,
 E. Howley **B.1890**
Edwards, Zachary **B.1900**
Edwardson, E. **A.1890**
Eliot, T. S. **B.1920**
Ellis, Thomas Evelyn (8th Baron Howard de
 Walden) **B.1900**
Emerson, Ralph Waldo **A.1840**
Emma, Cyril **B.1900**
Erskine, John **A.1920**
Evans, Sebastian **B.1870**
Eytinge, Pearl **A.1890**
Faraday, Wilfred Barnard **B.1930**
Fawcett, Edgar **A.1880**
Field, Eugene **A.1900**
Field, Michael (Katherine Harris Bradley and
 Edith Emma Cooper) **B.1910**
Fields, Herbert (with Lorenz Hart and
 Richard Rogers) **A.1920**
Foster, Harold R. **A.1940**
Frankland, Edward **B.1940**
Frere, John Hookham **B.1810**
Fry, Christopher **B.1940**
Fullarton, Ralph Macleod **B.1880**
Fuller, John G. **A.1940**
Furst, Clyde B. **B.1930**
Galloway, C. F. J. **B.1920**
Garrett, Erwin Clarkson **A.1950**
Gerhardie, William **A.1920**
Gillespy, Charlotte Ainsley **B.1910**
Glasscock, F. T. **B.1920**
Glennie, John Stuart Stuart **B.1860**
Gloag, John **A.1970**
Glynn, Elinor **B.1910**
Godwin, Parke **A.1980**
Goodchild, John Arthur **B.1910**
Gordon, Adam Lindsay **B.1860**
Gosse, Edmund **B.1870**
Gould, Gerald **A.1910**
Graff, Irvine **A.1920**
Graves, Alfred Percival **A.1910**
Greenslet, Ferris **A.1900**
Guthrie, Kenneth Sylvan **A.1910**
Hall, John Leslie **A.1890**
Hamilton (Lord), Ernest William **B.1920**
Hanemann, H. W. **A.1930**
Hardy, Thomas **B.1870**
Hare, Amory (Mrs James Pemberton
 Hutchinson) **A.1930**
Hawker, Robert Stephen **B.1860**
Hayes, James Juvenal **A.1920**
Heard, John Jr. **A.1910**
Hearne, Isabel **B.1910**
Heath-Stubbs, John **B.1970**
Heber, Reginald **B.1840**

Hemans, Mrs Felicia **B.1820**
Henry, Richard **B.1880**
Hewlett, Maurice **B.1900**
Hill, Geoffrey **B.1950**
Hill, Graham **B.1900**
Hilton, B. H. **B.1880**
Hollins, Dorothea **B.1910**
Hooker, Brian **A.1910**
Horne, Richard Henry (Hengist) **B.1840**
Horton, Douglas **A.1920**
Housman, Clemence **B.1900**
Hovey, Richard **A.1890**
Howard, Newman **B.1910**
Hughes, Ian **B.1970**
Hunt, Enid Leigh (Mrs D. E.
 Thornton) **A.1900**
Hunter, Jim **B.1970**
Hylton, John **A.1870**
James, Edwin Stanley **B.1920**
Jenkins, John **B.1870**
Johnson, Barbara **A.1970**
Jones, David **B.1930**
Jones, F. H. **B.1930**
Jones, Thomas Samuel Jr. **A.1900**
Joyce, James Augustus Aloysius **B.1930**
Kaplan, Freda, and Wheatley, Parker
 A.1930
Keith, Chester **B.1920**
Kendon, Frank **B.1930**
Kennedy, Charles Rann **A.1940**
King, Baragwanath **B.1920**
Kinross, Martha **B.1910**
Kobbé, Gustav **A.1880**
Koopman, Harry **A.1880**
Lang, Andrew **B.1860**
Lang, M. R. **B.1900**
Lathrop, George P. **A.1880**
Laubenthal, Sanders Anne **A.1970**
Lee, Thomas Herbert **B.1900**
Leslie, Vera **B.1900**
Levey, Sivori **B.1920**
Lewis, Charlton M. **A.1900**
Lewis, Clive Staples **B.1940**
Lindsay, (Nicholas) Vachel **A.1920**
Lindsay, Philip **B.1930**
Lounsbury, G. Constant **B.1900**
Lowe, Samuel E. **A.1910**
Lowell, James Russell **A.1840**
Lyman, Dean Belden Jr. **A.1920**
Lytton, Edward George, Earl Lytton Bulwer-
 Lytton **B.1840**
McCloskey, George V. A. **A.1920**
MacCormac, John **A.1940**
Macdonald, George **B.1890**
Machen (formerly Jones), Arthur **B.1910**
Macleod, Fiona (pseud. for William
 Sharp) **B.1920**
MacLeish, Archibald Flemming **A.1940**
Manley, William Ford **A.1930**

362

Manning, Frederic **B.1910**
Marquis, Don (Robert Perry) **A.1920**
Marshall, E. **A.1950**
Masefield, John **B.1920**
Masters, Edgar Lee **A.1910**
Menteath, Dora Stuart **B.1890**
Meredith, Owen (Edward Robert Bulwer-
Lytton) **B.1850**
Merrington, Marguerite **A.1910**
Meyerstein, Edward H. W. **B.1920**
Millard, Frederick **B.1870**
Millay, Edna St Vincent **A.1920**
Miller, Emily C. H. **A.1890**
Milman, H. H. **B.1810**
Mitchell, D. M. **B.1920**
Mitchell, S. Weir **A.1880**
Mitchison, Naomi **B.1950**
Monaco, Richard **A.1970**
Moore, George **B.1920**
Morgan, Charles **B.1930**
Morgan, Richard William **B.1860**
Morris, William **B.1850**
Muir, Edwin **B.1920**
Mumford, Ethel W. **A.1900**
Munn, H. Warner **A.1970**
Neilson, Frederick Brooke **A.1890**
Newbolt, Sir Henry **B.1890**
Newell, William W. **A.1900**
Newman, Sharan **A.1980**
Newson, Ranald **B.1930**
Noel, Roden **B.1900**
Norman, Diana **B.1980**
Norton, André **A.1970**
Noyes, Alfred **A.1910**
Nye, Robert **B.1970**
O'Donnell, Charles L. **A.1920**
O'Hara, Kane **B.1800**
Ormerod, James **B.1920**
Padmore, E. S. **B.1930**
Palfrey, Sara Hammond **A.1900**
Pallen, Condé Benoist **A.1900**
Parker, Dorothy **A.1930**
Paul, Evelyn **B.1920**
Peacock, Thomas Love **B.1810**
Percy, Walker **A.1970**
Percy, William Alexander **A.1940**
Peters, Elizabeth **B.1960**
Philibin, An (John Hacket Pollock) **B.1920**
Phillips, Douglas **B.1970**
Pomeroy, Florence M. **B.1950**
Porteous, Frances **B.1960**
Pound, Ezra **A.1950**
Powys, John Cowper **B.1930**
Price, Anthony **B.1970**
Priestley, J. B. **B.1960**
Prince, Aelian (Francis Carr) **B.1890**
Purnell, Charles William **B.1910**
Reade, John **C.1870**
Reed, Henry **B.1940**

Reynolds, Ernest Randolph **B.1930**
Reynolds, Marion Lee **A.1910**
Rhys, Ernest **B.1890**
Riethmuller, Christopher J. **B.1840**
Riley, James W. **A.1910**
Roberts, Dorothy James **A.1950**
Robinson, Edwin Arlington **A.1910**
Rope, H. E. G. **B.1920**
Rossetti, Dante Gabriel **B.1870**
Royle, Edwin M. **A.1920**
Ryan, W. P. **B.1930**
Saul, George Brandon **A.1960**
Scott, Sir Walter **B.1810**
Senior, Dorothy **B.1900**
Seton, Anya **A.1960**
Seymour, Alan **B.1920**
Sharpe, Ruth Collier **A.1940**
Sheehan, Perley Poore **A.1930**
Sheriff, R. C. **B.1950**
Shorthouse, J. Henry **B.1880**
Simcox, George Augustus **B.1860**
Skinner, Martyn **B.1950**
Smith, Arthur Saxon Dennett **B.1950**
Smith, Ken **B.1970**
Southworth, May E. **A.1900**
Sproston, S. **B.1910**
Steinbeck, John **A.1930**
Sterling, Sara H. **A.1900**
Stevens, Stanley **B.1890**
Stevenson, Francis Seymour **B.1920**
Stewart, Mary **B.1970**
Steynor, Morley **B.1900**
Sutcliff, Rosemary **B.1960**
Sweetman, Elinor **B.1890**
Swinburne, Algernon Charles **B.1850**
Symons, Arthur **B.1910**
Taft, Linwood **A.1920**
Tarkington, Booth **A.1910**
Tatum, Mrs Edith **A.1910**
Tax, Ervin H. **A.1940**
Taylor, Anna **B.1970**
Taylor, Bert Leston (B.L.T.) **A.1910**
Taylor, David ('Dave') **A.1930**
Taylor, T(homas) Hillhouse ('Toso
Taylor') **C.1900**
Teasdale, Sara **A.1910**
Tennyson, Alfred **B.1830**
Thelwall, John **B.1800**
Thomas, Edward **B.1920**
Thompson, Francis **B.1960**
Todhunter, John **B.1920**
Toynbee, Philip **A.1940**
Treece, Henry **B.1950**
Trevelyan, Robert C. **B.1900**
Tucker, Irwin St John **A.1910**
Turnbull, E. Lucia and H. Dalwey
Turnbull **B.1930**
Turton, G. **B.1960**
Twain, Mark (Samuel L. Clemens) **A.1880**

Vansittart, Peter **B.1970**
Veitch, John **B.1880**
Vere, D. B. **B.1930**
Viney, J. **B.1970**
Waite, Arthur Edward **B.1920**
Ward, Christopher **A.1930**
Watts, Alaric Alexander **B.1850**
Weston, Jessie L. **B.1890**
Westwood, Thomas **B.1860**
White, Terence Hanbury **B.1930**
Wibberley, L. **A.1950**
Wilbur, Richard **B.1950**
Williams, Antonia **B.1900**
Williams, Charles Walter Stansby **B.1930**
Williams, W. S. G. **B.1920**

Wills, W. G. **B.1890**
Wilmer, Lambert A. **A.1820**
Winters, Yvor **A.1950**
Wodehouse, P. G. **A.1920**
Wordsworth, William **B.1830**
Wright, S. Fowler **B.1920**
Yeames, Rev. James **A.1910**
Yeo, Margaret **B.1910**
Yonge, Charlotte M. **B.1850**
Young, Francis Brett **B.1950**
Young, J. W. ('An Old Harrovian') **B.1860**
Young, Stark **A.1900**
Young, W. W. **A.1880**
Zelazny, Roger **A.1970**

364

Notes

Place of publication is London unless otherwise stated

Prologue
The Nature of the Arthurian Stories

1 All references to Malory are to Caxton's edition of *Le Morte D'Arthur*, by book and chapter, and not to Vinaver's edition of the Winchester manuscript of Malory's *Works*, which was not discovered until 1934.
2 *Memorials of Edward Burne-Jones*. By G.B.-J. 2 vols. (1904) Vol. I, p. 211.
3 See Anne Wilson, *Traditional Romance and Tale: How Stories Mean* (1976) p. 50ff.
4 For those who wish to visit the places associated with Arthur, there is a *Guidebook to Arthurian Britain* by Geoffrey Ashe (1980).
5 The superstition has, of course, attached itself to many other national heroes (including the late John F. Kennedy—see B. A. Rosenberg, 'Kennedy in Camelot: the Arthurian Legend in America', *Western Folklore*, 35 (Jan. 1976), 52–9, and instances have occurred in many different cultures. See R. F. Hobson, *Arthurian Legend and British Mythology* (The King Who Will Return), an essay in Arthurian legend and British mythology (Guild of Pastoral Psychology. Guild Lecture 130) 1965.

1
The Return of Arthur
Nineteenth-Century British Medievalism and Arthurian Tradition

1 On the work and significance of the English antiquarians of the eighteenth century, see Arthur Johnston, *Enchanted Ground: The Study of Medieval Romance in the Eighteenth Century* (1964).
2 Kenneth Clark, *The Gothic Revival: An Essay in the History of Taste*, 3rd ed. (1962), pp. 146–47.
3 A. O. J. Cockshut, *The Achievement of Walter Scott* (New York 1969), p. 90.
4 Letter to Clough, February 1849, *The Letters of Matthew Arnold to Arthur Hugh Clough*, ed. H. F. Lowry (1932), p. 99.
5 Newspaper clipping attached to *Tournaments or, the Days of Chivalry, Its Origin, Nature and Effects*, 1839; in Widener Library, Harvard Univ.; cited by Helene E. Roberts, 'Victorian Medievalism: Revival or Masquerade?' *Browning Institute Studies*, 8 (1980), 25.
6 William J. Fox, review of *Poems, Chiefly Lyrical, 1830*, in *Westminster Review*, 14 (Jan. 1831), 210–24; in *Tennyson: The Critical Heritage*, ed. John D. Jump (1967), p. 23.

7 Hallam Tennyson, *Alfred Lord Tennyson: A Memoir* (1897), I, 453; hereafter cited in the text as *Memoir*.

8 John Sterling, review of *Poems, 1842*, in the *Quarterly Review*, 70 (Sept. 1842), 385–416; in *Tennyson: Critical Heritage*, p. 119.

9 Walter Bagehot, review of *Idylls of the King*, 1859, in the *National Review*, 9 (Oct. 1859), 368–94; in *Tennyson: Critical Heritage*, pp. 225–26.

10 John Ruskin, 'Of Modern Landscape', *Modern Painters*, III, in *The Works of John Ruskin*, V, ed. E. T. Cook and Alexander Wedderburn (1904), 321–22.

11 Letter to Frances Arnold, 17 Dec. 1860, *Letters of Matthew Arnold, 1848–1888*, ed. George W. E. Russell (1896), I, 147.

12 James Knowles, 'Aspects of Tennyson, II: A Personal Reminiscence', *The Nineteenth Century*, 33 (1893), 170.

13 Letter to Richard Watson Dixon, 27 Feb. 1879; in *Tennyson: Critical Heritage*, p. 334.

14 Letter to Elizabeth Barrett, 31 Jan. 1846, *The Letters of Robert Browning and Elizabeth Barrett Barrett, 1845–1846*, ed. Elvan Kintner (Cambridge, Mass. 1969), I, 429.

15 Morse Peckham, 'Historiography and *The Ring and the Book*', *Victorian Poetry*, 6 (1968), 249.

16 Letter to his son Charles, 21 Nov. 1821, *The Letters of Sir Walter Scott*, VII, ed. H. J. C. Grierson (1934), 34.

17 Review of Henry Neale's *The Romance of History: England*, in *Edinburgh Review*, 47 (May 1828), 331–67; in *Scott: The Critical Heritage*, ed. John O. Hayden (New York 1970), p. 309.

18 'Sir Walter Scott', *The Works of Thomas Carlyle*, XXIX (New York 1969), 77–8.

19 'The Diamond Necklace', *Works*, XXVIII, 327.

20 Kathleen Tillotson, 'Tennyson's Serial Poem', *Mid-Victorian Studies*, Geoffrey and Kathleen Tillotson (1965), p. 82.

21 Ibid., p. 96.

22 *Memoir*, II, 128–29; and *The Poems of Tennyson*, ed. Christopher Ricks (1969), p. 1660.

23 See Tom Peete Cross, 'Alfred Tennyson as a Celticist', *Modern Philology*, 18 (1920–21), 485–92; and P. G. Scott, 'Tennyson's Celtic Reading', *Tennyson Research Bulletin*, no. 2 (Nov. 1968), paper 2.

24 Charles Tennyson, *Alfred Tennyson* (New York 1949), pp. 441–42.

25 Lionel Trilling, *Matthew Arnold*, rev. ed. (New York 1949), p. 368.

26 Letter to Edward Burne-Jones, 4 Nov. 1869?, *The Swinburne Letters*, II, ed. Cecil Y. Lang (New Haven 1959), 51.

27 Ibid.; and letter to R. H. Horne, 13 Feb. 1882, *Letters*, IV (1960), 260.

28 Letter to Herbert Hill, 5 Nov. 1852; *Times Literary Supplement*, 19 May 1932; printed in C. B. Tinker and H. F. Lowry, *The Poetry of Matthew Arnold: A Commentary* (1940), p. 109.

29 Sir Walter Scott, review of 'Reliques of Robert Burns', *Quarterly Review*, 1 (1809), 30.

2

Reawakening Tradition

British Literature, 1800–1830

1 On Arthurian literature of the seventeenth and eighteenth centuries, see Roberta F. Brinkley, *Arthurian Legend in the Seventeenth Century*, Johns Hopkins Monographs in Literary History, 3 (New York 1970); and James Douglas Merriman, *The Flower of*

Kings: A Study of the Arthurian Legend in England between 1485 and 1835 (Lawrence, Kansas, 1973).

2 See Wordsworth's note to *The Egyptian Maid*, *The Poetical Works of William Wordsworth*, III, ed. Ernest de Selincourt and Helen Darbishire (Oxford 1946), 232; and *The Keats Circle: Letters and Papers, 1814–1879*, ed. Hyder Rollins, 2nd ed. (Cambridge, Mass., 1965), I, 259.

3 *Table Talk*, 4 Sept. 1833, in *Coleridge's Miscellaneous Criticism*, ed. Thomas M. Raysor (Cambridge, Mass., 1936), p. 429; and 12 May 1830, p. 405.

4 *Selections from the Letters of Robert Southey*, ed. John W. Warter (1856), II, 27; III, 49–50; II, 27.

5 Reply to the editor of the Pall Mall Gazette, *c.* 22 Jan. 1886, in *The Swinburne Letters*, V, ed. Cecil Y. Lang (New Haven 1962), 134.

6 J. G. Lockhart, *Memoirs of Sir Walter Scott*, I (1900), 339; 480.

7 Milman may have read Thelwall's work and referred to it in his preface as the 'modern Poem' which had, like his own, shown characters consulting a Northern deity in the icy infernal regions (Preface).

8 Lockhart, *Memoirs of Scott*, I, 287ff.

9 Ibid., pp. 480, 482. See Arthur Johnston, *Enchanted Ground: The Study of Medieval Romance in the Eighteenth Century* (1964), pp. 190–91.

10 Johnston, p. 180.

11 Lockhart, *Memoirs of Scott*, I, 361.

12 On the ruse of anonymity, see Lockhart, *Memoirs of Scott*, II, 227–28, 257–60.

13 Lockhart, *Memoirs of Scott*, I, 391.

14 Ibid., 381–82.

15 Bartle Frere, 'Memoir of John Hookham Frere', in *The Works of the Right Honourable John Hookham Frere*, I (1874), 166.

16 R. D. Waller, ed., *The Monks and the Giants* (Manchester 1926), p. 35.

17 On the political satire, see Merriman, *Flower of Kings*, p. 257, note 14; on the history, see G. M. Trevelyan, *British History in the 19th Century and After, 1782–1919*, 2nd ed. (New York 1937), pp. 122ff.

18 Bartle Frere, 'Memoir', p. 166.

19 Ibid., p. 170.

20 On Peacock's sources, see Herbert Wright, 'The Associations of Thomas Love Peacock with Wales', *Essays and Studies by Members of the English Association*, 12 (1926), 24–46; and David Gallon, 'Thomas Love Peacock and Wales: Some Suggestions', *Anglo-Welsh Review*, 17 (1968), 125–34.

21 *Calidore and Miscellanea*, ed. Richard Garnett (1891), pp. 19–20; cited in Carl Dawson, *His Fine Wit: A Study of Thomas Love Peacock* (Berkeley 1970), p. 242.

22 *Cambrian Quarterly Magazine*, 1 (April 1829), 231.

23 J. B. Priestley, *The English Comic Characters* (New York 1925).

24 See Lionel Madden, *Thomas Love Peacock* (1967), p. 62; and Dawson, pp. 244–45.

25 *Westminster Review*, 10 (April 1829), 434.

26 'The Four Ages of Poetry', in *Memoirs of Shelley and Other Essays and Reviews*, ed. Howard Mills (New York 1970), p. 125.

27 Letter to R. J. Wilmot, 10 June 1812, in Amelia Heber, *The Life of Reginald Heber* (New York 1830), I, 357.

28 Ibid., p. 476.

29 William Hazlitt, 'My First Acquaintance with Poets', in *The Complete Works of William Hazlitt*, XVII, ed. P. P. Howe (1933), 118.

30 Notes dictated to Isabella Fenwick, reproduced in *The Poetical Works of William Wordsworth*, III, 502.

3
Arthur Redux
British Literature of the Mid-Nineteenth Century

1. Tennyson was twenty-third in Rossetti's list; see G. H. Fleming, *Rossetti and the Pre-Raphaelite Brotherhood* (1967), pp. 78–9.
2. Letter of 1 May 1853, cited in Jack Lindsay, *William Morris: His Life and Work* (1975), p. 50.
3. J. W. Mackail, *The Life of William Morris* (1899; repr. 2 vols. in 1, New York 1968), p. 45.
4. John Sterling, review of *Poems, 1842*, *Quarterly Review*, 70 (Sept. 1842), 385–416; in *Tennyson: The Critical Heritage*, ed. John D. Jump (1967), p. 119.
5. John Wilson Croker, review of *Poems, 1833*, *Quarterly Review*, 49 (April 1833), 81–96; in *Tennyson: Critical Heritage*, p. 71.
6. See Kathleen Tillotson, 'Tennyson's Serial Poem', in Geoffrey and Kathleen Tillotson, *Mid-Victorian Studies* (1965), pp. 82ff.
7. James Anthony Froude, review of *Poems, 1853*, *Westminster Review*, 61 (1 Jan. 1854), 146–59; in *Matthew Arnold, The Poetry: The Critical Heritage*, ed. Carl Dawson (1973), p. 89.
8. See Charles Tennyson, *Alfred Tennyson* (1949), p. 33.
9. Letter of 10 Oct. 1832, cited in Hallam Tennyson, *Materials for the Life of Alfred Tennyson* (4 vols. privately printed, 1895), I, iii; cited (with minor errors) in Kathleen Tillotson, p. 86.
10. Hallam Tennyson, *Alfred Tennyson: A Memoir* (1897), I, 117; subsequently cited as *Memoir* in the text.
11. *The Poems of Tennyson*, ed. Christopher Ricks (1969), p. 354; and *Rossetti Papers, 1862–1870*, ed. William Michael Rossetti (1903), p. 341, cited in Ricks, p. 354.
12. See L. S. Potwin, 'The Source of Tennyson's The Lady of Shalott', *Modern Language Notes*, 17 (1902), 474–77; and D. Laurance Chambers, 'Tennysoniana', *Modern Language Notes*, 18 (1903), 227–28.
13. Journal entry 1813, in *Byron's Letters and Journals*, III, ed. Leslie A. Marchand (Cambridge, Mass. 1974), 220–21.
14. Letter to W. B. Donne, 22 June 1833, cited in Ricks, p. 505.
15. Ibid., pp. 502–03.
16. Richard Garnett, review of *The Defence of Guenevere, and Other Poems (1858)*, *Literary Gazette*, 42 (March 1858), 226–27; in *William Morris: The Critical Heritage*, ed. Peter Faulkner (1973), p. 32.
17. Unsigned review of *The Defence of Guenevere, and Other Poems (1858)*, *Saturday Review*, 6 (20 Nov. 1858), 506–07; in *Morris: Critical Heritage*, p. 45; and Garnett, *Morris: Critical Heritage*, p. 32.
18. Victor Bulwer-Lytton, *The Life of Edward Bulwer, First Lord Lytton* (1913), II, 71.
19. Ibid., pp. 430–31.
20. *Revue de Paris*, 3rd series, 34 (1841), 266–82.
21. Letter to A. C. Swinburne, 26 July 1882, in *The Times Literary Supplement*, 19 (12 Aug. 1920), 517; in *The Swinburne Letters*, IV, ed. Cecil Y. Lang (New Haven 1960), 289.
22. Yale MS, cited in *The Poems of Matthew Arnold*, ed. Kenneth Allott, 2nd ed. rev. Miriam Allott (1979), p. 233.
23. Letter to Arthur Hugh Clough, 14 Dec. 1852, *The Letters of Matthew Arnold to Arthur Hugh Clough*, ed. H. F. Lowry (1932), p. 126.
24. Letter to Herbert Hill, 5 Nov. 1852, in *The Times Literary Supplement*, 31 (19 May 1932), 368; cited in C. B. Tinker and H. F. Lowry, *The Poetry of Matthew Arnold: A Commentary* (1940), p. 124.

25 *Revue de Paris*, 2nd series, 41 (1837), 45–62; and Southey's Preface to *The Byrth, Lyf, and Actes of King Arthur* (1817), pp. xiv–xlvi.

26 Some years later in 'Stanzas from Carnac' (wr. 1859, pub. 1867) Arnold again used the Merlin figure to contrast with flux and suffering, suggesting that the wizard charms Brittany 'from his forest-grave'.

27 Letter to his mother, 5 June 1869, *Letters of Matthew Arnold, 1848–1888*, ed. George W. E. Russell (New York 1896), I, 10.

28 C. E. Byles, *The Life and Letters of R. S. Hawker* (1905), pp. 190–91, 193.

29 S. Baring-Gould, *The Vicar of Morwenstow* (1903), p. 70.

30 Byles, *Life and Letters*, p. 415.

31 Hallam Tennyson, *Memoir*, I, 456.

32 Byles, *Life and Letters*, p. 412.

33 Ibid., p. 446.

34 Ibid., pp. 390, 414.

35 Ibid., p. 558.

36 Ibid., p. 418.

4

An Epic in 'the Fashion of the Day'
Idylls of the King

1 See, for example, the review by Gladstone in the *Quarterly Review*, 106 (October 1859), 454–85; in *Tennyson: The Critical Heritage*, ed. John D. Jump (1967), pp. 241–66, esp. p. 260.

2 Hallam Tennyson, *Alfred Lord Tennyson: A Memoir* (1897), II, 124–25. Subsequently cited as *Memoir*.

3 *Idylls of the King, the Works of Alfred Lord Tennyson*, III, ed. Hallam Tennyson (1908), 436. See also *Memoir*, I, 166.

4 *Memoir*, II, 123.

5 *Memoir*, II, 126–27.

6 *Memoir*, II, 337.

7 *Memoir*, II, 127.

8 *Memoir*, II, 125.

9 Wright's edition of Malory, I, 5; cited in J. M. Gray, *Thro' the Vision of the Night: A Study of Source, Evolution and Structure in Tennyson's Idylls of the King* (Montreal 1980), p. 141, n. 83.

10 Tennyson's departures from his early prose draft for the idyll show how he increased the optimism. In the draft Bellicent sends Gareth to Camelot to confirm rumours of Guinevere's adultery, thereby justifying her own. Tennyson deleted this motive to heighten the purity of the court.

11 *The Poems of Tennyson*, ed. Christopher Ricks (1969), p. 1510 n.

12 *Memoir*, II, 122–23.

13 John D. Rosenberg suggests that Tennyson divided the Enid story when he abandoned plans for a twelfth idyll projected but never written; *The Fall of Camelot: A Study of Tennyson's Idylls of the King* (Cambridge, Mass., 1973), p. 157, n. 33.

14 *The Diary of Alfred Domett, 1872–1885*, ed. E. A. Horsman (1953), p. 79.

15 *Memoir*, I, 456–57; see also II, 126.

16 *Memoir*, II, 90.

17 *Poems of Tennyson*, ed. Ricks, p. 1661; see also *Memoir*, II, 131.

18 On Tennyson's use of Malory, see J. M. Gray, pp. 26–7.
19 *Poems of Tennyson*, ed. Ricks, p. 1661.
20 John Pfordresher, *A Variorum Edition of Tennyson's Idylls of the King* (New York 1973), pp. 42–3.
21 Hallam Tennyson, *Materials for a Life of Alfred Tennyson* (4 vols. privately printed, 1895), II, 220; cited in Pfordresher, p. 43.
22 *Poems of Tennyson*, ed. Ricks, p. 1687.
23 See Kathleen Tillotson, 'Tennyson's Serial Poem', in *Mid-Victorian Studies* (1965), p. 84 n.
24 On Tennyson's use of Malory's details, see J. M. Gray, pp. 34–7.
25 Charles Tennyson, *Alfred Tennyson* (1950), p. 297.
26 A. C. Swinburne, 'Under the Microscope', in *Swinburne Replies*, ed. C. K. Hyder (Syracuse 1966), p. 57.
27 Pfordresher, p. 55; see also *Memoir*, II, 129.
28 *Memoir*, II, 133. Tennyson also emphasised this point by changing his original title, 'The Death of Arthur'.
29 *Works of Tennyson*, ed. Hallam Tennyson, III, 508.
30 *Memoir*, II, 131.
31 Gladstone, in *Tennyson: The Critical Heritage*, p. 250.
32 Charles Tennyson, p. 518. Also *Materials*, IV, 242 n. 1.
33 *Memoir*, I, xii.
34 *Memoir*, I, 340.

5

The Pre-Raphaelites

Morris and Swinburne

1 *The Literary Gazette*, 6 March 1858, p. 226.
2 *The Saturday Review*, 20 November 1858, p. 507.
3 In a letter to William Allingham, 23 January 1855. In *Letters of Dante Gabriel Rossetti to William Allingham, 1854–1870*, ed. George Birkbeck Hill (1897), pp. 97–8.
4 In G.B.-J., *Memorials of Edward Burne-Jones* (1904), II, 248.
5 Quoted by L. L. A. Parry in 'The Tapestries of Edward Burne-Jones', *Apollo* November 1975, pp. 324–28.
6 'Moral Aspects of Mr Tennyson's "Idylls of the King"', *Macmillan's Magazine*, I, November 1859, pp. 63–72.
7 'Poems by Matthew Arnold', *Fraser's Magazine*, XLIX, February 1854, pp. 140–49.
8 *Chronicles of England, France, and Spain, and The Adjoining Countries by Sir John Froissart* translated from the French Editions by Thomas Johnes, Esq., 2 vols. (1852).
9 Quoted by J. W. Mackail, *The Life of William Morris* (1899), I, 83–6.
10 Ibid., p. 111.
11 *Le Morte D'Arthur*, Book XXI, Chap. 9.
12 *The Fortnightly Review*, July 1867, viii, pp. 20–1.
13 Ibid.
14 *The Westminster Review*, October 1868, xc, p. 302.
15 *Le Morte D'Arthur*, Book XX, Chap. 3.
16 Mackail, op. cit., p. 45.
17 *The Spectator*, February 1858, xxx, p. 238.
18 From a letter to Isabel Blagden, 19 January 1870, in *Letters of Robert Browning*, ed. T. L. Hood (1933), p. 134.

[19] *The Literary Gazette*, 6 March 1858, p. 227.

[20] In *Literary Remains of J. H. Shorthouse*, ed. S. Shorthouse (1905), pp. 108–9.

[21] Leonée Ormond, 'A Mid-Victorian Parody: George du Maurier's "A Legend of Camelot"' in *Apollo*, January 1967, pp. 54–8.

[22] All quotations from the poems of Swinburne are from the Bonchurch edition, ed. Sir Edmund Gosse and Thomas James Wise, *The Complete Works of Algernon Charles Swinburne* (1925).

[23] Letter to Rossetti, 22 December 1869 in Thomas Hake and Arthur Compton-Rickett, eds., *The Letters of Algernon Charles Swinburne with Some Personal Recollections* (1918). Samuel Chew in his *Swinburne* (1931) says that the letter was drastically expurgated by the editors.

[24] See Stoddard Martin, *Wagner to the Waste Land: A Study of the Relationship of Wagner to English Literature* (1982) p. 32.

[25] Anne Wilson, *Traditional Romance and Tale: How Stories Mean*, Ipswich 1976, p. 50.

[26] In 'Malory and the Grail Legend' from *The Dublin Review*, April 1944. Reprinted in *Charles Williams: The Image of the City and Other Essays* Selected by Anne Ridler (1958), p. 187.

[27] *The Saturday Review*, 29 July 1882, pp. 156–57.

[28] *The Spectator*, 12 August 1882, p. 1056.

[29] J. W. Mackail, op. cit., II, 74–5.

[30] Letter to Frederick Greenwood, 1 January 1873. In ed. C. L. Cline, *The Letters of George Meredith* (Oxford 1970) I, 475.

[31] *The Nineteenth Century*, January 1893, p. 98.

[32] Oliver Elton, *Modern Studies* (1907), pp. 208–27.

[33] Ibid., pp. 223–25.

6

Arthur's 'Return' in the New World

American Literature of the Nineteenth and Early Twentieth Centuries

[1] See Alice P. Kenney, 'The Necessity of Invention: Medievalism in America', *The Literary Review*, 23 (1980), 562.

[2] J. G. Lockhart, *Memoirs of Sir Walter Scott* (1900), III, 136.

[3] For these Arthurian references in Southern novels, I am indebted to Susan Page Ward, *The Development of the Theme of Chivalry in Nineteenth-Century Southern Literature*, a 1980 Ph.D. dissertation at Duke University.

[4] The increased number of tournaments held in the South may reflect this change in attitude. While there were two tournaments held in 1840, the year after the Eglinton tournament, the number of jousts peaked in the 1890s. Rare tournaments were held as late as the 1930s. See John Mills Turner, 'Tournament Riding in the South', *South Atlantic Quarterly*, 35 (1936), 399–410; and G. Harrison Orians, 'Walter Scott, Mark Twain, and the Civil War', *South Atlantic Quarterly*, 40 (1941), 342–59.

[5] Page also referred to the *Idylls* in *Red Rock: A Chronicle of Reconstruction* (1898), where a character shifts his attention from heroines in Tennyson's love stories to a real woman.

[6] Sidney Lanier, *Poems and Poem Outlines, Centennial Edition of the Works of Sidney Lanier*, I, ed. Charles R. Anderson (Baltimore 1945), xlii. (Lanier, characteristically, used a description of Malory to turn a gallant compliment to his wife; see *Letters, 1869–1873, Centennial Edition*, VIII, ed. Charles R. Anderson and Aubrey Starke, pp. 112–13.)

7 See Nancie Campbell, *Tennyson in Lincoln: A Catalogue of the Collections in the Research Centre*, I (Lincoln 1971).

8 Kenneth Walter Cameron, *Transcendental Climate* (Hartford 1963), III, 857–58.

9 'The Age of Fable', in *The Early Lectures of Ralph Waldo Emerson, I, 1833–1836*, ed. Stephen E. Whicher and Robert E. Spiller (Cambridge, Mass., 1959), p. 259.

10 *The Journals and Miscellaneous Notebooks of Ralph Waldo Emerson, XIV, 1854–1861*, ed. Susan Sutton Smith and Harrison Hayford (Cambridge, Mass., 1978), pp. 287–89.

11 *Early Lectures*, I, 240.

12 *The Journals and Miscellaneous Notebooks of Ralph Waldo Emerson, I, 1819–1822*, ed. William H. Gilman, *et al.* (Cambridge, Mass., 1960), p. 188.

13 *The Journals and Miscellaneous Notebooks of Ralph Waldo Emerson, II, 1822–1826*, ed. William H. Gilman, Alfred R. Ferguson, Merrell R. Davis (Cambridge, Mass., 1961), pp. 63–4.

14 *Letters of James Russell Lowell*, II, ed. Charles Eliot Norton (New York 1893), 85.

15 See his 'Essay on Chaucer'.

16 See Leon Howard, *Victorian Knight-Errant: A Study of the Early Literary Career of James Russell Lowell* (Berkeley 1952), p. vii.

17 Charles Oran Stewart, *Lowell and France* (Nashville 1951), p. 28.

18 'Essay on Chaucer', in *My Study Windows* (Boston 1887), p. 243; *Letters of James Russell Lowell*, II, 85.

19 'A Word About Tennyson', *The Critic*, 7 (1 January 1887), 1–2; in *Tennyson: The Critical Heritage*, ed. John D. Jump (1967), p. 350.

20 All quotations and background information pertaining to *Connecticut Yankee* are drawn from the introduction, text, and notes in *A Connecticut Yankee in King Arthur's Court*, ed. Bernard L. Stein, intro. Henry Nash Smith (Berkeley 1979).

21 Unsigned review, London *Daily Telegraph* (13 January 1890); in *Mark Twain: The Critical Heritage*, ed. Frederick Anderson (New York 1971), p. 160.

22 All material from Hovey's notes and fragments and from Mrs. Hovey's commentary is taken from her edition of *The Holy Graal and Other Fragments by Richard Hovey* (Boston 1907). This statement appears in Mrs Hovey's introduction, p. 13.

23 Hovey's notes for a lecture at Barnard College, cited in Allan H. Macdonald, *Richard Hovey: Man and Craftsman* (Durham, N.C. 1957), p. 81.

24 Published in the *Independent*, 47 (1895), 1125; cited in Macdonald, pp. 138–39.

25 See Laurence Perrine, 'The Sources of Robinson's Arthurian Poems and His Opinions of Other Treatments', *Colby Library Quarterly*, series 10 (1974), 336–46; and Perrine, 'The Sources of Robinson's *Merlin*', *American Literature*, 44 (1972), 313–21.

26 Unpublished letter cited in Charles T. Davis, 'Robinson's Road to Camelot', in *Edwin Arlington Robinson Centenary Essays*, ed. Ellsworth Barnard (Athens 1969), p. 94.

27 Hermann Hagedorn, *Edwin Arlington Robinson: A Biography* (New York 1938), pp. 320–21.

28 *Untriangulated Stars: Letters of Edwin Arlington Robinson to Harry DeForest Smith*, ed. Denham Sutcliffe (Cambridge, Mass. 1947), p. 214.

29 Hagedorn, p. 38.

30 *Selected Letters of Edwin Arlington Robinson*, ed. Ridgely Torrence (New York 1940), pp. 160, 112.

31 Perrine, 'The Sources of Robinson's Arthurian Poems', *Colby Library Quarterly*, series 10 (1974), 336–46.

32 *Selected Letters*, p. 97; *Edwin Arlington Robinson's Letters to Edith Brower*, ed. Richard Cary (Cambridge, Mass. 1968), p. 169.

33 Perrine, 'The Sources of Robinson's Arthurian Poems', 336–46.

34 *Selected Letters*, p. 113.

35 Ibid.

36 *Letters to Edith Brower*, p. 169; *Selected Letters*, p. 107. One can only wonder that

Robinson, who liked the Arthurian poems of Morris and Tennyson, did not find their queens 'interesting'.

[37] Hagedorn, p. 320.
[38] Hagedorn, p. 340.
[39] *Selected Letters*, p. 160.
[40] Hagedorn, pp. 199–200. On his interest in Wagner, see also p. 162; Davis, pp. 97–8; *Selected Letters*, p. 124.
[41] *Selected Letters*, p. 145.
[42] Davis, p. 101.
[43] Davis, p. 97.
[44] Hagedorn, p. 343.
[45] *Selected Letters*, p. 124.
[46] *Untriangulated Stars*, p. 247.
[47] *Letters to Edith Brower*, p. 186; *Selected Letters*, p. 112.
[48] See Frank L. Baer, 'The Finding of G. Ogyrvan Gawr', *Kalki*, 3, i (1969), 15.
[49] For Cabell's discussion of these 'attitudes', see *Beyond Life: Dizain des Démiurges*, Storisende ed., I (New York 1927), 36–8, 101–2.
[50] See *Beyond Life*, pp. 88ff.
[51] James P. Cover, *Notes on Jurgen* (New York 1928), p. 30. On Cabell's exchange of information with Cover, see *The Letters of James Branch Cabell*, ed. Edward Wagenknecht (Norman, 1975), p. 233.
[52] See *Let Me Lie* (New York 1947), pp. 146–47.
[53] *Letters of James Branch Cabell*, p. 233.
[54] *Preface to the Past* (New York 1927–36), p. 96.
[55] *Letters of James Branch Cabell*, p. 30.
[56] *The Delight of Great Books* (Indianapolis 1928), p. 71.

7

Dramatic New Developments

Early Twentieth-Century British Literature

[1] P. Fitzgerald, *Life of Henry Irving* (1906), p. 233.
[2] Ibid., p. 234.
[3] In *King Arthur: A Drama in a Prologue and Four Acts* by J. Comyns Carr (1895), p. 67.
[4] Clement Scott, *From 'The Bells' to 'King Arthur': A Critical Record of the First-Night Productions at the Lyceum Theatre from 1871 to 1895* (1897), pp. 372–84.
[5] *King Arthur*, op. cit., p. 38.
[6] *Saturday Review*, January 19th, 1895. No. 2047, 79, p. 93.
[7] F. B. Money Coutts, *King Arthur* (1897), Introduction p. xi.
[8] Ibid., p. vii.
[9] Ibid., p. 40.
[10] Ibid., p. 81.
[11] F. B. Money Coutts, *The Romance of King Arthur* (1907), p. 206.
[12] John Davidson, *The Last Ballad and Other Poems* (1899).
[13] *Collected Poems of Laurence Binyon: Lyrical Poems* (1931), p. 66.
[14] Graham Hill, *Guinevere* (1906), p. 63.
[15] J. Comyns Carr, *Tristram and Iseult* (1906), p. 63.
[16] Ibid., p. 65.
[17] Ibid., p. 67.
[18] Martha Kinross, *Tristram and Isoult* (1913), p. 39.

[19] See Stoddard Martin, *Wagner to The Wasteland: A Study of the Relationship of Wagner to English Literature* (1982).

[20] Arthur Symons, *Tristan and Iseult* (1917), p. 33.

[21] Laurence Binyon, *Arthur: A Tragedy* (1923), p. 32.

[22] *Le Morte D'Arthur*, Book XVIII, Chap. xix.

[23] Gordon Bottomley, ed., *The Madness of Merlin* (1947), p. vi.

[24] Ibid., pp. viii–ix.

[25] John Masefield, *Tristan and Isolt* (1927), p. 38.

[26] 'Isolt my blood, Isolt my breath,
In you my life; in you my death.' (p. 132)

[27] Margaret J. C. Reid, *The Arthurian Legend; a comparison of treatment in modern and medieval literature; a study in the literary value of myth and legend* (1938). Repr. 1970. p. 55.

[28] John Masefield, *Midsummer Night and Other Tales in Verse* (1928). 'The Begetting of Arthur', p. 13.

[29] F. B. Pinion, ed., in a note to the New Wessex edition (1977).

[30] Quoted by F. B. Pinion in the above, p. 236.

8

The Waste Land *and After*

[1] In 'Malory and the Grail Legend' from *The Dublin Review*, April 1944. Reprinted in *Charles Williams: The Image of the City and Other Essays* Selected by Anne Ridler (1958), pp. 186–87.

[2] p. 203.

[3] Ibid., p. 75.

[4] *Tradition and the Individual Talent*, in *Selected Essays 1917–1932* (1932), pp. 12–22.

[5] Quoted by the late Professor Theodore Spencer during a lecture at Harvard University, and recorded by the late Henry Ware Eliot, Jr, the poet's brother, in *T. S. Eliot: The Waste Land: a Facsimile and Transcript*, ed. Valerie Eliot (1971).

[6] Dame Helen Gardner, *The Waste Land 1972*. The Adamson lecture, 3 May 1972, University of Manchester.

[7] *The Great Return*, pp. 78–9.

[8] Page references are to the paperback reprint by Wm. B. Eerdmans Publishing Co., Michigan 1978.

[9] Page references are to the paperback reprint of Charles Williams and C. S. Lewis, *Taliessin through Logres, The Region of the Summer Stars* and *Arthurian Torso* (Michigan 1974). The first two titles are reprinted in *The Arthurian Poems of Charles Williams* (Cambridge 1982).

[10] In 'Malory and the Grail Legend', op. cit. pp. 186–87.

[11] Explaining his choice of Byzantium as background to the poems in an article on *The Making of Taliessin* in the *Poetry Review* for April 1941, Williams says, 'Mr Yeats had not then written his Byzantium poems, or if so, I had not read them.'

[12] *The Masks of God: Creative Mythology*, p. 542.

[13] Williams and Lewis (op. cit.), p. 292.

[14] Ibid., p. 286.

[15] Williams explains the symbolic significance of the Dolorous Blow in *The Figure of Arthur* (op. cit.) p. 269. When Balin uses the lance for his own self-preservation, he is turning the most sacred mysteries to the immediate security of the self and it is this that is the 'catastrophic thing'. In wounding the Keeper of the Hallows, man wounds himself: it is an image of the Fall. When subsequently Balin kills his own brother and is himself killed by him, the 'natural pieties begin to be lost'.

[16] *Le Morte D'Arthur*, Book XVII, Chap. xi.

[17] I Corinthians 12.4.

[18] Op. cit. p. 552.

[19] The significance of this event is suggested by Wordsworth's images of stone and shell referred to in *The Prelude* Book V, 1–165. In this episode, the poet dreams that in a desert he sees a Bedouin carrying a stone which is 'Euclid's elements' and a shell which is also a book and 'full of prophetic sound', both of which he is about to bury, to save them from an impending flood. In *The Prelude*, stone and shell represent Intellect and Poetry: for Williams, they symbolise a complex of complementary values. In Galahad himself, the shell has been fitted to the stone; the complementarities, once disjunct, are now united.

[20] Williams and Lewis, op. cit. p. 360.

[21] Ibid., p. 364.

[22] References are to *That Hideous Strength*, 1st edition (1945), but also apply to the edition of 1955, abridged by the author.

[23] *The Anathemata* (1952), p. 198, Note 1.

[24] *Le Morte D'Arthur*, Book XX, Chap. ix.

[25] Page references are to the first edition (1937).

[26] 'You ought to ask . . . roof-tree. Cf. the Welsh *Percivale* story, *Peredur ap Evrawc*: "Peredur, I greet thee not, seeing that thou dost not merit it. Blind was fate in giving thee favour and fame. When thou wast in the Court of the Lame King, and didst see the youth bearing the streaming spear, from the points of which were drops of blood . . . thou didst not enquire their meaning nor their cause. Hadst thou done so, the King would have been restored to his health and his dominion in peace. Whereas from henceforth he will have to endure battles and conflicts and his knights will perish, and wives will be widowed, and maidens will be left portionless, and all this is because of thee." See also Jessie Weston, *From Ritual to Romance*, ch. ii.'—Author's note, op. cit. p. 210, Note M.

[27] Preface to *Anathemata*, p. 20ff.

[28] 'The Myth of Arthur' in *Epoch and Artist* (selected writings, edited by Harman Grisewood) (1959) p. 243.

[29] Ibid., p. 245.

[30] *The Sleeping Lord and Other Fragments* (1974), p. 91.

[31] *Le Morte D'Arthur*, Book XVII, Chap. xx.

[32] *Epoch and Artist*, p. 247.

[33] Letter to Harriet Shaw Weaver, 7 April 1935, in *Letters of James Joyce* ed. Stuart Gilbert (1957), p. 362.

[34] Edmund Wilson, *Axel's Castle* (New York 1931) p. 221.

[35] Page references are to the 1975 edition of *Finnegans Wake* of which the text has been fully amended in accordance with the manuscript corrections compiled by Joyce himself. The publishers claim that it is the most accurate ever published.

[36] Christine Brooke-Rose, *A ZBC of Ezra Pound* (1971). See Chapter 10, pp. 183–207.

[37] Page references are to the Picador edition (1975), which contains J. Cowper Powys's 'Preface to the New Edition' of 1953.

[38] Page references are to the 1974 edition.

9

Arthurian Literature since World War II

[1] See Geoffrey T. L. Ashe, *King Arthur's Avalon: The Story of Glastonbury* (1957); *From Caesar to Arthur* (1960); *Camelot and the Vision of Albion* (1971); *The Quest for Arthur's Britain* (with L. Alcock and C. A. R. Radford etc., 1971). See also *Guidebook to*

Arthurian Britain (1980). Leslie Alcock, in *Arthur's Britain; History and Archaeology A.D. 367–634* (1971); '*By South Cadbury is that Camelot . . .*', *the excavation of Cadbury Castle, 1966–70* (New Aspects of Antiquity) (1972); *Dinas Powys; an Iron Age, Dark Age and early medieval settlement in Glamorgan* (University of Wales Board of Celtic Studies, Cardiff 1963), takes a more archaeological approach. See also John Robert Morris's comprehensive *The Age of Arthur; a History of the British Isles from 350 to 650* (1973).

[2] All page references are to the first edition of *The Book of Merlyn* (1977).

[3] p. 127. All references are to the 1958 edition.

[4] Letter to L. J. Potts, 6 December 1940, quoted by Sylvia Townsend Warner in her Prologue to *The Book of Merlyn*, p. xvi.

[5] References are to the 1979 paperback edition.

[6] References are to *Lancelot* (1978).

[7] References are to *Percival and the Presence of God* (1978).

[8] For a discussion of Charles Williams's concept of 'substitution' see Chapter VIII, p. 253.

[9] J. F. A. Heath-Stubbs, *Artorius* (1973) (limited edition).

[10] Emma Jung and Marie-Louise von Franz: *The Grail Legend* (1960).

[11] References are to the Penguin edition (1979).

[12] See the above edition, back cover.

Index

378

107, 108, 110, 117, 119, 120ff., 134, 136,
137–40, 141ff., 146, 156, 164, 168, 175ff.,
178–79, 182, 183, 185ff., 195, 196, 197,
199–201, 205–6, 207, 208–9, 210, 211, 213,
216, 217, 221ff., 229–31, 247, 248, 252,
255, 256–57, 260, 293, 294, 295, 298, 299,
302, 304, 305, 306, 309, 314, 316, 319
Gurteen, Stephen Humphreys, 182

Hallam, Henry, 27
Halliwell, James O., 29, 167
Hanson, Charles Henry, 197
Hardy, Thomas, 17–8, 216, 232–34
Harrison, William, 42
Hawker, Robert Stephen, 86–8, 110, 235
Hawthorne, Nathaniel, 162
Heath-Stubbs, John, 311–13, 315
Heber, Reginald, 29, 38, 44, 60–4, 68, 128,
176
Heber, Richard, 38, 39, 60
Hill, Graham, 213, 222
Historia Meriadoci, 47
Historical Clubs and Societies, 26, 178
History of Taliesin, 55
Hoare, Richard Colt, 55, 78
Hopkins, Gerard Manley, 15, 24
Hovey, Richard, 174–79, 184, 319
Howel, 190–91
Hughes, Arthur, 132
Hunt, William Holman, 69, 131–32
Hunter, Jim, 310
Hurd, Richard, 16, 162

Igerna (Igraine, Ygraine), 43, 92, 93, 192–93,
202, 226, 319
Irving, Henry, 204–5, 207, 217, 221
Irving, Washington, 162–63
Iseult (Isolt, Isolde, Izonda, Isoud, Isoult),
43, 65, 81, 119, 151ff., 179, 188ff., 193,
201–2, 208, 212, 214–20, 226–27, 231–33,
248, 254–55, 258, 280, 300
Iseult of Brittany, 80–1, 84, 155–57, 168, 188,
190–92, 201, 212, 215–17, 219–20, 233–34,
296
Iseult (Queen, mother), 155, 217, 275

Johnson, Barbara Ferry, 318
Jones, David, 12, 225, 237–39, 265–72
Jones, Edward, 55
Jones, Owen, 55–6, 166
Joseph of Arimathea, 113, 168, 279
Joseph of Exeter, 30
Joyce, James, 12, 237, 265, 268, 272–77, 301

Kay (Kai, Kei), 8, 97, 101, 226, 255, 290,
293, 298, 309
Keats, John, 36–7, 155, 231
Kennedy, John Pendleton, 163
'King Arthur's Death', 28
'King Ryence', 28

Kingsley, Charles, 134–35
Kinross, Martha, 216–17
Koopman, Harry Lyman, 168

Lady of the Lake, 40, 63–4, 66, 93, 97, 102,
166, 197–98
Lamorak, 180, 183, 208, 252, 256
Lancelot (Launcelot), 3, 5, 7–9, 36, 38, 43,
44, 46, 51, 60–1, 64, 70–2, 76–7, 85–7, 94,
97, 100, 102, 106ff., 117–19, 121, 136, 138,
141ff., 146, 156, 164, 172, 175ff., 179,
181–82, 185ff., 190–91, 193, 195, 197,
199–201, 205–13, 221ff., 229–31, 242, 248–
49, 255, 258–61, 280, 290, 293–95, 297–
301, 304, 306, 308–9, 311, 315, 317–19
Lancelot (Vulgate), 47, 60, 76, 111, 176
Lanier, Sidney, 164, 170, 175, 194
Laubenthal, Sanders Ann, 315–16
Launfal (Lanval), 167–68
Lavayne, 5, 110, 144, 221
Layamon, 28, 78, 164–65, 197, 277
Lee, T. H., 215–17
'Legend of King Arthur', 28
Le Grand, P. J. B., 76, 78
Le Morte D'Arthur, see Malory
Leodogran (Leodegrance, Leodegrance), 91–
4, 102, 120, 299
Lewis, C. S., 11, 245, 247, 251, 256–58, 260–
64, 312, 316
Leyden, John, 44, 48, 68
Lindsay, Vachel, 179
Lionel (Lyonel), 144, 298
Lionors, 318
Llywarch Hen, 166
Loathly Lady, 63, 165, 298, 317
Lohengrin, 308–9
Lot, 304
Lowell, James Russell, 167–68
Lucius, Emperor, 177
Lynette, 95, 96, 101, 317

Mabinogion, The, 28, 31, 77–8, 89, 98–100,
164–65, 178, 319
Macaulay, Thomas Babington, 26–7, 110
Machen, Arthur, 241–42
Maclise, Daniel, 69, 131
Macpherson, James, 162
Mador, 199
Malory, Sir Thomas, *Le Morte D'Arthur*,
1–13, 15–16, 28–34, 38, 40, 43–4, 47, 51,
53, 60, 62–5, 67, 69–71, 74, 78, 80–4, 86–9,
91–6, 98, 101–26, 128–37, 139–43, 145–47,
150, 156, 160–67, 169–70, 175–80, 182,
184–87, 189–99, 201–2, 205, 208, 210–11,
213, 220–22, 224–25, 227–28, 230–31, 236,
247, 258, 260–61, 265–66, 268, 270–71,
279, 285, 290–91, 294–300, 302, 304,
314–18, 321
Margawse, 93, 151, 176
Marhaus (Marhalt), 170, 297–98

379

Marie de France, 167
Mark (Marc), 8, 80, 106, 119, 153–55, 158, 176, 188–91, 193, 201–2, 208, 212–20, 226–27, 231, 233, 254–55, 274, 279, 296
Markale, Jean, 318
'Marriage of Sir Gawain', 28, 63, 165, 298
Masefield, John, 225–32
Masters, Edgar Lee, 179
Meliagrance (Meliagraunce, Meliagrant), 199, 294, 299
Melot, 190
Meredith, George, 159
Meredith, Owen, see Bulwer-Lytton, Edward Robert
Meriadoc, 217–19
Merlin (Myrddin, Myrddhin, Merlyn), 13, 35, 37–8, 42–3, 46, 54, 56–7, 62–6, 72, 77, 83–4, 87, 93–4, 97–8, 100, 104ff., 128, 153, 160–1, 165, 169–71, 175, 178, 181ff., 186, 191–93, 195–96, 201–2, 210, 213–14, 225, 250–53, 258–60, 262–64, 277–78, 280, 282, 286–90, 292–95, 297, 299, 303–5, 311–14, 316–20
Merlin (Auchinleck Ms. Arthour and Merlin), 60
Merlin, Ystoire de (Vulgate), 32, 47, 104, 179, 182, 183, 196
'Merlinus Anglicus, jun.', 65
Michel, Françisque, 31, 87, 167, 178
Millais, John Everett, 131, 149
Millay, Edna St Vincent, 179
Milman, Henry Hart, 38, 42–4, 60, 62, 68, 79, 128
Milton, John, 34, 36, 42, 44, 50, 69, 75, 135, 315
Mitchison, Naomi, 296
Monaco, Richard, 307–9
Monty Python and the Holy Grail, 315
Moore, Thomas, 162
Mordred (Modred, Medrawd, Medrawt, Medraut), 46, 47, 89, 94, 125, 153, 167, 181, 182, 187–88, 206, 207–9, 210, 213, 222, 229, 230, 254, 260, 265, 270, 286, 289, 290, 293, 294, 295, 300, 302, 303, 304, 306, 308, 309, 314, 317, 318
Morgan le Fay (Morgana, Morgance, Morgaine, Morgue), 40, 61, 132, 169, 173, 191, 198, 210, 211, 300, 308, 314, 316, 317, 318
Morgause (Morgawse), 252, 255, 292, 296, 299, 304, 306, 316
Morold (Morhold, Moraunt), 214, 217
Morris, John, 290, 309, 318
Morris, William, 1, 3, 7, 16, 20, 22, 32, 38, 62, 68, 69, 71, 75, 129, 131, 133, 134, 146, 149, 150, 159, 161, 179, 209, 235; Defence of Guenevere and Other Poems, 15, 129, 130, 135–48, 149, 184 ('The Chapel in Lyonness', 145–46; 'The Defence of Guenevere', 131, 134, 137–41, 146, 231; 'King Arthur's

Tomb', 130, 131, 141–44, 146; 'Sir Galahad, A Christmas Mystery', 131, 134, 144–45, 146, 150, 310)
Munn, H. Warner, 316
Myvyrian Archaiology of Wales, 55, 56, 166

Nennius, 28, 40, 42, 295, 304, 320
Newbolt, Henry, 207–10, 218
Newman, Sharan, 319–20
Nimuë, 104, 105, 114, 116, 175, 178, 196, 198, 202, 213–14, 251, 280, 304, 317
Norton, André, 316, 317
Nye, Robert, 11, 313–15

Once and Future King (motif), 6, 8, 10, 71, 73, 270, 312
Owein, 54
Owen, William, 166
Ozana le Cure Hardy, 145

Page, Thomas Nelson, 164
Palgrave, Francis, 78
Palomydes (Palomides, Palamede), 144, 201–2, 248, 249, 250, 254, 258–59
Partridge, John, 35
Pater, Walter, 143, 147, 209
Peacock, Thomas Love, 17, 20–1, 39, 49, 53, 54–60, 68, 79, 128, 163, 166, 169, 180, 198
Pellam, 5, 103, 106, 119, 160, 266, 319
Pelleas, 100, 107, 114ff., 119, 120, 192, 195, 207, 208
Pelles, 251, 252, 253, 260, 280, 319
Pellinore, 300
Perceval (Percival, Parsival), 43, 46, 87, 110, 111, 113, 114, 115, 122, 126, 144, 165, 167, 178, 242, 252, 255, 256, 269, 280, 298, 300, 301, 307–9, 310, 317
Perceval's sister (Blanchefleur, Dindrane), 113, 256, 257, 306, 319
Percy, Thomas, 16, 28, 45, 47, 63, 162
Percy, Walker, 301
Peredur, 269, 271, 306, 319
Peredur, 54, 165, 178
Perlesvaus, 166
Pinkerton, John, 29
Pocock, Isaac, 49
Pound, Ezra, 277
Powys, John Cowper, 12, 239; A Glastonbury Romance, 7, 242, 244, 277–85, 291; Porius, 285–89
Pre-Raphaelites, 2, 3, 69, 71, 72, 79, 129ff., 136, 142, 145, 147, 148, 149–50, 154, 161, 211, 220, 268
Prester John, 243, 245
Pritchard, T. J. L., 55
Pughe, William Owen, see Owen, William
Pugin, Augustus Welby, 17, 18, 33

Queste del Saint Graal, 164, 246

380

Vinaver, Eugène, 297
Vivian (Viviane, Vivien, Niniane), 83–4, 102, 104ff., 116, 122, 169, 181ff., 186, 189, 213, 304
Voltaire, 15
Vortigern, 40, 42, 43, 320
Vulgate Cycle, see *Estoire del Saint Graal*; *Lancelot*; *Merlin, Ystoire de*; *Queste del Saint Graal*

Wagner, Richard, 179, 308; *Parsifal*, 10, 31, 132; *Tristan und Isolde*, 10, 31, 81, 150–51, 188–91, 212, 215, 217, 238
Waite, A. E., 240–43, 247
Walpole, Horace, 17
Warton, Thomas, 16, 29, 165
Waste Land, 6, 12, 103, 111, 153, 160, 202, 225, 235–39, 242, 261, 265, 268–70, 278, 280, 308
Way, Gregory Lewis, 76, 78
Weddynge of Sir Gawen and Dame Ragnell, 63, 165, 298

Weston, Jessie, 235ff., 240, 242, 269, 295
Westwood, Thomas, 88, 110
Whitaker, John, 42
White, T. H., 2, 56, 290–95, 299, 300, 304, 314, 321
Whitman, Walt, 168
Williams, Charles, 12, 157–58, 235, 239, 240, 262, 283, 293, 310, 314, 315; *Taliessin through Logres* and *The Region of the Summer Stars*, 7, 11, 245–61; *War in Heaven*, 242–45, 262
Wills, W. G., 204
Wolfram von Eschenbach, 31, 111, 168, 178, 236, 300, 307, 308
Wordsworth, William, 29, 36, 39, 50, 64–6, 68, 75, 135, 165
Wright, Thomas, 28, 93

Yeats, William Butler, 240, 246, 255
Yonge, Charlotte, 33, 133
Ywaine (Ewein, Ewain), 297–98